The Theory and Development of Common-Law Actions

The Theory and Development of Common-Law Actions

BY

THOMAS ATKINS STREET, A.M., LL.B.

BeardBooks
Washington, DC

Reprinted 1999 Beard Books, Washington, D.C.

Printed in the United States of America

ISBN 1-893122-25-5

PREFACE

The volume now before the reader is concerned with the law of actions. In the first part of the book this subject is dealt with in its broad and general aspects. The matter here presented forms a sort of general introduction to the succeeding part, which treats of the several actions in particular.

There is a saying long current in the legal profession, and still justly credited by learned lawyers, to the effect that no man can master the science of common-law pleading without thereby of necessity becoming profoundly versed in the fundamental principles of the common law. So astonishing a claim has not been put forth concerning any other branch of legal knowledge. If not absolutely true, the saying in question is to be taken as containing a very important element of truth. One who would now become a truly efficient lawyer must of course labor in many other departments of legal science than that of common-law pleading, but it is still true that in this particular field important aspects of legal truth are directly presented which elsewhere are either entirely hidden or much obscured.

The learning connected with the common-law actions cannot be forgotten without serious loss to knowledge, and wherever the significance of the several forms of action is not duly appreciated obscurity in judicial reasoning is bound to appear. This is indeed one of the commonplaces of legal learning. The principles underlying the subject of common-law pleading do not lose their value with the abolition of the forms of action. The truth of this assertion is generally admitted, but the reason of it does not lie on the surface and is not always perceived. It is not enough to say that those principles are "founded on truth and sound reason and have been matured by the wisdom of ages."

We apprehend that the reason why the principles underlying the common-law actions are of permanent worth is to be found in the fact that those principles are indissolubly associated with fundamental conceptions of legal liability. It is true that the forms of action are the vestments or trappings of substantive rights of action. But they are more than this. Historically they are the vehicle in which substantive principle has been conveyed to the teachable mind, and such conceptions of fundamental liability as those actions were capable of conveying are the conceptions which have been accepted in our law.

Under the system of common-law pleading, lawyers and judges were compelled to do exact thinking. In choosing the form of action, in framing the pleadings, as well as in the instruction of juries, and even in the rendition of the judgment, it was necessary in each case to anatomize the cause of action in order to ascertain the exact nature of the legal liability upon which the suit was based. Each particular species of liability had, or was supposed to have, its peculiar and appropriate remedy. A mistake in the diagnosis of the nature of the liability would lead to the adoption of the wrong form of action, and this at a later stage would certainly lead to a wreck of that particular lawsuit and perhaps to a loss of the right of action itself. Every cause of action was therefore certain under the common-law system to be subjected, at one stage or another, to the closest scrutiny to ascertain the exact nature of the liability involved. The discussions to which this gave rise tended vastly to elucidate the principles underlying our law, and they form one of the richest elements in our court decisions.

In our own day, notwithstanding the abolition of the forms of action in many jurisdictions, it remains as necessary as ever that a plaintiff should have at least one certain and definite ground of action upon which to proceed, and this ground must be such as would in theory have been a sufficient basis at common law for the maintenance of some one of the several actions. Consequently, when a plaintiff under the modern procedure shows that his cause of action is such as was formerly remediable in some one of the several actions, he has thereby conclusively established his right to maintain his action. On the other hand, a defendant who demonstrates that his opponent's ground of action is not such as might have been enforced by any common-law remedy thereby establishes his title to immunity from that proceeding. In applying this doctrine, allowance must of course always be made not only for statutory innovations, but also for such extension of the field of legal liability as is incident to the natural growth of law.

Consideration of the truth just presented convinces the mind that in the law of actions is to be found the most workable and most productive mine to which those who would become conversant with the fundamental principles of common-law liability can resort. The law of actions has heretofore been a veritable quarrying ground for students of legal theory, and such it will continue to be in the future. The period in which our system of law can begin in good earnest to take an account of all its riches seems finally to have dawned. In the largeness of view incident to such a process we cannot afford, either as philosophic students or as practical lawyers, to relegate to the dust heap a mass of learning which sheds more light on fundamental conceptions of liability than any other equal mass of legal learning. The huge pile of knowledge pertaining to the more recondite and less practical parts of the law of pleading may well go. That which deals with the nature of the remedy and with the conception of legal liability which underlies it must be retained. No reflected or second-hand knowledge is here sufficient. The student must be brought into contact with the conceptions, as they took shape in the minds of judges and lawyers, as they found expression in the practice of the courts, and as they daily became operative in determining the rights of individual litigants.

In the light of this conviction the following chapters on the several actions have been prepared. We have not attempted to present the whole or even an imposing part of the law pertaining to the subjects treated. To do so within tolerable limits would have been impossible. We have merely endeavored to present to the enlightened reader a consistent account of the origin, evolution, and ultimate scope of the various remedies; and at the same time we have striven to impart in a suggestive way a sufficient knowledge of the conception of legal liability on which they are founded. This end being accomplished, we have always laid the pen aside, however inviting the field then opening upon our view appeared to be.

In writing these pages we have constantly been impressed with the fact that, while the subject of actions lies at the gateway of truth, still this branch of learning is after all only an approach to fuller and broader knowledge. Up to a certain point the law of actions is not only the best, but, we almost dare to say, the exclusive vehicle of legal truth. Beyond that point the law of actions becomes a hindrance rather than an aid to progress. When this point is reached the study of the actions must be put aside. But only he who has forced the actions to yield up their maximum of truth can afford to spurn these instruments by which he reached his higher knowledge.

The plan of the present book is such as to involve, to a certain extent, the repetition of some fundamental ideas that have been presented in the preceding volumes, since, in going over the various actions, one is compelled to canvass anew the fundamental principles of liability which underlie substantive law as well as the law of actions. The chapters on the action of assumpsit are marred by this blemish — if blemish it be — to a greater extent than those on the other actions. At one time it occurred to us to abridge the treatment of the several actions by omitting all reference to a matter which had been elsewhere presented; but this plan did not commend itself. It was thought best to present a rounded and systematic view of each of the actions even at the cost of some inevitable repetition. We take that to be a sound pedagogical principle which goes upon the idea of imparting truth by presenting it in different aspects and from different approaches. If the idea on which this volume was planned be sound, such repetition of fundamental principles as is incident to the carrying out of that idea is proper and may well prove helpful to the serious student.

In conclusion, we here take the occasion again to acknowledge special indebtedness to Professor Ames. His essays on the history of the actions of assumpsit and trover have been of the very greatest assistance to us. His paper on assumpsit truly marked an epoch in legal scholarship, and no subsequent investigator in the same field can fail to take account of his labors. Professor Langdell's remarks on the subject of accounting, which form a part of his Brief Survey of Equity Jurisdiction, proved of much value to us in writing our chapter on the action of account.

In our observations on the natural history of remedial law and in our treatment of the remedy of distress, we have introduced a few quotations of some length from the writings of Professor Maine. This has been done chiefly with an eye to relieving the monotony of subjects which will strike some readers as rather dull. We trust that the perusal of these passages will stimulate the reader who is so unfortunate as to be unacquainted with the works of this brilliant scholar, forthwith to familiarize himself with them.

Before closing this preface the author wishes to acknowledge a sense of obligation to the Edward Thompson Company. The generous support given by this company first made it possible for him to undertake the laborious task which is now accomplished, and the unwavering patience manifested by the officials of the company during the progress of the work has been a source of constant encouragement.

CONTENTS

PART I

ACTIONS AND RIGHT OF ACTION.

CHAPTER I

NATURAL HISTORY OF REMEDIAL LAW.

PAGE

Early Procedure.. 1

CHAPTER II

NATURAL HISTORY OF REMEDIAL LAW.—*Continued.*

Legal Actions.. 13

CHAPTER III

NATURAL HISTORY OF REMEDIAL LAW.—*Continued.*

Early Remedial Law in England.................................... 22

CHAPTER IV

NATURAL HISTORY OF REMEDIAL LAW.—*Continued.*

Classification of Actions in Common-law System.................... 36

CHAPTER V

NATURAL HISTORY OF REMEDIAL LAW.—*Continued.*

Right and Remedy.. 48

CHAPTER VI

NATURAL HISTORY OF REMEDIAL LAW.—*Continued.*

Actio Personalis Moritur cum Persona............................ 60

CHAPTER VII

NATURAL HISTORY OF REMEDIAL LAW.—*Continued.*

Assignment of Right of Action.................................... 76

CHAPTER VIII

NATURAL HISTORY OF REMEDIAL LAW.—*Continued.*

PAGE
Venue of Actions 90

CHAPTER IX.

Action of Account 99

PART II

COMMON-LAW ACTIONS.

CHAPTER X

COMMON-LAW ACTIONS.

Action of Covenant 114

CHAPTER XI

COMMON-LAW ACTIONS.—*Continued.*

Action of Debt 127

CHAPTER XII

COMMON-LAW ACTIONS.—*Continued.*

Action of Detinue 144

CHAPTER XIII

COMMON-LAW ACTIONS.—*Continued.*

Action of Trover 159

CHAPTER XIV

COMMON-LAW ACTIONS.—*Continued.*

Action of Special Assumpsit 172

CHAPTER XV

COMMON-LAW ACTIONS.—*Continued.*

Action of Indebitatus Assumpsit 182

CHAPTER XVI

COMMON-LAW ACTIONS.—*Continued.*

PAGE
Action of Replevin........ 207

CHAPTER XVII

COMMON-LAW ACTIONS.—*Continued.*

Action of Trespass........ 223

CHAPTER XVIII

COMMON-LAW ACTIONS.—*Continued.*

Action of Trespass on Case........ 245

CHAPTER XIX

COMMON-LAW ACTIONS.—*Continued.*

Action on Case........ 268

CHAPTER XX

REMEDY OF DISTRESS.

Distress in Early Law........ 278

CHAPTER XXI

REMEDY OF DISTRESS.—*Continued.*

Distress for Rent........ 298

CHAPTER XXII

REMEDY OF DISTRESS.—*Continued.*

Distrainable Things........ 304

CHAPTER XXIII

REMEDY OF DISTRESS.—*Continued.*

Distress Damage Feasant........ 309

TABLE OF CASES........ 315
INDEX........ 403

PART I

ACTIONS AND RIGHT OF ACTION

AN ESSAY ON THE NATURAL HISTORY OF REMEDIAL LAW

FOUNDATIONS OF LEGAL LIABILITY

CHAPTER I

NATURAL HISTORY OF REMEDIAL LAW.

Chapter I

THE theme indicated in the heading of this chapter takes us at once to the threshold of a great subject, remedial law; and even the most meagre treatment of it would require at our hands some investigation of very fundamental questions. What indeed could not be said under the title 'Actions'? Early law hardly has any other place to bestow its slender stock of legal principle. Bracton has fifty times as much on actions as he has on the law of persons, and it is under this head that we must search in his pages for much of what we now call substantive law. The close association thus observed between pure legal doctrine and matter of procedure is characteristic of all early law.

Prominence of the law of actions in early jurisprudence.

Only in comparatively recent times has any attempt been made to separate substantive and adjective law from each other. Procedure has now lost its former prominence. Forms of action are gone or are fast disappearing. A single civil action on the facts of the case supplants the ancient forms as an instrument for the enforcement of legal rights. Legal principle is thus stripped of luggage and can be discussed in abstract terms. Remedies thenceforth no longer stand in the forefront as a subject of legal investigation and are properly relegated to a minor position. To the modern mind no line of cleavage is more clearly marked than that between substantive and adjective law. It was not always so. The very term 'adjective law' was first used by Bentham. In early stages of legal growth the two elements are inseparable. Indeed, substantive law is born of procedure, being secreted, as has been said, in the interstices of form.[1]

Procedure less important in modern law.

[1] Maine, Early Law and Custom, 389.

Volume III

Relation between substantive and adjective law.

No more instructive chapter in legal history can be written than that which would give an adequate account of the long and intimate association that has existed between legal doctrine and legal procedure, between the *jus* and the *remedium*, and of their mutual interplay in shaping and stimulating the development of each other. In point of time procedure is undoubtedly entitled to the concession of priority. Nursing substantive law to maturity, or at least to independence, procedure is gradually severed from substantive principle and moves into the background. As one increases the other decreases.

Interplay of the two factors.

Though it is unquestionably true that procedure is thus the older element and has indeed been the bringer in of substantive doctrine, long before the period of definite history commences, the two elements are found inextricably blended. It is not until a society has arrived at legal consciousness and has begun mentally to conceive 'oughtness,' or duty, as a sort of incident to the primitive remedies that legal history properly begins at all. From this time the two elements act continuously upon each other, each sometimes retarding and sometimes stimulating the progress of the other. The result of this interaction between procedure and substantive principle is that body of law which at any particular time actually is, as distinguished from that which might be; a body of rules not so flexible or so advanced as theory would have it, nor yet so stable as the apparent inflexibility of legal machinery might lead us to expect.

Scope of present treatment.

In the following pages we shall endeavor to ascertain what insight may be gained into the evolution of law by viewing it from the standpoint of the long and necessary connection between right and remedy. We proceed with the consciousness that the subject is a large one. We shall try to say things that others have left unsaid; and accordingly these pages will be chiefly concerned with an account of the development of the civil action. Incidentally we must say something about the growth of law in general, in order to ascertain just what place remedial law occupies in legal science and the true function which it performs.

Chapter I

Taking up at random a book on speculative jurisprudence, our eye falls on this statement: "A system of laws promulgated by a lawgiver of sufficient wisdom and illimitable foresight would undoubtedly commence with a definition of rights, and thence proceed to prescribe duties, thence to prohibit wrongs, and finally to provide legal remedies." [2]

Process of historical development of legal conceptions.

To the analytical jurist it may well seem that the ideal code might be framed in such order. It cannot, however, escape observation that the method of unfolding legal truth here indicated is exactly the reverse of the process by which law has, as a matter of fact, historically developed. To the finite, human mind legal truth has come as a sort of gradual revelation. Form, which is so conspicuous in early law, serves as a vehicle for the abstract. As the mind is gradually educated to the point of grasping the abstract, formality disappears. In legal thought, as in philosophic speculation, we must move through the concrete up to the higher abstractions, and if we would conduct the reader over the true path of legal knowledge we must take a course exactly the reverse of that which the analytical jurist pursues in his speculations. In other words, instead of beginning with 'right'— a term so highly abstract as even now to defy attempts at successful definition [3]— we must begin with the phenomenon of adjudication. The order in which the different conceptions appear is somewhat as follows: judge, court, adjudication, legal proceeding (action or remedy), wrong, duty, right.

Adjudication embodies first step in legal evolution.

It may at first seem strange that historically adjudication should precede the development of the conception of law, for according to existing ideas adjudication is only an application of law and presupposes the existence of a body of legal principle; yet it is nevertheless true that law is built up inductively by observing and comparing particular decisions. This conclusion is borne out to the utmost degree of certainty by all that we know of legal development in early society. What the early communities must have is a decider or arbitrator of disputes. It is obvious that the reverend and wise man, the

[2] Robinson, Elements of American Jurisprudence, 155.
[3] Markby, Elements of Law, § 149.

Volume III

The early judge.

priest, or the king, one who by virtue of his wisdom, power, and position can command the love and obedience of all, would be the first to fulfil the function of judge. The desire peacefully to settle disputes instead of resorting to violent modes of redress would gradually make itself felt throughout the community. The decisions of this primitive judge must inevitably reflect the current ideas of justice, and in course of time the points of likeness in many cases are observed and teach the community its first lessons in law.

As the sinews of society come to be knit more firmly together, it becomes necessary to concede theoretical infallibility to the organ of justice. In order to give plausibility to this dogma, resort is had to the theory of divine inspiration. Thus, in the Homeric poems, as Professor Maine has shown, when the king decided a dispute, his judgment was attributed to inspiration. The divine agent suggesting such decrees the early Greeks personified in Themis, and the awards themselves were called 'themistes.' These are isolated judgments corresponding to the 'dooms' of the Teutonic people.[4]

The 'dooms.'

Whether institutions develop slowly as among the Aryans, or with rapidity as among the Hebrews, the judge always precedes the lawgiver. It is instructive to find the great Hebrew leader engaged in judging his people before he becomes legislator. Indeed, law can only be formulated as a result of experience gained by contemplating a mass of individual cases.[5] Judgment is a phenomenon which precedes the conception of law. This is a universal principle, and is found to be true whether we appeal to Hindoo, Greek, Hebrew, Roman, Teu-

Judge precedes the legislator.

[4] See Maine, Ancient Law, 5th ed., 3–5.

[5] *The Judge Precedes the Lawgiver.*—The sage advice given by Jethro, and the direct result of following it, is an instructive incident in the evolution of law. He finds Moses, in his capacity of judge, overwhelmed with a mass of litigation entirely beyond the capacity of any one judge, however wise and skilful. Jethro's solicitude for his son-in-law causes him to advise a division of labor. "Thou shalt provide out of all the people able men, such as fear God, men of truth, hating covetousness, . . . and let them judge the people at all seasons." Accordingly judges were chosen, "rulers of thousands, rulers of hundreds, rulers of fifties, and rulers of ten," who judged Israel at all seasons, bringing only the hard cases for Moses's personal decision. Presently the wise and experienced judge separates himself

tonic, or Celtic civilization.[6] The prayer of the Psalmist is that God may give the king His judgments so that the people may be judged with righteousness and the poor with judgment.[7] The themistes, the dooms, the judgments, these are the chief and tangible end of adjudication. They always contain just so much of divine wisdom as particular communities are able to embody in their ideals and in their life. From these isolated judgments must legal truth be worked out.

The court the first legal institution.

We find, then, that legal development begins with or presupposes an institution, namely, a judge or court, competent to pass upon and to decide all disputes that may be brought before it. We next find the court exercising this function. Its judgments are bound, of course, to exhibit some consistency. Upon like cases, similar judgments or awards must be made; for the very life of the judicial office is necessarily contingent upon a certain approximation to social and religious ideals. In course of time the sage men of the community come to know something of judicial sequences, and the end of any ordinary dispute, if carried to the tribunal of justice, may be foretold. Thus it comes to be known that on a certain state of facts, judgment will or will not be given in favor of the complainant. The mind thus becomes acquainted with the distinction between remedy and absence of remedy, between cases in which there is a right of action and disputes wherein the judge will not interefere.

Conception of law emerges.

Conceptions of wrong, duty, etc.

In this connection appear the conceptions of legal wrong and of legal duty. Legal interference, if it be not altogether vain and fruitless, necessarily involves the exercise of coercive power. It is the debtor, or person owing the legal duty, who comes under this coercion. He is the centre of interest in the legal drama. How instinctive it is for the mind to conceive of law from the standpoint of the party feeling its power, any one may verify for himself. The natural interest and sympathy felt by the onlooker in behalf of a child under the correction of the paternal rod is perhaps an illustration of this.

from his people and after a time produces the ten tables. Exodus xviii. 13-26; xix., xx.

[6] Maine, Ancient Law, ch. I; Early Law and Custom, ch. VI.

[7] Psalms lxxii. 1, 2.

Volume III

From the fact of legal coercion as incident to the enforcement of a judgment the mental inference is drawn that a wrong was done or act committed which called for punishment or redress. The conception of legal wrong is thus perhaps even more fundamental than the idea of duty. The former is an act or omission and we can become acquainted with its actual consequences. The idea of a wrong, however, necessarily leads to the abstraction of duty, that obligation which can only be known in its breach. One who does certain acts termed wrongful renders himself amenable to law and violates a duty. The early codes of law must be framed in terms apprehensible by ordinary minds. They consequently define the acts which constitute wrongs. No mind, however rudimentary, could contemplate the law promulgated by Moses without seeing that 'shalt not' imposes obligation and forever fixes a duty upon the subject. Duty to act or to refrain from acting is the first commentary that the intelligent human mind can make on the Decalogue.

Conception of wrong precedes that of duty.

This early code, which indeed is typical and the simplest of all, exhibits the legislative mind still far removed from that higher abstraction 'right,' which is the correlative of 'duty.' The idea of a right is scarcely deducible from the Mosaic code. The fifth commandment, which is exceptional in more ways than one, most nearly embodies it, and yet it stops short of lodging in the father and mother a right to that honor and obedience which is due from the offspring. It will be further observed that in the stage of development to which the Mosaic code belongs the distinction between moral and legal duties is not yet drawn.

Conception of right not familiar in early law.

The conception of right as the correlative of duty is an entirely modern acquisition in legal science. Bentham and Austin contributed more than any one else to familiarize the term. Since their day most schemes of law have substituted or have attempted to substitute 'right' in the place of 'duty' as a basis of legal classification.

Modernity of this conception.

Legal conceptions have consequently been largely recast and the attempt has been made to define everything in terms of 'right.' The Roman lawyers could not classify from this

Chapter I

point of view because they had not attained to it. They knew nothing of 'a right' or 'rights,' though, of course, they had an accurate notion of law in general, of particular laws, and of things that are right. The circumstance that the modern continental systems of law have only one word for 'rights' and 'law'[8] serves as a reminder of the fact that Roman law stopped short of the notion embodied in 'right.' In that system the conception of duty or legal obligation apparently occupies the point of central interest. Modern law, on the other hand, rightly or wrongly, prefers to look at legal rules from the standpoint of rights. Possibly political speculation in the eighteenth century had something to do with this transition, for the talk about rights comports well with democratic tendencies.

Right and duty correlative.

It is to be observed that the terms 'right' and 'duty' are substantial correlatives.[9] They are, in fact, only different names for different aspects of that legal obligation (*vinculum juris*), by which men are held in jural relations. The term 'duty' is the name applied to the legal tie when it is viewed from the standpoint of the person who is bound to do; while the term 'right' is used when the same tie is viewed from the standpoint of the person entitled to performance. The use of these terms can be illustrated as follows: The law, we may say, insists that if B harms A by publishing a libel concerning him, he must make reparation. The analytical jurist expresses

[8] The Latin 'jus,' the German 'recht,' the Italian 'diretto,' and the French 'droit' are used in both senses. This is a source of much ambiguity.

[9] But the terms are not precise correlatives of each other. Duty, according to the better view, is the broader expression. No right can exist unless there is a duty to correspond with it. But it is not necessary that all duties should have corresponding rights, nor do they. "For example," says Professor Markby, "there are duties imposed upon us to abstain from cruelty to animals, to serve certain public offices when called upon, and to abstain from certain acts of immorality; but there are no rights corresponding to these duties, at least none belonging to any determinate person. If it is asserted that a right exists at all in the cases I have put, it must be meant that it belongs to society at large; but as used by lawyers, the term 'right' indicates something which is attributed to a determinate person or body of persons." Markby, Elements of Law, § 150. See also 1 Austin, Jurisprudence, Campbell's ed., 353. Compare Robinson American Jurisprudence, 136.

Volume III

Illustration of use of the terms 'right' and 'duty.'

this in two ways. Looking at the situation from one point of view, he says that B owes A the duty to forbear publishing concerning him a defamatory writing; or that B owes A the duty not to harm him by such means. Looking at the situation from the other point of view, the analytical jurist says that A has the right to have his reputation untarnished by the publication of a libel. In either case, if the duty resting on B is breached or the right of A is violated, a cause of action accrues to A and damages may be recovered.

A little consideration of the meaning of the terms 'right' and 'duty' will teach us that they stand for legal abstractions which cannot be of much help to one who engages in research into the principles of legal liability along inductive and historical lines. 'Right' and 'duty' are not in any way explanatory of legal phenomena, but themselves require explanation. The conceptions of right and duty form a part of the general problem to be worked out. No man can safely say upon *a priori* reasons that a particular legal right or duty exists. The existence of a legal right or duty must be proved by reference to cases in which it has been recognized.

Path of the law.

The foregoing observations are enough to indicate the path pursued in the usual course of legal development. Legal evolution begins in the phenomenon of adjudication. It begins with a legal institution, like the court or judge, and the law is a product of the operations of that institution. High abstractions like right and duty are to be reached only by a process of generalization which presupposes a certain degree of maturity in legal thought. It is all very well for the analytical jurist to reverse the process by which the law is evolved and to classify the whole in accordance with his own mature conceptions. Such a method of study has its value, for it enables us to look down upon the whole system from its highest pinnacle, and thus we may grasp it in its entirety. We must not, however, conceive that such analytical process has any connection, other than that of direct reversal, with the actual process of historical growth.

That which to the analytical jurist seems most fundamental

Chapter I

The concrete precedes the abstract.

usually appears late in point of historical development. Nor can it be otherwise. The concrete must precede the abstract. A generalization that will bind many facts together cannot be made until the individual cases have been separately scrutinized. The law, like other sciences, is built up by induction: but this truth does not lie on the surface; for the decision of individual cases always involves a process of deduction, the major premise of the syllogism being an abstract principle of law. The most conspicuous feature in the administration of law, adjudication, being thus a process of deduction, the truth that the doctrine applied is obtained by induction is rendered obscure. But before the syllogism can be framed induction must supply the major premise, and no advance at all can be otherwise made.

Function of form in early law.

What has now been said will prepare the reader to understand the function of form in early law. In the absence of the higher abstractions, it serves as a nucleus around which the growing conceptions of duty and right can crystallize. It also has a value as a mnemonic. Thought is fugitive, but that which acquires an institutional character may endure forever. A principle once imbedded in form will be transmitted as long as it can answer a human need; sometimes indeed it may thus live long after its true mission is fulfilled.

Makes problem of adjudication simple.

The absence of a trained body of professional lawyers perhaps goes far to explain the prominence of form in early procedure. The lay mind which can easily understand a dramatic legal action, or learn to repeat a solemn formula in a legal proceeding, would be altogether incapable of discussing the law of the same case in abstract terms, or even of apprehending it. The formal action assists the mind in knitting together, in an orderly way, mental threads which would become tangled. In this respect it is of no less value to the early judge than to the early litigant.

Formality a necessary phenomenon in early law.

From what has been said above it becomes apparent that form in early remedial law is not a mere accident of legal history. It is a strictly necessary phenomenon. This is certainly true so far as the people of the Aryan race are concerned, and these people, it may be added, are the only ones whose

Volume III

legal institutions have developed fully enough and gradually enough to enable us to study the underlying principles of growth to any advantage.

Exemplified in Roman and Teutonic law.

The Roman law of course supplies the most instructive field of investigation, for that system exhibits an orderly and almost undisturbed development extending over fully a thousand years before it reached maturity. Teutonic institutions also shed much light on the evolution of remedial law, but during its formative period the Teutonic civilization was subjected to the shock of migration and conquest, and later to the powerful disturbing influence of feudalism — circumstances which sensibly disturbed the course of legal growth. It has been shown by Professor Maine that the Hindoo civilization has contributions in the same field which are not to be put aside as valueless. But the institutions of this remote people have been explored by few. Among all these races, Romans, Teutons, Hindoos, every scrap of procurable evidence shows that form occupies a commanding position in early remedial law.

Hindoo civilization.

Development of the Hebraic Code.

Hebrew law furnishes a striking exception to the course of development just indicated. But aside from the fact that this civilization is non-Aryan, the Hebrew state was evolved under very singular conditions. When but few in numbers and practically without social organization, save such as was incident to the patriarchal tribe, the Hebrew people were moved into an extraneous civilization and there reduced to slavery. When the nation was finally led out of bondage it afforded an exceedingly favorable and plastic material for the hand of the social, religious, and legal organizer. Their leader was a statesman equal to the task before him, and in forty years he did for them a work which under other conditions must have extended over centuries. For purposes of casual observation the legal system which he gave his people may be literally said to have been struck off in one generation. In this system of law, at least so far as its secular provisions are concerned, form plays no important part. The reason why it could be dispensed with is apparent. The nation was in a highly teachable state. Law came to it with a religious sanction, and pro-

Rapidity of growth.

vision was made for a class of men whose sole function it was to keep the knowledge of that law fresh in the minds of the people. Consequently, in the Hebrew state legal truth did not have to be slowly worked out through institutional processes extending over ages.

Chapter I

Broadly speaking, the history of the development of legal remedies falls into three stages marked with more or less clearness in different systems of law. First, there is an epoch beginning in prehistoric times when the strictly formal actions appear. The growing body of legal principle during this period is gradually integrated in or around these forms. Then follows a second stage, in which the strictly formal legal action gives way to forms of action based on the judicial formula, or writ. During the period of the supremacy of the writ, legal principle crystallizes around the many nuclei afforded by the different kinds of writs. As the association becomes more and more intimate both legal principle and the forms of action which are its vehicle become fixed and unyielding.

Epochs of legal development:

1. Formal actions.

2. Judicial writs.

This crystallization of the formulary remedies would inevitably put an end to all legal growth were it not that certain other factors are now brought into play for the purpose of extending and supplementing the forms of action. These factors are found in the subtle influence of fiction, in the principle that underlies the action on the case, and in the principles which appear and gain recognition under the name of equitable doctrine. Last but not least of the factors which operate to keep remedial law in some sort of harmony with social requirements is legislation.

Crystallization of the formulary remedies.

When all these elements have done their peculiar work and the interstices of remedial law are approximately filled, it becomes possible to abolish all forms of action whatsoever. Accordingly sooner or later the state intervenes, and in place of the many actions substitutes the single civil action on the facts of the case. This step, the establishment of the formless action, introduces the third and final stage in the evolution of remedial law. In this period legal principle is no longer integrated around the forms of action, for substantive law hav-

3. The action on the facts.

Volume III

Successive stages of development.

ing reached substantial maturity, no longer needs to be discussed under the head of the various actions. It will now be seen that forms of action and the universal formless action stand at the culmination of two successive stages of legal integration. The main facts in the course of this evolution we shall proceed to trace. As we are concerned with a universal principle of jurisprudence we must begin by taking some account of the phenomena revealed by an examination of the Roman law.

CHAPTER II

NATURAL HISTORY OF REMEDIAL LAW (CONTINUED).

Legal Actions (Legis Actiones).

Chapter II

Recovery of the Institutes of Gaius.

THE long-lost Institutes of Gaius, which were recovered by Niebuhr in 1816, brought to light much important matter concerning the earliest stages of Roman procedure, that of the *legis actiones.* The most important of the legal actions was the *actio sacramenti,* about which a few words must be said. It was highly formal and dramatic in its character and was a general remedy available where no other remedy was appointed by law.[1] Professor Maine has strikingly characterized it as the undoubted parent of all the Roman actions and consequently of most of the civil remedies now in use in the world.[2] Though we may not admit that this form of action was in any sense the progenitor of actions in other systems than that of Rome, it was certainly a predecessor and forerunner of all. This circumstance gives to it great interest. The action, as described by Gaius, gives a valuable clue to the manner in which the state at first peacefully intervened as an arbitrator in disputes and finally developed the power to enforce its jurisdiction.

Actio sacramenti.

The proceedings in the *actio sacramenti* began with a feigned dispute or combat over the property involved. The claimant held a wand and, grasping the slave or thing over which he claimed dominion, said: "This [man] I claim as proprietor, by the law of the Quirites by the title I have shown. Lo, thus upon him I lay my lance (*ecce tibi vindictam imposui*);" whereupon he touched the man with his wand. The adversary then said the same words and performed the same acts. The wand was typical of the lance, which itself symbolized the dominion or title acquired by conquest. This formal-

The feigned combat as reflected in *manuum consertio.*

[1] Gaius, Inst., Lib. IV., § 13. [2] Maine, Early Hist. Inst. 252.

Volume III

ity was called the *manuum consertio,* or hand-grapple, and was a sort of judicial reminiscence of an actual combat between the disputants.

In the next stage of the action, after both had claimed dominion, the pretor said: "Both claimants quit your hold," and both quitted hold. This intervention of the officer illustrated the state as interposing its authority for the preservation of peace. This was followed by a verbal altercation between the parties, ending in a friendly wager of fifty or five hundred asses on the validity of their respective titles. This stake was called the *sacramentum,* from which word the action took its name.

Intervention of pretor.

The *sacramentum.*

It is worthy of note that the stake did not go to the winner in the action, but was originally deposited with the pontifex and was consecrated to sacred uses, partly perhaps as an assurance of good faith and partly as compensation to the state for settling the dispute. The pretor then referred the disputed question to a private person (*judex*), who acted as arbitrator and exercised a function somewhat analogous to that of the English jury. The proceeding before the pretor was said to be *in jure;* that before the *judex* was termed a proceeding *in judicio.* The action proper ended with the award of the *judex.*

Subsequent steps in the trial.

The import of the whole proceeding has been expounded by Professor Maine with much insight in language which it would be impertinent to change: "It is impossible, I think, to refuse assent to the suggestion of those who see in it [the *actio sacramenti*] a dramatization of the origin of justice. Two armed men are wrangling about some disputed property. The pretor, *vir pietate gravis,* happens to be going by and interposes to stop the contest. The disputants state their case to him, and agree that he shall arbitrate between them, it being arranged that the loser, besides resigning the subject of the quarrel, shall pay a sum of money to the umpire as a remuneration for his trouble and loss of time. This interpretation would be less plausible than it is, were it not that, by a surprising coincidence, the ceremony described by Gaius as the imperative course of proceeding in a *legis actio* is substantially the same with one of the two subjects which the god Hephæstus is de-

Chapter II

Professor Maine's explanation of the significance and import of the various steps in the *actio sacramenti.*

scribed by Homer as moulding into the first compartment of the shield of Achilles. In the Homeric trial scene, the dispute, as if expressly intended to bring out the characteristics of primitive society, is not about property, but about the composition for a homicide. One person asserts that he has paid it, the other that he has never received it. The point of detail, however, which stamps the picture as the counterpart of the archaic Roman practice is the reward designed for the judges. Two talents of gold lie in the middle, to be given to him who shall explain the grounds of the decision most to the satisfaction of the audience. The magnitude of this sum as compared with the trifling amount of the *sacramentum* seems to me indicative of the difference between fluctuating usage and usage consolidated into law. The scene introduced by the poet as a striking and characteristic, but still only occasional, feature of city life in the heroic age has stiffened, at the opening of the history of civil process, into the regular, ordinary formalities of a lawsuit. It is natural therefore that in the *legis actio* the remuneration of the judge should be reduced to a reasonable sum, and that, instead of being adjudged to one of a number of arbitrators by popular acclamation, it should be paid as a matter of course to the state, which the pretor represents. But that the incidents described so vividly by Homer and by Gaius, with even more than the usual crudity of technical language, have substantially the same meaning, I cannot doubt; and in confirmation of this view, it may be added that many observers of the earliest judicial usages of modern Europe have remarked that the fines inflicted by courts on offenders were originally *sacramenta*. The state did not take from the defendant a composition for any wrong supposed to be done to itself, but claimed a share in the compensation awarded to the plaintiff simply as the fair price of its time and trouble. Mr. Kemble expressly assigns this character to the Anglo-Saxon *bannum* or *fredum*." [3]

[3] Maine, Ancient Law, 363–365.

Concerning the same ancient and curious remedy this brilliant writer, in his Early History of Institutions, says: "Almost every gesture and almost every set of formal words in the *legis actio sacramenti* symbolize something which, in some part of the world or another, in some Aryan society or another, has developed

Volume III

Its symbolic elements antedate historic knowledge.

The *actio sacramenti* thus occupies a unique position in the history of remedial law. It clearly embodies symbolic elements belonging to a period antedating historic knowledge. The value of its dramatic features as a mere means of perpetuating the memory of legal truth cannot escape observation. That it should become a purely formal and highly technical remedy was inevitable. When the law had definitely settled that this action would lie upon one particular state of facts, it was taken to follow as a necessary consequence that other debatable causes of action must come into the same category or the action would not lie. Thus, the Twelve Tables having recognized the action as a remedy for cutting trees, one who would sue for the cutting of vines must call them trees or go without redress.[4]

A formal and technical remedy.

Other legal actions described by Gaius.

In addition to the *sacramentum*, Gaius (after giving an account of the *judicis postulatio*, in a passage which is lost) mentions three other forms of *legis actiones* — the *condictio*, *manus injectio*, and *pignoris capio*. The *condictio* was introduced B. C. 244 by the *lex Silia* and was used for the recovery

into an important institution. The claimant places his hand on the slave or other subject of dispute, and this grasp of the thing claimed, which is reproduced in the corresponding procedure of the ancient Germans, and which from them was continued in various modified forms far down into the middle ages, is an early example of that demand before action, on which all civilized systems of law insist. The wand, which the claimant held in his hand, is stated by Gaius to have represented a spear, and the spear, the emblem of the strong man armed, served as the symbol of property held absolutely and against the world, not only in the Roman but in several other western societies. The proceedings included a series of assertions and reassertions of right by the parties, and this formal dialogue was the parent of the art of pleading.

"The quarrel between plaintiff and defendant, which was a mere pretense among the Romans, long remained a reality in other societies, and, though its theory was altered, it survived in the wager of battle, which as an English institution, was only finally abolished in our fathers' day. The interposition of the pretor and the acceptance of his mediation expanded into the administration of justice in the Roman state, one of the most powerful instrumentalities in the historical transformation of the civilized world." Maine, Early Hist. Inst. 254, 255.

[4] Gaius, Inst., Lib. IV., § 11.

For instances of this literalism in the early Teutonic law, compare the term 'leader of the herd' as applied to the bull; the 'arrow'-finger as applied to the forefinger, and the 'browser upon leeks' as applied to the goat. See Maine, Early Hist. Inst. 256.

of a determinate sum of money. Subsequently it was extended, B. C. 234, so as to be maintainable for any determinate thing. The *manus injectio* (arrest) and the *pignoris capio* (distress) were modes of execution rather than legal actions. The former was originally the Roman mode of execution against the person of the judgment debtor; the latter was at first an extrajudicial species of self-help. It is not important to enter into details as to either. The *condictio* was the only one of the *legis actiones* which really had an important future.

Legal actions become discredited.

The defects of the early forms of action were many. Gaius attributes their falling into desuetude to the excessive subtlety of the ancients. Owing to the excessive technicality of the actions and the literalism with which they were applied the remedies became discredited. The slightest error was fatal One who failed in the smallest item lost his case.[5]

Explanation found in their unbending character.

But there were other reasons. The *legis actiones* belonged to a primitive society and had become fixed before the period of legal growth had well begun. Legal knowledge was monopolized by the higher classes and carefully withheld from the public at large. The old patricians and such jurisconsults as were accessible doubtless served an important but very limited function. In the nature of things the remedies were absolutely fixed and unyielding. No provision was made for representation by an agent or attorney, and the personal appearance of the parties was required.

Legal actions available only among Roman citizens.

In addition to this we note the circumstance that none but Roman citizens could avail themselves of these forms. The Roman state, however, was continually extending its jurisdiction over foreigners, and the constant influx of aliens into the city made it necessary to provide some sort of justice for them. This necessity led to the adoption of an expedient which pointed a way out of the meshes of strict legal formalism.

Formulary process originated by the pretor.

From an early day the jurisdiction over disputes in which aliens were concerned had been vested in the *pretor peregrinus*, and he it was who devised, as a substitute for the *legis actiones*, a formulary process. He followed, it seems, so far as prac-

[5] Gaius, Inst., Lib. IV., § 30.

Volume III

ticable, the analogy of the Roman system and departed from it only when it was necessary or highly convenient to do so. For the judex of the legal system he substituted the *recuperatores*, or arbitrators, and did not undertake to decide issues himself. For the strict formalism of the actions he substituted a formula, or writ. This comprised plain written instructions to the arbitrators that, in the event they found the facts to be so and so, they should order the defendant to do such and such an act. By a simple variation of the language of the formula it became lawful to permit an agent or attorney to exact whatever was due to the plaintiff, and the principal was then no longer required to concern himself about the proceedings.

Nature of the *formula*, or writ.

Such is the generally accepted view of the origin of the formulary process. It grew up side by side with the older system of legal actions and did not at once supplant it. The gap between the alien and the citizen could not be crossed in a day. Consequently we find that the substitution of the formulary process for the old legal actions, which was begun by the *lex Æbutia*,[6] was only completed a hundred and fifty years later by the *leges Juliæ*.[7]

Formulary process finally substituted for legal actions.

Notwithstanding the decay and gradual disintegration of the old forms of action, fragments of the ceremonies and proceedings peculiar to them long remained imbedded in sundry out-of-the-way places, to testify, as fossils, to the existence of the ancient legal formation. The ceremony attending adoption, the form of manumitting slaves, the ceremony of emancipating sons, and the forms of conveying by means of the *in jure cessio*, as well doubtless as process of legal execution, are such fragments of the ancient remedies.[8]

Relics of the ancient procedure.

A comparison of the formulary process with the remedial system which it superseded shows that both systems belong

[6] *Cir.* 170 B. C.

[7] *Cir.* 45 B. C. and 25 B. C.

The exact effect of the *lex Æbutia* and *leges Juliæ* is not clear. Whether, as Gaius says, those statutes abrogated the *legis actiones*, or, as is now generally understood, only introduced the formulary process, leaving the older remedies to their chances of survival in competition with the new, it is clear that by the time Gaius wrote the *legis actiones* were all but obsolete.

[8] Gaius, Inst., Poste's ed., Lib. IV., § 30, and note.

alike to the period of formal actions. The formulary process no less than the old process (*legis actiones*) was quite literally interpreted, and in course of time it also became rigid and had to be laid aside. After a period of five hundred years it was brought into discredit, supposedly by the ingenuity of lawyers. The defect was not, however, due to the subtlety and ingenuity of the learned profession, but to the inherent weakness of the system. The formulary process came into existence in a much more complex society than that which had originated the *legis actiones.* It was therefore much better fitted to the needs of a highly organized civilization.

Formulary process becomes hardened.

It is further to be observed that the writ itself (formula), by which the pretor delegated to the arbitrator the jurisdiction of hearing and deciding a cause, was framed after both parties had been heard (*litis contestatio*), and the chances that the writ should be adapted to the facts of the case were greatly enhanced. By the adoption of the formulary process the pretor was in fact given power to invent new forms of action, a step exactly analogous to that by which, in the English system, the chancery was allowed to issue writs *in consimili casu.* Both in Rome and in England, the new power did not involve any radical departure from the system of forms of action and did not authorize a disregard of all form, as in the later exercise of the extraordinary jurisdiction of the pretor and chancellor in the two systems. Alike under the formulary process and the English writ system, the actions depended on the form of the writ and were capable of being distributed into different classes of actions in exactly the same manner. Doubtless the pretor was freer in framing his formula than the English clerks in chancery afterwards were in framing their writs; or at least the pretor in response to the remedial needs exercised greater freedom.

Comparison of the formulary process with the English writ system.

It is apparent that the establishment of the formulary process represents a great advance in the theory and practice of remedial law. The pretor was able to make effective various rights that had been without remedy, could recognize as valid certain defenses (*exceptiones*), which could not have been set up at law; and in many instances by the subtle use of fiction

Formulary system represents considerable advance in legal theory.

Volume III

was able so to extend the ancient remedies as virtually to create new rights.

Notwithstanding the liberal exercise of the pretor's power of framing appropriate writs, the formulary system in course of time tended to harden. This was inevitable, and, while this process went on, there was a corresponding expansion of the extraordinary jurisdiction of the pretor. About this we need not speak at length, but the way in which this branch of remedial law finally subverted and supplanted the formulary process, as that had previously supplanted the statute process, may be briefly indicated.

Extraordinary jurisdiction of the pretor:

While the formulary system was in full vogue there had been certain classes of cases which the pretor had himself decided without the assistance of a judge or arbitrator. Such proceedings were spoken of as *extra-ordinariæ cognitiones.* This jurisdiction was analogous to the extraordinary jurisdiction of the English chancellor. Among the cases in which the magistrate acted thus summarily were those where it was desirable that parties should be restored *in integrum,* or put, as we would say, *in statu quo,* and those involving *fidei commissa.* Thus by a *restitutio in integrum* the pretor could make void a disadvantageous bargain made by a minor under twenty-five. In cases of fraud, violence, innocent error, excusable absence, and the like, he intervened to avoid transactions between persons of any age.

1. Restoration *in integrum;*

2. Administration of trusts.

In all these cases the pretor heard the parties and made the appropriate decree without referring the matter to a judex. Possibly the ground upon which an appeal was most frequently made to the extraordinary power of the pretor was the enforcement of judgments, especially after the Julian law permitted the debtor to avoid arrest by giving up his goods (*cessio bonorum*). If the debtor could not be found the pretor intervened and ordered a compulsory sale (*missio in bonorum possessionem*).

Procedure before the pretor in such cases.

Under the Empire, the extraordinary process began to make serious inroads on the formulary system. By a constitution of A. D. 294, Diocletian authorized all provincial magistrates to decide causes for themselves instead of commissioning others

The extraordinary process makes inroads on the formulary system.

to hear them.[9] In A. D. 342, Constans extended the system of *extraordinaria judicia* throughout the whole Empire, and thus abolished the formulary system, root and branch. Legal formulas with their syllabic snares and pitfalls were thereby abolished in every action.[1]

Abolition of formulary system.

Thereafter the summary jurisdiction of the pretor was the only jurisdiction exercised. The magistrate and judge are henceforth the same person, and in the Institutes the term 'judex' means a magistrate deciding a cause. The stage of legal development was thus reached in which all actions were to be decided on the facts of the case. The plaintiff who wished to bring a suit furnished to the magistrate a short statement of his case, usually in writing, but not necessarily so. An officer of the court (*viator, executor*) served this on the defendant. Both parties by themselves or attorneys then appeared before the magistrate, who decided the dispute on the facts set forth in the statement of the cause of action and established by the proof.

The single civil action on the facts.

Nothing could be simpler than such a method of procedure, and no step could have been taken more calculated to bring into prominence matter of substantive principle and at the same time to push mere questions of form into the background. The step could not, of course, have been taken at all had not legal science already reached an approximate degree of maturity. Eleven hundred years had elapsed since the founding of Rome — a period sufficiently long to serve as a reminder that Roman law was not, as is sometimes supposed, marked by any notable rapidity of growth. From the union of the Saxon heptarchy under Egbert (A. D. 827) to the passage of the Judicature Act (A. D. 1873) is a somewhat shorter period, during which English remedial law passed through approximately the same stages. To be sure, part of this period belongs to modern times, when legal growth might be expected to be rapid; but the early common law encountered many obstacles against which Roman law did not have to contend.

Simplicity of the procedure.

The step becomes possible by development.

[9] Cod. 3. 3.

[1] "Juris formulæ, aucupatione syllabarum insidiantes cunctorum actibus radicitus amputentur." Cod. 2. 58.

CHAPTER III

NATURAL HISTORY OF REMEDIAL LAW (CONTINUED).

Early History of Remedial Law in England.

Volume III

English common law reproduces the history of Roman remedial law.

WE pass to the history of remedial law in England. We shall be better able to understand it by reason of what has just been learned about the course of development in the earlier and rival system. We shall find the common law substantially reproducing the same phenomena which were there observed. The similarity is in the large features and does not descend into details. There has been no copying and very little of conscious imitation. Indeed it is this very circumstance which renders the analogy highly instructive and gives it more than passing interest.

Three stages: 1. Formalism in actions; 2. Actions based on writ process; 3. Abolition of forms.

At the outset it is to be premised that the several threads are decidedly more tangled than in the history of Roman law. The various elements run into each other and exhibit that vitality which is characteristic of customary law. The successive waves are the same: first, formalism in actions; second, forms of action based on the writ, modified by the use of the action on the case and by the extraordinary jurisdiction of the chancery court. In the third stage, the evolution of remedial law culminates in the final abolition of the forms of action and in the establishment of the action on the facts of the case. The effect of none of these impulses dies away with the approach of its successor. The dramatic formalism of the earliest actions lives on in a world which recognizes only actions based on the royal writ, and the theory of rights and duties worked out under the writ system will survive in the reign of the civil action. Indeed, the time is even now not far distant when one casting his eye over the field of English remedial law could see obtrusive fossils, like the wager of law [1] and the

Complexity of the historical factors.

[1] Abolished in 1833 by Stat. 3 & 4 Wm. IV., c. 42, § 13.

wager of battle,[2] coexisting with the well-known common-law actions in a judicial system wherein equity had already attained a well-defined and perfectly stable position. By reason of the perdurance of the factors which have operated upon it, English remedial law fails to exhibit that clearness of definition which marks the history of Roman actions, and as a consequence it is characterized by much greater complexity.

There was no English Gaius to give us a photograph of the early formalism as it was just ready to pass away. Scholars have therefore been compelled to reconstruct the edifice by putting together details gathered here and there from the remains of many Teutonic tribes. This work of reconstructing the ancient procedural system of our ancestors has not proved attractive, and much has consequently been left undone. We have abundance of fragmentary evidence of a stage of strict formalism corresponding with the Roman *legis actiones*, but it cannot be neatly gathered together under such concise and suggestive names of actions as those used by Gaius.

Early stages not clearly made out.

The remedy by distress is the most striking relic of this period. It corresponds with the Roman *pignoris capio* and has remained until modern times as a unique illustration of the antiquity and permanence of the right of self-help. The obsolete action for the recovery of stolen goods, the *actio furti* of Bracton, also bears a resemblance to some features of the Roman *sacramentum*.

Distress as a relic of early legal formation.

Action of theft.

For instance, when the owner, not being upon fresh trail, found his chattel, he laid his hand thereon and claimed it.[3] This reminds one of the touch with the wand by which the Roman citizen asserted his ownership and title to the contested thing. In both the remedies a great part of the legal procedure was extrajudicial and took place before any appeal had been made to a court. In our early procedure there is abundance of material to prove the truth of Professor Maine's statement that formalism and legal technicality are not, as is often supposed, diseases incident to the decrepit age of legal systems. They

Analogy to the *actio sacramenti*.

[2] Abolished in 1819 by Stat. 59 Geo. III., c. 46.

[3] 2 Poll. & Mait. Hist. Eng. Law, 2d ed., 157.

Volume III

are inevitably associated with the early history of legal institutions.[4]

Manifestation of formalism in early English law.

It is to be noted that in England formalism manifested itself under an aspect somewhat different from that in which formalism was exhibited in early Roman law. There we contemplated a number of formal actions available under varying conditions for the enforcement of specific duties. Here the formalism is found not in the action, but in the mode of proof. Perhaps the distinction is not so much one of substance after all. Early Roman law has its *legis actiones.* Early English law has its formal modes of trial or proof.

Affects the mode of proof.

Fore-oath.

There was indeed from the beginning one piece of formalism in English law which lies at the inception of the action. This is the fore-oath of the complainant or the statement of his complaint witness. The fore-oath, according to our notion, belonged to the preliminary stage of the proceeding and would not now be considered a part of the trial at all. But originally this was not so clear. Much depended on the testimony of the complaint witnesses, or *secta,* and the whole proceeding might be nipped in the bud by the failure of the witnesses to go through the required formula aright. The defendant might, if he chose, stand on the answers of the *secta,* and if the witnesses disagreed among themselves he was discharged. The usual function of the fore-oath or statement of the *secta* was to determine on whom the right of proof, or of fulfilling the formalities prescribed by law, should fall. In the course of time the actual production of the *secta* became obsolete, but the concluding phrase in the old declaration, *inde producit sectam,* long retained its place and was not finally suppressed until the passage of the Common Law Procedure Act in 1852.[5]

The *secta.*

Right of proof.

Aside from this old fore-oath, or, as it later became, the statement of the *secta,* there were in English law after the Norman conquest, four well-known modes of trial. These were[6] trial by the defendant's oath, with or without the supporting oath of his compurgators (wager of law); trial by

[4] Maine, Early Law and Custom, 170.

[5] 15 & 16 Vict., c. 76, § 55.

[6] Thayer, Preliminary Treatise on Evidence, 16-46.

ordeal; trial by witnesses; and trial by battle. The history of these has been accurately traced by Professor Thayer. The learning on the subject does not properly belong to the law of actions in the modern sense, and it would be unprofitable now to go into it with any fulness. It is sufficient to indicate that in this field is to be found the formalism corresponding to that found in the *legis actiones*. The trial by witnesses would seem to have most in common with modern methods of legal procedure, yet its purely formal character is abundantly shown. The object of the production of the witnesses was not so much to instruct the intelligence of the court as it was simply to comply with a legal rule upon which judgment would be given for the party fulfilling the law.[7]

Early modes of trial: 1. Defendant's oath; 2. Ordeal; 3. Witnesses; 4. Battle.

It will be observed that along with the ordeal, compurgation, and trial by battle, another institution, the trial by inquest or jury, was slowly growing up. This mode of trial was, of course, destined to supersede all the others. This institution, however, did not reach anything like maturity until another epoch, and is not to be classed as a formal mode of trial. The jurors in the end come to be judges of questions of fact.

The trial by inquest, or jury.

The ceremonies attendant upon the trial by battle have some features in common with the *sacramentum* which have attracted attention. Thus, in the *sacramentum* the parties grasped hands over the subject claimed. In the trial by battle, the champions, armed with batons, the wand of the *sacramentum*, repaired to the lists or place of combat. Then the champion of the tenant took his adversary by the hand and swore that the lands in question were not the right of the demandant. The other champion, taking the other by the hand, swore that they were. Circumstances like this show that the hand-grasp and the *manuum consertio* are heritages in the Teutonic and Roman law from a common Aryan source. It is not a case where the less mature Teutonic system has borrowed from the Roman; for the trial by battle belongs to a much more archaic seam of legal thought than the *sacramentum*. In the latter action the law has already interposed to prevent the resort to violence. Trial by battle is evidently an instance of reversion

Analogy of the trial by battle to the *actio sacramenti*.

[7] *Ib.*, 17.

Volume III

to primitive self-help, with an appeal to heaven to assist the cause of the just.

The Forms of Action.

Passing now from the subject of the formal actions or formal modes of trial, traces of which may be expected to be found here and there in our law even down to our own day, we come to speak of the development of the forms of action. This branch of the subject is intimately connected with the growth of the writ process.

Did forms of action antedate the Norman writ process?

If our information were sufficiently full it would doubtless be found that there were well-known forms of action before the advent of the royal writ of the Norman kings. Professor Bigelow insists upon this, saying that the common-law forms of action are the direct lineal descendants of the Germanic formulas of pre-Norman and Norman England.[8] This writer truly tells us that in the earlier stages of the history of actions, the plaint, or formula, in which the plaintiff stated his grievance, occupied the position and exercised the same function in fixing the limits and conditions of liability that the writ subsequently did.

Formality of the early count.

Just to what extent the different actions or forms of counts were differentiated from each other before the Conquest is, however, not very clear. They were framed in formal language determined by long usage, and required exactness of statement. In a system where the slightest deviation from the recognized formula was fatal it was highly important that the language should be easily retained. This need led the ancient pleaders to frame the count in poetical form. Rhyme and alliteration thus came to the assistance of the human memory, a fact of much importance when pleadings were verbal. "An ear any way accustomed to Anglo-Saxon poetry will easily detect," says Mr. Thorpe, "the disjointed members of their poetic formulæ and instinctively arrange them in the order in which they ought to stand."[9]

Its poetic form.

There can be no doubt that, in the formalism of the plaint,

[8] Bigelow, History of Procedure, 147.

[9] 1 Anc. Laws & Inst. 178, note.

forms of action existed; but to say that they existed as distinctly as in modern law[1] presupposes a maturity in the remedial law of Anglo-Saxon and early Norman times which it did not possess. It may of course be said, without much violence to facts, that the forms of action in the writ period were descended from those of the previous epoch.[2] But apparently the relation is one of succession rather than of derivation. The count with its peculiar verbal formalism evidently belongs to the stratum of formal actions (*legis actiones*) rather than to that of forms of action (formulary period). This will be the more apparent as we come to study the development of the writ process and learn the secret of the flexibility which it for a time possessed.

Principle of political organization in pre-Norman England.

The principle of political organization in England was wholly changed by the Norman Conquest. The invaders found a community in which, in true accordance with Teutonic genius, organization had normally taken place from below. In studying such a community we must begin with the popular assemblies and work up to the state. This principle of growth had run its logical course in the Anglo-Saxon world with the result that the structure below was democratic, while the political power of the state was embodied in an organ not sufficiently powerful to keep the proper balance between all the elements of national life. The executive was too weak.

Principle of political organization in Norman England.

The Norman rulers were of course compelled to begin political organization at the top of the conquered society. They instituted a government strong enough to hold the unruly in subjection. At the same time this government afforded a nucleus around which the various elements of political life could arrange and perpetuate themselves. The state now had

[1] Bigelow, History of Procedure, 247.

[2] Professor Bigelow says: "There was never any sudden change from the Germanic to the modern formulæ. A gradual progress from the one to the other may be traced from the pre-Norman through the Norman period to the time of Edward I., when the modern forms of action may be considered to have assumed their definite type." Hist. Proc. 247.

Again, says he, "The writ and count are two converging forces, approaching almost to contact by the time of Glanvill, fully meeting only in the next century. But the count is unbroken from Alfred to Victoria." *Ib.*, 148.

a much-needed head — something that the Anglo-Saxon kingship had been unable to supply. This fact soon manifested itself in the judicial system. The Normans found a world in which judicial power was divided — it could hardly be said to be distributed — among a host of local private and feudal jurisdictions. Now the king had a court of his own, a court destined in time to draw to itself jurisdiction over nearly all sorts of contentions.

The king's court gives unity to the judicial structure.

The great instrument for the reconstruction of the judicial administration was the king's writ. The history of the work done by this engine of centralization cannot be told at large in this place. Suffice it here to say that the writ was a missive by which the king, at the instance of a party litigant, directed the parties to appear in the royal court or ordered the sheriff or feudal lord to do right in the county or seignorial court. Sometimes it was used in important cases to institute a commission for the purpose of trying a particular controversy. Soon after the Conquest we find the ruler exercising the unquestioned power of interfering in this way with the administration of justice.[3]

The writ becomes engine of centralization.

Nature and function of the writ.

The writ usually specified with some particularity the subject-matter of the complaint. But its primary function was to sanction the institution of a suit under the royal authority. At first its wording had no particular connection with the form of action, as the plaint, or count, according to Professor Bigelow, embodied whatever formalism the action involved.[4]

It was, however, inevitable that, as the royal interference became more and more regular, the wording of the writ should gradually become of critical importance as a statement of the cause of action and foundation of the suit. The work of penning the writ naturally fell to the royal secretary *(cancellarius)* or his assistants. Copies of the writ were preserved and used as precedents. The various forms were thus capable of comparison and amendment. As business increased they

Importance of the wording of the writ.

The writ issues from the chancery.

[3] See Bigelow, History of Procedure, ch. IV. Professor Maine has an interesting discussion of The King in His Relation to Early Civil Justice, in Early Law and Custom, ch. VI.

[4] History of Procedure, 196, 197.

Chapter III

became more rigid. Writs which once gained a secure place on the record of writs *(registrum brevium)* were thenceforth issued as of course to all applicants upon the payment of the required fee. Others could only be had on application to the chancellor. These were the *brevia magistralia*, or magisterial writs. To frame and issue them required an exercise of magisterial discretion.

Writs of course; magisterial writs.

Having thus become the source of writs, the chancery thereby also became the mother of actions. Subsequently these writs will be found capable of classification, more or less inaccurate, and they will be distributed under several heads. The outcome of it all will be the common-law theory that there are a certain number of definite and mutually exclusive causes of action expressed in appropriate forms. To test the question of legal liability under this theory it is only necessary to ascertain whether the facts of a particular case are such as to bring it under one of the recognized forms. Thus once again are we confronted with the spectacle of substantive principle becoming involved in the meshes of form.

The common-law theory of actions. No right of action unless there is a recognized form by which it may be enforced.

The similarity between the transition to the writ process in England and the advent of the formulary system at Rome will not escape notice. In both cases the change is from one system of formalism to another, but the latter is of a newer and higher type. The Roman *legis actiones* gave way to what was at first the flexible formula of the pretor. In England "the old oral and traditional formalism is in part supplanted and in part reinforced by a written and authoritative formalism." [5]

Analogy to Roman legal history.

In both cases the merit of the new plan was the same. The formulary system and the writ process came into existence at a time when the old forms had become manifestly inadequate as an expression of the legal consciousness of the nation. Now, if it was not possible to contrive a new system that would respond to all future needs, it was at least possible to contrive one that would be in harmony with existing notions of law and right. This is what was done. Neither the pretor nor the chancellor would have framed a writ plainly contrary to what

Adjustment to existing notions of law and justice.

[5] 2 Poll. & Mait. Hist. Eng. Law, 2d ed., 558.

Volume III

seemed to them to be lawful and just; but, in determining what was law and justice, they were at least free from the shackles of the old forms. All of the early writs were thus in a sense framed on the facts of the special case. Neither the chancery which issued the writs nor the courts which entertained suits upon them could at first have imagined that they were originating forms of action which would serve to mark the boundaries of legal liability. Yet this is what they were doing.

Relation between the 'jus' and the 'remedium.'

In studying the growth of the English actions it is important to ascertain just how soon the list of known writs became commensurate with the conceptions which lawyers and judges had of legal right. When could one say that remedies had been approved and were in actual existence sufficient to enforce any known duty? When did that state of theoretical equilibrium between right and remedy arrive which is embodied in the maxim *ubi jus ibi remedium?* The answer to this can be given with reasonable certainty.

Glanvill's treatise on writs.

When Glanvill wrote there was already a collection of writs. His book in fact is written about them. Some of them already had a past, dating from the time when the Norman kings first began to encroach upon the communal and feudal courts;[6] but before Glanvill wrote (*temp.* Henry II), there could hardly be said to be any register, and hence there was no well-defined body of writs. There is a coincidence between the order in which Glanvill treats the writs and the order in which they are subsequently found on the Register, but this circumstance is of doubtful import. The writer may have followed the order of some existing collection or the Register may have been put together on his plan as a matter of convenience.

The early Register.

The first Register known to Professor Maitland comes from 1227. It was promulgated by the king to be used in Ireland. There is another of almost equal antiquity to which the same writer directs attention.[7] Together these Registers no doubt reflect the existing state of royal justice with some fidelity.

[6] See Bigelow, Placita Anglo-Norm., Introduction, p. xxvi; Register of Original Writs, by F. W. Maitland, 3 Harv. L. Rev. 107.

[7] The contents of both Registers are fully set out by Professor Maitland in Register of Original Writs, 3 Harv. L. Rev. 110–115.

Chapter III

They show a distinct advance over the state of law in Glanvill's day. Each contains about sixty writs, framed, as we would now say, *in case*, for the enforcement of as many different rights of action. The recital of the missive accompanying the Irish Register, to the effect that the form of these writs of course *(formam brevium de cursu)* is to be followed in the cases to which they are applicable, gives a hint of that crystallization of principle around form which was to take place within the next fifty years.

The tale of writs.

Twenty-five years later the Register contains more than twice as many writs as are found in the copy dispatched to Ireland.[8] No one as yet supposed that such a Register embodied an exhaustive scheme of justice. Many writs were there conveniently docketed to be subsequently used in similar cases. New writs could be framed for the enforcement of rights not yet catalogued, but after a form was once fixed it was hard to change it.

State of the Register at middle of thirteenth century.

Some of the most important writs known to the common law date from this period. For instance, there is no case of trespass prior to the middle of the thirteenth century. In the plea rolls of 1252–53 actions of trespass are abundant.[9] The chancery was not unwilling to exercise the inherent prerogative of the king in framing new writs in appropriate cases, and even the judges in the king's courts, who were evidently in touch with the chancery, were able to influence the development of remedial law by suggesting, from time to time, the issuance of new writs.

Issuance of new writs.

The last years of the reign of Henry III have been called the golden age of forms. The number of forms then actually in use was at its maximum. "Very few of the writs that had as yet been invented had become obsolete, and, on the other hand, the common law's power of producing new forms was almost exhausted."[1] The occasions which called for new writs from the chancery were becoming less and less frequent. Messrs. Pollock and Maitland, after analyzing the rolls of

Golden age of forms.

[8] Maitland, Register of Original Writs, 3 Harv. L. Rev. 169, 175.
[9] Ames, History of Trover, 11 Harv. L. Rev. 282.
[1] 2 Poll. & Mait. Hist. Eng. Law, 2d ed., 564.

Volume III

State of remedial law at time of accession of Edw. I.

actions in the Common Bench tried in Northumberland before the justices in eyre during the years 1256, 1269, 1271, 1279, say that there were then thirty or forty forms of action between which large differences existed, and that the catalogue might easily be raised to the hundreds if smaller differences are regarded.[2]

Bracton's scheme of remedial justice.

Bracton, writing near the middle of the thirteenth century, clearly contemplated a scheme of royal remedial justice that was fully commensurate with existing conceptions of legal rights and duties. "There are," says he, "certain writs framed upon particular cases which are granted as of course and which have been approved by the common council of the whole realm; and these can by no means be changed without their consent and will [i. e., of the council]. . . . There are certain other [writs] called *magistralia*. These are often varied according to the varying circumstances of the cases disclosed in the pleas of the plaintiff and defendant." [3]

The learned writer closes the passage from which we have quoted with the statement that there are writs to correspond with all rights or sorts of action. *"Tot erunt formulæ bre-*

[2] 2 Poll. & Mait. Hist. Eng. Law, 2d ed., 565.

[3] The entire passage of Bracton on the matter of the form and function of the writ is instructive. The judicial writs to which he refers are not original writs. These are issued by the courts from time to time as the state of the suit requires. They are a mesne process. In the Register the original and judicial writs are of course put in different divisions. The following are the words of the learned writer:

"Breve quidem cum sit formatum ad similitudinem regulæ juris, quia breviter et paucis verbis intentionem proferentis exponit et explanat, sicut regula juris, rem quae est breviter enarrat. Non tamen ita breve esse debeat quin rationem et vim intentionis contineat. Et sunt quaedam brevia formata super certis casibus, de cursu et de communi consilio totius regni concessa et approbata, quae quidem nullatenus mutari poterint absque consensu et voluntate eorum. Sunt etiam brevia ex eis sequentia quae dicuntur judicialia, et saepius variuntur secundum varietatem placitorum proponentis et respondentis, petentis, et excipientis, secundum varietatem responsionum. Sunt etiam quaedam quae dicuntur magistralia et saepius variuntur secundum varietatem casuum factorum et querelarum; et quaedam sunt personalia quaedam realia quaedam mixta secundum quod sunt actiones diversae et variae, quia tot erunt formulae brevium quot sunt genera actionum, quia non potest quis sine brevi agere, cum non teneatur alius sine brevi respondere nisi gratis voluerit, et ex hoc ei non injuriatur, cum scienti et volenti not fit injuria." Bracton 413*b*.

vium quot sunt genera actionum." To his mind *remedium* was in exact equilibrium with *jus.* So far as we can judge, this view was in a measure fully justified. As yet form had only served as a useful aid in attaining conciseness in the statement of grounds of action. It was a servant and had not yet become a master.

Chapter III

'Where there is a right there is a remedy.'

The stage now reached was certainly, from the theoretical standpoint, a notably mature one. Whatever formality existed in remedial law was capable of being supplemented by an appeal to the inherent prerogative of the king as the ultimate fountain of justice. The fatal weakness of the system is to be found in the manner in which the power thus invoked was applied.

A precocious stage.

It will be observed that the chancery office, from which the writs issued, was wholly separate from the court in which the suit was afterwards tried. It was completely out of touch with the parties to the litigation. The chancellor issued the writ without ever having heard from the opposite party, a practice in which the English law differed entirely from the Roman system. The pretor had heard both parties before the formula by which the controversy was to be solved was framed. Again, it was customary to charge fees, which were uncertain in amount, for the issuance of special writs.

Defect of the system.

The operation of this system was fraught with possibilities of abuse. A corrupt chancellor, or an unscrupulous king acting through a weak chancellor, could easily become a menace to the liberties of the subject. This became fully apparent in the Barons' War. Henry III had attempted to govern either without a chancellor or with a merely nominal one. Beginning in 1244 we hear mutterings of discontent against novel writs.[4] The spirit of the Council of Merton (1237), which had resolved with one voice that it would not change the hitherto approved and accepted laws of England, was coming to be applied to other questions than rules of descent. It was

Possibility of abuse under corrupt chancellor or unscrupulous king.

Complaint against issuance of novel writs.

[4] Thus at a council of the magnates at London in 1244, one of the grievances dwelt upon was the frequent issuance of writs *per defectum cancellarii contra justitiam.* Stubbs, Sel. Charters, 8th ed., 328; Chron. Matt. Paris 639.

Volume III

becoming apparent that the power of issuing other writs than those 'of course' operated radically to affect rights and might even change the law. The wording of the writ in many cases effectually predestinated the result of the litigation.

Accordingly when, as a result of the Barons' War, the royal power was put into commission by the Provisions of Oxford (1258), it was provided that the chancellor should not issue writs other than those 'of course' without the approval of the executive council as well as of the king.[5] This may be accepted as a sort of legislative declaration that the scheme of remedies was getting to be pretty fully worked out, or at least that the power of issuing new ones should be exercised only in very exceptional cases and with the sanction of the representatives of the nation. Bracton's pen was therefore hardly dry before we see events take a turn such as would soon upset that equilibrium between right and remedy which appeared to him necessary and permanent. The tendency of the writ system towards stability was thus hastened. It culminated, we may perhaps say, in the reign of Edward I. Political events were rapidly lodging the law-making power in the hands of Parliament.

Chancery deprived of power to issue new writs without approval of council.

Scheme of writs becomes settled.

The Provisions of Oxford were of course abrogated upon the re-establishment of the kingly power and the failure of the revolution. The trend of events, however, both in political and judicial affairs, was such as to make permanent the inhibition placed by those Provisions on the power of the chancery to issue new writs. In 1285 this was so fully settled that Parliament saw fit to relax the rigidity of the writ system by declaring that thereafter when no writ was found for a case similar in its facts to one for which a writ already existed, the clerks should frame a writ *in consimili casu* with the existing writ; or, if the clerks could not agree upon a form, the matter should be referred to the next Parliament.[6]

Parliament authorizes issuance of writs in 'case.'

The passage of this statute sheds a double light upon the state of remedial law at that time. It shows that the formulary system had already so hardened as to abridge and sub-

[5] Provisions of Oxford, Stubbs Sel. Char. 389.
[6] Stat. West. II., c. 24.

stantially take away the power of framing new writs altogether. The statute therefore marks an extension of remedial law and becomes a new point of departure in the history of the common-law actions. At the same time the power of framing writs sanctioned by it falls far short of that which had been exercised by the chancery from its establishment far down into the reign of Henry III. Formerly the chancery could issue writs in entirely new cases. Henceforth it can issue writs only in cases that are clearly within the principle of existing writs, and if there is any doubt about it, the matter must go to Parliament.

Import of this statute.

It has sometimes been said that the courts were not liberal in their interpretation of this statute. Doubtless it was not meant that they should be. In the time of Edward I men thought that existing remedies were quite adequate, and at that time this view was not very far wrong. It is subsequent social growth which makes this theory no longer tenable and gives to the provision in question a significance which it otherwise could not have possessed. In the fourteenth century it began to be seen that this enactment furnished remedial law almost the only means of escaping from a truly sorry plight.

Importance of the statute largely due to subsequent development.

CHAPTER IV

NATURAL HISTORY OF REMEDIAL LAW (CONTINUED).

Classification of Actions in the Common-law System.

Volume III

HAVING reached the culmination of the formative period in the history of the common-law actions, it is proper that we should now say something about their classification. This is the more necessary since we shall not here have much to say about the particular actions. The first remark we make is that there is probably no other branch of the law in which abstract theory has had less influence on growth. The manner in which the actions originated shows that practical convenience and not theory determined their birth, their growth, and in many cases their death. It is, however, true that any system of remedial law, in what manner soever produced, may be profitably viewed from the standpoint of abstract jurisprudence, and this is especially necessary when we come to study it with the purpose of finding out the degree of maturity reached at a particular epoch. If we are to learn much about the actions they must be classified.

Classification of actions determined by considerations of practical convenience.

The simplest and most formal way of doing this, the way in which the older masters of the common law like Fitzherbert and Coke would have gone about it, would be to make an exhaustive analysis of the writs found on the Register, and distribute the actions according to the verbal resemblances found in them.

Two types: 1. The *præcipe;* 2. The *si te fecerit.*

There were two types of writs containing well-marked differences. One was the *præcipe;* the other, the *si te fecerit securum.*[1] Of the *præcipe* there were three forms: *præcipe quod reddat, præcipe quod permittat,* and *præcipe quod faciat.* The sheriff was ordered by these words of the writ to bid the

[1] 3 Co. Litt., Thomas's ed. (350)*, note.

Chapter IV

The *præcipe* oldest type.

defendant to render, permit, or do something. The return of the sheriff showed whether the defendant complied; if he did not, the action proceeded in the king's court. The oldest of the writs belong to this class. The writ of right and other proprietary real actions, as well as debt, detinue, account, and covenant, were *præcipes*.

The *si te fecerit* belongs to maturer stage.

The writs beginning *si te fecerit securum* presupposed the existence of a complete cause of action and ordered the sheriff to command the defendant to appear and answer in the king's court, if proper security should be given by the prosecution. The four petty assizes, *novel disseisin, morte d'ancestor, assize utrum*, and *darrein presentment*, as well as the writ of trespass and the different forms of case, were of this type. The *si te fecerit securum* involved a more immediate and direct application of the royal power, and evidently belonged to a maturer stage than the *præcipe*. Nothing that is helpful can now be made out of this formal difference in the writs, but when English law was merely a commentary on writs the distinction was not without importance.

The common-law scheme a natural growth.

After canvassing the field of remedial law in Edward I's day Professor Maitland has put together a string of questions which would be helpful in determining the genera and species of the many actions. The results would hardly compensate at this late day for the labor expended in putting each particular action through such an examination. The common-law scheme of actions was not framed; it grew. The secret of all its defects, its irregularities, its incompleteness is found in this. Yet in time even the slow and unaided process of natural growth fills in nearly all the interstices and gives us a rounded whole such as no legislator or theorist with all imaginable human wisdom and foresight could possibly have supplied beforehand.

Bracton's division.

Let us now turn to the other scheme of classification which has commended itself to English lawyers from the time of Bracton. All actions, says he, are either *in rem, in personam*, or mixed.[2] Fleta and subsequent writers converted the

[2] "Sciendum quod omnium actionum sive placitorum (ut inde utatur

Volume III

phrases *in rem* and *in personam* into the terms *real* and *personal.*[3]

Genesis of this classification.

For the genesis of this classification of actions we must go back much further than to the time of Bracton. As has already been indicated, the Roman classification of actions turned upon the conception of legal obligation or duty. The action *in personam* lay against a particular person to enforce a personal obligation arising out of contract or tort; or, as it may be otherwise expressed, to enforce the plaintiff's right to some specific act or forbearance on the part of the defendant.

Actio in personam.

The expression *in personam* is said to be abridged from *in personam certam sive determinatam.* At any rate the obligation in cases of actions *in personam* exists against a definite person, a person ascertained either by the fact that he has made a contract or has done an act which constitutes a delict or tort. The expression *in rem,* which is used in connection with the other grand division of Roman actions, is overlaid with perplexities. Primarily the action *in rem* lies to enforce such rights as are available not against a particular individual, but against the whole world. But it has another meaning — that of an action directed against the thing itself. The action *in rem* is therefore either an impersonal action or an action against a thing. This latter sense is, however, a derived one and may be included under the other. In the *actio in rem* the plaintiff claimed that, as against all the world, a *res,* corporeal or incorporeal, was his. This action was used to vindicate a *jus in rem.* The personal action, on the other hand, asserted a *jus in personam.* Status, property or ownership, and servitudes are illustrations of *jura in rem.*[4] It will be seen that the notion lying at the basis of the Roman action *in rem* was an abstract one and not very clearly defined. The most conspicuous element in it is the conception of the *res,* corporeal or

Actio in rem.

aequivoce) haec est prima divisio, quod quaedam sunt in rem quaedam in personam et quaedam mixtae." Bracton 101*b*.

[3] "Placitorum aliud personale, aliud reale, aliud mixtum." Fleta, I., c. 1. The same distinction is made in Britton and the Mirrour, and is followed by Littleton, by Coke, and by Blackstone. Co. Litt. 284*b*; 3 Bl. Com. 117.

[4] For a discussion of the distinction between *in rem* and *in personam*, see 1 Austin, Jurisprudence, Campbell's ed., 374 *et seq.*

Chapter IV

incorporeal, which was the subject-matter of the right to be vindicated.

Now, Bracton's chapter on actions, as Professor Maitland fully shows,[5] is largely based on the Roman Institutes as the learning of that book filters through the mind of the mediæval commentator Azo. Bracton seems to have made but poor use of his material and was unable to make the English actions fit into the Roman classification. Azo gives a number of divisions. Of these apparently the most important — that which divides all actions into actions *in rem*, actions *in personam*, and mixed actions — Bracton adopts. The actions *in personam* do not give him a great deal of trouble, though even here the English writer does not fail to fall into some errors.[6] No one could fail to grasp the conspicuous truth that the personal actions lie to enforce obligations arising against a definite person out of a contract or tort. This feature Bracton perceives, and he accordingly brings the idea out clearly.[7]

Bracton adopts Roman division.

Turning to the actions *in rem*, Bracton brings with him from his excursion into Roman law only the expression itself, *actio in rem*, and one or two ideas which lie plainly on the surface. Thus he perceives that the action is not based upon obligation in the Roman sense, and that the plaintiff demands a certain thing, not the value or equivalent of it. But Bracton goes further than this, and in a bold though apparently casual utterance restricts the action *in rem* in English law to the recovery of immovables (real property) and interests incident

Difficulty of adjustment.

Bracton restricts action *in rem* to recovery of immovables.

[5] Bracton and Azo 134 *et seq.*

[6] *Ib.*, 169, note.

[7] "Personales vero actiones sunt quae competunt contra aliquem ex contractu, vel quasi, ex maleficio, vel quasi, cum quis teneatur ad aliquid dandum vel faciendum, et locum habent adversus eum qui contraxit, et heredem suum, nisi sint poenales: et dicuntur actiones nativae, eo quod nascuntur ex contractibus. Et omnes fere personales actiones sunt ex contractu, sicut mutui, commodati, depositi, mandati, ex empto vendito, locato et conducto. Personales vero actiones quae nascuntur ex maleficio, aliae persequuntur poenam tantum, ut actio furti, aliae vero persequuntur ipsam rem et poenam, sicut actio vi bonorum raptorum, et ita sunt duplices, eo quod sunt rei persecutoriae et poenae, et ita tam in rem quam in personam. Et, cum sint uno modo rei persecutoriae, competunt contra omnes qui possunt restituere, sive ille possideat qui spoliavit, sive alius. Secundum vero quod fuerint poenales, non persequuntur nisi tantum actores delicti." Bracton 102, Bracton and Azo, 168, 169.

Volume III

thereto, such as the right of advowson and right of common.[8]

This departure of Bracton from Roman ideas was perhaps due to a mere caprice of independence rather than to any necessary distinction between the Roman and English law of actions. This whim of Bracton, if it be a mere whim, has had far-reaching effects, and the marks of it are found to-day in that distinction between real and personal property which is peculiar to English law. What reason does he give for the proposition that, in English law, an action for the recovery of a specific chattel cannot be an action *in rem?* "If," says he, "the thing sought to be recovered is a movable, such as a lion, ox, ass, garment, or other thing determinable by weight or measure, it would seem at first sight that the action would be *in rem* rather than *in personam*, because a specific thing is sought and because the possessor is in duty bound to restore the thing sued for. But on the contrary, the action will be *in personam* only because he from whom the recovery is sought is not held exactly to the restoration of the thing, but, in the alternative, either to the return of the thing or its value; and by paying the value only, he will be discharged whether the thing is produced or not."[9]

Action for recovery of specific chattel not an action *in rem* according to Bracton.

Bracton here clearly missed the true principle of classifica-

[8] "Actiones vero in rem sunt quae dantur contra possidentem, qui nomine proprio possideat ex quacumque causa, et non alieno, quia habet rem vel possidet quam restituere potest, vel dominum nominare. Ut si quis petat ab alio rem certam, fundum aliquem vel terram, et se contendat inde dominum, et persequatur rem illam, et non eius pretium, nec eius aestimationem, nec tantundem quod sit eiusdem generis, et sit res corporalis immobilis quae petitur ex quacumque causa versus aliquem, qui nullo iure personali obligatus est. Et per hoc quod petens, rem petitam suam esse intendens, actionem instituerit versus tenentem, et tenens negaverit, in rem erit actio sive placitum, et hoc sive nomine proprio petat, sive ratione rei, quam ipse possidet, sicut viri religiosi vel rectores nomine ecclesiarum suarum, vel alii nomine alicuius universitatis sicut in rem communem: et hoc etiam sive principaliter petat ipsam rem, sive ius quod rei adhaereat sive tenemento, et quod a tenemento separari non possit. Ut si quis petat advocationem alicuius ecclesiae, vel communam pasturae, vel quod liceat ei ire agere, vel quid tale quod consistat in iure, in rem erit placitum sive actio; quia huiusmodi iura omnia sunt res incorporales et quasi possidentur et insunt corporibus, et adquiri non possunt nec retineri sine corporibus quibus insunt, nec aliquando sine corporibus ad quae pertineant." Bracton 102, 102*b*.

[9] Bracton 102*b*, § 4.

tion, for instead of determining the nature of the action by the duty which it is brought to enforce, he finds the criterion in the nature of the redress which was to be or might be obtained. It would seem that the proposition to which he was here committing English law was a principle erroneously deduced from the fact that in writs of debt in the *detinet*, the plaintiff was required to state the value of the chattel sued for.[1] To state the value was certainly highly proper, and indeed necessary; for it might transpire that the chattel was lost or destroyed, or animal dead, in which case it could not be restored. Movables are necessarily destructible, but this furnishes no reason why the action for their recovery should not be classed as an action *in rem*. In Roman law the circumstance that the plaintiff might be compelled, as a last resort, to accept a money compensation instead of the chattel sued for did not result in changing the action from one category to another. It still remained an action *in rem* because of the nature of the fundamental duty. If the defendant failed to restore the thing, he was condemned to pay its value as damages.[2] If Bracton had been content faithfully to copy from the Roman sources he could have said with perfect consistency that detinue is an action *in rem* and that it is based directly on ownership. Instead of this, our law of ownership in chattels blunders around for two or three centuries, and the right clue to the subject has hardly yet been discovered.

Nature of error thus made.

Cause of the mistake.

From the viewpoint which classifies according to the nature of the duties to be enforced, a triple division of civil actions is the only proper one — actions based on ownership, actions *ex contractu*, and actions *ex delicto*. The actions based on ownership might well be called proprietary actions, or, to use a Roman term, recuperatory actions. There is no reason in na-

Division based on ownership and obligation.

1 "Si quis rem mobilem vindicaverit ex quacunque causa ablatam vel commodatam, debet in actione sua definire pretium, et sic actionem proponere: Ego talis peto quod talis restituat mihi talem rem tanti pretii: vel, Conqueror quod talis iniuste mihi detinet vel robbavit talem rem tanti pretii. Alioquin non valebit rei mobilis vindicatio, pretio non apposito." Bracton 102*b*, Bracton and Azo 172.

2 Sandars, Institutes, 9th ed., 427.

Volume III

English law recognizes no proprietary writ for chattels.

ture or law why the proprietary actions should be restricted to actions for the recovery of immovable property, but such was the result of Bracton's theory. The English law consequently acknowledged no purely proprietary writ for chattels; and detinue, which ought by all means to have been placed in this lost category, has since wandered around among the common-law actions, unable to find its proper place in the procedural system.

Difficulty in placing detinue.

Bracton and those who came after him would have it that the only actions *in rem* were those brought to vindicate a right to immovables. The action *in rem*, being thus permanently associated with real property, came to be spoken of as a real action.

The term 'personal' was of course likewise substituted for *in personam*, and as detinue had been improperly forced into the category of personal actions, the meaning of the term personal as applied to actions has been much confused.

Origin of distinction between real and personal actions.

It has, in fact, included three distinct sorts of actions, i. e., actions *ex contractu*, actions *ex delicto*, and the proprietary action for the recovery of chattels. The original meaning of personal action, as the equivalent of *actio in personam*, was thus obscured, and by a curious perversion the action was finally supposed to be called personal because of the fact that chattels might be recovered by the use of such remedy. Now just as the term 'realty' had come to be used for the immovable property recovered in real actions, so 'personalty' came to be used for the chattels or damages recovered in the personal action.[3] The distinction between real and personal property which runs all through our law is thus in a measure an accidental development in the evolution of the common-law actions.

The differences of most practical importance between the real and personal actions are found in the process incident to the prosecution of them.

Process in real actions.

In the real actions the process was direct, and the tenements could, under varying conditions, be seized by the sheriff into the king's hand and turned over to the demandant. In personal actions the mesne, as distinguished

[3] Mr. T. C. Williams has collated several passages from Littleton and Coke, showing that this transition was complete at the end of the sixteenth century. 4 L. Quar. Rev. 405-407.

Chapter IV

Process in personal actions.

from the final, process was directed against the defendant personally in order to compel him to put in an appearance. His goods could be distrained or he could be taken on a capias. In trespass *vi et armis* this right of arrest existed by common law; in debt, detinue, account, and trespass on the case it had been given by statute. It was well into the nineteenth century before a plaintiff in a personal action could obtain a final judgment against a defendant who failed to appear.[4]

Mixed actions.

As the Roman law had its mixed actions, so the English lawyers were compelled to classify as mixed certain actions which partook of the nature of both. The necessity for recognizing such a class shows that the original classification was not satisfactory. "'Mixed' is a blessed word," say the historians of our early law. "The impatient student who looks down upon mediæval law from the sublime heights of general jurisprudence will say that most of our English actions are mixed, and many of them very mixed."[5]

Blackstone's summary.

Perhaps it will lead to a better understanding of the classification approved by Bracton to quote from the familiar pages of his modern successor. "With us in England," says Blackstone, "the several suits, or remedial instruments of justice, are from the subject of them distinguished into three kinds: actions personal, real, and mixed. Personal actions are such whereby a man claims a debt or personal duty, or damages in lieu thereof; and likewise whereby a man claims a satisfaction in damages for some injury done to his person or property. The former are said to be founded on contracts, the latter upon torts or wrongs. . . . Of the former nature are all actions upon debt or promises; of the latter, all actions for trespasses, nuisances, assaults, defamatory words, and the like.

"Real actions, . . . which concern real property only, are such whereby the plaintiff, here called the demandant, claims title to have any lands or tenements, rents, commons, or other hereditaments, in fee simple, fee tail, or for term of life. By these actions formerly all disputes concerning real estates were decided; but they are now pretty generally laid aside in

[4] Stat. 2 Will. IV., c. 39, § 16.

[5] 2 Poll. & Mait. Hist. Eng. Law, 2d ed., 572.

Volume III

practice, upon account of the great nicety required in their management and the inconvenient length of their process; a much more expeditious method of trying titles being since introduced by other actions, personal and mixed.

"Mixed actions are suits partaking of the nature of the other two, wherein some real property is demanded and also personal damages for a wrong sustained. As, for instance, an action of waste, which is brought by him who hath the inheritance, in remainder or reversion, against the tenant for life, who hath committed waste therein, to recover not only the land wasted, which would make it merely a real action, but also treble damages in pursuance of the Statute of Gloucester, which is a personal recompense; and so both being joined together, denominate it a mixed action." [6]

Difficulty of placing various actions in this classification.

To go through the catalogue of actions in order to place them properly in this classification would be unprofitable and the result unsatisfactory. We have a hint of the difficulties that would be encountered in such an undertaking when we learn that Bracton could hardly determine in his own mind whether the assizes of *novel disseisin* and *morte d'ancestor* were actions *in rem* or *in personam*.[7] We must, however, notice a few of the most important of the actions and observe where they belong.

The writ of right.

At the top of the scale of actions available for the recovery of lands and interests therein was the writ of right, the most real of the real actions, the great and final remedy for the recovery of proprietary interests in land. Closely associated with this remedy in procedure were certain other writs said to be in the nature of the writ of right. Such were the writ of right of dower, the formedon in descender and reverter, and the writ of right *de rationabili parte*.[8]

Actions in nature of writ of right.

Possessory real actions:

Below the writ of right were the possessory real actions known as the assizes and the writ of entry. In the assize of *novel disseisin* the plaintiff recovered both seisin and dam-

[6] 3 Bl. Com. 117, 118.
[7] See 2 Poll. & Mait. Hist. Eng. Law, 2d ed., 570.
[8] 3 Bl. Com. 194.

Chapter IV

ages, this being, says Blackstone, the only instance where damages were recoverable in a possessory action at common law.[0]

1. Assize.

The assizes were in the nature of statutory remedies, and available only under circumstances defined for each. The writ of entry, on the other hand, was the universal remedy for the recovery of possession wrongfully withheld from the owner. Its forms were many, "being plainly and clearly chalked out in that most ancient and highly venerable collection of legal forms, the *Registrum Brevium*."[1] Some form of this writ was available by a party ousted of his tenements by abatement, intrusion, or disseisin, and, in general, for deforcements. But the widow's writs for obtaining her dower had special names: writ of dower and writ of dower *unde nihil habet*. If too much were assigned for dower her holdings could be cut down by means of a writ for the admeasurement of dower, sued out at the instance of the heir or, his guardian. The writs of dower were analogous to the writ of right.

2. Writ of entry.

Writ of dower.

For disturbance or usurpation of the right of presentation to a benefice there was a scheme of real actions beginning with the writ of right of advowson and ending in the *quare impedit*, which latter remedy, in Blackstone's day, had supplanted the others and then remained almost the sole real action in common use. For disturbance in franchises, commons, ways, and tenures, the usual remedy was by an action on the case; but a real action for the admeasurement of common and an action upon a writ *quod permittat* were respectively available for surcharging and disturbing the common.

Writ of right of advowson. *Quare impedit.*

Admeasurement of common. *Quod permittat.*

The writs *de ejectione firmæ* and *quare ejecit infra terminum* were maintainable at the suit of a tenant for years who was dispossessed of his interest in the term. The former lay against the lessor, reversioner, remainderman, or any stranger who was himself the wrongdoer; the other against a person claiming under a wrongdoer. From the *quare ejecit* came the modern action of ejectment. These actions are, like waste, mixed, inasmuch as the plaintiff recovers the unexpired term and damages for the injury. Originally the recovery of dam ages was the chief object in ejectment, but as the remedy came

Writ of *ejectione firmæ.*

Ejectment.

[0] 3 Bl. Com. 187.

[1] 3 Bl. Com. 183.

Volume III

to be more and more real and was principally used to try questions of title, this object was lost sight of. The damages recoverable in the action of ejectment thus became nominal, and the plaintiff was allowed to sue for his actual damages in an independent action for mesne profits.

The personal actions.

Of personal common-law actions the most important are account, covenant, debt, detinue, assumpsit, trespass, case, trover, and replevin. These, as we have seen, are divided into two classes — actions *ex contractu* and actions *ex delicto;* a classification logical enough in itself, but made somewhat unsatisfactory by the supposed necessity of forcing the action of detinue into one or the other divisions.

Real actions become obsolete.

One who compares the treatise of Bracton with such a modern work as Chitty on Pleading will be struck with the fact that the comparative importance of the real and personal actions has been reversed in the period spanning the six intervening centuries. Bracton wrote a big book, and a large part of the really English law which he undertook to expound is found in connection with the subject of real actions. Of the personal actions he has little or nothing to say. In Blackstone's treatise only the personal actions are thought deserving of attention. The old real actions were practically obsolete when Chitty wrote (1808), and within the succeeding generation legislation abolished nearly every remaining vestige of them.[2] The procedure incident to their prosecution was too cumbersome.

Characteristic mode of development of common-law actions.

It was a toilsome and tedious process, that by which English remedial law was wrought out. Remedies conceived and partially developed in one field had to be warped and bent to strange uses. Ejectment, assumpsit, trover, all illustrate this. Wondrous are the mazes encountered even in a casual glance at the history of the various actions. That there has never been a logical classification in this field is not surprising. Before the time of Blackstone no man could have been in a

[2] 3 & 4 Will. IV., c. 27, § 36. In this statute a reservation was made in favor of the various writs for the establishment of dower rights, but these too were practically obsolete, and the Judicature Acts have of course done away with all. Cf. 23 & 24 Vict., c. 126, § 26.

position to see the subject in its entirety. Even when Coke wrote, many new things were yet to be done with such actions as assumpsit, detinue, trover, and replevin, and in Blackstone's day some parts of the long cavalcade of actions had already passed or were receding from view.

CHAPTER V

NATURAL HISTORY OF REMEDIAL LAW (CONTINUED).

Relation Between Right and Remedy.

Volume III

BUT after all, the most important question about actions is not one of classification. It matters not much how remedies are catalogued and arranged so long as the system taken in its entirety is sufficiently complete to supply some sort of remedy for all real grievances. Is the remedial law properly co-ordinated with the *jus?* This is always a vital question. It is one of the inherent defects of every system based on form that this co-ordination can never be perfect for any long period of time. Form is not elastic. It only changes by being bent or broken. Before this can happen, social pressure must increase until the tension of form can no longer resist it. Growth of remedial law follows, and cannot precede, social growth. Such certainly is always the case after forms have become settled. Nor does this principle impeach the idea elsewhere brought out, that in the development of early law, form is the chief means by which substantive truth is first made apprehensible to the popular mind.

Inelasticity of the forms of action.

We shall now take a general view of the history of our remedial law in order to ascertain the manner in which the adjustment between right and remedy has been preserved and the extent to which the proper balance has failed.

The statement of the question to be considered presupposes that there have been times when remedial law was inadequate, when the *jus* and *remedium* were not in harmony. Legal theory has always consistently denied the existence of any such state of facts, and a verbal consistency has been reached in the adoption of the maxim *ubi jus ibi remedium.* The word *jus* in this maxim is given a meaning exactly coextensive with that of *remedium.* Legal theory as to the relation between

Relation between *jus* and *remedium.*

Chapter V

Theoretical equilibrium.

the two elements is thus shut up within the limits of a convertible formula whose subject and predicate are coextensive.

That the relation between right and remedy ought to be as is indicated in the maxim no one will deny. As a statement of legal and historical truth it grievously errs by excess. During the greater part of the past the maxim has pointed to the ideal rather than to the actual. This is made clear when we remember a few illustrations of the inadequacy of early remedies. In referring to some of these we shall confine ourselves to the field covered in modern times by the personal actions.

Modern scholarship has lately been greatly puzzled to account for a phenomenon found in the development of the law of ownership. In the thirteenth century and until long afterwards, thieves and trespassers were said to have the property in chattels taken by them; and modern law has hardly yet been able to escape from this doctrine.

Origin of doctrine by which thief and trespasser are said to acquire property in the chattel taken.

This ascription of property to the wrongdoer had its origin in the inadequacy of our early legal remedies. There was no action at common law by which the restitution of a chattel could be certainly accomplished. Originally there had been a remedy, the *actio furti* of Bracton's day, by which a disseised owner might gain restitution of his chattels against a thief or trespasser, but this remedy became obsolete at an early day. The appeal of larceny by which the *actio furti* was supplanted, or rather into which it was changed, was chiefly criminal, and the restoration of the goods followed, if at all, merely as a matter of favor. Detinue was apparently the only remedy which might have been used to enforce the restitution of the chattel. This action, however, could be used only against bailees, and could not be maintained against a trespasser until near the end of the sixteenth century. Replevin, as is well known, was restricted to the narrow field of distress even down to Blackstone's day. It resulted that trespass *vi et armis* was the only civil remedy available to the disseised owner of a chattel. But this remedy sounded in damages only, and no restitution could be enforced by it. As a consequence it long remained law that where a chattel was tortiously taken the owner could not recover the specific chattel of the wrongdoer;

Common-law remedy of the owner defective.

Volume III

and, as against parties subsequently coming into possession under the trespasser, he had no remedy at all.[1]

In the law of bailment a similar, but not so extensive, defect of remedy appeared. The bailor could use detinue against the bailee, but not against the third hand — that is, against one who claimed under or through the bailee. The bailee, and the bailee only, could be held to answer. The bailor had to seek his 'faith' where he had placed it.

Incomplete remedy of bailor.

Now Bracton, who was writing in the shadow of Roman law and using Roman terms, seems to have appreciated the truth that neither the trespasser nor the bailee had the property in the chattels taken or bailed to him. The *dominium* was vested in the *dominus*. The mere use of significant words like these was enough to prevent the concession of anything more than mere possession *(custodia)* to the wrongdoer or bailee. As time went on this safeguard was lost, and the absence of a remedy to enforce restitution was taken to indicate that the property went away from the owner when he lost possession. Thus did failure of remedy strangulate the legal right. A right without a remedy is merely an abstract right and cannot long survive as a vital conception.

Absence of remedy leads to denial of owner's right.

Another striking instance of the absence of remedy in connection with the law of personal property is found in the principle that there can be no reversion or remainder in a chattel interest. It is just as easy to conceive of such an interest as it is to conceive of reversions and remainders in land. In case of realty the common law had the writs of formedon in remainder and reverter, and the Statute of Westminster II gave the remedy of formedon in descender.[2] There were no such remedies in case of chattels. Hence one who takes a life estate in chattels gets all.

No reversion in chattels.

It would be tedious and unprofitable to go through the several actions in order to point out instances where the remedy wholly failed or was imperfect. Every gap into which in their subsequent growth the various actions have run repre-

[1] See Ames, Disseisin of Chattels, 3 Harv. L. Rev. 313; 2 Poll. & Mait. Hist. Eng. Law, 2d ed., 167.

[2] West. II., c. 1; 2 Co. Inst. 336 (16).

sents just so much territory where remedial law, in the very fact that the extension took place, was thereby acknowledged to be inadequate. If right and remedy had always been in such equilibrium as is indicated in the maxim *ubi jus ibi remedium,* no changes would have been necessary and there would have been no growth. Neither would we be so often confronted with such recitals as that with which the Statute of Westminster II begins: "Considering that divers of this realm are disinherited by reason of the fact that in many cases where remedy should have been had, there is none provided."

Acknowledged inadequacy of remedies.

As is elsewhere fully shown, the principle underlying case supplied a means for the extension of the various remedies. Hence the action on the case has been a prominent instrument in preserving the proper balance between legal right and remedy.[3]

Function of case in preserving balance between right and remedy.

The most conspicuous of the forms of case was trespass on the case; but the principle underlying case really fertilized all the old stocks like deceit, debt, and detinue, as well as trespass, giving new life to each of them. From deceit came an action on the case in the nature of deceit. This supplies us with the earliest instance in which damages were awarded for the breach of a simple contract. In other words, deceit on the case was the true parent of assumpsit. From detinue came an action on the case in the nature of detinue (detinue *sur trover*), the forerunner of the action of trover, a remedy which finally became concurrent not only with detinue and trespass *de bonis asportatis,* but with replevin.

Trespass on the case.

Deceit on the case.

Trover.

The action on the case in the nature of debt was a rather late development, and when it did finally appear it came through assumpsit and is known as indebitatus assumpsit. In regard to replevin it is not historically so clear that the principle of case has been the means of extending the scope of the remedy so as to permit of its use against all who wrongfully take chattels from the owner. Originally replevin could be used only in cases of wrongful distress. It is obvious that, whatever causes may have effected the extension, and whatever reasons may have weighed upon the courts in bringing it about,

Case in nature of debt.

[3] See *post,* Trespass on the Case.

Volume III

Replevin.

the modern action of replevin, as a general remedy concurrent with trespass and, in America, with detinue, is truly an action on the case in the nature of the ancient action or replevin, and this although it may be of statutory origin.

Principle of case operates through long period.

The most casual glance at the work consciously or unconsciously done by the principle of case in the field of the common-law actions shows that this work was not only of vast importance, but that its efficacy extended over a period of several hundred years. Trespass was the first of the old stocks to respond to the influence, and from it soon issued trespass on the case. The reason for this is perhaps to be found in the fact that trespass was a new remedy, having originated about 1250, and was yet plastic when the Statute of Westminster II was passed. The more settled remedies were longer in yielding, and the extension was in most instances brought about gradually and by indirection. It was well into the seventeenth century before the action on the case in the nature of debt was developed, and trover was nearly as slow in reaching maturity. The action on the case for deceit was also of rather slow growth.

The written record as an impediment to legal growth.

A circumstance which contributed to embarrass the growth of the actions under the stimulus of case was the fact that the law was coming to be more and more a *lex scripta*. In the maturity of legal systems the written record operates with exactly the same effect on remedies as verbal and dramatic form in the earliest stages of legal growth. Being first a means of perpetuating knowledge, it tends in time to destroy flexibility, and thus the most powerful forward impulses are finally overcome.

Exhaustion of the principle of growth.

Even the principle underlying case could not be expected to continue to operate with the same effect indefinitely. Aside from the fact that it was of limited operation, being restricted to cases analogous to those where liability was already recognized, it was but natural that in time the principle of case would be fully worked out. Remedial law, as reflected in the common-law actions, was thus bound sooner or later to come to a state of rest. How much the technical rules of pleading in which the common law abounded would further contribute

Chapter V

to restrict the usefulness and paralyze the growth of the actions may be more easily imagined than stated.

Forms of action tend to fixity.

The fact to be impressed is that the legal forms of action, however stimulated by case, inevitably tended towards finality and fixity. In laying down the principle that writs might be framed in analogous but not in new cases, Parliament struck a blow at the principle of remedial growth which, as time would reveal, was to prove fatal to the whole common-law system of actions. The full effects of depriving the chancery of the power to issue new writs appropriate to causes of action then unknown were not at once manifest; but before a hundred years after the enactment of the Statute of Westminster II had passed, an ominous sign appeared. Litigants, being unable to obtain adequate redress through the common-law actions, now began an appeal by petition to the king himself, who was in theory the ultimate fountain of justice. For a time such petitions were entertained by the king in council, but as they increased in number a general order was made referring all such matters as were of grace to the decision of the chancellor.[1]

Origin of chancery jurisdiction.

It is no part of our purpose here to trace the growth of the extraordinary jurisdiction of the court of chancery. The occasion for its beginning and the cause of its marvelous expansion are to be found in the fact that, despite the maxim *ubi jus ibi remedium,* the legal actions were inadequate and the common law was powerless to give forth new remedies. The principle of case might help to fill in lacunæ in existing actions, but even this process was slow. Our English law had to pay dearly for the premature maturity which it had attained in the Bractonian epoch. Remedies had become substantially fixed too soon, and as time began to reveal their defects, relief was found in a principle which the common law could not recognize. An appeal had been taken to Cæsar.

No forms of action recognized in chancery.

From the beginning, it will be observed, the court of chancery adopted the mature conceptions of procedure which the Roman law had finally attained. In other words, it recognized no forms of action. Every grievance which made its way into the equitable forum was judged solely upon its merits and

[1] 22 Edw. III. (A. D. 1348-49); 1 Spence, Equitable. Jur., 337.

upon its own facts. All bills in equity are therefore in form actions on the case. This is not an instance of mere resemblance in procedure. Between the civil action on the facts of the case and the equitable bill there is an identity of principle. The legal action has certain restrictions, due to historical causes and to peculiarities of the legal forum, to which the bill is not subject; but that the action on the case is merely a form of equitable bill is manifest. Form in its proper sense does not enter into either. Indebitatus assumpsit is a form of case; and that indebitatus — especially in the form of the common count for money had and received — is in the nature of a bill in equity is everywhere recognized.

Analogy between the bill and the action on the case.

One who casts his eye over the field of English remedial law during the five hundred years which ends with the passage of the Judicature Acts will thus see two great factors working in entirely different fields for the expansion of that law. In the equitable forum is the conception of the single civil action as a sufficient instrument for the redress of all grievances of which that court has jurisdiction. In the legal forum we see the principle embodied in the action on the case, fertilizing the old stocks and causing them to put forth anew. To this circumstance is probably due the survival of the common-law forms of action until our own time; though no doubt the existence of the institution of the jury has largely contributed to the same result.

The two expansive forces operating on the law.

It has often been observed that the existence of a chancery court ever ready to welcome litigants who had no redress at law operated with great power on the judges in the law courts and at critical times caused important advances in legal theory. In 1481 Fairfax, J., speaking of the action on the case upon assumpsit, suggested that if more attention were given to its extension, there would not be so much occasion to resort to chancery.[5] This sensible advice was presently followed.

Law judges stimulated by rivalry of chancery.

The action on the case has thus been one of the chief bulwarks of the common-law system of procedure. In modern times, at least, it has sufficed to keep right and remedy in absolute equilibrium in all cases where the recovery of dam-

[5] Y. B. 21 Edw. IV. 23, pl. 6.

Chapter V

Action on the case available where damages only are sought.

ages is the only relief sought. *Ashby v. White* (1703)[6] well illustrates the manner in which the action on the case may be used to redress a legal wrong though the particular facts may never have arisen before. It is a classical and leading authority on the maxim *ubi jus ibi remedium*.

In this case a qualified elector brought an action to recover damages against a returning officer for refusing to admit his vote. In the Queen's Bench, the majority of the judges were of opinion that the plaintiff had no remedy at law. Holt, C. J., dissented, and on appeal to the House of Lords his opinion prevailed. The committee of the House of Lords appointed to report on the case was assisted by the chief justice himself, and the argument in favor of the right of action contained in the report was written by him.[7]

Holt's argument in Ashby v. White.

"It is a vain thing," said his lordship in the court below, "to imagine that there should be a right without a remedy; for want of right and want of remedy are convertibles. If a statute gives a right, the common law will give a remedy to maintain it; and wherever there is injury it imports damage." In the argument accompanying the report of the Lords' committee the same great jurist eloquently insisted that the novelty of a situation afforded no ground of objection to the maintenance of the action. "It is not," said he, "the novelty of the action that can be urged against it, if it can be supported by the old grounds and principles of the law. . . . The law of England is not confined to particular precedents and cases, but consists in the reason of them, which is made more extensive than this or that case. *Ratio legis est anima legis et ubi eadem ratio ibi idem jus.*"

In other words, as his lordship might have said, case lies

[6] Holt K. B 524, 2 Ld. Raym. 938, 1 Bro. P. C. 45 (in House of Lords), also 14 How. St. Tr. 695.

[7] See Lords' Journal, 27 March 1704–05, p. 597. For another report of the same decision, first published in 1837, see 25 Eng. Rul. Cas. 52.

The decision in Ashby v. White has in modern times been qualified on the point actually determined in that case, by the recognition of the principle that where the returning officer is clothed with a judicial discretion and exercises it in good faith, no action will lie for a refusal to receive a vote. Tozer v. Child (1857), 7 El. & Bl. 377, 90 E. C. L. 377. But this does not affect the general principle for which the case is here referred to.

Volume III

Case a residuary remedy.

to recover damages for any act, omission, or refusal done or permitted contrary to the obligation of the law, provided no other remedy is available. This view of function of case as a residuary remedy has of course been applied in the many modern decisions which, like *Ashby v. White*, recognize new sorts of liability. Such decisions do no less credit to the judicial vision of the courts than to the flexibility of the action on the case. *Winsmore v. Greenbank* (1745),[8] *Chapman v. Pickersgill* (1762),[9] *Pasley v. Freeman* (1789),[1] and *Lumley v. Gye* (1853),[2] are perhaps the most familiar instances of the use of case for the enforcement of forms of liability unknown before those respective cases were decided.

The Modern Formless Action.

We have seen that it was the theory of the common law that there is no right without a remedy. This would not have been so glaringly false if under the term 'right' equitable rights of action had been included. The common law would not have it so. *Jus* meant legal right. Now if we thus leave out of view the field of equitable rights as belonging to an altogether different world from that in which law, as distinguished from equity, moves and has its being, we must see that by the beginning of the nineteenth century the principle embodied in case, together with the natural broadening of the forms of action, had pretty well rounded out the field of remedies. There were possibly, here and there, a few uncultivated patches where rights might in theory be found without corresponding remedies; semi-occasionally the abolition of an old action had the appearance of leaving a barren right floating around helplessly in the world of abstract jurisprudence.[3]

Remedial law becomes approximately rounded and complete.

[8] Willes 577.

[9] 2 Wils. C. Pl. 145.

[1] 3 T. R. 51.

[2] 2 El. & Bl. 216, 75 E. C. L. 216.

[3] For instance, when real actions were abolished no remedy was left for the recovery of rent charges in fee in so far as the rent charge was based on the real obligation. It was held, however, in Thomas *v.* Sylvester (1873), L. R. 8 Q. B. 368, that after the abolition of the real remedy and consequent destruction of the real right, the action of debt might be maintained upon the personal duty of the owner of the land out of which the rent charge in fee issues. This personal obligation had never been recognized before, and Mr. T. C. Williams has vigor-

This conclusion is, however, generally avoided by means of the principle that the abolition of a sole remedy is sufficient evidence of a legislative intention to destroy the right also.

Chapter V

Abolition of actions.

In a legal world where right and remedy had thus again arrived at the state of theoretical equilibrium which Bracton had looked upon as actual and necessary six hundred years before, a course of legislation was entered upon, first in America (1848) and then in England (1873–75), which has altogether abolished the forms of actions in nearly all common-law jurisdictions.

The formless action.

The adoption of the formless action on the facts must inevitably result in the maintenance for all time of that equilibrium between right and remedy which is the goal of remedial law.

Theory of the new procedure.

In working out the new remedial system, judicial opinion has accepted as fundamental the principle that the legislation by which the change in question was effected did not intend to alter substantive law at all. It does not create new rights, but only gives a new means of enforcing the old, abolishing legal forms and consolidating legal and equitable modes of procedure.[4]

ously maintained that the decision in Thomas *v.* Sylvester was erroneous. The decision shows the strong predilection of the courts in favor of giving some remedy where there is really a right.

See Landowner's Liability to Pay Rent-charges in Fee, by T. C. Williams, 18 L. Quar. Rev. 288; and The Incidence of Rent, by the same writer, 11 Harv. L. Rev. 1.

[4] Lattin *v.* McCarty, 41 N. Y. 107; Cole *v.* Reynolds, 18 N. Y. 74; British South Africa Co. *v.* Companhia De Moçambique, (1893) A. C. 602, 628; Macdonald *v.* Tacquah Gold Mines Co., 13 Q. B. D. 535, 539; Westbury-on-Severn Rural Sanitary Authority *v.* Meredith, 30 Ch. D. 387.

Said Lord Esher in Britain *v.* Rossiter, 11 Q. B. D. 123, 129, "I think that the true construction of the Judicature Acts is that they confer no new rights; they only confirm the rights which previously were to be found existing in the courts either of law or of equity; if they did more they would alter the rights of parties, whereas in truth they only change the procedure."

As was said by Mr. Pomeroy, the passage of the Code of Procedure by the Legislature of New York in 1848 was a decided shock to professional opinion. Pomeroy, Code Remedies, 3d ed., 72. At first the courts hardly knew what to make of it. They did not apprehend the bearing of the legislation and could hardly be expected to apply it with fidelity. Accordingly it seemed for a time that an interpretation would be placed upon the provisions abolishing actions which would have reduced the code system to the level of a mere amendatory act regulating the minor details

Volume III

Distinction between law and equity not abolished.

By this it is not meant that the distinction between legal and equitable rights is abolished or that it is even to be disregarded in the practice of the courts; for the terms 'legal' and 'equitable' are worked into the fibre of all legal thought. As expressions indicative of the nature and source of liability the distinction between law and equity cannot be extinguished. The right of trial by jury, which has been indissolubly associated with the action at law and is still incident to legal rights of action, will also serve to keep alive the distinction.

Procedural difficulties abolished.

The principle being accepted that the adoption of the new procedure did not operate to create new rights, it is sometimes supposed that an action can be now maintained only in those cases where some sort of action either at law or in equity could be maintained under the old system. In a general sense this is true. It is necessary that the right now sought to be enforced should be such as formerly had recognition. But if it should appear that a legal duty has been violated, an action can now be maintained, though formerly it could not, provided the former absence of remedy was due to a procedural defect only. Thus, at common law the assignee of a chose in action could not sue thereon in his own name. The modern procedure has abolished this technical rule, either by express provision or necessary implication, and the assignee now sues, as he would formerly have sued in equity, in his own name.

Assignee of chose sues in his own name.

Partnership may sue firm having a common member.

Another illustration of the same idea is found in *Cole v. Reynolds* (1858),[5] where it was held that judgment could be recovered by one partnership against another firm, though they had a common member. A technical rule peculiar to the common law would have defeated such an action. A man, it was said, cannot sue himself, and as all the members of a firm must unite in bringing a suit, the action could not be maintained. In equity this rule was not followed. It thus

of practice. See Reubens v. Joel, 13 N. Y. 488; Voorhis v. Childs, 17 N. Y. 354.

But more liberal views prevailed in the end, and the courts of the several states have generally accepted the reformed procedure as embodying a radical departure from the old remedial system. See observations of Allen, J., in Bush v. Prosser, 11 N. Y. 354; also Pom. Code Remedies, 3d ed., 76.

[5] 18 N. Y. 74.

appears that under the reformed procedure a party may in some instances maintain an action where he could not have sued under the old system; but such cases are exceedingly rare and are limited, as was intimated above, to situations where, though a right was conceded at common law, the remedy was nevertheless either defective or entirely absent.

CHAPTER VI

NATURAL HISTORY OF REMEDIAL LAW (CONTINUED).

Actio Personalis Moritur cum Persona.

Volume III

Uncertain origin of the maxim.

Universality of the principle.

Principle repudiated in modern law.

IT is a principle of early law that the death of either party to a personal duty takes away all remedy and destroys the duty. In English law the principle is usually put in the form *actio personalis moritur cum persona*, an expression of uncertain but post-classical origin. The doctrine it embodies is not peculiar to the common-law system. The idea belongs to primary strata in universal law. In a mature jurisprudence the doctrine is of narrow application. Hence we find that in modern times it has been greatly limited by judicial decision and is now being still further restricted by legislation. So great a change has here supervened in modes of legal thinking that the rule is now generally looked upon as embodying hardship, and as not being founded in reason.[1] The only common-law doctrine which occurs to us as having gathered a richer harvest of animadversion is the old rule that part payment of a debt cannot operate as a legal satisfaction of the whole. Let us endeavor to ascertain what necessity there is in the constitution of things which causes a personal duty to terminate upon the death of either party.

Principle not limited to tort law.

In the first place it will be necessary to put out of our head ideas which the modern authorities make very obtrusive. "*Actio personalis*," said Willes, C. J., "is always understood of a tort."[2] This, however, is a modern gloss forced upon the maxim by the exigencies of a growing society, and nothing can be more certain than that the line of demarcation between contract and tort does not coincide with the line which separates actions which survive from those which perish with the

[1] See Poll. on Torts, 6th ed., 61 *et seq.*, where the doctrine is characterized as barbarous.

[2] Sollers *v.* Lawrence, Willes 413, 421.

person. The right of action to recover damages for a breach of promise to marry arises out of a pure contract, yet it does not survive.[3] On the other hand, the right of action for the wrongful appropriation of property does survive, though such action is founded purely upon a tort.[4]

Principle not confined to penal actions.

For a moment then let us strip ourselves of all the modern learning, remembering only with Bowen, L. J., that "we are left still in the dark as to the maxim's exact meaning or source."[5] So much at sea has scholarship been to account for the rule with which we are dealing, that some have indulged the fancy that *personalis* in the maxim must have originated in a misprint for *poenalis*.[6] Bracton, it is true, remarks that the rule applies with special force to penal actions; but he does not limit it to such actions,[7] and the conjecture in question is untenable.

Maxim applies to all personal obligations, both contractual and delictual.

No, as a statement of fundamental principle in early law the term *actio personalis* in the maxim under discussion has the same scope as *actio in personam* in Roman law, and the same scope as the term 'personal action' originally had in our law as the proper equivalent of *actio in personam*. In other words, *actio personalis* includes all rights of action founded on obligation in the Roman sense.[8] It accordingly applies to contractual as well as delictual duties or obligations.

The two-sidedness of the personal obligation.

It will be observed that there are two parties to every obligation. One is entitled to performance, the other owes a duty. That is to say, the obligation involves a bilateral relation, namely, that of debtor and creditor. From this double aspect, both of the contractual and delictual obligation, an important

[3] Finlay *v.* Chirney, 20 Q. B. D. 495.

[4] Phillips *v.* Homfray, 24 Ch. D. 439. But the action of trover does not survive because it is in form an action *ex delicto*. Hambly *v.* Trott, 1 Cowp. 371.

[5] Finlay *v.* Chirney, 20 Q. B. D. 503.

[6] Poste, Elements of Roman Law (Gaius), 2d ed., 493.

[7] "Item tollitur morte alterius contrahentium vel utriusque, maxime si fuerit poenalis." Bracton 101.

[8] The term 'obligation' in Roman law includes all rights and duties *in personam*. The Roman notion of obligation is that of a tie between two persons, of such nature as to confer on one a power of compelling the other to give, do, or make good.

"Obligatio est juris vinculum quo necessitate astringimur alicuius solvendae rei secundum nostrae civitatis jura." Inst. 3, 13.

Volume III

consequence is deducible which has operated with more or less effect in the development of both Roman and English law. This is the principle of the non-transferability of the mere right of action. If there were only one party to the personal obligation, or if we were permitted to contemplate it solely from the point of view of the creditor, no difficulty could arise in regard to his power of transferring it. But this is clearly an impossibility.

Non-transferability of the right of action.

Accordingly, in early law the mere right of action is not assignable among the living nor does it survive after death. The principle of the non-assignability of the chose among the living and the rule that the personal right of action does not survive after the death of either party, therefore have a common origin. The doctrine of the non-transferability of the personal obligation, of which the two principles just stated are merely two manifestations, is axiomatic in early law and is inherent in the bilateral nature of the obligation. The act of one party cannot change a relation which affects two; nor when one dies will the law of its own arbitrary power change the duty. If the creditor dies, it will not allow another to enforce the duty as against the debtor; nor, if the debtor dies, will the law saddle the obligation upon his representative, if there be one. "If one doth a trespass to me and dieth, the action is dead also, because it would be improper to recover against one who was not a party to the wrong."[0]

Axiomatic principle.

Gradual subversion of the doctrine.

Modern law has found or is finding ways to subvert the doctrine of the non-transferability of personal rights of action. One phase of the problem, to wit, that presented by the question of the assignability of the chose in action, will be specially dealt with in a subsequent chapter. Concerning the history of the gradual circumscription of the maxim *actio personalis moritur cum persona*, something must here be said.

Causes.

The development of a satisfactory theory of succession and representation in the estates of deceased persons undoubtedly contributed much to impeach the broad doctrine that a personal right of action perishes with the death of either party.[1] But

[0] Y. B. 19 Hen. VI. 66, pl. 10.

[1] On this subject see 2 Poll. & Mait. Hist. Eng. Law, 2d ed., 257, 258; Holmes, Common Law 346 *et seq.*

other forces have operated to the same end. One conception which seems to have been a potent factor from the first in limiting the maxim in question is the principle of the inherent transferability of things and of rights incident to things.

Inherent transferability of things and of property rights.

Ownership is good as against the world. All individuals are bound not to disturb me in my property rights, and when my lands or chattels are seized by another, I have a right to recover them in specie, regardless of the question as to who is guilty of the wrongful act. If the wrongdoer dies, this should not normally affect the rights of the owner. In other words, recuperatory actions, or actions founded on property rights, unlike personal actions, do not die with the person. This distinction, especially as regards actions concerning personalty, has been worked out somewhat slowly, and we would need take a long leap forward in order to get a clear judicial statement of the principle.

State of law in Bracton's day.

Let us bear the principle in mind that in the beginning of legal development contractual and delictual rights of action die, while rights of action founded on property do not. That such was the state of the English law in Bracton's day is clear. "The obligation," says this writer, "is tolled by the death of one or the other contracting parties, especially if it be of a penal nature and simple (*poenalis et simplex*). If, however, it is of a mixed penal and recuperatory character (*duplex, poenalis et rei persecutoria*), the obligation is destroyed in so far as it is penal, and the right of action neither survives to the heirs nor is available against them."[2] In speaking of the penal action, Bracton evidently had in mind the trespass (*transgressio*). This term was then just beginning to be applied to all wrongful acts which fell short of felony. It included both the misdemeanor and trespass of the later law.[3] It should be borne in mind that the contract which Bracton has in view as being terminated upon the death of either party is the debt. "Actions," says he, "especially the hoary debt, cannot be bequeathed and are not reckoned among the goods of the testator."[4]

[2] Bracton 101.

[3] *Ib.*, 101, 101*b*.

[4] "Actiones legari non possunt nec inter bona testatoris connume-

Volume III

Our law, then, as regards the survival of actions, starts from the doctrine that actions brought to enforce contractual and delictual obligations perish with the person, but that actions brought to enforce the duty to restore (recuperatory actions) do not. In our time it has come to this: all recuperatory actions, nearly all contractual actions, and most delictual actions survive. Natural forces at work in the common law sufficiently account for the change by which contractual rights have come to survive. Legislative action has largely accomplished the same end in the field of tort. Between the two forces legal doctrine on the point now being considered has been practically reversed. Survival, having once been the exception, is now the rule.

Modern doctrine.

Concerning detinue no doubt could ever have been entertained that it is founded on property. Bracton indeed denied the recuperatory character of the action, but its nature was not to be changed by a mistake of this kind. As soon as detinue became distinct from debt it was held that the remedy could be maintained against executors upon a bailment made to their testator. Consequently, if three are executors and one has possession, detinue lies against him without joining the others.[5]

Detinue survives because of its recuperatory nature.

In modern times the principle that recuperatory actions and actions founded on property right survive has been accepted. But difficulty has sometimes been encountered in determining whether a particular action is really of this nature. In *Hambly v. Trott* (1776),[6] the action of trover was subjected to scrutiny in order to ascertain whether it is so far recuperatory as to be maintainable after the death of the tortfeasor. Lord Mansfield saw that the remedy savored strongly of property,

Trover perishes with person because it is not an action of property.

rantur, maxime de antiquo debito;" also, "Actiones legari non possunt, nec judices ecclesiastici inde recognoscere, nec executores petere debitum quod in vita testatoris non est recognitum." Bracton 407*b*. To these propositions Bracton cites two cases (Bracton's Note Book, pls. 162, 550). The proposition in question is fully borne out by other authorities from the same source. Note Book, pls. 684, 810.

[5] Y. B. 11 Hen. IV. 46, pl. 20. See also Y. B. 41 Edw. III. 30, pl. 35; Y. B. 14 Hen. IV. 23, pl. 30; Brooke's Abr., *Detinue*, 12, 19; *Executors*, 28.

[6] 1 Cowp. 371.

but not sufficiently so to prevent the right of action from perishing with the person.

The action of waste is very similar in many respects to trover, since the act of waste often consists of an appropriation of property to the use of the person doing the waste. But the action is personal and, like trover, dies with the person, and hence cannot be maintained against executors,[7] or administrators,[8] for waste committed by the decedent in his lifetime. But this right of action which at common law died with the person is, subject to a time limitation, continued against the executor by 3 and 4 William IV.[9] Though the action of waste undoubtedly perished with the person at common law, yet in equity we find recognition of the principle that the estate of the deceased can be held liable,[1] on the ground and subject to the limitations set forth in *Phillips v. Homfray* (1883).[2]

Waste perishes with the person.

Statutory qualification.

The distinction between debt and detinue above indicated, i. e., that detinue survived but that debt did not, is the more remarkable for the reason that debt was the mother of detinue. Yet the true cause of wonder to the modern mind is that debt should perish, not that detinue should survive. The writ of debt was modeled after the writ of right, which as we know was the most real and recuperatory of all actions. Still, debt was used to enforce a contractual obligation, and there was no escape from the principle that the personal obligation is mortal.

Distinction between debt and detinue as regards survival.

The first debt to be recognized as an exception to the general rule of mortality was that in which the successor, usually the heir, was expressly bound. Such contracts were generally put under seal. The solemnity of the instrument and the fact that the obligor expressly bound his heir were accepted as

Debt does not perish if heir or successor is bound.

[7] Brooke Abr., *Waste*, pl. 138. Turner v. Buck, 22 Vin. Abr., *Waste*, 523, pl. 9. Bedel v. Bedel, Brownl. & Goldes. 238, pt. i., contains a statement to the contrary, but this is erroneous. The Register and F. N. B. both have a writ against executors, but it is for their own waste and not for the waste of their testator. Reg. Brev. Orig. 72b, F. N. B. 56 (B).

[8] Went. Executors 127.

[9] Chapter 42, § 2.

The waste must have been committed within six months of the testator's death and suit must be brought within six months after qualification of representative. See Woodhouse v. Walker, 5 Q. B. D. 404

[1] Garth v. Cotton, 1 Ves. 524, 3 Atk. 757; Bacon Abr., *Waste* (O).

[2] 24 Ch. D. 439.

Volume III

affording a sufficient reason for changing the ordinary rule.[3] This exception was recognized long before Bracton's day, at which period indeed the heir was apparently liable for the debts of his ancestor to the extent of the assets, although not specially named in any obligation.[4]

The specialty debt survives.

In course of time, as was natural, the specialty came to be treated as binding on the successor (now executor) without any express words. In the reign of Edward III the distinction that the specialty survived while simple debts did not was fully recognized.[5] At an earlier day the close kinship between the actions of debt and detinue had caused confusion, and some actions on simple debts were seemingly maintained against representatives or by them.[6] Also, it seems, debts were sometimes proved against executors by suit or tally and not by specialty;[7] but the exception was soon restricted to specialties.

Erroneous explanation of perishability of the simple debt.

In the later year-book period it became customary to explain the rule that simple contracts died with the person, by saying that the testator could have waged his law and that, as the executor could not, it was unjust to allow the plaintiff to proceed in debt. But this was a mistake. The question of procedure, so far as we can see, had nothing to do with the origin of the doctrine in question. If wager of law was a good reason for denying the action of debt to the creditor of a deceased person, we ought to find that detinue was denied to him on the same ground. Yet this was not so.[8]

Wager of law.

One of the earliest cases in which the right of the testator

[3] 2 Poll. & Mait. Hist. Eng. Law, 2d ed., 258.

[4] 2 Poll. & Mait. Hist. Eng. Law, 2d ed., 345.

In the time of Glanvill, the liability of the heir was general and was not limited to the amount of assets. "Si vero non sufficiant res defuncti ad debita persolvenda tunc quidem heres ejus defectum ipsum de suo tenetur adimplere." Glanvill, Lib. VII., c. 8.

[5] Y. B. 24 Edw. III. 40, pl. 22; Y. B. 41 Edw. III. 13, pl. 3; Y. B. 14 Edw. III. (Rolls ed.), 94, pl. 40.

[6] *Debt in Favor of Executor.*— Y. B. 20–21 Edw. I. (Rolls ed.) 375; Y. B. 21–22 Edw. I. (Rolls ed.) 258, 598; Y. B. 33–35 Edw. I. (Rolls ed.), 62, 294.

Debt Against Executor.— Y. B. 30–31 Edw. I., 238; Goffin, Testamentary Executor, 47 *et seq.*

[7] Y. B. 21–22 Edw. I. (Rolls ed.), 456.

[8] For illustrations showing when detinue was subject to wager of law and when not, see 2 Rolle Abr., *Ley Gager,* 108, 109.

Chapter VI

to wage his law and the inability of the executor to wage it for him was assigned as the reason for a denial of the action of debt as against the estate of a deceased person comes from 1433, and the explanation was not then old. Debt was sued against executors, alleging that the testator had retained one of the brothers in a convent to sing masses for the soul of the deceased for a certain sum, and that the masses had been sung. The objection was made that the contract was not by specialty, and it was said that in every case where the testator could have waged his law, the action cannot be maintained against his executor without specialty—"for executors cannot wage their law upon the contracts of others, because they cannot have knowledge." [9]

Origin of this explanation.

The explanation was plausible and subsequently gained currency. Fitzherbert was perhaps the last of the English judges who really knew that the simple debt died with the person merely because it is a personal obligation. On one occasion, in one of those judicial colloquies which give a lively interest to many otherwise dull pages in the year books, Knightly asked the learned judge whether an action on the case upon assumpsit would lie against executors having assets after debts and legacies were paid. "Fitzherbert: You shall have neither an action on the case nor any other remedy; for when the testator dies, the debt due by reason of the simple contract is dead also. Knightly: The reason that no writ of debt lies against executors is that the testator could have waged his law, and the executors cannot wage law for him." [1]

Fitzherbert's opinion.

Fitzherbert, it will be perceived, was sagacious enough not to commit himself to Knightly's explanation of the perishability of the debt. In this connection the learned judge pointed out that assumpsit was subject to the same perishability as debt. Referring to a case holding the contrary, in which he had been of counsel for the successful plaintiff, he added: "Put that case out of your books, for without doubt it is not law." [2]

Assumpsit perishes with the person.

[9] Y. B. 11 Hen. VI. 48, pl. 5.

[1] Y. B. 27 Hen. VIII. 23, pl. 21.

[2] The case referred to is reported in Y. B. 12 Hen. VIII. 11, pl. 3; Brooke Abr., *Accion sur Cas*, pl. 106. Brooke adds this note, "But

Volume III

Explanation founded on wager of law accepted as sound.

Nevertheless, when Fitzherbert was gone, and the true reason for the perishability of the simple debt had been forgotten, the question whether assumpsit can be maintained against executors was again raised. Knightly's explanation was now seized upon as affording a good basis for discriminating on this point between assumpsit and debt. In *Norwood v. Read* (1557),[3] the telling argument in favor of the maintenance of assumpsit against the executor was "the testator could not have waged his law."

Assumpsit survives.

Pinchon's Case (1611)[4] raised a still more difficult problem. Fitzherbert had said that the debt was dead, like the testator. *Slade's Case* (1602)[5] established the doctrine that assumpsit would lie upon any debt. The question now arose in *Pinchon's Case* whether assumpsit would lie upon a debt after the death of one of the parties. Coke, C. J., and other eminent judges, after many arguments and lengthy consideration, answered in the affirmative. To reach this conclusion it was necessary to resolve, and they did accordingly declare, that after the death of the testator the debt remained, although no longer actionable as a debt. The difficulty being thus resolved into one of procedure, it was proper that assumpsit should be maintained: "for it would be a defect in the law, if no remedy were provided."[6] Thus was the doctrine that per-

Assumpsit maintainable on a simple debt after death of the debtor.

it is now questioned in that court [King's Bench], and the Common Bench has always held that the action lies not." The language of Fineux, C. J., in this case shows that the idea that *actio personalis* in the maxim refers only to injuries to the person was now becoming current. Said he: "This action [assumpsit] is not within the rule *actio personalis moritur cum persona:* for that is where the hurt or damage is corporal, as if one commits a battery on me and dies, my action is gone; or if I die my executors shall have no action. The party cannot be punished, because he is dead."

[3] Plowd. 180.

[4] 9 Coke 86*b*.

[5] 4 Coke 92.

[6] In regard to the objection that trespass on the case upon a promise, being a personal action, dies with the person, it was said: "Although it is termed trespass, in respect that the breach of promise is alleged to be mixed with fraud and deceit to the special prejudice of the plaintiff, and for that reason it is called trespass on the case, yet that doth not make the action so annexed to the persons of the parties that it shall die with the persons; for then if he to whom the promise is made dies, his executors should not have any action, which no man will affirm. And an action sur assumpsit upon good consideration, without specialty to do a thing, is no more personal, i. e. annexed to the person,

sonal actions die with the person, impeached so far as contract law is concerned. Debt was heard of no more as a remedy upon simple contracts. The wager of law was abolished in the nineteenth century, and debt was then sanctioned as a remedy by and against representatives.[7] But this piece of legislation was of no practical moment and served merely as a re minder of a curious chapter in past history.

Let us now consider for a moment the inroads made upon the maxim *actio personalis moritur cum persona* in the field of tort. Here it has sometimes been necessary to invoke legislative aid.

Trespass perishes with person.

Trespass, chief of delictual remedies, long remained not only personal, but penal. To have entertained this action after the death of one of the parties would have flatly contradicted the doctrine embodied in the maxim. It was, however, obviously unjust that tortfeasors should escape punishment by the accident of death. Accordingly, as early as 1330 a statute was passed for the benefit of executors, reciting that whereas in times past they had no action for a trespass done to their testators as of goods and chattels carried away in their life, and that such trespasses had remained unpunished, wherefore it was enacted that the executors in such cases should have an action against the trespassers to recover damages in like manner as the testators should have if they were alive.[8]

Statutory qualifications.

By Statute of 25 Edward III [9] this provision was extended to the executors of executors; and by judicial construction it was held to apply to administrators as well. It did not give the executor a right of action for injuries to the person or character of the testator. The only wrongs to which these statutes extended were those where there was an asportation of chattels or damage done to such property.[1] Trespasses to freehold interests continued as before to perish with either party.

than a covenant by specialty to do the same thing."

[7] 3 & 4 Will. IV., c. 42, § 13.

[8] Stat. 4 Edw. III., c. 7.

[9] Stat. 5, c. 5.

[1] 1 Williams, Executors, 7th ed., 793; Hatchard v. Mege, 18 Q. B. D. 771; Twycross v. Grant, 4 C. P. D. 40.

Volume III

Action against estate of deceased trespasser.

The foregoing statutes gave the right of action to executors and not against them. The estates of decedents were not made liable for trespasses done by them until later; nor was this step effected by statute. It resulted from the application of the doctrine that actions based upon property do not die with the person. Hence it was subject to the limitation, so clearly stated in *Phillips v. Homfray* (1883),[2] that the tort complained of, in order to give a right of action as against the representative of the wrongdoer, must operate to increase his estate.

In this case Bowen, L. J., discussing the matter of the survival of rights of action originating in tort, said: "The only cases in which, apart from questions of breach of contract, express or implied, a remedy for a wrongful act can be pursued against the estate of a deceased person who has done the act, appear to us to be those in which property, or the proceeds or value of property, belonging to another, have been appropriated by the deceased person and added to his own estate or moneys. In such cases, whatever the original form of action, it is in substance brought to recover property, or its proceeds or value, and by amendment could be made such in form as well as in substance. In such cases the action, though arising out of a wrongful act, does not die with the person. The property or the proceeds or value which in the lifetime of the wrongdoer could have been recovered from him, can be traced after his death to his assets, and recaptured by the rightful owner there. But it is not every wrongful act by which a wrongdoer indirectly benefits that falls under this head, if the benefit does not consist in the acquisition of property, or its proceeds or value. Where there is nothing among the assets of the deceased that in law or in equity belongs to the plaintiff, and the damages which have been done to him are unliquidated and uncertain, the executors of a wrongdoer cannot be sued merely because it was worth the wrongdoer's while to commit the act which is complained of, and an indirect benefit may have been reaped thereby."

Action lies only where estate of trespasser has been enriched by unjust acquisition.

The doctrine here announced by Lord Bowen seems to

[2] 24 Ch. D. 439.

Chapter VI

have been first recognized in *Sherrington's Case* (1583),[3] where the defendant had cut and converted to his own use certain oaks and other trees growing upon lands belonging to the crown. Manwood, C. J., gave judgment against him on the ground that he was liable for the property or its proceeds, since his estate had been thereby enriched. For damage done by pure trespass without any corresponding accretion to the trespasser's estate, as by trampling herbage, his representative was held not to be liable.

Conversion of timber.

From what has now been said it will be perceived that from Bracton's age to our own the course of judicial and legislative action has tended constantly to narrow the scope of the maxim *actio personalis.* Injuries to the person and character represent the final intrenchment of a doctrine once applicable to all personal obligations, whether arising from contract or tort. Even from this small territory legislation, such as Lord Campbell's Act in England[4] and the many enactments in America authorizing actions by personal representatives in case of death by wrongful act, is driving the old doctrine into a field ever growing more narrow.

Final scope of the maxim.

Effect of Death of Person Injured upon Third Person's Right of Action for Consequential Damage.

It will be observed that the maxim *actio personalis moritur cum persona* comes into operation only when one of the parties to the obligation dies. If A commits a battery on B and either party dies, the right of action which accrued to B by reason of the battery is taken away. But if A commits a battery upon B, or does other injury to him, any right of action which accrues to a third person will not be affected by the death of B, so far as the application of the maxim in question is concerned. This proposition is apparently in conflict with authority and requires to be made clear.

As a matter of common-law principle it is settled that if A commits a battery upon B, who is servant to C, and thereby disables B from the performance of service which is due to C,

Action founded on loss of service.

[3] Savile 40.

[4] 9 & 10 Vict., c. 93.

Volume III

the latter has a right of action against A, founded upon the loss of service.[5] Similarly the husband has a right of action against one who seduces or abducts his wife, this action being founded upon the loss of consortium. The seduction of a daughter or other female dependent also gives a right of action to the parent or guardian.

Action not taken away by death of person immediately injured.

It will be perceived that the maxim *actio personalis* does not operate to take away the right of action of the master, husband, or parent, where the servant, wife, or daughter dies subsequent to the wrongful act which gives rise to the cause of action in favor of the master, husband, or parent. The legal relation involved in these respective rights of action exists between the wrongdoer and the master, husband, or parent, as the case may be, and the death of the person who is the immediate subject of the wrongful act can apparently have no bearing upon the right of action vested in the master, husband, or parent.

Maxim of *actio personalis* inapplicable.

This principle was recognized at an early day, for it was held in the fourteenth century that the right of action which accrues to a husband by virtue of the abduction of his wife, or which accrues to the parent or guardian by virtue of the abduction or rape of a daughter or ward, does not perish when the wife, daughter, or ward happens to die before suit is brought or judgment is obtained.[6]

When right of action merged.

There is, however, another principle which has to a greater or less extent restricted the right of action which accrues to the master, husband, or parent, and other persons occupying similar relations, by reason of a wrongful interference with such relations. This is found in the rule that wherever the wrongful act amounts to a felony, the civil right of action is merged in the felony and thereby lost. The typical case for the application of this principle is that of violent injury to a servant. Thus, if a servant is wrongfully beaten so that he dies of the beating, the master has no right of action for the loss of service thereby occasioned to him.[7]

[5] Hodsoll *v.* Stallebrass, 11 Ad. & El. 301, 39 E. C. L. 94.
[6] Y. B. 44 Ass. 285, pl. 13; Bellewe's Cases, *Ravishment*, pl. 3.
[7] Higgins *v.* Butcher, Yelv. 89.

Chapter VI

Obsolescence of doctrine of merger.

In modern times this idea of civil cause of action being merged in the felony has practically become obsolete. Furthermore, the doctrine can have no application where the fatal injury, though done by force, is yet not a felonious act, as where the killing results merely from negligence.

Action for consequential damage to husband by negligent injury to wife.

In *Baker v. Bolton* (1808),[8] this case arose: The defendants were the proprietors of a stage coach, on the top of which the plaintiff and his wife were traveling from Portsmouth to London. The coach was overturned and the plaintiff's wife was so badly hurt that she died a month later. The plaintiff brought an action for negligence and sought to recover for the loss of service and consortium. It will be noted that the maxim *actio personalis* did not apply, and there was nothing to show that the defendant's conduct was felonious. Hence the doctrine of merger was not applicable.

Recoverable damage limited to such as accrues in life of wife.

The simple question was therefore presented whether at common law the master or husband can recover for the breaking up of a relation of service or consortium, where the wrongful act causes the death of the servant or wife. Lord Ellenborough instructed the jury that the husband might recover for the loss of his wife's society and for his own distress of mind suffered on her account from the time of the accident till the moment of her dissolution. Concerning the loss of consortium subsequent to the death of the wife, his lordship observed that "in a civil court the death of a human being could not be complained of as an injury." "The damages as to the plaintiff's wife must," said he, "stop with the period of her existence."

The decision in question cannot be said of itself to have much weight. It was merely a *nisi prius* ruling. No authority was vouched, and no process of reasoning by which the conclusion in question may be supported was stated. In fact the ruling in this case merely embodied a judicial impression. One argument which has sometimes been supposed to support the conclusion in question is based upon the fact that no case could at that time be found in the books where an action had been maintained for loss of service or consortium resulting

[8] 1 Campb. 493.

Volume III

from a death brought about by a wrongful negligent act. But this argument cannot be considered to have much weight when we bear in mind the fact that the whole subject of negligence is very modern and the point in question had never arisen.

No action where wife or servant instantly killed.

Notwithstanding the fact that *Baker v. Bolton* is thus very unsatisfactory, it is nevertheless true that its doctrine has been generally accepted, and the law is settled that in the absence of statute, an action for loss of service or consortium does not lie where the servant or wife is instantly killed. But if, instead of being instantly killed, the servant or wife lives for a while and then dies, an action lies for loss of service or consortium during the interim.[9]

Doctrine criticised by Bramwell, B.

Basis of the doctrine explained by Christiancy, J.

It would perhaps be somewhat presumptuous to say that the courts have gone entirely wrong on this question, though it should be noted that no less learned a judge than Bramwell, B., has lately dissented from the accepted doctrine.[1] In *Hyatt v. Adams* (1867),[2] Christiancy, J., undertook to explain the rule which was applied in *Baker v. Bolton*. In so doing he used the following language: "For myself I think . . . that the reason of the rule is to be found in that natural and almost universal repugnance among enlightened nations to setting a price upon human life, or any attempt to estimate its value by a pecuniary standard; a repugnance which seems to have been strong and prevalent among nations in proportion as they have been or become more enlightened and refined, and especially so where the Christian religion has exercised its most beneficent influence, and where human life has been held most sacred. . . . To the cultivated and enlightened mind, looking at human life in the light of the Christian religion as sacred, the idea of compensating its loss in money is revolting, and it can only become reconciled to such an idea by the strong necessity which has grown out of the new modes of travel and business in modern times, by which great num-

[9] Osborn *v.* Gillett, L. R. 8 Exch. 88; Carey *v.* Berkshire R. Co., 1 Cush. (Mass.) 475; Hyatt *v.* Adams, 16 Mich. 180; Eden *v.* Lexington, etc., R. Co., 14 B. Mon. (Ky.) 165; Kearney *v.* Boston, etc., R. Co., 9 Cush. (Mass.) 108; Whitford *v.* Panama R. Co., 23 N. Y. 465.

[1] Osborn *v.* Gillett, L. R. 8 Exch. 93.

[2] 16 Mich. 180.

bers are compelled to trust their lives to the skill and vigilance of the servants of corporations, and others in similar positions of responsibility — a state of things which seemed to call for a remedy which should make railroad corporations, steamboat managers, and parties to whom others are compelled to trust for safety, more sensible of their responsibilities, and more careful to secure a high degree of vigilance in protecting the lives intrusted to their care, and at the same time afford relief for cases of great individual hardship, which might otherwise be suffered by those dependent upon the person whose life may be lost. Statutes of this kind have been passed in England and in many of the States of the Union."

The doctrine perhaps had its origin in a misconception of the application of the maxim *actio personalis,* or in a misconception of the application of the obsolete doctrine of merger. But whatever its origin or source, the doctrine in question is retained because the judges have thought it reasonable and just that the law should be so.

CHAPTER VII

NATURAL HISTORY OF REMEDIAL LAW (CONTINUED).

Assignment of Right of Action.

Volume III

IN this chapter we shall deal with the question of the assignability of the right of action. Legal theory here begins with the principle that rights of action cannot be assigned at all. The history of the subject consists merely of an account of the process by which this principle has been in great part subverted.

Analogy to doctrine discussed in preceding chapter.

It will be noted that the principle that the right of action cannot be assigned is a congener of the principle embodied in the maxim *actio personalis moritur cum persona.* The first principle refers to transfers by the act of the parties, and hence is concerned only with transfers or assignments among the living; while the other principle has reference to transfers happening at death and resulting from the act of law. It may be remarked that in giving an account of the two doctrines we are confronted in each case by the same obstacles. Both principles have their origin in the same stratum of legal thought. The same factors have operated to limit and impeach each of them in modern times, and both have had the curious fortune to be almost completely misunderstood. In no field of legal inquiry do we find a more pronounced confusion in legal reasoning. Indeed, it is no exaggeration to say that as these two principles have been actually dealt with by the courts they are practically unintelligible.

In beginning let us inquire into the reason for the existence of the principle that the right of action cannot be assigned. What natural necessity is there in the structure of legal ideas which makes the early law accept this principle as a matter of course? The answer to this question is not difficult to give, yet until very recent years it has been almost entirely overlooked.

Chapter VII

Reason for non-transferability of the right of action.

The right of action is not assignable among the living for the reason that every legal obligation, that is to say, every right of action, contemplates the existence of two persons as necessary parties, while the assignment or transfer contemplates an act of only one of them. Every right of action is inherently and of necessity two-sided. There cannot be a creditor without a debtor. There cannot be a right of action vested in one man without there being a corresponding duty or obligation resting on the person against whom the right of action exists. This being true, the law naturally hesitates about recognizing the validity of the assignment. If A commits a tort against B or violates a contract with him, thereby becoming subject to an action for damages, and B assigns this right of action to C, the law, or at least the early law, cannot, or does not, recognize the assignment as valid. As a matter of fundamental principle, one who claims as the mere assignee of a right of action must fail in the attempt to enforce the right because he is not in privity with the person against whom the obligation exists. This we say is the fundamental principle, which it requires the work of ages in the course of legal evolution to attenuate and destroy. The non-transferability of the right of action is planted in the very nature of things and constitutes a starting point in legal theory.

Lack of privity on part of assignee.

Another aspect of the reason underlying the non-transferability of the right of action can be gotten from a consideration of the fact that the mere right of action is an intangible thing. Professor Maitland has well said that in early law there is a mental incapacity to conceive the proposition that a mere right can be transferred or can pass from one person to another. "Things can be transferred; that is obvious: but how rights? You have not your rights in your hand or your pocket, nor can you put them into the hand of another nor lead him into them and bid him walk about within their metes and bounds."[1] In other words, only those things of which the transferee may have seisin can be conceived as transferable. Only where there is 'thingliness' or 'corporeity' may we expect also to find transferability.

Intangibility of the right of action.

[1] The Mystery of Seisin, 2 L. Quar. Rev. 489.

Volume III

What has just been said brings us into contact with a principle which has in all ages competed more or less effectively with the doctrine of the non-transferability of the right of action. If bare rights of action are inherently non-transferable, things which a man can own and handle are, on the other hand, inherently transferable. Whatever is a man's property he may transfer, grant, sell, or give to another at his pleasure. The bare right of action, as we have seen, always concerns two parties; but there are no two sides to the matter of ownership, at least where the owner has actual possession of the thing. A moment's consideration of these two ideas — the inherent non-transferability of the mere right of action and the inherent transferability of property — will suggest to the reader the possibility that, in the course of ages, as the faculty of legal abstraction is sharpened and as men become able to conceive and realize rights of action as a species of property, the old idea of non-transferability must give way. Indeed it is chiefly in this very fact of the changed point of view that, in our opinion, is to be found the true clue to the obsolescence of the old doctrine.

Inherent transferability of things and of property rights.

Realization of rights of action as species of property.

It is to be observed that since the day when the French was the familiar language of our courts, the term 'chose in action' has been generally used to convey the same idea as 'right of action.' But it cannot be said that this phrase, however ancient and familiar, is a happy one. Chose in action literally means 'thing in action,' and 'right of action' does not embody the idea of 'thing' at all. Indeed, it is the very absence of the notion of 'thing' which is the chief characteristic of the mere right of action. In its essence the mere right of action is an intangible entity.

The chose in action.

In modern times the difficulty in using the term chose in action as synonymous with right of action has become practically insuperable. This is due to the fact that of late it has become necessary, or at least convenient, to use the term chose in action to indicate certain intangible property rights which have nothing whatever in common with that right of action which is the subject of this chapter. Still the use of the expression in the sense of right of action continues, and conse-

Extension of meaning of chose in action.

quently a great deal of confusion exists in the minds of modern legal writers over the meaning of the term.

Chapter VII

The principle that mere rights of action are not assignable or grantable in life goes almost without saying in the early law. Fleta expressly enumerates actions (i. e., rights of action) among the things which can by no means be granted away (*a nullo dari debent*).[2] Bracton before him had explicitly said that rights of action could not be disposed of by will.[3]

Early doctrine.

Rastell's Termes de la Ley is a book which, like St. Germain's Doctor and Student, reflects the common law at the close of the year-book period with much fidelity. In it is to be found a definition of chose in action which is worth noting. It is there said: "Chose or thing in action is when a man hath cause or may bring an action for some duty due to him; as an action of debt upon an obligation, annuity, or rent, action of covenant or ward, trespass of goods taken away, beating or such like; and because they are things whereof a man is not possessed, but for recovery of them is driven to his action, they are called things in action."[4]

Definition of chose in action.

If we let the mind dwell upon the situations which this old book fits to the term chose in action, it must strike us that 'chose' in sense of thing is a misnomer, and at most can be used only in a metaphorical sense. What is here meant is the *cause* or *right* of action, a conception as far removed from that of material thing as can possibly be. Still, it must be observed that there has always been a sort of mental difficulty in conceiving of the right of action in this highly abstract and immaterial sense. The vizualizing faculty constantly impels us to think of the thing to be recovered, albeit only damages, as a specific material thing. Even Blackstone seems to have been unable to conceive of the chose in action in any other sense than that of a specific chattel wrongfully withheld and recoverable by a proper action.[5] Joshua Williams, a lucid and

Confusion as to meaning of the term.

[2] Fleta, 183.

[3] Bracton, 407 *b*.

[4] Termes de la Ley, *s. v. Chose in Action*.

[5] "Thus money due on a bond is a chose in action, for a property in the debt vests at the time of forfeiture mentioned in the obligation, but there is no possession till recovered by course of law. If a

Volume III

accurate writer, says, with perfect truth, that the chose in action is "the liberty of proceeding in courts of law either to recover pecuniary damage for the infliction of a wrong or the nonperformance of a contract, or else to procure the payment of money due."[6] According to this definition the term chose in action includes all personal rights of action arising either from the breach of a contract or from a tort, and there can be no question that such is its true import.

True import of the phrase.

The following passage from the pen of a living writer gives so much insight into the nature of the chose in action that we here reproduce it: "If we examine the nature of things in action, we shall soon see that they are merely claims enforceable at law, and that a man entitled to a thing in action has no *thing* (in the primary sense), and has not even anything which he can take. For example, in the case of a chose in action proper, as a debt, what is the thing, which is or lies in action, and which the person entitled thereto is said to have? It cannot be anything tangible, for the contracting of a debt (otherwise than by judgment and except to the crown) gives the creditor no interest whatever in, or charge upon, any money or other property of the debtor. If the debtor refuse payment, the creditor cannot take the amount due to him out of the debtor's money without committing theft; he has no legal remedy but to sue the debtor. When a debt is paid, the creditor ceases to have a chose in action: but the true effect of payment is not that the thing, which he had before in action, is handed over to him and so becomes a thing in possession. It is that the debtor's obligation is discharged and extinguished, and the former creditor (if paid in cash) acquires the ownership of certain coins, in which he previously had no interest at all. The thing therefore which lies in or is to be exacted by action, and which

Exposition of the nature of the chose in action (T. C. Williams).

man promises or covenants with me to do an act, and fails in it, whereby I suffer damage, the recompense for this damage is a chose in action; for though a right to some recompense vests in me at the time of the damage done, yet what and how large such recompense shall be can only be ascertained by verdict, and the possession can only be given me by legal judgment and execution." 2 Bl. Com. 396.

[6] Williams on Personal Property 63.

the creditor has, appears to be no tangible object, but to be the debtor's duty to pay the amount owing." [7]

Right of action to be distinguished from the fruits of the suit.

From what has been said it appears that the mere right of action or the true chose in action is sharply distinguished from the thing which is recoverable by means of an action. Still, as is shown by the quotation already made from Blackstone, judicial usage has always oscillated more or less between the idea of the mere naked right of proceeding — which is the proper meaning of chose in action — and the idea of the recoverable thing. Clearly the legal mind is here struggling to realize the abstract in the concrete.

Assignment of debt ineffectual in early common law.

An early year-book case which gives recognition to the principle that a right of action or chose in action is not assignable comes from 1459.[8] It appeared in this case that a bond had been given for an assignment of certain debts. The obligee of the bond sued upon the same. The obligors pleaded that the bond was invalid because not supported by a sufficient *quid pro quo*. The plea was held to be good. The assignment of the debts, being an assignment of mere choses in action, was ineffectual to transfer the debts to the assignee. Hence there was no *quid pro quo* to support the obligation given for the transfer. In *Mowse v. Edney* (1599),[9] the same principle was recognized, and it was said, in a case involving the assignment of a bill of debt, that "notwithstanding the assignment of the bill, the property in the debt remained all the time in the assignor."

Assignment of right of action to or by the king is valid.

One prominent exception to the principle that a chose in action is not assignable is to be noted as having prevailed from the earliest day. The king can sue on a right of action assigned or granted to him, and the assignee or grantee of the king can do likewise.[1] "Where the king by his letters gives or grants a duty which is due to him from any one, the grantee

[7] Property, Things in Action, and Copyright, by T. Cyprian Williams, 11 L. Quar. Rev. 228, 229.

[8] Y. B. 37 Hen. VI. 13, pl. 3.

[9] 1 Rolle Abr. 20, pl. 12. Compare: "A debt which I have by obligation cannot be granted over, for this is a chose in action." 2 Rolle Abr. 46 (G), pl. 1.

[1] Brooke Abr., *Chose in Action*, pls. 1, 2, 4, 6.

Volume III

of this debt shall have a good action in his own name, and so can no other one do." [2]

It is to be observed that in the cases involving the validity of the assignment of choses in action which arose prior to the beginning of the seventeenth century the courts did not, generally speaking, put their decisions on the ground that the assignment is bad because of maintenance. They seem to have proceeded on the idea that the assignment of a right of action is a thing which is *per se* impossible. This was at least the correct view.

When assignment bad for maintenance.

Still, it must be admitted that cases may arise where the invalidity of the assignment can well be said to follow from the policy of the laws against maintenance and champerty. In *Lampet's Case* (1611),[3] it was said in a casual dictum that the reason why the law does not recognize the validity of an assignment of a right of action is that it would be the occasion of multiplying contentions and suits, to the great oppression of the people. From this language it would appear that the whole explanation of the invalidity of the assignments is to be found in the policy of the laws against maintenance and champerty. But this is clearly a mistake. An assignment may in particular cases be bad because the transaction is infected with maintenance or champerty; but the laws against maintenance and champerty fall far short of supplying an inclusive reason for the ancient principle that the chose in action is not assignable. The ultimate explanation, as we have already said, is to be found in considerations of the inherent nature of the act of assignment and lack of privity on the part of the assignee.

Currency of the explanation based on policy of law against maintenance.

Notwithstanding the purely artificial character of the explanation which is deduced from the policy of the laws against maintenance and champerty, this explanation has had currency from Coke's day to our own, and in all judicial discussions of the law concerning the assignment of rights of action, it is taken for granted that the sole reason why the chose in action cannot be assigned at common law is to be found in the

[2] Y. B. 39 Hen. VI. 26, pl. 36; Y. B. 2 Hen. VII. 9, pl. 25.
[3] 10 Coke 48*a*.

tendency of such a transaction to promote litigation. The consequence is that the idea of maintenance and champerty has been grievously overworked. Surely if this explanation were true to the full extent, then it certainly would appear that "our ancestors got into very odd notions" on this subject, and it could also be truthfully said that the common law had a "prodigious jealousy" of permitting rights to be transferred from one man to another.[4]

Legal history summed up.

Perhaps the course of early legal history in regard to this matter of the assignment of the chose in action can be truthfully stated as follows: The law starts, we may say, from the principle that the chose in action is not assignable at all. As time passes, this principle is found to be untenable as a matter of practical law, and so the original doctrine is circumscribed and limited. In the course of this process the idea emerges that the assignee of a chose in action does get a qualified right by virtue of the assignment, provided the transaction is not in fact objectionable for maintenance or champerty. This seems to be the stage of development which is reflected in the dictum of *Lampet's Case*. The idea of maintenance does not supply the point of origin, but merely represents a temporary point of lodgment in the history of the circumscription of the original broad doctrine.

Horn v. Foster (1455)[5] is perhaps the most instructive of all the early cases on the subject of the assignment of choses in action, for here we find the germ of that device by which the principle of the non-transferability of the chose in action was to be effectually impeached as a general rule of common law. It appeared in this case that one Francis was creditor of Horn to the extent of one hundred pounds. Francis was at the same time himself a debtor to one Foster in a like sum. In full satisfaction of the latter debt Francis assigned to Foster the obligation evidencing the debt against Horn. The latter was alleged to have consented to the transfer. Francis died, and suit was then brought at the instance of Foster against Horn in the name of the administrators of the deceased creditor,

Assignee may lawfully maintain suit in name of assignor where value is given.

[4] See Goodright v. Forester, 1 Taunt. 613.
[5] Y. B. 34 Hen. VI. 30, pl. 15.

Francis. Horn was evidently cast in this suit, for he afterwards brought an action for maintenance against Foster. The court held that this latter action would not lie. A man to whom a debt is assigned for value thereby acquires such an interest in it that it is not maintenance on his part to instigate and procure an action to be brought on the debt in the name of the original creditor or his representative.

Debt assignable "in satisfaction."

Fitzherbert says this case is authority for the doctrine that "a debt can be assigned in satisfaction."[6] Brooke, commenting on a similar case from a somewhat later period, said that "a chose [in action] can be assigned for lawful cause, such as a just debt, but not for [the purpose of] maintenance."[7]

Action in name of assignor to use of assignee.

Thus did the principle gain admittance into the law that the assignee of a debt who has given a consideration may lawfully instigate and maintain a suit thereon in the name of his assignor. Naturally this idea was too valuable to be lost, and accordingly we find that before many years had passed, the right of an assignee of a chose in action to sue to his own use in the name of his assignor was fully accepted. "If one be indebted to me and delivers to me in satisfaction of this debt an obligation to him, I shall bring an action in the name of my debtor [the assignor] and shall pay my counsel and all the [expense] incident to the suit."[8]

Custom has its origin in actual power of attorney.

There is reason to suppose that the recognition of the right of the assignee of a chose in action to sue in the name of his assignor to his own use had its origin from a custom by which the making of the assignment was originally accompanied by the execution of a power of attorney by the assignor, expressly authorizing the assignee to sue in the name of the assignor. In *Penson v. Hickbed* (1589),[9] Gawdy, J., observed that the assignment of a debt accompanied by a letter of attorney to sue for it is in no wise subject to objection on the ground of maintenance, "except it be assigned to be recovered and the party to have part of it."

Letter of attorney becomes unnecessary.

As was but natural, in course of time the actual execution of the letter of attorney came to be

[6] Fitz. Abr., *Maintenaunce*, pl. 14.

[7] Brooke Abr., *Chose in Action*, pl. 3.

[8] Y. B. 15 Hen. VII. 2, pl. 3.

[9] Cro. Eliz. 170, 4 Leon. 99.

Chapter VII

considered superfluous, and the act of assignment itself was construed as giving an implied authority to the assignee to use the name of the assignor.

The agreement by which a debt is assigned merely for the purpose of having suit brought upon it, and with the understanding that the assignee is to have part of the proceeds when the debt has been recovered, has always been considered as being champertous and unlawful. But an exception has been recognized even to this rule. Thus at an early day it was held that where the owner of a debt is an alien and ignorant of our language it is not champertous to prosecute the claim for him for a part of the recovery.[1] This exception proceeds upon the idea that it is charitable to assist a person so circumstanced, and hence this act of maintenance is held to be lawful.

The champertous assignment.

When prosecution of claim for alien not champertous.

By means of the device of suing in the name of the assignor, the assignee of a chose in action acquired a standing in the courts of common law. The assignment is not so far recognized as a perfect transfer of a right of action as to enable the assignee to sue in his own name. The assignee stands in the place of the assignor, so to speak, but does not displace him. Of late years statutes have been passed in many jurisdictions declaring that actions shall always be brought in the name of the party beneficially interested in the suit. These statutes of course operate to give the assignee a right of action in his own name. But it will be observed that the change thus effected is purely a procedural one, and the statutes in question do not operate to extend the power of assigning.

Present position of assignee of chose in action.

The chose in action which first became so far transferable as to admit of the bringing of a suit by the assignee in the name of the assignor (suing to the use of the assignee) was the debt. The question naturally arises, How far has this idea of the qualified transferability of the chose in action been extended? Can a man now transfer a claim arising out of the breach of an ordinary contract or arising from the commission of a tort, so as to permit the assignee to sue on such claim in the name of the assignor? How far has the ancient

[1] Y. B. 15 Hen. VII. 2, pl. 3. See also authorities cited in vol. 1, p. 340

Volume III

principle of the non-transferability of the chose in action been impeached?

Tendency towards extension of right to assign.

This is a very difficult question to answer with precision, because the decisions are not uniform; but it may be said that the general tendency has constantly been towards the extension of the right to assign. The ancient argument based on the idea of preventing litigation by discouraging assignments has ceased to appeal to the courts, and consequently that idea is looked upon as a mere legal curiosity and relic of the past.[2]

Actions founded on personal wrongs not assignable in any sense.

As regards particular results, it is pretty generally held in America that the only causes or rights of action which are not transferable or assignable in any sense are those which are founded upon wrongs of a purely personal nature, such as slander,[3] assault and battery,[4] negligent personal injuries,[5] criminal conversation, seduction,[6] breach of marriage promise, malicious prosecution,[7] and others of like nature. All other demands, claims, and rights of action whatever are generally held to be transferable.[8]

Illustrations of assignable rights of action.

In conformity with the principle just stated the following demands, claims, and rights of action have been held to be assignable: causes of action arising from the breach of a contract of any kind [9] (except the breach of a promise to marry); causes of action arising from torts which affect the estate

[2] See language of Buller, J., in Master *v.* Miller (1791), 4 T. R. 340, 341; Waties, J., in Parker *v.* Kennedy (1794), 1 Bay (S. Car.) 404, 406; Freeman, J., in East Tennessee, etc., R. Co. *v.* Henderson, 1 Lea (Tenn.) 4.

[3] Renfro *v.* Prior, 25 Mo. App. 402; Miller *v.* Newell, 20 S. Car. 123; Dillard *v.* Collins, 25 Gratt. (Va.) 343.

[4] McGlinchy *v.* Hall, 58 Me. 152; Averill *v.* Longfellow, 66 Me. 237.

[5] Central R., etc., Co. *v.* Brunswick, etc., R. Co., 87 Ga. 386; Stone *v.* Boston, etc., R. Co., 7 Gray (Mass.) 539.

[6] Howard *v.* Crowther, 8 M. & W. 601; People *v.* Tioga C. Pl., 19 Wend. (N. Y.) 73.

[7] Brewer *v.* Dew, 11 M. & W. 625; Lawrence *v.* Martin, 22 Cal. 174; Hunt *v.* Conrad, 47 Minn. 557; Noonan *v.* Orton, 34 Wis. 259.

[8] McKee *v.* Judd, 12 N. Y. 625; Hoyt *v.* Thompson, 5 N. Y. 320; North *v.* Turner, 9 S. & R. (Pa.) 248, 249.

[9] Pickering *v.* Ilfracombe R. Co., L. R. 3 C. P. 235; Savage *v.* Gregg, 150 Ill. 161; Morris *v.* Cheney, 51 Ill. 451; Felt *v.* Reynolds Rotary Fruit Evaporating Co., 52 Mich. 602; Sepp *v.* McCann, 47 Minn. 364; Salisbury *v.* Keigher, 47 Minn. 367; Hooker *v.* Eagle Bank, 30 N. Y. 83; Carver *v.* Creque, 46 Barb. (N. Y.) 507; Gilmore *v.* Westerman, 13 Wash. 390.

Chapter VII

rather than the person of the individual who is injured. Under the latter head are claims arising from the carrying away, or conversion, of personal property,[1] from the fraudulent misapplication of funds by the officer of a bank,[2] from negligent or intentional injury done to personal property[3] or upon real estate.[4]

Right of action for deceit not assignable.

In view of the general tendency to recognize the transferability of rights of action growing out of injuries done in respect of one's property or estate, it is somewhat curious to note that it is commonly held that the right of action for fraud and deceit is not assignable.[5] But where *property* is obtained by a deceit or fraudulent device of any sort, the cause of action is assignable,[6] for here the injury is done in respect of the particular property which is wrongfully acquired.

Assignability determined by reference to survival.

Some assistance in determining whether a particular right of action is assignable may sometimes be gotten from considering the question whether that right of action is so far of a personal nature as to perish upon the death of one of the parties. As we have already pointed out, the rule which prohibits the assignment of rights of action among the living is the exact counterpart of the rule that the personal action dies with the person. Consequently, assuming that in both fields the law has developed along similar lines, we ought to be able to determine the assignability of a right of action by reference to its perishability. Indeed, there is abundance of modern authority to the effect that the perishability of an action is a

[1] Lazard *v.* Wheeler, 22 Cal. 139; Final *v.* Backus, 18 Mich. 218; Smith *v.* Kennett, 18 Mo. 154; Jordan *v.* Gillen, 44 N. H. 424; Sherman *v.* Elder, 24 N. Y. 381; Tyson *v.* McGuineas, 25 Wis. 656; McArthur *v.* Green Bay, etc., Canal Co., 34 Wis. 139.

[2] Grocers' Nat. Bank *v.* Clark, 48 Barb. (N. Y.) 26.

[3] Everett *v.* Central Iowa R. Co., 73 Iowa 442; Butler *v.* New York, etc., R. Co., 22 Barb. (N. Y.) 110; East Tennessee, etc., R. Co. *v.* Henderson, 1 Lea (Tenn.) 1.

[4] More *v.* Massini, 32 Cal. 590; Chouteau *v.* Boughton, 100 Mo. 406; Fried *v.* New York Cent. R. Co., 25 How. (N. Y.) 285; Weire *v.* Davenport, 11 Iowa 49.

[5] Tufts *v.* Matthews, 10 Fed. Rep. 609; Morris *v.* Morris, 5 Mich. 171; Brush *v.* Sweet, 38 Mich. 574; Dickinson *v.* Seaver, 44 Mich. 624; Smith *v.* Thompson, 94 Mich. 381; Zabriskie *v.* Smith, 13 N. Y. 322; Shoemaker *v.* Keeley, 1 Yeates (Pa.) 245.

[6] Clews *v.* Tracr, 57 Iowa 459; Johnston *v.* Bennett, 5 Abb. Pr. N. S (N. Y.) 331.

Volume III

test of the assignability of such action.[7] "The power to assign and to transmit to personal representatives are convertible propositions." [8]

Difficulty of applying this test.

The value of this test is greatly lessened by reason of the fact that it is often quite as difficult to determine whether the maxim *actio personalis moritur cum persona* is applicable in a given case, as it is to determine the matter of assignability viewed as an independent problem. Besides, there is reason to believe that the rule concerning the perishability of actions and the rule concerning assignability have not developed *pari passu*. Thus, as we learned in the last chapter, before an action grounded upon a pure tort can survive to the personal representative the tort must be such as to bring about an increase of the estate of the tortfeasor. Such at least is the English rule, declared in *Phillips v. Homfray* (1883).[9] It is evident that if a similar rule were applied in regard to assignment very different results would have been reached from that indicated in some of the American cases cited above. It is clear that the law in both these branches has developed with great irregularity. Modern remedial statutes have played and will continue to play a large part in shaping the law of these subjects. Even if it were a feasible thing to attempt to work out the common-law doctrines applicable here, it is doubtful if the results would compensate for the labor expended. This department of law has always been more or less in a state of change. The difficulty has been greatly increased by the inability of the courts to perceive the original ground of the rule which here constitutes the starting point in legal theory.

Irregularity of legal development in this field.

Bearing of novation upon law of assignment.

The form of contract which is known as the novation furnishes a means by which, in modern times, effect can be given to the assignment of a debt or other chose in action in certain situations. Thus if A is indebted to B, and B to C, and the three agree that A shall pay C and that B shall in turn be

[7] Comegys *v.* Vasse, 1 Pet. (U. S.) 213; Tufts *v.* Matthews, 10 Fed. Rep. 609; Finn *v.* Corbitt, 36 Mich. 318; Zabriskie *v.* Smith, 13 N. Y. 322; Galveston, etc., R. Co. *v.* Freeman, 57 Tex. 156; Stewart *v.* Houston, etc., R. Co., 62 Tex. 246.

[8] Zabriskie *v.* Smith, 13 N. Y. 334; Byxbie *v.* Wood, 24 N. Y. 611.

[9] 24 Ch. D. 439.

discharged from his debt to C, the contract is binding.[1] The effect of such a novation is to transfer the obligation owing by the debtor A from creditor B to creditor C, so that the latter is enabled to sue upon it in his own name.

But it is to be noted that the novation is enforced as a new contract supported by the consideration of the discharge of one of the parties, and it is not to be treated as a mere assignment at all, though it is often spoken of as such. Where there is a true novation perfected by a new promise by the debtor to the assignee, the latter sues in his own name.[2] The novation is a comparatively late form of contract which, as we have elsewhere seen, derives its validity from the mutuality of the promises of the several parties. It follows that assignments put into the form of novations could not be given effect prior to the recognition of the validity of the bilateral contract. As a means of effectuating assignments of ordinary debts and other choses in action the novation is evidently of quite narrow compass.

Distinction between novation and assignment.

[1] Willmot *v.* Prigget, 1 Rolle Abr. 29, pl. 60; Fairlie *v.* Denton, 8 B. & C. 400, 15 E. C. L. 247.

[2] Clarke *v.* Thompson, 2 R. I. 146.

CHAPTER VIII

NATURAL HISTORY OF REMEDIAL LAW (CONTINUED).

The Venue of Actions.

Volume III

THE subject of the venue of actions is one of some practical importance, and the solution of certain difficulties connected with venue has given rise to the distinction between local and transitory actions, about which a few words may profitably be said.

Action triable in county where cause of action arises.

As a question of first impression it must strike one as rational and proper that all suits should be tried in the county where the particular cause of action arises. There is an ancient maxim to the effect that neighbors are presumed to know about the acts of one another: *vicini vicinorum facta praesumuntur scire.*

It has been supposed that the old system of frank-pledge, by which, for purposes of police, the various communities were divided into decennaries whose members served as a sort of collective bail for each other, was based partly on the idea embodied in the above maxim.[1] This is perhaps doubtful, but there can be no question that our early jury system did rest on such a notion. The jurors were drawn from the neighborhood

Corollary from system of jury trial.

(*vicinetum*) where the controversy arose or where the land in question lay, and their verdict was based upon their own personal knowledge or upon facts gathered by them. This peculiar institution served to wed actions to place. Hence that English predilection for local and rural justice which Henry I pledged himself in his *Leges* to maintain.

It being assumed as a general principle that actions should be tried in the county where the action arose and by the verdict of men actually acquainted with the case, it followed that

Venue to be laid in writ.

the writ should always contain a description of the district, hundred, or vill, where the transaction occurred. This

[1] Gilbert, Hist. Common Pleas, ch. 7.

Chapter VIII

was necessary in order that the sheriff might summon the jury from the proper neighborhood. That the rule requiring an accurate statement of the venue was strictly insisted upon will be apparent to any one who examines the old authorities on pleading. Thus, it was once said that even in assumpsit the plaintiff must allege the place where the promise was made.[2] But a little later in the same sort of action it was said, in a case where the promise was made in one county and the breach occurred in another, that the defendant could take issue either on the promise or on the breach, and that the venue would be thereby determined.[3] It is no doubt true that this particularity in stating the venue also fulfilled the requirement of certainty in pleading;[4] but the chief basis of the rule was undoubtedly found in the peculiar nature of the early jury.

Certainty of pleading required.

However strict in the theory the early common law may have been in the requirement of the statement of a venue, it was inevitable that the rule should in many cases be evaded. Some causes of action are of such character that it is not practicable and indeed hardly possible to localize them. The simple duty to pay money and the duty to compensate for damage done to the person are often of this character. The duty follows the debtor, and the place where the duty originates is wholly immaterial. As was said in *Byron v. Byron* (1596),[5] every debt follows the person of the debtor.

Debt follows person of debtor.

The distinction between local and transitory actions was perceived at a very early day, and the line of demarcation between the two sorts of actions coincided very nearly with the older division of real and personal actions. The mixed actions, when we come to consider them with regard to the question of venue, are to be treated as local, for they are partly based on rights *in rem*. Only actions which are purely *in personam* are transitory.

Distinction between local and transitory action.

One of the first forms of obligation to become recognized as transitory was the sealed obligation. Such an instrument

[2] Y. B. 48 Edw. III. 6, pl. 11.
[3] Brooke Abr., *Visne*, pl. 117.
[4] 3 Co. Litt., Thomas's ed., (464)* note.
[5] Cro. Eliz. 472, pl. 25 (Hil. 38 Eliz.).

Volume III

Sealed obligation is transitory.

was binding even though no place was named in it. Consequently, in order to make it ambulatory so that it could be sued on in any county where the defendant might subsequently be found, it became customary to omit the name of the place and begin the instrument with the words *noverint universi.*[6] In this way the hardship and inconvenience of the old rule in regard to venue was avoided.

All contractual obligations become transitory.

The idea that certain actions are of a transitory character spread further than the specialty, and in the time of Coke this truth was put into the maxim *debitum et contractus sunt nullius loci.*[7] As authority for this maxim Coke cites a number of decisions from the year books. The idea had evidently been familiar for a long period, and Coke seems to have looked upon it as representing a starting point in the common-law history of actions. In this he was probably mistaken. All actions were originally local in the sense that a particular venue had to be alleged and proved. The maxim that debts and contracts are of no particular place therefore appeared as an exception to the old doctrine.

The fictitious venue.

However this may be, the custom of the courts to allow certain of the personal actions to be maintained in any county in contravention of the rule concerning venue had become well established before the end of the fourteenth century. Fictitious venues were laid in counties remote from the defendant, and litigious plaintiffs were thus able greatly to harass those against whom they had claims. In such case the defendant had to repair with his witnesses to the court where the venue was laid, however remote it might be.

Early statutes.

Abuses of this kind caused Parliament to pass a statute in 1383 which aimed to restore the old and strict practice under which all actions were required to be brought in the county where the transaction giving rise to the action occurred. This enactment provided that henceforth writs of debt, account, and all other such actions, should be directed to the sheriffs of the county where the contract arose on which the action was

[6] Gilbert, Hist. Common Pleas, ch. 7, p. 90.
[7] Bulwer's Case, 7 Coke 3*a*.

based, and that in case of a violation of this rule the writ should be abated.[8]

This statute did not prove effective, since no penalty was imposed save the abatement of the writ. Consequently a few years later, attorneys were required to take an oath to the effect that "they would make no suit in a foreign county."[9] The court rules of 15 Elizabeth and of A. D. 1630 made it penal for attorneys to transgress this statute.

Impropriety of venue pleadable in abatement.

After the passage of the statute of 4 Henry IV it became customary to plead the impropriety of venue in abatement of the writ even before the plaintiff had declared. At first the courts of their own motion examined the plaintiff on oath as to the truth of the venue alleged;[1] but this did not prove adequate, and in the time of James I[2] it became customary for the courts to order changes of venue upon the application of the party defendant. An affidavit was required, since if the application prevailed it operated with the same effect as a plea in abatement so far as the original forum was concerned. The motion for the change of venue and the affidavit supporting it were called the common rule and common affidavit.[3]

Change of venue.

The power of changing venue was exercised by the court under and by virtue of the intent or, as it was called, the equity of the statutes of Richard II and Henry IV, above referred to, and hence the power does not extend to purely local actions. In these a change of venue seems never to have been granted save under very special circumstances.[4]

Local actions.

It will be observed that in the transitory actions the use of a fictitious venue does not vitiate the cause of action. In local actions the question of venue is implicated with that of jurisdiction as well. The purely local actions are such as are of a criminal character and such as involve the title to land or arise

[8] Stat. 6 Rich. II., c. 2.

[9] Stat. 4 Hen. IV., c. 18.

[1] See note by J. W. Smith to Mostyn *v.* Fabrigas, 1 Smith Lead. Cas. (8th ed.) 1047; Bacon's Abr., *Actions, Local and Transitory.*

[2] Knight *v.* Farnaby, 2 Salk. 670.

[3] Gerrard *v.* Floyd, 1 Sid. 185.

[4] Power was given by 3 & 4 William IV., c. 42, § 23, to change the venue even in local actions, and this right was confirmed and extended by the Common Law Procedure Act, 1852, §§ 41, 182.

Volume III

out of injuries to realty. The fictitious venue accordingly has never been used in these actions.[5]

Venue as question of jurisdiction.

The distinction between venue as a mere question of procedure and venue as a question of jurisdiction is fully developed in the opinions of the several judges in *British South Africa Co. v. Companhia de Moçambique.*[6] This case arose after the rules of practice established in conformity with the provisions of the Judicature Act had done away with venue as a mere matter of procedure,[7] and the question presented for decision was whether the courts of England had, by the abolition of local venue, acquired jurisdiction of a cause of action arising out of a trespass to realty in a foreign land. The case was ably and fully presented by counsel, and the several opinions contain much historical matter pertaining to the venue of actions. A perusal of those opinions will supply the reader with most of the learning on a somewhat complicated subject, or at least put him on the track of it. Suffice it to say that, in the view which finally prevailed, it was declared to be law that the disability of the courts of one country to entertain a suit for damages to realty in a foreign land is due to want of jurisdiction of the subject-matter. Consequently the abolition of local venues, as it only affects a matter of procedure, does not confer authority to entertain such a suit. "No two questions," said Lord Halsbury, "can be more distinct than the question whether a matter is in the jurisdiction of the English courts at all, and whether a matter undoubtedly within the

[5] See language of Lord Esher, M. R., (1892) 2 Q. B. 404.

[6] (1893) A. C. 602. In the Queen's Bench Division and in the Court of Appeal the case is reported as Companhia de Mocambique *v.* British South Africa Co., (1892) 2 Q. B. 358.

[7] Rule 1 of Order XXXVI. is as follows: "There shall be no local venue for the trial of any action except where otherwise provided by statute." Construing this rule Lord Herschell said: "The rule does not purport to touch the distinction between local and transitory actions —between matters which have no necessary local connection, and those which are local in their nature. It deals only with the place of trial, and enables actions, whatever their nature, to be tried in any county. But it is, in my opinion, a mere rule of procedure, and applies only to those cases in which the courts at that time exercised jurisdiction." British South Africa Co. *v.* Companhia de Mocambique, (1893) A. C. 627.

jurisdiction of the courts shall be assigned for trial to particular courts in England."[8] Lord Herschell, referring to the fact that the English courts had by means of a fictitious venue entertained suits upon transitory causes of action arising in foreign lands, but had refused to entertain suits upon local causes of action arising in foreign lands, said: "The rule that in local actions the venue must be local did not, where the cause of action arose in this country, touch the jurisdiction of the courts, but only determined the particular manner in which the jurisdiction should be exercised; but where the matter complained of was local and arose outside the realm, the refusal to adjudicate upon it was in fact a refusal to exercise jurisdiction, and I cannot think that the courts would have failed to find a remedy if they had regarded the matter as one within their jurisdiction, and which it was proper for them to adjudicate upon."[9]

[8] (1893) A. C. 631.

[9] *Ib.*, 619

PART II

COMMON-LAW ACTIONS

CHAPTER IX

THE ACTION OF ACCOUNT.

FOR several hundred years the action of account occupied no mean place among common-law remedies. In modern times the bill in equity for an accounting has been found to be better adapted to the enforcement of the obligation to render an account, and the old legal remedy has consequently fallen into disuse. The count in assumpsit for money had and received has also been extended into the field formerly occupied by the action of account. Chapter IX

Where the accounts are complicated or the parties numerous this latter remedy is manifestly unavailable; and consequently where it is necessary to proceed against a defendant upon the legal obligation to render an account, the bill in equity is now the only remedy. The obligation to account is therefore a good illustration of a perfect legal right for the enforcement of which the legal remedy is obsolete. The principles which underlie the old action still remain in our law. They cannot be neglected by the court of equity, for its jurisdiction in matters of account is determined largely by them.[1] We shall also presently see that the common-law courts cannot safely forget the ancient learning, except at the risk of doing violence to legal principle. **Account obsolete as legal remedy.**

The common-law action of account is founded directly on the legal duty to render an account, and this duty does not arise out of contract in the modern sense.[2] It belongs to the **The obligation to render account.**

[1] In an article entitled A Brief Survey of Equity Jurisdiction, 2 Harv. L. Rev. 242, 267, Prof. C. C. Langdell has made an admirable statement of the compass and function of the common-law remedy of account. His paper has been of material assistance in the preparation of what is here said on the subject.

[2] The form given in the Register for the writ of account against the bailiff and receiver contains no allegation of any contract. "Rex vicomiti etc., salutem. Praecipimus tibi quod justicies Johannem Brown

Volume III

stratum of real contract law rather than to the field of assumpsit. This will become manifest by an examination of the circumstances upon which the law imposes the duty to account.

The common-law accountants.

There are but three classes of common-law accountants — guardians, bailiffs, and receivers;[3] and the duty of accounting is imposed on these persons by virtue of the fact that under certain conditions they have the legal possession of property belonging to another. As was said by one of the judges in the latter part of the fifteenth century, "in every case where one has a thing in his keeping he is chargeable in an action of account if he has it not to his own use."[4]

Analogy to relation of bailor and bailee.

The relation between creditor and accountant is analogous to that between bailor and bailee. In fact, as we shall see, bailees are one sort of accountants; and the action of account has always been concurrent with detinue as a common-law remedy for the bailor. As in the case of the ordinary bailees, accountants have possession only while ownership remains in the proprietor. This severance of ownership and possession at once distinguishes bailees and accountants from persons (debtors) who acquire title at the time the obligation to reimburse or restore is incurred, and from tortfeasors who acquire the property by conversion. As one must always have possession before he can become liable as an accountant, it follows that the action cannot be maintained against a mere servant who has custody but not possession in law.[5]

Accountant, like bailee, has possession.

The term 'bailiff' as applied to one class of accountants is

quod juste et sine dilatione reddat B. rationabilem computum suum, de tempore quo fuit ballivus suus in N. et receptor denariorum ipsius B. sicut rationabiliter monstrare poterit quod ei reddere debeat." Reg. Brev. Orig. 135.

The writ between merchants counted upon a contract, but the expression used ("*ex quacumque causa et contractu*") shows that the duty arose out of the transaction and not out of agreement or promise. "Praecipimus tibi quod justicies A mercatorem quod juste etc., reddat B mercatori rationabilem computum suum de tempore quo fuit receptor denariorum ipsius B ex quacumque causa et contractu ad communem utilitatem ipsorum A et B pervenientium, sicut per legem mercatoriam rationabiliter monstrare poterit quod ei reddere debet." Reg. Brev. Orig. 135.

[3] Y. B. 2 Hen. IV. 12, pl. 50; Co. Litt. 172*a*; 2 Inst. 379; 1 Rolle Abr., *Accompt*, 117 (D); Com. Dig., *Accompt* (A 1).

[4] Keble, J., in Y. B. 10 Hen. VII. 6, pl. 12.

[5] Com. Dig., *Accompt* (D).

Chapter IX

of rather indefinite scope. In its proper legal signification it is applied to any agent who has possession of the lands, goods, or chattels of another and who is charged with the duty of using and administering them for the benefit of the owner.[6] But its meaning is sometimes restricted to a narrower compass. Thus bailiff is often particularly used to indicate the representative of the lord of a manor,[7] or a petty officer or magistrate in a hundred, or a deputy appointed by the sheriff. But it is also applicable to all agents charged with handling for profit the money or goods of another. Factors and commission merchants fall within this class.

The bailiff.

In the strict theory of the early law the bailiff is distinguishable from the bailee by the circumstance that the bailiff receives the property either for the purpose of selling it or for the purpose of using it in order to produce an income for the owner. The bailee, on the other hand, does not handle or manage for the profit of the owner the goods committed to his keeping. He holds solely for the purpose of keeping, conveying, managing, or performing work upon the thing bailed, with the ultimate object of restoring it to the owner when the purpose of the bailment is accomplished, or of delivering it to his order. However, since the action of account has fallen into disuse this distinction is no longer regarded. Accordingly, bailiffs and ordinary bailees are classed together.[8]

Distinction between bailiff and bailee.

[6] Co. Litt. 172*a*.

[7] F. N. B. 116 P.

[8] *The Factor a Bailee by Modern Usage.* — There was an active controversy in the early part of the nineteenth century between Judge Story and Chancellor Kent as to whether the term bailment is properly to be applied to cases in which no redelivery to the owner or his agent is contemplated. Judge Story gave the term bailment sufficient latitude to include a consignment of goods to a factor to be sold. Story on Bailments, § 2, note. Chancellor Kent, in his Commentaries, said: "Mr. Story . . . shows sufficiently from the books that bailment is a term sometimes applied to the delivery of goods to another for sale, without any expectation of redelivery;" "but I apprehend this is extending the definition of the term beyond the ordinary acceptation of it in the English law." 2 Kent Com. 558, note.

Strictly speaking, the factor is one of the common-law accountants, and Judge Kent evidently had the ancient distinction between bailiffs and bailees in his mind. When the question was mooted, however, the law of account had long ceased to be familiar and the term 'bailiff' in its broad sense had dropped out of use. It was therefore necessary to extend the term 'bailee' so as to cover this case. The legal liability

Volume III

The receiver.

The receiver at common law is strictly the *receptor denariorum*, or custodian of money. He has no other duty to perform than that of keeping the money safely and paying it over at the proper time to the party entitled. As he is not accountable for profits, he has no right to use the money in any way except to preserve it. If he otherwise uses or converts it, the obligation is changed into a personal debt. While he is thus answerable for the identical fund received by him, he is not required to have forthcoming the specific coins or bills committed to his custody.[0] It sometimes happens that one makes another his bailiff and also his receiver, in which case the accountant is liable in both capacities.[1]

Early history of action of account.

Turning now for a moment to the early history of the remedy, we find that the action of account first came into use in Bracton's age. The earliest instance of its use comes from the year 1232.[2] The writ is found on the Register near the end of the reign of Henry III, being used for the purpose of bringing manorial bailiffs to account.[3]

Guardians required to account for estate of ward.

During the Barons' War a concession to them was embodied in the Provisions of Westminster (1259) to the effect that guardians in socage should preserve the estate unimpaired for the benefit of the heir and render a lawful account upon his attaining majority.[4] This innovation was subsequently incorporated in the Statute of Marlborough (1267).[5]

The lawful age of the heir of a tenant in socage at common law is fourteen years, and consequently that was the age at which he was entitled to an accounting. Coke tells us that this provision in the Statute of Marlborough was only a declaration of the common law, but modern research has shown that he was mistaken. The action of account was very new when this statement was passed, and guardians in socage were

is substantially the same as regards both bailiffs and bailees, and no inconvenience resulted. Judge Story's view has therefore prevailed in modern times.

[0] A Brief Survey of Equity Jurisdiction, 2 Harv. L. Rev. 247.

[1] F. N. B. 116 P.

[2] Bracton, Note Book pl. 859; 2 Poll. & Mait. Hist. Eng. Law, 2d ed., 221.

[3] Register of Original Writs, F. W. Maitland, 3 Harv. L. Rev. 173, 214.

[4] Provisions West., c. 12.

[5] Chapter 17. See 2 Co. Inst. 135.

probably not liable at all before the enactment of the Provisions of Westminster.[6]

Remedy given by statutes of Marlborough and Westminster II.

Chapter twenty-three of the Statute of Marlborough gave a new remedy, by attachment of the body and imprisonment, against defaulting bailiffs who had no lands or tenements out of which the claim could be made good.[7] This statute, although only the term 'bailiff' was used, was interpreted to extend to guardians in socage and receivers. The Statute of Westminster II went much further, and allowed process of outlawry against "servants, bailiffs, chamberlains, and all manner of receivers, which are bound to yield account." This was very rigorous, and was interpreted not to extend to guardians in socage.[8]

Accounting among partners.

In the reign of Edward I the action of account was found to be useful in the settlement of partnership affairs, and as trade and commerce expanded largely under the influence of foreign merchants and capitalists, the remedy attained a very prominent position in English law. During the year-book period the action was nearly as common as debt, and apparently about twice as often used as detinue.[9]

Privity of relation essential to right of account.

One of the striking features of the obligation to account is that notwithstanding it is based directly on legal obligation and not on agreement, it is always necessary, before the law will raise the duty to account, that there should be direct privity between the parties. One must hold possession under or for another. If the guardian, bailiff, or receiver acquires and claims the property as his own, account will not lie.[1] As might be inferred from analogies in other departments of the common law, the privity existing between the parties to this relation was of a purely personal character and could not be transferred. Death severed it, and a duty to account could no

[6] 1 Poll. & Mait. Hist. Eng. Law, 2d ed., 323.

[7] 2 Co. Inst. 143.

[8] 2 Co. Inst. 378 *et seq.*

[9] Fitzherbert reports some 184 pleas under the title *Dette* in his Abridgment, 133 under the title *Accompt*, and 64 under the title *Detinue*.

[1] Com. Dig., *Accompt* (D).

"Account lies not against disseisors, for then the disseisee could avoid the descents at his pleasure; and also the defendant was never his receiver for to render account, for this cannot be without privity in law or in deed." Brooke's New Cases, pl. 454.

Volume III

more be enforced by or against a personal representative than could the duty to make reparation for a tort.[2] This defect was remedied slowly and by piecemeal. By chapter 23 of Westminster II, executors were enabled to maintain an action of account to the same extent as the testator might have done. In 1350 this relief was extended to the executors of executors,[3] and in 1356 to administrators.[4]

Strangely enough, in case the person liable to account died, no recourse could be had against his executor or administrator until an act of Parliament, passed after repeated efforts in 1705, gave such relief.[5] This immunity of the personal representative of a deceased accountant, together with the circumstance that his heir was not liable to suit unless expressly bound by the sealed obligation of his ancestor, left creditors without remedy in many cases.[6]

Effect of death of one of parties.

A similar defect existed in regard to joint tenants and tenants in common. It had always been held that where one of these tenants actually appointed his companion in the tenancy to be his bailiff, an action of account could be maintained against him as such. Where this was not done, no action lay[7] prior to the Statute of 4 Anne, which remedied this evil along with the other.

In the relation of guardian and ward privity was created by law. In the case of joint tenants and tenants in common privity resulted from the legal relation of the parties, and the statute created the obligation to account which had been unknown at common law. In other cases the privity resulted from the act or agreement of the parties.

In some situations the law recognized the principle that privity might result from the ratification of a previous unau-

[2] Coke tells us that *per legem mercatoriam* an action of account could be maintained by executors and that the successor of a prior could have the action against an accountant of his predecessor because the house did not die. 2 Co. Inst. 404; also F. N. B. 117 E.

[3] 25 Edw. III., c. 5.

[4] 31 Edw. III., c. 11.

[5] 4 Anne, c. 16, § 27.

[6] Littleton observes: "And in this case where the guardian in socage dieth before any account made by him to the heir, of this the heir is without remedy, for that no writ of account lieth against the executors but for the king only." Litt. Tenures, § 125.

[7] Co. Litt. 200*b*.

thorized act. Thus where one assumed to act as the bailiff or representative of another without appointment as such, he could be held liable as a bailiff.[8] The same rule applied to one who entered upon land claiming to be guardian of an infant.[9] The liability here recognized is analogous to that enforced against the executor *de son tort*. It is obvious that this rule could not be applied where the person upon whom liability was to be fixed entered as a mere trespasser.[1] The principle in question was, however, so extended as to vest a right of action in a third person, on a transaction entered into for his benefit. Thus if A delivered money to B to deliver to C, or delivered money to B for C's use, C could maintain an action of account against B;[2] though a defaulting custodian or depositary could of course also be called to account by the person who intrusted the money to him.

Ratification of unauthorized act.

Right of third party to enforce accounting on agreement made for his benefit.

This recognition of the right of action in a third person, to sue, as we would now say, on a contract made for his benefit, is worthy of more than passing notice. The right to maintain the action of account is based, as we have seen, directly on legal duty, and since B in the case supposed is under legal obligation to deliver the money to C, there is no impropriety in holding that C may have an action of account. The common-law theory of contract, as developed in modern times in connection with the action of assumpsit, was not broad enough to admit of this, and it was well settled that only those in privity with the consideration can maintain an action of assumpsit on the promise. It will be observed that the action of account, like the modern count for money had and received, is restricted to cases where there is a simple legal duty to turn over money received. Hence neither of these remedies was broad enough to serve as a general remedy for the beneficiary of a contract who is not in privity with the consideration.

Distinction here between account and assumpsit.

Since the duty to render account is created by law, it follows that where the relation to which the law attaches the

[8] F. N. B. 117 A; Brooke Abr., *Accompt*, pl. 8.

[9] F. N. B. 117 B.

[1] Brooke Abr., *Accompt*, pl. 93.

[2] F. N. B. 116 Q.

Volume III

liability to account exists, an express promise to render the account is not necessary; but if such a promise is actually made, assumpsit on the promise will lie.[3] Likewise, where the engagement to account is in the form of a bond or covenant, action can be maintained on it.[4] But, as was said in *Hawkins v. Parker*,[5] the express agreement to account does not take away the right to maintain an action of account on the pre-existing legal duty.

The express promise to account.

The common law did not fix the same degree of responsibility upon the different accountants. The bailiff intrusted with the prosecution of mercantile enterprises was required to account for profits from the time of his receiving the money or goods.[6] He was also chargeable with profits which he might have made; as where he retained money in his hands, when he might have improved it; or where he did not invest as profitably as he might in the exercise of prudence, or where he sold the goods for less than their value.[7] But he was excused from accounting for profit where he made oath that he found nothing to buy without hazard of loss.[8]

Degree of responsibility of different accountants:

1. Bailiff.

A receiver *ad computandum* or to deliver over was in no case charged with profits, since he had no authority to invest.[9] On the other hand, he was given no allowance for expenses.[1] Guardians and bailiffs were entitled to have credit before the auditors for their reasonable costs and expenditures, such as for the maintenance of their ward or for expenses incurred in the discharge of duty.[2] A bailiff of his own wrong, however, was not entitled to credit for his expenditures, and where loss was incurred by a bailiff from making a sale upon credit when he was only authorized to sell for cash, he was held liable for such loss.[3]

2. Receiver.

3. Guardian.

[3] Spurraway *v.* Rogers, 12 Mod. 517.

[4] Vere *v.* Smith, 2 Lev. 5.

[5] 2 Bulst. 256.

[6] Com. Dig., *Accompt* (E. 10); 1 Rolle Abr., 125, pl. 15.

[7] 1 Rolle Abr., 125, pl. 16.

[8] *Ib.*, pl. 17.

[9] 1 Rolle Abr., 125, pls. 12, 13, 14. See also Bellewe's Cases, *Accompt*, p. 7-9.

[1] 1 Rolle Abr., 119 (H), pl. 3.

[2] Com. Dig., *Accompt* (A 2). Coke tells us that in some cases the rule which denied to the receiver an allowance for his expenses had been relaxed in favor of trade and commerce. 1 Co. Litt. 172*a*.

[3] Com. Dig., *Accompt* (E 12, 13); Anonymous, 12 Mod. 514.

The action of account, it may be noted, could be used by the bailor in enforcing the liability of the bailee, if the bailor preferred to pursue such remedy rather than to sue in detinue. In this connection a noteworthy distinction existed between the degree of liability enforced in applying the respective remedies. The bailee when sued in detinue was treated as a debtor, and was originally held absolutely liable for the chattels bailed or their value. Hence loss by robbery was no defense in his behalf.[4]

Chapter IX

Account concurrent with detinue as against bailee.

Now the action of account, unlike detinue, is in the nature of an equitable remedy, both as regards the conception which underlies it and the procedure by which it is enforced. Accordingly it has always been accepted as law that the accountant will be discharged before the auditors where he shows that the money or goods committed to him were lost by robbery and without negligence on his part.[5]

Procedure in actions of account:

The common-law procedure in the action of account was not ill adapted to the purpose intended to be served. The obligation resting on the accountant was that of rendering an account, and this duty was specifically enforced. The action therefore necessarily involved two stages. The declaration, in the first place, charged the defendant as guardian, bailiff, or receiver. To this the defendant might plead that he had not occupied such a relation (*ne unques*), or that he was released, or had already accounted (*plene computavit*).[6] If the issue thus raised was decided for the plaintiff, an interlocutory judgment *quod computet* was entered against the defendant. At this stage the defendant was required to give bail or go to jail until the account was taken and judgment satisfied. In the event he did not appear to account after judgment *quod computet*, a *capias ad computandum* could issue for his apprehension.

1. Issue on question of liability to account.

Two clerks were usually assigned as auditors by the court, and before them the account was taken. By chapter 11 of

[4] See vol. 2, p. 255.

[5] Y. B. 9 Edw. IV. 40, pl. 22; Fitz. Abr., *Accompt*, pl. 111; 1 Rolle Abr., 124 (O), pl. 3; Goswill *v.* Dunkley, 1 Stra. 680.

[6] 3 Reeves, Hist. Eng. Law, Am. ed., 279; Com. Dig., *Accompt* (E 2-16).

Volume III

2. Accounting before the auditors.

Westminster II the right of the lord to appoint auditors to take the accounts of his own servants was recognized. The lord could also take the account himself, but in this case the balance due became a debt and he could not avail himself of the remedy given by statute where the account was taken before auditors.[7] Before the auditors only such matters could be pleaded in discharge as could not originally have been pleaded in bar; for to admit matters which could have been so pleaded would contradict the judgment *quod computet*.[8]

3. Judgment.

The mode of proceeding before the auditors was not substantially different from the practice observed in proceedings in chancery on reference to the master, and when the account had been stated by the auditors and delivered into court, final judgment was rendered in favor of the plaintiff for any balance found to be due him. The law of account was defective in the circumstance that judgment could not be rendered in favor of a defendant if it transpired that the balance was in his favor. But as the act of accounting converted the balance into a debt, he could sue and recover it in debt or indebitatus assumpsit without further difficulty.[9]

There are early evidences of a tendency of the action of account towards dissolution. The growth of the chancery jurisdiction and the development of the action of indebitatus assumpsit so as to allow recovery upon purely equitable claims in the common count for money had and received, were the two factors which contributed most to render the action of account unnecessary. Other forces also operated to this end. In 1505 Frowike, C. J., said that where money was committed to a man to deliver over to another and he converted it to his own use, the person who delivered the money could maintain an action on the case or an action of account, at his election.[1] Instances when it would be preferable to sue on the tort were no doubt numerous, for in account, as in debt and detinue, the defendant, if charged as receiver, was always en-

When accountant entitled to wage law.

[7] 3 Reeves, Hist. Eng. Law, Am. ed., 276.

[8] Godfrey *v.* Saunders, 3 Wils. C. Pl. 73.

[9] Gawton *v.* Dacres, 1 Leon. 219, Owen 23.

[1] Anonymous, Keilw. 77, pl. 25.

titled to wage his law where the money came to his hands directly from the plaintiff.[2]

Again, the distinction between debt and account was not always clear, and as account could not be maintained against the representatives of a deceased person when the obligation was under seal, it sometimes became necessary for the plaintiff to sue in debt, or remain without redress. The difference between the two forms of action in this respect, and the tendency of the courts to construe the law favorably to the cause of justice, are illustrated in *Core's Case* (1536).[3] Here B received a sum of money for investment at Rouen in goods which were thence to be shipped by him to the plaintiff in England. For some reason the money was not invested, and after B's death the plaintiff sued in debt to recover. The normal remedy in such a case was clearly by an action of account, but as this action was not then maintainable against an administrator, the plaintiff sued in debt, the contract being under seal. The majority of the court favored the maintenance of the action, on reasoning which was certainly not very clear.[4] It was admitted by all parties that if the money had actually been invested, account would have been the only available remedy.

Debt maintainable in lieu of account.

By the end of the sixteenth century the principle recognized in *Core's Case* was well established, and debt became concurrent with account in all cases where the plaintiff sought to recover a specific sum of money intrusted to a bailee but not invested by him.[5]

When remedies concurrent.

Concerning the action of account in modern times but little need be said. As indebitatus assumpsit has inherited the jurisdiction formerly possessed by account in all cases

[2] Y. B. 13 & 14 Edw. III. (Rolls ed.), 289, pl. 24.

[3] 1 Dyer 20*a*.

[4] See opinions of Spilman and Portman, JJ., and of Fitzjames, C. J., in 1 Dyer 22*a*. Luke, J., dissented, on the ground that account was the only remedy, saying: "If a man bail money to one to traffic with, if he do not lay out the money, he shall have account against him; and shall have the account for the increase and profit which he hath gained or might have gained by using the money: for in these cases he is a receiver and accountable; and no action of debt lies without a contract." 1 Dyer, 21*b*.

[5] Lincoln *v.* Topcliff, Cro. Eliz. 644.

Account superseded by indebitatus and by bill in equity.

where the amount due can be determined by means of legal machinery, so the chancery court has fallen heir to its jurisdiction in all cases where the accounts are complicated or parties numerous. The power to compel discovery by means of an answer under oath was doubtless the chief consideration which made it desirable for parties to proceed in the chancery court in these cases. At any rate, parties were inclined to resort thither, and the court of equity from an early time assumed jurisdiction to compel an accounting, going on the theory that the action of account at law was not an adequate remedy. For this reason account fell into disuse and in the eighteenth century became practically obsolete.

Ground of equitable jurisdiction.

The action of account was revived in *Godfrey v. Saunders* (1770).[6] The reason disclosed for the adoption of this ancient mode of procedure in that case is worth noting, as it throws light upon the lamentable state of affairs then confronting litigants in the chancery courts. It appears that the plaintiff had been fruitlessly litigating for twelve years in chancery, seeking to recover the sum of £12,000 on a meritorious cause of action. Finally, in despair of obtaining justice in that forum, he betook himself to the legal tribunal. He received a warm welcome, and Wilmot, C. J., in delivering his opinion in the case, said he was glad to see the ancient remedy revived. Be it said to the credit of the legal tribunal, the plaintiff obtained redress within a reasonable time.

Action of account revived in latter part of eighteenth century.

A large part of the learning of the subject of account was resurrected and put in a clear light in this case. The proceedings, record, and opinion in *Godfrey v. Saunders* therefore constitute, as said by Tilghman, C. J., in *Gratz v. Phillips* (1813),[7] a rich mine of information in regard to this action. Being thus revived, the action of account was frequently used in England during the early part of the nineteenth century, to the great advantage of litigants.[8] Account, however, is an action that cannot compete with the equitable remedy, when

[6] 3 Wils. C. Pl. 94.

[7] 5 Binn. (Pa.) 568.

[8] See Topham *v.* Braddick, 1 Taunt. 572; Owston *v.* Ogle, 13 East 538; Thomas *v.* Thomas, 5 Exch. 28; Sturton *v.* Richardson, 13 M. & W. 17; Baxter *v.* Hozier, 5 Bing. N. Cas. 288, 35 E. C. L. 114; Clarance *v.* Marshall, 2 Cromp. & M. 495.

Chapter IX

Equity regains the lost ground.

the chancery court is not hopelessly disabled as it was a century ago. In *Sturton v. Richardson* (1844),[0] one of the counsel urged the court to sanction the action of account as a remedy against a cotenant in a case where the necessary allegation that the defendant had received more than his share of the profits was lacking, saying that if this view were not adopted tenants in common would be driven into equity. Alderson, B., remarked that parties had already long been going by preference into the court of equity and that the legal remedy was inconvenient.[1]

Account render serves office of bill in equity in Pennsylvania.

Where no equitable machinery whatever is available, the legal remedy by means of the action of account must necessarily be used. This is well illustrated in the history of the action of account render in the state of Pennsylvania. In that state it was seen at an early day that the remedy of account must be freely extended, for in many cases the action of assumpsit was wholly inadequate, and there was no court of chancery to grant equitable relief. In *James v. Browne* (1788)[2] McKean, C. J., extended the remedy of account to all cases of partnership affairs, remarking that if the chancery court in England had not assumed jurisdiction, the Court of King's Bench would have been compelled to extend the common-law remedy, as the Pennsylvania court had done. In the decisions of this state we find an abundance of proof that the ancient action of account is capable of being put to excellent use where the general condition of remedial law is such as to force the courts to resort to it.[3]

[0] 13 M. & W. 17.

[1] In those American jurisdictions where the chancery courts exist these have generally exercised a concurrent jurisdiction over all matters of account. Nelson *v.* Allen, 1 Yerg. (Tenn.) 360; Mitchell *v.* Great Works Milling, etc., Co., 2 Story (U. S.) 648; Jones *v.* Bullock, 2 Dev. Eq. (17 N. Car.) 368; Bruce *v.* Burdet 1 J. J. Marsh. (Ky.) 80. In Stannard *v.* Whittlesey, 9 Conn. 556, it was held that the legal remedy of account was adequate for the purpose of giving relief against a guardian, and that this was fatal to the exercise of equitable jurisdiction.

[2] 1 Dall. (Pa.) 339.

[3] See Crousillat *v.* M'Call, 5 Binn. (Pa.) 432; Gratz *v.* Phillips, 5 Binn. (Pa.) 564; Whelen *v.* Watmough, 15 S. & R. (Pa.) 153; McCall *v.* Crousillat, 3 S. & R. (Pa.) 7.

Volume III

Owing to the almost complete obsolescence of the common-law action of account in modern times the courts have sometimes overlooked important principles connected with the remedy. A remarkable illustration of this is found in a line of American decisions which hold that the custodian of public funds is absolutely liable for money received by him in his official capacity. This is a plain and manifest violation of the rule which permitted all common-law accountants to show before the auditors that the money or goods were lost from their custody by inevitable disaster or by the felonious act of a third person — a principle which was in no danger of being lost so long as the action of account remained in vogue.

Liability of custodian of public funds.

This mistake was first made in *U. S. v. Prescott* (1845),[4] where a receiver of public moneys and his bondsmen were held liable for funds stolen from him without negligence on his part. Mr. Justice McLean said: "This is not a case of bailment and consequently the law of bailment does not apply." Strictly speaking this was true. There was no technical bailment, but the officer was a receiver and as such his liability at common law was substantially the same as that of a bailee. But this aspect of the case was not presented to the court, and the officer was treated as a debtor. This resulted in the establishment of the principle of the absolute liability of the public officer for funds committed to his keeping.

American doctrine.

The principle laid down in this case has been accepted, it seems, by the majority of the American courts. In 1853 it was said in Massachusetts that an officer charged with the custody of public funds is a "debtor and accountant,"[5] but at common law the two functions are distinct and incompatible. The effect of the rule declared in *U. S. v. Prescott* is to fix upon the custodian of public funds a stricter liability than that imposed on the common carrier, who is at least excused by

[4] 3 How. (U. S.) 578. See also Smythe *v.* U. S., 188 U. S. 156, where the superintendent of the mint at New Orleans was held liable for moneys lost by fire. In this case the former decisions of the United States courts are reviewed and the doctrine of U. S. *v.* Prescott followed.

[5] Hancock *v.* Hazzard, 12 Cush. (Mass.) 112. To the same effect see Perley *v.* Muskegon County, 32 Mich. 132; Ramsay *v.* People, 197 Ill. 572.

the act of God or of the public enemy. Such a doctrine could never have gained currency had the principle governing the liability of receivers and other bailiffs at common law been in the minds of the judges.[6]

Chapter IX

[6] For a statement of the positions of the various courts of this country on the point in question see article, Liability for Loss of Public Funds, by Gustav Stein, 1 Mich. L. Rev. 557 *et seq.*

CHAPTER X

THE ACTION OF COVENANT.

Volume III

COVENANT lies to recover damages for the breach of a sealed promise (covenant) to do some particular act. "Covenant lies when a man covenants with another by deed to do something and does it not; or that he has done it, when it is not done."[1] This remedy is the exact analogue of assumpsit, the only difference between the two actions being that the latter action lies for the breach of a simple promise, while covenant is maintainable only upon a specialty.

Scope of remedy.

It must not be imagined that the requirement of a seal distinguished the engagement of covenant in its early stages. The first covenants were merely promises to do or to refrain from doing a particular thing, and the engagement was based simply upon the agreement or convention of the minds of the respective parties. Neither a consideration, nor a writing, nor a seal was deemed to be a material requisite in its make-up. Such being the broad notion at first embodied in the covenant, it is to be surmised that the king's courts would be rather slow in admitting its legal validity. Such we find to have been the case.

The early contract of covenant.

We infer from the language of Glanvill that the only enforceable covenant known to him was that which was made of record (recognizance), and he expressly says that the king's court did not bother itself to enforce mere private covenants.[2] Accordingly no writ of covenant was then in existence. Hardly a generation, however, elapsed before the king's courts began to enforce some private agreements by means of a writ

Writ of covenant appears.

[1] Com. Dig., *Covenant* (A 1). In *Termes de la Ley*, s. v. *Covenant*, it is said: "Note well, no writ of covenant shall be maintainable without especialty, except in the city of London, or in some other place privileged by custom and use."

[2] "Privatas conventiones non solet curia domini regis tueri." Glanvill, Lib. X., c. 18.

Chapter X

of covenant. The industry of scholars has discovered a specimen of such a writ from the year 1201, and it was possibly a few years older. In 1227 the writ of covenant appears on the Register.[3]

The writ was undoubtedly originally confined to covenants concerning tenements. It was the chief, if not sole, remedy of the lessee as against his lessor, and was strictly an action upon a lease.[4] From the tenor of the writ it would be surmised that specific performance of the covenant was always granted;[5] but evidently this could only be done when the covenant concerned realty or specific chattels. Where the covenant was in fact capable of being specifically enforced, either movables or immovables could be recovered.[6] Where the covenant was purely personal, only damages could be awarded; for the king's court, it seems, did not exercise that power of personal coercion which at a later period was exercised by the court of chancery.

When specific performance granted.

Although the plaintiff in a writ of covenant might recover specific property where such was the subject-matter of the covenant, it did not follow that the action was a proprietary

Remedy sounds purely in contract.

[3] Register of Original Writs, 3 Harv. L. Rev. 113. See Rolls of the King's Court (Pipe Roll Soc., 1194), 53; Select Civ. Pleas (1201), 89; 2 Poll. & Mait. Hist. Eng. Law, 2d ed., 216.

[4] "Nota, per Littleton, that if I lease land to another for a term of years by indenture and oust him he shall have against me a writ of covenant. But if he be ousted by a stranger he shall have a writ of *ejectione firmæ* against the stranger." Y. B. 32 Hen. VI. 32, pl. 27.

[5] "Breve de convencione. Rex vic. salutem. Precipe A quod juste et sine dilatione teneat B convencionem inter eos factam de uno mess. X acris terre," etc. Stat. Wall. 12 Edw. I., c. 6. See also Note Book, pl. 1739 (A. D. 1226), "et ideo consideratum est quod convencio teneatur et quod Hugo habeat seisinam suam usque ad terminum suum decem annorum." 2 Poll. & Mait. Hist. Eng. Law, 2d ed., 106.

Observe the language of Blackstone: The writ of covenant "directs the sheriff to command the defendant generally to keep his covenant with the plaintiff (without specifying the nature of the covenant), or show good cause to the contrary; and if he continues refractory, or the covenant is already so broken that it cannot now be specifically performed, then the subsequent proceedings set forth with precision the covenant, the breach, and the loss which has happened thereby; whereupon the jury will give damages in proportion to the injury sustained by the plaintiff, and occasioned by such breach of the defendant's contract." 3 Bl. Com. 156.

[6] See 1 Stat. Realm 66.

remedy like detinue, or possessory like the assizes. It was conceived to be founded purely on the obligation created by the contract.

Bracton, writing near the middle of the thirteenth century, observed that the covenant was then acquiring some sort of standing in the king's courts.[7] It would have been impossible in his day to lay down any general principle by which the validity of a particular covenant could be determined; for no general limitation as regards either the form or the subject-matter of the engagement had as yet been imposed upon it. All that he could safely say was that the courts might enforce a covenant as a matter of favor.

Covenants at first enforced merely of royal favor.

One feature of the contract of covenant which impressed the lawyer of the thirteenth century was its remarkable scope. Bracton said that there were as many sorts of covenants as there are things to contract about.[8] The Statute of Wales (1284) has an observation to the same effect and assigns the infinite variety of covenants as an excuse for not going into details about this form of engagement.[9] Yet as a matter of fact, few actions of covenant could have been brought prior to that time which did not involve a lease or transfer of tenements.

The fifty years which ended approximately with the termination of the reign of Edward I (1307) were most important in the development of the law pertaining to covenants; for during this period the distinction between real and personal covenants took shape, and it was also determined at this time that the valid covenant is that which is in writing and under the seal of the covenantor. Concerning these two events a few words may well be said.

As has already been observed, the covenant which most frequently found its way into the royal courts during the thirteenth century was that which touched land and interests which, like advowsons, pertain to land. The fact that the

[7] Bracton 100, § 6.

[8] "Quarum totidem sunt genera quot paene rerum contrahendarum." *Ib.*

[9] "Quia infiniti sunt contractus conventionum, difficile est facere mentionem de quolibet in speciali." 1 Stat. Realm 66.

writ of covenant could be utilized in this field caused it to become popular as a means for levying a fine. Being personal rather than real, the action of covenant was not so heavily encumbered with troublesome rules of procedure as were the ancient real and possessory actions which had been used for the same purpose. It consequently afforded an expeditious method of securing that great and almost universal assurance of title, the fine. When covenant was used in this connection, the declaration merely alleged a previous covenant, either real or fictitious, to convey the premises in question. As the transaction was friendly, no proof of such allegation was required, and judgment was entered for the plaintiff upon default and without inquiry.[1]

Covenant used as means of levying fine.

This use of the writ of covenant brought into prominence the distinction between the real covenant, which is intended to pass land or is annexed to land and runs with it,[2] and the covenant which is purely personal, as where one covenants with another to serve him, or to build a house.[3] In modern times the learning pertaining to covenants real has grown to be an imposing mass. This matter, however, belongs to the department of real property and not to the law of actions, and hence is not within the scope of our present subject.

Covenants real and personal.

As above stated, the principle that the covenant must be in writing and under seal was settled by the close of the reign of Edward I. This rule first appeared, of course, as a mere rule of evidence. How must the plaintiff in the writ prove his covenant? Is the *secta* sufficient, or must there be a writing? Good reasons for an affirmative answer to this latter question can no doubt be given. The *secta* as a mode of proof was falling into disrepute. Jury in the modern sense there

Covenant must be evidenced by a writing.

[1] 3 Reeves, Hist. Eng. Law, Am. ed., 280. Upon searching the rolls of the Common Bench for the Easter Term 1271, Professor Maitland found thirty-five actions of covenant pending, most of which he tells us were brought merely to obtain assurance of title. See 2 Poll. & Mait. Hist. Eng. Law, 2d ed., 567.

[2] Bac. Abr., *Covenant*.

[3] F. N. B. 145 A. An early illustration of the personal covenant to build a house is found in Y. B. 21–22 Edw. I. (Rolls ed.), 111, where the court sustained a writ of debt brought to recover the amount which the covenantor had agreed to pay in the event of his failure to comply with his covenant to build.

Volume III

was none. As a consequence legal machinery was wholly unequal to the task of sifting human testimony and arriving at the truth concerning a disputed verbal agreement. Truly it would have been a dangerous innovation had the king's courts decided in Edward's day to meddle with all sorts of covenants. Considerations of this nature were decisive, and accordingly the courts imposed the condition that the covenant must appear in a sufficiently solemn form to preclude dispute as to the terms of the promise.[4] Thereafter the making of a contract in this form required technical learning and the service of a clerk.

Writing must be under seal.

The requirement of a writing (and in this period writing meant a sealed instrument) is the only condition which has ever been imposed on the covenant. But this condition was more than enough. It had the effect of turning the covenant into a strictly formal contract, a circumstance which is of momentous import in the history of English contract law. By this caprice, or at least by this turn of legal history, the course of legal evolutions was entirely changed and covenant thus missed the distinction of being the most important contract known to the common law. Heretofore the term 'covenant' had included promises of every kind, whether oral or in writing; and being founded on agreement this contract might under dif-

The covenant becomes a formal contract.

[4] Professor Maitland has shown that the question whether the covenant must be proved by a deed remained open practically during the whole of the thirteenth century. In 1274-75 a plea of covenant was dismissed because the plaintiff had no deed. 2 Poll. & Mait. Hist. Eng. Law, 2d ed., 220. But it seems still to have been debatable in 1292 whether a writing was necessary. This appears from Corbet's Case, Y. B. 20-21 Edw. I. (Rolls ed.), 223, where covenant was brought on a promise by the defendant to pay £20 for a horse lent by the plaintiff, in the event the defendant should fail to restore the animal safe and sound at a day specified. It appearing that the promise was not evidenced by a writing, the defendant craved judgment whether he should answer. The ruling of the court is not reported, but the point was no doubt well taken.

In Y. B. 32-33 Edw. I. (Rolls ed.), 296, the lease which contained the covenant declared on was properly in writing.

In London and Bristol, by special custom, the action of covenant can be maintained although the contract be not under seal. See Y. B. 22 Edw. IV. 2, pl. 6; Priv. Lond. 149; F. N. B. 146 A; Com. Dig., *London* (N 1). Such a custom is to be taken strictly and will not bind executors. Wade *v.* Bemboe, 1 Leon. 2.

ferent conditions have covered the field subsequently occupied by assumpsit, as well as that to which it was itself restricted. But "a man cannot have a clerk to make a deed for every little thing," [5] and consequently lawyers and judges were compelled to go afield into the law of torts to find an engine by which to redress the breach of a simple promise.

Considera-tion not necessary to support covenant.

After the covenant became a formal contract there was of course no necessity for requiring the presence of any element corresponding to the *quid pro quo* in debt or to consideration in assumpsit; nor even before the covenant became formal was there any evidence of a tendency towards such a requirement. No doubt such an element was present in the agreements which were actually enforced, and the king's courts would doubtless have refused to entertain a writ founded on a purely gratuitous covenant. But the presence of consideration or *quid pro quo* was not conceived as being a test of the validity of the promise. Perhaps the fact that the covenant was originally either a contract of lease or a stipulation subsidiary to a lease tended to obscure the need of such a test of liability as consideration, since the making of a lease, in most cases, involves reciprocal engagements. Where the covenant was merely collateral to the contract of lease, it was of course supported by the principal engagement, and no need for any further consideration was likely to be felt.

Covenant not main-tainable upon sealed ob-ligation of indebted-ness.

Inasmuch as the contract of covenant includes all sealed promises to do or to refrain from doing a particular act, the term may well be applied to the sealed obligation of indebtedness, for this is merely a promise to pay a specified sum of money. Accordingly there was no theoretical objection to the extension of the action of covenant into the field of debts created by specialty. Still, there was little or no necessity for such a step, since in debt upon a sealed obligation the plaintiff could not wage his law. Indeed in some respects debt was the preferable remedy, as in this action, we are told, final judgment is given in the first instance if the plaintiff fails to plead.[6] At any rate, whether moved by such reasons or by a natural

[5] Candish, J., in Y. B. 48 Edw. III. 6, pl. 11.
[6] 1 Chitty Pl. 132.

Volume III

parsimony in the allowance of apparently unnecessary remedies, the common-law courts did not encourage the use of the writ of covenant where debt will lie.[7]

Near the beginning of the seventeenth century it seems the action was maintained for the recovery of debts evidenced by a deed or indenture, provided the deed or indenture contained an express covenant to pay the debt.[8] As a rival of debt the action had little to commend it, and consequently covenant was destined to have no great career in this field.

Debt proper remedy upon all sealed promises to pay sum certain of money.

It should be noted that the use of the action of covenant upon a sealed debt is not to be confounded with the use of the action of debt upon covenants for the payment of an ascertained sum of money. The fact that a promise under seal is made for the payment of a sum certain makes such obligation technically a debt, and this though the term 'covenant' is the operative word. In such case debt is the proper remedy, and not covenant.[9] In the light of this distinction it will appear that the instances in which debt and covenant have actually been held to be concurrent remedies are very few in number.

It will be observed that the extension of covenant into the

[7] That the promise to do or to refrain from doing a particular act, other than the payment of an ascertained sum of money, is the proper field of covenant is shown by the illustrations of the covenant given by Blackstone: "If a man covenants to be at York by such a day, or not to exercise a trade in a particular place, and is not at York at the time appointed, or carries on his trade in the place forbidden, these are direct breaches of his covenant, and may be perhaps greatly to the disadvantage and loss of the covenantee. The remedy for this is by a writ of covenant." 3 Bl. Com. 155.

[8] In Anonymous (1585), 3 Leon. 119, there is a broad dictum to the effect that covenant is concurrent with debt upon sealed obligations. But the later authorities show that there must be an express covenant to pay the debt. Stronge *v.* Watts, 1 Rolle Abr. 518, pl. 2; *ib.*, pl. 3.

In Mordant *v.* Wats (1620), Brownl. & Goldes. (pt. i) 19, Sir Edward Coke drew this distinction: "Where an express covenant is made to pay the rent at divers days, an action of covenant will lie before all the days of payment be past; but an action of debt will not lie until all the days be passed."

In charter-parties where there are reciprocal covenants, the action of covenant is a proper remedy even upon the covenant for the money to be paid for the freight. Frere *v.* ——, Style 133. *Compare* Atty *v.* Parish, 1 B. & P. N. R. 104.

[9] See Chawner *v.* Bowes, Godb. 217; Browne *v.* Hancocke, Hetley 111, where it is said that upon a 'covenant' to pay a sum certain of money only debt will lie.

Chapter X

field of specialty debts as above indicated was entirely analogous to the process by which assumpsit was extended into the field of simple debt. In the case of covenant upon a sealed debt, however, legal development seems never to have gone further than to permit the use of the remedy where there is an express covenant to pay the debt, or where there are words which can be construed to operate as such.[1] No case has here laid down the broad principle that the law will imply a covenant to pay a debt from the mere creation of a sealed debt.

Covenant lies only at instance of a party to the covenant.

Inasmuch as the covenant is based on the agreement of the respective parties to it, strangers to the covenant are not bound by it and at common law can have no right of action for its breach. In *Gilby v. Copley* (1684),[2] an attempt was made by a third person to recover upon a covenant made for his benefit, but the point was not actually decided. Whatever the law may have been in that day, it has in modern times been settled beyond all question that covenant will lie only at the instance of one who is a party to the covenant. The rule here applied is exactly the same as that which maintains in debt and assumpsit. Neither a specialty nor a simple contract can give to a third person the right to sue upon it.

In *Colyear v. Mulgrave* (1836),[3] this doctrine was applied under circumstances which involved some hardship to the plaintiffs, but the point was too well settled to admit of doubt. It appeared that a father, who had four natural daughters and a legitimate son, entered into an agreement with the son, evidenced by certain deeds, whereby the father covenanted to transfer the sum of £20,000 to a trustee for the benefit of his four natural daughters, and the son covenanted to pay the debts of the father. The son paid some of the father's debts, and died before the covenant on the part of the father was per-

[1] In Norrice's Case (1661), Hardres 178, an action of covenant was brought upon these words, viz: "I oblige myself to pay so [much] money at such a day, and so much at another day." And *per curiam*, clearly an action of covenant lies, especially if both days are not passed. But the Chief Baron doubted how the law would have been if the words were *teneri et firmiter obligari;* for that those words sound in debt and not covenant.

[2] 3 Lev. 138.

[3] 2 Keen 82.

Third person for whose benefit covenant is made has no action.

formed, having by his will given the whole of his property to his father, who became the son's personal representative. One of the daughters having filed a bill to have the covenant performed as against the estate of the deceased son, a demurrer thereto was sustained on the ground that where two persons for a valuable consideration as between themselves covenant to do some act for the benefit of one who is a stranger to the covenant, that stranger cannot enforce the covenant, though either of the two parties to the covenant might do so against the other.[4]

Party to covenant may sue though covenant is not signed by him.

While it is essential that one who seeks to enforce a covenant should be a party thereto, it is not necessary that the contract should actually be signed and sealed by him. Thus it has been held that the covenantee in an ordinary indenture may sue the covenantor who executes it, although he himself has not executed it;[5] and it has even been said that a covenantee may be sued upon the covenant where he has enjoyed the whole term though he has not himself executed the contract.[6] But this cannot be accepted as law.

Subsidiary covenant fails if principal contract fails.

As we have already seen, the sealed covenant is older than the common-law doctrine of consideration. Hence when a covenant is properly executed it is binding regardless of the presence of such element. To this principle an exception, or apparent exception, is found in the rule that where the covenant is collateral or subsidiary to another contract such as a lease, and the principal contract is not executed, the covenant fails also. Thus if a lease be agreed upon and the lessee exe-

[4] See Barford *v.* Stuckey, 8 Moore 88, 1 Bing. 225, 8 E. C. L. 483; Berkerley *v.* Hardy, 5 B. & C. 355, 11 E. C. L. 251; Southampton *v.* Brown, 6 B. & C. 718, 13 E. C. L. 303; Chesterfield, etc., Silkstone Colliery Co. *v.* Hawkins, 3 H. & C. 677.

In Com. Dig., *Covenant* (A), it is said that if A covenants generally to indemnify B the latter may maintain an action of covenant against A though the covenant be not with him. This, however, is not accepted as law in more recent years. 1 Chitty Pl. 4. Certainly not where the deed is *inter partes* and not by deed-poll. Smith *v.* Emery, 12 N. J. L. 53.

[5] Morgan *v.* Pike, 14 C. B. 473, 78 E. C. L. 473.

[6] Cooch *v.* Goodman, 2 Q. B. 580, 42 E. C. L. 817. See *contra*, Cardwell *v.* Lucas, 2 M. & W. 111, and compare Master *v.* Hansard, 4 Ch. D. 718; Pitman *v.* Woodbury, 3 Exch. 4; Swatman *v.* Ambler, 8 Exch. 72.

cutes his part, but the lessor does not, whereby there is no lease, the covenants in the indenture sealed by the lessee, and also the bond for performance of the covenants, are void.[7] But it is not necessary to say even in this class of cases that the covenant is rendered nugatory by failure of consideration for the promise. The execution and validity of the main contract are conditions of the validity of the collateral covenant rather than a mere consideration for it.[8]

Assumpsit not maintainable upon a covenant.

Inasmuch as assumpsit and covenant are supplemental remedies, the one lying for the breach of a promise under seal, the other for the breach of a simple promise, very little confusion has arisen between them in practice. In modern times, however, some attempts have been made to extend general assumpsit into the field of covenant. Thus, in *Bulstrode v. Gilburn* (1736),[9] assumpsit was brought for the breach of a covenant to account. It was held that, inasmuch as the sealed covenant gave the plaintiff a remedy of a higher nature than assumpsit, the latter remedy would not lie.

In *Toussaint v. Martinnant* (1787),[1] the plaintiff, a surety, sought to recover in assumpsit money paid to the defendant's use. It seems that the plaintiff had taken a sealed bond from the defendant, covering the expenditure in question, and this was held fatal to the right of action in assumpsit. In *Barber v. Harris* (1839),[2] it was likewise held that if covenant lies, assumpsit cannot be maintained. It is consequently well settled that where there is a contract between two parties under seal, one cannot sue the other as upon a simple contract in respect of the subject-matter of such obligation.[3]

Plaintiffs who have sued in case for an independent tort involved in the breach of covenant have been more successful than those who have sought to maintain assumpsit upon an

[7] Com. Dig., *Covenant* (F); Soprani *v.* Skurro, Yelv. 18; Morgan *v.* Pike (1854), 14 C. B. 486, 78 E. C. L. 486; Rose *v.* Poulton, 2 B. & Ad. 828, 830, 22 E. C. L. 193, 194.

[8] See language of Parke, J., in Rose *v.* Poulton, 2 B. & Ad. 830, 22 E. C. L. 194.

[9] 2 Stra. 1027.

[1] 2 T. R. 100.

[2] 9 Ad. & El. 532, 36 E. C. L. 193.

[3] Edwards *v.* Bates, 7 M. & G. 590, 49 E. C. L. 590, 8 Scott N. R. 406; Schlencker *v.* Moxsy, 3 B. & C. 789, 10 E. C. L. 227.

Volume III

express or implied promise to perform the covenant. Thus, in *Kinlyside v. Thornton* (1776)[4] an action on the case in the nature of waste was maintained though there was a covenant not to commit waste. De Grey, C. J., said: "I have no difficulty upon this question. The tenant for years commits waste and delivers up the place wasted to the landlord. Had there been no deed of covenant, the action of waste or case in the nature of waste would have lain. Because the landlord by the special covenant acquires a new remedy, does he therefore lose his old?" In *Marker v. Kenrick* (1853),[5] it was held that case in the nature of waste was concurrent with covenant, where damage resulted to a mine from the removal of the barrier or boundary between it and the adjoining mine, contrary to the terms of a sealed indenture of lease.

When case lies for breach of covenant.

In *Burnett v. Lynch* (1826),[6] an action on the case was successfully maintained by a lessee against his assignee, under circumstances which precluded the right to sue upon the covenant, inasmuch as the assignee was not a party to the contract. The duty, however, for breach of which suit was maintained was created by the covenant, and the defendant was held liable in case because by accepting the assignment of the lease he had become legally bound for the fulfilment of its terms. The court was of the opinion that either case for breach of the legal duty or assumpsit for the breach of a promise implied by law could be maintained by the plaintiff, an election which could not have been conceded to the plaintiff if there had been a right of action in covenant.

The contract of covenant is primarily based upon agreement, and it is a formal contract only to the extent of the requirement that it must be under seal. It follows that no particular form of words is necessary to constitute a valid covenant, and any words in a deed which show an agreement to do a thing will be allowed to operate as a covenant.[7]

No particular form of words necessary to make covenant good.

Likewise a covenant will be implied from language which

[4] 2 W. Bl. 1111.

[5] 13 C. B. 188, 76 E. C. L. 188.

[6] 5 B. & C. 589, 12 E. C. L. 327.

[7] Com. Dig., *Covenant* (A 2). If by articles of agreement it is said that it is intended a fine shall be levied, this amounts to a covenant to levy it. Hollis *v.* Carr, 2 Mod. 91.

Chapter X

Implied covenant.

is clearly intended to impose a duty. Thus if by a sealed writing it is agreed that A shall give B a stipulated sum for his house, an action of covenant lies against B upon his failure or refusal to convey the house.[8]

Words importing covenant in law.

Some words import a covenant in law though there be no words of promise. Thus the word *demisi* in a lease has long operated as a covenant that the lessor has a right to let the premises demised; and if the lessee be ousted, covenant lies.[9] The word *concessi* in a demise or assignment of a lease is said to have the same effect as *demisi.* So with *dedi;*[1] and if a lessor does any act which defeats the effect of his grant, covenant will lie against him.[2] But where the lessor covenants that the lessee shall enjoy without eviction by him or any who claim under him, the action will not lie against him upon eviction by a stranger.[3]

The covenant does not die with the person.

It is worthy of notice that from the time of its first recognition the obligation incurred by covenant survived the death of either party. In this respect it differed from the early debt and such rights of action as are founded on tort. The reason for this is doubtless to be found in the fact that the covenant did not gain full recognition as a true formal contract until near the beginning of the fourteenth century, at which time the sealed obligation of indebtedness had come to be a well-recognized exception to the maxim *actio personalis moritur cum persona.* The covenant, being also evidenced by the seal of the covenantor, was treated in the same way. At any rate, the covenant does not perish with the person.

Nor is this principle limited, as one might imagine, to covenants which run with land. In 1354 Littleton said: "If I

[8] Pordage *v.* Cole, 1 Sid. 423, 1 Saund. 320. Com. Dig., *Covenant* (A 2).

[9] Com. Dig., *Covenant* (A 4). The doctrine that the mere act of letting for a term of years raises an implied warranty seems to be a corollary from the personal character of the contract of demise. The lessor does not grant an estate to the lessee, but merely contracts that he shall enjoy it for the stated period; and consequently if the lessee be evicted, he is entitled to recover damages for the breach of the covenant. 2 Poll. & Mait. Hist. Eng. Law, 2d ed., 107. Bracton, Note Book, pl. 106, 638.

[1] Pincombe *v.* Rudge, Hob. 3, 4.

[2] Pomfret *v.* Ricroft, 1 Saund. 321.

[3] Noke's Case, 4 Coke 80*b.*

Volume III

covenant by indenture with another to build a house and I do not make it in my life, he shall have an action of covenant against my executors." [4] But, as was pointed out at a later day, where the covenant stipulates for the performance of purely personal service, death of course puts an end to the contract.[5] As the executor can be sued on a covenant made by his testator, so also he can maintain an action where his own testator was the party entitled to performance.[6] Heirs may recover upon a covenant in which they are expressly named and upon such as run with the land.[7] So may they likewise be bound.[8]

Covenant terminated by death, when.

As with heirs so with assigns. They may sue and may be sued upon covenants running with the realty and upon covenants in which they are expressly mentioned.[9] At common law a grantee or assignee of a reversion or of rent could not maintain covenant for lack of privity. To remedy this the Statute of 32 Hen. VIII [9*] gave the same remedy to the assignee of a reversion against the lessee or his assignee or their personal representative, upon covenants running with the land, as the lessor or his heir or their successor had.

Covenant binding on assignee.

[4] Y. B. 32 Hen. VI. 32, pl. 27. See also Y. B. 47 Edw. III. 22, pl. 50, for a still earlier instance of the writ of covenant used against executors.

[5] "A covenant, as by indenture to repair, can be performed by another as well as by the [covenantor] himself, in which case the covenant is not discharged by death; . . . but where the covenant is to be performed by the covenantor during his own life, the executors cannot be charged." Keble and Mordant, JJ., in Y. B. 10 Hen. VII. 18, pl. 4.

[6] F. N. B. 145 F. Com. Dig., *Covenant* (B 1). See Reg. Brev. Orig. 165 B, for the form of the writs for and against the personal representative.

[7] 1 Rolle Abr., 520 (H); Y. B. 42 Edw. III. 3, pl. 14; Brooke Abr., *Covenant*, pl. 28.

[8] Com. Dig., *Covenant* (C 2).

[9] Com. Dig., *Covenant* (B 3), (C 3).

[9*] Chapter 34.

CHAPTER XI

THE ACTION OF DEBT.

Chapter XI

THE action of debt is certainly the broadest of the contractual remedies and is perhaps the broadest of all the common-law remedies; that is to say, it can be used to obtain satisfaction of duties of more diversity than any other action. By nature debt is an action of contract, but it is also the normal remedy upon duties created by custom or record, and is therefore broader than the field of pure contractual duty. In other words, it is a remedy upon quasi-contractual as well as contractual duties.

Broad scope of the action of debt.

Diverse as are the duties which the action of debt can be used to enforce, it is after all one of the simplest, as it is the very oldest of common-law remedies. One primary conception — that of pure legal duty — was originally at the foundation of the action, and it has never departed from it. Hence debt will be found to be one of the most inflexible of common-law remedies.

Its nature can perhaps best be defined by saying that the action of debt lies to enforce legal duty created by contract, by custom, or by record. The sole limitation upon such legal duty is the requirement that the duty be one for payment of a sum certain of money or for the delivery of an ascertained amount of ponderable or measurable chattels. Debt then, we may say, lies to recover money or chattels due and made certain in amount by contract, by custom, or by record. In this definition the term 'contract' has a technical meaning which is not so broad as that now commonly attached to it. The term here means such a contract as was sufficient at common law to create a debt. Accordingly it must be either a simple contract in which a *quid pro quo* passes to the debtor at the time the debt is created, or it must be a contract in the form of a specialty. Negatively, the contract which creates a debt is not

Lies to recover any duty created by contract, by custom, or by record.

Volume III

the simple promise upon which the action of assumpsit alone will lie, as where mutual promises are given, or where a promise is made by A to B upon a consideration moving from B to C.

The action of debt is necessarily coextensive with the common-law conception of a debt. Whatever duties can be classed as debts are recoverable in the action of debt. Accordingly, in the course of these chapters the subject of discourse will at times be debts conceived as legal duties for which the action of debt lies; at other times it will be debt conceived as the remedy for the enforcement of such duties.

Debt as remedy upon the early contract *re.*

The earliest legal duty upon which debt could be maintained was the duty which arose from the simple real contract. The nature of this duty has elsewhere been considered, and it is not necessary to go over the same ground again. Suffice it here to say that the situation involved in the early simple debt supposes one person to have possession of a thing (*res*) which he *owes*, and hence ought to turn over, to the owner. The obligation to restore is imposed by law upon the mere circumstance that the debtor has acquired the property of another by means of a contract *re*. The action of debt, being founded on such a duty, was originally of a proprietary character and lay for the recovery of the *res* which was the subject-matter of the contract.

As we have elsewhere seen, the *commodatum, depositum, mutuum, locatum,* and *pignus,* as well as the bargain and sale and contract of suretyship, created typical debts in the early law. The early conception of debt thus included situations which are clearly to be distinguished. For instance, the duty to return a borrowed implement of husbandry, or a specified amount of barley consumed by the borrower, was placed in the same legal category as the duty to return a loan of money. The law of the twelfth century had but one theory to fit cases where the thing itself was to be returned and where it was returnable only in kind by number, weight, or measure. The debtor owed the creditor the chattel, and the action of debt was his remedy.

Before long, however, the law began to separate these

Chapter XI

ideas, and as this progressed the action of debt split up into two forms, the action of debt in the *debet et detinet* being used for the recovery of money debts and for the recovery of a specified amount of ponderable or measureable chattels, while debt in the *detinet* was used for the recovery of specific chattels. This latter form of the action gradually acquired a distinct character, being known by the name of detinue. The recognition of detinue as a separate action thus narrowed the scope of debt proper (in the *debet et detinet*) to the limits indicated in the definition above given.

Debt in the *debet et detinet.*

Debt in the *detinet.*

In modern times the money debt has become by far the most conspicuous and important form of the simple contract debt, but in legal theory there has been no severance between the money and chattel debt. They are both enforced by the same form of the action; and after all, money is only one sort of chattel. In early law it is clear that these two debts were mentally assimilated to each other. One who owed money or chattels was conceived as wrongfully withholding from the creditor property which belonged to such creditor, and he was not viewed merely as being bound by the obligation of law to make compensation. In other words, the debt, whether of money or chattels, was viewed as a real and substantive thing. There is indeed reason for suspecting that such even to this day is the popular conception of a debt.[2]

The money debt.

In view of what has just been said it is not surprising that the precedents afford instances in which a count for money owing is joined with a count for chattels unlawfully detained.[3]

[2] "To all appearances our ancestors could not conceive credit under any other form. The claimant of a debt asks for what is his own. After all, we may doubt whether the majority of fairly well-to-do people, even at this day, realize that what a man calls 'my money in the bank' is a merely personal obligation of the banker to him." 2 Poll. & Mait. Hist. Eng. Law, 2d ed., 205.

"A debt according to the popular conception of the term is a sum of money belonging to one person [the creditor], but in the possession of another [the debtor]." Langdell on Contracts, § 100.

[3] "Quod reddat £20 argenti quas ei debet et dimidium sacci lanae quod ei injuste detinet." Y. B. 7 Edw. II. 241.

Writ of Debt for Money and Chattels.—"Quod reddat B centum solidas quos ei debet et quandam zonam vel quendam librum vel equum precii tanti et catalla ad valenciam tanti; quos, vel quem, ei injuste detinet ut dicit, etc." Reg. Brev. Orig. 39.

Volume III

Joinder of counts for money and chattels.

But it is evident that there is an appreciable and important difference between the chattel debt and the money debt. The latter can, at least by the trained mind, be conceived as a mere personal obligation, and when used to enforce it the action of debt is a purely personal remedy. When used to enforce the chattel debt the action is more clearly an action of property. It will be observed that when recovery is had in a suit for a chattel debt, a money judgment for the value of the chattels is always entered, and not a judgment for the delivery of the specific chattels due.[4] Specific performance of the duty to pay the chattel due is not attempted.

Proprietary character of the action of debt.

Evidences of the proprietary character of the action of debt are conspicuous throughout all its history, but this feature is more prominent in the early stages of its growth. It is plainly manifest in the wording of the early writ. The creditor complained that the debtor unjustly deforced him of the subject-matter of the debt, and the debtor was commanded that justly and without delay he render it to its owner.[5] By the time of Bracton the word detains (*detinet*) had supplanted the word deforce as descriptive of the wrongful exclusion of the owner from his property.[6] As in the writ of right for land, the action was based on ownership; and the writ of debt

[4] "If rent-corn be reserved upon a lease for years and it is behind for two or three years, the lessor may have debt for the corn and shall make his declaration of so much corn, and the same shall be in the *detinet;* but yet he shall not have judgment to have corn, but so much money as the corn was worth, every several year being accounted." Cheney's Case, 3 Leon. 260.

[5] "The King to the Sheriff, Health. Command N., that justly and without delay, he render to R. one hundred marks which he owes him, as he says, and of which he complains that he has justly deforced him. And unless he does so, summon him, by good Summoners, that he be before me or my Justices at Westminster in fifteen days from the Pentecost, to show wherefore he has not done it. And have there the Summoners and this Writ. Witness, etc." Glanvill, Bk. X., c. 2.

[6] The illustrations of the plea of debt found in Bracton's Note Book contain the formula *debet et detinet.* See Note Book, pl. 52, 177, 325, 381, 568, 645, 732, etc.

The form of the writ of debt for money in the county court which is given in the Register does not contain the word *detinet*, which was apparently necessary to give the king's court jurisdiction:

"Praecimus vobis quod justitietis A quod juste et sine dilatione reddat B mille marcas quas ei debet ut dicit sicut rationabiliter monstrare poterit quod ei redere debeat, etc." Reg. Brev. Orig. 139.

has been aptly called the "writ of right for money."[7] The analogy between debt and the proprietary action for land is shown in the further circumstance that in both there might be trial by battle;[8] but the offer of proof by battle has not actually been found in actions of debt.

Distinction between debt and detinue as regards perishability.

The proprietary character of the action being much more plainly marked in the *detinet* form of the action, it is not surprising to find that while the simple duty to pay a debt was originally conceived as an obligation so purely personal as to perish with the person, the duty to pay chattels did not so perish. Accordingly when the debtor died, the writ, in order to be maintainable, always had to be framed in the *detinet* solely, whether the debt was for money or chattels.[9]

Distinction between simple and specialty debts.

The most common means of creating a debt otherwise than by simple real contract is by the execution and delivery of a sealed obligation of indebtedness. Evidently the conception of obligation thus derived is quite different from that which is embodied in the real contract. The sealed obligation may of course originate in such a transaction and may indeed merely be evidence of it. Still in law, the sealed debt is conceived to be based on grant, the promise being made binding by reason of its form only. Accordingly it is not permissible for a plaintiff who counts upon a grant for £200 to prove by specialty to the extent of £140 and by simple contract for the other £60.[1]

The deed.

The sealed debt is created by the act or deed (*fet*) of the obligor, and is consequently referred to in the old authorities as his deed. The word 'deed,' which is of Anglo-Saxon origin (*dæd*), is doubtless cognate with the Latin *do, dedi.* The latter term has always been treated as a word of grant.

[7] 2 Poll. & Mait. Hist. Eng. Law, 2d ed., 206.

[8] Glanv., Bk. X., c. 12.

[9] "If debt be brought by the creditor against executors for the debt of the testator, the writ shall be *which they detain from him* and not *owe and detain,* although by the writ he demand money." F. N. B. 119 M. The rule was the same where the action was brought by the representatives of a decedent creditor. *Ib.* But the writ against heirs could be in the *debet et detinet* where the obligation which created the debt contained the word 'heirs.' 3 Bl. Com. 155.

[1] Y. B. 3 Edw. II. 78 (Dette).

So with the English deed which creates the specialty debt. It is evidence of a grant. The contract is good by reason of its form only, and no *quid pro quo* is required, as in simple debts.

Early local courts have jurisdiction over debts.

Prior to the time of Bracton the enforcement of debts was largely a matter for the local courts; but with the development of commerce and with the influx of foreign capital which took place in the thirteenth century, the royal courts were called upon to entertain such suits with some frequency. During the time of Edward I the action was chiefly and almost exclusively used for the recovery of money lent, the price of goods sold, arrears of rent due upon a lease for years, money due from a surety, and a debt confessed by a sealed instrument.[2] But there is nothing in the nature of the remedy to prevent the use of it in all cases where there is a legal duty to pay an ascertained amount of money or chattels, whether such duty arises from simple contract or grant by specialty or from covenant.[3]

Actions of debt entertained in common-law courts.

Debt as remedy for penalties and customary duties.

Statutory penalties, amerciaments, customary duties, and debts acknowledged of record are also well within the scope of the remedy. Thus debt lies for a penalty nominated in a lease,[4] for a fine due by custom for pound breach,[5] and for an amerciament recovered in a court baron or in a court leet.[6] Where an act of Parliament imposes a forfeiture of five pounds for practicing medicine in London without a license, the College of Physicians, to which the forfeiture inures, can maintain debt to recover the same, though no action is expressly given by the statute.[7]

Judgments.

Likewise after damages in a real action are reduced to certainty by judgment, debt can be maintained thereon.[8] So, where damages are recovered in the courts of London in an action there brought on a custom of the city, debt can subse-

[2] 2 Poll. & Mait. Hist. Eng. Law, 2d ed., 210.

[3] Anonymous, 1 Leon. 208, pl. 290; Com. Dig., *Debt* (A 8).

[4] Cibel *v.* Hill, 1 Leon. 110.

[5] Y. B. 11 Hen. VII. 13, pl. 8.

[6] Castle *v.* Oldman, 1 Leon. 203.

[7] 1 Rolle Abr. 598, pl. 18. So upon a statute imposing a treble value for not setting out tithes. *Ib.*, pl. 19.

[8] Y. B. 43 Edw. III. 2, pl. 5; Com. Dig., *Debt* (A 2); 1 Rolle Abr. 600 (N), pl. 1.

quently be maintained upon such judgment though the courts of Westminster had no jurisdiction of the original action.[0] There is no objection to the use of the remedy as a means of recovering on a judgment previously recovered in an action of debt; and the balance found due in an action of account can also be recovered in debt.[1] Putting any claim into a money judgment turns it into a legal duty, and debt can therefore be subsequently maintained upon such judgment. Hence it is not material that the original claim was not founded upon contract or covenant.[2]

Debt available upon quasi-contractual duty.

In *Speake v. Richards* (1618),[3] debt was brought against a sheriff to recover money taken by him under execution and wrongfully withheld from the plaintiff. It was argued for the defendant that debt would not lie, because there was no contract between the plaintiff and the sheriff. This was held to be immaterial, the court saying that "though there was no actual contract yet there was a kind of contract in law, so it is *ex quasi-contractu.*" Thus was the term 'quasi-contract' adopted as the appellation for those legal duties which are remediable in debt although they do not originate in contract in the modern sense (assumpsit).

Debt as remedy for recovery of rent.

One of the most characteristic and one of the most important obligations for the enforcement of which the action of debt has been immemorially used is the duty to pay rent. Rent, it is said, is a real obligation imposed primarily on land.[4] But it must be paid through the hands of the tenant, and from the earliest time debt has been used to enforce the duty to pay the rent.

About the propriety and fitness of the remedy as a means of recovering rent granted or reserved for years or at will

[0] 1 Rolle Abr. 600 (N), pl. 8.

[1] 1 Rolle Abr. 600 (N), pl. 6, 7.

[2] The case in Y. B. 43 Edw. III. 2, pl. 5, is an early and, it would seem, leading authority on the right to recover in debt upon a money judgment. The test of the right to maintain debt, according to the argument of the plaintiff in that case, is whether the demand has been turned into a 'duty.'

[3] Hob. 206, pl. 260; 1 Rolle Abr. 598, pl. 17.

[4] See article by Mr. Cyprian Williams on Landowners' Liability to Pay Rent Charges in Fee, 13 L. Quar. Rev. 288; also 2 Poll. & Mait. Hist. Eng. Law, 2d ed., 131.

Volume III

there has been no question.[5] Where, however, the rent was reserved for life, the action could not be maintained at common law until after the estate of freehold was determined. Debt could then be brought for the arrears.[6] Before the life estate determined a real action could be used to enforce the payment of the rent, and the existence of such remedy was fatal to the maintenance of debt.

Rent reserved for life recoverable only in real action.

For a similar reason debt could not at common law be used at all for the recovery of a rent reserved in fee or charged in fee. The same was true of rents in tail. In such case the estate could never determine, and accordingly the plaintiff was always compelled to resort to a real action.

So of rent reserved or charged in fee.

Now when real actions were abolished by statute,[7] the question naturally arose whether the owner of the rent charge in tail or fee had been deprived of all remedy and the right thereby destroyed. In *Varley v. Leigh* (1848),[8] Pollock, C. B., adverting to this question by way of dictum, said that, since there was now no remedy by real action for the recovery of rent charges in fee, debt would probably lie. Rolfe, B., did not concur in this view, and inclined to the opinion that the right was no longer enforceable. He remarked that the owner of a rent charge in fee was probably left like the owner of rent seck, who formerly had no remedy for the recovery of such rent.

Debt held to be maintainable in these cases after abolition of real actions.

Finally, in *Thomas v. Sylvester* (1873)[9] the question came up for decision, and it was held that debt would lie. The court considered that existence of the higher remedy by real action had constituted the main, if not the sole, obstacle to the maintenance of debt at common law, and that therefore, this obstacle being removed, debt could be maintained.[1]

[5] 1 Selwyn N. P., 13th ed., 539; Com. Dig., *Debt* (A 5). The action had to be brought where the land lay. Thursby *v.* Plant, 1 Sid. 401. Debt lies for rent though the lease call for corn or other chattel. Cheney's Case, 3 Leon. 260, pl. 347.

[6] 1 Rolle Abr. 596, pl. 11; Y. B. 10 Hen. VI. 11, pl. 38; Y. B. 11 Hen. VI. 15, pl. 4; Y. B. 19 Hen. VI. 41, pl. 85; Y. B. 39 Edw. III. 22*a*.

[7] 3 & 4 Will. IV., c. 27, § 36.

[8] 2 Exch. 446.

[9] L. R. 8 Q. B. 368.

[1] The decision is no doubt to be commended, as it operated to bring remedial law into harmony with substantive law at this point. Mr. T. C. Williams has, however, shown

Chapter XI

In the early history of the action of debt the requirement that the claim sued on should be for a sum certain of money or for an ascertained amount of ponderable chattels was rigidly insisted upon. It resulted that the plaintiff must always prove his claim to the exact extent sued for or he recovered nothing at all. To allege a debt for one amount and to prove for another was a fatal variance.[2] This was apparently the rule, at least in theory, as late as Blackstone's day, and this writer tells us that if one brought an action of debt for thirty pounds and only proved twenty pounds he could no more recover than if in detinue he sued for a horse and proved that the defendant detained his ox.[3]

Debt lies only for sum certain.

It seems that this rule requiring strict conformity between the allegation and proof as to the amount of the debt was also at first applied when assumpsit was used in suing upon a debt;[4] but this stringency was soon abandoned. In *Vaux v. Mainwaring* (1715)[5] it was declared that while in debt a variance in the proof from the amount stated in the declaration was fatal, in indebitatus assumpsit the plaintiff could recover so much as he proved.

Different rule applicable in indebitatus.

This decision supplied an entering wedge, and about seventy years later it was held that in simple debt the plaintiff can recover though he proves less than he has demanded in his declaration.[6] It was said the rule requiring that there

that the existence of the higher remedy by real action was probably not the only impediment to the maintenance of debt at common law on such a cause of action. See 13 L. Quar. Rev. 292. Probably the decision in Thomas *v.* Sylvester was more radical than the judges who made it supposed. It has since been followed. *In re* Blackburn, etc., Bldg. Soc., 42 Ch. D. 343.

[2] Y. B. 21 Edw. IV. 22, pl. 2. In Bladwell *v.* Sleggein, 2 Dyer 219*b*, Catlin, C. J., directed the jury to find for the defendant where the plaintiff sued in debt for £20 and the defendant proved that the debt was only for 20 marks.

[3] 3 Bl. Com. 154.

[4] Bagnal *v.* Sachaverell, Cro. Eliz. 292, pl. 5.

[5] Fortescue 197.

Said Parker, C. J.: "If you bring indebitatus assumpsit for £10 for a horse sold, if it was sold for more or less, yet the plaintiff shall recover what it was sold for; but if debt be brought on that contract, if it come out to be more or less, the plaintiff cannot recover; for it [the writ of debt] is a *praecipe quod reddat* for so much money in particular."

[6] M'Quillin *v.* Cox (1789), 1 H. Bl. 249. See to same effect, Lord *v.* Houstoun, 11 East 62; Aylett *v.* Lowe, 2 W. Bl. 1221; Emery *v.*

Volume III

shall be no variance between the amount named in the writ and the amount proved was applicable only to debts of record, specialties, and statutory penalties. The rule now is that debt will lie for any pecuniary demand which can be reduced to certainty.[7]

Debt personal and transitory.

At common law the right of action for a debt, except in the case of rent, was personal and transitory. In this respect it was like account and covenant. Consequently if a plaintiff brought an action by original writ in one county he might declare on a contract made in another, for the rule is *debitum et contractus sunt nullius loci*, and every duty is a duty in every county. This rule was not allowed to operate in favor of the jurisdiction of local courts, as where one had particular jurisdiction to hold pleas of debt in a manorial court. In such case the jurisdiction extended only to a cause of action arising within the limits of the manor.

Requirement as to venue.

By a statute of 6 Richard II[8] the general principle of the common law stated above was changed, and it was enacted that in debt and certain other actions the declaration should allege the contract to have been made in the county where the suit was instituted.[9] This operated in a measure to destroy the transitory character of the obligation to pay a debt.

Defect as regards venue pleadable in abatement only.

The fictitious venue.

In course of time, however, the statutory requirement that contracts should be sued on in the county where made was evaded. At first it seems to have been held that the question could only be raised by a plea in abatement; or the court might, upon motion, have inquired whether the cause of action arose in that county. But this practice fell into disuse, it being held that where the obligation or specialty was dated at large, i. e., stated no particular place of performance, it could be sued upon in any county. In such cases a plea that the obligation was made elsewhere than in the county where sued on was held bad. Finally, it was held that the effect of the statute was merely to require that the declaration should fol-

Fell, 2 T. R. 28; Van Deusen *v.* Blum, 18 Pick. (Mass.) 229.

[7] 1 Chitty Pl. 127.

[8] Chapter 2.

[9] 2 Co. Inst. 231.

Chapter XI

low the writ and that the statement of a fictitious venue in a transitory action made for the purpose of giving a court jurisdiction could not be traversed.[1] Thus was the rule in question circumvented in many cases.

In *Dutch West-India Co. v. Van Moses* (1725),[2] an action was brought for money borrowed in Amsterdam and payable in that place. The debtor was sued in London, and the plaintiff alleged that the debt originated "at Amsterdam in Holland, to wit, at Cheapside in the parish of St. Mary in London." It was held that this was good and that the venue could not be traversed.

Liability of heir upon debt of ancestor.

Although, as a matter of common-law principle, the action of debt is not available against a personal representative to recover a debt due from the estate of a deceased person, the remedy is available against an heir where the bond or specialty evidencing the debt expressly purports to bind the heir. But the liability of the heir is limited to the amount of assets actually descending to him. The law considers the bond of the ancestor, wherein the heir is bound, as becoming, upon the death of the ancestor, the heir's own debt in respect of the assets which the heir has in his own right, and holds him liable on such bond to the value of the land descended, "because the inheritance of the ancestor, which creates a lien upon the heir, is possessed by the heir *jure proprio* and not *alieno,* as the personal estate is by the executor."[3] The debt is not, however, a lien upon the land from the ancestor's death, but is only capable of being made so at the suit of the creditor. Although the heir is bound by the obligation of his ancestor, yet he is only liable to the extent of the value of the lands acquired by descent from the ancestor; and as soon as he has paid the ancestor's debt to the value of the land, he is not further liable.[4]

From what has been said it follows that in an action against an heir at law for a debt of his ancestor due by spe-

[1] Shalmer *v.* Slingsby, Aleyn 17.

[2] 1 Stra. 612.

[3] Gilbert, Treatise on the Action of Debt (printed in Gilb. Cas.), 401.

[4] Buckley *v.* Nightingale, 1 Stra. 665.

Volume III

cialty, the heir can plead *riens per descent* (nothing by descent), or that he received only so much. Formerly, if this plea was found false, he was charged personally for the whole debt, though he might have received only one acre. This severe rule was not applied as against an executor, who is charged only to the extent of assets coming to his hands, notwithstanding the plea of no assets be found false; and the rule as against the heir has been changed.[5]

Liability limited to value of land descended.

At the common law, if the heir had made a *bona fide* alienation of the lands descended, before action was brought upon the obligation of his ancestor, he was discharged and there was no remedy against him at law. But by a statute of 1 William IV,[6] heirs alienating descended lands are personally liable to the extent of the value of the lands alienated before action brought against them. The same statute gives the same remedy against devisees jointly with the heirs, and against devisees solely where there are no heirs.

Effect of alienation of land by heir.

A feature of debt which doomed the action to obsolescence so soon as assumpsit could be used in its stead, was found in the fact that the defendant could wage his law. All simple debts were subject to this mode of defense,[7] but the specialty and debts of record were not. When the right of the defendant to wage his law was indirectly taken away by the decision in *Slade's Case* (1602),[8] which permitted assumpsit to be used in suing upon simple debts, the old practitioners looked upon the innovation as a great hardship. The venerable Jenkins, in the time of the Commonwealth, enumerated this among the abuses which had crept into the common law in his day.[9] A little later Vaughan, C. J., inveighed with considerable show of feeling against what seemed to him to be an 'illegal resolution.'[1] Such protests as these were of no avail.

Action on simple debt subject to wager of law.

Martin *v.* Martin, 1 Ves. 211, 1 Will. IV., c. 47.

[6] Chapter 47.

[7] This rule, however, did not apply in the Exchequer. 1 Chitty Pl. 127.

[8] 4 Coke 92.

[9] Jenkins Centuries, ed. 1777, xxi.

[1] Edgcomb *v.* Dee, Vaugh. 101. The notion, said he, that every contract executory implies a promise, which was at the basis of Slade's Case, was a false gloss thereby to turn actions of debt into actions on the case.

The circumstance that the action of debt could not be used against the representatives of a deceased person also contributed to the popularity of assumpsit as a remedy upon debts.

When the wager of law became obsolete in the eighteenth century, debt gave some indications of a power to recover some of its lost ground,[2] for debt was more expeditious than assumpsit, judgment being final in the first instance, if the defendant did not appear. By statute in 1833 the wager of law was totally abolished,[3] and at the same time the action of debt was permitted to be brought against the representatives of deceased persons. But it was too late to bring the action back into frequent use, for a few years later all forms of action shared a common fate upon the passage of the Procedure Acts.

Modern effort at rehabilitation of the remedy.

In America, it should be observed, the wager of law never gained recognition as a legal mode of defense,[4] and modern constitutional provisions guaranteeing the right of trial by jury are of course inconsistent with the existence of such right. The action of debt, in this country, has not therefore been hampered by the limitations imposed upon the action by the wager of law.

Debt as a Remedy upon Bills and Notes.

As has elsewhere been shown, the first actions in the common-law courts on bills of exchange were in special assumpsit.[5] But when the principle was accepted that the custom of merchants is capable of creating a legal duty, special assumpsit had to give way to a specialized action on the case in the nature of assumpsit. At first this was not very obvious. Thus in *Oaste v. Taylor* (1612)[6] the declaration was clearly in case upon the custom of merchants, and there was no allegation of either promise or consideration. Nevertheless the action was spoken of as assumpsit. In truth it was a special

Normal mode of declaring on bills.

[2] King *v.* Williams, 4 D. & R. 206.

[3] 3 & 4 Will. IV., c. 42, § 13.

[4] See Childress *v.* Emory, 8 Wheat. (U. S.) 642, 675.

[5] See vol. 2, p. 343.

[6] Cro. Jac. 306.

Volume III

action on the case in the nature of assumpsit. No definite form of declaring was attained during the time of James I,[7] but later the action upon the case upon the custom was recognized as the correct form.[8]

Taking this as our point of departure and coming down to the present, we perceive from time to time a disposition to use debt and assumpsit to enforce the liability of various parties to the bill. We shall now endeavor to ascertain how far the action of debt has been so extended. The use of assumpsit as a remedy upon bills and notes is elsewhere considered.[9]

Tendency to adoption of debt and assumpsit as remedy on bills.

By way of general preface it may be observed that the extension of debt and assumpsit into the field of bills and notes was rendered possible by an extension of legal theory whereby the idea of duty derived from the law merchant was assimilated to the idea of duty imposed by law and to that of duty derived from simple promise. Debt, it will be borne in mind, is the proper remedy to enforce the pure legal duty to pay a sum certain of money; while duty derived from simple promise is enforced by assumpsit.

In *Anonymous* (1668),[1] otherwise commonly referred to as *Milton's Case*,[2] debt was brought by the payee against an acceptor. Hale, C. J., was anxious to sustain the action. He remarked that if debt would lie it would prove a short cut to a desired end, for then indebitatus assumpsit for so much money could be used on an accepted bill. The question was whether the duty involved had, really and in fact, become a common-law duty. "Without doubt," said Lord Hale, "if the common law or the custom of a place create a duty, debt lies for it without more ado, as in the case of a toll due by cus-

Debt not available by payee against acceptor.

[7] So said by Holt, C. J., in Starke *v.* Cheeseman, 1 Ld. Raym. 538. The arguments in Vanheath *v.* Turner (1622), Winch 24, display uncertainty on the question as to whether the action was purely in case or not.

[8] Starke *v.* Cheeseman (1700), 1 Ld. Raym. 538; Simmonds *v.* Parminter (1747), 1 Wils. C. Pl. 185. "By the custom of merchants no remedy was given on foreign bills of exchange but by action on the case. The statute of 9 & 10 Will. III., c. 17, gave the same remedy upon inland bills; and 3 & 4 Anne, c. 9, upon promissory notes." Welsh *v.* Craig, 8 Mod. 373.

[9] See Indebitatus Assumpsit, *post.*

[1] Hardres 485.

[2] Rainsford, C. J., in Browne *v.* London, 1 Mod. 286, 2 Keb. 695, 713.

tom; and so in cases of a certain sum due by custom for pound breach to the lord of the manor, or to a jailer for bar fees. But the great question here is whether or no a debt or duty be hereby raised. . . . The acceptance of the bill amounts clearly to a promise to pay the money, but it may be a question whether it amounts to a debt or not." The precedents were ordered searched. All the clerks of Guild Hall certified that there was no precedent in London of debt in such a case, and the opinion of some former chief justice was produced to the effect that debt lay not.

The whole court thereupon unanimously decided that an action of debt would not lie upon an accepted bill of exchange against the acceptor, but that a special action on the case must be brought against him. The absence of affirmative precedents on this question might alone have defeated the action in this instance, but another reason was also supposed to be conclusive against it. This was the erroneous notion that the drawee, in accepting a bill, thereby promises to pay the debt of another (the drawer). In this view the promise of the acceptor is collateral or secondary to the liability of the drawer, and a collateral promise or guaranty could never be enforced by debt. *Milton's Case* settled the law for some time. It was followed in *Brown v. London* (1670),[3] but it was there suggested that if A delivers money to B, and B draws a bill upon himself and accepts the same payable to C, then C can sue B in indebitatus assumpsit for so much money received to his use. Here there is a common-law right of action, and liability is not derived solely from the law merchant.

When indebitatus available against acceptor.

Inasmuch as the maker of a note has been generally considered as occupying the same position in law as the acceptor of a bill of exchange, it was held in *Welsh v. Craig* (1724),[4] that debt would not lie on a promissory note. This rule was much impaired by the decision in *Bishop v. Young* (1800),[5] in which case debt had been brought by the payee of a promissory note against the maker. The note recited a consideration, i. e., value received. Lord Eldon cautiously, even tim-

When debt available against maker of note.

[3] 1 Vent. 152, 2 Keb. 695, 713, 1 Mod. 285.

[4] 8 Mod. 373.

[5] 2 B. & P. 78.

Volume III

idly, upheld the declaration, yielding to the able argument of Sergeant Bailey for the plaintiff.

In *Stratton v. Hill* (1816),[6] the drift of Lord Eldon's previous holding was perceived. Mr. Chitty insisted that the old authorities were shaken. Accordingly it was decided that debt could be maintained by an indorsee against a party drawing, accepting, and indorsing a bill upon himself. The subsequent indorsement by the actual drawer of the bill does not render him less amenable on that account to any liability to which he is already subject.

Debt held to be available against acceptor.

In *Priddy v. Henbrey* (1823),[7] it was decided that the drawer could maintain debt against the acceptor where the bill purported to be drawn for value. The acceptance of such a bill is an admission of the receipt of assets and that the acceptor is debtor to that extent to the drawer.

Debt available by indorsee against immediate indorser,

Finally, in 1841 it was held that debt could be maintained by an indorsee against his immediate indorser.[8] The indorsement, like acceptance in *Priddy v. Henbrey*, was taken as an admission of the existence of a debt created by the passage of value given for the indorsement. Parke, B., said that the indorsement, in addition to being an admission of a debt, operated also as an implied promise to pay if the acceptor did not.

About the same time it was decided that the failure to recite value received does not in any way affect the right of the payee of a promissory note to sue the maker in debt; or of the drawer of a bill to sue the acceptor in the same form of action.[9]

but not against remote parties.

Having reached the conclusion that debt will lie at the instance of any holder against his immediate indorser, the English courts paused. Thus it is well settled in England that debt will not lie against the acceptor of a bill of exchange at the instance of any holder other than the immediate payee.[1]

[6] 3 Price 253; Sharpe *v.* Fowlkes, 7 Humph. (Tenn.) 512.

[7] 1 B. & C. 674, 8 E. C. L. 284.

[8] Watkins *v.* Wake, 7 M. & W. 488.

[9] Hatch *v.* Trayes (1840), 11 Ad. & El. 702, 39 E. C. L. 207.

[1] Powell *v.* Ancell (1841), 9 Dowl. 893; Cloves *v.* Williams (1837), 3 Bing. N. Cas. 868, 32 E. C. L. 360. See also Eales *v.*

Chapter XI

The difficulty encountered in using the action of debt as against a party not in immediate juxtaposition is the want of privity.[2]

As might be surmised, the action of debt has been used in America as a remedy on bills and notes more extensively than in England. In *Raborg v. Peyton* (1817),[3] Judge Story permitted the action of debt to be maintained at the instance of a remote indorsee against the acceptor, thus advancing where the English judges had paused. The objection urged was want of privity; but it was said, "Wherever the common law raises a duty, debt lies." In this decision the identification of duty imposed by the law merchant and duty imposed by common law becomes complete. The doctrine there laid down has been generally followed in this country.[4]

American doctrine.

Dicker (1829), M. & M. 324, 22 E. C. L. 323.

[2] Bishop *v.* Young, 2 B. & P. 78.

[3] 2 Wheat. (U. S.) 385.

[4] Kirkman *v.* Hamilton, 6 Pet. (U. S.) 20; Carroll *v.* Meeks, 3 Port. (Ala.) 226; Willmarth *v.* Crawford, 10 Wend. (N. Y.) 341; Onondaga County Bank *v.* Bates, 3 Hill (N. Y.) 53; Anderson *v.* Crockett, 6 Yerg. (Tenn.) 330; Regnault *v.* Hunter, 4 W. Va. 257.

CHAPTER XII

THE ACTION OF DETINUE.

Volume III

THE action of detinue is that form of the action of debt which is used for the recovery of specific chattels, together with damages for the wrongful detention. Though in modern times debt and detinue are treated as distinct actions, their affinity is shown by the fact that their properties, their form, and the process incident to each are substantially the same, and a money count in debt upon contract can be joined in detinue if the situation warrants. But the conclusion that detinue is only a form of debt does not rest merely upon inference from such similarities. It is a known fact in legal history and is shown by the form of the writ.[1]

Action derived from debt.

The separation between debt and detinue seems to have been accomplished by the end of the reign of Edward I, the line of cleavage being determined by the distinction between the duty to pay a definite amount of money or chattels by number, weight, or measure, and the duty to deliver specific chattels.[2] The action of detinue is accordingly substantially identical with the early debt in the *detinet*.

As the action of detinue is used for the recovery of specific chattels and is thus founded upon the legal duty to deliver such chattels to the plaintiff, it becomes necessary to inquire in what manner the duty which is enforced by this action can originate. To this it can be answered that the duty to deliver could, in the early stages of the development of the action, have no other origin than in contract. There must, in other words, be a common-law debt. The action of detinue was the proper remedy of the bailor, and for a long period it was chiefly used in the field of bailment.

Remedy chiefly used in field of bailment.

The scope of the action is illustrated in the following

[1] Reg. Brev. Orig. 139 *et seq.;* F. N. B. 138, 119.

[2] 3 Reeves, Hist. Eng. Law, Am. ed., 47; 2 Poll. & Mait. Hist. Eng. Law, 2d ed., 206.

Fitzherbert's statement of the scope of the action.

language of Fitzherbert: "Where a man delivereth goods or chattels unto another to keep and afterwards he will not deliver them back again, then he [the bailor] shall have an action of detinue of those goods and chattels; and so if a man deliver goods or money put up in bags, or in a chest, or in a cupboard, unto another to keep and he will not redeliver the goods or the money in the bags, he to whom they should be delivered shall have a writ of detinue."[3]

Detinue in bargain and sale.

Though detinue upon bailment (*sur bailment*) was the most conspicuous form of detinue, because the real contract of bailment was the most conspicuous of early contracts, the remedy was a proper one in all cases where a duty to deliver chattels was raised by any form of contract known to the common law. The bargain and sale was not strictly speaking a real contract, but detinue could nevertheless be used by the purchaser to enforce delivery. At first this was only permitted where the purchase price was paid or a sealed obligation therefor delivered to the seller.[4] But at a later day this was not required.[5]

Detinue as remedy on sealed obligation.

There could be no objection in point of principle to the maintenance of detinue upon a duty to deliver specific chattels, created by a sealed obligation or an indenture of lease, since such contracts create debts. Usually, however, such contracts call for the delivery of indeterminate chattels by number, weight, or measure, and debt in the *debet et detinet* is then used instead of detinue.[6] Furthermore, as debts may be created by a contract of record or by custom, there would be no objection to the use of detinue as a remedy upon a customary duty, provided the record or custom should impose a duty to deliver specific chattels. But this could seldom or never happen.

Accordingly, in studying the early history of detinue we

[3] F. N. B. 138.

In an action of detinue *sur bailment* a denial of the bailment is a good plea without answering to the detention. Y. B. 3 Edw. II. 78 (Detinue); Y. B. 6 Edw. II. 192 (Detinue).

[4] Y. B. 21 Edw. III. 12, pl. 2.

[5] Y. B. 20 Hen. VI. 35, pl. 4; Y. B. 21 Hen. VI. 55, pl. 12; Edgcomb *v.* Dee, Vaugh. 101.

[6] Y. B. 20 & 21 Edw. I. (Rolls ed.), 139; Y. B. 50 Edw. III. 16, pl. 8.

Volume III

Detinue *sur bailment.*

are chiefly concerned with it as the remedy of the bailor. In this connection we find one limitation upon the right to use detinue to recover a chattel bailed. The remedy was available only against the bailee and such persons as claimed under him by testate or intestate succession. It would not lie at the instance of the bailor against a third person who bought, bailed, stole, or took the chattel from the bailee.

Explanations.

This limitation upon the action has proved very puzzling to students of legal history. The simplest explanation is this: The contract of bailment created a debt. Consequently the bailee owed the chattel to the bailor, and was absolutely answerable for it or its value to him. When the bailor brought an action of detinue against the bailee, the latter could not be freed from liability upon proof that some third person had stolen or otherwise taken possession of the chattel. A right of action against the bailee being thus always conceded to the bailor, the law accordingly denied the bailor's right to sue the third person. The bailee was the one entitled to go upon him.

Another way of explaining the phenomenon is by saying that the action of detinue was a contractual action and it could not be maintained against the third person for lack of legal privity. At any rate the bailor had to seek redress from the person with whom he had trusted his property.[7] This limitation on the action is more surprising when we consider that the language of the ordinary writ of detinue was broad enough to include any case of wrongful detention.[8]

Detinue *sur bailment* available against representative of deceased bailee.

The first exception ingrafted on the general doctrine that detinue *sur bailment* could be maintained only against the bailee personally was the rule that the action would lie against the legal representative of the bailee after the latter's death.[9] The recognition of this exception took place at a very early day, and there is perhaps room for doubting whether the con-

[7] Y. B. 24 Edw. III. 41, pl. 22.

[8] "Quod reddat B decem quarteria avenarum et his similia, precii viginti solidorum, quae ei injuste detinet ut dicit." Reg. Brev. Orig. 139. "Command A, etc., that he render to B one charter which he unjustly detains from him," etc. F. N. B. 138 B.

[9] Y. B. 16 Edw. II. 490; Y. B. 43 Edw. III. 29, pl. 11.

Chapter XII

trary principle ever found expression in an actual decision.

Bailor permitted to sue sub-bailee in life of bailee.

In the early part of the fifteenth century the bailor was allowed to sue a sub-bailee while the bailee was yet alive.[1] "A man bails goods to one who bails them over to another. He may here have a detinue upon the bailment against the first bailee, and also he may have an action of detinue against the second bailee upon a *devenerunt ad manus*." [2]

Detinue upon allegation of *devenerunt ad manus*.

Presently a plaintiff, who could show that he had bailed property to A, was permitted to recover it from any one in whose possession soever it might be found, merely by alleging generally that the property came to the hands and possession of the defendant (*ad manus et possessionem devenerunt*), but without showing how he acquired it.[3]

The allegation of a *devenerunt ad manus* was doubtless originally used in cases where the property had come into the hands of the defendant as executor.[4] But if this be so, it was soon used in cases where the defendant occupied no such relation. By this means the action of detinue could be used by the bailor to recover chattels bailed, regardless of the manner in which the defendant acquired them. Still at this stage of the action there must have been a bailment to begin with.[5]

Detinue *sur trover*.

In its next stage the remedy was extended beyond this limit. The first situation in which the action of detinue was maintained without proof of any actual bailment was where the plaintiff lost and the defendant found the chattels in question. "If a man finds my goods which I have lost, I may have a writ of detinue of them." [6] This extension of detinue

[1] Y. B. 11 Hen. IV. 46, pl. 20; Y. B. 10 Hen. VII. 7, pl. 14.

[2] Coke, C. J., in Isaack *v.* Clark, 2 Bulst. 313.

[3] Y. B. 33 Hen. VI. 27, pl. 12.

[4] Wagworth *v.* Halyday, Y. B. 29 Edw. III. 38 B.

[5] Fairfax: "I bail goods to W, who loses them. If B finds them he is chargeable to me in an action of detinue." Brooke Abr., *Detinue*, pl. 40.

[6] F. N. B. 138 E.

In Y. B. 7 Hen. VI. 22, pl. 3, detinue was brought for charters against a finder. There being several claimants, the court forced them to interplead. It was said: "If one finds my goods I can have a general writ or a writ on the matter." By this we are to understand that the plaintiff could elect to bring either detinue on a general *devenerunt ad manus* or detinue *sur trover*. The action on the case *sur trover* had not yet appeared.

Volume III

took place apparently in the latter part of the sixteenth century, but the subject is not clear. As late as 1455 Prisot, J., thought detinue would not lie against a finder unless there had been a bailment to some one to begin with. A plaintiff who had himself lost the chattels could not, in the opinion of this judge, maintain detinue against the finder.[7] In the same case Serjeant Littleton, doubtless basing his opinion on the case from 7 Hen. VI, agreed with counsel for the plaintiff that any loser could maintain detinue against a finder. The plaintiff apparently failed in that case, but Littleton's view was subsequently accepted, and the loser was permitted to use detinue against a finder, or trespass, after unsuccessful demand, at his election.[8]

Loser may maintain detinue against finder.

It was in this case from 1455 that Littleton remarked that the mode of declaring *per inventionem* was a newly discovered boon ("a new-found haliday"), "the old allegation and entry having always been that the goods *ad manus et possessionem defendentis devenerunt* generally without showing how." He believed that the innovation extended so far as to do away with the necessity of alleging an original bailment; but as we have seen, Prisot, J., did not agree with him on this point.[9]

At any rate, detinue *sur trover* as a remedy against an actual finder was soon firmly established. There is no evidence that at this stage detinue *sur trover* could be maintained

Fictitious finding not recognized in fifteenth century.

[7] Y. B. 33 Hen. VI. 26, pl. 12. Where the owner himself loses the chattels, he can, said Prisot, J., maintain trespass against a finder if the latter should refuse to give them up on demand. "But if one A has [i. e., apparently as bailee] deeds of my land and loses them, and one B finds them, I shall have detinue against him without demand."

[8] Y. B. 2 Rich. III. 15, pl. 39.

Two reasons why detinue was not extended to cases of losing and finding at an earlier day have been assigned by Professor Ames. In the first place, the local courts supplied a remedy in the action for a *chose adirree (res adirata,* lost chattel); and, secondly, where a finder of property refused to give it up upon demand of the owner, he could be sued in an action of trespass *de bonis asportatis.* 11 Harv. L. Rev. 288, 381.

[9] Professor Ames remarks: "The innovation [referred to by Littleton] was not in allowing detinue where there was no bailment, but in describing the defendant as a finder." 11 Harv. L. Rev. 382, note. It is true that this was the only innovation which Prisot was willing to sanction, but Littleton's dictum went further.

upon an allegation of a fictitious finding. That the fictitious trover was as yet unknown appears from the fact that the defendant could traverse the finding in the action of detinue *sur trover.*[1] From what has been said it appears that the two classic counts in detinue are the counts upon bailment (*sur bailment*) and upon a finding (*sur trover*).

Chapter XII

There is still further evidence of a tendency to extend the action of detinue beyond the limits of bailment in the fifteenth century. Brooke cites a case from 1402 to the effect that where a bailment is alleged by a plaintiff suing in detinue, the fact of such bailment is not traversable, inasmuch as the defendant should be required to answer for the wrongful detention.[2] In other words, the allegation of a bailment was there treated as a fictitious averment. In modern times, the action of detinue having been extended to all cases of unlawful detention, the rule stated by Brooke has been fully applied, and where a bailment is alleged it need not be proved if an unlawful detention is otherwise shown.[3]

Detinue available for any unlawful detention.

It is obvious that neither detinue *sur bailment* nor detinue *sur trover* can be used to recover the possession of chattels tortiously taken by a trespasser, unless either the finding in the one case or the bailment in the other is treated as a fictitious averment. But notwithstanding the statement from Brooke which is referred to above, it is clear that the notion that the allegation of bailment could be treated as fictitious was not commonly accepted. Nor as yet had the principle been recognized that the finding in detinue *sur trover* could be treated as fictitious. Accordingly, no form of detinue could be maintained against one who tortiously took chattels. In other words, the action was not a concurrent remedy with trespass *de bonis asportatis.* But this extension of the remedy did occur, and it constituted the last step in the development of the remedy.

Extension of remedy to case of asportation.

[1] Y. B. 21 Edw. IV. 19, pl. 21; Y. B. 21 Edw. IV. 80, pl. 28.

[2] Brooke Abr., *Detinue de Biens*, pl. 50. This is contrary to what appears to have been the earlier ruling on this point. See Y. B. 3 Edw. II. 78.

[3] Gledstane *v.* Hewitt, 1 Cromp. & J. 565; Whitehead *v.* Harrison, 6 Q. B. 423, 51 E. C. L. 423.

Volume III

The change in legal theory by which this was rendered possible seems to have occurred near the end of the fifteenth century; but the subject has not been fully cleared up. The argument in a case from 1491 is instructive. Brian, C. J., stated the previously accepted doctrine in declaring that one from whom goods are taken by a trespasser cannot recover them in an action of detinue. The reason assigned for this was that only an owner could maintain detinue, and the tortious taking put the property in the trespasser. In detinue the plaintiff must allege, said he, that the defendant came into possession of the goods lawfully.[4]

Brian's view at close of fifteenth century.

In the same case, however, Vavisor, J., stated emphatically that an action of detinue would lie against a trespasser, as well as the actions of trespass and replevin. However unsound this proposition may have been so far as previous practice is concerned, it was in entire harmony with subsequent theory. It is obvious that the form of declaring in such an action would be in detinue *sur trover,* the finding being treated as a fictitious and non-traversable averment

Contrary doctrine.

In view of the language of Vavisor, J., in the case just cited we naturally expect presently to find express decisions to the effect that detinue *sur trover* can be maintained against trespassers. But there seems to have been no such decision for many years. The reason is not only to be found in the fact that trespass was a sufficient remedy in such case, but in the further fact that the action on the case was coming into use as a remedy both against bailees and trespassers at large.

Period of atrophy in the development of detinue.

There are several reasons why the action on the case was a more satisfactory remedy for the bailor than detinue. The plaintiff who sued in detinue could not in that action recover

[4] Y. B. 6 Hen. VII. 9, pl. 4. The language of the learned judge in this case seems to be somewhat inconsistent, for notwithstanding he asserts that the action lies only where the defendant comes into legal possession, he nevertheless admits that the bailment in detinue *sur bailment* and the finding in detinue *sur trover* may be treated as non-transferable fictions. Says he: "In detinue one ought to allege that the defendant came to the chattels lawfully, but if he brings detinue and counts on a finding or bailment it is not traversable."

Brooke in reporting this case accepts the statement of Brian, C. J., as good law. Brooke Abr., *Detinue,* pls. 36, 53.

damages incurred by reason of the bailee's negligence, provided the bailee chose to surrender the specific chattels in their deteriorated condition. In such case the owner was compelled to bring a separate action for such damages.[5] By suing in case the plaintiff could recover full damages in one suit.[6] Case was, of course, the sole remedy where the goods were without suit surrendered on demand in a damaged condition. Then, besides, detinue, like debt, was subject to a procedural difficulty which was fatal to its usefulness and effectually prevented its extension into other fields. The action could be defended by the wager of law. This rule applied even where the finding in detinue *sur trover* was fictitious.[7]

Chapter XII

Explanation of the phenomenon.

For the reasons above given the action on the case became concurrent with detinue as a remedy of the bailor,[8] and in the form of the modern action of trover came to be commonly used against trespass at large.[9] The result was that Vavisor's utterance remained fruitless, and detinue *sur trover* as a remedy against trespassers was not in practice adopted.

Detinue *sur trover* superseded by action on the case *sur trover*.

The appearance of the action on the case (trover) as a competing remedy not only prevented the further extension of detinue *sur trover* in the manner just indicated, but it also caused the action of detinue in all its forms to fall into disuse.[1] Just as the action of debt was superseded by assumpsit, so in the end was detinue superseded by trover.

Detinue falls into desuetude.

In course of time, when the wager of law had become obsolete, and detinue, like debt, began to emerge from the adumbration which it had suffered, the ancient limitations of the

[5] Keilw. 160, pl. 2; Holmes on Common Law 183.

[6] Y. B. 12 Edw. IV. 13, pl. 10; Y. B. 2 Hen. VII. 11, pl. 9; Y. B. 18 Edw. IV. 23, pl. 5.

[7] Y. B. 6 Hen. VII. 9, pl. 4; Brooke Abr., *Detinue*, pl. 40.

[8] Y. B. 2 Hen. VII. 11, pl. 9; Keilw. 160, pl. 2; Wheatly *v.* Lowe, Cro. Jac. 668.

"If I bail goods to you and you burn them or otherwise suffer them to be eaten by moths, I may elect to bring detinue or case." Spellman, J., Y. B. 27 Hen. VIII. 25, pl. 3.

[9] Bishop *v.* Montague, Cro. Jac. 50; Basset *v.* Maynard, 1 Rolle Abr. 105, 5.

[1] In Compleat Attorney (1666) it is said of trover: "The action is now very usual and takes place instead of actions of detinue, for in them the defendant was at liberty to wage his law, whereas this debars him." Compleat Attorney, ed. 1774, *Trover and Conversion*, 140.

Volume III

Rehabilitation of detinue.

Scope of the modern action.

action, whereby it was restricted to cases where the defendant had acquired lawful possession, seem to have been forgotten; or at least they were disregarded. Accordingly when the action of detinue came again into prominence in modern times, it was permitted without question to be maintained in all cases of tortious taking. In other words, it followed trover into the field of trespass *de bonis asportatis;* and any owner can now maintain the action of detinue where his property is wrongfully withheld from him by the defendant, regardless of whether the latter originally obtained possession lawfully or unlawfully.[2] This end has been accomplished by the recognition of the principle that in detinue the gist of the action is unlawful detention. As said by Bayley, B., in *Gledstane v. Hewitt* (1831):[3] "The plaintiff must make out that he was entitled to the delivery of the article and that the defendant wrongfully detained it. . . . He is not bound to show the circumstances under which the article came into the defendant's hands."

Available in case of asportation and generally for any unlawful detention.

Wrongful detention the gist of the action.

Wrongful detention being recognized as the foundation of the action, it followed that the allegation of an actual bailment was no longer essential. The allegation of bailment was, however, prior to the abolition of the actions, still common in declarations in detinue even where the action was brought to recover goods wrongfully taken. Like the allegation of a finding in trover, the bailment, in such case, was a fiction and could not be traversed.[4]

Allegation of fictitious bailment.

Requisites of plaintiff's title.

It is to be added that the plaintiff in detinue must have a general or special ownership and be entitled to immediate possession. But if the plaintiff has the general property he can maintain the action without ever having had actual possession.[5]

To sum up in a few words the various stages through which detinue has passed, we may say that the action first appeared as a form of debt, and before the reign of Edward I

[2] See Peirce *v.* Hill, 9 Port. (Ala.) 151.

[3] 1 Cromp. & J. 570.

[4] Whitehead *v.* Harrison, 6 Q. B. 423, 51 E. C. L. 423; Gledstane *v.* Hewitt, 1 Cromp. & J. 565; Brodbent *v.* Ledward, 11 Ad. & El. 209, 39 E. C. L. 48.

[5] 1 Chitty Pl. 137. See Reese *v.* Harris, 27 Ala. 301.

was not distinguishable from the mother action. It was the remedy by which the bailor enforced his rights against the bailee (detinue *sur bailment*); and though theoretically broad enough to be used in all cases where there was a contractual duty (debt) to surrender a specific chattel, it was in practice limited strictly to the field of bailment and was used only against the bailee. By degrees the action was permitted to be used against the heirs, representatives, and finally against sub-bailees.

Summary of steps in development of detinue.

Later, upon alleging a bailment and generally that the goods had thereafter come to the hands of the defendant (*devenerunt ad manus*), the bailor was permitted in this action to recover from any one who obtained the chattels unlawfully from the bailee, as by theft or trespass. By this means the remedy could be used by the bailor to recover his chattels wherever they might be found.

The next step in the development of the action was that by which the owner of goods (and not merely the bailor) was permitted to maintain detinue against one who came into possession by finding (*per inventionem*), the finder being treated as a sort of quasi-bailee. This was detinue *sur trover.* This form of the remedy was, by its nature, readily adapted to extension into the field of trespass; for it is easily seen that one who takes by trespass or theft can be held at least to the civil liability of a finder, such person not being permitted to take advantage of his own wrong and to show that the taking was unlawful. Detinue *sur trover* was thus in theory available against trespassers at large, but in practice it was not so used until quite modern times, detinue having been largely superseded by the action on the case. When in the nineteenth century detinue emerged from its long eclipse the old limitations on the action were forgotten, and it was properly used concurrently with replevin, trover, and trespass *de bonis asportatis,* in all cases of the wrongful detention of chattels, and regardless of whether the defendant originally acquired possession lawfully or otherwise.

Hitherto we have considered detinue as a contractual rem-

Volume III

edy, and that it is such in its origin is clear. Detinue *sur bailment* is manifestly such as appears from the history and scope of the action. This principle is illustrated in early decisions to the effect that detinue *sur bailment* does not lie against a husband and wife upon a bailment to them both, because of her inability to bind herself by contract.[6] So where goods were bailed to a married woman and she died, it seems to have been conceded, in the early years of the fifteenth century, that detinue could not be maintained against her husband, because he was not privy nor party to the delivery and the action would not lie for the detention only.[7] Likewise where there is a bailment to several jointly they must be joined as defendants.[8]

Detinue originally a contractual action.

In the modern case of *Atwood v. Ernest* (1853),[9] it was held that where two or more are interested in a chattel and they jointly deposit it with a stranger, a demand by one in his own name only, and not on behalf of all, will not entitle the demandant to maintain detinue So where one person bails a thing belonging to several, the actual bailor is the only person who can maintain detinue on such bailment.[1] The contract and delivery by the bailor in such case make the bailee answerable to him, and not to the owners who are not parties to the delivery.[2]

Detinue as remedy for one of several joint bailors.

[6] Y. B. 38 Edw. III. 1, pl. 1; Isaack *v.* Clark, 2 Bulst. 308.

[7] In such a case the owner was forced to file a bill in chancery alleging that he was without remedy at law. Sel. Cas. Ch. (Selden Soc.) 113, pl. 116.

[8] Y. B. 7 Hen. IV. 6, pl. 37.

[9] 13 C. B. 881, 76 E. C. L. 881.

[1] Y. B. 49 Edw. III. 13, pl. 6.

[2] Bellewe's Cas. 134, *Detinue de Charters.*

An interesting debate from 1292 shows that detinue was then considered in the light of a contractual remedy. A chattel was delivered (bailed) for safe keeping to a married woman. After the death of her husband she was sued in detinue for its detention. For the plaintiff it was argued that she was liable for the tortious detainer and not as upon the contract of bailment. For the defendant it was insisted that the bailment arose out of contract and that a married woman could not be held liable upon a contract. This argument seems to have prevailed, but the actual result is not stated. The colloquy in question is reported as follows: "*Huntingdon:* Sir, our plaint is of a tortious detinue of a charter which this lady is now detaining from us. We crave judgment that she ought to answer for her tort. *Lowther:* The cause of your action is the bailment, and at that time she could not bind herself. We crave judgment if she must now answer for a thing about which she could not bind herself. *Spigurnel:* If you had bailed to the lady thirty marks for safe custody while she

Chapter XII

Notwithstanding the contractual character of detinue *sur bailment* is thus manifest, it must further be said that it is such in a special sense only. The contract upon which detinue lies is the ancient debt, and not the modern assumptual contract. The duty is a duty imposed by law upon the circumstance that one party has acquired possession of the chattel of another and is bound to deliver it up. Accordingly, with the development in modern times of the idea that contractual liability is derived from the obligation of promise, men have ceased to realize that detinue was ever a contractual remedy at all.[3]

Detinue no longer viewed as purely contractual remedy.

The chief reason why detinue is no longer to be viewed exclusively as a contractual action is found in the fact that the remedy has been so broadened as to be available in case of any wrongful detention. The theory underlying the remedy has thereby in fact been revolutionized. The extent of the transformation has not always been fully appreciated and confusion has resulted. Some writers clinging to the older authorities persist in classifying the remedy as one of contract purely; while others, having an eye to what the remedy has become rather than what it was in the past, say that it is a proprietary remedy and founded directly on legal duty. Consequently, they say, if the action must be forced into one or the other categories it must now be classed as a remedy *ex delicto* rather than *ex contractu*.

Change in nature of remedy as result of extension of doctrine.

These two opposing views are well illustrated in the respective opinions of Denman, J., and Bramwell, L. J., at the

was *coverte* for return to you when you should demand them, would she be now bound to answer? I trow not. And so in this case. *Howard:* The cases are not similar; for in a writ of debt you shall say *debet*, while here you shall say *iniuste detinet*. And again, in this case an action arises from a tortious detainer and not from the bailment. We crave judgment. *Lowther:* We repeat what we have said." Y. B. 20 & 21 Edw. I. (Rolls ed.) 180, 191. See 2 Poll. & Mait. Hist. Eng. Law, 2d ed., 180.

[3] Thus, Mr. Tidd treats detinue as an action of tort. 1 Tidd's Pr. 4. The Common Law Procedure Act of 1852 also classed the action with remedies founded on tort. 15 & 16 Vict., c. 76, Sched. B (29).

But Wentworth and Chitty refrain in their forms from stating a cause of action in tort. 2 Chitty Pl. 429; 7 Went. 635. Chitty doubtfully classes the remedy as an action *ex contractu*, 1 Chitty Pl. 136; and the County Court Act of 1850 did likewise. 13 & 14 Vict., c. 61, § 11.

Volume III

Conflicting views concerning nature of detinue:

different hearings of *Bryant v. Herbert* (1878),[4] where the question was raised whether detinue was an action of contract or of tort within the meaning of a statute regulating the taxation of costs. The first of the judges above mentioned, in entire harmony with early theory and precedents, said that if we look into the history of detinue we find that it was based on the theory of a bailment, real or fictitious, imposing upon the defendant an obligation to return the chattel bailed when his right to retain it as bailee had ceased to exist. "A contract, real or fictitious, was the foundation of this obligation, and although his breach of it was a wrong, it was so only in the sense in which every breach of every contract is a wrong. In theory the action was founded on contract, and not on wrong independently of contract."

1. Contract theory.

In the Court of Appeal the judgment rendered in conformity with the foregoing view was reversed, Bramwell, L. J., saying: "One may observe that there is no middle term; the statute supposes all actions are founded either on contract or on tort. So that it is tort, if not contract; contract, if not tort. Then is this action on the face of the statements of claim and defense founded on contract or on torts. All that is alleged is that the plaintiffs are owners of the picture and that the defendant detains it. This means wrongfully detains it, not merely has in his possession, and negatively does not give it up. . . . Suppose the plaintiffs had sold the picture to A B; he might have maintained this action. On what would it then have been founded? Clearly not on contract; therefore on tort. So it is now."[5]

2. Tort theory.

The decision in the Court of Appeal is obviously correct. Where unlawful detention is the foundation of the action, the action sounds in tort rather than in contract. It is thus apparent that in some instances detinue may be an action *ex contractu*, in others an action *ex delicto*, according as the duty which it is brought to enforce is derived from contract or is imposed by law regardless of contract. The distinction here indicated has been expressed by an American court in the fol-

Remedy sometimes sounds in contract, sometimes sounds in tort.

[4] 3 C. P. D. 189; on appeal, 3 C. P. D. 389.
[5] 3 C. P. D. 390, 391.

Chapter XII

lowing language: "Detinue cannot always be considered an action *ex contractu.* Conceding that such is its character when the defendant's possession commences under a contract of bailment, yet where the taking is tortious, the detention must be alike wrongful. . . . Wherever there is a tortious taking the action in *ex delicto.*"[6]

Detinue a recuperatory action for chattels.

From what has just been said it follows that all efforts to classify detinue as being in strictness either on an action of contract or of tort are doomed to be more or less futile. Detinue clearly occupies a unique position in English remedial law, and must be considered solely as an action *in rem* for the recovery of chattels. Its proprietary character in modern times is manifest, for it is now a universal remedy for the recovery of chattels by the owner. In the early common law also its character as a proprietary remedy was sufficiently apparent; but there were two reasons which caused Bracton to deny that it was an action *in rem* in the full and complete sense.

In the first place, the legal machinery incident to the action was not equal to the task of compelling the defendant to deliver the chattels for which judgment was recovered, if he chose to remain obdurate. Every judgment in detinue was in the alternative, and the defendant could pay the assessed damages if he preferred to withhold the chattels. For this reason it seemed to the learned law writer of the thirteenth century that detinue was not an action *in rem.*[7]

A further circumstance, already considered, pointed to the same conclusion. This is found in the fact that detinue could not in the early period be maintained by the bailor against sub-bailees and trespassers who invaded the possession of the bailee; nor by the owner against trespassers at large. Although the defect and limitations mentioned did hamper and circumscribe the action, yet within its particular scope detinue was evidently founded on property. This quality indeed it inherited from debt. And now since the defect which struck Bracton as being an insuperable objection to classifying det-

[6] Salter *v.* Pearce (1843), 4 Ala. 669.
[7] See, *ante,* p. 40.

Volume III

inue as an action *in rem* has been removed,[8] and since the action can now be maintained upon any unlawful detention, the remedy should be allowed to take its true place in the field of remedial law as an action founded on property.

[8] This defect was not cured in England until the middle of the nineteenth century, when it was enacted that a plaintiff who recovered in detinue should have an order for the specific delivery of the chattel detained. Common Law Procedure Act (1854), c. 78.

CHAPTER XIII

THE ACTION OF TROVER.

Chapter XIII

THE action of trover is a specialized form of case devised for the purpose of recovering damages for the conversion of chattels.[1] It was differentiated from case somewhat later than assumpsit, and is consequently the youngest of the personal common-law actions.

Genesis of the action.

The close resemblance between the form of declaring in detinue *sur trover* and in the action on the case *sur trover* has given rise to the opinion that the latter was derived from the earlier form of action. In a qualified sense this is true, as the younger action was conceived for the purpose of redressing a wrong similar to that to which the older was applied. It seems better to say, however, that the relation between the modern trover and detinue *sur trover* is one of resemblance rather than of derivation. Indeed it is of the essence of all forms of case to be framed in analogy to the settled actions rather than to be derived directly from them. This is true in the instance before us. Detinue *sur trover* and trover have always been distinguishable, and there was never a time when the former changed into the latter remedy. In framing his count in trover the early pleader certainly had before him the form of the count in detinue *sur trover* and followed its pattern.[2] But after all, trover is merely an action on the case in the nature of detinue *sur trover*,[3] and is distinct from it.

Trover is an action on the case in nature of detinue.

The most curious feature of the action of trover is the fact that it is encumbered with more fictions than any other per-

[1] See opinion of Martin, B., in Burroughes *v.* Bayne, 5 H. & N. 296.

[2] "Add to the precedent [for detinue *sur trover*] in the 'Liber Intrationum' (1510) the single averment that the defendant converted the chattel to his own use, and we have the count in trover." Prof. J. B. Ames, 11 Harv. L. Rev. 382.

[3] "Here . . . detinue lieth and if [so] then also this action [trover] lieth, for this is the nature of it." Popham, Attorney General, in Russel *v.* Prat (1600), 4 Leon 44.

Volume III

The fictions.

sonal action. The declaration alleges a losing by the plaintiff and a finding by the defendant, but neither of these allegations need be proved. Furthermore, if a bailment is alleged as a means of indicating the manner in which the defendant acquired possession, it need not in modern times be proved. A refusal to surrender on demand is also often alleged in the declaration, but this allegation is likewise immaterial where the taking is tortious.

Conversion.

The gist of the action is found in the allegation that the defendant "converted the goods to his own use." [4] But oddly enough, even this allegation is also a sort of fiction; for if words mean anything, a conversion to one's own use implies an appropriation under such circumstances as to result in benefit to the converter. But nothing is better established than that this is not necessary. Conversion in law does not mean acquisition of property.[5] It is enough that the owner or person having the right to possession has, under conditions more or less clearly defined, been deprived of dominion over the goods.[6] A withholding of possession under an inconsistent claim of title is sufficient.[7]

Disseisin of chattel gist of the tort for which trover lies.

Diversion from the owner or possessor would therefore be a more accurate term than conversion to the defendant's use. The idea is perhaps still better brought out by the use of the expression 'disseisin of chattels,' which we have elsewhere adopted to indicate the gist of the wrong.[8] Legal liability here has its root in a principle analogous to that which underlies the doctrine of consideration in the law of contract. There

[4] "*In usum suum proprium convertit et disponit*—these are the words that make a conversion." Coke, C. J., in Isaack *v.* Clark, 2 Bulst. 313.

[5] Keyworth *v.* Hill (1820), 3 B. & Ald. 685, 5 E. C. L. 422.

[6] If one person dispose of the goods of another for the benefit of a third person this is a conversion; for the injury to the owner of the goods is the same as if they had been disposed of for the benefit of the disposer. Perkins *v.* Smith, Say. 41; Bac. Abr., *Trover* (B).

[7] To constitute a conversion, such as will sustain an action of trover, there must be a destruction of the plaintiff's property; or some unlawful interference with his use, enjoyment, or dominion over it; or an appropriation of it by the defendant to his own use, in disregard or defiance of the owner's rights; or a withholding of the possession from the owner, under a claim of title inconsistent with his own. Conner *v.* Allen, 33 Ala. 515.

[8] See vol. 1, c. 16.

Chapter XIII

it is detriment to the promisee and not benefit to the promisor which is the test of liability. Here detriment to the owner or possessor and not benefit accruing to the converter is the test of liability. In both situations the true ground of action has been made obscure, so far as truth can be hidden by the misuse of words. 'Conversion to his own use' is certainly an unhappy expression in which to charge the defendant in trover. But as the formula has always been used, it has been found necessary to warp it from its original import in order to keep it in harmony with the actual state of the law. As a result, only the legal expert knows the meaning of the term 'conversion' as used in the action of trover.[9]

Characteristic features of trover.

The existence in any action of fictions and incongruities of language such as those above enumerated would be strongly suggestive of flexibility and growth. It is so in trover. The flexibility of the action is due to the fact that it is a form of case. Its remarkable growth is due largely to the circumstance that detinue, the principal action which might successfully have competed with it, was hampered by grave defects of procedure. We shall now briefly consider the steps by which the action reached its present compass.

Stages in development of the action.

The history of the action of trover during its formative period can best be understood by examining the action on the case in four aspects. Accordingly, we briefly consider — I, Case as a remedy against the bailee; II, Case *sur trover* as a remedy against the finder; III, Case *sur trover* as a remedy against the trespasser *de bonis asportatis;* and IV, Case *sur trover* as a remedy against bailees.

I. Detinue, the ancient and time-honored remedy of the bailor, was subject to some limitations, and accordingly bailors were often driven to use the action on the case as a means of

[9] *Conversion a Technical Term.* —"Undoubtedly in the great majority of cases where an action of trover is brought, no conversion, in one sense, has taken place; the goods are in the same state in which they always were; there is no actual conversion in the sense in which a person not a lawyer might possibly understand the term. . . . But the word 'conversion,' by a long course of practice, has acquired a technical meaning. It means detaining goods so as to deprive the person entitled to the possession of them of his dominion over them." Martin, B., in Burroughes *v.* Bayne, 5 H. & N. 301.

Volume III

Case as remedy against bailee.

enforcing reparation against bailees. In this connection case could often be used to advantage where detinue would also lie and in some instances where it either could not be maintained at all or was inadequate. Thus detinue at an early day could not for lack of privity be maintained by the bailor against a sub-bailee who destroyed the chattels; but case would lie.[1]

So the bailor, it was held, ought to sue in case where the bailee negligently injured but did not destroy the goods bailed, for the reason that in the action on the case full damages could be recovered in the first instance, whereas in detinue the deteriorated goods could be recovered, but no damages for the impairment of value.[2] Again, where the bailee of a horse borrows or hires the animal to go to a stated destination and goes beyond to another place, the action on the case is maintainable against him, even after the return of the horse, while detinue is not.[3] During the fifteenth and sixteenth centuries the action on the case against a bailee for negligent injury to goods seems to have been common enough.

Case as substitute for detinue.

In 1479 an action on the case was maintained against a bailee who failed to produce silver cups which had been left with him for safe-keeping.[4] Detinue would have been a proper remedy, but as the silver appeared to be entirely missing and not merely wrongfully withholden, it seemed to the court unnecessary to remit the plaintiff to that action, since in the end he would have to be content with a judgment for damages.

Conversion by bailee to his own use.

The defendant in this case was charged with breaking and converting the property to his own use (*le defendant eux enfreint et eux convert a son oeps*). This is said to be the earliest instance in which a defendant was charged with a conversion.[5] The sale of bailed chattels makes the bailee liable in an

[1] Y. B. 12 Edw. IV. 13, pl. 9.

[2] Keilw. 160, pl. 2.

[3] See Y. B. 21 Edw. IV. 76, pl. 9 (by Nele). In Y. B. 18 Edw. IV. 23, pl. 5, Catesby said if one obtained a horse to ride to York and went beyond to Calbrught, case would lie against him "to recover damages for the labor of the horse beyond the agreement."

[4] Y. B. 18 Edw. IV. 23, pl. 5. Compare Bowser *v.* Cheseman, Y. B. 20 Hen. VII. 4, pl. 13.

[5] 11 Harv. L. Rev. 384.

action on the case, like any other negligent loss or injury done to them.[6]

Chapter XIII

Negligent destruction or injury by bailee.

By such decisions as those just noted, it was established that case is a proper remedy against a bailee who in any way destroys or negligently injures the goods committed to his custody, though for many years this action was not deemed a proper remedy where the bailee still retained the goods uninjured in his hands and refused to give them upon demand. Such a bailee was merely guilty of a breach of contract. Detinue was adequate and case was not felt to be necessary. In other words, a mere refusal to surrender bailed chattels according to the terms of the agreement is not a conversion. Conversion then, in the early actions against the bailee, meant a change in the nature of the goods or an actual appropriation by the defendant to his own use.

Case not available in case of mere detention by bailee.

It will be observed that in the early actions on the case against the bailee for a conversion there is no allegation of a fictitious finding (trover). Nor is any such allegation necessary. The mere statement of the fact of bailment shows how the defendant acquired possession and that his possession was lawful. It is clear, then, that if the action on the case had never been extended beyond the field of bailment no such allegation as that of a finding, real or fictitious, would ever have made its way into declarations of this sort.

II. One who finds lost goods and takes them into his possession is not exactly a bailee, but his legal duties are in some respects similar, and there is no difficulty in treating him as a quasi-bailee or bailee in law. He cannot, it is true, be held liable for failing to take the goods into his keeping, nor if he takes them into his keeping is he liable for loss resulting from a mere nonfeasance.[7] But he is liable for a direct or negligent injury, and in respect to the principal duty of returning the goods to the owner on demand he is on the same footing as other bailees. Accordingly, as we have already seen, the early law permitted the owner to sue the finder in detinue

Case *sur trover* against finder.

[6] "The bailee misdemeans himself in selling the goods to another." Keilw. 160, pl. 2.

[7] Walgrave *v.* Ogden, 1 Leon. 224.

Volume III

sur trover.[8] And of course it was only a question of time until case should also be recognized as a proper remedy against a finder who refuses to surrender or who injures the chattel. But the process was slow.

The occasions when it was necessary for the owner to bring an action against the finder of a chattel were doubtless rather infrequent, for it was not until 1596 that the question was raised whether the action on the case will lie at the instance of the owner against a finder who refuses to give up the chattels. It was held that the action could be maintained.[1] The action on the case against a finder who refuses to surrender the goods can be looked upon as being *in consimili casu* with either trespass or detinue, according to the point of view.

The fictitious finding.

III. But finders of goods actually lost are not the only 'finders' known to our law. As was acutely said by Coke, C. J., one may take goods when they are in no danger of being lost, and may thus find them before they are lost.[2] In other words, any one who takes possession of the goods of another lawfully or unlawfully can be treated as finder by a fiction of law. The owner is certainly no less a 'loser' by reason of the fact that the goods are taken by another and are not merely lost by fortuitous oversight or accident. Nor is the taker any less a 'finder' in law merely by reason of the fact that he wrongfully seizes upon a chattel which does not belong to him.

Trover becomes available in case of asportation.

The allegation of a fictitious finding (trover) thus supplies a means of extending the action on the case so as to make it available against trespassers at large (*de bonis asportatis*). The defendant cannot show that the allegation of finding is fictitious, because to permit him to do this would result in giving him the advantage of his own wrong. The plaintiff's case is made out by showing that the property in question was his,

[8] Y. B. 7 Hen. VI. 22, pl. 3; Y. B. 33 Hen. VI. 26, pl. 12.

[1] East *v.* Newman, Gouldsb. 152, pl. 79; Eason *v.* Newman, Cro. Eliz. 495.

[2] 2 Bulst. 312. Note a similar remark in the case of Kinaston *v.* Moor (1628), Cro. Car. 89. "The losing is but a surmise and not material, for the defendant may take it in the presence of the plaintiff or any other who may give sufficient evidence."

that it came to the hands of the defendant, and that the latter converted it. Chapter XIII

The mode of acquisition is not material. The theory underlying the fictitious trover was tersely stated, in *Bishop v. Montague* (1600),[3] to be this: "One may qualify a tort, but not increase a tort." In other words, where a plaintiff makes out a cause of action in case *sur trover* he cannot be defeated by proof on the part of the defendant which goes to show that the cause of action had its origin in a graver wrong.

Modern action of trover.

It is obvious that when a fictitious trover is incorporated in the declaration in case, and the action in that form used against trespassers at large, we have the modern action of trover, and not until then. Just when this was first done is not clear upon the authorities, but the process by which the end in question was reached is plain.

Obscurity of historical development.

Hypothetically we should expect to find the action on the case *sur trover* used first against finders in fact, and then against finders in law (trespassers). Such would be the natural course of development. But inasmuch as exactly the same form of declaring was used in both situations, the early reported cases are ambiguous. Thus when we find a plaintiff declaring in trover for a jewel or a hawk we cannot be certain whether there was an actual losing and an actual finding or a mere taking by trespass or even by larceny.[4] But when we find a plaintiff suing in trover for twenty barrels of butter[5] we cannot doubt that the finding in that case is a fiction. In several cases from the closing years of the sixteenth and early years of the seventeenth century, the defendant had evidently acquired possession by a tortious taking, or had obtained the goods from one having no title.[6]

[3] Cro. Eliz. 824.

[4] In Mounteagle *v.* Worcester (1555), 2 Dyer 121*a*, the plaintiff supposed by the writ and count that whereas he was possessed of a chain of gold, etc., and casually lost the said chain, which afterwards came to the hands and possession of the defendant by finding, who knowing that the said chain was the chain of the plaintiff, but contriving, etc., there sold the chain to divers persons unknown. Such sale was held to be a conversion. A similar declaration in trover for a hawk is found in Fines *v.* Spencer (1572), 3 Dyer 306*b*.

[5] Mulgrave *v.* Ogden (1591), Cro. Eliz. 219.

[6] In Vandrink *v.* Archer (1590), 1 Leon. 222, trover was maintained against an innocent purchaser who

Volume III

Trover concurrent with trespass *de bonis asportatis.*

In 1596 trover was held to be concurrent with trespass, where one without leave took and rode a horse, and this although the animal had been redelivered before the institution of the suit. The redelivery, it was said, could be proved in mitigation of damages.[7] A few years later it was fully accepted that case in the form of trover lies for any ordinary unlawful asportation of chattels.[8]

Fictitious finding alleged in actions against bailee.

IV. In adding the action on the case to the number of remedies available by the owner of goods tortiously taken, the fictitious allegation of finding accomplished its great and indeed only function. Being necessary in this class of cases, the allegation became a permanent feature of the action, and inasmuch as the allegation did not have to be proved, and inasmuch as the action of trover when used against a trespasser is identical, so far as legal principle is concerned, with the action on the case as used against bailees, it soon came to pass that the allegation of a finding (trover) was inserted into declarations against bailees. In this class of cases the allegation was entirely superfluous as well as fictitious, for the only purpose it can ever serve is to supply an explanation of the defendant's possession. In bailments the mere statement of the facts would always show how the defendant's possession originated, and that it is a lawful possession.

In *Isaack v. Clark* (1615),[9] a finding (trover) by the defendant of the goods alleged to have been converted was alleged. The defendant pleaded that they came into his possession by bailment. Dodderidge, J., was of the opinion that

had himself sold and thereby converted goods obtained by him from one having no title. In a similar case from the preceding year Anderson, J., said: "The plaintiff may choose to have his action against the first finder or against any other which gets the goods after by sale, gift, or trover." Galliard *v.* Archer (1589), 1 Leon. 189.

[7] 1 Rolle Abr. 5 (L), pl. 1.

[8] Basset *v.* Maynard, Cro. Eliz. 819, 2 Rolle 699, 1 Rolle Abr. 105 (M), pl. 5; Bishop *v.* Montague (1600), Cro. Eliz. 824. In this case the remedy was used for the unauthorized seizure of oxen for heriots.

Leveson *v.* Kirke (1611), 1 Rolle Abr. 105, pl. 10, has been referred to as an early instance of trover against a trespasser, but the action was purely in case, being brought by a master against his servant for bringing goods ashore before the custom duties were paid, whereby they were forfeited.

[9] 2 Bulst. 306.

Chapter XIII

this plea was entirely good, and pointed out that in such situation the proper remedy was detinue or case simply. But the application of this doctrine would have resulted in holding that the trover is traversable, whereas it had been held in a number of previous cases that the trover is a non-traversable fiction. These were actions against trespassers, but it would only have confounded confusion to have held that in some cases the finding is traversable but in others not. Accordingly Haughton, J., was of opinion that the allegation of trover in an action against the bailee did no harm, the conversion being the gist of the action. On this point Coke, C. J., evidently agreed with Haughton, and Croke, J., let the matter pass without animadversion. The case was decided against the plaintiff, but on another question, to wit, on the ground that the terms of the bailment, which was a pledge, had not been complied with.

Isaack v. Clark.

From this time on the propriety of alleging a fictitious trover in actions against the bailee was not questioned. But for more than half a century the law of conversion in the field of bailment was not in harmony with the principles applied in cases of actual finding and in trespass. This point is illustrated in the case to which reference was just made. In *East v. Newman* (1596), it had been held that a refusal by an actual finder to surrender to the owner on demand constituted a tortious conversion.[1] The same rule would of course apply in trover against a trespasser.[2] The question now arose in *Isaack v. Clark* (1615)[3], whether a mere refusal by a bailee to surrender the chattels according to the terms of the bailment constituted a conversion in law. The court was unanimously of the opinion that it did not. "A bare denial shall not make a conversion, neither shall there be any conversion so long as the privity of the bailment remains; but destroy this, and then otherwise it shall be." [4]

Refusal by trespasser or by finder to surrender chattel makes a conversion.

Refusal by bailee does not make a conversion.

[1] Gouldsb. 152, pl. 79. "If one finds my goods, and knowing them to be mine, refuses and denies to deliver them to me on demand, it is a conversion in law." Easton *v.* Newman, 1 Rolle Abr. 5 (L), pl. 2.

[2] "The denying to deliver upon request is a conversion." Wilson *v.* Chambers (1634), Cro. Car. 262.

[3] 2 Bulst. 306.

[4] Croke, J., 2 Bulst. 311. So Coke, C. J.: What shall make a

Volume III

Obviously you cannot treat the bailee, like the finder, as trespasser *ab initio* merely upon his refusal to surrender possession, for this would contradict his admittedly lawful possession. So in *Isaac v. Clark* it was held necessary to show an act of conversion changing the nature of the goods. In conformity with this doctrine it was held in several subsequent cases during the first half of the seventeenth century that trover will not lie merely upon unlawful detention by the bailee.[5] This was the doctrine accepted in 1650 by the author of the Compleat Attorney.[6]

Trover lies not against bailee who refuses to surrender.

A few years later, however, the inconsistency of holding a refusal to be a conversion in one class of cases and not in another produced its inevitable result, and it was said (1675) that trover could be maintained "on bare demand and denial against the bailee."[7] In 1704 Lord Holt said (in a case where the defendant after acquiring lawful possession, or at least lawful custody, had refused to deliver to the owner on demand): "The very denial of goods to him that has a right to demand them is an actual conversion, and not only evidence of it, as has been holden; for what is a conversion but an assuming upon oneself the property and right of disposing another's goods? and he that takes upon himself to detain another man's goods from him without cause, takes upon himself the right of disposing of them."[8]

This doctrine controverted by Lord Holt.

From that day the unlawful detention of goods has in all situations been treated as a conversion for the purpose of supporting trover. The only distinction between the rule as ap-

conversion? "As to this, there ought to be an act done to convert one thing to another: and [as to] whether a denier only shall make a conversion, by this you will confound all form, for then every action of detinue shall be an action upon the case upon a trover, because there is a denier." *Ib.*, 313.

But it was held that the refusal of the bailee to surrender the goods is admissible in evidence as tending to show a conversion. *Ib.*, 314.

The roots of this distinction between the effect of a mere refusal by bailees and trespassers are of course to be found in still older authorities. The bailee who refused to surrender could originally be sued only in detinue and not in trespass. Y. B., 16 Hen. VII. 3, pl. 7.

5 Holdsworth's Case (1638), Clayton 57, pl. 99; Walker's Case (1647), Clayton 127, pl. 227; Strafford *v.* Pell (1650), Clayton 151, pl. 276.

6 Compleat Attorney, ed. 1724, 139.

7 Sykes *v.* Walls, 3 Keb. 282.

8 Baldwin *v.* Cole, 6 Mod. 212.

Chapter XIII

plicable to bailees on the one hand and trespassers on the other is this, namely, that where a party is rightfully in possession of property belonging to another, he does not unlawfully detain it until after a demand by the true owner and a refusal.[9] But if the taking is tortious no such demand is necessary. This principle, it may be further observed, applies to the actions of detinue and replevin in their enlarged modern scope, as well as to the action of trover.[1]

Trover now available in case of any unlawful detention after demand.

A different line of decisions, also beginning in the early seventeenth century, illustrates another limitation on trover as a remedy against bailees. "If I bail goods to a common carrier to transport to a place and they are stolen from him, this is no conversion in the carrier to charge him in trover and conversion. But an action on the case lies against him as carrier upon the custom of the realm." [2] The rule that trover will not lie against a carrier where the goods are lost or stolen from him, and he is thereby disabled from delivering them ever after remained law.[3] In modern times, assumpsit on the contract, as well as case on the custom of the realm, affords sufficient means of redress. In 1772 an effort was made to maintain trover against a carrier in a case where the goods had been lost or stolen from his possession. But Lord Mansfield said: "In order to maintain trover there must be an injurious conversion. . . . They [the carriers] cannot deliver them. It is not in their power to do it. It is a bare omission." [4]

Trover lies not against carrier when goods are lost or stolen from him.

Case or assumpsit the remedy here.

By decisions already noted it was fully settled by the beginning of the seventeenth century that trover is generally concurrent with trespass *de bonis asportatis* for a tortious taking

[9] Where the possession of the defendant has had a lawful inception, as by loan, a demand for the chattel, in order to make a refusal operate as a conversion, must be a demand for delivery at the place where the borrower is bound by law to deliver it. Thus where a sled was lent, a request on the part of the owner that the borrower return it to the lender's house is not a sufficient demand. Farrar *v.* Rollins, 37 Vt. 295.

[1] Galvin *v.* Bacon, 11 Me. 28; Gates *v.* Gates, 15 Mass. 311.

[2] 1 Rolle Abr. 6, pl. 4.

[3] In Owen *v.* Lewyn (1673), 1 Vent. 223, Hale, C. J., said, "If a carrier loseth goods committed to him, a general action of trover doth not lie against him."

[4] Ross *v.* Johnson, 5 Burr. 2825.

Volume III

Trover formerly not available in case of unlawful distress or unlawful seizure under process.

of goods. One or two not very important exceptions to this rule persisted for many years. Thus the wrongful taking of goods in distress,[5] illegal seizure by an officer under execution,[6] and illegal seizures by collectors of the customs revenue,[7] were held not to constitute a conversion for which trover would lie. But it was held that a wrongful seizure for heriot service,[8] and illegal seizure for prisage[9] were sufficient to support the action.

The rule that trover will not lie for a wrongful distress was apparently merely a perpetuation of a similar rule which had once denied the remedy of detinue to the injured party,[1] replevin being of course the proper remedy. In applying this rule to trover the courts assigned the further reason that when chattels are distrained and impounded they are in the custody of the law. Hence there is no conversion to the distrainor's own use. Similarly the customs officer who seizes without authority acts for the government, and likewise cannot be said to have converted the goods to his own use. This was in harmony with the opinion entertained in the early part of the seventeenth century, that conversion meant something more than unlawful deprivation. This was true enough in the field of bailment. But the doctrine was impeached in all cases where trover was used against a trespasser. Accordingly, inasmuch as trespass had become concurrent with replevin as a remedy against wrongful distrainors, it should have been held, now that trover had become concurrent with trespass, that trover would lie for an illegal distraint and for any illegal taking by officers of the law. This ought to have become entirely clear to the judges in the early eighteenth century; and the decisions, noted by Bunbury from that period, which fail to give effect to the change, are therefore erroneous.

Explanation.

This fact was observed by Lord Mansfield in *Tinkler v.*

[5] Salter *v.* Butler (1602), Noy 46; Agars *v.* Lisle (1614), Hutton 10; Dee *v.* Bacon (1596), Cro. Eliz. 435.

[6] Ascue *v.* Sanderson, Cro. Eliz. 433.

[7] Etriche *v.* Officer of Revenue (1720), Bunb. 67; Israel *v.* Etheridge (1721), Bunb. 80.

[8] Bishop *v.* Montague (1600), Cro. Eliz. 824.

[9] Kenicot *v.* Bogan (1611), Yelv. 198.

[1] Y. B. 27 Hen. VIII. 22, pl. 15.

Poole (1770),[2] where the question was finally decided in favor of the right to maintain the action against officers for illegal seizures. "Nothing is clearer," said his lordship, "than that trover lies. It is a wrongful conversion, let the property be in whom it will." That is, it is immaterial to whose use the seizure is made. A few years later trover was recognized as being a proper remedy whereby to recover damages for a wrongful distraint.[3]

Chapter XIII

Subversion of this doctrine.

By the successive extensions that have been noted in these pages, trover, by the end of the eighteenth century, had become concurrent with detinue, replevin, and trespass *de bonis asportatis;* though each of these remedies has peculiar features and trover is not apparently entirely coextensive with them. Trespass will doubtless lie for acts of interference with goods, where trover will not.[4] The same may be said of detinue and replevin.[5]

Final scope of the action of trover.

The question whether the action of trover will lie in any particular case is to be determined solely by the test of conversion. Has the plaintiff done an act which constitutes a conversion in fact or in law? If so, trover is a proper remedy. This brings us to the threshold of the question, What is a conversion? What acts are sufficient to constitute this wrong? How far is the character of such acts affected by the intention of the wrongdoer? Enough has been said on this topic in another part of the present work.[6]

Lies for any conversion.

[2] 5 Burr. 2657.

[3] Shipwick *v.* Blanchard (1795), 6 T. R. 298.

[4] Kirk *v.* Gregory (1876), 1 Ex. D. 55.

"Where a dispute arises between the master of a ferryboat and a passenger, and the master refuses to carry the passenger and puts his goods on shore, this may be a trespass, but it is not of itself a conversion." Poll. on Torts, 6th ed., 343, citing Fouldes *v.* Willoughby, 8 M. & W. 540.

See, however, comments of J. W. Salmond, 21 L. Quar. Rev. 52, 53.

[5] If one loads my cart with corn or my boat with coal, I may take the cart or boat away without being liable in trespass or trover. But the owner of the corn or coal could replevy the chattels, or it seems could maintain detinue. Anonymous (1611), 1 Bulst. 96, note.

[6] See vol. 1, p. 231–262.

CHAPTER XIV

THE ACTION OF ASSUMPSIT.

Special Assumpsit.

Volume III

ONE who undertakes to give a sketch of the action of assumpsit may well feel embarrassed by the richness of the field which opens before him. The history of assumpsit is largely the history of modern contract law, and one who writes the history of contracts finds himself chiefly occupied in narrating the progress of this remedy and in bringing the reader into contact, at the proper juncture, with the new conceptions which were sharers in its triumphs. But this very circumstance will serve greatly to lessen the particular task now before us, as the development of English contract law is fully treated elsewhere in this work. Our present purpose is merely to trace the development of assumpsit in its most general features, with a view to the ascertainment of the scope and function of the remedy. So much must be done even at the cost of some repetition. It may be here observed that in so far as this chapter treats of matter which has already been dealt with in connection with the development of contract law, it is founded upon a new and independent survey of the authorities, and it therefore has a corroborative value where it lacks in novelty.

Scope of this chapter.

The action of assumpsit is a specialized form of case which gradually acquired recognition and individuality in the fifteenth century as a proper remedy for the breach of a simple promise. It was not from any subtle perception of the tie resulting from the making of the oral promise that the courts were led to countenance this form of case. The advance was due to a very natural extension of the older delictual remedy which we will now trace. The fact that the step by which assumpsit was differentiated from case was taken is not more surprising than the fact that the courts were so long about it.

Genesis of the action of assumpsit.

By way of anticipation it may be said that the conception which is at the root of liability in assumpsit is that of damage done by deceitful artifice. Thus if A contrives to obtain a thing of value from B on the faith of a promise to do some act for B in the future, and A subsequently refuses to fulfil the promise, it is not difficult to look upon A's refusal or failure to perform as being the culmination of a false pretense.

Fundamental notion underlying the action.

The situation here conceived discloses the existence of a detriment to B, the promisee, which in later times is dominated the consideration for the promise, and also an actionable deceit on the part of A. This deceit is of an *ex post facto* nature, it is true, since the presumption of deceitful intent does not arise until the subsequent breach. But in a legal system where simple promises were pressing for recognition as a source of legal duty, this objection could not stand; and accordingly an action on the case in the nature of deceit was permitted to be maintained upon the promise. Such was assumpsit. The full and final establishment of the remedy did not take place until near the end of the fifteenth century.

The detriment to the promisee.

Assumpsit is an action on the case in the nature of deceit.

Inasmuch as the action of assumpsit is derived from case we naturally turn, for the early history of assumpsit, to those examples of case found in the older books wherein a breach of promise on the part of the defendant is alleged.

From the time when the action on the case first came into prominence, the pleader often found it necessary or proper to state, among other things, that the wrong complained of was done by the defendant while engaged in performing an undertaking or agreement. But this statement merely served to show that the injury complained of was done under such circumstances as excused the plaintiff from suing in trespass and from alleging that the wrong was done with force and arms. Negligent injury to property which had lawfully come into the defendant's care was the gist of the action, and the breach of the promise was merely incidental and collateral to the true ground of liability. In such cases the plaintiff generally alleged that the defendant undertook *(enprise)* [1] or as-

Case as remedy for negligent performance of lawful undertaking.

[1] Y. B. 11 Hen. IV. 33, pl. 60.

Volume III

Allegation of the assumption.

sumed *(assuma sur luy)*[2] to do a particular act. Liability was not derived from the promise, and where the fact that the defendant did enter upon the enterprise sufficiently appeared on the facts of the case, no allegation of assumpsit was, as a matter of law, necessary.[3]

Emergence of idea of obligation of promise.

As was natural, it came to pass in time that in cases where an assumpsit or undertaking on the part of the defendant was alleged, the cause of action was occasionally viewed as being in some way based on the promise. Thus in 1373 an action for malpractice was brought against a surgeon for a negligent failure to cure the plaintiff as he had undertaken to do. It occurred to Candish, J., that the maintenance of such an action looked very like giving recognition to a parol covenant. But said he: "This action of covenant is of necessity maintainable without specialty, because for every little thing a man cannot have a clerk to make a deed."[4] This observation seems to show that the purely tortious character of the action was being overlooked.

That the action on the case, for injury resulting from a misfeasance in the performance of an undertaking or promise, is in one aspect an action on the promise is illustrated in still another case against a surgeon for malpractice, which comes from the same period. The point arose on the question of the venue of the action. The agreement to cure had been made in one county and the injurious medicines given in another. The court held that either the assumpsit or tort could be negatived in the plea, and that the venue of the suit should be in one county or the other in conformity with the plea.[5]

[2] Y. B. 19 Hen. VI. 49, pl. 5.

The equivalent Latin expression was *super se assumpsit.* "If I bail my goods to a man to keep safe and he takes the custody thereof upon himself, and my goods for lack of safe keeping are lost or destroyed, I shall have an action of detinue or on my case at my pleasure and shall charge him by this word *super se assumpsit.*" Keilw. 77, pl. 25.

It will be observed that this formula is somewhat ambiguous to the modern mind, since the use of the word *assumpsit* naturally leads to the inference that the legal duty on which liability is based in the particular instance is derived from the promise. But prior to the sixteenth century at least, it meant no more than that the defendant actually entered upon the enterprise.

[3] Y. B. 46 Edw. III. 19, pl. 19.

[4] Y. B. 48 Edw. III. 6, pl. 11.

[5] Bellewe Cas., *Accion sur le Case,* 5.

Chapter XIV

Inadequacy of the idea of liability for misfeasance.

Still, it must be conceded that however near the conception of liability for misfeasance may come to supplying a means of redress for the breach of an assumptual obligation, it does not quite reach the goal. Commencing about the year 1400, the courts began to strain legal theory at this point, but without much success.

In the first case a carpenter was sued for the breach of a promise to build a house.[6] The action failed because it was upon a promise (*conventio*, covenant) not proved by a writing under seal. Subsequent cases from the same period in which a similar question was raised, were decided in the same way and upon substantially the same ground.[7]

Action on case in nature of deceit against deceitful real-estate broker.

Much more flexible than the conception of liability for misfeasance was the notion which underlay the action on the case for deceit. In a case from 1432 [8] the defendant, who had agreed to purchase a manor for the plaintiff, was held liable on the ground of deceitful conduct. The writ alleged that, having undertaken to buy the manor, he by collusion with another, contriving to defraud the plaintiff, disclosed the latter's evidence and falsely and fraudulently became of counsel with a third party and bought the premises for him instead of for the plaintiff. Cotesmere, J., observed that a matter lying wholly in promise could be converted *ex post facto* into a deceit. "When he became of counsel for another that was a deceit; and changed all that was before only a covenant [promise], as between the parties [into a deceit], for which deceit he shall have an action on his case."

It is not explicitly stated in the report of this case that the plaintiff had parted with a thing of value or that he had done any act which might have constituted a detriment to himself at the time the promise was made to him. But this factor was clearly essential. In a case which arose a few years later

In Y. B. 19 Hen. VI. 49, pl. 5, it was also held that a traverse of the assumpsit is good.

[6] Watton *v.* Brinth, Y. B. 2 Hen. IV. 3, pl. 9; 3 Reeves, Hist. Eng. Law, Am. ed., 435.

[7] Y. B. 11 Hen. IV. 33, pl. 60; Y. B. 3 Hen. VI. 36, pl. 33.

[8] Y. B. 11 Hen. VI. 18, pl. 10; 24, pl. 1; 55, pl. 26.

Volume III

such an element was present, but no collusion was alleged. Some of the judges in the Court of the Exchequer Chamber were in favor of sustaining the action. Here the defendant, for one hundred pounds cash in hand paid, had promised to enfeoff the plaintiff, but had conveyed to another instead.[0]

Two elements were present in this case out of which liability might arise: the prepayment of the one hundred pounds, and the defendant's misfeasance in putting title into a third person when he had undertaken to enfeoff the plaintiff. The first element was entirely adequate, but this was not clearly perceived by any of the judges. The second element supplied no adequate theory, since there is no substantial difference in

Detriment to promisee makes parol promise binding.

law between a mere refusal to convey to the plaintiff and such a refusal aggravated by conveyance to a third person. Accordingly some of the judges were of the opinion that this was not a misfeasance sufficient to support the action. The point where the theory of misfeasance failed is found in the fact that the situation in question did not reveal any damage to property of the plaintiff; for it must be borne in mind that the doctrine of liability for a negligent misfeasance properly applies only to cases where damage is done to person or property.

But however unsatisfactory the theory of misfeasance may have been as applied to cases like that just considered, so urgent was the necessity for the recognition of the validity of the simple promise, that the judges continued to assign it as a reason for holding the defendant liable where a promise to enfeoff one was followed by the enfeoffment of another, at least in those cases where money was paid to the promisor on the faith of his promise.[1]

State of law of assumpsit at beginning of sixteenth century.

As we can now see, it was the latter element which really vitalized the promise. But the true rationale of these decisions seems not to have become manifest until 1505. In that year Frowike, C. J., made a somewhat elaborate résumé of the

[0] Y. B. 20 Hen. VI. 34, pl. 4. The case was passed without decision and the ultimate disposition of it is not indicated.

[1] Y. B. 3 Hen. VII. 14, pl. 20; Y. B. 2 Hen. VII. 12, pl. 15; Y. B. 16 Edw. IV. 9, pl. 7.

Chapter XIV

cases bearing on the actionability of simple promises.[2] The language then used by him finally and clearly differentiates misfeasance in doing a thing which one has undertaken to do, from the mere refusal to embark upon the performance of an executory promise. Case lies for a misfeasance resulting in damage to the plaintiff's person or property regardless of any other element, but it is only where detriment has been incurred or where consideration has been given that mere nonperformance of a promise becomes actionable. Misfeasance and nonfeasance are therefore distinct roots of liability and have not since been confounded.

The promise supported by the executed consideration.

By reason of the identity between the early action of assumpsit and the action on the case for a deceit, assumpsit could be used only where the consideration was given or detriment incurred by the promisee at the time the promise was made. The "taking of the money beforehand" by the promisor,[3] or the assumption of a charge by the promisee,[4] was the thing which made the promise binding. The promise, then, which was actionable in assumpsit during the first part of the sixteenth century was as purely a unilateral obligation as is the obligation known as a debt. Just as the debt could only be created by the passage of a *quid pro quo*, so the actionable promise had to be supported by an executed consideration.

The promise to pay existing debt.

Having reached this stage, the development of assumpsit apparently paused for a time; but before the century passed it had undergone important changes. A sufficiently full account of these is given elsewhere.[5] The two most important extensions came about by the recognition of existing indebtedness as a sufficient consideration for an actual promise to pay the debt

[2] Keilw. 77, pl. 25; 69, pl. 2. See also Y. B. 20 Hen. VII. 8, pl. 18; Y. B. 21 Hen. VII. 41, pl. 66; Brooke Abr., *Disceit*, pl. 29.

[3] "If a man promise and take upon him to make for another man certain carts for carriages, or other thing, and take money beforehand to do the same, and afterwards he do not make them according to his promise and undertaking, the other may have an action upon the case against him." F. N. B. 94 A; F. N. B. 145 G.

[4] "If he to whom the promise is made have a charge by reason of the promise which he hath also performed, then in that case he shall have an action for that thing that was promised, though he that made the promise have no worldly profit by it." Doctor & Student, Dial. II., c. 24.

[5] See vol. 1, p. 36, 46, 52, 61.

Volume III

Mutual promises.

and the recognition of mutual promises as a sufficient consideration to support each other. By these two steps assumpsit was put in a position of vantage by reason of which it soon obtained almost undisputed supremacy in the field of simple contract law. That it was a great and necessary engine of legal progress is obvious from the fact that the older contractual remedy of debt was soon giving way before it, and from the fact that the courts, by means of fiction, were presently busy in throwing wide the doors to permit of its extension into new and remote fields.

Assumpsit maintainable upon any simple debt.

At the beginning of the seventeenth century, so great a change had supervened in legal thought that the courts were able to take up the metaphysical conception of obligation resulting from promise, and place it side by side with the older notion of contractual duty embodied in the debt. This movement culminated in *Slade's Case* (1602),[6] wherein it was held that the creation of a debt operated to raise an implied promise actionable in assumpsit as well as to impose an obligation of debt. In other words, assumpsit thereby became, with unimportant exceptions, a concurrent remedy with debt upon simple contract, and it was no longer necessary for a plaintiff suing in assumpsit upon a debt to prove an express promise to pay a precedent debt made subsequent to the creation of the debt, as had previously been required.[7] Though the action of assumpsit was originally of delictual origin, it had now become a contractual remedy. But some traces of its early character remained. Thus, *non assumpsit* is the proper plea in this action, but in *Corbyn v. Brown* (1595)[8] the court refused to arrest judgment where the plea of *not guilty* had been put in, on the ground that, as a deceit was alleged, the plea of *not guilty* was an answer to the tort and good after verdict, though it might have been ground for a demurrer.

Assumpsit becomes a purely contractual remedy,

In *Pinchon's Case* (1611),[9] the question was raised whether assumpsit could be maintained upon a debt after the

[6] 4 Coke 92*a*.

[7] Turges *v.* Beacher, Moo. K. B. 694; Maylard *v.* Kester, Moo. K. B. 711; Estrigge *v.* Owles, 3 Leon. 200; Edwards *v.* Burre, Dal. 104, pl. 45.

[8] Cro. Eliz. 470.

[9] 9 Coke 86*b*, 89*a*.

death of a party to the contract. It was decided in the affirmative. This decision deprived the action of assumpsit of substantially all vestiges of its delictual origin, for by this time it was generally accepted that rights of action *ex contractu* survived, but that rights of action *ex delicto* did not.

Chapter XIV

and does not perish with the person.

Although the main features of special assumpsit were settled for all time during the early years of the seventeenth century and the distinction between this remedy and case generally observed, the action was still frequently spoken of as 'case' or 'case upon an assumpsit.' This appellation showed the genealogy of the action, and as may be seen from *Everard v. Hopkins* (1614),[1] the line of division between assumpsit and the mother action may sometimes be very fine. There a master who had hired a doctor to cure his servant brought suit to recover damages *per quod servitium amisit,* resulting from the giving of unwholesome medicines. The court recognized that the servant had a right of action in case and that the master had a right of action for the damages resulting to him. It is not, however, made clear whether this right of action was conceived to be in tort for unlawful interference with the status of master and servant, or whether it rested upon the idea of breach of contract.

Assumpsit and case.

Assumpsit has never been extended into the field of formal contracts, for the very obvious reason that here the actions of covenant and debt have always afforded ample relief. Sealed obligations of indebtedness and contracts of covenant survive after death, and the actions of debt and covenant upon such contracts cannot be met by the wager of law. As a result, no attempt has ever been made to substitute assumpsit for either debt or covenant when the contract is under seal.[2]

Assumpsit not available for breach of sealed contract.

For similar reasons assumpsit will not lie upon a judg-

[1] 2 Bulst. 332.

[2] *Assumpsit Not Maintainable upon a Covenant.*— Baber *v.* Harris, 9 Ad. & El. 532, 36 E. C. L. 193; Bulstrode *v.* Gilburn, 2 Stra. 1027.

"Assumpsit does not lie if the promise be by deed, for then covenant will lie." Com. Dig., *Action upon the Case upon Assumpsit* (F 1).

"If one promises by deed and for a good consideration to refrain from doing a certain thing, no action on the case lies upon this

Volume III

ment[3] or recognizance. The duty to pay rent is in the same category, and this is true though the duty to pay the rent originates in a simple contract. Rent not being subject in any case to the wager of law, it was unnecessary to resort to assumpsit to recover it.[4] In all of these cases the obligation is said to be of a higher nature than the simple assumpsit.

At one time the courts seemed to be on the point of recognizing assumpsit as the proper remedy upon an express promise to pay a debt evidenced by a sealed instrument.[5] While this would not have been inconsistent with the theory underlying indebitatus assumpsit, yet it was entirely unnecessary. Accordingly it became a settled rule that assumpsit would not lie upon an express promise to pay a debt evidenced by a bond; nor upon a promise to perform a covenant or to pay a judgment; nor upon a promise made by a tenant to pay his rent.[6]

Assumpsit lies not upon a promise to pay a debt evidenced by seal.

promise, but a writ of covenant." Bemishe *v.* Hildersley, 1 Rolle Abr. 11, pl. 20.

The making of an express contract by deed excludes any implied contract. See Schlencker *v.* Moxsy, 3 B. & C. 789, 10 E. C. L. 227.

[3] But indebitatus assumpsit will lie on a foreign judgment. Lawes on Plead. (448*); Crawford *v.* Whittal, 1 Dougl. 4; Walker *v.* Witter, 1 Dougl. 1.

[4] *Assumpsit Not Maintainable for Rent.*— Reade *v.* Johnson (1591), Cro. Eliz. 242, 1 Leon. 155; Brett *v.* Read, W. Jones 329; Green *v.* Harrington, Hob. 284; Shuttleworth *v.* Garrett, Comb. 151. In the last case it was said by Holt, C. J.: "It doth not follow that an indebitatus assumpsit lies because debt lies. Where wager of law doth not lie, there an indebitatus assumpsit does not lie; and it is mischievous to extend it further than Slade's Case, for an indebitatus assumpsit is laid generally and the defendant cannot tell how to make his defense. But debt is laid more particularly."

[5] *Indebitatus Assumpsit upon the Sealed Debt.*— "If one be bound in an obligation and afterwards promiseth to pay the money, assumpsit lieth upon this promise; and if he recover all in damages, this shall be a bar in debt upon the obligation." Ashbrooke *v.* Snape (1590), Cro. Eliz. 240.

[6] Langdell on Contracts, § 48. Slack *v.* Bowsal (1623), Cro. Jac. 668, note.

But of course if there is some new collateral consideration for the promise to pay the bond or judgment, assumpsit might be maintained upon such independent promise. Lawes on Plead. (450*).

Action on Case for Use and Occupation.— In the seventeenth century some inroad was made into the rule that assumpsit will not lie upon an express promise to pay rent, by holding that if, at the time of the making of the contract of lease, the tenant made an additional or, as it was called, a collateral express promise to pay the rent, assumpsit could be maintained on this promise. This extension of assumpsit, like that which was marked by Slade's Case, first took place in the King's Bench and thence made its way into the Ex-

The Court of King's Bench was in favor of permitting assumpsit to be maintained upon a promise to pay a debt of any kind, whether simple or specialty. But the Exchequer Chamber successfully stood out against this needless extension of the remedy, and required that in declaring in assumpsit upon a debt, the nature of the debt should be set forth so that the court could see whether the duty was such that assumpsit could be maintained upon it.[7]

chequer, Trever *v.* Roberts (1664), Hardres 366; and later into the Common Pleas, Johnson *v.* May (1683), 3 Lev. 150.

By statute of 11 Geo. II., c. 19, § 18, Parliament, in order to remove the difficulty of proving an express collateral promise in actions of assumpsit for rent not evidenced by a specialty, and to remove the difficulty in cases where the amount of the rent had not been fixed, authorized the bringing of an action on the case for use and occupation, and declared that the parol demise might be given in evidence on the question of damages. The action on the case for use and occupation thereby sanctioned is evidently an action in the nature of assumpsit and may properly be classed as a statutory form of indebitatus assumpsit. See Assumpsit for Use and Occupation, by Prof. J. B. Ames, 2 Harv. L. Rev. 377.

[7] Woodford *v.* Deacon (1609), Cro. Jac. 206; Buckingham *v.* Costendine (1606), Cro. Jac. 213.

In case of Gardiner *v.* Bellingham (1613), Hob. 5, it was held that an allegation that the debt was for "the agistment and feeding of beasts, and for wheat and other merchandise had and received" by the defendant, sufficiently showed the nature of the debt and that it originated in simple contract.

CHAPTER XV

THE ACTION OF ASSUMPSIT (CONTINUED).

Indebitatus Assumpsit.

Volume III

SPECIAL assumpsit is thoroughly identified in modern times with the general subject of contract, and such points concerning special assumpsit as are of general interest have consequently been fully treated elsewhere. In truth, special assumpsit has undergone no radical change in theory or application since the recognition of the bilateral contract. Accordingly the remainder of our treatment of assumpsit will be concerned solely with assumpsit in its general forms: indebitatus, quantum counts, count for money had and received, count for money lent, count for money paid, and the count upon an account stated.

Scope of this chapter.

At the outset it should be understood that the term 'indebitatus assumpsit' is used in two senses. In its narrow and specific sense it is applied to that form of assumpsit which is available for the recovery of any simple common-law debt. The expression 'indebitatus assumpsit' is indeed nothing more than a fragment of the ancient declaration in assumpsit upon a debt. In such actions the plaintiff counted that *the defendant, being indebted, did promise;* and from the Latin form of these vital words in the declaration the name of the action is taken.

Indebitatus assumpsit.

In this its narrow sense, the action of indebitatus assumpsit has passed through two, and only two, stages. In its first stage the remedy was available to recover upon an express promise to pay a simple debt, given after the debt was created. In its second stage the remedy became available to recover upon any simple debt without regard to any express promise to pay the debt. In both these stages of the remedy, the existence of an actual debt is essential to the maintenance of the action.

Narrow use of term.

Assumpsit upon simple debt.

Chapter XV

Broader use of term.

In its broader and more general sense the expression 'indebitatus assumpsit' is applied to the various counts above mentioned, to wit, the quantum counts, the count for money had and received, etc. These forms of general assumpsit are, indeed, derived from indebitatus, and represent a tertiary stage in the development of the remedy. But there is this peculiarity of the counts referred to, namely, they are maintainable upon facts and circumstances which do not, according to earlier notions, result in the creation of a common-law debt. Hence there seems to be a sort of impropriety in classifying the various common counts as species of indebitatus proper. Still, if one keeps clearly in mind the different senses of indebitatus there seems to be no solid reason why the term should not be used in the broader inclusive sense.

The common counts.

Genesis of the action.

Indebitatus assumpsit originated near the middle of the sixteenth century,[1] and for about fifty years it could be maintained only upon an express promise to pay a pre-existing debt.[2] By the end of the century efforts were being made to use assumpsit for the recovery of simple debts without proving an express promise subsequent to the creation of the debt.

Attitude of Queen's Bench.

The Court of Queen's Bench was the first to countenance this notion.[3] This was due to the fact that this court had jurisdiction to entertain the action of assumpsit, that being a form of trespass on the case, but it had no original jurisdiction over actions of debt. By recognizing assumpsit as a proper remedy for the recovery of debts the Queen's Bench was thus enabled to extend its jurisdiction. For many years the Court of Exchequer Chamber refused to sanction this position, and on appeal several times reversed the Queen's Bench on this question.[4] The more liberal view, however, soon prevailed,

[1] Brooke Abr., *Accion sur Case*, pl. 105 (citing an unreported case from 33 Hen. VIII.); *Ib.*, pl. 5.

[2] Anonymous, Dal. 84, pl. 35; Maylard *v.* Kester (1601), Moo. K. B. 711; Manwood *v.* Burston (1588), 2 Leon. 203, 204.

[3] Edwards *v.* Burre (1573), Dal. 104, pl. 45. "If such action [assumpsit] be brought and the plaintiff declares upon an indebitatus, then if the plaintiff prove the debt it is not material to prove the promise." Estrigge *v.* Owles (1588), 3 Leon. 200.

[4] Turges *v.* Beacher, Moo. K. B. 694; Paramour *v.* Payne, Moo. K. B. 703.

Volume III

and in 1602 it was held by all the justices of England and Barons of the Exchequer that the law raises an assumpsit upon the creation of every simple debt.[5]

There would seem to be some subtlety in saying that the assumpsit on which the action of indebitatus assumpsit was here allowed to be sustained was a fictitious one, yet this is the view that was taken. The creation of nearly every debt involves the making of a promise in fact, but it was conceived that the efficacy of this promise was exhausted in creating the debt. Accordingly it was held that the creation of the debt raised an implied promise on which indebitatus assumpsit was now permitted to be maintained. In other words, in addition to the liability involved in the creation of the debt, which liability originated in the act and agreement of the parties, the law gave recognition to a new sort of liability predicated upon the assumpsit or promise implied by law. This liability was *in consimili casu* with the liability previously enforced by debt and special assumpsit, but was not identical with either.

Promise implied from creation of simple debt.

It will be observed that when this the second stage of indebitatus assumpsit was reached, and the action was permitted to be maintained upon all simple debts, it was no longer necessary to take account of any express promise that might at any time be made to pay the debt. Consequently, assumpsit could not thereafter be maintained upon such a promise, and the plaintiff always sued on the assumptual obligation imposed by law on the creation of the debt.

Express promise to pay debt unnecessary.

After the decision in *Slade's Case* indebitatus assumpsit became a very common action. It superseded debt by reason of the facts that it could be maintained by and against representatives[6] and was not subject to the wager of law. It is of course chiefly used in recovering money debts, but it lies for a simple debt for specific chattels as well.[7] Inasmuch as chattels cannot be recovered in specie by use of indebitatus, but only damages for the breach of the duty to supply them, it is

[5] Slade's Case, 4 Coke 92*b*.

[6] Pinchon's Case, 9 Coke 86*b*.

[7] Falmouth *v.* Penrose, 6 B. & C. 385, 13 E. C. L. 205; Cock *v.* Vivyon (1733), 2 Barnard. 243, 384.

always necessary, in declaring on a chattel debt, to specify the value of the chattels due.[8]

Chapter XV

Indebitatus not available upon mutual promises.

From the foregoing it appears that the scope of indebitatus in its proper and narrow sense is bounded by the limits of the action of debt upon simple contract. Therefore indebitatus assumpsit lies not upon mutual promises.[9] As the wager derives its validity solely from the fact of the mutuality of the promises, indebitatus assumpsit will not lie to recover money won on a bet.[1] Special assumpsit is the winner's exclusive remedy.

Indebitatus lies not upon collateral guaranty.

Likewise indebitatus assumpsit will not lie upon a collateral guaranty, for it creates no debt. Accordingly it has been held that if one promises in consideration that another marries his kinswoman, to give her a sum of money, the promisor is not liable in indebitatus assumpsit. The plaintiff must declare specially on the contract.[2] Similarly the plaintiff cannot declare in indebitatus on a collateral promise to pay for goods sold to a third person. It is otherwise if the defendant is debtor for the goods.

As before observed, the classic count in indebitatus assumpsit alleges that the defendant, *being indebted, did promise.* In the first stage of the development of the remedy both these allegations corresponded with the actual facts. In the second stage, the promise alleged was fictitious, or, if the allegation corresponded with the facts, it did not have to be proved.

We come now to consider the origin of the so-called quantum counts *(quantum meruit, quantum valebant)*, which are respectively used to recover for work and labor done, or service rendered, and for goods sold and delivered. These counts are derived directly from indebitatus assumpsit, and the form of declaring is substantially the same.[3] They were devised to

[8] Reading *v.* Clarke, 4 B. & Ald. 268, 6 E. C. L. 479.

[9] Lawes on Plead. (451*).

[1] Smith *v.* Airey, 2 Ld. Raym. 1034, 6 Mod. 128, Holt K. B. 329; Walker *v.* Walker, Holt K. B. 328, 5 Mod. 13; Hard's Case, 1 Salk. 23, pl. 3; Bovey *v.* Castleman, 1 Ld. Raym. 69.

[2] Anonymous, 1 Ventr. 268. But see Cockram's Case, cited by Wild, J., in Kent *v.* Deaubeny, 3 Keb. 757.

[3] After reciting the particular facts out of which the cause of action arises, the count alleges, as in indebitatus assumpsit, that *the defendant, being indebted, did prom-*

Volume III

Origin of the common counts.

enable a plaintiff to recover for a benefit conferred under such circumstances as did not create either a true debt or an actionable assumpsit, but which benefit was nevertheless intended by both parties to be paid for.

Limitations of debt and assumpsit.

The difficulty which was intended to be remedied can be appreciated by reference to the limitations of debt and assumpsit. In order to maintain the action of debt it was necessary that the plaintiff should prove a debt for a sum certain.[4] In 1471 Brian, C. J., said: "If I carry cloth to a tailor to have a robe made, and the price which I shall pay for the making be not fixed beforehand, he cannot maintain an action of debt against me."[5] On the other hand, special assumpsit could not be maintained without proof of a promise in fact,[6] and of course indebitatus assumpsit was as yet limited to cases where a true debt could be shown. The situation manifestly called for remedy, and equity for a time was compelled to intervene in such cases for the purpose of giving relief.[7] But

ise. But the words *being indebted* are sometimes omitted. See e. g., 2 Encyc. of Forms 298, Forms 2521, 2522.

[4] Young *v.* Ashburnham, 3 Leon. 161.

[5] Y. B. 12 Edw. IV. 9, pl. 22.

In the same case Pigot expressed the opinion that if one comes to a tavern to drink and goes away without paying, the taverner can have an action of trespass, "for he did not do that which was incident to coming to a tavern." This notion was repudiated by Brian, C. J., who thought that in such case debt might be maintained, "for in the case of victuals and wine at a tavern the price is put in certain by the clerk of the tavern."

[6] Thursby *v.* Warren, W. Jones 208.

[7] The following passage from Spence is pertinent on this point: "The jurisdiction of the Court of Chancery appears to have been anciently called into action in respect of executory promises and implied obligations now designated under the name of assumpsits, by reason of the courts of law not having at first acted upon the Statute of Westminster II., so as to give a remedy by the action on the case, in cases intended to be embraced within its provisions." 1 Spence, Eq. Jur. 694.

The learned writer adds that "in the time of Edward IV. many suits founded on equitable assumpsits were still instituted." In the same connection he mentions the case of the executrix of a tailor who sued in chancery in 1567 to recover the value of clothes furnished by the tailor. The case was referred to the queen's tailor to report what was due. On his report a decree for payment was made. The author adds that "there were suits for wages and many others of like nature." In the case of the executrix of the tailor the necessity for resorting to equity arose chiefly, no doubt, from the fact that the tailor was dead. It had not then been settled that the action of as-the defect was too glaring to be long tolerated even in a court of law.

Implied promise of guest of innkeeper. The *quantum meruit* count.

The adaptability of assumpsit to other uses than for suing upon express promises had been shown in *Slade's Case,* and this flexibility of that action now afforded a means for the necessary extension of remedial law. In 1609 it was said by way of dictum that there is an implied promise on the part of the guest of an innkeeper to pay all the duties and charges which he incurs at the inn.[8] This concession was made to the innkeeper because the law laid upon him the duty to receive those who applied to him, and it was manifestly just that a corresponding duty to pay should be imposed upon those who were accommodated.

Extension of doctrine.

Presently the benefit of this innovation was extended to all persons whether they plied one of the so-called common callings, like that of innkeeping, or not.[9] That the right of action thus sanctioned was *in consimili casu* with debt was clearly perceived. The action was "a special action of debt;" or rather, it was a special action on the case in the nature of debt.[1]

sumpsit could be maintained by a personal representative.

[8] Warbrook *v.* Griffin (1609), Brownl. & Goldes. 254 (pt. ii.). This dictum seems to have come from Foster, J. It was said: "It is an implied promise . . . of the part of the innkeeper that he shall preserve the goods of his guest; and of the part of the guest, that he will pay all duties and charges which he caused in the house." Coke, C. J., took part in the decision of this case.

In the report of the same case under the style of Watbroke *v.* Griffith, Moo. K. B. 876, it is said to have been resolved that the hostler has lien on the horse of his guest for the provender, and that he may hold the animal therefor or he may have an action on the case for the feeding.

[9] Recovery by tailor for labor and materials, see Six Carpenters Case (1610), 8 Coke 147*a*. Recovery for work and labor done by laborer (1632), Shepp., *Actions on the Case,* 2d ed., 50. Carrier may recover on a *quantum meruit* reasonable compensation for carrying. Nicholls *v.* More (1661), 1 Sid. 36. *Quantum meruit* for value of personal services. Russel *v.* Collins, 1 Sid. 425, 1 Mod. 8, 1 Vent. 44, 2 Keb. 552.

[1] In Six Carpenters Case (1610), 8 Coke 147*a*, the right of a tailor to sue for the value of services and materials expended upon a gown was recognized: "The tailor in such a case shall have a special action of debt; *scil.,* that A did put cloth to him to make a gown thereof for the said A, and that A would pay him as much for making and all necessaries thereto, as he should deserve; and that for

Volume III

Quantum valebant.

The doctrine having been once admitted that the law may raise a promise on the facts of the case, new applications of the principle soon followed. The *quantum valebant* count for wares and merchandise or for goods sold and delivered belongs to this period,[2] being based on exactly the same principle as the *quantum meruit* count.

Other common counts.

The other so-called common counts came into use about the same time. The most important are the counts for money lent,[3] for money paid at the defendant's request,[4] for money had and received,[5] and the count upon account stated (*insimul computassent*).[6]

Nature of these counts.

In all these cases the plaintiff, after setting out the facts, alleged that the defendant had thereby become indebted to the plaintiff and that he thereupon promised to pay. But there was no true common-law debt, and the promise was not necessary to be proved. The common counts, then, in form are a species of indebitatus assumpsit. In substance they differ materially from indebitatus in its original sense, because they are maintainable without proof of a common-law debt. It will be observed that in the implied contracts enforced by the common quantum counts the factors of agreement and consideration are both present. A promise is therefore all that is necessary in order to make the contract perfect. This element the law now supplied by implication.

Simplicity of pleading in indebitatus.

The invention of the common counts was a great boon to the pleader. In declaring upon a debt the plaintiff had always been held to the facts with much strictness, and the whole ground of action had to be set out in detail. In indebitatus assumpsit, however, it was only necessary to set out the debt or cause of indebtedness generally as matter of inducement, for the law raised the promise which was the foundation of

making thereof and all necessaries thereto he deserves so much, for which he brings his action in debt."

[2] See Gardiner *v.* Bellingham (1613), Hob. 5.

[3] Holms *v.* Tostwood, Cro. Jac. 690; Rooke *v.* Rooke (1610), Cro. Jac. 245; Rock *v.* Rock (1610), Yelv. 175.

[4] Moore *v.* Moore (1611), 1 Bulst. 169.

[5] Babington *v.* Lambert, Moo. K. B. 854.

[6] Colimore *v.* Jenson, Moo. K. B. 854; Brinsley *v.* Partridge (1612), Hob. 88; Vale *v.* Egles (1606), Yelv. 70, Cro. Jac. 69; Bard *v.* Bard (1621), Cro. Jac. 602.

the suit. As was said in *Gardiner v. Bellingham* (1613),[7] pleading the assumpsit "requires not so much certainty as if it were an action of debt upon the very contract."

Indebitatus assumpsit lies for money due by custom or for penalties forfeited under by-laws. The decisions which established this doctrine come from the later years of the seventeenth century.[8] Recovery is here permitted on the theory of a promise implied by law. The decisions in question embody a principle analogous to that which underlies *Slade's Case,* namely, that where there is an actual debt the law will imply a promise to pay it. Here there is merely a granting of an additional remedy, and no new liability is created. Decisions like these illustrate the process by which legal theory in the field of contract was gradually brought into harmony with the modern conception of assumptual law, under which liability is derived from the obligation of promise as distinct from duty imposed by law (debt).

Indebitatus a remedy for customary duties and legal penalties.

As the action of debt had supplied a sufficient remedy upon customary dues and fines imposed by by-laws, it is not surprising that the extension of indebitatus assumpsit into this field was resisted by some. Lord Holt was decidedly opposed to it. It was hard, thought he, that questions concerning customary duties and fines incurred under by-laws or charters should be left to juries, a thing which was supposed to be a necessary and inevitable consequence of the adoption of indebitatus.[9] It was certainly somewhat curious that a contractual remedy supposed to be based upon privity, agreement, consideration, promise, should be used to recover a fine imposed upon a man against his will.

Opposition to extension of indebitatus in this field.

[7] Hob. 5.

[8] Indebitatus assumpsit available to recover money due and ascertained in amount by custom. London *v.* Gorry (1677), 2 Lev. 174. In this case it appeared that by the custom of London, persons exposing foreign goods for sale, which had been entered at the custom house, were required to pay a certain amount for showing them, and it was held that the action would lie for the custom dues although there was no contract express or implied.

Indebitatus assumpsit for recovery of penalties forfeited under by-laws. Barber Surgeons *v.* Pelson, 2 Lev. 252. See also Duppa *v.* Gerrard, 1 Show. 78.

[9] York *v.* Toun, 5 Mod. 444, 1 Ld. Raym. 502.

Volume III

Equitable nature of count for money had and received.

In the form of the equitable count for money had and received indebitatus assumpsit sounds in pure legal duty. As the common counts embody an extension of the action into a field where no debt had existed and no assumpsit could be shown, so likewise the count for money had and received is maintainable where money can be said to be legally due notwithstanding there is no true debt and no actual promise. The distinction between the count for money had and received and the other common counts is that whereas those counts belong to the field of promises implied as of fact, the count for money had and received belongs to the field of true quasi-contract, or contract implied of law. Here the obligation to pay is imposed without regard to the factor of agreement. The typical situation to which the count for money had and received is applicable is where there has been a payment of money under mistake, or on a consideration which has failed, and the plaintiff seeks to recover it back.[1]

A substitute for action of account.

Indebitatus assumpsit in the form of the count for money had and received seems to have first come into prominence as a substitute for the old action of account, and the fact that it became concurrent with account in all cases except where equitable interposition was necessary, was the chief cause of the obsolescence of that ancient and useful remedy. But assumpsit for money had and received outgrew the scope of account, and became available in all cases where the law would raise a duty to pay money.

At first the courts were inclined against allowing indebitatus where account was maintainable. Thus in *Lincoln v. Parr* (1672)[2] it was said that indebitatus assumpsit would not lie for money delivered to a factor, as he would often have discharges and this would involve the court in confusion. But this opposition did not prevail.

In 1678 the action was sustained against a usurper in office to recover the emoluments that had been received by him during his tenure of the office. The court said that in such a case

[1] Bonnel *v.* Foulke (1657), 2 Sid. 4, is probably the earliest reported case where money was recovered as having been paid under mistake. 2 Harv. L. Rev. 66.

[2] 2 Keb. 781.

account would lie, and that wherever the plaintiff could sue in account indebitatus assumpsit could also be maintained.[3] Presently it was held that indebitatus was available as a general remedy on a failure to account, and it was declared not to be necessary to allege or prove a promise to account.[4]

Complicated accounts must go into equity.

Accounts can of course be so complicated as to render the action of indebitatus assumpsit altogether inadequate and inappropriate; but just where the line should be drawn is not so easy to say. Wherever that line is, it now marks the limits between the legal and equitable jurisdiction. In *Scott v. M'Intosh* (1809)[5] it was held that indebitatus assumpsit would not lie on running accounts between merchants, and that account was the proper remedy in such case. But later, Gibbs, C. J., criticised that decision and said: "If, by subtracting the amount of six articles on the one side, from the amount of nine articles on the other, the plaintiff can make out that a balance is due to him, it is impossible to say that the action of assumpsit will not lie for that balance."[6]

Indebitatus available in case of running accounts.

Not available as between cotenants.

In *Thomas v. Thomas* (1850)[7] the court refused to permit one tenant in common to recover in assumpsit against his cotenant, on the ground that the Statute of 4 and 5 Anne[8] gave the action of account only. Being based on statutory grounds, the decision is not to be accepted as constituting a reversion to the ancient doctrine that a bailiff is liable for money received by him as such bailiff only in an action of

[3] Arris *v.* Stukely, 2 Mod. 260. See also Woodward *v.* Aston, 2 Mod. 95.

[4] Wilkyns *v.* Wilkyns (1689), Carth. 89; Tomkins *v.* Willshear, 5 Taunt. 431, 1 E. C. L. 145. In the first of these cases there was an express promise to account. But Lord Holt thought this not material, and thereafter the action was maintained regardless of any promise to account.

[5] 2 Campb. 238.

[6] Tomkins *v.* Willshear (1814), 5 Taunt. 431, 1 E. C. L. 145, 1 Marsh. 115.

See also Arnold *v.* Webb, 5 Taunt. 432, note, 1 E. C. L. 146, note, where Dampier, J., held that whatever doubts might have been entertained upon the subject a century back, the action of indebitatus assumpsit for the balance due on the result of numerous mercantile transactions had been so long maintained that it was now too late to make any objection to it. Said he, "How long is the account to be which is to prevent assumpsit from being maintained? If assumpsit will lie for the price of one parcel of goods, or to recover one sum lent, why not for two, and why not for twenty?"

[7] 5 Exch. 28.

[8] Chapter 16, § 27.

Volume III

account, though on its face the decision might seem to countenance that view.

During the latter part of the seventeenth century the submission of a dispute to arbitration was held to imply a promise to perform the award; on which assumpsit would lie for the nonperformance of the award. This decision for the first time gave to the successful party to an arbitration a general remedy where the award was for the performance of some other act than the payment of money. Theretofore debt could be maintained for an award of money, or assumpsit upon an award for the performance of some other act, provided there had been an express promise to perform the award. But where no such promise was made and the award was not for the payment of money, the successful arbitrant was without remedy.[9] The submission to arbitration, it was now said, operated as a contract of mutual promises, binding the parties to performance of the award.[1]

Indebitatus available to enforce performance of an award.

Although, as already stated, Lord Holt was averse to the extension of indebitatus so as to permit the use of it as a remedy for penalties and customary duties, he did not hesitate to hold, in *Holmes v. Hall* (1705),[2] that the count for money had and received to the plaintiff's use would lie for the recovery of money paid upon a promise to do an act which the defendant subsequently refuses to perform; in other words, wherever there can be said to be a failure of consideration.

Failure of consideration.

Lord Mansfield seems to have been the first fully to appreciate the marvelous flexibility of the count for money had and received. He repeatedly said that he was a great friend of the action, and he observed, in *Longchamp v. Kenny* (1779),[3] that

[9] Penruddock *v.* Monteagle (1613), 1 Rolle Abr. 7 (N), pl. 3.

[1] "The award of payment of money vests a duty in the party and is a bar in debt, or trespass, or assumpsit. And the old books are that upon a parol submission, if any collateral matter be awarded to be done other than the payment of money, as the making a release or the like, no action lay for nonperformance. Yet it has been otherwise adjudged since; for when two persons submit, they actually promise to perform the award, and an action lies on the mutual promises." Holt, C. J., in Squire *v.* Grevett (1704), 2 Ld. Raym. 961. See also Purslow *v.* Baily, 2 Ld. Raym. 1039; Freeman *v.* Bernard, 1 Ld. Raym. 248.

[2] 6 Mod. 161, Holt K. B. 36.

[3] 1 Dougl. 137. See also Weston *v.* Downes, 1 Dougl. 23.

great benefit arose from its liberal extension, because "the charge and defense in this kind of action are both governed by the true equity and conscience of the case."

Chapter XV

The fact that the count for money had and received is in the nature of a bill in equity was recognized by him on several occasions, notably in *Moses v. Macferlan* (1760).[4] In this case the equitable character of the action was fully expounded. Among other things his lordship said: "This kind of equitable action, to recover back money, which ought not in justice to be kept, is very beneficial, and therefore much [to be] encouraged. It lies only for money which, *ex æquo et bono*, the defendant ought to refund. It does not lie for money paid by the plaintiff, which is claimed of him as payable in point of honor and honesty, although it could not have been recovered from him by any course of law; as in payment of a debt barred by the statute of limitations, or contracted during his infancy, or to the extent of principal and legal interest upon an usurious contract, or for money fairly lost at play; because in all these cases the defendant may retain it with a safe conscience, though by positive law he was debarred from recovering. But it lies for money paid by mistake; or upon a consideration which happens to fail; or for money got through imposition (express or implied), or extortion, or oppression, or an undue advantage taken of the plaintiff's situation, contrary to laws made for the protection of persons under those circumstances. In one word, the gist of this kind of action is, that the defendant upon the circumstances of the case is obliged by the ties of natural justice and equity to refund the money."[5]

Lord Mansfield's exposition of the nature of the count for money had and received.

In this case it was insisted for the defendant that indebitatus assumpsit can only be maintained where the action of debt will lie. This proposition is certainly true of indebitatus in its primary and secondary stages.[6] But that this argument should have been made in an action for money had and received is suggestive of the great confusion with which the

Debt and indebitatus

[4] 2 Burr. 1005.

[5] *Ib.*, 1012.

[6] Hard's Case, 1 Salk. 23; Browne *v.* London, 1 Mod. 285, 1 Lev. 298; Bovey *v.* Castleman, 1 Ld. Raym. 69.

Volume III

subject of indebitatus assumpsit is everywhere overlaid. Lord Mansfield brushed the argument aside as clearly untenable. "There is no foundation for it," says he; "assumpsit will lie in many cases where debt does not lie." [7]

Form of the count for money had and received.

It will be observed that the ordinary count for money had and received alleges that the money sued for was received by the defendant "to the plaintiff's use." Evidently this allegation was originally framed to fit the situation where money was delivered by A to B to be turned over to C. The ancient action of account was maintainable under such circumstances by C, and as indebitatus for money had and received was first devised largely as a substitute for account, the allegation of a receipt to the plaintiff's use was natural and proper.

Incongruity of the technical words of the count.

If it is taken literally, this allegation imports a relation of trusteeship between the defendant and plaintiff in respect to the money sued for, and this on its face is in flat contradiction of the allegation 'being indebted' which is also usually found in the count; for it is obvious that a custodian of money can never be a debtor and a trustee at the same time. This incongruity is also manifested in those cases where the

[7] 2 Burr. 1008.

In Walker *v.* Witter (1778), 1 Dougl. 1, there was a curious perversion by some of the judges of the true historical relation between the actions of indebitatus assumpsit and debt. The normal remedy upon a judgment of record has of course always been the action of debt. In Crawford *v.* Whittal (1778), 1 Dougl. 4, note, it was held that indebitatus assumpsit might be maintained on a foreign judgment. The court proceeded upon the idea that such a judgment did not import absolute verity like a domestic judgment in a court of record. Hence it seemed reasonable to allow the plaintiff to declare in assumpsit upon an indebitatus and offer the judgment as only *prima facie* evidence of the debt. This left it open for the defendant to impeach the judgment by showing that it was irregularly or unduly obtained. On the whole, this was satisfactory enough.

In Walker *v.* Witter, 1 Dougl. 1, the question was raised whether debt could be maintained upon a foreign judgment. About this there ought to have been little or no question. But Ashurst and Buller, JJ., assigned as a conclusive reason for permitting debt to be maintained the fact that indebitatus would lie, and "whenever indebitatus assumpsit is maintainable debt also lies." This was a mistaken view. It would have been correct to say that indebitatus would lie because debt was originally the proper remedy upon a judgment, and the foreign judgment is only a simple debt and not a conclusive record like the judgment of a domestic court.

defendant has unrighteously acquired the money sued for. "Where a receipt depends merely on a tort there can be no contract or privity, and without them no debt." [8]

Allegation of receipt 'to plaintiff's use' is surplusage.

Consequently when the count for money had and received is used against a mere tortfeasor, the allegation that the money was received by the defendant to the plaintiff's use must be treated either as surplusage, or as a legal fiction, or as the mere statement of a legal conclusion. At first common-law pleaders were inclined either to omit the allegation where the receiving did not originate in a bailment or trust, or to allege, in conformity with the facts, that the defendant received the money to his own (the defendant's) use. This practice was upheld in a few cases.[9]

Origin of this allegation.

It thus appeared that the allegation of a receipt to the plaintiff's use was not always necessary, but the distinction between the cases where it should and should not be used was left somewhat vague. Accordingly out of abundant caution practitioners began to insert the allegation of a receipt to the plaintiff's use in all actions for money had and received. This practice in its turn was questioned. Thus in *Lamine v. Dorrell* (1705),[1] the usual count for money received to the plaintiff's use was used against a pretended administrator who converted chattels by selling them. It was objected that by selling the chattels under a claim of title and interest in them the defendant had converted the proceeds to his own use and hence could not be said to have received the money to the plaintiff's use. But this view did not prevail. Indebitatus assumpsit in the form of the count for money had and received thus became concurrent with trover in all cases where the tortfeasor converts chattels by selling and receives value.[2]

Count for money had and received available in case of conversion of chattels.

[8] Howard *v.* Wood, T. Jones 127.

[9] Noseworthy *v.* Wildman (1671), 2 Keb. 615; Palmer *v.* Stavely (1701), 12 Mod. 510. In the first of these cases it was observed that if A delivers money to B to deliver to C, and C sues B for the money, the allegation that B received it to his own use would be fatal.

[1] 2 Ld. Raym. 1216. See also Howard *v.* Wood, 2 Lev. 245, T. Jones 126.

[2] In Philips *v.* Thompson (1675), 3 Lev. 191, the contrary had been held.

The extension of indebitatus assumpsit which was sanctioned in Lamine *v.* Dorrell occurred at the very point where in previous years the courts had refused to extend

Volume III

This was undoubtedly one of the most remarkable perversions of a common-law remedy that has ever been permitted, yet so gradually had legal theory approached this goal that the extraordinary nature of the holding was hardly perceived. In trover for conversion by selling, the plaintiff alleges that the defendant converted the goods to his own use. In indebitatus assumpsit upon the same facts the plaintiff alleges that the proceeds came to the hands of the defendant to the plaintiff's use. A more inconsistent use of two apparently incompatible legal fictions cannot be found elsewhere.

Indebitatus for recovery of proceeds of conversion.

Powell, J., showed a clear appreciation of the difficulty of turning into a contract that which is in its nature tortious, and he placed the decision in *Lamine v. Dorrell* on the ground that where one sells the goods of another, the owner can ratify the act and suppose the sale was made by his consent, the defendant being disabled from taking advantage of his own wrong and showing that his act was really tortious. This is doubtless the true rationale of the decision. The step was analogous to that by which the fiction of finding was used in order to extend trover to cases of taking by the trespasser.

Waiving the tort.

Lamine v. Dorrell is thus important as having established on a firm basis the right of a plaintiff to 'waive the tort' in cases of this kind and to sue in indebitatus assumpsit for money had and received. One circumstance made it highly expedient that this conclusion should be reached. Trover, the competing remedy, being delictual in form, could not be maintained against a personal representative after the death of the tortfeasor.[3] The action for money had and received, on the other hand, is contractual in form and death is therefore no impediment to its maintenance.

Advantage of this right of election.

We now proceed to consider a limitation to which the action of indebitatus assumpsit is subject where the plaintiff waives the tort and sues on the contract. In the leading case

the action of account: "If an account be brought against one as receiver, he ought to be charged with the receipt of the money; and an account doth not lie where the party pretends to be owner," i. e., against a wrongdoer. Tottenham *v.* Bedingfield, 3 Leon. 24.

[3] Hambly *v.* Trott, 1 Cowp. 371.

Chapter XV

of *Lamine v. Dorrell* the conversion was accomplished by selling, and the action was brought to recover the proceeds. In theory such actual conversion into money or its value is always necessary.[4]

Limitation of the money count as used against converter.

There are two reasons for this. The count for money or goods had and received is founded on equitable theory, and it is necessary that there should be a property right on which liability can be predicated. The converter is held liable in respect to the proceeds acquired by him in exchange for the property, as a sort of trustee *ex maleficio*. Again, being *in consimili casu* with debt, this count has inherited from that action the limitation that it can be maintained only where there is a duty to turn over money or goods ascertained in amount or capable of being reduced to certainty. This requirement is fully met in situations where there has been a sale or exchange of the converted goods, but it is not met in the absence of actual sale or exchange.

Explanation of this limitation.

It will thus be perceived that the duty upon which the implied contract is here predicated is a duty to disgorge the proceeds of an unlawful acquisition, and not upon the mere general duty to compensate for injury done. From this it follows that in actions of this kind the plaintiff can recover of the defendant only so much as he has actually received for the goods irrespective of their actual value.[5]

Recovery limited to amount received by converter.

While it is clear that the count for money had and received is maintainable only where the chattels in question have been thus sold or exchanged, it is equally clear that indebitatus in another form may be maintained where the conversion consists merely in an appropriation of the goods by the defendant and is not accompanied by a sale or exchange. Thus, if one asserts dominion over the horse of another, and thereby converts it to his own use, the original owner may declare in

The count upon fictitious sale available in case of any conversion.

The action for money had and received will not lie to recover the value of property unless there is evidence that the property has been sold and the money received, or its equivalent, or unless a sufficient time has elapsed to raise the inference of fact that it has been converted into money. Lytle *v.* Bowdon, 107 Ala. 361; Moody *v.* Walker, 89 Ala. 619.

[5] King *v.* Leith, 2 T. R. 144; Lindon *v.* Hooper, 1 Cowp. 419.

Volume III

assumpsit as for goods bargained and sold, the sale of course being a fiction like the finding in trover.[6]

Theoretically it might appear that in such situation the plaintiff might declare in assumpsit as for goods delivered by the plaintiff to the defendant to be held to the plaintiff's use and to be surrendered to him upon demand. Here the statement of the cause of action would set forth substantially a fictitious bailment, and the action would thereby inevitably become in its essence a form of trover. Hence indebitatus cannot take the form of a count upon a fictitious bailment.

Count on fictitious sale.

In England the count upon a fictitious sale seems to have hardly ever been used, though there are intimations to the effect that it might properly be adopted as a remedy against converters.[7] Where one of the parties dies, the action of indebitatus assumpsit counting upon a fictitious sale is the only remedy available, for trover is not then maintainable at all.[8]

American doctrine.

In America judicial opinion is divided. In a majority of the states the count in assumpsit upon a fictitious sale is fully sanctioned as a broad remedy concurrent with trover in all cases where the tortfeasor actually appropriates and uses the chattels as his own.[9]

In other states it has been held that the count for money had and received is the only form of assumpsit which will lie against a pure tortfeasor; and since this action can be maintained only where there is a subsequent sale and conversion into money or its equivalent, it follows that in such jurisdictions a tortfeasor who appropriates but does not sell the personalty of another cannot be held liable upon an implied contract.[1]

[6] *Assumpsit Against Tortfeasor upon a Fictitious Sale.*— Bradfield *v.* Patterson, 106 Ala. 397; Fratt *v.* Clark, 12 Cal. 89; Roberts *v.* Evans, 43 Cal. 380; Newton Mfg. Co. *v.* White, 53 Ga. 395; Toledo, etc., R. Co. *v.* Chew, 67 Ill. 378; Gordon *v.* Bruner, 49 Mo. 570; Terry *v.* Munger, 121 N. Y. 161; Kirkman *v.* Philips, 7 Heisk. (Tenn.) 222.

[7] See Bennett *v.* Francis, 2 B. & P. 550; Hill *v.* Perrott, 3 Taunt. 274.

[8] Hambly *v.* Trott, 1 Cowp. 371.

[9] Walker *v.* Duncan, 68 Wis. 624. See cases cited in third preceding note.

[1] Bowman *v.* Browning, 17 Ark. 509; Moses *v.* Arnold, 43 Iowa 187; Mann *v.* Locke, 11 N. H. 246. See also Thompson *v.* Banks, 43 N. H. 540.

Chapter XV

The decisions holding to this view are generally based on the authority of a Massachusetts case.[2] And it must be considered that the doctrine is erroneous. There is no theoretical difficulty in supporting an action upon a fictitious sale, in a legal system where fiction has played so important a part as in our own. The only question to be considered is whether the step is necessary to effect the ends of justice. Trover, of course, is adequate until one of the parties dies.

Indebitatus for service rendered by person unlawfully imprisoned.

In conformity to the theory of those cases in which the fiction of a sale is indulged, as against persons who appropriate but do not sell or exchange the chattels, it has been held that assumpsit upon an implied contract can be maintained to recover the value of services rendered, or work and labor done, by one who is illegally imprisoned.[3] In other words, the indebitatus count for services rendered or for work and labor can be maintained upon the fiction of a contract for service.

Enticement of apprentice.

It has been held that one who entices the apprentice of another is liable to the master for the value of the service rendered by the apprentice.[4]

On general principle the rule is that wherever one person commits a wrong or tort against the property of another, with

[2] Jones *v.* Hoar (1827), 5 Pick. (Mass.) 285.

This Massachusetts case m... perhaps be considered good law on its particular facts. It merely went to this extent, namely, that one who enters upon land and cuts timber thereon is not liable in assumpsit for the value of the wood upon carrying it away without subsequently selling it. Here the appropriation of the wood is merely accessory to the principal cause of action, which is for trespass to the realty. Hence it may well be conceived that the nature of the cause of action is in nowise changed merely by this circumstance of aggravation. See U. S. *v.* Lynah, 188 U. S. 474; Balch *v.* Patten, 45 Me. 41; Rogers *v.* Greenbush, 57 Me. 441. But the court declared in the principal case that assumpsit will in no case lie upon an implied promise unless there is a subsequent sale of the property converted. This is perfectly true of assumpsit in the form of the count for money had and received, but it has no application to assumpsit in the form of the count for goods sold and delivered. The decision on this point is undoubtedly wrong.

[3] Patterson *v.* Prior, 18 Ind. 440. In this case the lessee of convicts was charged as upon an implied contract for the service of one imprisoned upon a void judgment. But the warden was held not to be liable as upon a contract, because he had derived no profit from the wrong and was a bare trespasser.

[4] Lightly *v.* Clouston, 1 Taunt. 112.

Implied contractual duty to compensate for benefit.

the result of benefiting his own estate, the law will, at the election of the party injured, impose a contractual duty on the wrongdoer to pay the party injured the full value of the property appropriated; [5] and this duty may be enforced by the action of indebitatus in some of its forms.

No contractual duty to compensate for damage unaccompanied by enrichment of estate of wrongdoer.

The proposition just stated indicates the point beyond which the fiction of contract cannot be indulged. No form of indebitatus will lie to recover damages for a merely destructive trespass. It is essential that there should be an unjust enrichment of the estate of the tortfeasor. This limitation will be found to be inherited from the action of debt. To create a common-law debt, the *quid pro quo* must accrue as a benefit to the debtor, and at the same time it must move from the creditor. So here the loss of the plaintiff must be the gain of the defendant. It is not sufficient that the plaintiff suffers a detriment. The legal duty to make reparation for damage does not by implication raise a promise to pay such damage.[6]

Illustration of this doctrine.

The distinction now being considered has not, as might be imagined, lost its importance with the abolition of forms of action, for it is implicated with the question whether the right of action survives after the death of a party; and apart from statute the survival of rights of action is unaffected by the abolition of forms. This aspect of the matter was fully examined in *Phillips v. Homfray* (1883).[7] It appeared in this case that a trespasser had entered upon the premises of the plaintiff and had appropriated minerals and transported them over the plaintiff's roadways. The defendant having died, it was held that the action for damage done to the realty and for the user of the roadways in transporting the mineral could not be maintained, as the injury complained of was purely in tort; but it was also held that the plaintiff could recover for the minerals actually appropriated by the defendant, for here he could be held on the implied contract.

From what has been said it is manifest that the action of

[5] Fanson *v.* Linsley, 20 Kan. 239.
[6] Cooper *v.* Cooper, 147 Mass. 373.
[7] 24 Ch. D. 439.

Chapter XV

indebitatus assumpsit because of its affinity to the action of debt is the proper remedy upon all quasi-contractual duties which are in the nature of debt. For the same reason it is not normally the appropriate remedy by which to enforce those quasi-contractual obligations which are in the nature of true assumpsits. The reader who has perused chapter XXV of the second volume of this work will recall the fact that among such obligations are the following: the duty of the innkeeper to entertain, the duty of the carrier to transport, and the duty of officials to fulfil the functions of their office. All statutory and customary duties are of the same type. The implied warranty, wheresoever it arises, is also an obligation in the nature of assumpsit. Upon all these obligations the action on the case, or special assumpsit, or an action on the case in the nature of special assumpsit, is the appropriate remedy.

Indebitatus general remedy upon quasi-contractual duties in nature of debt,

but not upon quasi-assumpsit.

But there is one class of cases in which the action of indebitatus assumpsit has been used to enforce an obligation in the nature of assumpsit. This is where one man is compelled to expend money for the benefit of another under such circumstances that the law will imply a promise to repay it. The right of a surety to enforce exoneration and contribution furnishes a good illustration here. Where a surety is forced to pay off the principal's debt the law implies a promise on the part of the latter to repay the money so expended; likewise a surety who has paid off the secured claim can maintain an action against a co-surety for contribution. It has been held that a stranger whose goods are distrained for rent, and who is compelled to pay the rent to get them back, may maintain an action against the party primarily liable for the rent. In all cases of this kind indebitatus assumpsit in the form of the count for money paid is the appropriate remedy.[8]

Count for money paid to defendant's use.

Obligations which are incurred under the law merchant are of an assumptual or quasi-assumptual nature. Hence the action of special assumpsit or an action on the case in the

[8] Decker *v.* Pope, 1 Selwyn N. P., 13th ed., 91; Toussaint *v.* Martinnant, 2 T. R. 100; Cowell *v.* Edwards, 2 B. & P. 268; Exall *v.* Partridge, 8 T. R. 308.

Volume III

nature of special assumpsit is the proper and normal remedy on a negotiable instrument. As we have elsewhere learned, special assumpsit was first used in this connection; but this form of declaring was cumbersome and was generally abandoned as soon as the action on the case upon the custom was sanctioned.[9]

Effect of statutes on form of declaring on bill.

In England the action of special assumpsit or an action in the nature of special assumpsit came into common use as a remedy upon bills in the early part of the nineteenth century.[1] The Hilary Rules (1833) abolished the plea of non-assumpsit in actions upon bills of exchange and promissory notes. The defendant, being no longer able to plead the general issue, was thereby compelled to plead all matters of defense specially. In 1852 the Common Law Procedure Act[2] prohibited all immaterial and fictitious statements in pleading, such as "promises which need not be proved." The effect of the rules and statutes is to drive pleaders more and more back to that special action on the facts, in the nature of assumpsit, which is the normal and proper remedy upon these instruments. This was the remedy used when the custom of merchants was first sanctioned by the common law, and it is destined to be the remedy finally prevailing.

It has been generally held in America that a bill of ex-

[9] See vol. 2, p. 349; also *Action of Debt, ante.*

[1] Masters *v.* Ibberson, 8 C. B. 100, 65 E. C. L. 100; Bailey *v.* Bidwell, 13 M. & W. 73; May *v.* Chapman, 16 M. & W. 355.

Professor Ames observes that in the United States the following distinction maintains: In counts against a drawer, acceptor, and indorser, the implied promise is alleged; but as against the maker the implied promise is omitted, the idea being that in this case the express promise which is stated in describing the note is sufficient. 2 Ames Cases on Bills and Notes, 252, note.

In Henry *v.* Burbidge (1837), 3 Bing. N. Cas. 501, 32 E. C. L. 222, the declaration was in assumpsit against a drawer, and it was held to be necessary to allege a promise on the part of the drawer, though this promise was raised by implication of law and, of course, did not have to be proved. Tindal, C. J., pointed out a difference in this respect between drawing and accepting a bill. Accepting *per se* imports and includes an express promise to pay the bill; so with the making of a promissory note. Drawing a bill implies a promise in law, not in fact, to pay if the drawee does not. In this case the promise must be alleged; in the others, only the facts need be shown.

[2] 15 & 16 Vict., c. 71, § 49.

Chapter XV

change or promissory note will support the common counts for money against any previous party liable thereon; e. g., for money lent by the holder to the defendant, for money paid by the holder at the request of the defendant, or for money had and received by the defendant to the plaintiff's use.[3] This follows as a sort of corollary from the extension of the action of debt into the field of the law merchant, which has been noted elsewhere.[4] But that some of these decisions in which the money counts have been thus maintained do violence to legal principle is clear.

Use of common counts in suing on commercial paper.

The error which is here involved arose from a failure to distinguish between assumpsit brought to recover a debt (pure indebitatus assumpsit) and the money counts mentioned. The fact that assumpsit, or debt, can be maintained in a particular case is not conclusive that these counts are proper. Whether or not the money counts are applicable depends upon the particular facts of the case. The drawer of a dishonored bill, for instance, is liable in debt, in case, in indebitatus assumpsit, or in a count for money had and received, when sued by a remitter paying value. The acceptor is liable in debt, indebitatus assumpsit, and in case upon the custom, but it is a violation of legal principle to sustain a count for money had and received against him. So in regard to an indorser. The money counts have always been more or less confused with indebitatus assumpsit in its narrower sense, to the great embarrassment of all who seek to fathom the subject of remedial law in the field of contract and quasi-contract.[5]

Confusion between money counts and indebitatus.

[3] Penn *v.* Flack, 3 Gill & J. (Md.) 369; Ellsworth *v.* Brewer, 11 Pick. (Mass.) 316; Wild *v.* Fisher, 4 Pick. (Mass.) 421; Edgerton *v.* Brackett, 11 N. H. 218; Olcott *v.* Rathbone, 5 Wend. (N. Y.) 491; Pierce *v.* Crafts, 12 Johns. (N. Y.) 90.

[4] See *Action of Debt, ante.*

[5] In Appendix, note A, 1 Cranch (U. S.) 421, will be found a lengthy argument in favor of the use of the money counts in a suit by the holder of a note against a remote indorser. Judge Cranch, the author of this paper, combats the conclusion reached in Mandeville *v.* Riddle, 1 Cranch (U. S.) 290, where it was held that, in Virginia, a count for money had and received cannot be maintained by a holder against any other indorser than the one from whom he receives the note and to whom he pays value. Upon this particular point the decision was certainly correct. In this decision, however, it is also assumed that an indorser

Volume III

We have now dealt with the most important features of the truly protean action of indebitatus assumpsit, and a few general observations on the nature of the remedy are now in place. That indebitatus assumpsit is an action on the case in the nature of debt is abundantly illustrated in what has gone before. To one familiar with the manner in which the conception which is at the foundation of the action on the case operated to extend the common-law actions, it may be a cause of surprise that an action of debt on the case was not developed earlier and also directly from debt. We are familiar with trespass on the case and with detinue on the case (trover). Furthermore, assumpsit itself is an action on the case in the nature of the action of deceit. Why should we not also have had an action of debt on the case developed directly from debt?

General observations on nature of indebitatus assumpsit.

The reason is no doubt to be found in the fact that debt was the most ancient of common-law remedies, and consequently its scope and character had become definitely fixed before the courts began to exercise with freedom the power of framing writs *in consimili casu* with the fixed forms. When the action on the case in the nature of debt finally appeared it had to issue from assumpsit, and not directly from the action of debt.

It will be observed that as the action of assumpsit was perverted and extended into the field of quasi-contract the remedy approximated more and more in feature and in character to the original action on the case, which was the mother of assumpsit. Indeed, indebitatus assumpsit in its specialized modern forms supplies a most remarkable instance of reversion to primitive type. Although it is an action of debt on the case derived from assumpsit, it probably has more in common with

Reversion to primitive type.

is not liable to a remote holder in any form of action; in other words, that there is no liability at all. This conclusion is partially reached upon interpretation of an early Virginia statute, but it also rests upon the erroneous assumption that Lord Holt's view of the status of notes at common law was correct. The court was right in holding that the indorsement of a note is not a general admission of money had and received in favor of any subsequent holder. If any remedy exists it is by an action on the case. The error into which the court fell, if any, was in denying that any liability existed.

case than with either assumpsit or debt. Like case, indebitatus assumpsit is based directly on legal obligation; and to the circumstance that it is really a pure action on the case in disguise, the action owes that remarkable flexibility which has enabled the courts to extend it with such freedom into the field of pure legal duty.

Affinity to other actions.

The action of indebitatus assumpsit is therefore at the point of confluence of the three actions — assumpsit, debt, and case; and it derives important features from each of them. Its form, its theory, its procedure, it gets from assumpsit. From debt it obtains the substantial limitation involved in the fact that it can be maintained only when there is a claim for money or chattels in the nature of a debt. Its flexibility and power are largely derived from the fact that it is an action on the case. Inasmuch as the action now being considered shows plain evidence of an almost complete reversion to case, it is a just cause of wonder that the remedy was not originally derived directly from case. Why, for instance, did it not occur to lawyers and judges that a person who refused to pay what was reasonable for entertainment at an inn, where there was no previous agreement as to the price to be paid and no promise actually given, was guilty of a deceit, and that case could be maintained against him? But relief did not come from this direction. This circumstance is characteristic of common-law growth. Legal development was here, as always, along lines of least resistance. It is much easier to bridge a chasm in legal theory by means of such a fiction as that of an implied promise than it is to say, once and for all, the defendant *ought* to pay this money *ex aequo et bono*, consequently he is under a legal duty to pay and an action on the case accordingly lies.

At point of confluence of three actions.

Inasmuch as indebitatus assumpsit constitutes a reversion to case, it is free from one limitation to which the action of special assumpsit has always been subject. It is an inflexible rule that special assumpsit cannot be maintained by any other person than the one from whom the consideration moves. Being founded directly on the legal duty to pay money, indebitatus is not subject to this restriction. In this respect it resembles the old action of account. Thus if A pays money to

When indebitatus available by stranger to consideration.

Volume III

B that it may be turned over to C, the latter may sue in account or indebitatus, but not in special assumpsit. It thus appears that indebitatus supplies in some instances a remedy available to a stranger to the consideration where performance under the contract is due to him.[6] But from debt the action has inherited the requirement that the duty must be in the nature of a debt; that is, the duty must be one which calls for the delivery or payment of something specific. A mere promise to pay money to a third person, though upon good consideration, gives such third person no right of action in indebitatus assumpsit. A general remedy for the stranger to the consideration for whose benefit a contract is made was not found until all actions were abolished and the modern civil action on the facts of the case substituted in their stead.[7]

Limitation of the action.

[6] See Mellen *v.* Whipple, 1 Gray (Mass.) 322.

[7] See vol. 2, p. 158.

CHAPTER XVI

THE ACTION OF REPLEVIN.

LIKE most of the common-law actions, replevin in the course of the ages has undergone important changes. It had its roots in the remedy of distress, and for several hundred years was used for no other purpose than to restore to the owner chattels that had been wrongfully distrained. To-day replevin is a universal remedy for the recovery of chattels wrongfully taken upon any pretext, and in some jurisdictions, as we shall perceive, the remedy lies for any unlawful detention. In jurisdictions where the remedy is given this extreme scope it has of course ceased to be a purely possessory remedy and has become a true action *in rem,* being founded on property as well as possessory right.

Chapter XVI

Scope of replevin.

At present replevin is distinguished from detinue chiefly by the circumstance that in the latter remedy possession is not recovered until the action is terminated, while in replevin the chattels in dispute are, upon the giving of bond for their forthcoming, put into the hands of the plaintiff at the beginning of the suit.

The action of replevin had its origin in an immemorial custom by which a person distrained upon could have back his chattels from the distrainor upon tendering sufficient sureties to answer for the service distrained for.[1] The property having been replevied, it became the duty of the respective parties to appear in the local court and there present their contention. If it appeared that the original taking was unlawful, the plain-

Genesis of the action.

[1] One of the earliest instances of a replevin suit resulting from a distress for rent is given by Professor Bigelow. Abbot Faritius distrained upon Ermenold for non-payment of rent. The latter replevied the property with pledges. The replevin suit came on for trial, but the abbot obtained judgment by default. The matter was compromised, the sureties being friends of the abbot. This record belongs to the time of Henry I. Placita Anglo-Norm. 131.

Volume III

tiff in the replevin retained his chattels and the defendant was fined for the wrongful taking. If, however, the right of distraint was upheld, the chattels were then turned over to the distrainor unless, of course, the owner was content to satisfy the claim.

The right to replevy being thus sanctioned by custom and law, a writ was framed in the time of Glanvill, and perhaps by that very author, which could be used to compel the surrender.[2]

The writ of replevin.

In the time of Bracton the whole subject had been fully taken in hand by royal authority, on the theory that the refusal of the distrainor to permit the replevy was a breach of the king's peace. Hence, it was said, when the sheriff took cognizance of such matters it was by virtue of his authority as a royal justice and not as a sheriff. So if any other person claimed to exercise a similar authority, a special franchise was necessary, and the functionary acted, like the sheriff, as *justiciarius regis*.[3]

Proceedings in early action of replevin.

The proceedings in replevin during this period were of the following nature: When chattels were distrained and the owner saw fit to contest the claim, he might apply to the chancery for a writ *quod replegiari facias* commanding the sheriff to cause the goods (nearly always cattle) to be replevied.[4] The procedure by royal writ being tedious and doubtless expensive, the owner was also permitted to proceed without a

[2] *Writ of Replevin.*— The form of the writ was as follows: "The King to the Sheriff, Greeting. I command you, that justly and without delay, you cause G to have his beasts by gage and pledges, of which he complains that R has taken them, and unjustly detains them, for the customs which he exacts from him, and which he does not acknowledge to owe him; and, in the meantime, cause him justly, &c., least, &c." Glanv., Bk. XII., c. 12.

The Mirrour attributes this writ to Glanvill as the originator of it and this is certainly a safe conjecture. See Mirrour of Justice, c. 2, § 26.

[3] Bracton, 155*b*.

[4] The writ of replevin (*replegiari facias*) in Bracton's day was as follows: "Rex vicomiti, salutem. Praecipimus tibi quod sine dilatione replegiari facias tali averia sua quae talis cepit et injuste detinet ut dicit et postea cum unde juste deduci facias ne amplius inde clamorem audiamus pro defectu justitiae. Teste, &c." Bracton 157, § 6. In the Register the writ is given under the title *De Averiis Replegiandis* (Of the replevying of cattle), and from the term *replegiandum* the word replevin is derived.

writ and merely upon a direct verbal complaint to the sheriff. Chapter XVI

This officer, whether acting under a writ or merely by virtue of his own judicial authority, was forthwith required to replevy the chattels, provided the party complaining produced sufficient sureties. In order to do this he repaired in person or by deputy to the place where the chattels were impounded. A demand was there made for a view of the distress. If the right of inspection was denied, or any violence was done to prevent it, the sheriff immediately raised hue and cry and committed the offender or offenders to prison as persons acting in manifest violation of the king's peace. In this event he also forcibly took and restored the distress, if it could be found.

The replevy by the sheriff.

If the chattels could not be found, or if it appeared that they had been removed to prevent deliverance,[5] the sheriff was authorized to take counter-distress of the defendant's cattle, if he had any in the county to be distrained. This distress was called the 'withernam' and was to be in double the value of the property first taken. It was held by the sheriff until the original distress was restored. If the absconding distrainor had no chattels to be seized, recourse was had to process of attachment.[6]

Withernam.

If, on the other hand, the sheriff was not obstructed by the distrainor, he caused the cattle to be delivered to the complaining party on good security, and the parties were then bound to appear at the next term of the county court in order that the validity of the distress might then be judicially considered.[7] The refusal of the distrainor to submit to a view of the distress and to allow its restoration by the sheriff to the party complaining placed him in direct opposition to the royal authority and hence was considered a very grave misdemeanor. Indeed, this act of refusing or withholding the distress, *vetitum namium,* as it was called, was almost enough to convert the original taking into an *ex post facto* robbery.[8]

Vetitum namium

[5] Bracton 157, § 6.

[6] For the form of this writ see Bracton 157, § 7.

[7] Bracton 157*b*, § 8.

[8] "Cum injusta captio et detentio contra vadium et plegium dici poterit quaedam roberia." Bracton 157*b*.

There can be little doubt that in the early community, when the king through his sheriff had not yet undertaken to enforce replevins, it was considered a legal wrong for the distrainor to deny the chattels to an owner who tendered amends or sufficient sureties, but at any rate in the time of Bracton the refusal which constituted the great enormity in the eye of the law was that which thwarted the sheriff. Such act gave rise to a specific right of action which, like the early trespass, was criminal in its nature.[9] This plea, the *placitum de vetito namio,* receives much attention at Bracton's hand.[1] It gradually fell into disuse, being superseded in its civil aspect by the actions of trespass and replevin, and in its criminal aspect by the appeal of larceny or robbery.

Plea *de vetito namio.*

The Statute of Marlborough contains a number of provisions on the subject of distress. Particularly notable are those attaching heavy penalties for the taking of excessive distress and for the taking of distress on other grounds than those recognized by law.[2] Nothing was said in this statute concerning the proceedings in replevin; but later, at the second Westminster session (1285), Parliament passed a statute on the subject which embodied three important measures:

Excessive and unlawful distresses forbidden.

(1) It had previously been the law that where in a replevin suit the distrainor appeared in an inferior court and avowed that the distress had been lawfully taken to enforce the payment of service due in respect of tenements held by the plaintiff, the latter could at once terminate the proceedings merely by disowning the existence of the tenure. This gave to an unscrupulous plaintiff in replevin a great advantage; for, by entering such a plea though it were false, he was enabled to keep possession of the chattels and had judgment for the taking. The reason why the suit suffered this catastrophe merely upon the suggestion of nontenure was that such a plea raised a question

Effect of suggestion of nontenure in distress for rent.

[9] In Y. B. 30–31 Edw. I. (Rolls ed.), 222, it was said by Brumpton, J.: "The plea *de vetito namio* is properly had before the sheriff, and it is a matter against the king's crown and affects the king's peace in a high degree." In the same case it was said by Berrewik, J., that the plea *de vetito namio* was first invented in the time of King John.

[1] Bracton 155–159.

[2] Stat. Marl., c. 1–4; 2 Co. Inst. 101 *et seq.*

of title to the freehold and the local court had no jurisdiction to determine it.[3] This trouble was now remedied by permitting lords who seized for service due and who were attached to answer for the distraint in the local court, to remove the cause forthwith by a writ of *pone* into the king's court, which had ample jurisdiction to try the question of tenure.[4]

(2) The second measure adopted by this parliament for the protection of the distrainor was the requirement that the owner upon replevying should not only give sureties for the due prosecution of the suit, but should also give sureties for the return of the chattels in the event he should be cast in the suit. To effectuate this sheriffs and bailiffs were directed to require sureties in accordance with the statute before deliverance of the chattels, and were made personally liable for the value thereof if they failed to do so.[5] From the recitals of the statute it appears that the custom had previously been to give sureties for the prosecution of the suit only. Whether or not such custom was merely a lax innovation which was now corrected, or whether the practice had always been thus, we are unable to say with certainty.[6]

Sureties for return of property replevied.

(3) A further abuse was cured by a provision forbidding the institution of more than two successive replevin suits for the same distress. Theretofore some persons who had no good ground for replevying had adopted the device of making de-

Second replevin made final

[3] Bracton says that upon a plea denying the service the issue might come to trial by battle or the grand assize, and "it is manifest that a free man should no more be required to answer for such a service without a royal writ than for his freehold." Bracton 156, 156*b*.

[4] Stat. West. II., c. 2. Prior to this enactment there had been a rule of practice which prohibited removal of any plea to the higher court at the instance of the defendant. This provision apparently violated that rule, but the statute attempted to reconcile it with the previous practice by treating the distrainor as the plaintiff: "Though it *prima facie* appears that the tenant is plaintiff and the lord defendant, nevertheless having respect to the fact that the lord hath distrained and sueth for services and dues behind, he appeareth indeed to be rather actor than defendant."

[5] Stat. West. II., c. 2.

[6] In the case of Ermenold *v.* Abbot Faritius, Placita Anglo-Norm. 131, to which reference was made above, the sureties were evidently bound for the return of the property, as the abbot, after obtaining judgment by default, moved against the sureties for the restoration of the chattels: "Unde abbas praedictos plegios ascitos movit de habita re quaestionen."

Volume III

fault in the first suit and thereupon forthwith instituting a new suit before the property could be returned. By this means they were able to harass their opponents and keep possession indefinitely. To remedy this it was provided that when the writ for the return of the chattels (*de retorno habendo*) was issued after judgment for the defendant in any replevin proceeding, a clause should be inserted therein notifying the sheriff not to deliver the chattels to the same plaintiff upon a second replevin unless in obedience to a judicial writ. The second replevin instituted upon such writ (the so-called writ of second deliverance) was made conclusive, and the distress ever after remained irreplevisable.

Frequent use of the writ.

From this time on the action of replevin was common enough, as a glance at the proper headings in the old abridgments will show.[7]

Who is plaintiff?

It is to be observed that in the thirteenth century the law had hardly made up its mind as to who is really the plaintiff in such a proceeding. Bracton said that the owner of the distrained property was complainant (*querens*); the Statute of Westminster II treated the distrainor as such. Later both are said to be actors; the plaintiff in the replevin is said to be such because he seeks to be vindicated in his possession and to recover damages, while the distrainor seeks to have a return of the goods.[8] In his aspect as an actor the defendant in replevin who formally justifies the taking under a lawful right to distrain has always been called an avowant, and the pleading in which he so vindicates his conduct is known as an avowry.

Avowant.

Claim of property ousts jurisdiction of sheriff.

One rule obtained from an early day in the law of replevin which seriously impaired the efficacy of the remedy. If the defendant at the time when the officer appeared to replevy the property claimed it as his own, the jurisdiction of the sheriff or bailiff at once ceased and he could not deliver it to the

[7] See in Fitzherbert, titles *Avowrie, Replevyn;* in Brooke, *Avowrye, Propertie and Proprietate Probanda, Replegarie des Avers* (*Replevin*).

[8] Hodgkinson *v.* Snibson, 3 B. & P. 603; Bac. Abr., *Replevin and Avowery* (A).

plaintiff.[9] In such case the plaintiff was driven to an action of trespass or appeal of larceny.[1]

Chapter XVI

The reason for the astonishing rule that the distrainor could totally abate the replevin merely by claiming property is due to the fact that the action of replevin was designed purely for the protection of the right to the possession of chattels, and a disputed question of property could not be tried in it. Replevin thus occupies a place in the law of personalty entirely analogous to that occupied by the possessory assizes in the field of real property.

Reason for this rule.

That replevin is a remedy designed to protect the right of possession merely is obvious from the fact that a possessory right only is sufficient to maintain it. Thus if the beasts of another are agisting upon my land and manuring it, I shall have replevin against a stranger who takes them.[2] Hence also it follows that in any case the bailee may sue in replevin against one who seizes the chattels out of his possession.

Replevin a possessory remedy.

It was, indeed, customary in ancient times to say that it is necessary for the plaintiff in the replevin to have property in the goods sought to be replevied, and cases where the bailee maintained replevin were explained by saying that the bailee has a special property which will sustain the writ.[3] But in truth, what the older writers call a special property is nothing more than the right of possession, and this is all that is necessary to support replevin when the property has been in the first instance wrongfully taken from the person suing. Accordingly, "ownership cannot be tried in this writ."[4] The replevin writ in terms commands the sheriff to replevy the goods of the plaintiff which have been taken and unlawfully detained by

Property right not necessary to support the action.

[9] Britton, I., 55, § 4.

See Y. B. 21–22 Edw. I. (Rolls ed.), 106, where the right to prevent delivery by a mere claim of ownership is referred to.

[1] Y. B. 5 Edw. III. 3, pl. 11.

[2] Y. B. 42 Edw. III. 18, pl. 32; 2 Rolle Abr. 430 (C), pl. 1.

[3] 2 Rolle Abr. 430 (C), pl. 2; Y. B. 21 Hen. VII. 14, pl. 23; Y. B. 11 Hen. IV. 17, pl. 39; Y. B. 1 Edw. IV. 9, pl. 18; 1 Co. Litt. 145*b*.

[4] Howard, J., in Y. B. 32–33 Edw. I. (Rolls ed.), 54.

It is true the defendant in replevin may plead that the property was in a third person at the time of the alleged taking and not in the plaintiff. Y. B. 2 Hen. VI. 14, pl. 10. But it is conceived that this can only be good where the plea is taken as also negativing the plaintiff's right of possession at the time of the taking.

Volume III

Ownership not triable in replevin.

the defendant. It confers no authority on the sheriff to deliver to the plaintiff any goods belonging to the defendant. Neither does it confer on the sheriff any jurisdiction to try a controverted question of title. Hence when the defendant asserted ownership of the property which was sought to be replevied, the sheriff's power terminated and the replevin was thereby blocked. Even if the defendant failed to put in a claim of ownership at the time the replevy was accomplished, he might subsequently have the advantage of it by plea in court.[5]

Nevertheless there was one recognized limitation on the right to plead ownership in court. This was found in the rule that where the defendant was present at the replevy and permitted the sheriff to make deliverance of the chattels, he thereby acknowledged property in the plaintiff and was thereafter estopped to plead ownership in himself.[6]

Special writ for trial of property invented.

The recognition of the general principle that the defendant could defeat the action merely by claiming ownership and without proof certainly rendered the action of replevin a little hazardous. In the latter part of the fourteenth century the difficulty was largely removed by the invention of the writ for the trial of property (*de proprietate probanda*). This writ authorized the immediate trial of the right of property, and the fate of the replevin suit was made to depend upon the result.

Concerning the procedure connected with the trial of the right of property, a distinction is to be observed. If the replevin had been made upon verbal complaint to the sheriff without a writ from the chancery, then the writ *de proprietate* authorized the sheriff who would have effected the replevy and before whom the claim of property was made, to try the truth

[5] "If the property be claimed before the sheriff he cannot replevy, but if it be claimed in court it shall be tried by issue." Brooke Abr., *Propertie*, pl. 1, citing language of Brian, C. J., in Y. B. 21 Edw. IV. 64, pl. 35.

[6] Y. B. 32-33 Edw. I. (Rolls ed.) 54; Y. B. 5 Edw. III. 3, pl. 11. Professor Ames is of the opinion that after 1331 the defendant was in no case allowed to abate the writ by plea of ownership in court. 3 Harv. L. Rev. 32. But taken all together the cases hardly go further than to hold that the plaintiff may estop himself by standing by and seeing delivery made without asserting his title.

of the claim. If upon this inquest of office the sheriff found in favor of the defendant, the replevin proceedings were dropped.[7] If he found in favor of the plaintiff he proceeded to replevy the property as if no interruption had taken place. When, however, the replevin suit was begun by original writ, the writ *de proprietate* was not issued until the return of the replevin writ showing that the property was claimed by the defendant.

Proceedings in trial of property.

The writ for the trial of property could issue either from the chancery or from the King's Bench or Common Bench. The chancery issued the writ upon the return of the *alias* replevin; the other courts issued it only upon the return of the *pluries* replevin, for the reason that the *pluries* alone was returnable into those courts.[8] When the question of property was raised by plea in court at the trial of the replevin suit, the issue was tried by judge and jury.[9]

Issuance of writ.

The writ *de proprietate*, it will be observed, could be had only at the instance of one named as a party in the writ of replevin. Consequently if the beasts of a stranger are taken in replevin, he cannot have a writ for the trial of property.[1]

Who entitled to writ for trial of property.

In regard to the scope of the remedy, replevin presents one rather remarkable feature even down to the time of Blackstone. In theory it was broad enough to be used for the recovery of goods in any case of wrongful taking. But in fact it was used only in cases of alleged wrongful distress. The writ of replevin, as shown by the form in the Register, merely alleged an unlawful taking and withholding by the defendant,[2]

[7] Y. B. 7 Hen. IV. 28, pl. 5; Y. B. 1 Edw. IV. 9, pl. 18.

But the plaintiff was not absolutely precluded by the finding of the sheriff in this inquest of office. He could still sue out a replevin, and when the sheriff returned claim of property on this writ the issue was disposed of in the court. Co. Litt. 145*b;* Bac. Abr., *Replevin* (E 4).

[8] St. John *v.* Saunders, 2 Dyer 172*b*, 173*a*. See also Weaver *v.* Lawrence, 1 Dall. (Pa.) 156.

[9] So said by Brian, C. J., in Y. B. 21 Edw. IV. 64, pl. 35. Brooke Abr., *Propertie*, pls. 1, 32.

[1] Y. B. 14 Hen. IV. 25, pl. 32; 2 Rolle Abr. 431 (F).

[2] "Cepit et injuste detinet." Reg. Brev. Orig. 81 (*de averiis replegiandis*). The form given by Bracton contains the same language. The expression "taken and unjustly detained" characterizes the writs as given in Fitzherbert's Natura Brevium, 68–70.

Volume III

Does replevin lie for all unlawful takings?

and no hint is anywhere to be found in the early law to the effect that replevin is in theory limited to the field of distress. The fact that the writ and declaration contain no suggestion that the property was taken in distress affords indisputable evidence that such taking was not in theory the sole foundation of the action. The form of the writ and pleadings has always been taken as good evidence of what the law is. Again, where property in the defendant is pleaded in the replevin suit, it can never appear in the record that the goods were taken in distress. The consequence would be that if replevin lies only in cases of distress the plaintiff could not have had judgment when the issue of property was found in his favor, since the record would fail to show an essential requisite for the maintenance of the action.[3]

In conformity therefore with true legal theory, there is from the earliest times an abundance of judicial dicta to the effect that replevin may be maintained upon any wrongful taking. In this view replevin, as was said by Gascoigne, C. J., in 1406,[4] becomes concurrent with trespass.

In theory, action concurrent with detinue and trespass.

Accordingly, in theory, one who is disseised of a chattel may elect to sue in trespass, replevin, or detinue. If he sues in trespass damages to the full value of the chattel taken can be recovered, for that action proceeds on the theory that the property has vested in the tortfeasor. If replevin be chosen, the plaintiff reacquires the chattel as his own and recovers damages for the wrongful detention.[5] In modern times trover

[3] Vaiden *v.* Bell, 3 Rand. (Va.) 452.

[4] Y. B. 7 Hen. IV. 28*b*, pl. 5.

[5] In Y. B. 6 Hen. VII. 8*b*, pl. 4, Vavisor, J., said "When one takes possession from me he does not at the same time strip me of the ownership: for the fact that I can maintain replevin proves the property entire in me, and if he claims property it will be found against him and in my favor. . . . Furthermore one can have a writ of detinue, which proves that the property is not out of him if he chooses; but he can, if he will, bring an action of trespass, for he can waive the property."

So in Y. B. 10 Hen. VI. 65, pl. 5, Newton, J., observed: "If you have taken my chattels it is in my election to sue in replevin, which supposes the property to be in me; or to sue a writ of trespass, which supposes the property to be in you who took it. Thus it is my choice to waive property or not."

In Y. B. 14 Hen. VII. 12, pl. 22, an action of trespass was brought for the tortious seizing of a horse. The defendant pleaded that an action of replevin was then

was added to the number of remedies available against a trespasser who takes and converts chattels to his own use.[6]

In practice, action restricted to field of unlawful distress.

Notwithstanding the fact that replevin was judicially conceded to be concurrent with trespass in all cases of tortious caption and detention, the remedy did not come into general use for the purpose of recovering property in such cases.[7] Just why replevin did not become popular as a concurrent remedy with trespass is obscure. Wager of law was a common mode of defense in the trial of a replevin suit in Bracton's day,[8] and this circumstance may partially explain the failure to use the remedy more extensively. Then, too, the possibility that the plaintiff might be temporarily side-tracked by an inquest into the matter of ownership must have operated with deterrent effect.

Reason for restriction of remedy.

At any rate, replevin has been in practice so completely and exclusively associated with distress, that when Blackstone wrote (*cir.* 1765) he declared the remedy obtained in no other case of unlawful taking than that of wrongful distress.[9] This proposition undoubtedly stated the law of replevin correctly so far as previous usage was concerned, but it certainly was not in harmony with legal theory.[1]

Scope of action in Blackstone's day.

Strange as it may seem, the question whether replevin will lie for property tortiously taken on other pretexts than that of distress was not settled by judicial decision until the nineteenth century. Even as late as 1853 replevin was said in

pending in the King's Bench for the same horse and grounded upon the same wrong. The plea was held good.

[6] Bishop *v.* Montague, Cro. Eliz. 824.

[7] Professor Ames says there is no reported case where replevin was used to recover property taken otherwise than in distress, prior to the last century. 3 Harv. L. Rev. 32. This seems to be true. In Y. B. 14 Hen. VII. 12, pl. 22, such a suit was alleged to be pending in another court.

[8] Bracton 156; Note Book, pl. 477, 741.

[9] 3 Bl. Com. 145.

[1] In Comyn's Digest, which was published about the same time as Blackstone's Commentaries, it is said that replevin lies for all goods and chattels unlawfully taken, regardless of their nature. Com. Dig., *Replevin* (A). Viner likewise said: "If a trespasser takes beasts, replevin lies for this taking at election." Vin. Abr., *Replevin* (B).

Buller says that the action of replevin may be brought in any case where a man has had his goods taken from him by another. Bull. N. P. 52.

Volume III

England to be a very unusual form of action to recover chattels taken by ordinary wrongful trespass.[2]

Modern doctrine.

The opinion of Lord Redesdale, who delivered the judgment of the Irish High Court of Chancery in the case of *Shannon v. Shannon* (1804),[3] may be said to have dissipated the last vestiges of the notion, to which Blackstone had given currency, that replevin is limited to cases of wrongful distress. This opinion of his lordship has since been accepted, both in England and most of the American jurisdictions, as embodying the true common-law doctrine.

Pangburn v. Patridge (1810)[4] has the distinction of being one of the first reported cases, if indeed not the very first, in which replevin was actually used successfully in an ordinary case of trespass to recover chattels wrongfully taken. Thus at length has the action of replevin become really and practically concurrent with trespass *de bonis asportatis.*[5]

Replevin not available where goods are taken under process,

Ordinarily, in the absence of statute, replevin will not lie to recover goods which have been taken under execution or by virtue of a distress warrant issuing from a court of competent jurisdiction, and this for the reason that goods so taken are in the custody of law.[6] If, however, the seizure is a pretended one, or is made under the authority of a court hav-

[2] Mellor *v.* Leather, 1 El. & Bl. 618, 72 E. C. L. 618.

[3] 1 Sch. & Lef. 324. In this case the right of the plaintiff to maintain replevin was directly involved. Judgment was given against the right to maintain the action on another ground; but Lord Redesdale, upon consideration of the authorities, declared that Blackstone's conception of the remedy was too narrow and that replevin would certainly lie in favor of any one wrongfully disseised of chattels.

[4] 7 Johns. (N. Y.) 140.

[5] In a number of American jurisdictions, however, replevin has a more limited scope. In Alabama there is a statutory action in the nature of detinue which combines the qualities of both detinue and replevin, Rich *v.* Lowenthal, 99 Ala. 487; but there is properly speaking no action of replevin as the remedy is understood at common law. In Connecticut replevin is limited to attachment and distress. Watson *v.* Watson, 9 Conn. 140, 10 Conn. 75. So in South Carolina it is limited to cases of wrongful distress. Hewitson *v.* Hunt, 8 Rich. L. (S. Car.) 106. In Mississippi it lies only in case of distress for rent. Wheelock *v.* Cozzens, 6 How. (Miss.) 279. So likewise in Virginia by statute. Vaiden *v.* Bell, 3 Rand. (Va.) 448.

[6] Ilsley *v.* Stubbs, 5 Mass. 283; Gardner *v.* Campbell, 15 Johns. (N. Y.) 401.

ing no jurisdiction, replevin can be maintained by the party aggrieved.[7]

unless the taking is wholly unauthorized.

Likewise it is settled that where an officer clothed with power to seize the goods of one person under legal process, wrongfully levies on the goods of a third person, the latter may institute replevin. In this case, the authority of law not having been pursued, the officer is a mere trespasser and the goods taken by him cannot be said to be *in custodia legis.*[8] Nor is it material that the goods happen to be found in the possession of the actual defendant in the execution and are taken by the officer from him.[9] In a number of states statutes have been passed expressly declaring that a judgment debtor may have replevin to recover exempt property wrongfully seized under execution.[1]

Unlawful taking a prerequisite to maintenance of replevin.

The principle being now generally accepted that replevin lies for any wrongful taking, it becomes necessary to inquire for a moment what constitutes a taking within the meaning of the rule. In this connection it will be observed that the taking must be accompanied by a change of possession. Replevin therefore will not lie for a constructive taking merely, such, for instance, as is involved in an unlawful detention. As was said by Coleridge, J., in *Mennie v. Blake* (1856),[2] there must first be a taking out of the possession of the person suing.

The scope of the action was explained by Lord Redesdale in 1804 in these words: Replevin "is merely meant to apply to this case, viz., where A takes goods wrongfully from B and B applies to have them redelivered to him upon giving security until it shall appear whether A has taken them rightfully. But if A be in possession of goods in which B claims a property, this is not the writ to try that right."[3] In the

[7] George *v.* Chambers, 11 M. & W. 149; Mills *v.* Martin, 19 Johns. (N. Y.) 34.

[8] Thompson *v.* Button, 14 Johns. (N. Y.) 84; Clark *v.* Skinner, 20 Johns. (N. Y.) 467.

[9] Dunham *v.* Wyckoff, 3 Wend. (N. Y.) 281.

[1] See Settles *v.* Bond, 49 Ark. 114; Wilson *v.* Stripe, 4 Greene (Iowa) 551.

[2] 6 El. & Bl. 849, 88 E. C. L. 849.

[3] Matter of Wilson, 1 Sch. & Lef. 320, note.

Volume III

Plaintiff must once have had possession.

case where this language was used it was held that replevin was not maintainable for corn which the plaintiff claimed as his, but which had not been in his possession and was merely being detained by assignees in bankruptcy. So in *Ex p. Chamberlain* (1804),[4] the same learned chancellor refused to issue a writ of replevin, where the party complaining sought to acquire for the first time possession of a ship which had been assigned to him but which the master had refused to deliver.

Replevin lies not against fraudulent vendee;

nor against carrier;

In conformity with the doctrine that replevin lies only where the wrongful taking involves an actual trespass as against the person suing, the action cannot be used by the seller to regain possession of a chattel, title to which has been acquired by a fraudulent vendee.[5] Nor can the consignee of goods maintain replevin against a common carrier who refuses to deliver them up;[6] for the action cannot be used to enforce a merely contractual duty. In other words, unlawful detention alone is not sufficient to support the action.[7]

nor against vendee of a bailee.

Replevin a purely possessory action under common-law theory.

Consequently, if a special bailee without authority sells or pledges the goods in his possession and delivers them to his vendee, replevin cannot be maintained against the latter by the owner, because there is no trespass in his taking possession.[8] It thus appears that upon a common-law principle replevin is a purely possessory remedy. It contemplates the situation where property being in the peaceful possession of A is seized by B. The original possession of A justifies the presumption, ordinarily indulged by the law in favor of possession, that A is the owner, or at least is entitled as against a trespasser to be treated as such. The law therefore gives the writ of replevin to A, by which he recovers the property pending the settlement of the controverted right.

Now when replevin is extended beyond these limits and is used to recover property wrongfully detained, it at once be-

[4] 1 Sch. & Lef. 320.

[5] Shannon *v.* Shannon, 1 Sch. & Lef. 324.

[6] Galloway *v.* Bird (1827), 4 Bing. 299, 13 E. C. L. 443. *Contra*, Portland Bank *v.* Stubbs, 6 Mass. 422.

[7] Gardner *v.* Campbell, 15 Johns. (N. Y.) 401.

[8] Mennie *v.* Blake, 6 El. & Bl. 842, 88 E. C. L. 842.

Chapter XVI

Anomalous extension of remedy to cases of mere unlawful detention.

comes an anomalous remedy and goes against the presumption of law that one having lawful possession has also *prima facie* title.[0] Still, in a number of American jurisdictions this is permitted, either as a result of judicial decision or by statute. In Pennsylvania the innovation was recognized at an early day, and the right of a plaintiff to maintain replevin against any one wrongfully detaining goods has not there been questioned.[1]

A case decided by the Massachusetts court in 1819 seems to be a leading authority on the proposition that replevin lies for a wrongful detention even though the property may originally have come lawfully into the defendant's possession.[2] This decision apparently proceeds on the theory that one who wrongfully withholds possession is guilty of a constructive trespass. In most jurisdictions such extension of the remedy has been accomplished by statute.[3]

Remedy thus comes to be founded upon property as well as possessory right.

It will be observed that the adoption of the doctrine that replevin will lie for any unlawful detention operates at once to destroy its distinctive character as a possessory action. The remedy thereby comes to be founded on property as well as possession. The issue of ownership in the defendant is therefore no longer a collateral issue and is available as matter of defense at the trial of the replevin suit.[4] It results that though the plea of *non cepit* admits property in the plaintiff, such plea may be joined with a special plea of property in the defendant or other person.[5]

The Register contains a form of replevin to be used by executors for the recovery of chattels wrongfully taken from

[0] This circumstance was adverted to by Lord Redesdale in Shannon *v.* Shannon, 1 Sch. & Lef. 326, and by Coleridge, J., in Mennie *v.* Blake, 6 El. & Bl. 849, 88 E. C. L. 849.

[1] Weaver *v.* Lawrence (1785), 1 Dall. (Pa.) 157. Morris on Replevin, 3d ed., 52.

[2] Baker *v.* Fales, 16 Mass. 147. To the same effect see Portland Bank *v.* Stubbs, 6 Mass. 427; Simpson *v.* M'Farland, 18 Pick. (Mass.) 427; Page *v.* Crosby, 24 Pick. (Mass.) 211.

[3] Seaver *v.* Dingley, 4 Me. 315; Cullum *v.* Bevans, 6 Har. & J. (Md.) 469. See 24 Am. and Eng. Encyc. of Law (2d ed.) 495.

[4] Harrison *v.* M'Intosh, 1 Johns. (N. Y.) 380; Weaver *v.* Lawrence, 1 Dall. (Pa.) 156.

[5] Simpson *v.* M'Farland, 18 Pick. (Mass.) 427.

Volume III

Replevin at instance of executors.

their testator in his life.[6] In other words, the right of action which might be enforced by this remedy did not die with the person disseised. This is undoubtedly due to the fact that replevin, though only a possessory remedy, really afforded a means of protecting property right.

Ground of this concession.

If replevin had been conceived like trespass, as being founded merely upon the right to obtain redress for a tort, the right of the executor to sue in replevin could not have been admitted. The common law, in permitting the executor to maintain replevin for goods taken from the testator in the latter's lifetime, had its eye on property the recovery of which was the end and aim of the action. Then, too, at common law replevin was in practice used only where chattels had been distrained, and the distrainor, as will be recalled, gained no property by the taking. He held the property as belonging to the party distrained upon. Hence when the latter died there was no great difficulty in conceding the right of action to his representative. Still, it is obvious that the rule allowing executors to maintain replevin was somewhat exceptional.

No writ of replevin against executors.

There was no corresponding writ against executors; from which it seems that where the tortfeasor died, the law looked upon the cause of action as being founded on a tort and consequently as dying with him.[7] Nor did the common law have any writ for the assignee; for such a person of course could not show prior possession, and hence could not show that the property had been wrongfully taken from him.

[6] Reg. Brev. Orig. 81*b;* Fitz. Abr., *Executors,* pl. 106; *ib., Avowrie,* pl. 257.

"Executors shall have replevin for the taking of chattels distrained in the life of their testator, and this, it seems, by the common law, for the action affirms property to remain. Otherwise of trespass, for this disaffirms property." Brooke Abr., *Replevin,* pl. 59.

[7] Pitts *v.* Hale, 3 Mass. 321.

CHAPTER XVII

THE ACTION OF TRESPASS.

Chapter XVII

TO superficial observation it would appear that if there is any common-law remedy whose scope is definable with precision, that remedy should be found in the action of trespass. The contrary, however, is true, for no action has been more illogically used. In stating the scope and limits of the action of trespass no intelligible principle can be laid down which is absolutely and unqualifiedly true in the exact sense of the language employed. The precision which one can attain to here is at most only a sort of verbal precision. The scope of trespass cannot be set forth with exactness in any single proposition, for the reason that from time to time the courts have permitted the remedy to be used in situations where under strict theory it should not be available.

Difficulty in defining the scope of trespass.

At the outset we observe that the two remedies of trespass and case divide between them the entire field of tort. These are the two purely delictual remedies. If damage results from a wrongful act or omission other than a breach of contract, either trespass or case in some form must lie, if the act constitutes a wrong for which a civil action for damages will lie at all. There are other remedies besides trespass and case which are rightly classed as delictual. Detinue, for instance, is such in one aspect, but it is also an action of property, and hence is not purely delictual. The same can be said of replevin. Trover, though historically it has affinities with detinue, nevertheless sounds in damages merely, and is delictual; but then trover is merely a specialized form of case. We repeat, an act is no tort unless it be remediable in trespass or in some form of case.

Trespass and case supplemental in field of tort.

It requires but little insight to teach us that the conception of damage done to person or property by the direct and wrongful application of force supplies one of the first roots of delictual liability. Such injury is therefore, in a growing system of law, very naturally the first tort which is redressable purely as such in an action for civil damages. As a remedy for it the common law gave the writ of trespass.

Idea of forceful damage at root of trespass.

The primary notion underlying the action of trespass is therefore easily perceived, namely, the conception of damage done by the direct and wrongful application of force. As the action of trespass is available for the recovery of damage occasioned by an act which constitutes the wrong known as a trespass, it will at times be found convenient in the course of this discussion to treat the subject from the point of view of substantive law rather than from that of remedial law. In other words, we shall sometimes speak of the trespass rather than the writ of trespass.

Original meaning of trespass.

The term 'trespass' (old French, *trespasser*) primarily means any act which transcends or passes beyond the bounds of legal right. In this broad sense it is the equivalent of *transgressio,* the Latin word used by Bracton and other early writers on English law to convey the same idea. Both 'trespass' and 'transgression' are therefore terms either of which might well have been used in English law as the name of that legal wrong (not being a breach of contract) which is redressable in an action for civil damage; and it seems almost a caprice of language that one or the other of these expressions was not so used. The word 'tort' has, however, been adopted as the general term for legal wrong other than breach of contract. The reason for this is found in the fact that when in modern times a need was felt for such a general word, the early legal sense of the word *transgressio* had been forgotten, and the word 'trespass' had long since become permanently identified with injuries of a particular class, namely, those occasioned by a display of force. This led to the adoption from the old law French of the neat and expressive term 'tort' to indicate the breach of a duty fixed by law, as distinguished from the breach of a duty fixed by contract. The term trespass was thereby relieved of double duty and legal terminology was enriched in a corresponding degree. In modern times, therefore, the term is no longer used in the broad sense of legal wrong.

Term used in broad sense of legal wrong.

It is worth observing that the original broad meaning of trespass has adhered to it in the phrase 'trespass on the case.'

Importance of early history of writ of trespass.

The early history of the writ of trespass is of importance to the legal scholar, because here is to be found material for studying the beginnings of our law of tort. This action was the first and for some time the only common-law remedy which was based purely on the idea of giving compensation for damage resulting from wrongful acts. Of course the conception of liability for tortious acts antedated the earliest writ of trespass.[1] But into the early stages of the growth of this conception we cannot here enter. It is sufficient to observe that prior to the advent of the writ of trespass such 'law of torts' as existed was immature and in a highly confused state. No distinction whatever was made between public and private wrongs, for the rules applicable to crimes had not yet become a separate body of law. In addition to being ill defined in itself, such law of torts as existed during this early period was enforced only in the inferior local courts. These have left few written records, and there is very little extraneous evidence to show how far such courts could or did go in enforcing reparation for civil wrongs.

Beginnings of common-law theory of tort found in writ of trespass.

But when the chancery began to issue the writ of trespass and the royal justices began to entertain suits founded upon this writ, the obscurity which had previously enveloped the subject gradually disappeared. Then it was that the common law began to concern itself about a law of torts or, more particularly, about a law of trespasses; and before long it could be seen that the common law was arriving at some sort of theory concerning wrongs redressable in the civil action of trespass.

Appearance of the writ.

The writ of trespass (*breve de transgressione*) first came into common use near the middle of the thirteenth century; at about the time, that is to say, when Bracton was writing his famous book on English law. There is record of a few actions of trespass on the Rolls of the King's Bench for the reign of

[1] The first of Professor Wigmore's three papers on Responsibility for Tortious Acts, 7 Harv. L. Rev. 315 *et seq.*, seems to be the most suggestive article in English on this subject during the early

Volume III

John,[2] and Bracton's Note Book contains a number of such pleas from the first half of the reign of Henry III.[3] But the action of trespass seems not to have become common until after the first half of the century was gone.[4] The form of the writ did not appear upon the Register until during the time of Edward I.[5]

Form of writ incorporated in Register.

That two hundred years should have elapsed after the Conquest, before an action of trespass could be entertained by the royal courts for the redress of so common a wrong as the trespass of violence, is somewhat singular. The fact that the local courts had jurisdiction of such matters partly explains the late appearance of the action in the higher courts. The main reason, however, is to be found in the circumstance that before the advent of trespass certain other remedies were available in the king's courts for the redress of the more grievous wrongs which at a later day supplied a basis for the writ of trespass. These remedies were chiefly the assize of novel disseisin and the criminal appeals of larceny and felonious assault. A brief account of these is essential to an understanding of the early law of trespass.

Late appearance of writ explained.

Early substitutes.

period. His paper is based mainly on Dr. Brunner's article in the Proceedings of the Royal Prussian Academy of Sciences, vol. 35, July 10, 1890 — Ueber Absichtlose Missethat im Altdeutschen Strafrecht.

Judge Holmes has an instructive chapter on Early Forms of Liability, in his work on the Common Law, 1 *et seq.*

[2] See 3 Harv. L. Rev. 177, where Professor Maitland refers to these cases, citing 2 Rot. Cur. Reg. 34, 51, 120, 169, 260.

[3] See Note Book, pl. 85 (1220), a case of tortious intrusion upon land and asportation of chattels; pl. 287 (1228), trespass upon realty; pl. 314 (1229), trespass for false imprisonment; pl. 378 (1230), trespass upon realty; pl. 465 (1230), imprisonment. For other pleas of trespass noted in the same work, see vol. 1, pls. 567, 616, 821, 835, 839, 843; vol. 2, pls. 1041, 1121, 1232, 1520, 1735.

[4] "After looking through some unprinted rolls we feel entitled to say that this action was still uncommon in 1250, but was quite common in 1272." 2 Poll. & Mait. Hist. Eng. Law, 2d ed., 525, note 2.

The Abbrevatio Placitorum contains no reference to an action of trespass during the period from 1194 to 1252. The same record for the succeeding year however (1252–53) shows, as Professor Ames has pointed out, no less than twenty-five cases of trespass. From that time on the action is common enough. See 11 Harv. L. Rev. 282.

[5] Register of Original Writs, F. W. Maitland, 3 Harv. L. Rev. 179.

Chapter XVII

When a trespass upon land was of such nature that it could be treated as constituting a disseisin, the writ of novel disseisin was available to the person aggrieved. If this remedy had been restricted exclusively to cases where there was an actual amotion from possession, it would of course have been of no benefit to one who was damaged by a wrongful intrusion not amounting to an actual ouster. But the action was not so limited. The writ of novel disseisin could be maintained against any one who harassed the possessor in his possession, provided the possessor chose to treat the wrongful act as a disseisin.[6] This was particularly true where the interference was repeated or made under a claim of right.

Function of the writ of novel disseisin.

This broadening of the scope of the writ of novel disseisin resulted, of course, from the effort to supply a remedy for which no special action then existed. Consequently, as trespass came into use this anomalous extension of the writ of novel disseisin was less necessary. Bracton observed the difference between a mere trespass and a true disseisin, saying that to constitute the latter it was necessary that one who merely intruded or hindered another should claim an interest in the tenement, and that if he claimed nothing he was only guilty of a trespass.[7] This distinction having become clear, it resulted that in an action of novel disseisin it might appear that the defendant's intrusion fell short of being a disseisin by reason of the absence of an intent to usurp the right of the owner.[8]

Distinction between the disseisin and the mere trespass.

Where this issue was raised it became a question for the judge whether the wrongful act in question amounted to a disseisin or constituted merely a trespass. In other words, the question of intent in these cases was for the court. If the court was of the opinion that the act complained of amounted

[6] Bracton 161*b*, 216*b*; 2 Poll. & Mait. Hist. Eng. Law, 2d ed., 53.
"If one be prevented from ploughing his land by reason of his plough being carried off, or from sowing his land, he is disseised." Y. B. 20-21 Edw. I. (Rolls ed.) 392.

[7] Bracton 161*b*.

[8] "Omnis disseisina est transgressio sed non omnis transgressio est disseisina. Et si eo animo forte ingrediatur fundum alienum non quod sibi usurpet tenementum vel jura, non facit disseisinam sed transgressionem." Bracton 216*b*, § 5.

only to a trespass, the novel disseisin failed; but the matter of the trespass itself required further proceedings.

Inquiry into matter of trespass in proceedings under writ of novel disseisin.

If the defendant now chose to deny the act constituting the trespass altogether, this question of fact had to be determined by triers. The assizemen were of course present in court, having been summoned to respond on the question of disseisin. They were accordingly incompetent to try the question of trespass as an assize. Hence the issue was submitted to them in their capacity as jurors. The assize was then said to be turned into a jury.[9] If the defendant was now found guilty of the trespass he was of course fined, and before long it became customary for the damages incurred by the plaintiff by reason of the trespass to be thereupon assessed against the defendant.[1]

Assize turned into jury.

It will be perceived that this proceeding was not founded upon any writ of trespass. It was merely an incident in the trial of the older action. The novel disseisin was originally of a purely possessory character, but even before Bracton's day it had become permissible for the recognitors in the assize to estimate the damage which had been inflicted; and the plaintiff was given judgment for this at the same time that he recovered his possession.[2] In this way the idea of awarding damages in a civil action as compensation for a wrong done was gradually strengthened. When the action of trespass made its appearance this conception for the first time found a vehicle destined to bring it to full maturity.

Damages given in compensation.

In the early days of the common law one from whom chattels were wrongfully taken could avail himself of the criminal appeal of larceny. But this remedy was somewhat restricted in its scope, and the prosecution of it was hampered by highly technical rules. Besides, the mode of trial, which was by battle, was perilous in fact and of doubtful issue. Still, in the days when there was no action of trespass *de bonis asportatis*,

Scope of the appeal of larceny.

[9] Bracton 216*b*, § 5; *ib.*, 217, § 6.

[1] Britton, Bk. I., 133*b*.

[2] Select Civ. Pleas (Sel. Soc.), pl. 4; 2 Poll. & Mait. Hist. Eng. Law, 2d ed., 524.

a plaintiff might choose to prosecute an appeal in the king's court, and if successful the chattels were returned to him.

The technical appeal of larceny seems to have been maintainable only when the plaintiff could charge a felonious taking, in which case the trial took place in the king's court; but the remedy seems to have shaded off into what Bracton calls the *actio furti*, or action of theft. This action was maintainable in divers inferior courts, and it was not necessary in this action that the plaintiff should charge a felonious taking. He might if he saw fit proceed civilly to recover the chattel as lost (*adirata*), although it had been in fact stolen.[3] The action could thus be used to recover chattels tortiously taken by the defendant. It afforded an unsatisfactory substitute for the later remedy of trespass *de bonis asportatis*, and differed from the latter in being recupatory in its character, while trespass lies for the recovery of damages only.[4]

The action of theft.

In the department of personal injury the criminal appeal for felonious assault (*de plaga facta*) was clearly the predecessor of the action of trespass for assault and battery. If the injury inflicted was not of a serious nature the royal court had no jurisdiction. For mere bruises the injured party could recover damages (*bot*) according to a fixed scale in the local court.

Criminal appeal for felonious assault.

What has been said above directs attention to the particular types of injury for the redress of which an action like trespass was much needed. Accordingly, when the remedy appeared we find it used to recover for damage done by violence to the plaintiff's land, or for the asportation of his chattels, or for injury violently inflicted upon his person.

The threefold function of the early action of trespass.

Looking for a moment to the contents of the writ of trespass when it finally came to issue from the chancery, we find

[3] Bracton 150*b*.

[4] The recupatory character of the appeal was commented upon by Hussey, C. J., in Y. B. 4 Hen. VII. 5, pl. 1: "The appeal," says he, "is for the recovery of the chattels and affirms property continually in the party [who brings the appeal]; but it is otherwise of trespass, for this [action] is not for the recovery of the goods, but is for the damages."

Volume III

Contents of early writ of trespass.

that it directed the sheriff to cause the defendant to appear in the King's Bench to answer for the wrong complained of. The ground on which the royal court was thus given jurisdiction to entertain the action was indicated in the wording of the writ, for it charged that the trespass was done by force and arms and against the king's peace.[5]

Jurisdiction of royal court based on charge of violence.

If the words *vi et armis* and *contra pacem* were omitted the writ was not returnable in the King's Bench. Such a writ was merely an authority for the sheriff to determine the cause in his own court and was called a vicontiel writ.[6] As the local courts already had jurisdiction of trespasses, the issuance of the vicontiel writ did not involve new principle. It merely illustrated the supervision which royal authority had now come to exercise over the proceedings of the inferior courts.

Action supplants the criminal appeal.

As a remedy for personal injuries and for the asportation of chattels the writ of trespass, as has already been stated, supplied a much-needed supplement and substitute for the criminal appeals. The new action had many points of resemblance to the appeal, and a recognition of these has led to the observation that trespass is only a sort of attenuated appeal.[7] This suggestion is borne out by the fact that the language of the writ of trespass is substantially identical with the corresponding language of the appeal, the chief difference being

[5] *Form of the Writ of Trespass.*— The first returnable writ of trespass appearing in the Register is one to recover damages for an assault and battery: "Rex vicomiti, &c. salutem. Si A fecerit te securum de clamore suo prosequendo, tunc pone per vadium et salvos plegios B quod sit coram justitiariis nostris apud Westmonasterium in octavis sancti Michaelis, vel sic, &c., ostenturus quare vi et armis in ipsum A apud N insultum fecit et ipsum verberavit, vulneravit, ei male tractavit, ita quod de vita ejus desperabatur et alia enormia ei intulit ad grave dammum ipsius A et contra pacem nostram." Reg. Brev. Orig. 93.

For illustration of the form of the pleadings in trespass see 1 Ryley Plac. Parl. 2, 5; also 2 Reeves Hist. Eng. Law, Am. ed., 566–568.

[6] The form of the vicontiel writ was as follows: "Rex &c. Questus est nobis A quod B in ipsum A apud N insultum fecit et ipsum verberavit et male tractavit et alia enormia ei intulit ad dammum ipsius A non modicum et gravamen. Et ideo tibi praecipimus quod loquelam illam audias et postea eum inde juste deduci facias; ne amplius inde clamorem audiamus pro defectu justitiae." Reg. Brev. Orig. 92. See F. N. B. 85 *et seq.*

[7] 2 Poll. & Mait. Hist. Eng. Law, 2d ed., 526.

that in the writ of trespass the words charging a felony and the offer of battle are omitted. Instead of these an allegation is inserted to the effect that the act was done *vi et armis* and damages are claimed for the consequent injury.

Chapter XVII

Points of analogy to the criminal appeal.

The action of trespass was of a semi-criminal character, this being in fact the very ground on which the royal court acquired jurisdiction over the wrong. The process and procedure of the action aimed at the outlawry of the defendant if he should prove obstinate. When convicted of the trespass he was fined, and was subject to imprisonment if the fine were not paid. The civil aspect of the remedy appeared in the assessment of damages in favor of the plaintiff.

Criminal features of trespass.

The superiority of the action of trespass over the criminal appeal is obvious. The trial in the king's court was by jury and the proceedings were comparatively swift. Writing in the latter years of the thirteenth century, and consequently not long after the action of trespass had come into common use, the author of Britton advises prospective litigants to sue a writ of trespass when possible rather than to bring an appeal, in order thereby to avoid "the perilous risk of battle."[8]

Advantage of trespass over the criminal appeal.

Though the affinity of the action of trespass to the criminal appeal is obvious, one point in the early history of the action seems to be as yet obscure. It was logical enough to use a writ which was closely akin to an appeal as a remedy for bodily blows and for the asportation of chattels; but how did it come to pass that the same writ could be used to recover for a mere trespass upon realty? There was never at any time such a thing as an appeal of felony for a simple entry upon land unaccompanied by a battery or an asportation.[9]

Origin of trespass as a remedy for injury to real property.

The solution of the problem is perhaps this: The writ of trespass was first used in cases of battery and in cases of the asportation of chattels (*de bonis asportatis*). In charging a taking and carrying away of chattels it often happened that the plaintiff would allege an unlawful entry upon his premises. Certain it is that in the early records the count for the aspor-

[8] Britton I., 49.
[9] See Sel. Pleas Crown (Seld. Soc.), pl. 35.

Volume III

tation of chattels is usually coupled with the allegation of an unauthorized entry upon the plaintiff's premises.[1]

Trespass *quare clausum.*

This conjunction of the two wrongs in one writ suggested the propriety of holding that the writ of trespass might be used for the breaking of a close alone. In this form the writ is known as trespass *quare clausum fregit.* As will be remembered, the idea that an intrusion upon land is wrongful was familiar in the law of disseisin; for the party injured could, as we have seen, bring an assize of novel disseisin and thereby force the defendant into a collateral proceeding before a jury, in which damages could be assessed for the trespass. A direct and swifter remedy was now obtained by adopting the action of trespass as an appropriate remedy. The alternative to the view here suggested as to the historical connection between trespass *quare clausum* and trespass *de bonis* is to suppose that the former remedy had an entirely independent origin. This does not seem adequately to account for the similarity in the forms of the writs and for the identity of procedure.

Trespass lies for forceful damage of any kind.

However this may be, in the end it all comes to this: that the action of trespass is available in some form to recover compensation for damage directly done by violence, whether such damage is in the form of injury to person or is done to land or consists of the asportation of chattels. Such is the form of the proposition in which we must formulate the theory of trespass.[2]

But the law did not define the amount of force which is necessary to constitute a trespass, and very little is enough. "By force and arms and against the king's peace" has a mighty sound, but in ultimate theory any unlawful touching of the person,[3] or the slightest intrusion upon land,[4] or any improper intermeddling with chattels (which results in damage) is sufficient to constitute a technical trespass.

Indeed, it is not always necessary that force complained

[1] Bracton's Note Book, pl. 85 (1220).

[2] "Every trespass is in law done with force and arms." Doctor & Student, Dial. II., c. 54.

[3] Cole *v.* Turner, 6 Mod. 149.

[4] See Lord Ellenborough's observations in Pickering *v.* Rudd, 1 Stark. 56, 2 E. C. L. 32; also U. S. *v.* Appleton, 1 Sumn. (U. S.) 492; Smith *v.* Smith, 110 Mass. 302.

Chapter XVII

of should be actually applied. The unlawful display of violence, as where one assaults another but does not commit a battery, is actionable in trespass.[5] But in the beginning the actions of trespass which were actually litigated were based on very simple facts and the force element was conspicuous enough. Beating, taking and carrying away chattels, cutting and carrying away growing trees or grain, depasturing tenements, and seizing and abducting one's wife along with his goods, are illustrations of the trespasses with which the king's courts were at first busied. Such were the wrongs which appeared to the early judges fit objects of censure.

Extension of doctrine leads to recognition of assault.

For reasons above indicated the writ of trespass, being obtainable as of course (*de cursu*), became exceedingly popular, and during the time of Edward I the use of it threatened to overwhelm the royal courts with a host of petty suits. As a result, by the Statute of Gloucester (1278) it was enacted that no one should thereafter have a writ of trespass *de bonis asportatis* returnable before the justices unless he should swear that the goods taken away were worth at least forty shillings. Naturally, a limitation based on money value could not be placed on trespasses involving blows and bruises. These were accordingly excepted out of the statute, but the plaintiff who complained of a beating was required to make oath that his plaint was true.[6]

Popularity of action of trespass.

Restriction of remedy by statute.

From what has been stated herein it appears that the early actionable trespass against personalty consisted of an asportation, or the taking away thereof from the possessor. This wrong is analogous to the true disseisin of realty, for the effect of both is to strip the owner of control and effectually to deprive him of the benefit of his legal rights. It is readily seen that a recognition of the principle that one may recover damages for an asportation is bound presently to lead to the recognition of the right to recover damages for the destruction; for the effect of both is the same. Accordingly the destruc-

[5] 2 Rolle Abr. 545, pls. 9, 10.

[6] Stat. Gloucester, 6 Edw. I., c. 8.

Volume III

tion of personalty, like the taking of it away, gives a good right of action in trespass.[7]

Trespass for damage falling short of asportation or destruction.

This being granted, we naturally expect also to find a recognition of the right to recover for damage to chattels falling short of destruction or asportation. But the authorities here are not very explicit. The Register contains no form of a writ for damage to chattels not amounting to a destruction. The reason, perhaps, is that such wrongs were in the early common law redressed in the lower courts [8] and were thought too trivial to claim the attention of the higher jurisdiction. But it is manifest that upon principle trespass *vi et armis* should be maintainable for damage directly done by the application of force to chattels, just as it is maintainable for an entry upon realty or for battery of the physical body. Inferentially there is recognition of this doctrine in the early authorities. Thus we are told by Brooke that an action of trespass lies for the mutilation of a deed by the tearing off of the seal.[9] So for the unlawful chasing of beasts.[1] The right to recover for damage resulting from an act not amounting to a total deprivation is likewise implicitly recognized in the proposition that trespass lies for a taking although the goods are restored to the owner, the restoration in such case being admissible only in mitigation of the damages.[2] But whatever doubts may have arisen on this point in early times, it has long been settled that trespass will lie for damage violently done to personalty.[3]

Trespass Violates Possession.

For centuries it has been common learning that the action of trespass *vi et armis* lies only where there is a wrongful invasion of possession. The conception of trespass, so far as it concerns injuries to personal or real property, embodies the

[7] Reg. Brev. Orig. 100 (*de equo interfecto*).

[8] Compare Select Pleas in Manorial Courts (Seld. Soc.), 10: "William, Eve's son, is at his law against R. [to prove] that he did not beat his mare to his damage 5s."

[9] Brooke Abr., *Trespass*, pl. 29.

[1] Brooke Abr., *Trespass*, pl. 421.

[2] Brooke Abr., *Trespass*, pl. 221; Y. B. 1 Hen. VI. 7, pl. 30; Y. B. 11 Hen. IV. 24*b*; 2 Rolle Abr. 569, pls. 3, 6.

[3] Dand *v.* Sexton, 3 T. R. 37; Bull *v.* Colton, 22 Barb. (N. Y.) 94.

idea of the violation of possessory right as well as the idea of forceful damage. Hence if one who has acquired a lawful possession of the property of another does damage to it he is not liable in an action of trespass though the application of force be direct and immediate. If there is any one principle upon which the common law seems to have committed itself fully and unequivocally it is upon this principle that the wrong of trespass is predicated upon the idea of the violation of possessory right. Trespass will not lie unless the right of possession be somehow violated or invaded.

Trespass embodies idea of violation of possession.

Now why should this be true? Is this principle grounded in the very nature of this action of trespass, or is it an artificial and accidental rule? Why cannot trespass be maintained against any one who does violent injury to the property of another, without regard to the question whether the one or the other has the legal possession of the property? Why is not the bailee of chattels or the lessee of land liable in trespass where he forcefully damages the chattels of his bailor or commits waste upon the premises of his landlord? The question is one deserving attention.

Explanation.

The explanation of the rule is to be found, as might be expected, in certain facts of legal history. The action of trespass was in its origin a criminal action, and hence it would not lie for an act which did not constitute a breach of the peace or manifestly tend to a breach of the peace. This was the very ground on which the King's Bench assumed jurisdiction over the wrong. In the light of this idea it is easy to see how the law arrived at the proposition that only those acts which involve a violation of possessory right are trespasses.

Other remedies available for injuries done by force without violation of possession.

It was comparatively easy to reconcile the law with this conclusion, for the reason that there were other remedies which were available for the commonest injuries done by persons who have lawful possession of the property of others. Thus the writ of waste lay against the lessee or tenant who committed waste upon the estate of the lessor or remainderman. Against the bailee who lost or destroyed the chattel committed to his care the bailor had his writ of detinue, and at a later day the action on the case.

Volume III

The principle that the action of trespass is maintainable only against one who violates possession manifests itself in various aspects. In regard to real property we note this consequence, to wit, that if land is in the possession of a lessee or of a tenant, and a stranger does an injury to the premises, the lessee or the tenant is the person who is entitled to maintain trespass against the stranger.[4] The landlord or remainderman must seek redress in some other remedy, such as the action on the case. He cannot maintain trespass, because the tortfeasor has not violated his possession, but that of the tenant. "Only the person who has the possession in fact of the real property to which an injury has been done can maintain an action of trespass *quare clausum.*"[5]

Only one having possession in fact of realty can maintain trespass *quare clausum.*

In the field of personal property the doctrine that trespass lies only at the instance of one whose possessory right is violated manifests itself in the early rule that the action of trespass is available only against the immediate wrongdoer or those who are so connected with the tortious act as to be liable as principals with him. In the case of an asportation of chattels the remedy could not be used against a 'third hand,' that is, against one who got the goods from the original tortfeasor. It made no difference whether such third person claimed as a purchaser from the trespasser or had obtained the property by a second trespass. The principle in question is illustrated in a charge once given by Brian, C. J., and his fellow judges to a jury in these words: "If one takes my horse with force and arms and then gives it to S, or S takes it with force from him

Rule in trespass on personalty.

[4] 2 Rolle Abr. 551 (N); Y. B. 2 Hen. IV. 12, pl. 49; Y. B. 19 Hen. VI. 45, pl. 94.

In the year-book cases just cited there is a dictum to the effect that the action can be maintained not only by the tenant who is disturbed in his possession, but by the owner also, thus subjecting the trespasser to liability in two actions of trespass for the same wrong. But this is shown to be incorrect by other decisions. The owner, if he is out of possession, must sue in case and not in trespass for the wrong done in respect of his right of ownership. Thus a freeholder not having actual possession cannot maintain trespass, nor can an heir before entry; and one who has been disseised cannot without re-entry have trespass against a stranger for any trespass done pending the disseisin. 2 Rolle Abr. 553 (S), pl. 1, 3, 5; Y. B. 19 Hen. VI. 28*b*, pl. 49. Compare Brooke Abr., *Trespass*, pl. 38.

[5] Bac. Abr., *Trespass* (C3).

who took from me, in this case S is no trespasser to me and I shall have no action of trespass against him for such horse, because the possession was out of me by the first taking." [6]

This limitation upon the action of trespass was exceedingly unfortunate, for detinue could not in the early period be maintained by the original owner against a trespasser of any sort. The result was that one who lost his chattels by a trespass had no remedy whatever against one who subsequently acquired them. This defect proved to be highly embarrassing to the common-law theory of ownership, for the absence of remedy naturally led to the inference that the tortious taking stripped the owner not only of possession but of the property, and thereby vested the ownership of the disseised chattel in the tortfeasor. As a result, lawyers got into the habit of ascribing property to tortfeasors and even to thieves.[7] This is well illustrated in a gloss of the digester Brooke on the very passage above quoted from Brian, C. J. The learned judge, it will be observed, said that the first trespasser gained possession by his tortious taking. This proposition is in no way objectionable; but Brooke, reporting that observation in the next century, observes, " for the first offender acquired property by the tort." [8]

Consequence of this doctrine.

Ascription of property to tortfeasor.

Now it was certainly in a measure in conformity with the theory of trespass to hold that the tortfeasor acquired not only the possession but even a sort of property in the goods taken by him; for the remedy contemplates the recovery of damages as the equivalent of their value. But the point here to be noted is this, viz., the property acquired by the trespasser is not the absolute substantive ownership. Property is merely ascribed to him for remedial reasons and for the purpose of holding him liable in damages to the extent of the value of the goods. Consequently this ascription of ownership to the tortfeasor should never have been made elsewhere than in the particular field of trespass.

The distinction, however, was not clear to the early judges,

[6] Y. B. 21 Edw. IV. 74. pl. 6.
[7] 2 Poll. & Mait. Hist. Eng. Law, 2d ed., 168.
[8] Brooke Abr., *Trespass*, pl. 358.

Volume III

Idea that trespasser acquires property retards extension of detinue.

and we therefore find that when the time came for the extension of detinue so as to permit of the use of that remedy against trespassers and those claiming under them, such extension was resisted on the very ground that, as the trespasser acquires the property by his wrongful taking, an action of property is not available to the person injured. The true distinction was seen and stated by Vavisor, J., in 1490, namely, that the tortfeasor gains possession by his trespass, but not the absolute property. Consequently the disseised owner has an election to assert property in himself by bringing detinue, or, on the other hand, by bringing trespass, to treat the trespasser as owner.[9]

Trover also retarded by same notion.

But this view did not at once prevail. The learned Brian was of the contrary opinion, and the extension of detinue that would have followed from the acceptance of the principle stated by Vavisor was effectually blocked. It was only by the invention of trover during the following century that the owner acquired substantially an action *in rem* for the vindication of his property right. But trover had a close affinity to detinue, and so deeply rooted was the notion which had been expressed by Brian that we even find some of the judges resisting the adoption of trover as a remedy against a trespasser.[1] The action of detinue was not used against trespassers until in the nineteenth century; and this extension was accomplished by the use of a fictitious and non-traversable allegation of bailment.[2] Such were some of the fruits of accepting too literally the doctrine that the trespasser acquires title by his tortious taking.

Rule in field of bailment.

The rule denying the right of the owner to bring trespass against the third hand was naturally applied in cases of bailment, for in the theory of the early law the bailee was debtor to the bailor for the chattel, and the bailor had to look to him, and to him only. Thus if I bail goods to B and the latter

[9] Y. B. 6 Hen. VII. 8*b*, pl. 4. Compare the similar observation of Danby, J., in Brooke Abr., *Replevin*, pl. 39.

[1] Bishop *v.* Montague, Cro. Eliz. 824, Cro. Jac. 50.

[2] See *ante*, c. 12, *The Action of Detinue*.

sells or gives them to a stranger, I have no action of trespass against such third party. Chapter XVII

Likewise, originally, the same limitation applied where a stranger acquired possession by a tortious taking from the bailee. This may be explained by saying that the trespass is a wrong against the possession of the bailee, and his possession cannot ordinarily be treated as the possession of the bailor. At an early day, however, the doctrine just stated was so far relaxed as to allow a bailor to bring trespass against one who disseised his bailee. This made the tortfeasor in such case liable to suit at the instance of either bailor or bailee; but it was said that the one who first sued ousted the other of his action.[3]

The making of the concession just indicated resulted in this distinction: If I bail goods to a man and he makes delivery to a vendee or donee, then I shall have no writ of trespass against such person; but if the stranger takes them without such delivery by way of gift or sale, he is a trespasser and I shall have a writ of trespass against him.[4] Trespass allowed against one who disseises bailee.

The right of the bailor to bring trespass against one who invades the possession of his bailee seems to be recognized only in those cases where the possession of the bailee can be considered in some sort the possession of the bailor. This is true in the ordinary bailment at will and in bailments for carriage.[5] It does not apply to pledgors,[6] nor to bailees for a definite term.[7] Limitation on this concession.

As was indicated above, the clue to the origin of the doctrine that there can be no trespass where there is no violation of

[3] Y. B. 48 Edw. III. 20, pl. 8; Brooke Abr., *Trespass*, pl. 67.

In 1482 counsel say: "If I bail to you my goods and another takes them out of your possession, I shall have good action of trespass *quare vi et armis.*" Y. B. 22 Edw. IV. 5, pl. 16.

[4] Note by Fineux, C. J., and Tremayle, J., Y. B. 21 Hen. VII. 39, pl. 49; also Y. B. 16 Hen. VII. 3. pl. 7.

[5] "The carrier is considered in law as the servant of the owner, and the possession of the servant is the possession of the master." Buller, J., in Ward *v.* Macauley, 4 T. R. 489.

[6] Y. B. 10 Hen. VI. 25, pl. 86 (incorrectly numbered 16 in Maynard).

[7] Ward *v.* Macauley, 4 T. R. 489.

Volume III

possession is found in the criminal character of the early action of trespass. Now it will be noted that in the course of ages the action of trespass has lost its criminal character and has become, like the other personal remedies, simply an action for the recovery of civil damages. It would appear that with this change in the character of the remedy, the theory of the action might well have been so far changed as to permit of its use against all tortfeasors who do damage to the person or property of another by means of the immediate or direct application of violence.

Doctrine that trespass lies only where possession is violated maintains in modern law.

But here the principle of parsimony comes into operation and prevents the extension of doctrine. If the question were raised, the law, it would be said, gives other remedies to those whose property is damaged by force under conditions where possession is not violated, and hence trespass is restricted to its original bounds. But the artificial nature of the limitation in modern times at least is manifest. Clearly we are here confronted with a principle which, though it originated in social and legal conditions long since passed, has nevertheless contrived by one means or another to retain a hold on life. Tradition and history have at this point plainly triumphed over any impulse of innovation that may have manifested itself.

As might be expected in the history of a rule thus derived and retained, the principle embodied in it has not always been consistently applied. At certain points considerations of policy and convenience have operated to impeach the rule or limit its application. The doctrine concerning the breaking of bulk is clearly an instance of this.

Larceny and trespass.

It is a principle of the criminal law that a man cannot be guilty of the larceny of goods unless the alleged criminal act of taking involves a trespass.[8] The well-known case from 1473 illustrates this point. It appeared that one A had employed B to transport certain bales of goods to Southampton. The bailee, B, took the goods to another destination and converted them to his own use. B was thereupon prosecuted for

[8] 2 Bish. New Crim. Law, §§ 799, 835.

larceny. It was held that the taking was not felonious.[9] Said Brian, C. J.: "Where one has possession from the party by bailment and delivery lawfully, it cannot thereafter be called felony nor trespass, for no felony can be but with violence and *vi et armis,* and what he himself has he cannot take with *vi et armis* nor against the peace. Therefore it cannot be felony nor trespass, for he may not have any other action for these goods but the action of detinue."

Breaking of bulk by bailee involves trespass.

In the same case Choke, J., drew a distinction, to wit, that where the bailee converts the entire subject of the bailment he cannot be held for a larceny, but that if he breaks the bulk and takes out a part only, he is guilty. This idea has been accepted in modern times, with the consequence that while it is no offense for a bailee to steal the entire parcel committed to his care, it is a larceny for him to break bulk and steal only a part.[1]

Explanation.

This exceptional doctrine, whereby the bailee is held to be a trespasser and therefore a thief when he breaks the bulk and takes out part but not when he disposes of the whole bailment, is generally explained by saying that the breaking of bulk is a violation of the contract of bailment and terminates the relation of bailor and bailee. This leaves the bailee a naked trespasser. The artificial nature of the explanation is obvious.

The true import of the matter in question is apparently this: The principle that there must be a violation of possession in order that there may be a trespass is really no longer a vital principle, and in permitting the bailee to be held liable for larceny when he breaks bulk and appropriates a part of the goods, the law shows a natural tendency to break away from that principle. But the breaking away from the old doctrine is only partial.

In the law of real property we find evidence of a similar tendency to break away from the rule that there must be a violation of possession before there can be a trespass. This is found in the proposition that the action of trespass can be maintained against a tenant at will who commits voluntary waste.

[9] Y. B. 13 Edw. IV. 9, pl. 5.

[1] Robinson *v.* State, 1 Coldw. (Tenn.) 120, 78 Am. Dec. 487; State *v.* Fairclough, 29 Conn. 47.

Volume III

Voluntary waste by lessee involves a trespass.

The doctrine is stated in *Shrewsbury's Case* (1600),[2] in these words: "If a lessee at will commits voluntary waste, *scil.*, in abatement of the houses, or in cutting of the woods, there is a general action of trespass lies against him; for . . . when tenant at will takes upon him to do such things which none can do but the owner of the land, these amount to the determination of the will, and of his possession, and the lessor shall have a general action of trespass without any entry."

Doctrine of trespass *ab initio*.

The peculiar doctrine of trespass *ab initio* also represents a distinct breaking away from the idea that violation of possession is essential to the maintenance of the action of trespass. The principle underlying this branch of the law was first clearly enunciated in the *Six Carpenters Case* (1610).[3] Here it was held that wherever one person, by reason of an authority vested in him by the law, acquires a lawful possession of the chattels of another or enters lawfully upon the premises of another, an abuse of that authority will make such person liable, as a trespasser *ab initio*, for all the damage which he does. Illustrations of the operation of this rule have been given elsewhere.[4] It applies, it will be observed, only in those cases where there is an abuse of authority conferred by law, and it has no application in cases where the authority abused has been conferred by an individual.

The doctrine of trespass *ab initio*, wherever applicable, effectually impeaches the principle that trespass will not lie unless the plaintiff can show a violation of his possession by the tortfeasor. But the fact that it does not violate this principle has been obscured by the resort to an artificial presumption of intent.[5]

The true explanation of the doctrine of trespass *ab initio* is apparently to be found in considerations of policy and convenience. It appeared to the early judges that the power which under one condition or another the law bestows upon

[2] 5 Coke 13*b*.

[3] 8 Coke 146.

[4] See vol. 1, p. 46.

[5] "The reason of this difference is that in the case of a general authority or license of law, the law adjudges, by the subsequent act, *quo animo*, or to what intent, he entered; for *acta exteriora indicant interiora secreta*." Six Carpenters Case, 8 Coke 146*a*.

Chapter XVII

one individual to seize the chattels or invade the premises of another is a power that is capable of resulting in great hardship where it is abused. Therefore it was highly expedient that the law should furnish a quick and even punitory remedy to one who is injured by an act which is done under the color of legal authority but which nevertheless is not within the purview of that authority. For this reason the action of trespass was sanctioned by the courts. The only objection to the use of this remedy was found in the principle that trespass lies only where there is a trespassory invasion of possession. But, as we have seen, this rule was a mere accident of legal history and was based upon an idea that long ago ceased to have any real ground for its support. As a result, the extension of trespass into the field of wrong, indicated by the expression 'abuse of authority conferred by law,' was comparatively easy. The step taken was in a measure made plausible by the false ground upon which it was justified. The episode well illustrates the manner in which "a slight preponderance of feeling rather than of articulate reason" can operate to obtain recognition for legal principle.[6]

Basis of doctrine of trespass *ab initio*.

It will be observed that the only effect of the doctrine of trespass *ab initio* is to enable the person injured by an abuse of legal authority to maintain the action of trespass against the tortfeasor. If this concession had not been made, the per-

Doctrine involves question of remedial law only.

[6] Matthew Bacon, in his explanation of the doctrine of trespass *ab initio*, substantially puts the rule on the ground of legal policy. Says he: "Where the law has given an authority it seems reasonable that the law should, in order to secure such persons as are the objects thereof from abuse of the authority, when it is abused, make everything done void, and leave the abuser in the same situation as if he had done everything without any authority. And this agrees with the maxim *actus legis nemini facit injuriam*. In the other case, where a man, who was under no necessity of giving an authority to any person, has thought proper to give an authority to any person, and this person is guilty of an abuse of the authority, there is no reason that the law should interpose, so as to make everything done under it void; because it was his own folly to trust a person with an authority who has shown himself not fit to be trusted therewith. The interposition of the law in such case would, moreover, be contrary to the maxim, *vigilantibus non dormientibus servit lex*." 9 Bac. Abr. 451. This explanation is commended in Allen *v.* Crofoot, 5 Wend. (N. Y.) 506.

Volume III

son injured would have been compelled to resort to the action on the case. The doctrine of trespass *ab initio* consequently does not result in the creation of liability where otherwise none would exist, but merely sanctions the use of the remedy of trespass in situations where otherwise the plaintiff would use case.

Finder treated as trespasser *ab initio.*

The doctrine of trespass *ab initio* was at one time thought to be applicable to the case of a finder of lost goods who refused upon demand to surrender possession to the rightful owner. Thus in 1455, Prisot, C. J., said that if one lost chattels and another found them, the finder could be sued in trespass if, upon demand, he refused to deliver; "for by the finding he does no wrong, but now the wrong commences by the detention when the owner is known."[7] But the development of the modern action of trover made it unnecessary to press the doctrine of trespass *ab initio* to the extent indicated in this remark of the learned judge.[8]

[7] Y. B. 33 Hen. VI. 26, pl. 12.
[8] Bishop *v.* Montague, Cro. Eliz. 824, Cro. Jac. 50.

CHAPTER XVIII

THE ACTION OF TRESPASS ON THE CASE.

WE now come to consider the great residuary remedy of trespass on the case or the action on the case. To be entirely accurate and precise we must distinguish between trespass on the case and the general action on the case. Trespass on the case, we should say, is that form of the action on the case which is strictly *in consimili casu* with the action of trespass. It is used to redress wrongs which are analogous to the wrong of trespass, but which yet are not identical with the trespass. The general action on the case, on the other hand, is used to redress wrongs in general which have no resemblance to the trespass whatever.

Chapter XVIII

Distinction between special action of trespass on the case and the broad action on the case.

The distinction here drawn can be made clear by reference to the categories of wrong established in the first volume of this treatise. The action of trespass is the proper and normal remedy in which redress is to be sought for all wrongs which fall within the primary formation of trespass, such as assault and battery, trespass upon realty, and all direct injuries to person or property.

The action of trespass on the case is the proper and normal remedy for all wrongs which fall within the secondary trespass formation. These, as we have seen, are wrongs in which liability is based on the idea of responsibility for independent agents of harm, and their affinity to wrongs of the primary trespass formation is revealed in the circumstance that here, as in trespass proper, the harm element commonly manifests itself in forceful injury to person or property.

Trespass on the case normal remedy in field of secondary trespass.

The broad action on the case is used to redress injuries which do not fall within either of the two trespass formations. This remedy is available, for instance, to obtain redress for an actionable slander or for a libel, wrongs which, as will readily

Where case in general lies.

Volume III

be seen, have hardly any sort of affinity whatever for the true common-law trespass.

We are bound to add that the authorities do not make the explicit distinction which is here drawn between trespass on the case and the general action on the case, and in the books the expressions 'trespass on the case' and 'action on the case,' or simply 'case,' are used interchangeably. The propriety of the distinction cannot, however, be doubted; neither can there be any doubt that the authorities themselves point to the distinction in that vague and obscure way which is indicative of inadequate analysis. In truth, if we push analysis far enough we shall perceive that under this head of trespass on the case, or action on the case, have been grouped together a number of really different remedies which have only the feature in common that they are all derived by an identical process of extension from the several distinct common-law remedies. Just as there is a specific action on the case in the nature of trespass (trespass on the case), so there are such specific actions as the action on the case in the nature of deceit, the action on the case in the nature of waste, the action on the case in the nature of nuisance, the action on the case in the nature of detinue (trover). And in addition to these specific forms of case there is, as was indicated above, the general residuary action which lies to recover redress for wrongs for which no specific remedy existed. In the succeeding pages we shall attempt to portray the process by which the principle of growth which is embodied in the action on the case has manifested itself in the development of legal principle.

Case a general head for several specific remedies.

The various actions on the case are formless actions based directly on legal duty. In conformity with common modes of speech we should speak in the singular, and say that the action on the case is a formless action based directly on legal duty. As indicated above, it is the great residuary remedy in the field of tort, just as indebitatus assumpsit is the residuary remedy in the field of contract. Wherever the law upon a particular state of facts imposes a pure legal duty, as distin-

Case a formless action.

Chapter XVIII

guished from a contractual duty, the action on the case lies to enforce that duty or to recover damages for its breach provided no other form of action is available. Accordingly we may say that case lies to recover damage incurred by reason of any act done, or permitted, or omitted to be done, contrary to the obligation of the law. "In all cases where a man has a temporal loss or damage by the wrong of another, he may have an action upon the case to be repaired in damages."[1]

Lies for any act or omission contrary to law.

In the evolution of the common-law remedies the action on the case has served to keep remedy measurably abreast with the expanding conception of right, and to the existence of this remedy is largely to be attributed whatever truth is to be found in the ancient legal maxim *ubi jus ibi remedium*. Inasmuch as the action on the case is a formless action and is founded directly on legal duty, an attempt to assign limits to its scope would be as vain as an attempt to define the limits of legal liability. The limits of legal liability are being constantly extended with the growth of society, and as long as there exists any sort of equilibrium between substantive and remedial law the scope of the action on the case must be likewise extended.

Principle of growth embodied in action on the case.

From a practical standpoint the importance of the remedy may be appreciated when we observe that it is the action by which the greater number of legal rights in the field of tort have been vindicated. A glance at the most prominent heads in this branch of the law will show the truth of this statement.

Importance of the action.

[1] Com. Dig., *Action upon the Case* (A).

"Where from a given state of facts the law raises a legal obligation to do a particular act, and there is a breach of that obligation, and a consequential damage, there . . . an action on the case founded in tort is the more proper form of action, in which the plaintiff in his declaration states the facts out of which the legal obligation arises, the obligation itself, the breach of it, and the damage resulting from that breach." Littledale, J., in Burnett *v.* Lynch, 5 B. & C. 609, 12 E. C. L. 335, 8 Dowl. & R. 381.

Conversely, it is said that the action on the case will not lie where there is no legal liability, a proposition which is in the nature of a truism. Thus, where a defendant refused to administer the sacrament, Clovell *v.* Cardinall, 1 Sid. 34; or to read divine service, 5 Coke 73*a*; the action on the case, it was held, could not be maintained, for no legal right had been infringed. Nor would it lie for a legacy due only by the spiritual law. Nicholson *v.* Shirman, 1 Sid. 46.

Volume III

Thus the wrongs which are grouped under such titles as Negligence, Fraud, Malice, Slander and Libel, Slander of Title, Waste, Conversion, Conspiracy, Nuisance, Escape of Dangerous Things, are all redressed by the action on the case in some form or other.

In the general part of this volume we have given a brief sketch of the origin of the common-law actions, and have directed attention to the power of the English chancery, during the formative period of our law, to issue new writs (*brevia magistralia*) upon new cases from time to time arising where no existing writ (*brevium formatum*) was applicable to particular states of facts. This power was originally vested in

Issuance of new writs in case.

the chancery in the exercise of the inherent prerogative of the king. We have also seen how in the thirteenth century political and social conditions, as well as the actual state of the law itself, all concurred in causing the exercise of this power of the chancery to become less and less common. As the field covered by the *brevia formata* was extended, the occasions for framing magisterial writs became fewer; and as it became more and more apparent that the granting of new writs operated to create new legal rights, it was recognized that the power of issuing them was one which ought to be exercised, if at all, only under the supervision of Parliament.

The chancery thus came to be more and more a mere clerical department, and as soon as Edward I contrived to get legislative machinery into a working condition it was thought well to stimulate rather than to curtail the ancient power of chancery to issue new writs. This was cautiously done by

Statute of Westminster II.

Statute of Westminster II (1285).[2] The important general clause at the close of that statute is in the following language: "Whenever from henceforth it shall happen in the chancery that in one case a writ is found, and in like case falling under like law and requiring like remedy no writ is found, the clerks of the chancery shall agree in framing the writ, or the plaintiff may adjourn it until the next Parliament; and the cases in which they cannot agree shall be reduced to writing and re-

[2] Chapter 24.

ferred to the next Parliament, and there by consent of men learned in the law writs shall be framed, lest in the future the king's court should fail in administering justice to complainants."

Chapter XVIII

From this language it is clear that the power of creating entirely new legal remedies had now definitely and finally passed to the Parliament. In so far as the statute recognized the right of the chancery to frame writs for cases slightly different from others, but within their principle, it was declaratory of common law; but as this enactment shows, the chancery was becoming conservative and the power in question needed stimulation.

Power of issuing new writs vests in Parliament.

The general clause above quoted, authorizing writs *in consimili casu,* followed an enumeration of certain specific instances in which writs were specifically directed to be issued. Consequently this clause was for a time construed, under the rule *ejusdem generis,* to apply only to cases like those expressly enumerated. A good illustration of what was considered at that time as being a similar case within the meaning of the act is found in the writ granted to a reversioner to recover possession from one to whom the tenant in curtesy had aliened. The Statute of Gloucester (1278)[3] had directed the issuance of a writ for the heir or reversioner to recover lands alienated by the tenant in dower. This was known as the writ of entry *in casu proviso.*[4] And now after the enactment of Westminster II the situation of the reversioner of the tenant by curtesy was looked upon as being analogous to that of the heir or reversioner of the tenant in dower, and a writ on the case was consequently granted to him under the authority of this statute.[5]

Writs in like case.

Illustration.

It was about a hundred years before the common law began to feel the full effect of the important provision in the Statute of Westminster II, which authorized the issuance of writs *in consimili casu* with the established forms. The action of trespass was one of the first and one of the most important actions

Appearance of various actions on the case.

[3] Chapter 7.

[4] 2 Co. Inst. 310, note (5).

[5] 2 Reeves, Hist. Eng. Law, Am. ed., 510.

Volume III

to feel its stimulus. But trespass was by no means the only remedy to show the results of this influence.

Trespass on the case.

Deceit on the case.

From the old common-law action of deceit was developed deceit on the case, or an action on the case in the nature of deceit, which was of much wider scope than the older remedy and altogether supplanted it. The name of the old action of deceit was, however, retained and applied to the broader action. Deceit thus acquired a greatly extended scope. It was here that the action of assumpsit had its origin. From the ancient common-law action of detinue, trover was developed in somewhat the same way, for trover, historically, is merely an action on the case in the nature of an action of detinue.

Trover.

Again, there are instances where writs on the facts of the case were framed for the enforcement of rights that had found no previous recognition in the king's courts and which, strictly speaking, bore little or no analogy whatever to the rights protected by the older actions. The best illustration of this is found in the action on the case for slanderous words. The king's court in the time of Bracton, and indeed for a long period thereafter, gave no remedy for defamation.[6] The first instance of an action for slanderous words comes from the middle of the fourteenth century.[7] It may seem curious that a wrong of such frequent occurrence as slander should be so late in finding recognition in the higher tribunals, but this is explained by the fact that the local courts and the ecclesiastical tribunals had from an early day punished offenses of this kind. It was therefore rather late before the common-law courts began to sanction the action on the case for words. When the action was recognized it was, as must be admitted, a remedy that had little analogy to any existing writ. In such situations as this we come into contact with the action on the case in its most general form.

Action for slander.

No real analogy to any existing writ.

One of the earliest instances where the action of trespass on the case was maintained is found in a suit against a ferryman who undertook to transfer the plaintiff's horse across the

[6] 2 Poll. & Mait. Hist. Eng. Law, 2d ed., 537.
[7] Y. B. 30 Ass. 177, pl. 19.

Chapter XVIII

river Humber. It was alleged that he had overloaded the boat and that the animal was thereby drowned.[8] The action was sustained on the idea that there was a misfeasance on the part of the defendant in the performance of a lawful undertaking, to wit, in his improperly overloading the boat, and that he was liable for the consequences of this misfeasance. The action was in substance based on the defendant's negligence. Actions of this kind mark the advent of the action on the case, for it will be perceived that the wrong here complained of clearly falls short of the wrong of trespass, inasmuch as the defendant did not directly compass the drowning of the plaintiff's animal, and furthermore he did not violate the plaintiff's possession.

Early instance of trespass on the case.

Negligent misfeasance.

Other early instances of the use of the action of trespass on the case are found in an action against a surgeon who treated a plaintiff's arm with such lack of skill as to cause him to be permanently maimed;[9] against a veterinarian for the unskilful treatment of the plaintiff's horse;[1] and against a barber for the negligent shaving of the plaintiff with an unwholesome razor.[2]

Among early instances of the use of the action on the case as a general remedy for violation of legal duty may be noted the following: The action could be maintained against a sheriff for quashing the plaintiff's essoin in a plea of replevin without the assent of the suitor;[3] against a slanderer for calling the plaintiff a traitor, felon, and robber;[4] against an escheator for a false return;[5] against a clerk for negligent failure to enter a *nisi prius* record;[6] against one who by the negligent keeping of fire caused his neighbor's house to be burned;[7] against a common victualer or innkeeper who refused to feed or lodge the wayfarer;[8] and against the keeper

Early instances of case in broadest form.

[8] (1348) Y. B. 22 Ass. 94, pl. 41.

[9] Y. B. 48 Edw. III. 6, pl. 11.

[1] Y. B. 19 Hen. VI. 49, pl. 5; Powtuary *v.* Walton, 1 Rolle Abr. 10, pl. 5.

[2] Rastell Entries 2*b*, 1.

[3] Y. B. 26 Ass. 129, pl. 46.

[4] Y. B. 30 Ass. 177, pl. 19.

[5] Y. B. 9 Hen. VI. 60, pl. 9.

[6] Y. B. 34 Hen. VI. 4, pl. 12.

[7] Y. B. 28 Hen. VI. 7, pl. 7.

[8] Y. B. 39 Hen. VI. 18, pl. 24.

of a dog known to be addicted to the killing of sheep, where the neighbor's flock suffers from its depredations.[0] The action against the vendor of chattels upon a false warranty of title[1] may be noted as supplying an instance of an action on the case in the nature of the ancient action of deceit.

Reference to the heading of Action on the Case (*Accion sur Case*) in the abridgments of Fitzherbert and Brooke, and to the tables of the year books, will show that by the middle of the fifteenth century this action was one of the most frequently used of all common-law remedies.

Frequent use of the action.

In regard to its substance it may be observed that the writ in actions on the case contains merely a recital of the facts which constitute the basis of the action. This recital is substantially repeated or perhaps abridged in the declaration. It is of course from the circumstance that the simple facts of the case are thus set forth in the pleading, that the action derives its name. The action on the case is a formless action based on the particular facts of the case.[2]

The contents of declaration in case.

Trespass and Trespass on the Case.

Let us now direct our attention for a few moments to the matter of the distinction between the action of trespass and the action of trespass on the case, in their adaptation to the end of redressing wrongs which fall within the primary and secondary trespass formations.

In *Reynolds v. Clarke* (1725),[3] this illustration was put by Fortescue, J.: "If a man throws a log into the highway and in that act hits me, I may maintain trespass, because it is an immediate wrong; but if as it lies there I tumble over it and receive an injury, I must bring an action upon the case, because it is only prejudicial in consequence." In the same case Chief Justice Raymond observed: "The distinction in law is, where the immediate act itself occasions a prejudice, or is an injury to the plaintiff's person, house, land, etc., and

The immediate and the consequential injury.

[0] Y. B. 28 Hen. VI. 7, pl. 7.

[1] Y. B. 42 Ass. 259, pl. 8.

[2] Com. Dig., *Action upon Case* (C 2).

[3] 1 Stra. 636.

where the act itself is not an injury, but a consequence from that act is prejudicial to the plaintiff's person, house, land, etc. In the first case trespass *vi et armis* will lie; in the last it will not, but the plaintiff's proper remedy is by an action on the case."[4]

Chapter XVIII

In conformity with the foregoing language the doctrine is generally stated to be that where the damage which results from a particular act is direct or immediate, trespass is the proper remedy, but that if the damage is of a consequential nature the action on the case must be used. In *Day v. Edwards* (1794),[5] Lord Kenyon said that the distinction between trespass and case is perfectly clear; that if the injury be committed by the immediate act complained of, the remedy is trespass; but if the injury be merely consequential upon that act, case is the proper remedy.

When trespass and trespass on the case respectively maintainable.

As a mere matter of words this statement is sufficiently precise, and superficially it might appear that this distinction, founded on the nature of the damage and its degree of remoteness from the wrongful act, would be of very simple and easy application. But appearances are here deceptive, and as a matter of actual experience hardly any problem has proved more difficult to solve. In truth, this distinction between 'direct' and 'consequential' damage considered in and of itself is specious and misleading. All actions are brought rather for the consequences of acts than for acts themselves, and some actions of trespass, as has been observed, are for consequences more remote from the defendant's act than in other instances where the remedy would be by the action on the case.[6]

Distinction between direct and consequential damage difficult of application.

But however illusory the distinction between direct and consequential damage may appear to be as a criterion of the applicability of the respective actions of trespass and case, a certain important truth lurks in this distinction. That truth is this, namely, that the action of trespass is the normal remedy

[4] Reynolds v. Clarke, 2 Ld. Raym. 1402. Compare Howard v. Bankes, 2 Burr. 1114; Harker v. Birkbeck, 3 Burr. 1559.

[5] 5 T. R. 648.

[6] Holmes, Common Law 91.

Volume III

Trespass normal remedy in primary trespass. Trespass on the case normal remedy in secondary trespass.

for torts which come within the conception of primary trespass, while trespass on the case is the normal remedy for torts which fall within the category of secondary trespass. That is to say, wherever a man is to be held liable for the immediate consequences of his own forceful acts the action of trespass must be brought, but wherever he is to be held responsible for harms done by independent agents, case is the proper remedy. In this idea of responsibility for independent agents, and in this idea alone, do we find the true clue to the meaning of that mysterious and baffling term 'consequential damage' which is so often used in the law books. Taken with this explanation and in this light, the import of the respective terms 'direct' and 'consequential' is intelligible and the distinction in question is instructive enough. The distinction is not so much one between the proximity and the remoteness of the damage as it is a distinction between the respective conceptions of liability which underlie the two types of wrong.

Principle not always consistently applied.

It cannot be pretended that the courts have consistently applied the principle that trespass is the proper remedy in primary trespass and case the proper remedy in the field of secondary trespass. But for this matter there is apparently no principle in the law of actions which has been applied consistently throughout. The actions have rightly been looked upon as instruments for the effectuation of justice and not as ends in themselves. There can be no doubt, however, that the distinction which we have pointed out, whereby the action of trespass is identified with wrongs of primary trespass, and trespass on the case is identified with wrongs of secondary trespass, embodies the true principle which has struggled for utterance throughout the entire history of the evolution of the common-law actions. It has been rather obscured than made clear by the distinction between direct and consequential damage. There was just enough truth in this latter distinction to cause the courts to cling to it even after they had been baffled in the effort to apply it.

The failure of lawyers and judges to generalize wrongs in which the harm element manifests itself in physical hurt or in damage to property, under some such distinct heads as primary and secondary trespass, has been a fruitful source of trouble. If the fundamental idea on which the classification is founded, that is, the distinction between liability for one's own acts and responsibility for the acts of independent agents, had once been fully and clearly grasped, most of the difficulty which was encountered in distinguishing the situations where the respective actions of trespass and case are applicable would have disappeared. But legal theory was not sufficiently mature to enable the legal mind to penetrate the mist. If by any fortunate chance in the formative period of the common law a distinct writ had gotten into the Register, adapted to the end of enforcing reparation for damage in cases where the idea of responsibility comes into operation, legal evolution would have gone right, and the distinction between torts attributable to the defendant in person and torts of responsibility would have been clearly perceived as a matter of course. But this did not happen. There was no nominate writ for torts of responsibility. The action of trespass or an action on the case in the nature of trespass consequently had to be used to recover the damage where the wrong was founded on the idea of responsibility. Hence followed that fatal confusion between trespass and trespass on the case, as applicable especially to the redress of wrongs of the first and second trespass formations, which is visible in the pages of the Register and which gave more or less trouble until our own day.

Chapter XVIII

Obscurity due to failure to recognize existence of secondary trespass formation.

No common-law writ for torts founded solely on idea of responsibility.

Let us now consider a few of the cases in which the courts have dealt with this question of the limits of trespass and trespass on the case as regards wrongs of the first and second trespass formations. In *Preston v. Mercer* (1656)[7] the plaintiff declared in trespass, and for cause of action showed that the defendant had dumped a quantity of dirt and filth so near to the walls of the plaintiff's dwelling house in Bishopsgate that the said walls became rotten, wasted, and broken; and also that the defendant did cause and make filthy water to

Preston v. Mercer.

[7] Hardres, 60.

run into the plaintiff's message, which water did pierce the walls of the plaintiff's dwelling and percolate into his cellar, to the plaintiff's damage. After judgment for the plaintiff it was moved in arrest that trespass would not lie upon the state of facts shown in this declaration.

The point was undoubtedly well taken. The judges seemed to be of opinion against the plaintiff and advised the parties to agree. Thereupon the matter was referred to arbitrament, but the reference proved ineffectual. Finally, "after great wavering in opinion and arguings *pro* and *con,*" judgment was allowed to stand against the defendant. The court here evidently strained principle somewhat in order to sustain the judgment. The cause of action was evidently based on the idea of the defendant's responsibility for the consequences of harmful agents. But the point was somewhat doubtful after all, and later Lord Raymond explained the decision by saying that the allegation that the defendant made the water to run was the same in effect as if it had been said that the defendant poured the water upon the plaintiff's premises.[8] This is certainly a rather strained inference, but it brings the tort within the conception of primary trespass and rationalizes the decision.

Improper use of trespass.

In *Reynolds v. Clarke* (1725),[9] an action of trespass was brought under these circumstances: The plaintiff was owner of a certain messuage and the defendant was the occupier of adjacent premises. The defendant had a right under the terms of his deed to have the rain, which fell from his eaves upon the land of the plaintiff, carried off over the said land; but it did not appear that the defendant had a right to collect his water and turn it on the plaintiff's land in a body. The defendant did, however, put up gutters and a spout by means of which in time of rain the water was turned upon the premises of the plaintiff in a considerable stream and damage was done. No actual trespass was done by the defendant in the act of putting up the gutters or the spout. It was held unani-

Turning water on land of neighbor.

[8] Reynolds *v.* Clarke, 2 Ld. Raym. 1403.

[9] 2 Ld. Raym. 1399, 1 Stra. 634, 8 Mod. 272.

mously by the judges that the action on the case was the only remedy here available. Raymond, C. J., cited as authority the case of *Loveridge v. Hoskins,* in which it had lately been held by Chief Justice Holt that if a man digs ditches on his own land whereby quantities of water are discharged upon the land of a neighbor, trespass will not lie, but case only. It was in this case of *Reynolds v. Clarke* that Fortescue, J., put the very apt illustration concerning the placing of a log in the highway, which has been already quoted.

The question of the limits of trespass and case was much stirred in the oft-cited decision of *Scott v. Shepherd* (1772),[1] but it may be doubted whether much light was shed upon the subject by the opinions of the several judges in this case. It appeared that a lighted squib had been tossed by the defendant into a market house. It alighted upon the stall of one A, and a bystander, in order to avert the threatened danger, took up the squib and tossed it across the market house. Another person near whom it fell likewise threw it in another direction. Thereupon the squib exploded and put out one of the plaintiff's eyes. An action of trespass was brought against the person who first threw the mischievous agent, and the action was sustained. Sir William Blackstone, who happened to be a member of the court, dissented, being of the opinion that case only would lie upon the facts stated.

The squib case.

It will be noted that the question raised in this case was purely one of remedy. The defendant was clearly guilty of a tort and could be held in one form of action or the other. He was either liable because he had directly occasioned a hurt by his own act, or he was liable because responsible for the harm done by the mischievous agent which he had set going. Now which view is the right one to take on the facts of this case? Does this wrong fall within the category of trespass proper or does it come under the head of secondary trespass? Upon the answer to this depends the solution of the problem concerning the matter of remedy.

Nature of the problem involved.

But to the judges who had to decide the case the problem

[1] 2 W. Bl. 892, 3 Wils. C. Pl. 403.

Volume III

was not presented in this simple form. The distinction between liability for one's own immediate acts and responsibility for the acts of independent agents, which seems to the present writer to be so fundamental and important, was not in their minds. On the contrary, they had to approach the problem by the way of the crude distinction between the direct and consequential, between the immediate and mediate. It cannot be surprising that under such conditions the judges should incline to support the form of action which had actually been adopted by the plaintiff. Blackstone's judicial instinct caused him to rebel at this, and he stoutly maintained that trespass would not lie. The reasoning by which the learned judge supported this conclusion cannot be said to be satisfactory. His argument was built of very rickety material.

Remedy for direct and immediate injury negligently done.

The action of trespass on the case has always been considered the proper remedy where the action is grounded solely upon negligence.[2] This is as it should normally be, for the normal tort in which liability is founded exclusively upon negligence is a secondary trespass. But as we have elsewhere learned, negligence is a factor which often figures in wrongs of primary trespass. The typical case is that in which hurt or damage results from the negligent driving of a vehicle.

The first thought of the common-law judges on the question of the remedy for such a tort is indicated in *Day v. Edwards* (1794),[3] where it was alleged that the defendant negligently drove his cart furiously along the highway, in consequence of which the plaintiff's landaulet was struck and damaged. An action on the case was brought to recover the damage. It was held that this was not the proper remedy.[4]

[2] 1 Rolle Abr. 1–4; 1 Com. Dig., *Action upon the Case for Misfeasance*, also *Action upon the Case for Negligence.*

[3] 5 T. R. 648.

[4] Tripe *v.* Potter (1767) was cited by Espinasse, in Savignac *v.* Roome, 6 T. R. 128, as authority on the same point. The plaintiffs in an action on the case alleged that they were fishermen and had thrown out their net in a certain part of the sea for the purpose of catching fish. Thereupon the defendant wilfully and maliciously rowed his boat into and against the net and sank it, to the plaintiffs' damage. Yates, J., at the assizes held that trespass and not case was the proper remedy.

Trespass and trespass only would lie, so it was held, because the injury was directly and immediately done.

Chapter XVIII

In *Leame v. Bray* (1803),[5] the same idea was consistently applied in a ruling to the effect that where a man drives on the highway on a dark night and negligently gets on the wrong side, whereby a collision occurs, the action of trespass is the proper remedy.[6]

Trespass lies for negligent injury directly done.

It must be confessed that if the technical distinction between trespass and case was to be strictly maintained these decisions were in conformity with principle, since the wrongs complained of in these cases were clearly referable to the head of primary trespass.

But it was neither necessary nor desirable that the distinction between the remedies should be closely observed. Remedial law is only a means to an end, and it is highly desirable that the actions should have a certain amount of flexibility. In the complications of life the combinations of fact out of which it is possible for legal liability to arise are infinite, and no system of remedial law based on form could be devised in which every action would be so nicely discriminated as to prevent all danger of confusion. Cases inevitably arise in which the lawyer who has to institute proceedings must have his doubts as to the proper remedy, and hence mistakes arise. It is but natural that under these conditions the courts should show a disposition to sustain, so far as possible, the particular action which is in fact chosen. It would not be creditable either to the law or to the judges if litigants with good causes of action should be dismissed on technical and frivolous pretexts.

Technical limits of actions not to be strictly observed.

It cannot therefore be considered surprising that the action on the case for negligence should in time be sanctioned as a concurrent remedy with trespass in all cases where the negligent act which results in damage involves an actual trespass. A disturbing factor which contributed to unsettle the rule laid

[5] 3 East 593.

[6] Compare Taylor *v.* Rainbow (1808), 2 Hen. & M. (Va.) 123, where it was held that whe a man negligently discharges a gun in a public place, one who is hurt thereby can recover only in an action of trespass.

Volume III

down in *Day v. Edwards*, that only trespass will lie where damage is directly and negligently done, is found in that class of cases where the injurious act is done by the servant of the person who is sought to be held liable. What form of action should be used against the master to recover for damage done by the negligence of his servant?

In *Jones v. Hart* (1698),[7] Holt, C. J., used this language: "If the servants of A with his cart run against another cart, wherein is a pipe of wine, and overturn the cart and spoil the wine, an action lieth against A. So where a carter's servant runs his cart over a boy, action lies against the master for the damage done by this negligence. And so it is if a smith's man pricks a hole in shoeing, the master is liable; for whoever employs another is answerable for him, and undertakes for his care to all that make use of him. The act of a servant is the act of his master, where he acts by authority of the master."

Master liable in case for negligent act of servant,

Confessedly so. The master is responsible for the negligent act of his servant done in the course of his employment; and the remedy is by the action on the case.[8] Trespass does not lie against the master for the negligent act of his servant, because the liability of the master is here founded upon the idea of responsibility. The direct act of the servant cannot be treated as the direct act of the master. This idea was expressed by Parke, B., in *Sharrod v. London, etc., R. Co.* (1849),[9] thus: "The maxim *qui facit per alium facit per se* renders the master liable for all the negligent acts of the servant in the course of his employment; but that liability does not make the direct act of the servant the direct act of the master."

because liability results from principle of responsibility.

Such is undoubtedly the general principle. The master is liable in case, and not in trespass, for the negligent act of his servant.[1] But it is to be noted that this rule does not apply where a servant acts with due care in carrying out the express commands of his master. Here the servant becomes, as it were, the passive instrument for registering his master's will,

Distinctions.

[7] Holt K. B. 642, 2 Salk. 441; Anonymous, 1 Ld. Raym. 739.

[8] Barnes *v.* Hurd, 11 Mass. 57.

[9] 4 Exch. 585.

[1] Morley *v.* Gaisford, 2 H. Bl. 442.

Chapter XVIII

and what he thus does in carrying out this will of his master is really as much the act of his master as if done by the latter's own hand. In this case if the act of the servant constitutes a trespass in fact, trespass will lie against the master. Thus if a servant is commanded to enter the close of another and he does so, this is a trespass as against the master who ordered the act to be done.

The commanded act.

The same is true where the servant is ordered to do an act which naturally and foreseeably might be expected to lead to the commission of a trespass though the trespass itself is not specifically authorized, but on the contrary is prohibited to be done. Here if the servant undertakes to carry out the master's order, and acting with ordinary care commits a trespass, the master must be taken to have commanded it, since he ordered something to be done which naturally involved the commission of the trespass. This is illustrated in *Gregory v. Piper* (1829).[2] In this case the master told his servant to lay down a quantity of rubbish near his neighbor's wall, but so that it might not touch the same. The servant used ordinary care in executing the orders of his master, but some of the rubbish naturally ran against the wall. It was held that the master was liable in an action of trespass.

The harm necessarily resulting from performance of commanded act.

In addition to the foregoing qualifications of the rule that case is the proper remedy as against the master for the negligent act of his servant, it is to be noted that the rule itself has sometimes been clearly violated; and indeed it frequently seems that the maxim *qui facit per alium facit per se* (which identifies the act of the agent or servant as the act of the principal or master) ought so far to operate as to make the principal liable in the same form of action as the servant himself who immediately does the wrong.

This idea is manifest in *Brucker v. Fromont* (1796),[3] though the remedy was not there in question. The declaration in this case set forth that the defendant so carelessly and negligently drove his cart along the highway that he collided with the plaintiff's vehicle, with the result that the shaft of

[2] 9 B. & C. 591, 17 E. C. L. 454.

[3] 6 T. R. 659.

Volume III

Principal identified with servant as regards legal consequences of acts.

the defendant's vehicle was driven into the body of the plaintiff's horse, from the effects of which the animal died. From the proof it appeared that the defendant's cart at the time the mischief occurred was being driven by a servant of the defendant, and not by the defendant himself, as was to be inferred from the language of the declaration. It was nevertheless held that this was not a fatal variance in the proof.

Savignac v. Roome (1794)[4] is worthy of note. Trespass on the case was brought against a master for damage resulting to the plaintiff's chaise from a collision with a coach which was being driven along the highway by the defendant's servant. It was alleged that the defendant by his said servant "wilfully drove" the coach and horse upon the plaintiff's chaise. It was held that the action could not be maintained. Three points are to be considered in this case; namely, the nature of the act which was done, the responsibility of the master for that act, and the matter of the remedy to be pursued. On the first point it is clear that the servant was guilty of a trespass.

Wilfulness of servant removes master's responsibility.

On the second it is to be noted that the wilfulness of the servant's act was a factor which might well be considered as sufficient to remove the responsibility of the master altogether. As was said a few years later in the well-known case of *M'Manus v. Crickett* (1800),[5] when a servant quits sight of the object for which he is employed, and without having in view his master's orders pursues that which his own malice suggests, he no longer acts in pursuance of the authority given him and his master will not be answerable for such act. This was the vulnerable point, if there was any, in the plaintiff's case in *Savignac v. Roome*, and it was to this point that Espinasse chiefly directed his argument in behalf of the defendant.

But it was not upon this point of the servant's departure from the course of his duty that the case was actually decided. The court held that the servant was clearly guilty of a forcible trespass, and that the plaintiff should have brought an action

[4] 6 T. R. 125. [5] 1 East 106.

Chapter XVIII

of trespass against the master if he wished to hold him liable. *Day v. Edwards* (1794)[6] was cited as authority, but that was a case where the tort was committed by the defendant himself and not by his servant. The decision in *Savignac v. Roome*, so far as the point on which it was actually determined is concerned, was clearly a judicial oversight. If any action at all was maintainable, no objection could properly be taken to the use of the action on the case as a remedy.[7]

Savignac v. Roome criticised.

In *Ogle v. Barnes* (1799)[8] the facts appeared to be these: The plaintiff was the owner of a ship called the Anne, and the defendants were the owners of the Acteon. While the two vessels were sailing near each other the defendants so incautiously, carelessly, and negligently managed and steered their vessel that it ran foul of the Anne and did damage. It appeared that the Acteon was at the time under the charge of one Barnes, who was himself one of the defendants, and certain servants of the defendants. It was held that the action would lie. Lord Kenyon discriminated *Day v. Edwards* and *Savignac v. Roome* by observing that in the first case it was alleged that the defendant *furiously*, and in the other that he *wilfully*, drove his cart against the plaintiff's chaise. "But," said he, "it cannot be said that in this case the defendants *vi et armis* did an injury to the plaintiffs, when it appears that they did not do any act at all. The charge imputed to these defendants is that they so carelessly and negligently steered their vessel that by reason of such negligence their vessel sailed against and ran foul of the plaintiffs'; and for that negligence they are liable in an action upon the case. In other words, to the mind of his lordship the wrong declared on was purely a tort of omission. And so indeed is every negligent injury, in one aspect. This is the first decision in which the

Case sanctioned as remedy for negligent direct injury.

[6] 5 T. R. 648.

[7] There is American authority to the effect that an action of trespass may be maintained against a master for a trespass committed by his servant, but from the cases here cited on this point the rule appears to be limited to corporations which of necessity act only through their agents and servants. Yahoola River, etc., Hydraulic Hose Min. Co. *v.* Irby, 40 Ga. 479; Mobile, etc., R. Co. *v.* McKellar, 59 Ala. 458.

[8] 8 T. R. 188.

Volume III

idea was sanctioned that case may be sustained against one who does injury by the immediate and negligent application of violence; and here the idea was not openly sanctioned, but only by indirection.

It is noteworthy that some of the defendants were here sued as owners only and that they had taken no part in the management of the ship. As to these, case was clearly the proper remedy and it certainly would have been nonsense to dismiss the action against Barnes because he had actual charge of the ship at the time the mishap occurred.

Extension of case into field of direct trespassory injury.

The innovation thus introduced found favor at once. In *Rogers v. Imbleton* (1806),[9] a declaration in case charged that the defendant "by and through mere negligence and inattention" drove his cart against the plaintiff's horse with such force and violence that the animal died. It was held that the action was maintainable. In *Huggett v. Montgomery* (1807),[1] it was held that if, by the negligence of a pilot while the owner is on board, one ship runs into another, the remedy against the owner is by an action on the case.

Moreton v. Hardern (1825)[2] presented facts very similar to those involved in *Ogle v. Barnes, ante.* Trespass on the case was brought against three defendants as proprietors of a stage coach. The declaration stated that the defendants so carelessly managed their coach and horses that the coach ran against the plaintiff and broke his leg. It appeared in the evidence that one of the defendants was driving at the time when the accident happened, and the jury found that the mishap was due to his negligence. It was held that the plaintiff might maintain case against all the proprietors, though he might also have maintained trespass against the one who drove the coach.

Right to elect between trespass and case.

In *Williams v. Holland* (1833),[3] the doctrine thus declared was accepted, and the intelligible rule was laid down that in all cases where the injury is occasioned by the carelessness and negligence of the defendant, the plaintiff may, if he sees proper, make the negligence of the defendant the

[9] 2 B. & P. N. R. 117.
[1] 2 B. & P. N. R. 446.
[2] 4 B. & C. 223, 10 E. C. L. 316.
[3] 10 Bing. 112, 25 E. C. L. 50.

ground of the action and declare in case, although the injury be caused by his immediate act. Here the injured party has an election of remedy.[4]

Notwithstanding the fact that the plaintiff is thus sometimes permitted to elect between trespass and case, the distinction between the two remedies is fundamental; and there is a misjoinder of counts if the plaintiff declares in both case and trespass in the same declaration,[5] in the absence of legislation to the contrary.[6] The right of election between trespass and case exists only where the wrong complained of consists of a negligent injury. If a person wilfully causes a direct and immediate injury to another, trespass is the only available remedy. This further distinction is also to be noted, and it marks not so much the limits of the action considered as an engine for redressing a legal wrong as it does a limit of legal responsibility. The principle referred to is this: If a servant while about his master's business turns aside from the object of his employment on purpose to inflict a wilful malicious injury on some other person, the master cannot be held responsible. This principle is deducible from the two cases of *Savignac v. Roome* (1794)[7] and *M'Manus v. Crickett* (1800).[8] In the first it was held that case would not lie against the master for a wilful trespass committed by his servant, and in the latter that trespass would not lie. On the question as to what constitutes a departure by the servant from the course of his employment such as will relieve the master of responsibility the authorities are not in harmony, and it is perhaps needless to caution the reader that so far as the matter of substantive principle is concerned the cases just referred to are not to be accepted as stating the law on this point as it

Trespass only remedy for wilful injury.

Departure of servant from course of employment relieves master.

[4] Knott v. Digges, 6 Har. & J. (Md.) 230; Blin v. Campbell, 14 Johns. (N. Y.) 432; Percival v. Hickey, 18 Johns. (N. Y.) 257; Claflin v. Wilcox, 18 Vt. 605; Jordan v. Wyatt, 4 Gratt. (Va.) 151, 158.

[5] Courtney v. Connet, Carth. 436; Sheppard v. Furniss, 19 Ala. 760; Dale Mfg. Co. v. Grant, 34 N. J. L. 138.

[6] Parsons v. Harper, 16 Gratt. (Va.) 64; Beckwith v. Mollohan, 2 W. Va. 477; Sawyer v. Goodwin, 34 Me. 419; Farnsworth v. Howard, 1 Coldw. (Tenn.) 215.

[7] 6 T. R. 128.

[8] 1 East 110.

now is generally held. But this matter of substantive principle is not a subject to be dealt with here.

In no department of tort is the distinction between trespass and case less tangible and less instructive than in the field of interference with domestic relations. No distinction of much importance can be deduced from the cases, but a moment's reference to the confusion of remedy which is perceptible in this field will possibly prove instructive. The subject has been incidentally dealt with in chapter XVIII of the first volume of the present work, and the authorities there collected will not be here repeated.

Form of action in wrongs of interference with domestic relations.

It will be recalled that the idea of trespass supplies the point of beginning in all wrongs of interference with domestic relation. It is the violent seizure and abduction of the wife or heir, or the violent beating of the servant, whereby the husband, parent, or master is deprived of consortium or of service, that the law first attempts to punish. Naturally the action of trespass is first used as the remedy.

Trespass and case.

As legal evolution proceeds these torts gradually transcend the theory of trespass, and the action on the case comes to be recognized as the proper remedy. A significant fact in connection with the use of the action of trespass in this field is that the principle that trespass lies only for direct injury is flatly repudiated. In all torts of interference with domestic relations the damage which results to the person whose right of consortium or service is interfered with is always of a purely consequential nature. If one's child or servant is beaten so that he is disabled from performing his accustomed duties, the injury which accrues to the child or servant can be said to be direct, but the consequential loss of service which falls upon the parent or master is not in any sense a direct injury. That the early courts never hesitated in permitting trespass to be brought for such consequential damage shows that the action of trespass was by no means originally restricted to the recovery of such damage as is directly done. It is manifest that the distinction between 'direct' and 'consequential' damage as a criterion for distinguishing between

Damage always of consequential nature in these torts.

trespass and case, which was so clearly stated in *Reynolds v. Clarke, ante,* is a comparatively modern distinction and, so far as it has any value at all, is restricted in its application to the field of primary and secondary trespass. It certainly is not true in these wrongs of interference. But there can be no question that a perception of the fact that in actions for the loss of consortium and for the loss of service the damage to be recovered is of a consequential nature, has been a potent cause of the gradual supersession of trespass by the action on the case.

CHAPTER XIX

THE ACTION ON THE CASE.

The Action on the Case for Waste.

Volume III

WE now pass to a consideration of certain other specific forms of the action on the case which are of less general interest and importance than that form of the remedy which we have just been considering. And first we shall speak of the action on the case in the nature of waste, or the action on the case for waste.

Waste is a tort very similar in many respects to the trespass *vi et armis* upon realty, because it involves the doing of damage by the direct use of violence; but the action of trespass cannot ordinarily be maintained for waste, because there is no violation of possession. Case therefore seems to be the appropriate remedy for this wrong. In the end it was adopted for such purpose, but originally there was a distinct common-law remedy for this injury — the writ of waste (*breve de vasto*). Some account of the ancient remedy and of the steps by which case finally superseded it must now be given.

The writ of waste.

The writ of waste is probably older than the writ of trespass itself, and was common enough in the first half of the thirteenth century.[1] Most of the early writs of waste were sued against tenants in dower or guardians. None appears against a tenant by curtesy, though no doubt such tenant would often be held as a guardian. The action could also be maintained against ordinary tenants for life who were bound by covenant not to commit waste.[2] It is possible that the writ might have been used against any tenant who committed posi-

Waste maintainable against tenants in dower, guardians, and others.

[1] Bracton's Note Book contains more pleas of waste than of trespass, and from the beginning the wrong is clearly defined. See Note Book, pls. 27, 56, 115, 388, 443.

[2] Note Book, pl. 115 (warranty against waste inserted in common recovery); *ib.*, pl. 443 (covenant contained in a fine).

Chapter XIX

tive waste though no express covenant against waste had been entered into;[3] but this is doubtful, and later opinion was to the effect that such action could be maintained only by virtue of the statute.[4]

Waste by guardians.

The right to hold guardians liable for waste was settled by Magna Carta.[5] The right to use the writ against tenants in dower was of different origin. Here, it seems, the king's court first assumed jurisdiction to issue, at the instance of the heir, a prohibition against threatened waste.[6] Having issued such prohibition, the court had the power subsequently to give damages for its violation. The early writ of waste against the dowress consequently contained the allegation that the waste was done *contra prohibitionem regis,*[7] an expression which served the same jurisdictional purpose as *contra pacem* in the writ of trespass. This allegation became unnecessary when the legislation of Edward I had expressly made waste done by all sorts of tenants actionable.[8]

The prohibition of waste.

Tenant and cotenant.

By the Statute of Westminster II[9] a right of action was conceded to a tenant in common as against his cotenant, for waste committed by such cotenant. From the recitals of this statute it appears that the courts did in fact have power, upon issuing the prohibition of waste, to inquire into the damage already done and to give judgment therefor; but this principle was not generally known, for which reason the writ of prohibition was by that statute abolished altogether and the

[3] In Note Book, pl. 607, a writ of waste against a termor was dismissed, not on the ground that the writ would not lie against such termor, but on the ground that the waste was too trivial to claim the attention of the court.

[4] 2 Co. Inst. 145, note.

[5] Magna Carta, art. 4.

[6] The form of this writ of prohibition is given in Bracton, 315*a*, 315*b*.

[7] Note Book, pls. 27, 1617, 1371. In plea No. 574 (1231) the omission of this allegation in a writ of waste was held fatal.

[8] Stat. Gloucester, c. 5. "It is provided also, that a man from henceforth shall have a writ of waste in the chancery against him that holdeth by law of England, or otherwise for term of life, or for term of years, or a woman in dower. And he which shall be attainted of waste, shall leese the thing that he hath wasted, and moreover shall recompence thrice so much as the waste shall be taxed at." 2 Co. Inst. 298. The earlier provision in the Statute of Marlborough applied only to fermors (*firmarii*), lessees for a term of life or years.

[9] Chapter 22.

Volume III

ordinary writ of waste sufficiently strengthened to answer every purpose.[1]

The statutory action of waste.

The statutory action of waste thus obtained a secure footing among common-law remedies. Its chief advantage lay in the fact that in this action the premises wasted could be recovered as well as the statutory penalty; for by the statutes the doing of waste operated as a forfeiture of the tenements.[2] As a means of recovering tenements the statutory action of waste was, however, found to be cumbersome and ineffectual,[3] and for recovering damages the action on the case furnished a more satisfactory remedy, since the plaintiff got his costs.[4] Besides, case would lie in some instances where waste would not.[5] Consequently an action on the case in the nature of waste gradually supplanted the action of waste.[6] After having been long obsolete in practice, the remedy by writ of waste was expressly abolished in England by statute,[7] the law on the subject of waste remaining otherwise unchanged.[8] The result was that the action on the case in the nature of waste was thereby left in almost exclusive possession of the field covered by waste, and this supremacy it maintained until the final abolition of all forms of action.

Action on the case in nature of waste supplants statutory action.

Trespass the remedy for destructive waste of tenant at will.

By a peculiar exception which had its analogies in the field of bailment, trespass and not case was the proper remedy for destructive waste committed by a tenant at will. The reason assigned for this was that the commission of waste by such tenant terminated his estate, just as the breaking of bulk by a carrier terminated his possession and made his taking a trespass, and just as a destruction of chattels by a bailee at will terminated the bailment and made the wrongdoer a trespasser.[9]

[1] Stat. West. II., c. 14.

[2] 2 Bl. Com. 283.

Where the term ended and the premises were surrendered before judgment was had, judgment was entered for damages only. 2 Rolle Abr., 835 (I), pl. 5.

[3] Greene *v.* Cole, 2 Saund. 252, note.

[4] Greene *v.* Cole, 2 Saund. 252, note.

[5] Jefferson *v.* Jefferson, 3 Lev. 130.

[6] Greene *v.* Cole, 2 Saund. 252, note; Kinlyside *v.* Thornton, 2 W. Bl. 1111; Stevens *v.* Rose, 69 Mich. 259.

[7] Stat. 3 & 4 Will. IV., c. 27, § 36.

[8] Woodhouse *v.* Walker, 5 Q. B. D. 404; Bacon *v.* Smith, 1 Q. B. 345, 41 E. C. L. 571.

[9] See Trespass, *ante*.

The Action on the Case for Nuisance.

The law of nuisance supplies another instance where a special action on the case was substituted for and gradually superseded the more ancient mode of proceeding. The original remedy for nuisance was by the assize of nuisance or by writ of *quod permittat*. But owing to inherent limitations the former remedy could not always be used and the latter was exceedingly cumbersome, since the writ of *quod permittat* was in the nature of a writ of right. Case was consequently substituted for those actions. At first it was only used where the assize could not be maintained at all, as where the nuisance was committed by one who had no freehold in the premises where the nuisance was created,[1] or where the nuisance, after being done against a testator in his life, was continued against his devisee.[2] So, where a nuisance created by one was continued against his heir, case lay.[3] The action on the case also had to be used where the nuisance consisted of a mere nonfeasance,[4] as where one who was bound to repair a bridge failed to do so, whereby it fell;[5] or where one who was bound to keep a ditch open failed to do so, whereby another's meadow was flooded.[6]

Assize of nuisance.

Writ of *quod permittat.*

Case competes with these remedies.

Distinctions.

It was at one time accepted that case would not lie where the nuisance consisted of a positive misfeasance, such as the destruction of a bridge[7] or the obstruction of a highway,[8] the proper remedy in these cases being by the assize.

Again, it was said, though not without misgivings, that where a road or right of way was entirely stopped the assize was the proper remedy, but if it was merely diverted the remedy was by an action on the case.[9] The reason for this was that only in case of a complete stoppage was there such a dis-

[1] Case for nuisance against lessee for years, F. N. B. 184 G.

[2] Some *v.* Barwish, Cro. Jac. 231.

[3] Com. Dig., *Action upon Case for Nuisance* (D 1).

[4] 1 Rolle Abr. 104 (L).

[5] Y. B. 11 Hen. IV. 83, pl. 29.

[6] *Ib.*

[7] *Ib.*

[8] 1 Rolle Abr. 104 (L), pl. 5; Yevance *v.* Holcomb (1565), Dyer 250*b*, 3 Leon. 13; Anonymous, 4 Leon. 167, pl. 273.

[9] Y. B. 11 Hen. IV. 25, pl. 48; Y. B. 11 Hen. IV. 83, pl. 29; Y. B. 33 Hen. VI. 26, pl. 10.

Volume III

seisin of the right of way as was necessary for the maintenance of the assize.

But these distinctions could not stand, and in the latter years of the sixteenth century it was established that a plaintiff may have case or a writ of assize, at his election, for a nuisance resulting from any positive act.[1] This extension of case was compared by Rolle to the extension of assumpsit into the field of debt, which occurred in the same period.[2] As a result of this step the assize of nuisance, like the *quod permittat,* fell into desuetude, though both these remedies were perhaps occasionally used until the need for them entirely disappeared, owing to the growth of the injunctive power of the court of equity.

Case supplants its rivals in field of nuisance.

Case and Assumpsit.

Inasmuch as the action on the case is a general residuary remedy and as such maintainable where any act or omission is done or permitted contrary to the obligation of the law, it follows that this action can sometimes be maintained for the breach of a contractual duty. This leads us to refer to a few cases wherein the question of the limits of the respective actions of assumpsit and case has been presented. We cannot promise the reader that much information of real importance is to be gotten in this connection, but certain ideas may be developed which should not be wholly lost.

The general principle upon which the law here proceeds is that if in any case a perfect contract exists or is stated in the declaration, the cause of action must be conceived and treated as being in assumpsit; while if for any particular reason the contract is not so far perfect as to present a case where assumpsit will lie, then the cause of action must be conceived and treated as being in tort, and the remedy is by the action on the case.

General principle.

Corbett v. Packington (1827)[3] illustrates the principle that

[1] Aston's Case (1586), 2 Dyer 250*b*, note; Villet *v.* Parkhurst (1587), 2 Dyer 250*b*, note; Stye *v.* Mordant, I Rolle Abr. 104, pl. 7; Loverett *v.* Townesend, 1 Rolle Abr. 104, pl. 8.

[2] 1 Rolle Abr. 104, pl. 6.

[3] 6 B. & C. 268, 13 E. C. L. 170.

where a perfect contract is stated the remedy is exclusively in assumpsit upon the contract. The declaration in this case averred that the plaintiff at the request of the defendant had caused to be delivered to him certain pigs to be safely kept for a reward and then to be returned to the plaintiff. A promise on the part of the defendant to care for and redeliver the pigs in consideration of the reward was alleged. The declaration then stated that by the carelessness of the defendant in keeping and feeding the pigs, they were wholly lost to the plaintiff. It was held that the count which set forth the foregoing facts was in assumpsit and could not be joined with a count in tort.

Chapter XIX

If contract perfect, remedy exclusively in assumpsit.

In *Gladwell v. Steggall* (1839)[4] an action on the case was brought by an infant against a surgeon for malpractice. The declaration alleged that the defendant was employed by the plaintiff. But it appeared from the evidence that he was really employed by the plaintiff's father. After verdict for the plaintiff it was objected on behalf of the defendant that the allegation of an employment by the plaintiff was not made out. It was held that considering the action as being in case it was immaterial by whom the defendant was employed. If the action had been in assumpsit the objection would doubtless have been fatal.

Plaintiff not in privity with contract sues in case.

In cases where the wrong complained of is done in the course of discharge, by the defendant, of a duty which rests upon him by virtue of his public calling as well as by virtue of his special contract with the plaintiff, either case for the breach of the public duty or assumpsit for the breach of the special agreement is maintainable at the election of the plaintiff. Thus in *Pozzi v. Shipton* (1838)[5] an action on the case was brought against a carrier for damage resulting from his negligence in the transportation of certain goods which had been delivered to him for carriage. No contract was alleged, but only that the defendant was a common carrier; that the goods in question were delivered to him; and that the damage was done while he had the goods in course of transportation.

Breach of duty incident to public calling remediable either in case or assumpsit.

[4] 5 Bing. N. Cas. 733, 35 E. C. L. 292.

[5] 8 Ad. & El. 963, 35 E. C. L. 574.

18

Volume III

It was held that the action was maintainable in this form. In cases of this kind the plaintiff has a right to sue in case or assumpsit, at his election, and before the right of election can exist it is essential that there should be a breach of the general duty as well as a breach of the special contract.[6]

In *Marzetti v. Williams* (1830),[7] it was held the relation between banker and depositor is such that the law imposes an obligation on the banker, apart from any question of special contract, to pay the check of his depositor, when there are sufficient funds to meet it, and that the action on the case will lie for the breach of this general duty. The real import of this decision is that the court here gave recognition to an implied obligation in the nature of a special assumpsit, and recognized the action on the case as a proper remedy for the breach of such obligation. Said Parke, J.: "The action being substantially founded on a contract, I think it can make no difference whether it is in form tort or assumpsit." [8]

Case as remedy for breach of implied obligation in nature of assumpsit.

In *Burnett v. Lynch* (1826),[9] it appeared that the assignee of a certain lease had taken it subject to covenants contained therein. The original lessee, having been held liable by the

[6] It was once thought that an action against a common carrier for loss of goods, even when framed in case for the violation of the duty imposed by the custom of the realm, is an action in contract. Accordingly it was held that such a count could not be joined with trover. Dalston *v.* Janson (1695), 5 Mod. 89.

Three-quarters of a century later Chief Justice Wilmot observed that the practice was then to the contrary, and he declared that the question of the right to join the count against a carrier for negligence with a count in trover was to be determined by the question whether like judgment could be given upon both. Dickon *v.* Clifton (1766), 2 Wils. C. Pl. 321.

Traces of the notion that the liability of the carrier arises exclusively out of contract are to be found in Buddle *v.* Willson (1795), 6 T. R. 369, where it was held that, in an action against a carrier in case on the custom of the realm, the defendant may plead in abatement the nonjoinder of his partners. The principle on which this decision proceeded was undermined in Govett *v.* Radnidge (1802), 3 East 62, by the reasoning of Lord Ellenborough, and in England the cause of action against a carrier, now that all forms of action are abolished, is to-day treated as being in tort whether the negligence charged is an omission on the part of the servants of the carrier, Kelly *v.* Metropolitan R. Co. (1895), 1 Q. B. 944; or the commission of some act amounting to a misfeasance. See Baylis *v.* Lintott, L. R. 8 C. P. 349.

[7] 1 B. & Ad. 415, 20 E. C. L. 412.

[8] *Ib.*, 425.

[9] 5 B. & C. 589, 12 E. C. L. 327.

Chapter XIX

lessor for breaches of the covenants during the time the assignee was in possession, brought an action on the case against his assignee and recovered. It was held that, upon his accepting the assignment of the lease subject to the performance of its covenants, the law imposed a duty on the assignee to fulfil those covenants, though the assignment was merely by deed poll and there was no contract, as by bond or covenant, that he should indemnify his assignor. Abbott, C. J., was of the opinion that assumpsit could be maintained on the promise implied by law and that case would also lie for the breach of the legal duty. Littledale, J., said: "Where from a given state of facts the law raises a legal obligation to do a particular act and there is a breach of that obligation and a consequential damage, there, although assumpsit may be maintainable upon a promise implied by law to do the act, still an action on the case founded in tort is the more proper form of action, in which the plaintiff in his declaration states the facts out of which the legal obligation arises, the obligation itself, the breach of it, and the damage resulting from that breach." In this decision the idea that case is a proper remedy upon implied obligations in the nature of assumpsit is quite manifest.[1]

Implied obligation of assignee of covenant of lease.

Case concurrent with special assumpsit, when.

The case of *Brown v. Boorman* (1844)[2] is rather peculiar, inasmuch as the English House of Lords here came very near recognizing the principle that case can be used in suing upon any breach of a simple assumptual contract. The facts in this case were these: The plaintiff employed the defendant to sell and deliver oil, on the terms contained in such contracts of sale as should be made by the defendant with the various persons who should become purchasers thereof. The defendant accepted the employment, and sold oil to C, to be paid for at the time of delivery. The defendant afterwards delivered the oil to C without insisting on the cash payment, as he might and should have done under the terms of his contract of sale. It

[1] For a discrimination between implied obligations in the nature of assumpsit and the implied duty in the nature of debt (the ordinary quasi-contract) the reader is referred to chapter XXV. of the second volume of the present work.

[2] 11 Cl. & F. 1 (in House of Lords), 3 Q. B. 511, 43 E. C. L. 843 (in Queen's Bench and Exchequer Chamber).

will be observed that the law did not impose on the defendant in his capacity of broker the duty of selling and delivering for cash only. That duty was imposed only by the contract of employment. Nevertheless it was held in the Exchequer Chamber, and afterwards in the House of Lords, that the principal might recover his damages of the broker in an action wherein the declaration merely set out the facts of the case. The point in the decision is that a declaration which sets forth a contract of employment, a consequent assumptual duty, and a subsequent breach, is a good declaration whether the action be called case or assumpsit. But it is clear that in this case the cause of action arose out of the breach of a contract. But it is also certainly true that by the majority of the judges the action, so far as its form is concerned, was treated as being purely an action on the case. Hence if this decision had been literally taken it would have resulted in the establishment of the principle that the action on the case can be maintained upon either the misperformance or nonperformance of any simple contract. But the court evidently intended to go no further than to hold that case will lie for the violation of a duty which exists by reason of a contract of employment. In other words, the decision is authority for the proposition that the relation between employer and employee, like that between the banker and depositor in *Marzetti v. Williams*, and like that between the assignor and assignee of a lease in *Burnett v. Lynch*, is of such a nature that the law will impose an independent legal duty, for breach of which case will lie. As a matter of technical learning the decision is unsound.[3]

Case for breach of duty incident to performance of contract of employment.

[3] By far the most instructive and most learned part of the reported proceedings in this case is found in the argument of Mr. J. W. Smith for the appellant in the House of Lords. So far as technical and legal theory is concerned he was entirely correct. Said he: "The action in this case is misconceived. The remedy was by an action of contract, and not by an action on the case. The obligation here, which is alleged to have been broken, is not one which would have existed at common law, and would have been implied at law to arise from the character of the broker as such. It is the result of a special contract. The breach stated is not that which relates to the common-law character of broker, but to the special duty of not delivering without payment of price. The action is therefore misconceived. . . . This action ought to have been brought in assumpsit

Chapter XIX

Import of Brown v. Boorman.

The case is chiefly suggestive as marking that point in the evolution of the common-law remedies when form has ceased to have its accustomed significance in legal theory. It belongs to the period of the senility of the actions, and was a precursor of the legislation which was soon destined to abolish forms of action altogether. If *Brown v. Boorman* were really sound there would have been little need to give further recognition to the action of assumpsit in any form, for every breach of contract could have been treated as a tort, and case could have been used to recover the damages.[4] However, it soon became apparent that the decision was not to be accepted as having established any such radical doctrine, and in *Courtenay v. Earle* (1850),[5] it was held that the action on the case will not lie for the breach of a simple promise supported by a consideration.

only; it is not maintainable in the form of case; and if treated as assumpsit, then the declaration cannot be supported, for it is defective in the statement of the promise and breach. However slight might have been originally the distinction between assumpsit and tort, it has been so long and so fully established, and has been so interwoven in the practice of the law, that the greatest inconvenience would follow from now disregarding it. . . . The rule is, that where there is a general relation and there is also a general duty, the plaintiff may have his election as to the form of action. But he cannot have that election where the supposed duty is altogether the creature of the convention and agreement of the parties. In such a case the cause of action is a contract and nothing else, and the action must be in the form of contract and none other." 11 Cl. & F. 4 *et seq.* The court proceeded on the idea that the existence of the relation of employer and employee operated to make the employee liable in an action on the case for a misfeasance done in the course of the employment, although the particular duty violated was created by contract.

4 "Since the decision of the Exchequer Chamber in Boorman *v.* Brown, it has been supposed that every action for a breach of contract may be considered as an action of tort." Williams, J., in Courtenay *v.* Earle, 10 C. B. 77, 70 E. C. L. 77.

5 10 C. B. 73, 70 E. C. L. 73.

CHAPTER XX

THE REMEDY OF DISTRESS.

Distress in Early Law.[1]

Volume III

DISTRESS occupied a prominent place in remedial law long before the modern forms of action were known. It belongs to the stratum of the *legis actiones,* and is a remedy rather than a form of action. The subject, however, as will fully appear in the course of this chapter, is of peculiar importance and must be treated along with the modern common-law actions which have supplemented and supplanted it. The history of the remedy illustrates in a striking way the normal growth of the conception of law in human society; for it shows how the unruly elements are gradually taught to bear the yoke first of custom and then of law.

Place of law of distress in legal theory.

The archaic character of distress as a remedy founded on the instinct and principle of self-help is made apparent in the definition of the remedy. "A distress," it is said, "is the taking of a personal chattel without legal process from the possession of a wrongdoer into the hands of the party aggrieved, as a pledge for the redress of an injury, the performance of a duty, or the satisfaction of a demand." [2]

Definition of distress.

[1] One unacquainted with Professor Maine's brilliant contributions to legal history and comparative jurisprudence would naturally suppose that a paper on distress would conduct him over a dry and recondite field of legal investigation. A perusal of what this writer has said concerning distraint of goods will entirely disabuse the mind of this opinion; for in his hands the subject becomes luminous with interest and full of instruction. Lectures IX. and X., in his Early History of Institutions, are devoted to this subject and will amply repay perusal. The extent of our indebtedness to this writer will become apparent to the reader of the present and succeeding chapters.

[2] Bradby on Distress 1.

Judicial Distress.— No account is taken in this article of the remedy of distress as used for the enforcement of recognizances or to compel the payment of fines and amerciaments. When used for such purposes the right to distrain is derived either from the agreement of the parties, as where a recognizance

Chapter XX

The first impulse of an injured man is to punish the wrong-doer and compel him to make immediate reparation. We have not yet brought this instinct into complete subjection. Nor indeed, it may be added, should the power of preserving one's personal equilibrium in a world of conflicting interests ever be wholly abdicated. Only when society has developed a complex and powerful legal organization can mankind safely surrender the right of self-redress. As the child brings his playmate to terms, forces a compromise, or compels him to do a particular act by the pressure of withholding a toy which chance, strength, or strategy has put in his possession, so the grown-up man living in a society not competent to adjust his grievances naturally adopts compulsion by distraint. One who would personally compel another must, of course, occupy a position of advantage. He must be able to exert leverage. This position the distrainor acquires by actually taking the distrainee's chattels into his custody. In a primitive society this naturally presupposes superior strength, skill, or valor.

Remedy of distress founded on idea of self-help.

In tracing the history of distress we must begin not with the right or law of distress, but with the disposition of impulse which naturally prompts an injured person to take from the wrongdoer, if he dare, whatever is seizable and transportable. Passing on from the impulse we come to the fact, then to the custom, and finally to the legal right of distraint. The conditions under which the act can be done and the formalities with which it must be attended are now defined. This represents a long step in advance. The law does not at first attempt directly to combat, but only to mitigate, the evils attendant upon the exercise of the power and custom of taking distress. The sovereign authority prefers to regulate what it dare not or cannot altogether forbid.

Right to distrain originates in immemorial usage.

Nor does the law at first assume complete jurisdiction over the quarrel which provokes the high-handed caption. It prescribes forms, limits the exercise of the right, and gives a new direction to the forces which are behind it. As might be ex-

Gradual ameliora-tion of remedy.

expressly specifies that the creditor may distrain, or from custom or statute. For an account of judicial distraint for the payment of fines and amerciaments, see Bradby on Distress, ch. 8.

Volume III

pected, the early utterances of the lawgiver are made up of denials, reservations, and limitations on the exercise of distraint. Clearly here was a force at work in society which needed to be guided and checked rather than stimulated. At most stages in the evolution of legal doctrines, the spokesmen of the law have had more sense than to lay emphasis upon the right of self-help. Human nature needs no prompting along this line.

Remedy of distress breaks down.

It is instructive to observe that the form of self-help with which we are now to deal was not extirpated by direct attack. It was gradually rendered ineffective by being burdened with too much form. It thus became a cumbersome remedy, dangerous even to the plaintiff who would pursue it. Under this weight the remedy broke down. Part of the law of distress has passed into the general body of modern law under the heads of attachment and distringas. That part of the law of distress pertaining to rent still retains vitality in some jurisdictions; but this is solely due to the fact that the remedy as a means of enforcing the payment of rent has been converted by statutes from an imperfect extrajudicial remedy by self-help into a perfect legal remedy. The full import of this will be apparent further on.

Distress in Roman Law.

Pignoris capio.

The universality of distraint and the wide field which it occupied in early law make it desirable to take a passing glance at the various forms which the remedy took among the different Aryan people of whose legal systems we have knowledge. Naturally the Roman law first claims attention. In this system we find a remedy, *pignoris capio,* corresponding with the English remedy by distress. Its existence is noted by Gaius, but he does not go into much detail.[3] It belonged, of course, to the early period of Roman law when the only legal remedies recognized were the *legis actiones.* The *pignoris capio* differed from the other remedies then known, in being extrajudicial. The pledge could be taken by the cred-

[3] Gaius, Inst., Lib. IV., §§ 26–29.

Chapter XX

itor in the absence and without the previous sanction of the pretor, and generally also in the absence of the debtor.[4]

Nature of this remedy.

The *pignoris capio* seems originally to have been a true instance of substantive distress; that is, the creditor could exercise it against a citizen regardless of the pendency of any suit. It will be observed that what is called auxiliary distraint, by which the chattels of a defendant in a lawsuit are attached and held, in order to enforce appearance or satisfaction of a judgment, is a late development. But it comes from the same root as the substantive right of distress. When auxiliary distress appears we may know that the courts have now become strong enough to bring into subjection, and to use as part of their machinery, the power of stripping a wrongdoer of his goods. This phenomenon appeared in the Roman law when the *pignoris capio* of the early law became, under the later formulary system, a mode of legal execution, then known by the slightly different name *pignoris captio.*

When available.

The extrajudicial right of seizure by an individual creditor, which we have noted, could be properly exercised only in a few cases. Soldiers could distrain against public officers bound to supply sustenance (*aes militare, aes equestre, aes hordearium*) for them or for their horses. In this case the right was older than the Twelve Tables, having originated in custom. The remedy could likewise be used against a man who purchased a sacrificial victim but refused to pay for it; also against one who failed to pay the hire for a beast of burden let out for the purpose of raising money to celebrate religious service. In these cases the remedy was granted by the Twelve Tables. Later[5] the remedy was extended by the Censorial law so as to permit of its use by the farmers of state revenue in collecting taxes.[6]

From the very meagre account of the remedy given by Gaius, and from the urgency of the cases to which it was applied, it is to be inferred that the property seized was, or might be, taken in satisfaction of the claim distrained for. If so it

[4] Hunter, Roman Law, 3d ed., 1044; Gaius, Inst., Lib. IV., § 29.

[5] Gaius, Inst., Lib. IV., § 28.

[6] Hunter, Roman Law, 3d ed., 1044.

was a more complete remedy than the common-law distress. There is no substantial reason for doubting that the history of the two remedies was substantially the same in Roman and English law. Beginning as a species of self-help and intended merely as a means of getting security or pledge for the performance of a duty, both the Roman and the English remedy finally came to be much more speedy and effective.

Distress Among Teutonic People.

Turning from Rome to Teutonic communities, we find, as might be expected, traces of the remedy on every hand. The *Leges Barbarorum* contain numerous references to 'pignoration,' which is easily identified with distraint of goods. The provisions of the Salic law are doubtless the most instructive. Here we see the law putting forth powerful efforts to bring distress under its sway. The remedy is still extrajudicial, but already it is burdened with a heavy weight of formal procedure.

Salic law.

A succession of demands had to be made in solemn form by the complainant. Three witnesses (*rachimburgs*) accompanied the creditor to the house of the debtor, and formal demand was there made. The accompanying witnesses, in addition to supplying proof of the demand, also identified the property subsequently to be distrained, and appraised its value. If payment was refused, the creditor summoned the defendant to the hundred court, where the president of the court (*thunginus*) appears to have laid an injunction upon the defendant not to dispose of the property which was intended to be distrained.[7]

Proceedings: 1. The demand. 2. The summons.

It was the duty of the creditor to give publicity to this judicial act of the *thunginus*. He was also required forthwith to proceed with witnesses to the debtor's house and there make another demand. If the debt was not then paid before sunset an additional sum of three shillings accrued against the debtor as a penalty. This same formal demand was again made by the creditor at the end of two successive weeks, with the result that nine shillings were now added to the debt. Upon refusal

3. Second demand. 4. Third demand.

[7] Bigelow, History of Procedure, 209, 210.

Chapter XX

of the last demand, distress followed in accordance with the appraisal made by the three witnesses who accompanied the creditor on his first demand. It will thus be seen that under the Salian Code the judiciary had apparently become strong enough to take full control of the remedy and direct the conduct of the distrainor in regard to minute details.

5. The caption.

Among others of the barbarous peoples the courts had not reached this degree of influence and power. The Lombard law, for instance, retained traces of the primitive license by which distress followed after a simple demand of payment. In the laws of the Bavarians and Ostrogoths, distress was prohibited unless the authority of the judge was obtained. Visigothic law expressly prohibited it. The lawmakers everywhere made war against the institution, and apparently sometimes forbade altogether what they could not control.

Distraint among other Teutonic people.

Details as to the law of distress in England prior to the Conquest are wanting. The old costumals show that distress was a well-known remedy, and the same effort to bring it into subjection to the courts is manifest. Professor Bigelow surmises that the English law of distraint resembled the Salic law in its most striking features. The laws of Cnut contain a passage to the effect that no distress should be taken before the creditor had thrice demanded his right in the hundred court. If the creditor did not obtain satisfaction of his claim upon the third demand, he was then required to appear in the shiremoot. A time for a fourth demand was then appointed, and if it failed he was given permission to distrain or seize his own.[8] In later ages English law did not exhibit this strict-

Early law of distress in England.

Probable resemblance to Salic law.

[8] Secular Dooms of Cnut, c. 19 (Stubbs, Select Charters 73).

Distress in Irish Law.—In Professor Henry Sumner Maine's Early History of Institutions there is a brilliant lecture on the Irish law of distress as found in the ancient Irish Code (Senchus Mor). The writer treats the subject from the standpoint of comparative jurisprudence, and conclusively demonstrates that the law of distress as found in the customs of the different Aryan races, such as the Romans, Celts, Teutons, and Hindus, is derived from a common Aryan source. Early Hist. Inst. 279-293.

The following epitome of the Irish law of distress is given by the editor of the first volume of the Ancient Laws of Ireland (Record

ness in regard to the requirement of notice, and we are told that notice of an intention to distrain was never essential at common law to the legality of a distress.[9] By statute, however, notice was at a late day made necessary in order to au-

Commission) and is reproduced by Professor Maine with approval: "The plaintiff or creditor, having first given the proper notice, proceeded, in the case of a defendant or debtor, not of chieftain grade, to distrain. If the defendant or debtor were a person of chieftain grade, it was necessary not only to give notice, but also to 'fast upon him.' The fasting upon him consisted in going to his residence and waiting there for a certain time without food. If the plaintiff did not within a certain time receive satisfaction for his claim, or a pledge therefor, he forthwith, accompanied by a law-agent, witnesses, and others, seized his distress. The distress, when seized, was in certain cases liable to a stay, which was a period varying according to fixed rules, during which the debtor received back the distress, and retained it in his own keeping, the creditor having a lien upon it. Such a distress is a 'Distress with time;' but under certain circumstances and in particular cases an 'immediate distress' was made, the peculiarity of which was that during the fixed period of the stay the distress was not allowed to remain in the debtor's possession, but in that of the creditor, or in one of the recognized greens or pounds. If the debt was not paid by the end of the stay, the creditor took away the distress, and put it in a pound. He then served notice of the distress on the debtor whom he had distrained, letting him know where what was distrained was impounded. The distress remained in the pound a certain period, fixed according to its nature (*dithim*, translated 'delay in pound,' is the name of this period). At the end of the delay in pound, the Forfeiting Time began to run, during which the distress became forfeited at the rate of three 'seds' per day, until entirely forfeited. If the entire value of the distress thus forfeited was exactly equal to the original debt and the subsequent expenses, the debt was liquidated; if it was less than this, a second distress was taken for the difference; and if more, the overplus was returned. All this proceeding was managed by the party himself, or his law-agent, with the several witnesses of the various steps, and other necessary parties. But if, instead of allowing his cattle to go to pound, the debtor gave a sufficient pledge, e. g., his son, or some article of value, to the creditor, that he would within a certain time try the right to the distress by law, the creditor was bound to receive such pledge. If he did not go to law, as he so undertook, the pledge became forfeited for the original debt. At any time, up to the end of the 'dithim' the debtor could recover his cattle by paying the debt and such expenses as had been incurred. But if he neglected to redeem them until the 'dithim' had expired, then he could only redeem such as were still unforfeited." For a fuller account see Ginnell's Brehon Laws, 156-176.

[9] *Notice of Intent to Distrain Unnecessary.*— If the lord distrains for rent or service he need not give notice to the tenant for what thing it is he distrains, for the tenant by intendment of law knows what is in arrear from his land by way of rent and service. Y.B. 45 Edw. III. 9, pl. 13. See also Trent *v.* Hunt, 9 Exch. 20.

thorize a sale of the property. The ordinance of Cnut evidently attempted to enforce too strict a rule and was for this reason premature.

Distress sinks to level of auxiliary process.

As a result of the continual struggle to bring distress into subjection to the law, the remedy had ceased to be an extrajudicial remedy long before the Norman Conquest. It seems at that epoch to have been almost wholly a species of auxiliary process. As such it was used to enforce attendance at courts or to enforce judgments, and in no case could a man distrain without the sanction of a court.[1]

Subsequent revival of substantive distress.

This was not true of the law during the subsequent ages, nor was it true during that earlier period of which our knowledge is more vague and in a degree hypothetical. The question then arises, How is the subsidence and subsequent revival of substantive extrajudicial distress to be accounted for? Having reached its lowest node at or near the time of the Conquest, why did not the institution wholly disappear as at Rome? The answer may be briefly indicated. The decay of the extrajudicial remedy was due entirely to a natural process of legal evolution. Its revival is to be attributed to feudalism.

Normal legal growth antagonistic to distress.

That normal legal growth must be fatal to the remedy of distress is apparent. It is not only extrajudicial; it is strictly anti-social and anti-legal. It is opposed to fundamental legal conceptions. It can never be tolerated that a man should at the same time be both judge and executive officer in his own behalf. But this is really what distress implies, and in this we see the reason why so much counterbalancing machinery has been built up around the institution wherever it survived. The first articulate voice of the law is against it. If a system of law fully adapted to the capacity and purpose of man could come into existence without regard to antecedent conditions, distress would certainly have no place in it. Legal evolution tends to bring all procedure into the category of legal process, and thus to eliminate self-help altogether. We therefore see early law gradually and surely disentangling itself from the

[1] Bigelow, History of Procedure 205 *et seq.*

Volume III

meshes of this primitive institution. Roman law developed with such rapidity that distress had already become a thing of the past when Gaius wrote, and later authorities on Roman law take no notice of it. Among Teutonic people development was slower. The Romans could dispense with self-help because their remedial law was highly elastic and very complete. Teutonic remedial law, on the other hand, developed with painful slowness. Nevertheless the process of eliminating self-help out of our remedial law had made such headway prior to the advent of feudalism that Professor Bigelow, looking to the testimony of the ancient codes and costumals, sees in distress a truly judicial remedy; and this aspect of distress is so conspicuous in that epoch that one needs to be cautioned against misinterpreting its past.[2]

Judicialization of the remedy.

[2] *Self-help in Early English Law.*— The following passage from Professor Bigelow's History of Procedure will indicate his point of view on this question: "There is no greater mistake, it is apprehended, than to suppose that private distraint as it has existed in modern times in England and in America — distraint made without judicial permission — is archaic, as having been transmitted in its present form from the period of supposed early Anglo-Saxon law. The time perhaps was, when non-judicial distress was exercised among the Germanic peoples; but that time was prehistoric, and is only matter of inference from the course of events in actual history, and not capable of proof. But whether private distress once prevailed or not, it is certain that from the time when the Germanic nations first appear in legal history until the period of which we are writing, distraint between freemen of the same *gau*, hundred, or (later) municipality, was lawful only when effected under judicial authority." History of Procedure 202, 203.

This language embodies the important truth that prior to the advent of the feudal system distress was under judicial control and had about lost its character as an independent remedy by self-help; but there can be little doubt of the validity of Professor Maine's hypothesis to the effect that when law first began to develop in human society, it found the field of remedies largely occupied by the custom of private distraint. The fact that the early codes denounce and regulate it is abundant proof of the existence of the institution. Nor can it be said that an institution is really prehistoric when we see it in the very process of being transformed from a private customary extra-judicial remedy into a truly judicial remedy.

Messrs. Pollock and Maitland have some remarks on the place of self-help in early remedial law which are instructive: "For a long time law was very weak, and as a matter of fact it could not prevent self-help of the most violent kind. Nevertheless, at a fairly early stage in its history it begins to prohibit in uncompromising terms any and every attempt to substitute force for judgment. . . . This at all events was true

Looking, too, at its future from the point of time marked by the Conquest, the enlightened observer would be tempted to predict the certain and speedy extinction of this primitive institution. Such a person would doubtless anticipate that the idea of stripping wrongdoers of their chattels might be utilized by the courts as a means of legal compulsion. He might thus anticipate the evolution of such process as attachment, execution, and distringas. But he would not expect to see that which was already discarded come into prominence again. Two things lay hid in the future — the slow growth of remedial law and the effect which the feudal organization of society was to have upon this ancient remedy.

Nature of the feudal tenure.

As a system feudalism was based upon a peculiar tenure of land, and the life of the tenant's estate was dependent upon the performance by him of certain feudal duties. Perhaps, in strict legal theory, upon the failure of the tenant to perform his part of the feudal obligation, the lord could enforce a forfeiture. An alternative to this was found in the exercise of the right to distrain the tenant's goods. Consequently distress was revived and became associated with feudalism as a remedy for the enforcement of the services due from the tenant. As such it took on new life. With the decay of feudalism, the remedy withered and lost many of its branches, but it did not wholly disappear. In our own day it still survives in many jurisdictions and furnishes the quickest remedy for the collection of rents. Even in this respect the modern distress is purely a survival from feudal law, for rent originated

of our English law in the thirteenth century. So fierce is it against self-help that it can hardly be induced to find a place even for self-defense. . . . This thought, that self-help is an enemy of law, a contempt of the king and his court, is one of those thoughts which lie at the root of that stringent protection of seisin on which we have often commented. . . . It would be a great mistake were we to suppose that during the later middle ages the law became stricter about this matter; it became laxer, it became prematurely lax. Some of the 'fist right,' as the Germans call it, that was flagrant in the fifteenth century, would have been impossible, if the possessory assizes of Henry II.'s day had retained their pristine vigor. In our own day our law allows an amount of quiet self-help that would have shocked Bracton. It can safely allow this, for it has mastered the sort of self-help that is lawless." 2 Poll. & Mait. Hist. Eng. Law 2d ed., 574.

Distress normal remedy for enforcement of feudal duties.

in tenure, and is the menstruum in which all other forms of feudal service have gradually dissolved. When feudal tenures were abolished [3] rent was left as almost the sole representative of the ancient feudal service, and distress has thus been brought down to modern times as a remedy for its collection.

Instead, then, of saying with Professor Bigelow that private distraint is prehistoric in early law and a modern innovation in modern law, we should say it is truly an archaic remedy which, after being once almost entirely banished from Teutonic legal systems, has been revived and brought down to modern times by social and historical conditions.

Distress for Feudal Services.

Structure of feudal society.

The organization of feudal society highly favored the adoption of distress as a remedy to enforce feudal service. The lords all had their seignorial and manorial courts. The vassals and retainers made up the suitors of these courts, and were bound to attend the sessions. It was consequently easy to comply with the condition that the distraint take place under the sanction and by the authority of a court.[4] The lord, being entitled to a particular service, proceeded by the judgment of his own court. Glanvill tells us that the law permitted a lord by the judgment of his court to call upon and distrain his homager to appear in court and render the service due.[5] Where the lords thus had a right to proceed by the judgment of their own courts to enforce attendance and service by distraining tenants, it was easy in time to assert the right to distrain without judgment. This indeed took place, and thus occurred that reactionary transition whereby distress again became substantially an extrajudicial remedy.[6]

Manorial courts.

But notwithstanding this measurable reversion to the an-

[3] 12 Chas. II., c. 24.

[4] *Leg. Henrici*, 51, § 3: "et nulli sine judicio vel licentia namiare liceat alium in suo vel alterius."

[5] Glanv., Bk. IX., c. 1. Compare: "With respect to the rendering of reasonable aids, lords may of right, without the king's precept or that of his justices, but by the judgment of his own court, distrain their tenants by such of their chattels as may be found within their fees." Bk. IX., c. 8.

[6] 2 Poll. & Mait. Hist. Eng. Law, 576.

Chapter XX

cient notion of self-help, the remedy still retained marks of its previous procedural and quasi-judicial character. When the goods were once taken they were in the custody of the law, and the distrainor had no right to use or control them in any way. The law did not allow the lord to seize whatever he could lay hands upon. Some things he might not touch at all, others only as a last resort. He could not sell or in any way dispose of the chattels taken, but held them strictly in pledge. Here was no complete self-help.

Distress retains quasi-judicial character.

The fact that the feudal services were not generally commutable into money demands partly accounts for the firmness of the notion that the lord could not convert the chattels to his own use or sell them for the purpose of turning them into money. Such incidents of tenure as homage, fealty, and knight service are personal in their character and cannot be arbitrarily changed into money charges. In course of time even these incidents were commuted into payments of money, and in modern times the term 'rent' has been used to include nearly all distrainable duties incident to the tenure of land.

Distress was undoubtedly a much quicker and more satisfactory remedy to the lord than a suit in the king's court for the enforcement of customs and services, and it must also have appeared to the tenant to be a milder remedy than the enforcement of the forfeiture on which the lord in many cases might have insisted. Besides, it was much to the interest of both parties that the service due should be satisfied and the tenure continued. To oust the tenant worked hardship on him and profited the lord but little. It was not long, however, until the remedy became a means of oppression, and during the twelfth and thirteenth centuries there were many outcries from the tenants.

Hardship incident to abuses of the right to distrain.

The Statute of Marlborough recites that many of the lords had been accustomed unlawfully to exact heavy ransoms and levy unlawful distresses, holding them for redemption at their own will and refusing to deliver up according to law what they had seized of their own authority.[7] It is plain they were

[7] Stat. Marl. (1267), c. 1.

Volume III

departing far from that theory according to which the distress ought to be accompanied or preceded by judicial action in their own courts, at least. The nobility had evidently turned it into a purely *ex parte* and extrajudicial proceeding.

Statute of Marlborough codifies law of distress.

An effort was accordingly made in the Statute of Marlborough to remedy the evil. This enactment is almost an attempt at a codification of the law of distress, so fully does it go into the matter. Nor indeed was further legislation necessary on the subject until far down into modern times. The statute apparently marks the period when the king's court finally got the law of distress well into hand and marked out its definite limits. It was expressly provided that no person should undertake to exact justice for himself without judgment of the king's court; and that distresses should not be taken in other cases than those allowed by law, and then they should be reasonable in amount. Otherwise the offender was to be heavily fined.[8] It was also provided that cattle distrained should not be driven out of the county where taken; and the right of taking distress at all was strictly limited to the boundaries of the fee.[9]

Right to distrain an incident of feudal jurisdiction.

A perusal of the statute will show that a close connection still existed in theory between the right to distrain and the possession of feudal jurisdiction. Bracton gives a lengthy dissertation upon the grounds available to the distrainor as a justification of his distraint. It is not necessary to specify them. But it is worth noting that first of all he places this ground, namely, that the seizure was justly made by the lord in pursuance of the judgment of his court, for a service owing by his tenant and unlawfully withheld. To prove this he might vouch his court to warranty.[1]

Proceedings in distress.

Let us now turn to the act of distress itself and follow up the steps which were necessary to be taken by the party dis-

[8] Stat. Marl., c. 4.

[9] Stat. Marl., c. 15.

[1] "Tunc dicat captor quod juste cepit et per considerationem curiae suae, pro servitio quod idem querens et tenens suus ei debuit et ei injuste detinuit; et inde poterit vocare curiam suam ad warrantum si voluerit." Bracton, 157*b*, § 8.

Chapter XX

The seizure.

training. Having, in a typical case, seized the cattle of his tenant, the distrainor drove the beasts to an inclosure, usually open to the sky and known as the village pound. There is no more ancient institution in the country, says Professor Maine, than the village pound. It is far older than the King's Bench and probably older than the kingdom.[2] While the cattle were

[2] Early Hist. Inst. 263.

Archaic Features of Distress.— Professor Maine in a singularly felicitous and graphic way has directed attention to the various features of the taking of distress which connect this transaction with the very earliest stages of legal development. So much light does the passage in question shed upon the development of early remedial law, that we take the liberty of quoting it here. Says he: "The comparative antiquity of the various steps in the procedure is not, I think, difficult to detect. Nothing can be more archaic than the picture presented by its more venerable details. The seizure of the cattle, the rescue and the counter-seizure, belong to the oldest practices of mankind. We were carried back, by the *legis actio sacramenti* of the Romans, to a sudden fight over disputed property barely stopped by a casual passer-by. Here, not in a city community, but among the ancient legal forms of a half-pastoral, half-agricultural people, we come upon plain traces of a foray. But the foray which survives in the old law of distress is not, like the combat of the ancient Roman action, a mere dramatic representation. Up to a certain point it is a reality, and the most probable account of its origin is that it is a genuinely disorderly proceeding which the law steps in to regulate.

"You will see presently that there are other independent reasons for thinking that some of the earliest interferences of the power which we call the Law, the State, or the King, with high-handed violence consisted, neither in wholly forbidding it nor in assuming active jurisdiction over the quarrel which provoked it, but in limiting it, prescribing forms for it, or turning it to new purposes. Thus the next series of incidents in the practice of distraint — the impounding, the stress laid upon pledge or security, and the acknowledgment of continuing ownership which is implied in the liability of the person distrained upon to feed the cattle, and in the rule that the distrainor shall not work them — belong to a newer range of ideas which dictate the first attempts to moderate reprisals and regulate revenge for wrong. Distress now becomes a semi-orderly contrivance for extorting satisfaction.

"Many vestiges of this ancient function remain. It has been observed by Blackstone and others that the modified exemption of certain classes of goods from distraint — plough-oxen, for example, and tools of trade — was not in its origin the least intended as a kindness to the owner. It was entailed by the very nature of the whole proceeding, since without the instruments of tillage or handicraft the debtor could never pay his debt. A passage in the 'Dialogus de Scaccario' (ii. 14), prescribing the order in which the goods of the king's debtors are to be sold, strongly bears out this view.

"Latest in the order of proceeding, and latest probably in date, came the direct interposition of the state. The king steps in, first, in what we should now call his ad-

Volume III

The impounding. Right of rescue.

on their way to the pound, the owner had a limited right of rescue if the distress was unlawful. But this restricted right could only be exercised with great caution, for if it resulted in a breach of the peace, the owner was criminally liable. When the pound was reached and once closed upon the cattle the owner had no right to free them unless perchance the pound was left unfastened. The pound could not be broken even though the distress had been wrongfully taken.[3]

Owner must furnish provender to impounded cattle.

The distrainor's part in the proceeding ended with the act of impounding and he was not required thereafter to supply the creatures with subsistence.[4] This duty was imposed on the owner. If he failed to feed the animals and they died, the distrainor could again seize other distress to enforce his claim.[5]

Distrainor cannot use the distress.

It is obvious that the distrainor acquires no sort of property in the things distrained. He does not even acquire possession in law. At most the chattels are merely in his custody prior to the impounding, and thereafter they are in the custody of law.[6] Consequently the distrainor ordinarily has no authority

ministrative capacity. His administrative deputy, the sheriff, on complaint made by their owner, follows up the cattle, demands a sight of them, raises the hue and cry if it be refused, and seizes twice their number if the beasts have been driven away. Even when he obtains his view, he can do nothing unless the cattle-owner, denying the right of his adversary to distrain, is prepared with security that he will try the question between them in a court of justice. Thus tardily does that power make its appearance which according to our notions should long since have appeared on the scene — the judicial power of the commonwealth. Its jurisdiction is obviously acquired through the act of the sheriff in restoring the cattle upon pledge given. The distrainor has lost his material security, the cattle. The owner of the cattle has become personally bound. And thus both are placed under a compulsion which drives them in the end to a judicial arbitration." Early Hist. Inst. 265–267.

[3] In a writ *de parco fracto*, "the defendant cannot justify breaking the pound and taking them out, though the distress was without cause, because they are now in actual custody of law; yet note, before impounding, he might have rescued." Cotsworth *v.* Bettison, 1 Salk. 247.

[4] Observe, however, the following distinction: "If cattle be impounded in a pound close, the impounder shall sustain them without allowance for it." Co. Litt. 47*b*. In this case the party distrained upon could not get at the beasts, and consequently was under no obligation to provide for them.

[5] Anonymous, 3 Dyer 280*b*.

[6] Rex *v.* Cotton, Parker 121.

Chapter XX

to use the chattels taken by him, as by working beasts of the plough, or by milking cows that are in milk.[7]

Use of distress by distrainor constitutes a trespass.

One who tans hides which have been distrained becomes a trespasser although the tanning be necessary to the preservation of the hides. Such use changes the nature of the goods and makes it impossible for the owner to identify his property. But one who distrains armor may scour it to prevent rust.[8]

Goods seized in withernam may be used by distrainor.

The strict rule which prohibited the distrainor from using the distress did not apply in counter-distress. "If one hath cattle delivered to him in withernam he may work them because he has them in lieu of his own beasts; and it is reasonable that he should have their labor and use for their pasture." [9]

Writ of *rescous.*

De parco fracto.

Having neither property nor possession, the distrainor could not bring trespass [1] or trover against one who seized the distress while he was on the way to the pound or took it therefrom after the impounding. Special remedies were accordingly provided, the writ of *rescous* in the first instance, the writ *de parco fracto* in the latter.[2] In these writs the plaintiff alleged no property in himself, and it was not even necessary for him to show whose chattels they were.

Inasmuch as the distrainor could proceed no further than merely to impound his debtor's cattle, his remedy was incomplete. Such in theory distress indeed is — an imperfect remedy originating in an instinctive act of self-help. With com-

[7] A quaint application of this doctrine is given by Rolle. "If one takes a cow for distress, he may n milk her, for though the cow would be the better by this, still he ought not to do a favor to the owner without the latter's consent; peradventure also the owner might appear before any damage comes to the animal by this; and if she perish, still the distrainor can distrain again, so he suffers no damage." Bagshawe *v.* Galliard (1606), 1 Rolle Abr. 673, pl. 8. But the same case is reported differently by Croke, "Of necessity the cow may be milked to prevent her being spoiled." Cro. Jac. 147.

[8] Duncomb *v.* Reeve (1601), Cro. Eliz. 783.

[9] Anonymous, 2 Dyer 280*b*, note; Almeskey *v.* Johnson, Owen 46. In the latter case, a party upon surrendering the counter-distress sought to charge the other for the sustenance of the cattle. It was said, "As to the meat [i. e. provender], he had the use of the cattle, whereby it was reason he should sustain them."

[1] Brooke Abr., *Propertie,* pl. 52.

[2] Y. B. 20 Hen. VII. 1, pl. 1; F. N. B. 100, 101.

Volume III

mendable stubbornness, the common law has refused to make the remedy legally effective. A situation sufficiently embarrassing to both parties might result where an obstinate debtor chose to let his beasts remain in the pound.

Distress falls into disuse.

With the decay of the system of tenure with which distress was so completely associated, and with the corresponding extension of the modern remedy of assumpsit, the ancient remedy inevitably tended to obsolescence. As a means of recovering rent it was saved by a statutory enactment which turned it into a complete legal remedy by giving the distrainor a power of sale.[3] It was, however, touched very little by legislation during the period when it was most in vogue.[4]

Very common remedy in middle ages.

Hardly any other remedy was more frequently used from the thirteenth to the seventeenth century. The year books contain an enormous number of cases on distress, and the old authors are full of learning on the subject.[5]

During the same period the remedy gradually grew more and more technical in response to judicial prejudice against it as an essentially *ex parte* remedy. Professor Maine has called

[3] 2 W. & M., Sess. 1, c. 5.

[4] The Statute of Westminster II. contains some provisions on the subject of distress, but these enactments belong to the same period as the Statute of Marlborough and are in furtherance of its policy. It appears that notwithstanding the protection given to tenants by the earlier statutes, the lords frequently drove the cattle distrained into their castles or fortresses, which were inaccessible to the king's officers, and it was impossible to replevy the distress. To remedy this it was provided by 13 Edward I., c. 17, that if such lords did not, upon being duly warned, make deliverance of the distress, the fortress should be demolished and the lord should restore double the value of the things distrained. Also, heavy fines were, by chapters 36 and 37 of the same act, imposed for using the remedy of distress on colorable grounds for the purpose of extorting illegal fines. In the reign of Mary a statute was passed which re-enacted the clause in the Statute of Marlborough making it unlawful to drive distress out of the hundred, or wapentake, except to a pound overt within the same shire and not above three miles distant from the place where taken. 1 & 2 Philip & Mary, c. 12. There was very little legislation on the subject, and no radical change until the statute of William and Mary above referred to.

[5] See *Distress* and kindred topics, like *Avowry* and *Replevin*, in the Digests of Brooke, Fitzherbert, Rolle, Comyn, Viner, and Bacon; also the essays by Gilbert, Bradby, and Bullen, on Distress. Its prominence as a remedy during the reign of Edward I. is indicated by the legislation of that period.

Chapter XX

Distress becomes burdened with technicalities.

attention to the fact that the analogous formal remedy in Roman law went through exactly the same process. Gaius, speaking generally of the *legis actiones,* says, "they fell into discredit because through the excessive subtlety of the ancient lawyers, things came to such a pass that he who committed the smallest error failed altogether."[6] With this language compare the entirely similar but wholly independent statement of Blackstone: "The many particulars which attend the taking of a distress used formerly to make it a hazardous kind of proceeding; for if any one irregularity was committed, it vitiated the whole."[7]

There is an abundance of matter in the old books which proves the correctness of Blackstone's statement. Truly the remedy is, as has been said, a two-edged sword by which one may bring down his antagonist, but not without danger to himself. In a case of trespass tried before Rolle, C. J., it appeared that the defendant had distrained a trunk for rent. Being informed that there were things of value in the trunk, he caused it to be corded as a precaution against loss or damage. It was adjudged that this interference with the chattels was unwarranted, and made the distress void.[8]

Doctrine of trespass *ab initio* largely associated with distress.

It is to be noted that the peculiar and exceptional doctrine of trespass *ab initio* no doubt had its origin largely in this prejudice against distraint. An irregularity in the distress made the distrainor a wrongdoer from the beginning and made him subject to the action of trespass. "If the lord who distrains for rent, or the owner for damage feasant, works or kills the distress . . . the law adjudges that he entered for that purpose; and because the act which demonstrates it is a trespass, he shall be a trespasser *ab initio.*"[9] This principle was modified in 1738 by a statute which provided that distresses should not thereafter be treated as being made alto-

[6] "Sed istae omnes legis actiones paulatim in odium venerunt; namque ex nimia subtilitate veterum qui tunc jura condiderunt eo res perducta est, ut vel qui minimum errasset litem perderet." Gaius, Inst., Lib. IV., § 30.

[7] 3 Bl. Com. 14.

[8] Cited by Twisden in Welsh *v.* Bell. 1 Vent. 37.

[9] Six Carpenters Case, 8 Coke 146*b*.

Volume III

gether unlawful and void merely because of some irregularity incident to the proceedings, but the party aggrieved was by the same statute permitted to maintain his action for such damage as actually resulted from the irregularity.[1] But when this act was passed feudalism was a thing of the past, distress had been restricted almost wholly to the recovery of rent, and an entirely different character had been given to the remedy by the statute of William and Mary.

Principal incidents of military tenures.

The incidents attached to the principal military tenures (knight service and grand serjeanty) were homage, fealty, aids, reliefs, primer seisin, wardship, marriage, fines for alienation, and escheat. For these the lord was generally entitled to enforce a forfeiture or to distrain. The Statutes of Westminster III (*Quia Emptores*)[2] and *De Prerogativa Regis*[3] prohibited mesne lords and tenants *in capite* from making subinfeudations of their lands, and thus operated to lessen the number and variety of legal services incident to the tenure of land. Still, during the whole of the middle ages services due from the tenant in demesne to the crown and to the ancient seignories were numerous enough. A great revolution was effected by a statute of 12 Charles II,[4] for by this enactment military tenures were virtually abolished and converted into tenures in free and common socage.[5] As a consequence all feudal incidents connected with them were discharged.

Abolition of the military tenures.

Reservations of the statute.

Nevertheless there was a reservation in this statute in favor of rents certain, heriots, and suits of court belonging to any tenure so abolished, and in favor, of course, of all services incident to common socage and the fealty and distress belonging thereto. Copyhold tenures and tenures in frankalmoign, as well as the honorary service in tenures by grand serjeanty, were also left untouched by the act. By reason of the modern enfranchisement acts, the copyhold tenures have become very much less important than formerly, while tenures in frankal-

[1] Stat. 11 Geo. II., c. 19.

[2] 18 Edw. I.

[3] 17 Edw. II., c. 6; 1 Edw. III., Stat. 2, c. 12; 34 Edw. III., c. 15.

[4] Chapter 24.

[5] 2 Bl. Com. 76.

moign and grand serjeanty have become practically obsolete. Only such of the old feudal incidents as were or might be attached to tenures in free and common socage therefore remained.

Surviving feudal incidents:

The three incidental services which so survived were fealty, heriots, and suit service, all of which have become of comparatively little importance. To fealty, distress is incident as of common right and is inseparable from it unless by an act of the law.[6]

1. Fealty.

There were two kinds of heriots — heriot service, which was never due save by particular reservation; and heriot custom, due by immemorial custom. It was an old rule that for heriot service distress could be levied; while for a heriot custom the lord should seize, and not distrain, for the property in the heriot vested in him at the moment of the tenant's death.[7] Hence he could seize the specific heriot, but could not distrain any other chattel for it.[8]

2. Heriots.

Suit of court was a third species of service spared by the statute of 12 Charles II. This was of two kinds — suit-real and suit-service. The first is that attendance which persons residing in the jurisdiction of a county court or court-leet owe to those courts. The defaulter was liable to a fine or amerciament which could be levied by distress. The other, suit-service, is that attendance which is due to the court baron by the freehold tenants of a manor and to the customary court by its copyhold tenants, in order to form the jury. For this service likewise the lord could distrain.[9]

3. Suit-service.

6 Co. Litt. 151*b*, 153*a*.

7 Y. B. 8 Hen. VII. 10, pl. 3.

8 Odiham *v.* Smith, Cro. Eliz. 589.

9 Suit of Court and Services, 3 Salk. 332.

The obligation on the customary and freehold tenants of a manor to repair to the lord's mill for the grinding of their grain, is also classed as a species of suit service. Distress would lie for subtraction of this service, or the lord could sue a writ *de secta ad molindinum* at his option.

Bradby on Distress 157; Reg. Brev. Orig. 153.

CHAPTER XXI.

THE REMEDY OF DISTRESS (CONTINUED).

Distress for Rent.

Volume III

TO inquire into the extent to which the incidents of socage tenure not abolished by the statute referred to above may now be recognized in English custom and law would take us too far afield. But it is very evident that judicial, social, and industrial evolution works steadily towards their extinction.[1] The result of this is that the remedy is now chiefly used to enforce the payment of rent. It is in this aspect that the remedy still has importance in modern times, and the fact that it furnishes an expeditious remedy for the recovery of rent has been the sole reason why it has been disencumbered of technicalities and made more effective. We shall accordingly say a few words of it as used for this purpose in modern times.

Distress now chiefly used for rent.

The subject of rent is involved in a great deal of technical learning into which, for our present purposes, it is unnecessary to enter. It must be borne in mind that at common law rent is a thing which issues out of land. The creation of a rent in money gives rise to a real obligation in which the duty to pay is primarily imposed upon the land.[2] It is therefore an incorporeal hereditament. A clearer comprehension of the

Rent a real obligation.

[1] It may be added that reliefs may be incident to socage, and, if so, were not taken away by the statute. Mr. Hargraves has a learned note or two on the subject; Co. Litt. 85*a*, note 1; *ib.*, 93*a*, note 2; and it is discussed in Bradby on Distress 158, 160.

[2] *Rent a Charge upon the Land.* — An interesting question has lately been discussed as to whether rent is at common law a charge upon the land out of which it issues or is merely a charge upon the income of the land. That it is a charge upon the land seems to follow necessarily from its feudal origin, and this conclusion is amply borne out by a number of facts apparently not to be reconciled with any other view than that the duty to pay rent rests upon the land from which it issues, just as if the land itself were the debtor. The payment,

Chapter XXI

subject will be obtained if we distinguish the three kinds of rents known to the common law.

Three types of rent:

The typical feudal form of rent, after which the others have clearly been modeled, is the rent-service, "so called because it hath some corporeal service incident to it, as at the least fealty or the feudal oath of fidelity." Thus, to use Blackstone's language further, "if a tenant holds his land by fealty and ten shillings rent, or by the service of ploughing the lord's land and five shillings rent, these pecuniary rents being connected with personal services, are therefore called rent-service."[3] In cases of this kind the lord could distrain as of common right provided he himself owned the reversion or future estate in the lands after the lease or particular estate expired.

1. Rent-service.

The rent-charge differs from the rent-service in that it is created in favor of one who has no future interest or reversion in the land, "as where a man by deed maketh over to others his whole estate in fee simple with a certain rent payable thereout, and adds to the deed a covenant or clause of distress, that if the rent be arrere, or behind, it shall be lawful to distrain for the same."[4] If the special clause of distress be wanting, the rent is said to be *reditus siccus,* or a dry rent, rent-seck, and its payment cannot be enforced by distress.

2. Rent-charge.

3. Rent-seck.

Though the classification of rents into rent-service, rent-charge, and rent-seck is the one most frequently used by the older writers, a little consideration will show that the division of rents into rents reserved and rents granted is perhaps more helpful. These are discriminated by Professor Langdell as follows: "A rent is created by a reservation when the owner

Twofold division of rent:

1. Rent reserved.

however, must of course be made through the hands of the tenant, and it is he who is primarily affected by the enforcement of the duty. In a learned article Mr. T. C. Williams has recently stated the case in favor of this view with much force. Landowners' Liability to Pay Rentcharges in Fee, 13 L. Quar. Rev. 288; see also The Incidence of Rent, by the same writer, 11 Harv. L. Rev. 1. These articles embody a criticism on the position of Professor Langdell, who had previously expressed the opinion that rent is an obligation chargeable, not on the *corpus* of the land, but upon its fruits. Brief Survey of Equity Jurisdiction, 10 Harv. L. Rev. 78.

[3] 2 Bl. Com. 41, 42.

[4] 2 Bl. Com. 42.

Volume III

of land grants it to another person for years, for life, in tail, or in fee, reserving to himself a rent out of the same, the estate in the rent reserved being generally of the same duration as that granted in the land. A rent is created by grant when the owner of land grants a rent out of the same to another person for years, for life, in tail, or in fee."[5]

2. Rent granted.

It should be noted that a grant of rent does not create a personal relation of landlord and tenant, and the grantee becomes merely a creditor, not of the obligee personally, but of the land upon which the payment of the rent is charged. Hence the right to distrain for rent granted does not exist unless the contract granting the rent expressly so provides.

Distress for rents granted.

In case of the rent reserved, the situation is different. Here there is not a mere contractual grant of rent, but a conveyance of land, and the reservation of the rent is merely an incident thereto. At common law every conveyance of land creates a feudal relation between the parties, the grantee holding the land from the grantor and the latter having a reversion, or at least a feudal seignory in the land. Hence it follows, as Professor Langdell proceeds to say, that every rent reserved is payable by a feudal tenant to his lord, and the rent is in the nature of feudal service. It results from this that the right to distrain is a legal incident of every rent reserved, inasmuch as it is incident to every legal service.

Distress for rent reserved.

In the case of the rent-charge, as we have seen, the right of distress did not exist unless the deed expressly provided for it, and in case of the rent-seck it did not exist at all. Both these species of rent and a few other kinds or rent of minor importance were finally put on the same footing as the rent-service and rent reserved, as regards the right to distrain, by the Statute of 4 George II,[6] by which it was enacted that there should be like remedy by distress in case of rent-seck, as in case of rent reserved upon a lease. Distress, therefore, now belongs, subject to certain conditions named in the statute, equally to all sorts of rent.

Connection between distress and rent.

[5] Brief Survey of Equity Jurisdiction, 10 Harv. L. Rev. 78, 79.
[6] Chapter 28, § 5.

The connection between rent and the right to distrain is so intimate at common law that if a man grants a mere right of distress in a particular manor to a certain amount, it operates to create a valid rent-charge.[7] So also it is settled that no rent can issue out of incorporeal hereditaments such as rights of common, piscary, and franchises, but only out of lands and tenements upon which the grantee might distrain.[8] Nor can an agreement of the parties change the law in this respect.[9]

Rent must be reducible to certainty.

As it is necessary that rent should be reserved out of a corporeal hereditament, so it is essential that the rent, or service, be certain in quantity, extent, and time of payment, or at least that it be capable of being reduced to certainty; for *id certum est quod certum reddi potest.*[1] For this reason the lord could not distrain upon failure of a tenant in frankalmoign to perform divine services uncertain in both time and number. But it was always sufficient if the rent could be reduced to certainty, as where a tenant held by the service of shearing all the sheep depasturing within the manor.[2]

Rent reserved to stranger cannot be distrained for.

It is a principle of the common law that rent cannot be reserved to a stranger.[3] If so reserved it cannot be enforced by distress. Privity of relation between the parties to a rent-service or rent-charge is therefore quite as essential as privity between the parties to an action of debt or assumpsit. This essential element in the creation of a distrainable rent was supplied by the relation between lessor and lessee, feoffor and feoffee, grantor and grantee. By reason of his prerogative the king was exempt from this rule and could reserve a rent to a stranger.

The requirement of privity between the person owing the rent and the party entitled to distrain therefor was not fatal to the transfer or assignment of the estate or interest to which the rent was incident. Consequently it did not prevent the

[7] 1 Co. Litt. 147*a*.

[8] 1 Co. Litt. 47*a*, 144*a*.

[9] Butt's Case, 7 Coke 23*b*.

[1] 1 Co. Litt. 96*a*.

[2] *Ib.*

[3] "No rent (which is properly said a rent) may be reserved upon any feoffment, gift, or lease, but only to the feoffor, or to the donor, or to the lessor, or to their heirs, and in no manner it may be reserved to any strange person." Litt. § 346; 2 Co. Litt. 213*b*.

Volume III

Obligation to pay rent assignable, and after attornment assignee could distrain.

assignment by the creditor of the obligation to pay rent. The rule requiring privity did, however, make it necessary that the tenant should attorn to the new lord or grantee. Otherwise the latter could not distrain. The attornment operated as a recognition of the new party, supplied the link necessary to create privity, and at the same time gave the new lord or grantee seisin of the rent. The statute of 4 Anne [4] made attornment unnecessary, and since then the doctrine of seisin with relation to distress for rent has become unimportant.

Rent reserved an incident to the reversion.

From the nature of rent reserved, it will be seen that it was closely associated with the reversion. If separated from the reversion it lost its character as rent reserved and became rent-seck. Thus, if a man being entitled to a rent-service granted it away by deed to another, retaining the reversion in himself, such rent-service became in the hands of the grantee a mere rent-seck, and the right to distrain at once ceased.[5]

Distress inseparable from fealty.

The same result followed where the rent was for any reason separated from the fealty or other feudal service. Thus, if a tenant held by fealty and a certain rent, and the lord, reserving the fealty to himself, granted the rent to another and the tenant attorned to the grantee, the remedy of distress did not follow the rent, but remained in the lord. "Distress is an incident inseparable from the fealty," and it is even said that a release of the right to distrain is void.[6] The rent might be separated from the fealty, but the right to distrain could not. Consequently the assignee of the rent could not distrain; otherwise the tenant would have been liable to two distresses by reason of one tenancy. This was not permitted.

Conveyance necessary to support reservation of rent.

It is to be observed that rent must either be reserved upon the making of a conveyance or granted by a sufficient deed; and the conveyance which will support a reservation of rent must be such as would convey an estate or interest in land. It followed, before the Statute of Uses, that rent could not be reserved upon a bargain and sale, since only a use in favor of the bargainee was thereby created. But after the passage

[4] Chapter 16. [5] Litt., §§ 227, 228. [6] 1 Co. Litt. 151*b*.

of that statute[7] the legal title vested in the bargainee, and the bargainor could then distrain for the rent.[8]

Conditions to right of distress.

From what has been said it will be seen that before the right to distrain for rent can exist at common law, several things are necessary: (1) The lord or lessor should have the reversion in himself. (2) The rent should be reserved out of a corporeal hereditament. (3) It must be certain in quantity and duration. (4) It should be properly reserved in respect of the persons to whom it is payable; that is, there must be privity between the parties to the relation. And, finally (5), it must be reserved upon the making of a sufficient conveyance.

[7] 27 Hen. VIII., c. 10.

[8] 1 Co. Litt. 144a.

CHAPTER XXII

THE REMEDY OF DISTRESS (CONTINUED).

Distrainable Things.

Volume III

CONCERNING things liable to be taken in distress, we find it laid down by Coke that nothing shall be distrained for rent which cannot be rendered again in as good plight as it was at the time of the taking of the distress.[1] Out of indulgence to the tenant and in order to enable him to perform the service or pay the rent due, certain further exemptions are recognized as existing in his favor. The law in regard to this question was fully and accurately stated by Lord Chief Justice Willes in the leading case of *Simpson v. Hartopp* (1744),[1*] thus: "There are five sorts of things," said he, "which at common law were not distrainable: (1) Things annexed to the freehold. (2) Things delivered to a person exercising a public trade, to be carried, wrought, worked up, or managed in the way of his trade or employ. (3) Cocks or sheaves of corn. (4) Beasts of the plough and instruments of husbandry. (5) The instruments of a man's trade or profession. The first three sorts were absolutely free from distress, and could not be distrained, even though there were no other goods besides. The last two are only exempt *sub modo*, that is, upon a supposition that there is sufficient distress besides.

Exemptions in favor of tenant.

Absolute exemption.

Qualified exemption.

"Things annexed to the freehold, as furnaces, millstones, chimney-pieces, and the like, cannot be distrained, because they cannot be taken away without doing damage to the freehold, which the law will not allow. Things sent or delivered to a person exercising a trade, to be carried, wrought, or manufactured in the way of his trade, as a horse in a smith's shop,

Reasons for exemption.

[1] 1 Co. Litt. 47; Gilbert on Distress 34, 48.

[1*] Willes 512.

materials sent to a weaver, or cloth to a tailor to be made up, are privileged for the sake of trade and commerce, which could not be carried on if such things under these circumstances could be distrained for rent due from the person in whose custody they are.

"Cocks and sheaves of corn were not distrainable before the Statute of 2 William and Mary, c. 5 (which was made in favor of landlords), because they could not be restored again in the same plight and condition that they were before upon a replevin, but must necessarily be damaged by being removed. Beasts of the plough, etc. [i. e. farming implements], were not distrainable, in favor of husbandry (which is of so great advantage to the nation), and likewise because a man should not be left quite destitute of getting a living for himself and his family. And the same reasons hold in the case of the instruments of a man's trade or profession. But these two last are not privileged in case there is distress enough besides; otherwise they may be distrained."

Implement of trade cannot be distrained while in use.

The question before the court in this case was whether a stocking frame could be taken in distress while it was actually being used by a weaver. It was held that, being an implement of trade, the stocking frame was liable to be distrained as a last resort if no other distress could be taken:[2] but that inasmuch as it was in actual use at the time of the seizure it was privileged. Two reasons were given for this: First, the implement would be apt to be injured in removing it, or at least, the stocking with which the worker was engaged at the time would be stopped and probably spoiled; consequently it could not be restored in the same plight and condition. Secondly, the taking of a stocking frame out of the custody of the person by whom it is in actual use tends, or may tend, to a breach of the peace. The latter is probably the true reason; for notwithstanding Blackstone, on the authority of *Webb v. Bell* (1670),[3] stated that a horse may be distrained damage feasant

Basis of the privilege.

[2] Vinkinston *v.* Elden, Carth. 358.

[3] 1 Sid. 440. In this case it appeared that the distrainee had his horses to a cart laden with oats. The distrainor seized the horses for rent arrere owing by the distrainee in respect of the premises where the horses were taken.

Volume III

though a man be riding him at the time,[4] the contrary is now law and there is no exception to the rule that things actually in use are privileged.[5]

Extent of exemption incident to use.

The protection afforded by the exemption just noted is extensive and important. Under it goods in the hands of a carrier, for carriage, or in the hands of a commission merchant, for sale, are not distrainable.[6] The same is true of things in the hands of an auctioneer for sale,[7] of silk delivered to a manufacturer to be made up,[8] and of chattels pledged in the usual course of business to a pawnbroker or left with a depositary.[9] A cab let at rent to a driver is exempt as his implement of trade.[9*]

When goods of stranger may be taken.

If a chattel which does not fall within some one of the various classes of exempt things is actually found in the tenant's possession, or even on the demised premises, it is liable to be taken in distress. The doctrine that the property of one man can be taken for the debt of another merely because it is found upon the premises, and regardless of the manner in which it came there, exhibits a disregard of fundamental justice which is curious. Such a rule could only originate in a society where, as under the feudal system, the rent is looked upon as a charge on the land rather than as a debt of the tenant. Even then the rule is hard to account for unless we bear in mind that live stock was the principal subject of distress and that the true owner ought to keep them either upon his own premises or under his control. It is possible also that the difficulty which the common law had in dealing with title to personal property, and its reluctance to go into what appeared to be collateral issues, may partly account for the survival of the rule.[1]

[4] 3 Bl. Com. 8.

[5] Simpson *v.* Hartopp, Willes 517.

[6] Gilman *v.* Elton, 3 Brod. & B. 75, 7 E. C. L. 355.

[7] Adams *v.* Grane, 3 Tyrw. 326.

[8] Gibson *v.* Ireson, 3 Q. B. 39.

[9] Swire *v.* Leach, 18 C. B. N. S. 479, 114 E. C. L. 479; Miles *v.* Furber, L. R. 8 Q. B. 77.

[9*] Lavell *v.* Richings, (1906) 1 K. B. 480.

[1] In Brown *v.* Sims (1828), 17 S. & R. (Pa.) 138, Chief Justice Gibson used the following striking language: "The right to distrain the property of a stranger rests on no principle of reason or justice; it is a feudal prerogative, handed

Chapter XXII

A rather novel application of the common-law doctrine on this point was involved in *Bull v. Horlbeck* (1793).[2] It appeared that a certain tenant of land in South Carolina was in arrears to his landlord for rent. A slave belonging to a third person casually came upon the premises and was seized by the landlord by way of distress to satisfy the rent. The owner brought an action of replevin for the slave. At the trial two of the judges, Rutledge, C. J. (afterwards chief justice of the United States), and Grimke, J., instructed the jury that in that state slaves casually found upon premises were liable to be distrained for rent owing in respect of such premises.[3]

Distraint of slave casually visiting on leased premises.

A third member of the trial court, Bay, J., was of a contrary opinion, and he told the jury that slaves must be considered an exception to the common-law principle by which chattels found upon premises are subject to be distrained for

down from the time when chattels were of little account, and when it may have been impolitic, if not unreasonable, to embarrass the lord with responsibility to one who had thrust his property in the way of the remedy to compel a performance of the services. But commerce, which wrought a change in the habits and pursuits of men, and gave an importance to personal transactions, necessarily produced a relaxation of the rule, so as to admit of a variety of exceptions, some of them of early origin, in favor of trade. These have been so often enumerated that it would be useless to pass them in review here, particularly as no two of the judges seem to have taken the same view of the principles applicable to them, or of the ground on which they were sustained. But be this as it may, there is little reason to doubt that the exceptions will, in the end, eat out the rule.

"The most plausible argument in support of it is that as the landlord is supposed to have given credit to a visible stock on the premises, he ought to be allowed recourse to everything he finds there. But this recourse cannot be presumed to have been in the view of the parties, where it would defeat the very object of the contract. The particular business for which the premises are let is always known to the landlord; and where the course of it will necessarily put the tenant in possession of the property of those who deal with or employ him, it is fair to presume the landlord intended to dispense with his prerogative, because to do so would be manifestly for his advantage."

In accordance with this view it was held in the case where this language was used that the goods of a third person placed on storage in a warehouse cannot be distrained for the rent of such warehouse.

[2] 1 Bay (S. Car.) 301.

[3] These judges, it should be added, justified this instruction on the ground that the point had been determined by former precedents in that state and they did not feel at liberty to depart from previous rulings. By a statute of December, 1799, slaves of third persons were expressly exempted from liability to be destrained.

rent. Slaves, argued this judge, have a will of their own, and it is not practicable for their masters to keep them from going abroad and visiting upon neighboring plantations. The jury took the same sensible view of the law and returned a verdict for the plaintiff.

American doctrine.

On the whole the modern decisions, especially in America, tend to restrict the operation of the rule by adding to the number of privileged things.[4] In *Youngblood v. Lowry* (1822),[5] Bay, J., observed that distress was a peculiarly feudal remedy and that the American courts ought originally to have held that it was not applicable to our state of society. Indeed, in some of the American states it has never been recognized.[6] In others it has been superseded by statutory remedies and is now wholly abolished.[7]

[4] Taylor on Landlord and Tenants, § 584; Riddle *v.* Welden, 5 Whart. (Pa.) 10.

Baron Parke's dissenting opinion in Muspratt *v.* Gregory, 1 M. & W. 650, contains a strong presentation of the view that exemptions should be favored.

[5] 2 McCord L. (S. Car.) 39.

[6] Folmar *v.* Copeland, 57 Ala. 588; Deaver *v.* Rice, 4 Dev. & B. L. (20 N. Car.) 431; Crocker *v.* Mann, 3 Mo. 472.

[7] Potter *v.* Hall, 3 Pick. (Mass.) 368; Fowler *v.* Rapley, 15 Wall. (U. S.) 328; Scruggs *v.* Gibson, 40 Ga. 518; Hosford *v.* Ballard, 39 N. Y. 150.

CHAPTER XXIII

THE REMEDY OF DISTRESS (CONTINUED).

Distress of Things Damage Feasant.

Chapter XXIII

THERE is reason to believe that in ancient Teutonic society distress was resorted to in many cases where modern law has refused to sanction it. In other words, it was doubtless a sort of universal remedy, and was not restricted to causes of action *ex contractu*. During historic times, however, the distress has generally been conceived as a remedy for the enforcement of contractual or quasi-contractual duties.[1] But there is one situation where the law recognizes the right to distrain in order to enforce reparation for a tort.

Distress chiefly associated with enforcement of contractual duties.

Distress damage feasant can hardly be said to have any history, for the law pertaining to it has never changed. We shall direct attention to a few points which will at once serve to illustrate its character and to emphasize its difference from feudal distress. If cattle or other things, animate or inanimate, be on the land of any other person than their owner, encumbering the land or otherwise doing injury thereto, they may be distrained and held until compensation be made for the injury.

Exception in case of cattle damage feasant.

This right is older than feudalism and hence is older than the right to distrain for feudal service, though it is not older than the ancient right to distrain for the breach of contractual duties in which feudal distress originated. As common right has always been said to support distress for feudal service, so the immemorial custom of the realm has always been assigned as the basis of the right to distrain things damage feasant. Nor, indeed, is any other explanation than the common in-

Antiquity of right to distrain for damage feasance.

[1] Under the *Lex Salica* only contractual duties could be distrained for. Bigelow, Hist. of Procedure, 201.

Volume III

stinct, common sense, and common custom of mankind necessary; for they all alike concur in permitting the injured party to take the damage-working thing into his custody. By this means he obtains irrefutable proof of the identity of the wrong-doer and at the same time puts himself in a position to force the owner of the chattel to compensate for the injury. It is also likely that the right to exercise the remedy found readier acceptance because it was in harmony with the archaic notion that an animate or inanimate thing doing injury to a man may itself be forfeited and appropriated by the injured party in satisfaction of his damage.

Who may distrain damage feasant.

The conception of privity which is necessarily involved in the feudal relation, and which is so important in distress for rent, is altogether absent in distress damage feasant. Hence the remedy is not confined to the owner of the soil, but extends to all who may be injured by the trespass, as commoners or other persons entitled to the use or produce of the land.[1*]

When commoner may distrain beast of his lord.

By custom a commoner may indeed distrain the beasts of his lord, as where the land is to lie fresh until a stated day, during which interim the lord is excluded from the land.[2] So also where by custom the lord should not put more than three horses on the land, the commoner may distrain additional horses to the same extent as if they belonged to a stranger.[2*] But if the lord has color of right for putting in his own cattle and the number admissible be not absolutely limited, the commoner cannot distrain, even though the lord put in more than he should.[3] The same rule applies in all cases of surcharging the common. Thus if the owner of cattle, having a right of pasture for two sheep to every acre of land, turns in too many, the excess cannot be taken in distress, for the proper number of cattle can be ascertained only by measuring the land.[3*] In such case the party aggrieved is not permitted to take immediate execution by distraining on his own judgment, and the

Surcharging the common.

1* 1 Rolle Abr. 405, pl. 5; Mary's Case, 9 Coke 112*b*; Hall *v.* Harding, 4 Burr. 2432.

2 Burt *v.* Moore, 5 T. R. 329, 335.

2* Kenrick *v.* Pargiter, Cro. Jac. 208, Yelv. 129; Dixon *v.* James, 2 Lutw. 1241; Ellis *v.* Rowles, Willes 638.

3 Hoddesdon *v.* Gresil, Yelv. 104.

3* Hall *v.* Harding, 4 Burr. 2426, 2431.

question must be submitted to the jury on a writ for the admeasurement of common.

Cattle may be distrained not only for injury done to the herbage and pasture, but for other damage of whatever kind. Hence an avowry by a defendant in replevin is good which avers generally that the cattle taken were doing damage on the premises, although it appear that the grass eaten belonged to others than the distrainor.[4]

When beasts to be taken.

It is ancient learning that distress damage feasant can be taken on the spot and at any time either day or night; "otherwise," as Coke says, "it may be the beasts will be gone before he can take them." [5] Distress for rent, on the contrary, can only be taken in the daytime — a rule adopted in order to give the tenant a chance to stop the proceeding by tendering the rent or service due.

No exemption save where chattel is in possession of individual.

As the right of taking distress damage feasant is exercised *in rem,* as it were — that is, against the thing doing injury — nothing is exempt unless it be in the possession of a man at the time. In this case to take the chattel might lead to a breach of the peace. Thus, as we have already seen, a horse with which a trespasser is riding down grain cannot be taken, nor a net in his hand.

Each beast to answer for its own damage.

Each particular animal distrained can be held only for the damage done by it. If ten cattle be damage feasant and only one be distrained, it can be held only for so much damage as itself may have occasioned. For the other damage trespass must be brought. Again, it is determined that animals can be taken damage feasant only for the injuries actually being done at the time of their caption. If they do damage to-day and go off, coming again at another time, the party cannot then hold them for the first damage. For reasons of this kind damage feasant is said to be the strictest distress that is.[6]

Beasts must be damage feasant at time of taking.

Coke illustrates the technical strictness of distress damage feasant in this connection in quaint language: "If a man come to distreyne for damage feasant, and see the beasts in his

[4] Hoskins *v.* Robins, 2 Saund. 324, 328.
[5] 1 Co. Litt. 142*a*.
[6] Vaspor *v.* Edwards, 12 Mod. 658.

Volume III

soyle, and the owner chase them out of purpose before the distresse is taken, the owner of the soyle cannot distreyne them, and if he doth, the owner of the cattle may rescue them; for the beasts must be damage feasant at the time of the distresse." [7]

Right to distrain damage feasant extends to inanimate things.

Finally, it is to be remarked that the right to distrain damage feasant is not restricted to living things.[8] A curious modern instance of distress of an inanimate object is found in *Ambergate, etc., R. Co. v. Midland R. Co.* (1853).[9] It appeared in this case that by act of Parliament it had been made unlawful for any one to use an engine upon a railway without a certificate of approval from the company whose railway was used; a penalty was imposed for violation of this provision, in favor of the company upon whose railway the unlicensed engine should be found. On one occasion the Ambergate Railway Company violated the statute in question by placing an unlicensed engine on the road of the defendant company. The latter thereupon distrained the engine damage feasant and impounded it. On an action being brought for a conversion it was held that the defendant company had an undoubted common-law right to distrain the engine, and consequently that the proper detention of the same to prevent the unlawful use of it could not be treated as a conversion.

Uncertainty of the damages.

Distress of things damage feasant is anomalous in respect to the fact that it lies to enforce an indefinite and uncertain duty. Who, for instance, is to fix the amount of compensation which should be paid in order to obtain a release of the things distrained? In losing possession the owner of the chattels taken loses the so-called nine points of the law and is apparently placed at a disadvantage. All the inconvenience of the proceeding is not on his side, however, for the party distraining may also be greatly embarrassed by the still more

[7] 1 Co. Litt. 161*a*; Clement *v.* Milner, 3 Esp. 95.

[8] In Bromhall *v.* Norton, T. Jones 193, it was held that turves encumbering a common cannot be burned by the owner of the premises, but it seems they may be distrained for the trespass.

[9] 2 El. & Bl. 793, 75 E. C. L. 793.

Chapter XXIII

exceptional rule that he must accept a tender of satisfaction made by the owner of the cattle at any time before the impounding[1] As a general rule a tender is not a good plea to a claim for unliquidated damages.

Distrainor must use due care.

It is perhaps needless to repeat in regard to distress taken damage feasant that the distrainor, as in case of distress for rent, acquires no right to use the chattels in any way; and if he negligently injures them, he is liable in trespass or case. Hence, he must drive animals to the pound with due care, gently leading those that are with young.[2]

[1] Vaspor *v.* Edwards, 12 Mod. 661.

[2] Anonymous, 3 Leon. 15: "A man brought an action of trespass against another for chasing of his ewes, being great with lambs, so as by such driving of them he lost his lambs. The defendant justified, because they were in his several damage feasans, wherefore he took them and drove them to the pound. And it was holden by the whole court to be no plea; for although he might take, yet he cannot drive them with peril."

TABLE OF CASES

CITED IN VOLUMES I, II, AND III.

A. F. Pike Mfg. Co. *v.* Cleveland Stone Co., 35 Fed. Rep. 896.......i. 425
Abbott *v.* Blossom, 66 Barb. (N. Y.) 353........................ii. 216
Abbott *v.* Doane, 163 Mass. 433...........................ii. 117, 120
Abbott *v.* Kimball, 19 Vt. 551...................................i. 47
Abbott *v.* Wolcott, 38 Vt. 666...................................i. 178
Abeles *v.* Western Union Tel. Co., 37 Mo. App. 554...............i. 452
Abrath *v.* North Eastern R. Co., 11 App. Cas. 247.................i. 331
Absor *v.* French, 2 Show. 28.....................................i. 23
Ackworth *v.* Kempe, 1 Dougl. 40...........................ii. 441, 466
Acton *v.* Blundell, 12 M. & W. 324...............................i. 198
Adams *v.* Adams, 17 Oregon 247..................................ii. 192
Adams *v.* Bafealds, 1 Leon. 240...................................i. 266
Adams *v.* Grane, 3 Tyrw. 326....................................iii. 306
Adams *v.* Irving Nat. Bank, 116 N. Y. 606........................ii. 229
Adams *v.* Lawson, 17 Gratt. (Va.) 250.............................i. 296
Adams *v.* Lee, 72 Miss. 281......................................ii. 293
Adamson *v.* Jarvis, 4 Bing. 66, 13 E. C. L. 344.............i. 244, 490
Addison *v.* Gandasequi, 4 Taunt. 574............................ii. 479
Agars *v.* Lisle, Hutton 10.......................................iii. 170
Agincourt, The, 1 Hag. Adm. 274..................................i. 40
Agra, etc., Bank, *In re,* L. R. 2 Ch. 391..........................ii. 402
Ahern *v.* Steele, 115 N. Y. 203...................................i. 223
Alabama G. S. R. Co. *v.* Crocker, 131 Ala. 584....................i. 160
Alabaster *v.* Harness, (1895) 1 Q. B. 339..........................i. 340
Aldred's Case, 9 Coke 57*b*.............................i. 202, 206, 218
Aldrich *v.* Wright, 53 N. H. 398...................................i. 18
Alexander *v.* Jenkins, (1892) 1 Q. B. 797..........................i. 277
Alexander *v.* Lewis, 47 Tex. 481.................................ii. 491
Alexander *v.* New Castle, 115 Ind. 51......................i. 121, 123
Alexander *v.* Southey, 5 B. & Ald. 247, 7 E. C. L. 85..............i. 246
Alleghany Fertilizer Co. *v.* Woodside, 1 Hughes (U. S.) 115........i. 424
Allen *v.* Bryson, 67 Iowa 596......................................ii. 87
Allen *v.* Cape Fear, etc., R. Co., 100 N. Car. 397...................i. 311
Allen *v.* Crofoot, 5 Wend. (N. Y.) 506...........................iii. 243
Allen *v.* Flood, (1895) 2 Q. B. 21.................................i. 348
Allen *v.* Flood, (1898) A. C. 1.......i. 318, 327, 344, 345, 347, 350, 353, 355, 356, 357, 358, 359, 361, 365, 478

Allen *v.* Hearn, 1 T. R. 57....ii. 111, 166
Allen *v.* Pryor, 3 A. K. Marsh. (Ky.) 305....ii. 173
Allsop *v.* Allsop, 5 H. & N. 534....i. 289, 290, 470
Allyn *v.* Boston, etc., R. Co., 105 Mass. 77....i. 138
Alsbrook *v.* Hathaway, 3 Sneed (Tenn.) 454....ii. 216
Alta Land, etc., Co. *v.* Hancock, 85 Cal. 219....i. 202
Ambergate, etc., R. Co. *v.* Midland R. Co., 2 El. & Bl. 793, 75 E. C. L. 793....iii. 312
American Print Works *v.* Lawrence, 21 N. J. L. 249....i. 23
Ames *v.* Union R. Co., 117 Mass. 541....i. 267
Amies *v.* Stevens, 1 Stra 128....ii. 301
Amoskeag Mfg. Co. *v.* Trainer, 101 U. S. 51....i. 423
Anchor *v.* Bank of England, 2 Dougl. 637....ii. 399
Anderson *v.* Clark, 155 Mass. 368....i. 170
Anderson *v.* Crockett, 6 Yerg. (Tenn.) 330....iii. 143
Anderson *v.* Gorrie, (1895) 1 Q. B. 668....i. 37
Anderson *v.* McPike, 86 Mo. 293....i. 414
Andrew *v.* Administrator, 11 Hen. VI....ii. 123
Andrew *v.* Boughey, 1 Dyer 75*a*....ii. 55, 90
Andrew *v.* Deshler, 45 N. J. L. 172....i. 323
Andrews *v.* Chapman, 3 C. & K. 289....i. 310
Andrews *v.* Mockford, (1896) 1 Q. B. 372....i. 397
Andrews *v.* Robertson, 111 Wis. 334....ii. 532
Andrews *v.* Woodmansee, 15 Wend. (N. Y.) 232....i. 300
Angle *v.* Alexander, 7 Bing. 119, 20 E. C. L. 71....i. 300
Annas *v.* Milwaukee, etc., R. Co., 67 Wis. 46....ii. 50
Anonymous, 1 Bulst. 96....iii. 171
Anonymous, 1 Comyns 43....ii. 383
Anonymous, Cro. Eliz. 10....i. 56
Anonymous, Dal. 84, pl. 35....iii. 183
Anonymous, 1 Dyer 25*b*, pl. 163....i. 54
Anonymous, 3 Dyer 280*b*....iii. 292, 293
Anonymous, Hardres 485....ii. 350, 351, 370, 376; iii. 140
Anonymous, Keilw. 77, pl. 25....iii. 108
Anonymous, 1 Leon. 208....iii. 132
Anonymous, 3 Leon. 15....iii. 313
Anonymous, 3 Leon. 119....iii. 120
Anonymous, 4 Leon. 81....ii. 97
Anonymous, 4 Leon. 167, pl. 273....iii. 271
Anonymous, 1 Ld. Raym. 739....iii. 260
Anonymous, 6 Mod. 25, 73....i. 330
Anonymous, 12 Mod. 514....iii. 106
Anonymous, Moo. K. B. 459, pl. 637....i. 316
Anonymous, Owen 57....ii. 299, 305
Anonymous, 1 Rolle Abr. 105, pl. 12....i. 183
Anonymous, 1 Salk. 280....ii. 176
Anonymous, 2 Salk. 655....i. 237
Anonymous, Skin. 119....i. 377, 392
Anonymous, Style 6....ii. 153
Anonymous, Style 392....i. 316

Anonymous, 1 Vent. 248....................................i. 207
Anonymous, 1 Vent. 264....................................i. 184
Anonymous, 1 Vent. 268....................................iii. 185
Antcliff *v.* June, 81 Mich. 477....................................i. 334, 335
Appilgarth *v.* Sergeantson, 1 Cal. Chan. 41....................................ii. 35
Appleton Bank *v.* McGilvray, 4 Gray (Mass.) 518....................................ii. 213
Arbouin *v.* Anderson, 1 Q. B. 498, 41 E. C. L. 642....................................ii. 407
Archambault *v.* Great North Western Tel. Co., 4 Montreal Q. B. 122..i. 298
Arend *v.* Smith, 151 N. Y. 502....................................ii. 120
Arkwright *v.* Newbold, 17 Ch. D. 325....................................i. 411, 413
Armory *v.* Delamirie, 1 Stra. 505....................................i. 252; ii. 317, 453
Arnold *v.* Norfolk, etc., Hosiery Co., 148 N. Y. 392....................................i. 414
Arnold *v.* Sprague, 34 Vt. 402....................................ii. 503, 504
Arnold *v.* Webb, 5 Taunt. 432, 1 E. C. L. 146....................................iii. 191
Arris *v.* Stukely, 2 Mod. 260....................................iii. 191
Arthur *v.* Griswold, 55 N. Y. 410....................................i. 393
Arthur *v.* Oakes, 63 Fed. Rep. 310....................................i. 366
Arthur Gordon, The, Lush. 270....................................i. 145
Artz *v.* Chicago, etc., R. Co., 34 Iowa 153....................................i. 141
Arundel *v.* Gardiner, Cro. Jac. 652....................................ii. 74
Ascue *v.* Sanderson, Cro. Eliz. 433....................................iii. 170
Ash *v.* Abdy, 3 Swanst. 664....................................ii. 169
Ashbrooke *v.* Snape, Cro. Eliz. 240....................................ii. 62; iii. 180
Ashby *v.* White, Holt K. B. 524, 2 Ld. Raym. 938, 1 Bro. P. C. 45.... i. 491; iii. 55
Ashmole *v.* Wainwright, 2 Q. B. 837, 42 E. C. L. 938....................................ii. 230
Aslin *v.* Parkin, 2 Burr. 665....................................i. 261
Assaby *v.* Manners, 2 Dyer 235*a*....................................ii. 42, 45
Astley *v.* Reynolds, 2 Stra. 915....................................ii. 230
Aston's Case, 2 Dyer 250*b*, *note*....................................iii. 272
Atchison *v.* Dullam, 16 Ill. App. 42....................................i. 83
Atchison *v.* Peterson, 20 Wall. (U. S.) 507....................................i. 201
Atherfold *v.* Beard, 2 T. R. 610....................................ii. 166
Atkins *v.* Banwell, 2 East 505....................................ii. 150
Atkins *v.* Hill, 1 Cowp. 284....................................ii. 144, 147
Atkins *v.* Johnson, 43 Vt. 78....................................i. 490
Atkinson *v.* Newcastle, etc., Waterworks Co., 2 Ex. D. 441......i. 174, 175
Atkinson *v.* Sinnott, 67 Miss. 502....................................i. 416
Atlas, The, 93 U. S. 302....................................i. 145
Atty.-Gen. *v.* Bouwens, 4 M. & W. 171....................................ii. 420
Atty.-Gen. *v.* Brighton, etc., Co-operative Supply Assoc., (1900) 1 Ch. 276....................................i. 227, 229
Atty.-Gen. *v.* Cambridge Consumers Gas Co., L. R. 4 Ch. 71.........i. 214
Atty.-Gen. *v.* Conservators, 1 Hem. & M. 1....................................i. 229
Atty.-Gen. *v.* Gee, L. R. 10 Eq. 131....................................i. 202
Atty.-Gen. *v.* Metropolitan R. Co., (1894) 1 Q. B. 384....................................i. 43
Atty.-Gen. *v.* Sheffield Gas Consumers Co., 3 DeG. M. & G. 304, 22 L. J. Ch. 811, 19 Eng. Rul. Cas. 273....................................i. 214
Atty.-Gen. *v.* Steward, 20 N. J. Eq. 415....................................i. 222
Atty *v.* Parish, 1 B. & P. N. R. 104....................................iii. 120

Atwill *v.* Macintosh, 120 Mass. 181....i. 311
Atwood *v.* Ernest, 13 C. B. 881, 76 E. C. L. 881....iii. 154
Atwood *v.* Fisk, 101 Mass. 363....i. 495
Auditor *v.* Ballard, 9 Bush (Ky.) 572....ii. 82
Austin *v.* Boston, etc., R. Co., 164 Mass. 282....i. 170
Austin *v.* Culpeper, Skin. 124....i. 291
Aveline *v.* Whisson, 4 M. & G. 801, 43 E. C. L. 414....ii. 172
Averett *v.* Booker, 15 Gratt. (Va.) 163....ii. 504
Averill *v.* Longfellow, 66 Me. 237....iii. 86
Avery *v.* Halsey, 14 Pick. (Mass.) 174....ii. 74
Awde *v.* Dixon, 6 Exch. 869....ii. 516
Ayerigg *v.* New York, etc., R. Co., 30 N. J. L. 460....ii. 467
Aylett *v.* Lowe, 2 W. Bl. 1221....iii. 135
Aynsley *v.* Glover, L. R. 10 Ch. 283....i. 209
Ayre *v.* Cravens, 2 Ad. & El. 2, 29 E. C. L. 11....i. 277
Ayres, *In re*, 123 U. S. 503....i. 36
Ayres *v.* Birtch, 35 Mich. 501....i. 7
Ayres *v.* Chicago, etc., R. Co., 52 Iowa 478....ii. 129

Babcock *v.* Terry, 97 Mass. 482....ii. 74
Baber *v.* Harris, 9 Ad. & El. 532, 36 E. C. L. 193....iii. 123, 179
Babington *v.* Lambert, Moo. K. B. 854....iii. 188
Back *v.* Stacey, 2 C. & P. 465, 12 E. C. L. 218....i. 210
Backhouse *v.* Harrison, 5 B. & Ad. 1098, 27 E. C. L. 276....ii. 407
Backus *v.* Danforth, 10 Conn. 297....ii. 387, 504
Bacon *v.* Smith, 1 Q. B. 345, 41 E. C. L. 571....i. 31; iii. 270
Bacon *v.* Woodward, 12 Gray (Mass.) 382....ii. 149
Bagge *v.* Slade, 3 Bulst. 162....ii. 106
Bagnal *v.* Sachaverell, Cro. Eliz. 292, pl. 5....iii. 135
Bagshawe *v.* Galliard, 1 Rolle Abr. 673....iii. 293
Bahel *v.* Manning, 112 Mich. 24....i. 83
Bailey *v.* Bidwell, 13 M. & W. 73....iii. 202
Bailey *v.* Bussing, 28 Conn. 455....ii. 240
Bailey *v.* Colby, 34 N. H. 29, 35....i. 240
Bailey *v.* Day, 26 Me. 88....ii. 69
Bailey *v.* Manchester, etc., R. Co., L. R. 7 C. P. 415....ii. 470
Baily *v.* Merrell, 3 Bulst. 95....i. 393, 415
Baker *v.* Bolton, 1 Campb. 493....iii. 73
Baker *v.* Fales, 16 Mass. 147....iii. 221
Baker *v.* Hill, 3 Keb. 627....ii. 370
Baker *v.* Metropolitan L. Ins. Co., 64 S. W. Rep. 913....i. 366
Baker *v.* Moore, cited in 1 Ld. Raym. 491....i. 229
Baker *v.* Portland, 58 Me. 199....i. 177
Baker *v.* Smith, Style 293....i. 463
Baker *v.* Sun L. Ins. Co., 64 S. W. Rep. 967....i. 366
Balch *v.* Patten, 45 Me. 41....iii. 199
Baldwin *v.* Cole, 6 Mod. 212....i. 233, 247; iii. 168
Baldwin *v.* Elphinston, 2 W. Bl. 1037....i. 297
Baldwin *v.* U. S. Tel. Co., 45 N. Y. 744....i. 450
Baldy *v.* Stratton, 11 Pa. St. 316....i. 272, 465

Ball, *Ex p.*, 10 Ch. D. 667....................i. 327, 495
Ball *v.* Bruce, 20 Ill. 161....................i. 270
Ball *v.* Dunsterville, 4 T. R. 313....................ii. 475
Ball *v.* Ray, L. R. 8 Ch. 469....................i. 218
Ballard *v.* Tomlinson, 29 Ch. D. 115....................i. 203
Ballew *v.* Alexander, 6 Humph. (Tenn.) 433....................i. 495
Ballingalls *v.* Gloster, 3 East 481....................ii. 552
Baltimore *v.* Warren Mfg. Co., 59 Md. 96....................i. 202
Baltimore, etc., R. Co. *v.* Jones, 95 U. S. 439....................i. 138
Baltimore, etc., R. Co. *v.* Washington Fifth Baptist Church, 108 U. S. 332....................i. 44
Bamford *v.* Turnley, 3 B. & S. 62, 66, 113 E. C. L. 62, 66....................i. 218, 219
Banes' Case, 9 Coke 94....................ii. 34
Bangs *v.* Little, 1 Ware (U. S.) 506....................i. 39
Bank of England *v.* Vagliano, (1891) A. C. 107....................ii. 511, 512
Bank of Ireland *v.* Archer, 11 M. & W. 383....................ii. 401
Banks *v.* Highland St. R. Co., 136 Mass. 485....................i. 180
Barber *v.* Fox, 1 Vent. 159....................ii. 77
Barber Surgeons *v.* Pelson, 2 Lev. 252....................iii. 189
Barclay *v.* New South Wales Bank, 5 App. Cas. 374....................ii. 94
Bard *v.* Bard, Cro. Jac. 602....................iii. 188
Barford *v.* Stucky, 8 Moore 88, 1 Bing. 225, 8 E. C. L. 483....................iii. 122
Barham *v.* Dennis, Cro. Eliz. 769....................i. 267
Barham's Case, 4 Coke 20....................i. 282
Baring *v.* Corrie, 2 B. & Ald. 137....................ii. 479
Barker *v.* Bucklin, 2 Den. (N. Y.) 45....................ii. 187
Barker *v.* Furlong, (1891) 2 Ch. 181....................i. 244
Barker *v.* Miller, 6 Johns. (N. Y.) 195....................i. 252
Barnard *v.* Coffin, 141 Mass. 37....................ii. 465, 477
Barnard *v.* Poor, 21 Pick. (Mass.) 378....................i. 481
Barnardeston *v.* Soame, 6 How. St. Tr. 1096....................i. 38
Barnes *v.* Bruddel, 1 Lev. 261....................i. 285
Barnes *v.* Chapin, 4 Allen (Mass.) 444....................i. 52
Barnes *v.* Hedley, 2 Taunt. 184....................ii. 144
Barnes *v.* Hurd, 11 Mass. 57....................iii. 260
Barnes *v.* Lloyd, 1 How. (Miss.) 584....................ii. 95
Barnes *v.* McCrate, 32 Me. 442....................i. 308
Barnes *v.* State, 88 Md. 347....................i. 300
Barnes *v.* Western Union Tel. Co., 27 Nev. 438....................i. 466, 473
Barnesville First Nat. Bank *v.* Western Union Tel. Co., 30 Ohio St. 555....................i. 450
Barr *v.* Essex Trade Council, 53 N. J. Eq. 101....................i. 367
Barr *v.* Gibson, 3 M. & W. 389....................i. 385
Barrington *v.* Turner, 3 Lev. 28....................i. 18
Bartlett *v.* Christhilf, 69 Md. 219....................i. 308
Bartlett *v.* Hoyt, 29 N. H. 317....................i. 252
Bartlett *v.* Tucker, 104 Mass. 336....................i. 405
Barton's Hill Coal Co. *v.* Reid, 4 Jur. N. S. 767, 3 Macq. H. L. 266....................ii. 462
Barwick *v.* English Joint Stock Bank, L. R. 2 Exch. 266....................ii. 465
Baseley *v.* Clark, 3 Lev. 37....................i. 19

Bass *v.* Chicago, etc., R. Co., 36 Wis. 450, 39 Wis. 636, 42 Wis. 654...i. 480
Bass *v.* Gregory, 25 Q. B. D. 481...i. 205
Bassell *v.* Elmore, 48 N. Y. 561...i. 288, 290
Basset *v.* Maynard, Cro. Eliz. 819, 2 Rolle 699...iii. 166
Basset *v.* Maynard, 1 Rolle Abr. 105, 5...iii. 151
Batavia Bank *v.* New York, etc., R. Co., 106 N. Y. 195...ii. 482, 486
Batchelor *v.* Fortescue, 11 Q. B. D. 474...i. 159
Baten's Case, 9 Coke 53*b*...i. 210, 215
Bates *v.* Nashville, etc., R. Co., 90 Tenn. 36...i. 160
Bates County Bank *v.* Anderson, 85 Mo. App. 351...i. 386
Bathrick *v.* Detroit Post, etc., Co., 50 Mich. 629...i. 309
Battersby *v.* Collier, 34 N. Y. App. Div. 347...i. 304, 305
Battersey's Case, Winch 48...i. 490; ii. 74
Baxter *v.* Hozier, 5 Bing. N. Cas. 288, 35 E. C. L. 114...iii. 110
Baxter *v.* Woodyard, Moo. K. B. 776, pl. 1075...i. 376
Bayley *v.* Homan, 3 Bing. N. Cas. 915, 32 E. C. L. 379...ii. 92
Bayliffe *v.* Butterworth, 1 Exch. 425...ii. 485
Baylis *v.* Lintott, L. R. 8 C. P. 349...iii. 274
Bays *v.* Hunt, 60 Iowa 251...i. 309, 315
Beach *v.* Hancock, 27 N. H. 223...i. 12
Beach *v.* Mullin, 34 N. J. L. 343...ii. 227
Beal *v.* South Devon R. Co., 3 H. & C. 337...i. 100
Beale *v.* Carter, Owen 98...i. 9
Bealey *v.* Shaw, 6 East 208...i. 202
Beamond *v.* Hastings, Cro. Jac. 240...i. 282
Bearce *v.* Bass, 88 Me. 521...i. 304, 305
Beasley *v.* Meigs, 16 Ill. 139...i. 290
Beaulieu *v.* Finglam, 2 Hen. IV...i. 56; ii. 443
Beaumont *v.* Reeve, 8 Q. B. 483, 55 E. C. L. 483...ii. 72
Beaumont's Case, Jenk. 348...i. 282
Baupre *v.* Pacific, etc., Tel. Co., 21 Minn. 155...i. 450
Bechuanaland Exploration Co. *v.* London Trading Bank, (1898) 2 Q. B. 658...ii. 416, 423
Beck *v.* Railway Teamsters' Protective Union, 118 Mich. 497...i. 367
Beckett *v.* Midland R. Co., L. R. 3 C. P. 82...i. 227
Beckwith *v.* Corral, 4 Bing. 444, 13 E. C. L. 44...ii. 406
Beckwith *v.* Oatman, 43 Hun (N. Y.) 265...i. 61
Beckwith *v.* Shordike, 4 Burr. 2092...i. 54
Bedan *v.* Turney, 99 Cal. 653...i. 264
Beecker *v.* Beecker, 7 Johns. (N. Y.) 99...ii. 148
Beedle *v.* Morris, Cro. Jac. 224...i. 189
Beers *v.* Arkansas, 20 How. (U. S.) 527...i. 35
Beirne *v.* Dord, 5 N. Y. 98...i. 389
Belknap *v.* Trimble, 3 Paige (N. Y.) 577...i. 202
Bell *v.* Midland R. Co., 10 C. B. N. S. 287, 100 E. C. L. 287...i. 481
Bell *v.* North, 4 Litt. (Ky.) 133...i. 47
Bell *v.* Stone, 1 B. & P. 331...i. 293
Bell *v.* Wood, 1 Bay (S. Car.) 249...ii. 73
Bellairs *v.* Tucker, 13 Q. B. D. 562...i. 394
Bemische *v.* Hildersley, 1 Rolle Abr. 11, pl. 20...iii. 180

Benjamin *v.* Storr, L. R. 9 C. P. 400....i. 227, 229
Bennett *v.* Allcott, 2 T. R. 166....i. 269, 271
Bennett *v.* Beam, 42 Mich. 349....i. 464
Bennett *v.* Francis, 2 B. & P. 550....iii. 198
Bennett *v.* New Jersey R., etc., Co., 36 N. J. L. 225....i. 141
Bennett *v.* Terrill, 20 Ga. 83....i. 415
Bentley *v.* Doggett, 51 Wis. 224....ii. 482
Bentley *v.* Whittemore, 18 N. J. Eq. 366....ii. 214
Berkeley *v.* Hardy, 5 B. & C. 355, 11 E. C. L. 251....ii. 474; iii. 122
Bernina, The, 12 P. D. 58, 89....i. 126, 142
Berry *v.* Da Casta, L. R. 1 C. P. 331....i. 464
Berry *v.* Donovan, 188 Mass. 353....i. 370
Berry *v.* Lake Erie, etc., R. Co., 70 Fed. Rep. 679....i. 144
Beseman *v.* Pennsylvania R. Co., 50 N. J. L. 235, 52 N. J. L. 221....i. 44
Besozzi *v.* Harris, 1 F. & F. 92....i. 55
Bessey *v.* Olliot, T. Raym. 467....i. 70
Best *v.* Jolly, 1 Sid. 38....ii. 34
Bestney's Case, Jenk. 361....i. 282
Beswick *v.* Chappel, 8 B. Mon. (Ky.) 486....i. 300
Beswick *v.* Cunden, Cro. Eliz. 402....i. 214
Bettisworth *v.* Campion, Yelv. 133....ii. 55, 135
Beven *v.* Cowling, Popham 183....ii. 34
Bibby *v.* Carter, 4 H. & N. 153....i. 196
Bigelow *v.* Baldwin, 1 Gray (Mass.) 245....ii. 95
Bilby *v.* Lumley, 2 East 469....ii. 211, 214
Bill *v.* Neal, 1 Lev. 52....i. 282
Bill *v.* Porter, 9 Conn. 23....ii. 390
Billings *v.* McCoy, 5 Neb. 187....ii. 212
Billings *v.* Wing, 7 Vt. 439....i. 276
Binford *v.* Johnston, 82 Ind. 426....i. 59, 172
Bingham School *v.* Gray, 122 N. Car. 699....i. 432
Binnington *v.* Wallis, 4 B. & Ald. 650, 6 E. C. L. 639....ii. 72
Birch *v.* Benton, 26 Mo. 153....i. 276, 290
Birdleback *v.* Wilkins, 22 Pa. St. 26....ii. 504
Bird *v.* Astcock, 2 Bulst. 280....ii. 301
Bird *v.* Brown, 4 Exch. 786....ii. 487
Bird *v.* Holbrook, 4 Bing. 628....i. 68
Bird *v.* Jones, 7 Q. B. 742, 53 E. C. L. 742....i. 14
Bird *v.* Monroe, 66 Me. 344....ii. 177
Birkhauser *v.* Schmitt, 45 Wis. 316....ii. 214
Birmingham *v.* Allen, 6 Ch. D. 284....i. 194
Birmingham First Nat. Bank *v.* Allen, 100 Ala. 476....ii. 248
Birmingham R., etc., Co. *v.* Allen, 99 Ala. 359....i. 170
Bishop *v.* Latimer, 4 L. T. N. S. 775....i. 301
Bishop *v.* Montague, Cro. Eliz. 824, Cro. Jac. 50....iii. 151, 165, 166, 170, 217, 238, 244
Bishop *v.* Young, 2 B. & P. 78....iii. 141, 143
Bishop Auckland Local Board *v.* Bishop Auckland Iron, etc., Co., 10 Q. B. D. 138....i. 221
Bittridge's Case, 4 Coke 19....i. 282

Bitz *v.* Meyer, 40 N. J. L. 252 .... i. 333
Bixby *v.* Dunlap, 56 N. H. 456 .... i. 346, 481
Black *v.* Ballymena Com'rs, 17 L. R. Ir. 459 .... i. 199
Black *v.* Lewiston, 2 Idaho 276 .... i. 178
Black *v.* Westminster First Nat. Bank, 96 Md. 399 .... ii. 531
Blackburn, etc., Bldg. Soc., 42 Ch. D. 343 .... iii. 135
Blackmore *v.* Fairbanks, 79 Iowa 282 .... i. 386
Blackwell *v.* Old Colony R. Co., 122 Mass. 1 .... i. 228
Blades *v.* Higgs, 10 C. B. N. S. 713, 10 E. C. L. 713 .... i. 8
Blake *v.* Barnard, 9 C. & P. 626, 38 E. C. L. 259 .... i. 12
Blanchard *v.* Hill, 2 Atk. 484 .... i. 419
Blanchard *v.* Ilsley, 120 Mass. 487 .... i. 270
Blanckenhagen *v.* Blundell, 2 B. & Ald. 417 .... ii. 510
Bland *v.* Moseley, 9 Coke 58*a* .... i. 207
Bland's Case, 1 Rolle Abr. 107, pl. 17, Hutton 136 .... i. 207
Bleaden *v.* Charles, 7 Bing. 246, 20 E. C. L. 119 .... ii. 233
Blin *v.* Campbell, 14 Johns. (N. Y.) 432 .... iii. 265
Bliss *v.* Hall, 4 Bing. N. Cas. 183, 33 E. C. L. 315 .... i. 220
Bliss *v.* Johnson, 73 N. Y. 529 .... i. 8
Block *v.* Standard Distilling, etc., Co., 95 Fed. Rep. 978 .... i. 426
Blofeld *v.* Payne, 4 B. & Ad. 410, 24 E. C. L. 87 .... i. 419
Blood *v.* Nashua, etc., R. Corp., 2 Gray (Mass.) 137 .... i. 228
Bloodworth *v.* Gray, 7 M. & G. 334, 49 E. C. L. 334 .... i. 277
Bloss *v.* Toby, 2 Pick. (Mass.) 320 .... i. 300
Blount *v.* Blount, 2 Law Repos. (4 N. Car.) 587 .... ii. 45
Blount *v.* Western Union Tel. Co., 126 Ala. 105 .... i. 468
Bloxam *v.* Saunders, 4 B. & C. 941, 10 E. C. L. 477 .... i. 253
Blyth *v.* Birmingham Waterworks Co., 11 Exch. 781 .... i. 97, 104
Blyth *v.* Topham, Cro. Jac. 158 .... i. 156
Boardman *v.* Meriden Britannia Co., 35 Conn. 402 .... i. 423
Boas *v.* Updegrove, 5 Pa. St. 516 .... ii. 213
Bobbett *v.* Pinkett, 1 Ex. D. 368 .... ii. 490
Bobbitt *v.* Shryer, 70 Ind. 513 .... ii. 244
Bodkin *v.* Western Union Tel. Co., 31 Fed. Rep. 134 .... i. 454
Bohn Mfg. Co. *v.* Hollis, 54 Minn. 223 .... i. 362, 366
Bolander *v.* Peterson, 136 Ill. 215 .... i. 424
Bolingbroke *v.* Local Board, L. R. 9 C. P. 575 .... ii. 456, 467
Bolling *v.* Kirby, 90 Ala. 215 .... i. 237
Bolton *v.* Hellersden, 1 Ld. Raym. 224, 3 Salk. 234, Holt K. B. 641, Comb. 450 .... ii. 453
Bolton *v.* Lambert, 41 Ch. D. 295 .... ii. 489
Bond *v.* Chapin, 8 Met. (Mass.) 31 .... i. 335
Bond *v.* Bunting, 78 Pa. St. 210 .... ii. 104
Bonion's Case, 8 Edw. II .... ii. 256
Bonnel *v.* Foulke, 2 Sid. 4 .... iii. 190
Bonney *v.* Bonney, 9 Manitoba 280 .... i. 398
Bonomi *v.* Backhouse, El. Bl. & El. 643, 96 E. C. L. 643 .... i. 211
Booth *v.* Ratcliffe, 107 N. Car. 6 .... ii. 221
Booth *v.* Rome, etc., Terminal R. Co., 140 N. Y. 267 .... i. 45
Boothe *v.* Fitzpatrick, 36 Vt. 681 .... ii. 87

Borland *v.* Barrett, 76 Va. 128....i. 486
Borough *v.* Perkins, 1 Salk. 131....ii. 380
Borradaile *v.* Brunton, 8 Taunt. 535, 4 E. C. L. 202....i. 446
Borrekins *v.* Bevan, 3 Rawle (Pa.) 23....i. 391
Bosden *v.* Thinne, Yelv. 40....ii. 84
Boson *v.* Sandford, 2 Salk. 440, 3 Mod. 321, 3 Lev. 258....i. 490; ii. 453
Boss *v.* Litton, 5 C. & P. 407, 24 E. C. L. 384....i. 134
Boston, etc., R. Corp. *v.* Dana, 1 Gray (Mass.) 83....i. 495
Boston Steel, etc., Co. *v.* Steuer, 183 Mass. 140....ii. 517, 521
Bosworth *v.* Swansey, 10 Met. (Mass.) 363....i. 179, 180
Bottomley *v.* Goldsmith, 36 Mich. 27....ii. 408
Boucher *v.* Lawson, Lee t. Hardw. 85, 94....ii. 453
Boughton *v.* Bishop, Anderson 119....i. 292
Bourlier *v.* Macauley, 91 Ky. 135....i. 346
Bourne *v.* Mason, 1 Vent. 6....ii. 153
Bovey *v.* Castleman, 1 Ld. Raym. 69....ii. 165; iii. 185, 193
Bowden *v.* Marlborough Electric Mach., etc., Co., 185 Mass. 549....i. 170
Bowen *v.* Hall, 6 Q. B. D. 333....i. 344, 345
Bowers *v.* Horen, 93 Mich. 420....i 18
Bowles's Case, 11 Coke 79*b*....i. 26
Bowman *v.* Browning, 17 Ark. 599....iii. 198
Bowman *v.* Carithers, 40 Ind. 90....i. 413
Bowser *v.* Cheseman, 20 Hen. VII....iii. 162
Boxsius *v.* Freres, (1894) 1 Q. B. 842....i. 297
Boyce *v.* Williams, 84 N. Car. 275....i. 252
Boyd *v.* Bopst, 2 Dall. (Pa.) 91....i. 384
Boyd *v.* Hind, 1 H. & N. 938....ii. 94, 131
Boyd *v.* Johnston, 89 Tenn. 284....ii. 148
Boyd *v.* Shiffer, 156 Pa. St. 100....i. 413
Boyd *v.* Wilson, 83 Pa. St. 319....i. 389, 391
Boyer *v.* Barr, 8 Neb. 68....i. 481
Boyson *v.* Thorn, 98 Cal. 578....i. 346
Brace *v.* Evans, 3 Ry. & Corp. L. J. 561, 35 Pittsb. L. J. 399....i. 367
Brackett *v.* Griswold, 112 N. Y. 454....i. 366, 393, 413
Bradfield *v.* Patterson, 106 Ala. 397....iii. 198
Bradford *v.* Manly, 13 Mass. 139....i. 389
Bradford *v.* Pickles, (1895) A. C. 587....i. 198, 355
Bradford *v.* Roulston, 8 Ir. C. L. 468....ii. 86
Bradlaugh *v.* Newdegate, 11 Q. B. D. 6....i. 338, 339, 340; ii. 164
Bradley *v.* Copley, 1 C. B. 685, 50 E. C. L. 685....i. 253
Bradley *v.* Methuen, 2 Ford 78....i. 293
Bradt *v.* New Nonpareil Co., 108 Iowa 449....i. 294
Brainerd *v.* New York, etc., R. Co., 25 N. Y. 496....ii. 501
Braithwaite *v.* Skinner, 5 M. & W. 313....ii. 149
Braithwaite *v.* Watson, 5 Times Rep. 331....i. 152
Brandao *v.* Barnett, 12 Cl. & F. 787....ii. 353, 421
Brantley *v.* Thomas, 22 Tex. 270....i. 388
Brayton *v.* Fall River, 113 Mass. 218....i. 229
Bree *v.* Marescaux, 7 Q. B. D. 434....i. 287
Brenner *v.* Brenner, 48 Ind. 263....ii. 192

Brenner *v.* Herr, 8 Pa. St. 106 ... ii. 102
Bret *v.* J. S., Cro. Eliz. 755 ... ii. 47
Brett *v.* Read, W. Jones 329 ... iii. 180
Brewer *v.* Dew, 11 M. & W. 625 ... iii. 86
Brewer *v.* Dyer, 7 Cush. (Mass.) 337 ... ii. 157
Brewster *v.* Shrader, 26 Misc. (N. Y.) 480 ... ii. 522
Brick Presbyterian Church, *In re*, 4 Bradf. (N. Y.) 503 ... i. 461
Bridge *v.* Langton, Lit. C. Pl. 193 ... i. 285
Bridgeford *v.* Masonville Mfg. Co., 34 Conn. 546 ... ii. 376
Bridges *v.* Hawkesworth, 7 Eng. L. & Eq. 424, 21 L. J. Q. B. 75 ... i. 252
Bridges *v.* Tennessee Coal, etc., Co., 109 Ala. 287 ... i. 170
Brierly *v.* Kendall, 17 Q. B. 937, 79 E. C. L. 937 ... i. 256
Briggs *v.* Boston, etc., R. Co., 6 Allen (Mass.) 246 ... i. 257
Briggs *v.* Garrett, 111 Pa. St. 404 ... i. 309, 315
Briggs *v.* Oliver, 4 H. & C. 403 ... i. 107
Brill *v.* Flagler, 23 Wend. (N. Y.) 354 ... i. 212
Brimsley *v.* Partridge, Hob. 88 ... iii. 188
Bringloe *v.* Morrice, 1 Mod. 210, 3 Salk. 271 ... ii. 282
Bringman *v.* Von Glahn, 71 N. Y. App. Div. 537 ... ii. 521
Brink *v.* Freoff, 40 Mich. 610 ... i. 256
Brisbane *v.* Dacres, 5 Taunt. 162, 1 E. C. L. 51 ... ii. 213
Bristol *v.* Burt, 7 Johns. (N. Y.) 254 ... i. 233
Bristol *v.* Warner, 19 Conn. 7 ... ii. 504
Bristol *v.* Wilsmore, 1 B. & C. 514, 8 E. C. L. 218 ... i. 259
Britain *v.* Rossiter, 11 Q. B. D. 123 ... ii. 177; iii. 57
British South Africa Co. *v.* Companhia De Mocambique, (1893) A. C. 602 ... iii. 57, 94
Brittain *v.* Lloyd, 14 M. & W. 762 ... ii. 233
Britton *v.* Turner, 6 N. H. 481 ... ii. 225
Brocas's Case, 3 Leon. 219 ... ii. 134
Brock *v.* Berry, 132 Ala. 95 ... i. 46
Brodbent *v.* Ledward, 11 Ad. & El. 200 ... iii. 152
Broke *v.* Abbot of Wobirne, 22 Hen. VI ... i. 184
Bromage *v.* Prosser, 4 B. & C. 247, 10 E. C. L. 321 ... i. 317, 323
Bromhall *v.* Norton, T. Jones 193 ... iii. 312
Bromwich *v.* Loyd, 2 Lutw. 1582 ... ii. 351, 352, 353, 379
Bronson *v.* Bruce, 59 Mich. 467 ... i. 309
Brooker *v.* Coffin, 5 Johns. (N. Y.) 188 ... i. 277
Brookline *v.* Mackintosh, 133 Mass. 215 ... i. 203
Brooks *v.* Haigh, 10 Ad. & El. 323, 309, 37 E. C. L. 115, 108 ... ii. 70
Brooks *v.* Martin, 43 Ala. 360 ... ii. 244
Brooks *v.* White, 2 Met. (Mass.) 283 ... ii. 103
Broschart *v.* Tuttle, 59 Conn. 1 ... i. 177
Brought *v.* Parkings, 2 Ld. Raym. 992 ... ii. 380
Brown *v.* Barry, 3 Dall. (U. S.) 365 ... **ii. 554**
Brown *v.* Boorman, 11 Cl. & F. 1, 3 Q. B. 511, 43 E. C. L. 843 ... iii. 275
Brown *v.* Carpenter, 26 Vt. 638 ... i. 17
Brown *v.* Castles, 11 Cush. (Mass.) 348 ... i. 393
Brown *v.* Collins, 53 N. H. 442 ... i. 105
Brown *v.* Conger, 8 Hun (N. Y.) 625 ... ii. 192

Brown *v.* Crump, 1 Marsh. 567, 4 E. C. L. 348....................ii. 86
Brown *v.* Edgington, 2 Scott N. R. 496....................i. 386
Brown *v.* Garborough, Cro. Eliz. 63....................ii. 47
Brown *v.* Giles, 1 C. & P. 118, 11 E. C. L. 337....................i. 54
Brown *v.* Harraden, 4 T. R. 151....................ii. 385
Brown *v.* Hawkes, (1891) 2 Q. B. 718....................i. 331
Brown *v.* Howard, 14 Johns. (N. Y.) 119....................i. 39, 40
Brown *v.* Kendall, 6 Cush. (Mass.) 292....................i. 79, 82
Brown *v.* Knapp, 79 N. Y. 136....................ii. 149
Brown *v.* London, 1 Vent. 152....................ii. 376
Brown *v.* Marsh, Gilb. Eq. 154....................ii. 388
Brown *v.* Marshall, 47 Mich. 577....................i. 61
Brown *v.* Nickerson, 5 Gray (Mass.) 1....................i. 277
Brown *v.* Perkins, 12 Gray (Mass.) 89....................i. 216
Brown *v.* Robins, 4 H. & N. 186....................i. 193, 197, 198
Brown *v.* Seidel, 153 Pa. St. 60....................i. 431
Brown *v.* Sims, 17 S. & R. (Pa.) 138....................iii. 306
Brown *v.* Swineford, 44 Wis. 289....................i. 480
Brown *v.* Western Union Tel. Co., 6 Utah 219....................i. 459
Browne *v.* Dawson, 12 Ad. & El. 624, 40 E. C. L. 137....................i. 9
Browne *v.* Hancocke, Hetley 111....................iii. 120
Browne *v.* London, 1 Mod. 285, 1 Lev. 298, 2 Keb. 695.....iii. 140, 141, 193
Brownlie *v.* Campbell, 5 App. Cas. 952....................i. 403
Bruce *v.* Burdet, 1 J. J. Marsh. (Ky.) 80....................iii. 111
Bruce *v.* Reed, 104 Pa. St. 408....................i. 298
Bruce *v.* Wyman, 17 Harv. L. Rev. 156....................i. 186
Brucker *v.* Fromont, 6 T. R. 659....................iii. 261
Brumby *v.* Smith, 3 Ala. 123....................ii. 224
Brunswick *v.* Rex, 2 H. L. Cas. 1....................i. 37
Brunswig *v.* White, 70 Tex. 507....................i. 60
Brush *v.* Sweet, 38 Mich. 574....................iii. 87
Bryan *v.* Harr, 21 App. Cas. (D. C.) 190....................ii. 531
Bryant *v.* Crosby, 40 Me. 9....................i. 386
Bryant *v.* Herbert, 3 C. P. D. 189, 389....................iii. 156
Bryant *v.* Lefever, 4 C. P. D. 172....................i. 205
Buchanan *v.* Smith, 10 Hun (N. Y.) 474....................ii. 282
Buck *v.* Hersey, 31 Me. 558....................i. 276
Buckingham *v.* Costendine, Cro. Jac. 213....................iii. 181
Buckley *v.* Nightingale, 1 Stra. 665....................iii. 137
Buckley *v.* Wood, 4 Coke 14*b*....................i. 283
Buckstaff *v.* Hicks, 94 Wis. 34....................i. 310
Buddle *v.* Willson, 6 T. R. 369....................iii. 274
Bull *v.* Colton, 22 Barb. (N. Y.) 94....................i. 16, 17; iii. 234
Bull *v.* Horlbeck, 1 Bay (S. Car.) 301....................iii. 307
Bullard *v.* Bell, 1 Mason (U. S.) 243....................ii. 371, 395
Bullard *v.* Harrison, 4 M. & S. 387....................i. 23
Buller *v.* Crips, 6 Mod. 29....................ii. 368, 385
Bullock *v.* Babcock, 3 Wend. (N. Y.) 391....................i. 4
Bullock *v.* Lloyd, 2 C. & P. 119, 12 E. C. L. 53....................ii. 185
Bulstrode *v.* Gilburn, 2 Stra. 1027....................iii. 123, 179

Bulwer's Case, 7 Coke 3*a*....iii. 92
Bunn *v.* Ahl, 29 Pa. St. 387....i. 415
Bunniworth *v.* Gibbs, Style 419....ii. 70
Bunting *v.* Hogsett, 139 Pa. St. 363....i. 117, 118
Burbank *v.* Gould, 15 Me. 118....ii. 159
Burby *v.* Bollett, 16 M. & W. 644....i. 379
Burchell *v.* Slowcock, 2 Ld. Raym. 1545....ii. 387
Burchfield *v.* Moore, 3 El. & Bl. 683, 77 E. C. L. 683, 23 L. J. Q. B. 261....ii. 412
Burgess *v.* Burgess, 3 DeG. M. & G. 896....i. 432, 433
Burgess *v.* Denison Paper Mfg. Co., 79 Me. 266....ii. 95
Burgess *v.* Wilkinson, 13 R. I. 646....i. 407
Burke *v.* Greene, 2 Ball & B. 517....i. 340
Burks *v.* Shain, 2 Bibb (Ky.) 341....i. 272, 465
Burn *v.* Miller, 4 Taunt. 745....ii. 221
Burnby *v.* Bollett, 16 M. & W. 644....i. 387
Burnett *v.* Lynch, 5 B. & C. 609, 12 E. C. L. 335, 8 Dowl. & R. 381.. iii. 124, 247, 274
Buron *v.* Denman, 2 Exch. 167....i. 36
Burr *v.* Mills, 21 Wend. (N. Y.) 290....i. 201
Burroughes *v.* Bayne, 5 H. & N. 296....i. 233, 239, 246; iii. 159, 161
Burroughs *v.* Housatonic R. Co., 15 Conn. 124....i. 57
Burrows *v.* March Gas, etc., Co., L. R. 7 Exch. 96....i. 123
Burt *v.* Advertiser Newspaper Co., 154 Mass. 242, 247....i. 288, 309
Burt *v.* Moore, 5 T. R. 329....iii. 310
Burton *v.* English, 12 Q. B. D. 218....i. 19
Burton *v.* Hughes, 2 Bing. 173, 9 E. C. L. 368....i. 252
Burton *v.* West Jersey Ferry Co., 114 U. S. 474....i. 119
Burton Lumber Co. *v.* Wilder, 108 Ala. 669....ii. 216
Bury *v.* Bokenham, 1 Dyer 8, 10*a*....ii. 42
Bury *v.* Pope, Cro. Eliz. 118....i. 207
Busby *v.* Holthaus, 46 Mo. 161....i. 197
Bush *v.* Brainard, 1 Cow. (N. Y.) 78....i. 157
Bush *v.* Prosser, 11 N. Y. 354....iii. 58
Bush *v.* Steinman, 1 B. & P. 404....ii. 472
Butler *v.* Maples, 9 Wall. (U. S.) 776....ii. 484
Butler *v.* Mercer, 14 Ind. 479....i. 481
Butler *v.* New York, etc., R. Co., 22 Barb. (N. Y.) 110....iii. 87
Butler *v.* Stockdale, 19 Pa. Super. Ct. 98....i. 460
Butner *v.* Western Union Tel. Co., 2 Okla. 234....i. 439, 467
Butterfield *v.* Forrester, 11 East 60....i. 125
Butt's Case, 7 Coke 23*b*....iii. 301
Buxendin *v.* Sharp, 2 Salk. 662....i. 53
Byam *v.* Collins, 111 N. Y. 143....i. 308
Byard *v.* Holmes, 34 N. J. L. 296....i. 393
Byram *v.* McGuire, 3 Head (Tenn.) 530....i. 482
Byrchley's Case, Jenk. 361, 4 Coke 16....i. 282
Byrd *v.* Rautman, 85 Md. 414....i. 396
Byrne *v.* Boadle, 2 H. & C. 722....i. 107
Byrne *v.* Jansen, 50 Cal. 624....i. 386

Byrne *v.* Stout, 15 Ill. 181 .... i. 241
Byron *v.* Byron, Cro. Eliz. 472, pl. 25 (Hil. 38 Eliz.) .... iii. 91
Byxbie *v.* Wood, 24 N. Y. 611 .... iii. 88

C. F. Simmons Medicine Co. *v.* Mansfield Drug Co., 93 Tenn. 119 .... i. 422, 425
Cabot *v.* Christie, 42 Vt. 121 .... i. 415
Cadman *v.* Markle, 76 Mich. 448 .... ii. 223
Cæsar *v.* Curseny, Cro. Eliz. 305 .... i. 282
Cahaba *v.* Burnett, 34 Ala. 400 .... ii. 214
Cahill *v.* Bigelow, 18 Pick. (Mass.) 369 .... ii. 188
Cahill *v.* Eastman, 18 Minn. 324 .... i. 63
Calder *v.* Dobell, L. R. 6 C. P. 486 .... ii. 480
Caledonian R. Co. *v.* Ogilvy, 2 Macq. H. L. 229 .... i. 494
Caledonian R. Co. *v.* Sprot, 2 Macq. H. L. 449 .... i. 193
Caledonian R. Co. *v.* Walker, 7 App. Cas. 259 .... i. 494
Callisher *v.* Bischoffsheim, L. R. 5 Q. B. 449 .... ii. 79
Callonel *v.* Briggs, 1 Salk. 112 .... ii. 137, 139
Callum *v.* Bevans, 6 Har. & J. (Md.) 469 .... iii. 221
Calthorpe's Case, 3 Dyer 336*b* .... ii. 38
Calumet Iron, etc., Co. *v.* Martin, 115 Ill. 358 .... i. 148
Calye's Case, 8 Coke 32 .... ii. 265, 294
Camden *v.* Green, 54 N. J. L. 591 .... ii. 214
Cameron *v.* Mount, 86 Wis. 477 .... i. 408
Cameron *v.* New England Telephone, etc., Co., 182 Mass. 310 .... i. 459
Campbell *v.* Boyd, 88 N. Car. 129 .... i. 158
Campbell *v.* French, 6 T. R. 200 .... ii. 553
Campbell *v.* Race, 7 Cush. (Mass.) 408 .... i. 23
Campbell *v.* Seaman, 63 N. Y. 568 .... i. 221, 222
Campbell *v.* Spottiswood, 3 F. & F. 426 .... i. 305
Campbell *v.* Spottiswoode, 3 B. & S. 769, 113 E. C. L. 769 .... i. 303
Campbell *v.* Talbot, 132 Mass. 174 .... i. 202
Candee *v.* Western Union Tel. Co., 34 Wis. 471 .... i. 450, 452
Cannon *v.* Barry, 59 Miss. 289 .... i. 31
Cannon *v.* Western Union Tel. Co., 100 N. Car. 300 .... i. 452
Capital, etc., Bank *v.* Henty, 7 App. Cas. 787 .... i. 318
Caples *v.* Branham, 20 Mo. 244 .... ii. 504
Card *v.* Case, 5 C. B. 622, 57 E. C. L. 622 .... i. 54, 55
Cardon *v.* McConnell, 120 N. Car. 461 .... i. 323
Cardwell *v.* Lucas, 2 M. & W. 111 .... iii. 122
Carew *v.* Rutherford, 106 Mass. 1 .... ii. 231
Carey *v.* Berkshire R. Co., 1 Cush. (Mass.) 475 .... iii. 74
Carlos *v.* Fancourt, 5 T. R. 482 .... ii. 392, 507
Carnwright *v.* Gray, 127 N. Y. 98 .... ii. 504
Carpenter *v.* Hale, 8 Gray (Mass.) 157 .... i. 239
Carr *v.* Hood, 1 Campb. 353 .... i. 304
Carr *v.* London, etc., R. Co., L. R. 10 C. P. 315-318 .... ii. 245
Carrington *v.* Roots, 2 M. & W. 248 .... ii. 177
Carrington *v.* Taylor, 11 East 571 .... i. 358
Carroll *v.* Meeks, 3 Port. (Ala.) 226 .... iii. 143

Carroll *v.* Welch, 26 Tex. 149....................ii. 226
Carson *v.* Chicago, etc., R. Co., 96 Iowa 583....................i. 160
Carter *v.* Crick, 4 H. & N. 412....................i. 383
Carter *v.* Downish, 1 Show. 127....................ii. 351
Carter *v.* Kingman, 103 Mass. 517....................i. 239
Carter *v.* Palmer, 12 Mod. 380....................ii. 379
Carter *v.* Towne, 98 Mass. 567....................i. 59
Carterville *v.* Cook, 129 Ill. 152....................i. 122, 123
Cartwright, *In re*, 41 Ch. D. 532....................i. 31, 33
Carver *v.* Creque, 46 Barb. (N. Y.) 507....................iii. 86
Case *v.* Barber, T. Raym. 450....................ii. 91, 92, 95
Case of Thorns, 6 Edw. IV....................i. 21
Case of Tithes, 21 Hen. VII....................i. 20
Casey *v.* Cincinnati Typographical Union No. 3, 45 Fed. Rep. 135....i. 367
Casey *v.* Suter, 36 Md. 1....................ii. 282
Cashill *v.* Wright, 6 El. & Bl. 891, 88 E. C. L. 891....................ii. 295
Cashion *v.* Western Union Tel. Co., 123 N. Car. 467....................i. 471
Cass *v.* Boston, etc., R. Co., 14 Allen (Mass.) 448....................ii. 284
Castle *v.* Duryee, 2 Keyes (N. Y.) 169....................i. 80, 82
Castle *v.* Houston, 19 Kan. 417....................i. 275
Castle *v.* Oldman, 1 Leon. 203....................iii. 132
Castlemain *v.* Craven, 22 Vin. Abr. 523, pl. 11....................i. 31
Castrique *v.* Behrens, 3 El. & El. 709, 107 E. C. L. 709....................i. 329
Caswell *v.* Fellows, 110 Mass. 52....................ii. 124
Catherine, The Schooner, *v.* Dickinson, 17 How. (U. S.) 170......i. 145
Cattlin *v.* Hills, 8 C. B. 130, 65 E. C. L. 130....................i. 141
Caughey *v.* Smith, 47 N. Y. 244....................i. 265
Cawthon *v.* Lusk, 97 Ala. 674....................ii. 485
Cayle's Case, 8 Coke 32....................ii. 296
Cayzer *v.* Carron Co., 9 App. Cas. 873....................i. 145, 146
Cellular Clothing Co. *v.* Maxton, (1899) A. C. 326....................i. 424, 428
Celluloid Mfg. Co. *v.* Read, 47 Fed. Rep. 712....................i. 424
Centaur Co. *v.* Marshall, 97 Fed. Rep. 785....................i. 431
Central Bank *v.* Laug, 1 Bosw. (N. Y.) 203....................ii. 513
Central, etc., R. Co. *v.* Letcher, 69 Ala. 106....................i. 128
Central Nat. Bank *v.* Copp, 184 Mass. 328....................ii. 519
Central R., etc., Co. *v.* Brunswick, etc., R. Co., 87 Ga. 386........iii 86
Central Sav. Bank *v.* Richards, 109 Mass. 413....................ii. 402
Central Trust Co. *v.* Bridges, 57 Fed. Rep. 753, 764....................ii 433
Certwell *v.* Hoyt, 6 Hun (N. Y.) 575....................i. 270
Cerveny *v.* Chicago Daily News Co., 139 Ill. 345....................i. 294
Chadwick *v.* Manning, (1896) A. C. 231....................i. 394
Challis *v.* McCrum, 22 Kan. 157....................ii. 415
Chamberlain, *Ex p.*, 1 Sch. & Lef. 320....................iii. 220
Chamberlain *v.* Boyd, 11 Q. B. D. 407....................i. 280, 286
Chamberlain *v.* Hazelwood, 5 M. & W. 515....................i. 271
Chamberlain *v.* Neale, 9 Allen (Mass.) 410....................i. 254
Chamberlain *v.* Reed, 13 Me. 357....................ii. 230
Chamberlain *v.* Williamson, 2 M. & S. 408....................i. 465
Chambers *v.* Baldwin, 91 Ky. 121....................i. 346

Chambers *v.* Caulfield, 6 East 245....i. 489
Chamblee *v.* Baker, 95 N. Car. 98....ii. 227
Champion *v.* Vincent, 20 Tex. 811....i. 18
Champlin *v.* Laytin, 6 Paige (N. Y.) 189....ii. 214
Chandelor *v.* Lopus, Cro. Jac. 4....i. 380, 381, 382, 386
Chandelor *v.* Lopus, 8 Harv. L. Rev. 284....i. 378, 383
Chaplin *v.* Hawes, 3 C. & P. 554, 14 E. C. L. 445....i. 132
Chapman *v.* Hughes, 61 Miss. 339....ii. 205
Chapman *v.* Keane, 3 Ad. & El. 193, 30 E. C. L. 69....ii. 540
Chapman *v.* New Haven R. Co., 19 N. Y. 341....i. 141
Chapman *v.* Pickersgill, 2 Wils. C. Pl. 145....i. 331; iii. 56
Chapman *v.* Rose, 56 N. Y. 140....ii. 408
Chapman *v.* Rothwell, El. Bl. & El. 169, 96 E. C. L. 169....i. 151
Chapman *v.* State, 78 Ala. 463....i. 12
Chapman *v.* Thumblethorp, Cro. Eliz. 329....i. 53
Chapman *v.* Western Union Tel. Co., 88 Ga. 763....i. 467
Chapman *v.* Western Union Tel. Co., 90 Ky. 265....i. 454, 466
Chase *v.* Fitz, 132 Mass. 359....i. 466
Chase *v.* Western Union Tel. Co., 44 Fed. Rep. 554....i. 467
Chasemore *v.* Richards, 7 H. L. Cas. 349, 5 H. & N. 982....i. 98, 493
Chatfield *v.* Paxton, cited in 2 East 471, *note*....ii. 211, 212
Chatfield *v.* Wilson, 31 Vt. 358....i. 204
Chattanooga Medicine Co. *v.* Thedford, 58 Fed. Rep. 347....i. 426
Chatterton *v.* Secretary of State, (1895) 2 Q. B. 189....i. 307
Chawer *v.* Bowes, Godb. 217....iii. 120
Cheetham *v.* Hampson, 4 T. R. 318....i. 223
Chemical Manure Co. *v.* London Docks Co., 9 Ch. D. 503....i. 64
Cheney's Case, 3 Leon. 260, pl. 347....iii. 130, 134
Cheny *v.* Watkins, 1 Har. & J. (Md.) 352....ii. 43
Cherry *v.* Call, 23 Ga. 193....i. 481
Cherry *v.* Colonial Bank, L. R. 3 P. C. 24....i. 406
Cherry *v.* Des Moines Leader, 114 Iowa 298....i. 305
Cherry *v.* Heming, 4 Exch. 631....ii. 172, 176
Chesapeake, etc., R. Co. *v.* Foster, 88 Tenn. 671....i. 148
Chesterfield, etc., Silkstone Colliery Co. *v.* Hawkins, 3 H. & C. 677..iii. 122
Chicago *v.* Tilley, 103 U. S. 146....ii. 222
Chicago City R. Co. *v.* Wilcox, 24 N. E. Rep. 419....i. 144
Chicago, etc., R. Co. *v.* Hall, 90 Ill. 42....i. 43, 44
Chicago, etc., R. Co. *v.* Krayenbuhl, 65 Neb. 889....i. 160
Chicago, etc., R. Co. *v.* Thompson, 19 Ill. 578....i. 89
Chicago G. W. R. Co. *v.* First M. E. Church, 102 Fed. Rep. 85....i. 218
Chichester *v.* Cobb, 14 L. T. N. S. 433....ii. 117
Child *v.* Affleck, 9 B. & C. 403, 17 E. C. L. 405....i. 311
Child *v.* Hearn, L. R. 9 Exch. 176....i. 52
Child *v.* Sands, Carth. 294....i. 490
Childress *v.* Emory, 8 Wheat. (U. S.) 642....iii. 139
Childs *v.* Harris Mfg. Co., 68 Wis. 231....ii. 207
Chillicothe Bank *v.* Dodge, 8 Barb. (N. Y.) 233....ii. 214
China Merchants' Steam Nav. Co. *v.* Bignold, 7 App. Cas. 512....i. 145
Chinery *v.* Viall, 5 H. & N. 288....i. 256

Chinn *v.* Morris, 2 C. & P. 361, 12 E. C. L. 171 .... i. 13
Chipley *v.* Atkinson, 23 Fla. 206 .... i. 346
Chisholm, etc., Mfg. Co. *v.* U. S. Canopy Co., 111 Tenn. 202 .... i. 448
Chope *v.* Detroit, etc., Plank Road Co., 37 Mich. 195 .... i. 44
Chouteau *v.* Boughton, 100 Mo. 406 .... iii. 87
Christie *v.* Sawyer, 44 N. H. 303 .... i. 341
Chubb *v.* Flannagan, 6 C. & P. 431, 25 E. C. L. 472 .... i. 298
Churchill *v.* Holt, 127 Mass. 165 .... ii. 240
Churton *v.* Douglas, Johns. Ch. (Eng.) 174 .... i. 433
Cibel *v.* Hill, 1 Leon. 110 .... iii. 132
Citizens Sav. Bank *v.* Greenburgh, 173 N. Y. 215 .... ii. 501
City of London Brewery Co. *v.* Tennant, L. R. 9 Ch. 212 .... i. 209
Claflin *v.* Wilcox, 18 Vt. 605 .... i. 190; iii. 265
Clarance *v.* Marshall, 2 Cromp. & M. 495 .... iii. 110
Claridge *v.* South Staffordshire Tramway Co., (1892) 1 Q. B. 422 .. ii. 315
Clark *v.* Bales, 15 Ark. 452 .... i. 481
Clark *v.* Boston, etc., R. Co., 64 N. H. 323 .... i. 172
Clark *v.* Chambers, 3 Q. B. D. 327 .... i. 65
Clark *v.* Downing, 55 Vt. 259 .... i. 17
Clark *v.* Evans, 66 Fed. Rep. 263 .... ii. 408
Clark *v.* Foster, 8 Vt. 98 .... i. 406
Clark *v.* Herring, 5 Binn. (Pa.) 33 .... ii. 148
Clark *v.* Keliher, 107 Mass. 406 .... i. 18, 69
Clark *v.* Molyneux, 3 Q. B. D. 237 .... i. 315
Clark *v.* Pinney, 6 Cow. (N. Y.) 297 .... ii. 231
Clark *v.* Skinner, 20 Johns. (N. Y.) 467 .... iii. 219
Clark *v.* Terry, 25 Conn. 395 .... ii. 227
Clark *v.* Whitaker, 19 Conn. 319 .... i. 238
Clarke, *Ex p.*, 3 Bro. C. C. 238 .... ii. 412
Clarke *v.* Dickson, 6 C. B. N. S. 453, 95 E. C. L. 453 .... i. 397, 414
Clarke *v.* Earnshaw, 1 Gow 30, 5 E. C. L. 448 .... ii. 277
Clarke *v.* Russell, 3 Dall. (U. S.) 425 .... ii. 554
Clarke *v.* Shee, 1 Cowp. 197 .... ii. 216, 404
Clarke *v.* Thompson, 2 R. I. 146 .... iii. 89
Clarke *v.* Zettick, 153 Mass. 1 .... i. 299
Clarkson *v.* Lawson, 6 Bing. 266, 19 E. C. L. 78 .... i. 301
Clason *v.* Bailey, 14 Johns. (N. Y.) 484 .... ii. 182
Claxton *v.* Swift, 1 Lutw. 878, 882*b* .... ii. 379
Claxton *v.* Swift, 3 Mod. 86, 2 Show. 494 .... ii. 362, 376
Clayards *v.* Dethick, 12 Q. B. 439, 64 E. C. L. 439 .... i. 131
Clayton *v.* Clark, 74 Miss. 499 .... ii. 102, 103
Cleary *v.* Booth, (1893) 1 Q. B. 465 .... i. 39
Cleary *v.* Sohier, 120 Mass. 210 .... ii. 224
Clement *v.* Chivis, 9 B. & C. 172, 17 E. C. L. 353 .... i. 294
Clement *v.* Lewis, 3 Brod. & B. 297, 7 E. C. L. 444, 3 B. & Ald. 702, 5 E. C. L. 427 .... i. 301
Clement *v.* Milner, 3 Esp. 95 .... iii. 312
Clement *v.* Western Union Tel. Co., 137 Mass. 463 .... i. 437
Clerke *v.* Martin, 2 Ld. Raym. 757, 1 Salk. 129 .... ii. 363, 384
Cleveland *v.* Citizens' Gaslight Co., 20 N. J. Eq. 201 .... i. 219, 220

Clews *v.* Tracr, 57 Iowa 459....iii. 87
Cloon *v.* Gerry, 13 Gray (Mass.) 201....i. 330
Clopton *v.* Cozart, 13 Smed. & M. (Miss.) 363....i. 413
Closson *v.* Staples, 42 Vt. 209....i. 333
Clotworthy *v.* Schepp, 42 Fed. Rep. 62....i. 426
Clovell *v.* Cardinall, 1 Sid. 34....iii. 247
Cloves *v.* Williams, 3 Bing. N. Cas. 868, 32 E. C. L. 360....iii. 142
Clowes *v.* Staffordshire Potteries Waterworks Co., L. R. 8 Ch. 125.. i. 43, 202
Clubb *v.* Hutson, 18 C. B. N. S. 414, 114 E. C. L. 414....ii. 73
Clutterback *v.* Chaffers, 1 Stark. 471, 2 E. C. L. 181....i. 296
Clutton *v.* Attenborough, (1895) 2 Q. B. 306, 707....ii. 511
Cobb *v.* Great Western R. Co., (1893) 1 Q. B. 459....i. 129
Cobbett *v.* Clutton, 2 C. & P. 471, 12 E. C. L. 221....i. 246
Cobleigh *v.* Pierce, 32 Vt. 788....ii. 131
Coburn *v.* Harwood, Minor (Ala.) 93....i. 285
Cochran *v.* Miller, 13 Iowa 128....i. 482
Cochrane *v.* Green, 9 C. B. N. S. 448, 99 E. C. L. 448....ii. 124
Cochrane *v.* Halsey, 25 Minn. 52....i. 394
Cochrane *v.* Rymill, 27 W. R. 777....i. 244
Cock *v.* Vivyon, 2 Barnard. 243, 384....iii. 184
Cockram's Case, cited in 3 Keb. 757....iii. 185
Cockroft *v.* Smith, 2 Salk. 642....i. 7
Coddington *v.* Bay, 20 Johns. (N. Y.) 637....ii. 522
Coffin *v.* Coffin, 4 Mass. 1....i. 307
Coggs *v.* Bernard, 2 Ld. Raym. 909......i. 187; ii. 16, 50, 257, 260, 262, 264, 267, 270, 275, 282, 285, 298, 300
Cogswell *v.* New York, etc., R. Co., 103 N. Y. 10....i. 41
Cohn *v.* People, 149 Ill. 486....i. 423
Coit *v.* Houston, 3 Johns. Cas. (N. Y.) 243....ii. 95
Coit *v.* Western Union Tel. Co., 130 Cal. 657....i. 438, 441
Colby *v.* Jackson, 12 N. H. 526....i. 9
Colby *v.* Reynolds, 6 Vt. 489....i. 291
Cole *v.* Atlanta, etc., R. Co., 102 Ga. 474....i. 470
Cole *v.* Cassidy, 138 Mass. 437....i. 407
Cole *v.* Reynolds, 18 N. Y. 74....iii. 57, 58
Cole *v.* Turner, 6 Mod. 149....i. 6; iii. 232
Colehan *v.* Cooke, Willes 393....ii. 392, 507
Coleman *v.* Chadwick, 80 Pa. St. 81....i. 192
Coleman, etc., Co. *v.* Dannenberg Co., 103 Ga. 724....i. 426
Colemore *v.* Jenson, Moo. K. B. 854....iii. 188
Coles *v.* Clark, 3 Cush. (Mass.) 399....i. 244
Coles *v.* Thompson, 7 Tex. Civ. App. 666....i. 315
Collen *v.* Wright, 8 El. & Bl. 647, 92 E. C. L. 647......i. 343, 404, 406, 407; ii. 237
Collier *v.* Coates, 17 Barb. (N. Y.) 471....ii. 227
Collier *v.* Simpson, 5 C. & P. 73, 24 E. C. L. 219....i. 277
Collins *v.* Blantern, 2 Wils. C. Pl. 341, 1 Smith Lead. Cas. (8th Am. ed.) 715....ii. 163
Collins *v.* Renison, Say. 138....i. 9

Collis *v.* Emett, 1 H. Bl. 313....ii. 412
Collobine *v.* Vinor, 1 Rolle Abr. 79, pl. 1....i. 284
Colls *v.* Home, etc., Stores, (1904) A. C. 179....i. 209
Collyer *v.* Moulton, 9 R. I. 90....ii. 127
Columbian Ins. Co. *v.* Ashby, 13 Pet. (U. S.) 331....i. 19
Colyear *v.* Mulgrave, 2 Keen 82....iii. 121
Com. *v.* Clark, 2 Met. (Mass.) 23....i. 9
Com. *v.* Costello, 1 Pa. Dist. 745....i. 310
Com. *v.* Donahue, 148 Mass. 529....i. 8
Com. *v.* Pierce, 138 Mass. 176....i. 96
Com. *v.* Randall, 4 Gray (Mass.) 36....i. 39
Com. *v.* Rubin, 165 Mass. 453....i. 47
Com. *v.* White, 110 Mass. 407....i. 12
Combes' Case, 9 Coke 76*b*....ii. 473
Comegys *v.* Vasse, 1 Pet. (U. S.) 213....iii. 88
Commercial Bank *v.* Jones, (1893) A. C. 313....ii. 125
Companhia de Mocambique *v.* British South Africa, (1892) 2 Q. B. 358....iii. 94
Comstock *v.* Hannah, 76 Ill. 530....ii. 408
Congress, etc., Spring Co. *v.* Edgar, 99 U. S. 651....i. 55
Conn *v.* Wilson, 2 Overt. (Tenn.) 233....i. 273
Connell *v.* Reed, 128 Mass. 477....i. 426
Connell *v.* Western Union Tel. Co., 108 Mo. 459....i. 467
Connelly *v.* Devoe, 37 Conn. 570....ii. 128
Connelly *v.* Western Union Tel. Co., 100 Va. 51....i. 467
Connolly *v.* Boston, 117 Mass. 64....i. 179
Connolly *v.* Eldredge, 160 Mass. 566....i. 170
Connolly *v.* Knickerbocker Ice Co., 114 N. Y. 104....i. 176
Connor *v.* Allen, 33 Ala. 515....iii. 160
Conrow *v.* Little, 115 N. Y. 387....ii. 217
Consolidated Co. *v.* Curtis, (1892) 1 Q. B. 495....i. 244
Constable *v.* Andrew, 2 Cromp. & M. 298....ii. 131
Constable's Case, 1 Dyer 102....ii. 42
Constitution, The, 4 P. D. 39....i. 37
Cooch *v.* Goodman, 2 Q. B. 580, 42 E. C. L. 817....ii. 172; iii. 122
Coogler *v.* Rhodes, 38 Fla. 240....i. 309
Cook *v.* Cox, 3 M. & S. 110....i. 300
Cook *v.* Darby, 4 Munf. (Va.) 444....i. 495
Cook *v.* McCabe, 53 Wis. 250....ii. 224
Cook *v.* Munstone, 1 B. & P. N. R. 351....ii. 221
Cook *v.* Oxley, 3 T. R. 653....ii. 54
Cook *v.* Patterson, 35 Ala. 102....i. 252
Cook *v.* Wright, 1 B. & S. 559, 101 E. C. L. 559....ii. 79
Cooke *v.* Eshelby, 12 App. Cas. 271, 16 L. J. Q. B. 505....ii. 479
Cooke *v.* Forbes, L. R. 5 Eq. 166....i. 214
Cooley *v.* Galyon, 109 Tenn. 1....i. 307
Coolidge *v.* Payson, 2 Wheat. (U. S.) 66....ii. 401
Coolidge *v.* Ruggles, 15 Mass. 387....ii. 508
Cooper *v.* Chitty, 1 Burr. 20....i. 239
Cooper *v.* Cooper, 147 Mass. 370....ii. 217; iii. 200

Cooper *v.* McJunkin, 4 Ind. 290 .... i. 39
Cooper *v.* Meyer, 10 B. & C. 468, 21 E. C. L. 116 .... ii. 412
Cooper *v.* Schlesinger, 111 U. S. 148 .... i. 407
Cooper *v.* Willomatt, 1 C. B. 672, 50 E. C. L. 672 .... i. 238, 248, 254
Cooper *v.* Witham, 1 Sid. 375 .... i. 495
Coover *v.* Davenport, 1 Heisk. (Tenn.) 368 .... ii. 110
Corbett *v.* Clark, 45 Wis. 403 .... ii. 503
Corbett *v.* Gilbert, 24 Ga. 454 .... i. 411
Corbett *v.* Packington, 6 B. & C. 268, 13 E. C. L. 170 .... iii. 272
Corby *v.* Hill, 4 C. B. N. S. 556, 93 E. C. L. 556 .... i. 157
Corbyn *v.* Brown, Cro. Eliz. 470 .... iii. 178
Core's Case, 1 Dyer 20*a* .... iii. 109
Cork *v.* Baker, 1 Stra. 34 .... ii. 190
Corliss *v.* E. W. Walker Co., 57 Fed. Rep. 434, 64 Fed. Rep. 280 .... i. 319
Corn Exchange Bank *v.* American Dock, etc., Co., 149 N. Y. 174 .... ii. 482
Cornfoot *v.* Fowke, 6 M. & W. 358 .... ii. 456
Cornish *v.* Abington, 4 H. & N. 549 .... ii. 248
Correio *v.* Lynch, 65 Cal. 273 .... i. 387
Corwin *v.* Wallace, 17 Iowa 374 .... ii. 221
Coryell *v.* Colbaugh, 1 N. J. L. 90 .... i. 464
Cotsworth *v.* Bettison, 1 Salk. 247 .... iii. 292
Cotterell *v.* Jones, 11 C. B. 713, 73 E. C. L. 713 .... i. 373
Cotton *v.* State, 31 Miss. 504 .... i. 7
Cotton *v.* Wood, 8 C. B. N. S. 568, 98 E. C. L. 568 .... i. 106
Cottrill *v.* Chicago, etc., R. Co., 47 Wis. 634 .... i. 134
Couch *v.* Steel, 3 El. & Bl. 402, 77 E. C. L. 402 .... i. 174; ii. 236
Couldery *v.* Bartrum, 19 Ch. D. 394 .... ii. 89
Countryman *v.* Lighthill, 24 Hun (N. Y.) 405 .... i. 20
Coupland *v.* Hardingham, 3 Campb. 398 .... i. 153
Coursin *v.* Ledlie, 31 Pa. St. 506 .... ii. 504
Courtenay *v.* Earle, 10 C. B. 73, 70 E. C. L. 73 .... iii. 277
Courtney *v.* Connet, Carth. 436 .... iii. 265
Courtney *v.* Doyle, 10 Allen (Mass.) 122 .... ii. 504
Coventry *v.* Barton, 17 Johns. (N. Y.) 142 .... ii. 74
Coverdale *v.* Eastwood, L. R. 15 Eq. 121 .... ii. 192
Covington Transfer Co. *v.* Kelly, 36 Ohio St. 86 .... i. 141
Cowan *v.* Hallack, 9 Colo. 572 .... ii. 504
Coward *v.* Baddeley, 4 H. & N. 478 .... i. 6
Cowell *v.* Edwards, 2 B. & P. 268 .... iii. 201
Cowen *v.* Simpson, 1 Esp. 290 .... i. 413
Cowie *v.* Sterling, 6 El. & Bl. 333, 88 E. C. L. 333 .... ii. 510
Cowley *v.* Newmarket Local Board, (1892) A. C. 345 .... i. 174
Cowley *v.* Pulsifer, 137 Mass. 392 .... i. 310
Cowlin *v.* Cook, Latch 151 .... ii. 34
Cox *v.* Blair, 76 N. Car. 78 .... ii. 293
Cox *v.* Burbridge, 13 C. B. N. S. 430, 106 E. C. L. 430 .... i. 53
Cox *v.* Matthews, 1 Vent. 237 .... i. 207, 208
Coxhead *v.* Richards, 2 C. B. 569, 52 E. C. L. 569 .... i. 312, 313
Coxon *v.* Chadley, 3 B. & C. 591, 10 E. C. L. 191 .... ii. 125
Coyle *v.* Baum, 3 Okla. 695 .... i. 388

Craft *v.* Parker, 96 Mich. 245....i. 387
Craker *v.* Chicago, etc., R. Co., 36 Wis. 657....i. 461, 480
Cramlington *v.* Evans, 1 Show. 5....ii. 383
Cramlington *v.* Evans, 2 Vent. 307....ii. 376
Crane *v.* Waters, 10 Fed. Rep. 619....i. 304
Cratty *v.* Bangor, 57 Me. 423....i. 179
Crawford *v.* Parsons, 18 N. H. 293....ii. 227
Crawford *v.* Whittal, 1 Dougl. 4....iii. 180, 194
Crawson *v.* Western Union Tel. Co., 47 Fed. Rep. 544....i. 467
Craythorne *v.* Swinburne, 14 Ves. Jr. 160....ii. 239
Credit *v.* Brown, 10 Johns. (N. Y.) 365....i. 17
Credit Co. *v.* Howe Mach. Co., 54 Conn. 357....ii. 408
Creed *v.* Fisher, 9 Exch. 472....i. 488
Cribbs *v.* Sowle, 87 Mich. 340....ii. 229
Cripps *v.* Hartnoll, 2 B. & S. 697, 10 E. C. L. 697....ii. 187
Crocker *v.* Gullifer, 44 Me. 491....i. 258
Crocker *v.* Manley, 164 Ill. 282....i. 414
Crocker *v.* Mann, 3 Mo. 472....iii. 308
Crockett *v.* McLanahan, 109 Tenn. 517....i. 308
Croft *v.* Alison, 4 B. & Ald. 590, 6 E. C. L. 614....ii. 453, 469
Croft *v.* Day, 7 Beav. 84....i. 420, 432
Crofts *v.* Brown, 3 Bulst. 167....i. 284
Crogate *v.* Morris, 1 Brownl. & Goldes. 197....i. 266
Cronsillat *v.* M'Call, 5 Binn. (Pa.) 432....iii. 111
Crook *v.* Jadis, 5 B. & Ad. 909, 27 E. C. L. 234....ii. 406
Crooker *v.* Bragg, 10 Wend. (N. Y.) 260....i. 204
Cropp *v.* Tilney, 3 Salk. 225, Holt K. B. 422....i. 293
Crosby *v.* Leng, 12 East 409....i. 495
Cross *v.* Andrews, Cro. Eliz. 622....i. 189
Cross *v.* Garnet, 3 Mod. 261....i. 382
Crossley *v.* Lightowler, L. R. 2 Ch. 478....i. 203
Crouch *v.* Credit Foncier, L. R. 8 Q. B. 374....ii. 422, 423
Crow *v.* Rogers, 1 Stra. 592....ii. 154
Crowhurst *v.* Burial Board, 4 Ex. D. 5....i. 20, 156
Crowther *v.* Farrer, 15 Q. B. 677, 69 E. C. L. 677....ii. 94
Crump *v.* Lambert, L. R. 3 Eq. 409....i. 220, 221
Cudahy Packing Co. *v.* State Nat. Bank, 134 Fed. Rep. 542....ii. 417
Culbreath *v.* Culbreath, 7 Ga. 64....ii. 214
Cullen *v.* Sears, 112 Mass. 299....ii. 221
Cumber *v.* Wane, 1 Stra. 426....ii. 100, 101
Cumberland County *v.* Pennell, 69 Me. 357....ii. 293
Cummings *v.* Cass, 52 N. J. L. 77....i. 395
Cumpston *v.* Lambert, 18 Ohio St. 81....ii. 74
Cundy *v.* Lindsay, 3 App. Cas. 459....i. 260
Cunningham *v.* Macon, etc., R. Co., 109 U. S. 446....i. 35, 36
Cunningham *v.* Reardon, 98 Mass. 538....ii. 205
Currie *v.* Misa, L. R. 10 Exch. 162....ii. 68
Curtin *v.* Western Union Tel. Co., 13 N. Y. App. Div. 253....i. 467
Curtis *v.* Williamson, L. R. 10 Q. B. 57....ii. 480
Curtis, etc., Mfg. Co. *v.* Williams, 48 Ark. 325....i. 386

Cutler *v.* Bonney, 30 Mich. 259 .... ii. 296
Cutler *v.* Dixon, 4 Coke 14*b* .... i. 283
Cutter *v.* Powell, 6 T. R. 320 .... ii. 224
Cutting *v.* Williams, 7 Mod. 155 .... ii. 384

Da Costa *v.* Jones, 2 Cowp. 729 .... ii. 111, 166
Dadirrian *v.* Yacubian, 98 Fed. Rep. 872 .... i. 424
Dale *v.* Hall, 1 Wils. C. Pl. 282 .... ii. 302
Dale Mfg. Co. *v.* Grant, 34 N. J. L. 138 .... iii. 265
Dale's Case, Cro. Eliz. 44 .... i. 382, 385
Dallas *v.* Hollingsworth, 3 Ind. 537 .... ii. 226
Dalston *v.* Janson, 5 Mod. 89 .... iii. 274
Dalton *v.* Angus, 6 App. Cas. 740, 791 .... i. 192, 193, 195
Dambmann *v.* Schulting, 75 N. Y. 55 .... ii. 212
Dana *v.* National Bank of Republic, 132 Mass. 156 .... ii. 248
Dand *v.* Sexton, 3 T. R. 37 .... i. 16; iii. 234
Daniel *v.* Metropolitan R. Co., L. R. 5 H. L. 45 .... i. 105
Daniels *v.* Keokuk Waterworks, 61 Iowa 549 .... i. 44
Daniels *v.* New York, etc., R. Co., 154 Mass. 349 .... i. 160
Daniels *v.* Potter, 4 C. & P. 262, 19 E. C. L. 375 .... i. 121
Dansey *v.* Richardson, 3 El. & Bl. 161, 77 E. C. L. 161 .... ii. 459, 466
Danville, etc., R. Co. *v.* Com., 73 Pa. St. 29 .... i. 44
Danville, etc., Turnpike Road Co. *v.* Stewart, 2 Met. (Ky.) 119 .... i. 141
Darcy *v.* Askwith, Hob. 234 .... i. 26, 27
Darling *v.* Williams, 35 Ohio St. 58 .... i. 8
Daskam *v.* Ullman, 74 Wis. 474 .... ii. 415
Daughtery *v.* American Union Tel. Co., 75 Ala. 168 .... i. 452, 453
Davenport *v.* Lynch, 6 Jones L. (51 N. Car.) 545 .... i. 332
Davey *v.* London, etc., R. Co., 12 Q. B. D. 70 .... i. 128
Davey *v.* Shannon, 4 Ex. D. 81 .... ii. 194
Davidson *v.* Goodall, 18 N. H. 423 .... i. 270
Davies *v.* Gardiner, 4 Coke 16*b* .... i. 283
Davies *v.* London, etc., Marine Ins. Co., 8 Ch. D. 469 .... i. 412
Davies *v.* Mann, 10 M. & W. 546 .... i. 134
Davies *v.* Snead, L. R. 5 Q. B. 608 .... i. 311, 312
Davies *v.* Williams, 16 Q. B. 546, 71 E. C. L. 546 .... i. 216
Daviess *v.* Fairbairn, 3 How. (U. S.) 636 .... ii. 499
Daviess County Distilling Co. *v.* Martinoni, 117 Fed. Rep. 188 .... i. 431
Davis *v.* Davis, 97 Mich. 419 .... i. 396
Davis *v.* Dodd, 4 Taunt. 602 .... ii. 375
Davis *v.* Gelhaus, 44 Ohio St. 69 .... i. 490
Davis *v.* Getchell, 50 Me. 602 .... i. 200
Davis *v.* Guarnieri, 45 Ohio St. 492 .... i. 61
Davis *v.* Hurt, 114 Ala. 147 .... i. 237
Davis *v.* Maxwell, 12 Met. (Mass.) 286 .... ii. 227
Davis *v.* Munson, 43 Vt. 676 .... ii. 121
Davis *v.* Preston, 6 Ala. 83 .... ii. 227
Davis *v.* Saunders, 2 Chit. 639, 18 E. C. L. 437 .... i. 80
Davis *v.* Shepstone, 11 App. Cas. 187 .... i. 303, 309
Davis *v.* Wright, 1 Vent. 120 .... ii. 77

Dawe *v.* Morris, 149 Mass. 188....i. 396
Dawkes *v.* Coveneigh, Style 346....i. 495
Dawkins *v.* Paulet, L. R. 5 Q. B. 94....i. 307
Dawkins *v.* Rokeby, L. R. 8 Q. B. 255....i. 308
Dawkins *v.* Sappington, 26 Ind. 199....ii. 82
Dawson *v.* Chamney, 5 Q. B. 164, 48 E. C. L. 164....ii. 295, 296, 297
Day *v.* Bream, 2 M. & Rob. 54....i. 298
Day *v.* Edwards, 5 T. R. 648....i. 16, 190; iii. 253, 258, 263
Day *v.* Gardner, 42 N. J. Eq. 199....ii. 117
Day *v.* Raguet, 14 Minn. 273....i. 389
Day *v.* Woodworth, 13 How. (U. S.) 489....i. 482
Dayton *v.* Hooglund, 39 Ohio St. 671....i. 389
Dean *v.* Keate, 3 Campb. 4....i. 97
Dean *v.* Peel, 5 East 45....i. 269, 271
Deaver *v.* Rice, 4 Dev. & B. L. (20 N. Car.) 431....iii. 308
De Beil *v.* Thomson, 3 Beav. 469....ii. 192
De Bodreugam *v.* Arcedekene, 30 Edw. I....i. 490
De Bussche *v.* Alt, 8 Ch. D. 286....ii. 477
Decker *v.* Gammon, 44 Me. 322....i. 52, 55
Decker *v.* Pope, 1 Selwyn N. P. (13th ed.) 91....ii. 238; iii. 201
Dee *v.* Bacon, Cro. Eliz. 435....iii. 170
Deeks *v.* Strutt, 5 T. R. 690....ii. 144, 150
Deering *v.* Austin, 34 Vt. 330....i. 239
Deering *v.* Winchelsea, 2 B. & P. 270....ii. 239
De Feriet *v.* Bank of America, 23 La. Ann. 310....ii. 248
Defreeze *v.* Trumper, 1 Johns. (N. Y.) 274....i. 384
Delacroix *v.* Thevenot, 2 Stark. 63, 3 E. C. L. 317....i. 296
Delaware, etc., R. Co. *v.* Reich, 61 N. J. L. 635....i. 160
Delegal *v.* Highley, 3 Bing. N. Cas. 950, 32 E. C. L. 398....i. 310
De Mesnil *v.* Dakin, L. R. 3 Q. B. 18....ii. 228
Dench *v.* Walker, 14 Mass. 500....i. 258
Denman *v.* Johnston, 85 Mich. 387....i. 181
Dennehy *v.* O'Connell, 66 Conn. 175....i. 314
Dennis *v.* Clark, 2 Cush. (Mass.) 347....i. 268
Denny *v.* New York Cent. R. Co., 13 Gray (Mass.) 481....i. 118
Dent *v.* Chiles, 5 Stew. & P. (Ala.) 383....i. 246
Denton *v.* Great North. R. Co., 5 El. & Bl. 860, 85 E. C. L. 860...i. 398, 412
Denver *v.* Dunsmore, 7 Colo. 328....i. 489
Derby *v.* Johnson, 21 Vt. 17....ii. 222
Dermott *v.* Jones, 23 How. (U. S.) 220....ii. 221
Derry *v.* Peek, 14 App. Cas. 337....i. 400, 402, 406, 455
Detroit Daily Post Co. *v.* McArthur, 16 Mich. 447....i. 481
Deuters *v.* Townsend, 5 B. & S. 613, 117 E. C. L. 613....ii. 501
Devaux *v.* Conolly, 8 C. B. 640, 65 E. C. L. 640....ii. 212
Devereux *v.* Barclay, 2 B. & Ald. 702....i. 248
Devine *v.* Edwards, 101 Ill. 138....ii. 212
Devine *v.* Rand, 38 Vt. 621....i. 481
Dew *v.* Parsons, 2 B. & Ald. 562....ii. 231
Dewey *v.* Field, 4 Met. (Mass.) 381....ii. 243
Dews *v.* Riley, 11 C. B. 434, 73 E. C. L. 434....i. 38

Deyo *v.* Thompson, 53 N. Y. App. Div. 9............ii. 504
Dickenson *v.* Seaver, 44 Mich. 624............iii. 87
Dickenson *v.* Watson, T. Jones 205............i. 79
Dickerson *v.* Colgrove, 100 U. S. 578............ii. 243
Dickon *v.* Clifton, 2 Wils. C. Pl. 321............iii. 274
Dickson *v.* McCoy, 39 N. Y. 400............i. 53
Dickson *v.* Reuter's Tel. Co., 2 C. P. D. 62............i. 438, 455
Dickson *v.* Reuter's Tel. Co., 3 C. P. D. 1............i. 406
Dillard *v.* Collins, 25 Gratt. (Va.) 343............iii. 86
Dillon *v.* Balfour, 20 L. R. Ir. 600............i. 307
Disbrow *v.* Tenbroeck, 4 E. D. Smith (N. Y.) 397............ii. 286
Ditcham *v.* Bond, 2 M. & S. 436............i. 266
Dixon *v.* Bell, 5 M. & S. 198............i. 58
Dixon *v.* James, 2 Lutw. 1241............iii. 310
Dixon *v.* Metropolitan Board of Works, 7 Q. B. D. 418............i. 493
Dixon *v.* Parsons, 1 F. & F. 24............i. 312
Dobell *v.* Stevens, 3 B. & C. 623, 10 E. C. L. 201............i. 413
Docker *v.* Voyel, Cro. Eliz. 885............ii. 81, 87
Dodd *v.* Holme, 1 Ad. & El. 493, 28 E. C. L. 128............i. 196
Dodge *v.* Hopkins, 14 Wis. 630............ii. 488
Dodwell *v.* Burford, 1 Mod. 24............i. 17
Doe *v.* Wright, 10 Ad. & El. 763, 37 E. C. L. 222............i. 261
Doherty *v.* Allman, 3 App. Cas. 709............i. 28
Dole *v.* Erskine, 35 N. H. 503............i. 7
Dole *v.* Lyon, 10 Johns. (N. Y.) 449............i. 294
Donahoe *v.* Wabash, etc., R. Co., 83 Mo. 560............i. 133
Donahue *v.* Shippee, 15 R. I. 453............i. 243
Donald *v.* Suckling, L. R. 1 Q. B. 585............i. 240, 256
Donellan *v.* Read, 3 B. & Ad. 899, 23 E. C. L. 215............ii. 176
Donford *v.* Ellys, 12 Mod. 138............i. 261
Dongal *v.* Wilson, cited in 2 Saund. 175*b*............i. 208
Dooling *v.* Budget Pub. Co., 144 Mass. 258............i. 324
Doolittle *v.* Shaw, 92 Iowa 348............ii. 288
Doorman *v.* Jenkins, 2 Ad. & El. 256, 29 E. C. L. 80............ii. 276, 280
Dorenius *v.* Hennessy, 62 Ill. App. 391............i. 372
Dorley *v.* Roberts, 3 Bing. N. Cas. 835, 32 E. C. L. 346............i. 277
Dorman *v.* Kane, 5 Allen (Mass.) 38............i. 238
Dorsey *v.* Manlove, 14 Cal. 553............i. 481
Doss *v.* Secretary of State, L. R. 19 Eq. 509............i. 37
Dougherty *v.* Stepp, 1 Dev. & B. L. (18 N. Car.) 371............i. 19
Dovaston *v.* Payne, 2 H. Bl. 527............i. 22
Doward *v.* Lindsay, L. R. 5 P. C. 338............i. 106
Dowling *v.* Livingstone, 108 Mich. 321............i. 304
Down *v.* Halling, 4 B. & C. 330............ii. 406
Downer *v.* Cheesebrough, 36 Conn. 39............ii. 178
Downey *v.* Sawyer, 157 Mass. 418............i. 170
Downing *v.* Wilson, 36 Ala. 717............i. 299
Downman *v.* Williams, 7 Q. B. 103, 53 E. C. L. 103............i. 405
Dows, David, The, 16 Fed. Rep. 154............i. 146
Doyle *v.* O'Doherty, C. & M. 418, 41 E. C. L. 230............i. 308

Doyle *v.* Vance, 6 Vict. L. Rep. 87 ... i. 54, 55
Dozier *v.* Gregory, 1 Jones L. (46 N. Car.) 100 ... i. 32
Drawn *v.* Cherry, 14 La. Ann. 705 ... ii. 506
Drayton *v.* Dale, 2 B. & C. 293, 9 E. C. L. 91, 41 Am. L. Reg. N. S. 562 ... ii. 412
Drinkall *v.* Movius State Bank, 11 N. Dak. 10 ... ii. 530
Drinkhorn *v.* Bubel, 85 Mich. 532 ... i. 8
Drope *v.* Theyar, Popham 179 ... ii. 473
Drummond *v.* Van Ingen, 12 App. Cas. 284 ... i. 388
Drury *v.* Macauley, 16 M. & W. 146 ... ii. 506
Duberley *v.* Gunning, 4 T. R. 656 ... i. 163
Du Bost *v.* Beresford, 2 Campb. 511 ... i. 294
Ducktown Sulphur, etc., Co. *v.* Barnes, 60 S. W. Rep. 593 ... i. 220
Dudley *v.* Briggs, 141 Mass. 582 ... i. 324
Dudley *v.* Kennedy, 63 Me. 466 ... i. 227
Duffany *v.* Ferguson, 66 N. Y. 482 ... i. 386
Duke *v.* Harper, 2 Mo. App. 10 ... i. 341
Dulieu *v.* White, (1901) 2 K. B. 669 ... i. 458, 460
Dull *v.* Bricker, 76 Pa. St. 255 ... ii. 401
Dun *v.* Weintraub, 111 Ga. 416 ... i. 311
Dunbar *v.* Alcalde, etc., 1 Cal. 355 ... i. 23
Duncan *v.* Baker, 21 Kan. 99 ... ii. 226
Duncan *v.* Findlater, 6 Cl. & F. 910 ... ii. 461
Duncan *v.* Fisher, 18 Mo. 403 ... i. 237
Duncan *v.* Maryland Sav. Inst., 10 Gill. & J. (Md.) 299 ... ii. 504
Duncan *v.* Scott, 1 Campb. 100 ... ii. 531
Duncan *v.* Spear, 11 Wend. (N. Y.) 54 ... i. 252
Duncombe *v.* Reeve, Cro. Eliz. 783 ... iii. 293
Dung *v.* Parker, 52 N. Y. 494 ... i. 406
Dunham *v.* Powers, 42 Vt. 1 ... i. 307
Dunham *v.* Wyckoff, 3 Wend. (N. Y.) 281 ... iii. 219
Dunn *v.* Birmingham Canal Nav. Co., L. R. 7 Q. B. 244 ... i. 493
Dunton *v.* Dunton, 18 Vict. L. R. 114 ... ii. 72, 76
Duppa *v.* Gerrard, 1 Show. 78 ... iii. 189
Durant *v.* Roberts, (1901) 1 Q. B. 629 ... ii. 490
Durden *v.* Barnett, 7 Ala. 169 ... i. 268
Durgin *v.* Gage, 40 N. H. 302 ... i. 249
Durkee *v.* Vermont Cent. R. Co., 29 Vt. 127 ... i. 438
Durland *v.* Pitcairn, 51 Ind. 426 ... ii. 504
Duryea *v.* National Starch-Mfg. Co., 79 Fed. Rep. 651 ... i. 432
Dutch West-India Co. *v.* Van Moses, 1 Stra. 612 ... iii. 137
Dutton *v.* Poole, 1 Vent. 318, 2 Lev. 211 ... ii. 153, 155, 157
D'Wolf *v.* Rabaud, 1 Pet. (U. S.) 501 ... ii. 181
Dwyer *v.* St. Louis, etc., R. Co., 52 Fed. Rep. 87 ... i. 489
Dyckman *v.* Valiente, 42 N. Y. 549 ... i. 240
Dye *v.* Denham, 54 Ga. 224 ... i. 488

Eagle *v.* Smith, 4 Houst. (Del.) 293 ... ii. 82
Eaglechild's Case, Hetley 167 ... ii. 350
Eales *v.* Dicker, M. & M. 324, 22 E. C. L. 323 ... iii. 142

Eason *v.* Newman, Cro. Eliz. 495 .... iii. 164
East *v.* Newman, Gouldsb. 152, pl. 79 .... iii. 164, 167
Eastin *v.* Stockton Bank, 66 Cal. 123 .... i. 333
East India Co. *v.* Sandys, 10 How. St. Tr. 525 .... ii. 334
East Indian R. Co. *v.* Mukerjee, (1901) A. C. 396 .... i. 105
Easton *v.* Newman, 1 Rolle Abr. 5 (I.), pl. 2 .... iii. 167
East Tennessee, etc., R. Co. *v.* Aiken, 89 Tenn. 245 .... i. 148
East Tennessee, etc., R. Co. *v.* Cargille, 105 Tenn. 628 .... i. 160
East Tennessee, etc., R. Co. *v.* Henderson, 1 Lea (Tenn.) 4 .... iii. 86, 87
Eastwood *v.* Holmes, 1 F. & F. 347 .... i. 304
Eastwood *v.* Kenyon, 11 Ad. & El. 438, 39 E. C. L. 137 .... ii. 146
Eaton *v.* Libbey, 165 Mass. 218 .... ii. 148
Eaton *v.* Lynde, 15 Mass. 242 .... ii. 314
Ecker *v.* McAllister, 54 Md. 362 .... ii. 113
Eckert *v.* Long Island R. Co., 43 N. Y. 503 .... i. 133
Eckhart *v.* Wilson, 10 S. & R. (Pa.) 44 .... i. 299
Edelsten *v.* Edelsten, 1 DeG. J. & S. 185 .... i. 421
Eden *v.* Chaffee, 160 Mass. 225 .... ii. 185
Eden *v.* Lexington, etc., R. Co., 14 B. Mon. (Ky.) 165 .... iii. 74
Edgar *v.* Chut, 1 Keb. 592, 636 .... ii. 369
Edgcomb *v.* Dee, Vaugh. 101 .... ii. 2, 27; iii. 138, 145
Edgerly *v.* Whalen, 106 Mass. 307 .... i. 243
Edgerton *v.* Brackett, 11 N. H. 218 .... iii. 203
Edgerton *v.* Brownlow, 4 H. L. Cas. 237 .... ii. 165
Edgerton *v.* Edgerton, 8 Conn. 6 .... ii. 504
Edgington *v.* Burlington, etc., R. Co., 116 Iowa 410 .... i. 160
Edie *v.* East India Co., 2 Burr. 1216 .... ii. 397, 398, 524, 525
Edmunds *v.* Bushell, L. R. 1 Q. B. 97 .... ii. 481
Edmundson *v.* Penny, 1 Pa. St. 334 .... ii. 153, 154, 155
Edsall *v.* Russell, 4 M. & G. 1090, 43 E. C. L. 560 .... i. 277
Edwards *v.* Bates, 7 M. & G. 590, 49 E. C. L. 590, 8 Scott N. R. 406 .. iii. 123
Edwards *v.* Baugh, 11 M. & W. 641 .... ii. 77
Edwards *v.* Burre, Dalison 104, pl. 45 .... ii. 63; iii. 178, 183
Edwards *v.* Hooper, 11 M. & W. 363 .... i. 238
Edwards *v.* Thomas, 66 Mo. 468 .... ii. 491
Edwards *v.* Trulock, 37 Iowa 244 .... ii. 390
Ehrlich *v.* Ætna L. Ins. Co., 88 Mo. 249 .... ii. 222
Eichholz *v.* Bannister, 17 C. B. N. S. 708, 112 E. C. L. 708 .... i. 384
Einstein *v.* Marshall, 58 Ala. 153 .... i. 409
Elderton *v.* Emmens, 4 C. B. 479, 56 E. C. L. 479, 6 C. B. 160, 60 E. C. L. 160 .... ii. 86
Elgin Nat. Watch Co. *v.* Illinois Watch Case Co., 179 U. S. 666 .... i. 424, 431
Elkins *v.* McKean, 79 Pa. St. 493 .... i. 60
Ellington *v.* Ellington, 47 Miss. 329 .... i. 269
Elliot *v.* Ailsberry, 2 Bibb (Ky.) 473 .... i. 276
Elliot *v.* Brown, 2 Wend. (N. Y.) 497 .... i. 7
Elliot *v.* Fitchburg R. Co., 11 Cush. (Mass.) 191 .... i. 198, 200, 201
Elliot *v.* Western Union Tel. Co., 75 Tex. 18 .... i. 450
Elliott *v.* Swartwout, 10 Pet. (U. S.) 137 .... ii. 214

Ellis *v.* American Tel. Co., 13 Allen (Mass.) 234....................i. 440
Ellis *v.* Cary, 74 Wis. 176....................ii. 223
Ellis *v.* Loftus Iron Co., L. R. 10 C. P. 10....................i. 20, 52
Ellis *v.* Rowles, Willes 638....................iii. 310
Elliston *v.* Berryman, 15 Q. B. 205, 69 E. C. L. 205....................ii. 74
Ellsworth *v.* Brewer, 11 Pick. (Mass.) 316....................iii. 203
Elmore *v.* Brooks, 6 Heisk. (Tenn.) 45....................i. 243
Elsee *v.* Gatward, 5 T. R. 143....................i. 187; ii. 49, 50
Eltham *v.* Kingsman, 1 B. & Ald. 683....................ii. 167
Elwell *v.* Martin, 1 Ware (U. S.) 53....................i. 39
Ely *v.* Stannard, 46 Conn. 124....................i. 416
Emblen *v.* Myers, 6 H. & N. 54....................i. 481
Emblen *v.* Myers, 30 L. J. Exch. 72....................i. 485
Embrey *v.* Owen, 6 Exch. 353....................i. 201
Embry *v.* Jennison, 131 U. S. 336....................ii. 223
Emery *v.* Fell, 2 T. R. 28....................iii. 135
Emmens *v.* Pottle, 16 Q. B. D. 354....................i. 298, 299
Emmerton *v.* Mathews, 7 H. & N. 586....................i. 388
Endriss *v.* Belle Isle Ice Co., 49 Mich. 279....................ii. 128
Engelhart *v.* Ferrant, (1897) 1 Q. B. 240....................i. 114
England *v.* Cowley, L. R. 8 Exch. 126....................i. 233, 236
England *v.* Davidson, 11 Ad. & El. 856, 39 E. C. L. 245....................ii. 121
English Spokane Commission Co., 57 Fed. Rep. 451....................i. 388
Enos *v.* Hamilton, 27 Wis. 256....................i. 227
Entick *v.* Carrington, 19 How. St. Tr. 1029....................i. 19, 24
Ephick *v.* Hoffman, 49 Conn. 331....................i. 414
Equitable Co-operative Foundry Co. *v.* Hersee....................ii. 218
Erb *v.* Brown, 69 Pa. St. 216....................ii. 129
Erickson *v.* Michigan Land, etc., Co., 50 Mich. 604....................i. 192
Ermenold *v.* Abbot Faritius, Placita Anglo-Norm. 131....................iii. 211
Escott *v.* White, 10 Bush (Ky.) 169....................ii. 221
Estrigge *v.* Owles, 3 Leon. 200....................ii. 34; iii. 178, 183
Eten *v.* Luyster, 60 N. Y. 252....................i. 89
Etriche *v.* Officer of Revenue, Bunb. 67....................iii. 170
Euler *v.* Sullivan, 75 Md. 616....................i. 220, 221
European, The, 10 P. D. 99....................i. 102
Evans *v.* Edmonds, 13 C. B. 777, 76 E. C. L. 777....................i. 394
Evans *v.* Gee, 11 Pet. (U. S.) 80....................ii. 552
Evans *v.* Gwyn, 5 Q. B. 844, 48 E. C. L. 844....................i. 277
Evans *v.* Powis, 1 Exch. 601....................ii. 95, 131
Evans *v.* Thompson, 12 Heisk. (Tenn.) 534....................i. 330
Evans *v.* Walton, L. R. 2 C. P. 615....................i. 268
Evans *v.* Western Union Tel. Co., 102 Iowa 219....................i. 450
Everard *v.* Hopkins, 2 Bulst. 332....................iii. 179
Everett *v.* Central Iowa R. Co., 73 Iowa 442....................iii. 87
Everett *v.* Saltus, 15 Wend. (N. Y.) 474, 20 Wend. (N. Y.) 267....i. 240
Everling *v.* Holcomb, 74 Iowa 722....................i. 415
Ewer *v.* Jones, 2 Ld. Raym. 937, 2 Salk. 415....................ii. 149
Ewing *v.* French, 1 Blackf. (Ind.) 354....................ii. 291
Ewing *v.* Pittsburgh, etc., R. Co., 147 Pa. St. 40....................i. 458

Exall *v.* Partridge, 8 T. R. 308..........iii. 201
Exchange Bank *v.* Tracy, 77 Mo. 594..........ii. 491
Exeter Bank *v.* Gordon, 8 N. H. 66..........ii. 552

Fairbank Canning Co. *v.* Metzger, 118 N. Y. 260..........i. 386
Fairbanks *v.* Kerr, 70 Pa. St. 86..........i. 103
Fairbanks *v.* Phelps, 22 Pick. (Mass.) 535..........i. 254, 260
Fairlie *v.* Denton, 8 B. & C. 400, 15 E. C. L. 247..........iii. 89
Fallon *v.* O'Brien, 12 R. I. 518..........i. 53
Falmouth *v.* Penrose, 6 B. & C. 385, 13 E. C. L. 205..........iii. 184
Fanning *v.* Russell, 94 Ill. 386..........ii. 148
Fanson *v.* Linsley, 20 Kan. 235..........ii. 215; iii. 200
Farley *v.* Lincoln, 51 N. H. 577..........i. 259
Farmer *v.* Arundel, 2 W. Bl. 824..........ii. 213
Farmers' Co-operative Mfg. Co. *v.* Albemarle, etc., R. Co., 117 N. Car. 579..........i. 223
Farnsworth *v.* Duffner, 142 U. S. 43..........i. 395
Farnsworth *v.* Howard, 1 Coldw. (Tenn.) 215..........iii. 265
Farrant *v.* Barnes, 11 C. B. N. S. 553, 103 E. C. L. 553..........i. 60
Farrar *v.* Beswick, 1 M. & W. 682..........i. 240
Farrar *v.* Rollins, 37 Vt. 295..........i. 249; iii. 169
Farwell *v.* Boston, etc., R. Corp., 4 Met. (Mass.) 49..........ii. 462, 470
Farwell *v.* Hanchett, 120 Ill. 573..........i. 259
Fauntleroy *v.* Wilcox, 80 Ill. 477..........i. 414
Faxon *v.* Faxon, 28 Mich. 159..........ii. 245
Fay *v.* Harrington, 176 Mass. 270..........i. 303, 304
Fay *v.* Parker, 53 N. H. 342..........i. 481
Fay *v.* Steamer New World, 1 Cal. 348..........ii. 305
Feather *v.* Reg., 6 B. & S. 296, 118 E. C. L. 296..........i. 37
Featherston *v.* Hutchinson, Cro. Eliz. 199..........ii. 73
Featherstonhaugh *v.* Johnston, 8 Taunt. 237, 4 E. C. L. 86..........i. 238, 241
Felburn *v.* People's Palace, etc., Co., 25 Q. B. D. 258..........i. 55
Felt *v.* Reynolds Rotary Fruit Evaporating Co., 52 Mich. 602..........iii. 86
Fenn *v.* Bittleston, 7 Exch. 160..........i. 248
Fenn *v.* Suckling, L. R. 1 Q. B. 614..........i. 248
Fent *v.* Toledo, etc., R. Co., 59 Ill. 357..........i. 117
Fenton *v.* Emblers, 3 Burr. 1281..........ii. 176
Fererro *v.* Western Union Tel. Co., 9 App. Cas. (D. C.) 455..........i. 450, 452
Fergusson *v.* Anglo-American Tel. Co., 178 Pa. St. 377..........i. 452
Fernald *v.* Chase, 37 Me. 289..........i. 236
Festerman *v.* Parker, 10 Ired. L. (32 N. Car.) 474..........ii. 120
Field *v.* New York Cent. R. Co., 32 N. Y. 349..........i. 57
Fields *v.* Stokley, 99 Pa. St. 306..........i. 23
Fildew *v.* Besley, 42 Mich. 100..........ii. 224
Filley *v.* Fassett, 44 Mo. 168..........i. 424
Filliter *v.* Phippard, 11 Q. B. 347, 63 E. C. L. 347..........i. 56
Final *v.* Backus, 18 Mich. 218..........iii. 87
Findon *v.* Parker, 11 M. & W. 675..........i. 310; ii. 164
Finer *v.* Jeffry, Style 57..........ii. 34
Fines *v.* Spencer, 3 Dyer 306*b*..........iii. 165

Finlay *v.* Chirney, 20 Q. B. D. 494....i. 465; iii. 61
Finn *v.* Corbitt, 36 Mich. 318....iii. 88
Firbank *v.* Humphreys, 18 Q. B. D. 54....i. 406
Fire Ins. Assoc. *v.* Wickham, 141 U. S. 579....ii. 71
Fischer *v.* Blank, 138 N. Y. 245....i. 431
Fish *v.* Chapman, 2 Ga. 349....ii. 306
Fish *v.* Ferris, 5 Duer (N. Y.) 49....ii. 286
Fisher *v.* Bristow, 1 Dougl. 215....i. 329
Fisher *v.* Golloday, 38 Mo. App. 540....i. 61
Fisher *v.* Hamilton, 49 Ind. 341....i. 460
Fisher *v.* Hildreth, 117 Mass. 558....ii. 223
Fisher *v.* Kamala Naicker, 8 Moo. Indian App. 170....i. 340
Fisher *v.* Kyle, 27 Mich. 454....i. 257
Fisher *v.* Western Union Tel. Co., 119 Wis. 146....i. 454
Fishmonger's Co. *v.* East India Co., 1 Dick. 163....i. 210
Fisk *v.* Soniat, 33 La. Ann. 1400....i. 307
Fitch *v.* Snedaker, 38 N. Y. 248....ii. 82
Fitch *v.* Sutton, 5 East 230....ii. 99, 105
Fite *v.* Dorman, 57 S. W. Rep. 129....i. 425, 434
Fitzgerald *v.* Allen, 128 Mass. 234....ii. 221, 222
Fitzgerald *v.* Cavin, 110 Mass. 153....i. 5
Fitzgerald *v.* Connecticut River Paper Co., 155 Mass. 155....i. 167, 170
Flagg *v.* Hudson, 142 Mass. 280....i. 131
Fleet *v.* Hollenkemp, 13 B. Mon. (Ky.) 227....i. 61
Flemming *v.* Ball, 1 Bay (S. Car.) 6....i. 40
Flemmington *v.* Smithers, 2 C. & P. 292, 12 E. C. L. 131....i. 268
Fletcher *v.* Ellis, Hempst. (U. S.) 300....i. 341
Fletcher *v.* Fletcher, 28 L. J. Q. B. 134....i. 9
Fletcher *v.* Rylands, 1 Exch. 265, 3 H. & C. 774....i. 62
Flewellin *v.* Rave, 1 Bulst. 68....ii. 123
Flight *v.* Gresh, Hutton 77....ii. 34
Flight *v.* Leman, 4 Q. B. 883, 45 E. C. L. 883....i. 339
Flight *v.* Reed, 1 H. & C. 703....ii. 145
Flint, etc., R. Co. *v.* Weir, 37 Mich. 111....ii. 50
Flockton *v.* Hall, 14 Q. B. 380, 68 E. C. L. 380....ii. 94
Foakes *v.* Beer, 9 App. Cas. 605....ii. 69, 101, 102, 104
Foley *v.* Holtry, 43 Neb. 133....i. 414
Folmar *v.* Copeland, 57 Ala. 588....iii. 308
Fonseca *v.* Hartman, 84 N. Y. Supp. 131....ii. 542
Fonville *v.* M'Nease, Dudley L. (S. Car.) 303....i. 296
Forbes *v.* Boston, etc., R. Co., 133 Mass. 154....i. 255
Forbes *v.* Parker, 16 Pick. (Mass.) 462....i. 256
Ford *v.* Caldwell, 3 Hill L. (S. Car.) 248....ii. 217
Ford *v.* Garner, 15 Ind. 298....ii. 113, 119
Ford *v.* Gourlay, 42 U. C. Q. B. 552....i. 271
Ford *v.* Surget, 46 Miss. 130....i. 23
Ford *v.* Surget, 97 U. S. 594....i. 23
Ford *v.* Taggart, 4 Tex. 492....i. 18
Forde *v.* Skinner, 4 C. & P. 239, 19 E. C. L. 364....i. 6
Forehand *v.* Jones, 84 Ga. 508....i. 237

Fores v. Wilson, Peake N. P. (ed. 1795) 55....i. 271
Forester v. Secretary of State, L. R. Indian App. (Supp. vol.) 10..i. 37
Fortman v. Rottier, 8 Ohio St. 548....i. 333
Fortune v. Harris, 6 Jones L. (51 N. Car.) 532....ii. 282
Forward v. Pittard, 1 T. R. 27....ii. 301, 302
Foshay v. Ferguson, 2 Den. (N. Y.) 617....i. 330
Foshay v. Ferguson, 5 Hill (N. Y.) 154....ii. 229
Foss v. Hildreth, 10 Allen (Mass.) 76....i. 275
Foster v. Collins, 6 Heisk. (Tenn.) 1....ii. 94
Foster v. Dawber, 6 Exch. 839....ii. 101, 102, 410
Foster v. Essex Bank, 17 Mass. 479....ii. 276
Foster v. Stewart, 3 M. & S. 191....ii. 215
Fotheringham v. Adams Express Co., 36 Fed. Rep. 252....i. 14
Foulger v. Newcomb, L. R. 2 Exch. 327....i. 277
Foulger v. Newcomb, L. R. 2 Exch. 327....i. 277
Fowler v. Rapely, 15 Wall. (U. S.) 328....iii. 308
Fowles v. Bowen, 30 N. Y. 20....i. 312
Fraley v. Bispham, 10 Pa. St. 320....i. 289, 391
Frambers v. Risk, 2 Ill. App. 499....ii. 212
Francis v. Cockrell, L. R. 5 Q. B. 184, 501....i. 151
Francis v. Deming, 59 Conn. 108....ii. 95
Francis v. Western Union Tel. Co., 58 Minn. 252....i. 467
Frank v. Lillienfeld, 33 Gratt. (Va.) 377....ii. 516
Franklin Wharf Co. v. Portland, 67 Me. 46....i. 45
Fratt v. Clark, 12 Cal. 89....iii. 198
Fray v. Blackburn, 3 B. & S. 576, 113 E. C. L. 576....i. 37
Frazer v. Hatton, 2 C. B. N. S. 512, 89 E. C. L. 512....ii. 75
Frazier v. Western Union Tel. Co., 45 Oregon 414....i. 439
Freeman v. Bernard, 1 Ld. Raym. 248....iii. 192
Freeman v. Cooke, 2 Exch. 663....ii. 247
Freeman v. Venner, 120 Mass. 424....i. 416
French v. Ryan, 104 Mich. 625....i. 395
French v. Vining, 102 Mass. 132....i. 388
Frere v. ———, Style 133....iii. 120
Fresh v. Cutter, 73 Md. 87....i. 312
Fried v. New York Cent. R. Co., 25 How. (N. Y.) 285....iii. 87
Frier v. Kinnersley, 15 C. B. N. S. 422, 109 E. C. L. 422....i. 315
Frisbie v. Fowler, 2 Conn. 707....i. 277
Fritz v. Hobson, 14 Ch. D. 542....i. 226, 227, 229
Frizzell v. Rundle, 88 Tenn. 396....i. 244
Frost v. Eastern R. Co., 64 N. H. 220....i. 160
Fuller v. Brown, 11 Met. (Mass.) 440....ii. 224
Fuller v. Colby, 3 Woodb. & M. (U. S.) 1....i. 39
Fuller v. Duren, 36 Ala. 73....ii. 216
Fuller v. McEwen, 17 Ohio St. 288....ii. 149
Fuller-Warren Co. v. Shurts, 95 Wis. 606....i. 387
Fullwood v. Fullwood, 9 Ch. D. 176....i. 418, 434
Furnis v. Leicester, Cro. Jac. 474....i. 382

Gaar v. Green, 6 N. Dak. 48....ii. 75
Gabriel v. Dresser, 15 C. B. 622, 80 E. C. L. 622....ii. 92

Gachet *v.* Warren, 72 Ala. 288 .... i. 385, 388
Gaffney *v.* Brown, 150 Mass. 479 .... i. 125
Gage *v.* Epperson, 2 Head (Tenn.) 669 .... i. 259
Gahan *v.* Western Union Tel. Co., 59 Fed. Rep. 433 .... i. 467
Gaines *v.* Green Pond Iron Min. Co., 32 N. J. Eq. 86 .... i. 26
Galena, etc., R. Co. *v.* Jacobs, 20 Ill. 478 .... i. 147
Galizard *v.* Rigault, 2 Salk. 552 .... i. 204
Gallagher *v.* Sharpless, 134 Pa. St. 134 .... ii. 221
Gallagher *v.* State, 3 Minn. 270 .... i. 7
Galliard *v.* Archer, 1 Leon. 189 .... iii. 166
Galloway *v.* Bird, 4 Bing. 299, 13 E. C. L. 443 .... iii. 220
Galveston, etc., R. Co. *v.* Freeman, 57 Tex. 156 .... iii. 88
Galvin *v.* Bacon, 11 Me. 28 .... iii. 169
Galvin *v.* Prentice, 45 N. Y. 162 .... ii. 227
Gandy *v.* Gandy, 30 Ch. D. 57 .... ii. 159
Gardiner *v.* Bellingham, Hob. 5 .... iii. 181, 188, 189
Gardiner *v.* Gray, 4 Campb. 144 .... i. 389
Gardiner *v.* Spurdance, 1 Rolle Abr. 71 (Z), pl. 1 .... i. 284
Gardner *v.* Campbell, 15 Johns. (N. Y.) 401 .... iii. 218, 220
Gardner *v.* Gardner, 5 Cush. (Mass.) 483 .... ii. 475
Gardner *v.* Slade, 13 Q. B. 796, 66 E. C. L. 796 .... i. 312
Garnet *v.* Clarke, 11 Mod. 226 .... ii. 391
Garret *v.* Taylor, Cro. Jac. 567 .... i. 346, 352
Garside *v.* Trent, etc., Nav. Co., 4 T. R. 581 .... ii. 302
Garth *v.* Cotton, 1 Ves. 524, 3 Atk. 757 .... iii. 65
Garton *v.* Bristol, etc., R. Co., 1 B. & S. 112, 101 E. C. L. 112 .... ii. 306
Gates *v.* Gates, 15 Mass. 311 .... iii. 169
Gates *v.* Parker, 43 Me. 544 .... ii. 402
Gautret *v.* Egerton, L. R. 2 C. P. 371 .... i. 158
Gawton *v.* Dacres, 1 Leon. 219, Owen 23 .... iii. 108
Gay *v.* Ballou, 4 Wend. (N. Y.) 403 .... ii. 204
Gay *v.* Burgess, 59 Ala. 575 .... i. 46
Gaylard *v.* Morris, 3 Exch. 695 .... i. 17
Gazzam *v.* Armstrong, 3 Dana (Ky.) 554 .... ii. 556
Gedge *v.* Minne, 2 Bulst. 60, 2 Rolle Abr. 558 .... i. 21
Gee *v.* Metropolitan R. Co., L. R. 8 Q. B. 161 .... i. 131
Gelley *v.* Clerk, Cro. Jac. 189 .... i. 189
Gelpke *v.* Dubuque, 1 Wall. (U. S.) 175 .... ii. 424
George *v.* Chambers, 11 M. & W. 149 .... iii. 219
George *v.* Clagett, 7 T. R. 355 .... ii. 479
George *v.* Skivington, L. R. 5 Exch. 1 .... i. 58, 61, 386, 387
Georgia Pac. R. Co. *v.* Lee, 92 Ala. 262 .... i. 181
Georgia R., etc., Co. *v.* Baker, 120 Ga. 991 .... i. 470
Gerard *v.* La Coste, 1 Dall. (Pa.) 194 .... ii. 503
German-American Bank *v.* Milliman, 31 Misc. (N. Y.) 87 .... ii. 537
Gerrard *v.* Floyd, 1 Sid. 185 .... iii. 93
Gerrarde *v.* Worseley, 3 Dyer 374*a* .... ii. 45
Gerrish *v.* New Market Mfg. Co., 30 N. H. 478 .... i. 204
Gerst *v.* Jones, 32 Gratt. (Va.) 518 .... i. 387
Gessler *v.* Grieb, 80 Wis. 21 .... i. 424

Geush *v.* Mynne, 1 Brownl. & Goldes. 224.......................i. 21
Gheen *v.* Osborne, 11 Heisk. (Tenn.) 61.......................ii. 244
Gibbon *v.* Paynton, 4 Burr. 2298.......................i. 89; ii. 301, 305
Gibbon *v.* Pepper, 2 Salk. 637, 1 Ld. Raym. 38.......................i. 81, 105
Gibbons *v.* Proctor, 64 L. T. 594.......................ii. 82
Gibbs *v.* Baltimore Gas Co., 130 U. S. 396.......................ii. 223
Gibbs *v.* Blanchard, 15 Mich. 292.......................ii. 186
Giblan *v.* National Amalgamated Labourers' Union, (1903) 2 K. B. 623.......................i. 353, 364
Giblin *v.* McMullen, L. R. 2 P. C. 318, 3 Eng. Rul. Cas. 613.......................i. 100
Giblin *v.* McMullen, L. R. 2 P. C. 318, 38 L. J. P. C. 25.......................ii. 275, 277
Gibney *v.* State, 137 N. Y. 6.......................i. 133
Gibson *v.* Ireson, 3 Q. B. 39.......................iii. 306
Gibson *v.* Minet, 1 H. Bl. 569, 625.......................ii. 403
Gibson *v.* Wells, 1 B. & P. N. R. 290.......................i. 30, 31
Gilbert *v.* People, 1 Den. (N. Y.) 41.......................i. 308
Gilbert *v.* Showerman, 23 Mich. 448.......................i. 219
Gilbert *v.* Stone, Aleyn 35, Style 72.......................i. 78
Gilbert *v.* Sykes, 16 East 150.......................ii. 167
Gilbert *v.* Woodbury, 22 Me. 246.......................i. 487
Gilby *v.* Copley, 3 Lev. 138.......................iii. 121
Giles *v.* Walker, 24 Q. B. D. 656.......................i. 129
Gill *v.* Cubitt, 3 B. & C. 466, 10 E. C. L. 154.......................ii. 405, 531
Gill *v.* Harewood, 1 Leon. 61.......................ii. 31
Gill *v.* Middleton, 105 Mass. 479.......................i. 100
Gillard *v.* Brittan, 8 M. & W. 575.......................i. 256
Gillet *v.* Roberts, 57 N. Y. 32.......................i. 236
Gillett *v.* Johnson, 30 Conn. 180.......................i. 199, 201
Gilley *v.* Gilley, 79 Me. 292.......................ii. 205
Gillott *v.* Esterbrook, 48 N. Y. 374.......................i. 423
Gilman *v.* Elton, 3 Brod. & B. 75, 7 E. C. L. 355.......................iii. 306
Gilman *v.* Hill, 36 N. H. 311.......................i. 238
Gilman *v.* Noyes, 57 N. H. 627.......................i. 116
Gilmore *v.* Driscoll, 122 Mass. 199.......................i. 196, 197
Gilmore *v.* Lewis, 12 Ohio 281.......................ii. 120
Gilmore *v.* Newton, 9 Allen (Mass.) 171.......................i. 230
Gilmore *v.* Westerman, 13 Wash. 390.......................iii. 86
Gilpin *v.* Fowler, 9 Exch. 615.......................i. 314, 315
Giroux *v.* Stedman, 145 Mass. 439.......................i. 387
Givens *v.* Van Studdiford, 86 Mo. 158.......................i. 228
Gladwell *v.* Steggall, 5 Bing. N. Cas. 733, 35 E. C. L. 292....i. 187; iii. 273
Glasscock *v.* Glasscock, 66 Mo. 627.......................ii. 504
Glasspoole *v.* Young, 9 B. & C. 696, 17 E. C. L. 474.......................i. 239
Gleason *v.* Dyke, 22 Pick. (Mass.) 393.......................ii. 87
Gledstane *v.* Hewitt, 1 Cromp. & J. 565.......................iii. 149, 152
Gleeson *v.* Virginia Midland R. Co., 140 U. S. 435.......................i. 108
Glencoe Land, etc., Co. *v.* Hudson Bros. Commission Co., 138 Mo. 439.......................i. 346
Glendon Iron Co. *v.* Uhler, 75 Pa. St. 467.......................i. 424
Glenn *v.* Kays, 1 Ill. App. 479.......................i. 21

Glover *v.* London, etc., R. Co., L. R. 3 Q. B. 25....................i. 119
Glyn *v.* Baker, 13 East 509....................ii. 419
Goddard *v.* Westcott, 82 Mich. 180....................i. 464
Godfrey *v.* Saunders, 3 Wils. C. Pl. 73....................iii. 108, 110
Goebel *v.* Linn, 47 Mich. 489....................ii. 128
Goetting *v.* Day, 87 N. Y. Supp. 510....................ii. 531
Goffin *v.* Donnelly, 6 Q. B. D. 307....................i. 308
Gokal Prasad *v.* Radho, Indian L. R. 10 Allahabad 358....................i. 320
Goldrich *v.* Ryan, 3 E. D. Smith (N. Y.) 324....................i. 388
Goldsmid *v.* Tunbridge Wells Imp. Com'rs, L. R. 1 Ch. 349....................i. 202
Goldsmith *v.* Preston, 1 Rolle Abr. 96, pl. 1....................i. 380
Goldstein *v.* Foss, 4 Bing. 489....................i. 300
Goldthwait *v.* Haverhill, etc., St. R. Co., 160 Mass. 554....................i. 170
Good *v.* Cheesman, 2 B. & Ad. 328, 22 E. C. L. 89....................ii. 94, 106, 131
Goodall, *In re*, 42 Ch. D. 566....................i. 425
Goodisson *v.* Nunn, 4 T. R. 761....................ii. 138
Goodman *v.* Chase, 1 B. & Ald. 297....................ii. 185
Goodman *v.* Gay, 15 Pa. St. 188....................i. 53
Goodman *v.* Harvey, 4 Ad. & El. 870, 31 E. C. L. 212....................ii. 407, 531
Goodman *v.* Pocock, 15 Q. B. 576, 69 E. C. L. 576....................ii. 222
Goodman *v.* Simonds, 20 How. (U. S.) 343....................ii. 408
Goodno *v.* Oshkosh, 28 Wis. 300....................i. 489
Goodrich *v.* Burbank, 12 Allen (Mass.) 459....................i. 201
Goodrich *v.* Davis, 11 Met. (Mass.) 473....................i. 299, 300
Goodright *v.* Forester, 1 Taunt. 613....................iii. 83
Goodrun *v.* State, 60 Ga. 509....................i. 6
Goodwin *v.* Gilbert, 9 Mass. 510....................ii. 173
Goodwin *v.* Robarts, 1 App. Cas. 476, L. R. 10 Exch. 76....................ii. 423
Goodwin *v.* Robarts, L. R. 10 Exch. 337....................ii. 323, 354, 386, 417
Goodwin *v.* Robinson, 30 Ark. 535....................i. 407
Goodwin *v.* Willoughby, Popham 177....................ii. 34, 77
Goodyear Dental Vulcanite Co. *v.* White, 2 N. J. L. 150....................i. 341
Gordon *v.* Bruner, 49 Mo. 570....................iii. 198
Gordon *v.* Butler, 105 U. S. 553....................i. 394
Gordon *v.* Gordon, 56 N. H. 171....................ii. 119
Gordon *v.* Harper, 7 T. R. 9....................i. 251, 253, 255
Gorgier *v.* Mieville, 3 B. & C. 45, 10 E. C. L. 16....................ii. 420
Gorham *v.* Gross, 125 Mass. 240....................i. 63
Gorham Mfg. Co. *v.* Emery-Bird-Thayer Dry-Goods Co., 104 Fed. Rep. 243....................i. 431
Goring *v.* Goring, Yelv. 10....................ii. 91
Gormely *v.* Gymnastic Assoc., 55 Wis. 350....................i. 395
Gorris *v.* Scott, L. R. 9 Exch. 125....................i. 174, 175
Goshen, etc., Turnpike-Road Co. *v.* Hartin, 9 Johns. (N. Y.) 217....................ii. 387, 504
Goss *v.* Nelson, 1 Burr. 226....................ii. 508
Goswill *v.* Dunkley, 1 Stra. 680....................iii. 106
Gott *v.* Pulsiver, 122 Mass. 235....................i. 324
Gotwalt *v.* Neal, 25 Md. 434....................ii. 230
Gough *v.* Goldsmith, 44 Wis. 262....................i. 290

Gould *v.* Oliver, 4 Bing. N. Cas. 142, 33 E. C. L. 305................i. 162
Goulding *v.* Davidson, 26 N. Y. 609................................ii. 87
Gout *v.* Alepoglu, 6 Beav. 69..i. 424
Government St. R. Co. *v.* Hanlon, 53 Ala. 70....................i. 144
Govett *v.* Radnidge, 3 East 62......................................iii. 274
Gower *v.* Capper, Cro. Eliz. 543............................ii. 55, 135
Grace Girdler, The, 7 Wall. (U. S.) 196..........................i. 145
Grady *v.* American Cent. Ins. Co., 60 Mo. 116..................ii. 476
Graham *v.* Western Union Tel. Co., 109 La. 1069.................i. 466
Grainger *v.* Hill, 4 Bing. N. Cas. 212, 33 E. C. L. 328............i. 239, 334
Grandona *v.* Lovdal, 70 Cal. 161......................................i. 20
Grand Trunk R. Co. *v.* Latham, 63 Me. 177..........................ii. 240
Granger *v.* Collins, 6 M. & W. 458....................................ii. 86
Grant *v.* Duluth, etc., R. Co., 61 Minn. 395........................ii. 117
Grant *v.* Vaughan, 3 Burr. 1516...........................ii. 369, 385, 394
Grant *v.* Willey, 101 Mass. 356..i. 464
Gratz *v.* Phillips, 5 Binn. (Pa.) 564...........................iii. 110, 111
Graves's Case, cited in Co. Litt. 53*a*..................................i. 28
Gray *v.* Combs, 7 J. J. Marsh. (Ky.) 478............................i. 8
Gray *v.* Gray, 2 J. J. Marsh. (Ky.) 21.................................ii. 227
Gray *v.* Jefferies, Cro. Eliz. 55...i. 267
Gray *v.* Merriam, 148 Ill. 179..ii. 277
Gray *v.* Western Union Tel. Co., 108 Tenn. 39...............i. 466, 473
Gray Eagle, The, 9 Wall. (U. S.) 505..................................i. 145
Great Northern R. Co. *v.* Swaffield, L. R. 9 Exch. 132..............ii. 234
Great Republic, The, 23 Wall. (U. S.) 20..............................i. 146
Greely *v.* Tremont Ins. Co., 9 Cush. (Mass.) 415...................i. 19
Green *v.* Ashland Water Co., 101 Wis. 258..........................i. 128
Green *v.* Button, 2 C. M. & R. 707...............................i. 323, 343
Green *v.* Chapman, 4 Bing. N. Cas. 92, 33 E. C. L. 288...............i. 306
Green *v.* Cresswell, 10 Ad. & El. 453..................................ii. 187
Green *v.* Dunn, 3 Camph. 215...i. 246
Green *v.* Harrington, Hob. 284...iii. 180
Green *v.* Kelley, 64 Vt. 309..ii. 117
Green *v.* Spencer, 3 Mo. 318...i. 464
Green *v.* Thomas, 11 Me. 321...ii. 40
Green *v.* Western Union Tel. Co., 136 N. Car. 489.............i. 466, 473
Greene *v.* Cole, 2 Saund. 252.................................i. 30; iii. 270
Greenland *v.* Chaplin, 5 Exch. 248.....................................i. 90
Greenleaf *v.* Barker, Cro. Eliz. 429, 1 Leon. 238.....................ii. 106
Greenway *v.* Fisher, 1 C. & P. 190, 11 E. C. L. 362.............i. 244, 245
Greeser *v.* Sugarman, 37 Misc. (N. Y.) 799..........................ii. 517
Gregg *v.* Coates, 23 Beav. 33..i. 30
Gregg *v.* Dunn, 38 Mo. App. 283...ii. 226
Gregg *v.* Wills, 10 Ad. & El. 90, 37 E. C. L. 54.......................ii. 242
Gregory *v.* Brunswick, 6 M. & G. 205, 46 E. C. L. 205.................i. 353
Gregory *v.* Lee, 64 Conn. 407..ii. 204
Gregory *v.* Piper, 9 B. & C. 591, 17 E. C. L. 454....ii. 453, 456, 469; iii. 261
Grey *v.* Paterson, 60 N. J. Eq. 385.......................................i. 44
Griffin *v.* Goldsboro Water Co., 122 N. Car. 206.......................i. 186

Griffin *v.* Moore, 43 Md. 246....i. 277
Grill *v.* General Iron Screw Collier Co., L. R. 1 C. P. 600....i. 100
Grinnell *v.* Wells, 7 M. & G. 1033, 49 E. C. L. 1033....i. 270, 271
Grissom *v.* Commercial Nat. Bank, 87 Tex. 350....ii. 538
Grocers' Nat. Bank *v.* Clark, 48 Barb. (N. Y.) 26....iii. 87
Gross *v.* Miller, 93 Iowa 72....i. 178
Grotton *v.* Glidden, 84 Me. 589....i. 7
Guerrant *v.* Guerrant, 7 Va. L. Reg. 639....ii. 517
Guest *v.* Reynolds, 68 Ill. 478....i. 208
Guild *v.* Baldridge, 2 Swan (Tenn.) 295....ii. 212
Guille *v.* Swan, 19 Johns. (N. Y.) 381....i. 88
Gulf, etc., R Co. *v.* Harriett, 80 Tex. 73....ii. 95
Gulf, etc., R. Co. *v.* Levy, 59 Tex. 542, 563....i. 468
Gulf, etc., R. Co. *v.* Wilson, 69 Tex. 739....i. 453
Gundry *v.* Feltham, 1 T. R. 334....i. 21
Gurratt *v.* Cullum, referred to in Willes 405....ii. 478
Gutta Percha, etc., Mfg. Co. *v.* Houston, 108 N. Y. 276....ii. 207
Guy *v.* Livesey, Cro. Jac. 501....i. 263
Gyre *v.* Culver, 47 Barb. (N. Y.) 592....i. 8

Habersham *v.* Lehman, 63 Ga. 383....ii. 515
Hackett *v.* Brown, 2 Heisk. (Tenn.) 264....i. 290
Haddrick *v.* Heslop, 12 Q. B. 267, 64 E. C. L. 267....i. 330
Hadley *v.* Baxendale, 9 Exch. 341....i. 445, 447
Haft *v.* New Castle First Nat. Bank, 19 N. Y. App. Div. 425....i. 315
Haile *v.* Texas, etc., R. Co., 60 Fed. Rep. 557....i. 458
Haines *v.* Finch, Aleyn 6....ii. 47
Haines *v.* Roberts, 7 El. & Bl. 625, 9 E. C. L. 625....i. 192
Hale *v.* Bonner, 82 Tex. 33....i. 474
Hale *v.* Lawrence, 21 N. J. L. 714....i. 23
Hales *v.* Freeman, 1 Brod. & B. 391, 5 E. C. L. 131....ii. 232
Halestrap *v.* Gregory, (1895) 1 Q. B. 561....i. 114
Hall *v.* Barrows, 4 DeG. J. & S. 150....i. 421
Hall *v.* Fearnley, 3 Q. B. 919, 43 E. C. L. 1037....i. 81
Hall *v.* Harding, 4 Burr. 2432....iii. 310
Hall *v.* Hennesley, Cro. Eliz. 486....i. 207
Hall *v.* Hollander, 4 B. & C. 660, 10 E. C. L. 436....i. 268
Hall *v.* Johnson, 41 Mich. 286....i. 396
Hall *v.* Marston, 17 Mass. 575....ii. 156
Hall *v.* Smith, 10 Iowa 48....ii. 95
Halliday *v.* Holgate, L. R. 3 Exch. 299....i. 253
Halsey *v.* Bird, 99 Fed. Rep. 525....i. 239
Halsey *v.* Brotherhood, 19 Ch. D. 386....i. 323
Hambly *v.* Trott, 1 Cowp. 371....iii. 61, 64, 196, 198
Hamburg Bank *v.* Wray, 4 Strobh. L. (S. Car.) 87....i. 406
Hamden *v.* Walsh, 1 Q. B. D. 189....ii. 223
Hamer *v.* Sidway, 124 N. Y. 538....ii. 72
Hamilton *v.* Lomax, 26 Barb. (N. Y.) 615....i. 272
Hamilton *v.* Marks, 63 Mo. 167....ii. 408
Hammack *v.* White, 11 C. B. N. S. 588, 103 E. C. L. 588....i. 104
Hammersmith, etc., R. Co. *v.* Brand, L. R. 4 H. L. 171....i. 42

Hancock *v.* Hazzard, 12 Cush. (Mass.) 112................ii. 293; iii. 112
Handcock *v.* Baker, 2 B. & P. 260........................i. 10
Handlan *v.* McManus, 42 Mo. App. 551, 100 Mo. 124..........i. 196
Handy *v.* Commander, 49 La. Ann. 1119......................i. 421
Hankinson *v.* Bilby, 16 M. & W. 442.......................i. 284
Hanks *v.* Barron, 95 Tenn. 275............................ii. 113
Hanover Nat. Bank *v.* American Dock, etc., Co., 148 N. Y. 612....i. 483
Hansard *v.* Robinson, 7 B. & C. 90, 14 E. C. L. 20.............ii. 375, 376
Hanson *v.* Elton, 38 Minn. 493.............................i. 464
Hardaker *v.* Idle Dist. Council, (1896) 1 Q. B. 335..............i. 154
Harding *v.* Freeman, 1 Rolle Abr. 91, pl. 8....................i. 382
Hard's Case, 1 Salk. 23, pl. 3......................ii. 165; iii. 185, 193
Hardy *v.* Reed, 6 Cush. (Mass.) 252.........................i. 254
Hargrave *v.* Le Breton, 4 Burr. 2422........................i. 323
Harker *v.* Birkbeck, 3 Burr. 1559...........................iii. 253
Harker *v.* Dement, 9 Gill (Md.) 7............................i. 252
Harland *v.* Person, 93 Ala. 273.............................ii. 149
Harman *v.* Delany, Fitzg. 254..............................i. 293
Harmon *v.* Harmon, 61 Me. 227.............................ii. 229
Harnett *v.* Maitland, 16 M. & W. 257........................i. 30
Harper *v.* Graham, 20 Ohio 115.............................ii. 103
Harrington *v.* Fall River Iron Works Co., 119 Mass. 82..........ii. 224
Harrington *v.* Long, 2 Myl. & K. 590........................i. 340
Harrington *v.* Victoria Graving Dock Co, 3 Q. B. D. 549..........ii. 73
Harriott *v.* Plimpton, 166 Mass. 585........................i. 311
Harris *v.* Bowden, Cro. Eliz. 90............................i. 376
Harris *v.* Brisco, 17 Q. B. D. 504.......................i. 340; ii. 164
Harris *v.* Carter, 3 El. & Bl. 559, 77 E. C. L. 559...............ii. 76
Harris *v.* Cassidy, 107 Ind. 158.............................ii. 119
Harris *v.* De Pinna, 33 Ch. D. 238, 262......................i. 205
Harris *v.* Mobbs, 3 Ex. D. 268..............................i. 113
Harris *v.* More, 70 Cal. 502................................ii. 121
Harris *v.* Ryding, 5 M. & W. 60..........................i. 192, 193
Harris *v.* Saunders, 2 Strobh. Eq. (S. C.) 370..................i. 238
Harris *v.* Terry, 98 N. Car. 131.............................i. 277
Harris *v.* Watson, Peake N. P. (ed. 1795) 72....................ii. 75
Harris *v.* Zanone, 93 Cal. 59...............................i. 296
Harrison *v.* Berkley, 1 Strobh. L. (S. Car.) 525.................i. 173
Harrison *v.* Bush, 5 El. & Bl. 344, 85 E. C. L. 344..............i. 308
Harrison *v.* Cage, Carth. 467, 5 Mod. 411, 1 Salk. 24...........i. 463
Harrison *v.* Cage, 1 Ld. Raym. 386...................ii. 175, 190, 191
Harrison *v.* Howe, 109 Mich. 479............................i. 323
Harrison *v.* M'Intosh, 1 Johns. (N. Y.) 380....................iii. 221
Harrison *v.* Rutland, 1 Q. B. 142............................i. 22
Harrison *v.* Thornborough, 10 Mod. 196......................i. 299
Harrison *v.* Western Union Tel. Co., 10 Am. & Eng. Corp. Cas. 600..i. 456
Harrop *v.* Hirst, L. R. 4 Exch. 43...........................i. 222
Hart *v.* Aldridge, 1 Cowp. 54...............................i. 265
Hart *v.* Western Union Tel. Co., 66 Cal. 579....................i. 452
Hartfield *v.* Roper, 21 Wend. (N. Y.) 615......................i. 142

Hartford Live Stock Ins. Co. *v.* Matthews, 102 Mass. 221 .... i. 415
Hartley *v.* Cummings, 5 C. B. 247, 57 E. C. L. 247 .... i. 266
Hartley *v.* Harriman, 1 B. & Ald. 620 .... i. 54, 55
Hartman *v.* Rogers, 69 Cal. 643 .... ii. 226
Hartop *v.* Hoare, 3 Atk. 44 .... ii. 313
Harvey *v.* Brydges, 14 M. & W. 442 .... i. 9
Harvey *v.* Epes, 12 Gratt. (Va.) 153 .... ii. 288
Harvey *v.* Martin, 1 Campb. 425, *note* .... ii. 411
Harvey *v.* Merrill, 150 Mass. 1 .... ii. 223
Haskins *v.* Royster, 70 N. Car. 601 .... i. 346
Hastings *v.* Lovering, 2 Pick. (Mass.) 214 .... i. 386
Hatch *v.* Searles, 2 Smale & G. 147 .... ii. 516
Hatch *v.* Trayes, 11 Ad. & El. 702, 39 E. C. L. 207 ..... ii. 382, 391; iii. 142
Hatch *v.* Vermont Cent. R. Co., 25 Vt. 49 .... i. 44
Hatchard *v.* Mege, 18 Q. B. D. 771 .... i. 322; iii. 69
Hatchell *v.* Odom, 2 Dev. & B. L. (19 N. Car.) 302 .... ii. 86
Hatlin *v.* Chapman, 46 Conn. 607 .... i. 464
Hatton *v.* Jones, 78 Ind. 466 .... ii. 148
Haubelt *v.* Rea, etc., Mill Co., 77 Mo. App. 672 .... i. 456
Havana Press Drill Co. *v.* Ashurst, 148 Ill. 115 .... ii. 113
Haven *v.* Foster, 9 Pick. (Mass.) 112 .... ii. 214
Hawarden *v.* Youghiogheny, etc., Coal Co., 111 Wis. 545 .... i. 366
Hawkes *v.* Saunders, 1 Cowp. 289 .... ii. 143, 144, 147
Hawkins *v.* Cardy, 1 Ld. Raym. 360 .... ii. 351, 379, 524
Hawkins *v.* Cooper, 8 C. & P. 473, 34 E. C. L. 485 .... i. 137
Hawkins *v.* Gilbert, 19 Ala. 54 .... ii. 225
Hawkins *v.* Parker, 2 Bulst. 256 .... iii. 106
Hawkins *v.* U. S., 96 U. S. 697 .... ii. 221
Hawse *v.* Crowe, R. & M. 414, 21 E. C. L. 477 .... i. 259
Hay *v.* Le Neve, 2 Shaw Sc. App. 395 .... i. 145, 146
Haycroft *v.* Creasy, 2 East 92 .... i. 393, 395, 409
Hayes *v.* Waldron, 44 N. H. 580 .... i. 202
Hayes *v.* Warren, 2 Stra. 933 .... ii. 84, 85
Haynes *v.* Clinton Printing Co., 169 Mass. 512 .... i. 299
Haynes *v.* Rudd, 102 N. Y. 372 .... ii. 230
Hazard *v.* Irwin, 18 Pick. (Mass.) 95 .... i. 407
Hazard Powder Co. *v.* Volger, 58 Fed. Rep. 152 .... i. 59
Hazel *v.* Clark, 3 Harr. (Del.) 22 .... i. 7
Hazelton Boiler Co. *v.* Hazelton Tripod Boiler Co., 142 Ill. 494 ...... i. 423
Head *v.* Georgia Pac. R. Co., 79 Ga. 358 .... i. 460, 474
Heake *v.* Moulton, Yelv. 90 .... i. 278
Heald *v.* Carey, 11 C. B. 977, 73 E. C. L. 977 .... i. 237
Hearn *v.* Shaw, 72 Me. 193 .... i. 334
Heathcote *v.* Crookshanks, 2 T. R. 24 .... ii. 94, 105
Heaven *v.* Pender, 11 Q. B. D. 503 .... i. 92, 94, 149
Hebden *v.* Rutter, 1 Sid. 180 .... i. 463
Hebditch *v.* McIlwaine, (1894) 2 Q. B. 54 .... i. 309, 312
Heckle *v.* Lurvey, 101 Mass. 344 .... i. 239
Hedges *v.* Tagg, L. R. 7 Exch. 283 .... i. 269, 270
Hedin *v.* Minneapolis Med., etc., Institute, 62 Minn. 146 .... i. 382

Hedley *v.* Barlow, 4 F. & F. 224.....i. 305
Hegeman *v.* Moon, 131 N. Y. 462.....ii. 504
Heine *v.* Meyer, 61 N. Y. 171.....ii. 224
Heland *v.* Lowell, 3 Allen (Mass.) 407.....i. 177
Helsham *v.* Blackwood, 11 C. B. 111, 73 E. C. L. 111.....i. 301, 302
Hemmens *v.* Nelson, 138 N. Y. 524.....i. 315
Henderson *v.* Broomhead, 4 H. & N. 569.....i. 307
Hendrick *v.* Lindsay, 93 U. S. 143.....ii. 157
Hennessy *v.* Braunschweiger, 89 Fed. Rep. 664.....i. 422
Henn's Case, W. Jones 296.....i. 23
Henry *v.* Burbidge, 3 Bing. N. Cas. 501, 32 E. C. L. 223.....iii. 202
Henry *v.* Henry, 11 Ind. 236.....ii. 207
Henry *v.* Henry, 27 Ohio St. 121.....ii. 192
Henwood *v.* Harrison, L. R. 7 C. P. 606.....i. 304, 306
Heriot *v.* Stuart, 1 Esp. 437.....i. 304
Herlakenden's Case, 4 Coke 62.....i. 26
Hern *v.* Nichols, 1 Salk. 289.....ii. 453
Herne *v.* Bembow, 4 Taunt. 764.....i. 31
Herring *v.* Boyle, 1 C. M. & R. 377.....i. 13
Herrmann *v.* Orcutt, 152 Mass. 405.....ii. 95
Herron *v.* Western Union Tel. Co., 90 Iowa 129.....i. 451
Hewitson *v.* Hunt, 8 Rich. L. (S. Car.) 106.....iii. 218
Heylyn *v.* Adamson, 2 Burr. 669.....ii. 397
Heywood *v.* Tillson, 75 Me. 225.....i. 366
Hickinbotham *v.* Leach, 10 M. & W. 363.....i. 301
Hickman *v.* Maisey, 1 Q. B. 752.....i. 22
Hickok *v.* Buck, 22 Vt. 149.....i. 254
Hicks *v.* Palington, Moo. K. B. 297.....i. 19
Hide *v.* Thornborough, 2 C. & K. 250, 61 E. C. L. 250.....i. 195
Higgins *v.* Butcher, Yelv. 89.....iii. 72
Higgins *v.* Senior, 8 M. & W. 834, 845.....ii. 480
Highmore *v.* Harrington, 3 C. B. N. S. 142, 91 E. C. L. 142.....i. 277
Hilbery *v.* Hatton, 2 H. & C. 822.....i. 239
Hill *v.* Bateman, 1 Stra. 710.....i. 38
Hill *v.* King, 8 Cal. 337.....i. 201
Hill *v.* Lewis, 1 Salk. 132.....ii. 378, 503
Hill *v.* New River Co., 9 B. & S. 303.....i. 111
Hill *v.* Perrott, 3 Taunt. 274.....iii. 108
Hill *v.* Rodgers, 2 Iowa 67.....i. 8
Hill *v.* Winsor, 118 Mass. 251.....i. 104
Hillhouse *v.* Dunning, 5 Conn. 391.....i. 294
Hilliard *v.* Richardson, 3 Gray (Mass.) 349.....ii. 472
Hills *v.* Street, 5 Bing. 37, 15 E. C. L. 358.....ii. 230
Hillyard *v.* Crabtree, 11 Tex. 264.....ii. 224
Hinde *v.* Whitehouse, 7 East 558.....ii. 175
Hindhaugh *v.* Blakey, 3 C. P. D. 136.....ii. 549
Hinkley *v.* Penobscot, 42 Me. 89.....i. 179
Hinson *v.* Burridge, Moo. K. B. 701.....ii. 63
Hinton's Case, 2 Show. 235.....ii. 383
Hiort *v.* Bott, L. R. 9 Exch. 86.....i. 233, 234

Hirschfeld *v.* London, etc., R. Co., 2 Q. B. D. 1....................i. 395
Hoadly *v.* McLane, 10 Bing. 482, 25 E. C. L. 208....................ii. 195
Hoag *v.* Hatch, 23 Conn. 585....................i. 277
Hoag *v.* Lake Shore, etc., R. Co., 85 Pa. St. 293....................i. 117, 118
Hoare *v.* Silverlock, 12 Q. B. 624, 64 E. C. L. 624....................i. 300, 310
Hobson *v.* Perry, 1 Hill L. (S. Car.) 277....................i. 18
Hoddesdon *v.* Gresil, Yelv. 104....................iii. 310
Hodge *v.* Vavisor, 1 Rolle 413....................ii. 87
Hodge *v.* Vavisour, 3 Bulst. 222....................ii. 63
Hodgeden *v.* Hubbard, 18 Vt. 504....................i. 8
Hodges *v.* Shuler, 22 N. Y. 114....................ii. 508
Hodges *v.* Steward, 12 Mod. 37, 1 Salk. 125..........ii. 351, 362, 372, 377, 379, 503
Hodgkinson *v.* Ennor, 4 B. & S. 241, 116 E. C. L. 241....................i. 203
Hodgkinson *v.* Snibson, 3 B. & P. 603....................iii. 212
Hodsoll *v.* Stallebrass, 11 Ad. & El. 301, 39 E. C. L. 94......i. 266; iii. 72
Hoe *v.* Sanborn, 21 N. Y. 556....................i. 387
Hoffman *v.* American Exch. Nat. Bank, 96 N. W. Rep. 112........ii. 521
Hoffman *v.* Carow, 22 Wend. (N. Y.) 285....................i. 244
Hoffman *v.* Eppers, 41 Wis. 251....................i. 9
Hoffman *v.* Planters Nat. Bank, 99 Va. 480....................ii. 547
Hogg *v.* Kirby, 8 Ves. Jr. 215....................i. 419
Hogle *v.* New York Cent., etc., R. Co., 28 Hun (N. Y.) 363.........i. 130
Holbrook *v.* Connor, 60 Me. 578....................i. 394
Holcomb *v.* Danby, 51 Vt. 428....................i. 179
Holcomb *v.* Noble, 69 Mich. 396....................i. 407
Holcroft *v.* Dickenson, Cart. 233....................i. 463
Holden *v.* Banes, 140 Pa. St. 63....................ii. 87
Holdom *v.* Ayer, 110 Ill. 448....................i. 414
Holdsworth's Case, Clayton 57, pl. 99....................iii. 168
Hole *v.* Barlow, 4 C. B. N. S. 334, 93 E. C. L. 334....................i. 219
Holliday *v.* Poole, 77 Ga. 159....................ii. 75
Hollins *v.* Fowler, L. R. 7 H. L. 757....................i. 244, 245, 246
Hollis *v.* Carr, 2 Mod. 91....................iii. 124
Holmes *v.* Hall, 6 Mod. 161, Holt K. B. 36....................iii. 192
Holmes *v.* Mather, L. R. 10 Exch. 261....................i. 79, 81
Holmes *v.* Tostwood, Cro. Jac. 690....................iii. 188
Holsman *v.* Boiling Spring Bleaching Co., 14 N. J. Eq. 335......i. 202, 203
Holt *v.* Clarencieux, 2 Stra. 937....................ii. 108
Holt *v.* Scholefield, 6 T. R. 691....................i. 300
Holton *v.* Noble, 83 Cal. 7....................ii. 95
Holzapfel's Compositions Co. *v.* Rahtjen's American Composition Co., 183 U. S. 1....................i. 426
Homans *v.* Boston El. R. Co., 180 Mass. 456....................i. 459
Honywood *v.* Honywood, L. R. 18 Eq. 306....................i. 26
Hood *v.* Bloch, 29 W. Va. 244....................i. 388
Hooker *v.* Eagle Bank, 30 N. Y. 83....................iii. 86
Hooker *v.* Miller, 37 Iowa 613....................i. 69
Hooper *v.* Mayor, 56 L. J. 457....................ii. 230
Hoover *v.* Peters, 18 Mich. 51....................i. 387

Hope *v.* Johnston, 11 Rich. L. (S. Car.) 138....................i. 102, 103
Hope *v.* Lawrence, 50 Barb. (N. Y.) 258....................ii. 245
Hopkins *v.* Drowne, 21 R. I. 20....................i. 323
Hopkins *v.* Logan, 5 M. & W. 241....................ii. 86
Hopkins *v.* Oxley Stave Co., 83 Fed. Rep. 912....................i. 366
Hopkins *v.* Tanqueray, 15 C. B. 130, 80 E. C. L. 130....................i. 380
Horn *v.* Foster, 34 Hen. VI....................iii. 83
Horn *v.* Fuller, 6 N. H. 511....................ii. 389
Horne *v.* Midland R. Co., L. R. 8 C. P. 131....................i. 449
Horner *v.* Watson, 79 Pa. St. 251....................i. 192
Horsely *v.* Branch, 1 Humph. (Tenn.) 199....................i. 258
Horsfall *v.* Thomas, 1 H. & C. 90....................i. 394
Horton *v.* Coggs, 3 Lev. 299....................ii. 329, 371, 372, 379, 384
Hosford *v.* Ballard, 39 N. Y. 150....................iii. 308
Hoskins *v.* Robins, 2 Saund. 324....................iii. 311
Hotchkiss *v.* Hunt, 49 Me. 213....................i. 239
Houck *v.* Wachter, 34 Md. 265....................i. 225
Houlden *v.* Smith, 14 Q. B. 841, 68 E. C. L. 841....................i. 38
Hounsell *v.* Smyth, 7 C. B. N. S. 731, 97 E. C. L. 731....................i. 158
Houston, etc., R. Co. *v.* Davidson, 15 Tex. Civ. App. 334....................i. 450
How *v.* Kemball, 2 McLean (U. S.) 107....................ii. 181
How *v.* Prinn, 2 Salk. 694....................i. 277
Howard *v.* Bankes, 2 Burr. 1114....................iii. 253
Howard *v.* Crowther, 8 M. & W. 601....................iii. 86
Howard *v.* Emerson, 110 Mass. 320....................i. 388
Howard *v.* Harris, 1 Cab. & El. 253....................i. 237
Howard *v.* Sheward, L. R. 2 C. P. 150....................ii. 485
Howard *v.* Wood, 2 Lev. 245, T. Jones 126....................iii. 195
Howes *v.* Rose, 13 Ind. App. 647....................i. 61
Howland *v.* Lounds, 51 N. Y. 604....................ii. 82
Hoyt *v.* Jeffers, 30 Mich. 181....................i. 112
Hoyt *v.* Thompson, 5 N. Y. 320....................iii. 86
Hubbard *v.* Martin, 8 Yerg. (Tenn.) 498....................ii. 214
Hubbard *v.* Weare, 79 Iowa 678....................i. 407
Huckle *v.* Money, 2 Wils. C. Pl. 205....................i. 484
Huff *v.* Watkins, 15 S. Car. 82....................i. 346
Huffman *v.* Hughlett, 11 Lea (Tenn.) 549....................ii. 218
Hugett *v.* Montgomery, 2 B. & P. N. R. 446....................iii. 264
Hughes *v.* Keene, Calth. 1....................i. 207
Hughes *v.* Keene, Godb. 183....................i. 207
Hughes *v.* Keme, Yelv. 215....................i. 207
Hughes *v.* Keymish, 1 Bulst. 115....................i. 207
Hughes *v.* Sloan, 8 Ark. 146....................i. 413
Hulbert *v.* Hartman, 79 Ill. App. 289....................ii. 296
Hulett *v.* Swift, 33 N. Y. 571....................ii. 296
Hummer *v.* Lockwood, 3 Greene (Iowa) 90....................ii. 221
Humphreys *v.* Stilwell, 2 F. & F. 590....................i. 311
Humphries *v.* Brogden, 12 Q. B. 739, 64 E. C. L. 739......i. 191, 192, 193
Humphries *v.* Parker, 52 Me. 502....................i. 488
Humphry *v.* Stanfeild, Cro. Car. 469, 1 Rolle Abr. 38, pl. 21.........i. 278

Hunt *v.* Bate, 3 Dyer 272a .... ii. 83
Hunt *v.* Conrad, 47 Minn. 557 .... iii. 86
Hunt *v.* Jones, 12 R. I. 265 .... ii. 178
Hunt *v.* Rousmanier, 8 Wheat. (U. S.) 174 .... ii. 492
Hunt *v.* Simonds, 19 Mo. 583 .... i. 366
Hunter *v.* Parker, 7 M. & W. 322, 344 .... ii. 474
Huntingdon *v.* Hall, 36 Me. 501 .... i. 384
Huntington *v.* Knox, 7 Cush. (Mass.) 371 .... ii. 480
Hurlbut *v.* McKone, 55 Conn. 31 .... i. 218, 219
Hurley *v.* Buchi, 10 Lea (Tenn) 346 .... i. 449
Hussey *v.* Jacobs, 1 Comyns 4 .... ii. 349
Hutchins *v.* Hutchins, 7 Hill (N. Y.) 104 .... i. 372, 373
Hutley *v.* Hutley, L. R. 8 Q. B. 112 .... i. 340
Hutson *v.* New York, 9 N. Y. 163 .... i. 36
Huttley *v.* Simmons, (1898) 1 Q. B. 181 .... i. 362
Hyatt *v.* Adams, 16 Mich. 180 .... iii. 74
Hyde *v.* Seyssor, Cro. Jac. 538 .... i. 263
Hygeia Distilled Water Co. *v.* Hygeia Ice Co., 70 Conn. 516 .... i. 424

Ide *v.* Stanton, 15 Vt. 685 .... ii. 195
Illidge *v.* Goodwin, 5 C. & P. 190, 24 E. C. L. 272 .... i. 66
Ilott *v.* Wilkes, 3 B. & Ald. 304, 5 E. C. L. 295 .... i. 69, 163
Ilsley *v.* Stubbs, 5 Mass. 283 .... iii. 218
Ilwaco R., etc., Co. *v.* Hedrick, 1 Wash. 446 .... i. 160
Imperial Gas-Light, etc., Co. *v.* Broadbent, 7 H. L. Cas. 600 .... i. 221
Indemaur *v.* Dames, L. R. 1 C. P. 274 .... i. 151, 157
Ingate *v.* Christie, 3 C. & K. 61 .... ii. 306
Ingraham *v.* Edwards, 64 Ill. 526 .... ii. 474
Inland, etc., Coasting Co. *v.* Tolson, 139 U. S. 551 .... i. 136, 139
Innes *v.* Wylie, 1 C. & K. 257, 47 E. C. L. 257 .... i. 11
Innis *v.* Cedar Rapids, etc., R. Co., 76 Iowa 165 .... i. 225
International Fraternal Alliance *v.* Mallalieu, 87 Md. 97 .... i. 298
International Ocean Tel. Co. *v.* Saunders, 32 Fla. 434 .... i. 467
International Trust Co. *v.* Wilson, 161 Mass. 80 .... ii. 408
Irving Nat. Bank *v.* Alley, 79 N. Y. 536 .... ii. 513
Irwin *v.* Dearman, 11 East 23 .... i. 269, 271
Irwin *v.* Phillips, 5 Cal. 146 .... i. 201
Irwin *v.* Sprigg, 6 Gill (Md.) 200 .... i. 153
Isaack *v.* Clark, 2 Bulst. 306 .... ii. 278; iii. 147, 160, 166, 167
Israel *v.* Etheridge, Bunb. 80 .... iii. 170
Itinerant, The, 2 W. Rob. 236 .... i. 145
Ivay *v.* Hedges, 9 Q. B. D. 80 .... i. 158
Ives *v.* Jones, 3 Ired. L. (25 N. Car.) 538 .... ii. 74
Iveson *v.* Moore, Holt K. B. 10 .... i. 494
Iveson *v.* Moore, 1 Ld. Raym. 486, 3 Ld. Raym. 291, Carth. 451 .... i. 226

J. H. Mohlman Co. *v.* McKane, 60 N. Y. App. Div. 546 .... ii. 521
Jackson *v.* Pittsburgh Times, 152 Pa. St. 406 .... i. 304
Jackson *v.* Rogers, 2 Show. 327 .... i. 185; ii. 237
Jackson *v.* Sebring, 16 Johns. (N. Y.) 515 .... ii. 43

Jackson *v.* Smithson, 15 M. & W. 563 .... i. 55
Jackson *v.* Wetherill, 7 S. & R. (Pa.) 480 .... i. 391
Jacobson *v.* Dalles, etc., Nav. Co., 106 Fed. Rep. 428 .... i. 146
Jager *v.* Adams, 123 Mass. 26 .... i. 107
James, *Ex p.*, L. R. 9 Ch. 609 .... ii. 214
James *v.* Browne, 1 Dall. (Pa.) 339 .... iii. 111
James *v.* Campbell, 5 C. & P. 372, 24 E. C. L. 367 .... i. 4
James *v.* David, 5 T. R. 141 .... ii. 92
James *v.* Hayward, Cro. Car. 184 .... i. 215
James *v.* Hayward, 2 Rolle Abr. 137 (C), pl. 1 .... i. 225
James *v.* Hodsden, 47 Vt. 127 .... i. 415
James *v.* James, L. R. 13 Eq. 421 .... i. 432
James *v.* Kerr, 40 Ch. D. 458 .... ii. 164
James *v.* LeRoy, 6 Johns. (N. Y.) 274 .... ii. 215
Jansen *v.* McCahill, 22 Cal. 563 .... ii. 475
Janson *v.* Brown, 1 Campb. 41 .... i. 18
J'Anson *v.* Stuart, 1 T. R. 748 .... i. 301
Jarvis *v.* Rogers, 15 Mass. 408 .... i. 240
Jarvis *v.* Wilkins, 7 M. & W. 410 .... ii. 506
Jarvis *v.* Wilson, 46 Conn. 90 .... ii. 401
Jay *v.* Ladler, 40 Ch. D. 649 .... i. 423
Jay *v.* Whitfield, cited in 3 B. & Ald. 308, 5 E. C. L. 207 .... i. 68
Jeames *v.* Rutlech, 4 Coke 17*b* .... i. 283
Jefferies *v.* Austin, 1 Stra. 674 .... ii. 388
Jefferies *v.* Duncombe, 11 East 226 .... i. 294
Jefferies *v.* Great Western R. Co., 5 El. & Bl. 802, 85 E. C. L. 802... i. 252; ii. 315, 317
Jefferson *v.* Hartley, 81 Ga. 716 .... i. 46
Jefferson *v.* Jefferson, 3 Lev. 130 .... iii. 270
Jeffrey *v.* Rosenfeld, 179 Mass. 506 .... ii. 547
Jeffries *v.* Williams, 5 Exch. 792 .... i. 196
Jencks *v.* Coleman, 2 Sumn. (U. S.) 221 .... i. 185
Jenkins *v.* Fowler, 24 Pa. St. 308 .... i. 366
Jenkins *v.* Hutchinson, 13 Q. B. 744, 66 E. C. L. 744 .... i. 405
Jenkins *v.* Reynolds, 3 Brod. & B. 14, 7 E. C. L. 328 .... ii. 180
Jenney *v.* Herle, 2 Ld. Raym. 1361 .... ii. 392
Jennings *v.* Broughton, 17 Beav. 234 .... i. 413
Jennings *v.* Carlucci, 87 N. Y. Supp. 475 .... ii. 532
Jennings *v.* Lyons, 39 Wis. 554 .... ii. 224
Jenoure *v.* Delmege, (1891) A. C. 73 .... i. 316
Jenne *v.* Ward, 1 B. & Ald. 653 .... ii. 411
Joannes *v.* Bennett, 5 Allen (Mass.) 169 .... i. 308
Joel *v.* Morrison, 6 C. & P. 503, 25 E. C. L. 512 .... ii. 470
John *v.* Saunders, 2 Dyer 172*b*, 173*a* .... iii. 215
John W. Lovell Co. *v.* Houghton, 116 N. Y. 520 .... i. 323
Johnson *v.* Chadbourn Finance Co., 89 Minn. 310 .... ii. 296
Johnson *v.* Clark, 39 N. Y. 216 .... ii. 402
Johnson *v.* Collings, 1 East 98 .... ii. 401
Johnson *v.* Gulick, 46 Neb. 817 .... i. 407
Johnson *v.* Lancashire, etc., R. Co., 3 C. P. D. 499 .... i. 255

Johnson *v.* McConnel, 15 Hun (N. Y.) 293....i. 9
Johnson *v.* May, 3 Lev. 150....iii. 181
Johnson *v.* Mitchell, 50 Tex. 212....ii. 515
Johnson *v.* Patterson, 14 Conn. 1....i. 18, 69
Johnson *v.* St. Louis Dispatch Co., 65 Mo. 539....i. 300
Johnson *v.* Sellars, 33 Ala. 265....ii. 113
Johnson *v.* Stear, 15 C. B. N. S. 330....i. 248
Johnston *v.* Bennett, 5 Abb. Pr. N. S. (N. Y.) 331....iii. 87
Jones *v.* Alabama Mineral R. Co., 107 Ala. 400....i. 181
Jones *v.* Andover, 10 Allen (Mass.) 18....i. 179
Jones *v.* Ashburnham, 4 East 455....ii. 77
Jones *v.* Barkley, 2 Dougl. 684....ii. 138
Jones *v.* Blocker, 43 Ga. 331....i. 346
Jones *v.* Boyce, 1 Stark. 493, 2 E. C. L. 189....i. 132
Jones *v.* Bright, 5 Bing. 533, 15 E. C. L. 529....i. 386, 387
Jones *v.* Brown, 1 Esp. 217....i. 268
Jones *v.* Brown, 54 Iowa 74....i. 38
Jones *v.* Bullock, 2 Dev. Eq. (17 N. Car.) 368....iii. 111
Jones *v.* Chappel, L. R. 20 Eq. 539....i. 27, 28
Jones *v.* Cooper, 1 Cowp. 227....ii. 188
Jones *v.* Downman, 4 Q. B. 235, 45 E. C. L. 234....i. 405
Jones *v.* Fay, 4 F. & F. 525....i. 98
Jones *v.* Gordon, 2 App. Cas. 628....ii. 407
Jones *v.* Hart, 2 Salk. 441, Holt K. B. 642....ii. 453, 465; iii. 260
Jones *v.* Hill, 7 Taunt. 392, 2 E. C. L. 392....i. 31
Jones *v.* Hoar, 5 Pick. (Mass.) 285....ii. 216; iii. 199
Jones *v.* Hough, 5 Ex. D. 128....i. 233
Jones *v.* Jones, 1 H. & C. 1....i. 216
Jones *v.* Judd, 4 N. Y. 411....ii. 224
Jones *v.* Just, L. R. 3 Q. B. 197....i. 388, 389
Jones *v.* Morgan, 90 N. Y. 4....ii. 291
Jones *v.* Powell, Hutton 135....i. 206
Jones *v.* Powell, Palmer 539....i. 218
Jones *v.* Randall, 1 Cowp. 37....ii. 111, 166
Jones *v.* Stanly, 76 N. Car. 355....i. 346
Jones *v.* Testiniog R. Co., L. R. 3 Q. B. 733....i. 57
Jones *v.* Waite, 5 Bing. N. Cas. 341, 35 E. C. L. 130....ii. 103
Jones *v.* Williams, 11 M. & W. 176....i. 216
Jordan *v.* Alabama G. S. R. Co., 81 Ala. 220....i. 330, 331
Jordan *v.* Barloe, 3 Salk. 67....ii. 379
Jordan *v.* Gillen, 44 N. H. 424....iii. 86
Jordan *v.* Wyatt, 4 Gratt. (Va.) 151....iii. 265
Jorden *v.* Money, 5 H. L. Cas. 185....i. 394
Jordon *v.* Pickett, 78 Ala. 331....i. 414
Joscelin *v.* Skelton, 3 Leon. 4, Benloe 57, Moo. K. B. 13....ii. 40, 45
Josceline *v.* Lassere, Fortescue 281....ii. 391
Joseph *v.* Macowsky, 96 Cal. 518....i. 426
Josselyn *v.* Lacier, 10 Mod. 294....ii. 504
Judd *v.* Ballard, 66 Vt. 668....i. 83
Judge *v.* Cox, 1 Stark. 285, 2 E. C. L. 114....i. 54

Judkins *v.* Walker, 17 Me. 38....................ii. 226
Julian *v.* Hoosier Drill Co., 78 Ind. 408....................i. 424
Justh *v.* National Bank of Commonwealth, 56 N. Y. 478....................ii. 212
Juzan *v.* Toulmin, 9 Ala. 662....................i. 394, 399

Kallisto, Bark, The, 2 Hughes (U. S.) 128....................i. 146
Kaltenbach *v.* Lewis, 10 App. Cas. 617....................ii. 479
Kann *v.* Diamond Steel Co., 89 Fed. Rep. 706....................i. 431
Kansas City *v.* Orr, 62 Kan. 61....................i. 178, 179
Kansas City, etc., R. Co. *v.* Little, 66 Kan. 378....................i. 460
Karger *v.* Rich, 81 Wis. 177....................i. 315
Karr *v.* Parks, 44 Cal. 46....................i. 268
Kaye *v.* Dutton, 7 M. & G. 807, 49 E. C. L. 807, 8 Scott N. R. 495....ii. 86
Kearney *v.* Boston, etc., R. Co., 9 Cush. (Mass.) 108....................iii. 74
Kearney *v.* Clutton, 101 Mich. 106....................i. 248
Kearney *v.* Lloyd, 26 L. R. Ir. 268....................i. 362
Kearney *v.* London, etc., R. Co., L. R. 5 Q. B. 411....................i. 108
Keasby *v.* Brooklyn Chemical Works, 142 N. Y. 467....................i. 424
Keates *v.* Cadogan, 10 C. B. 591, 70 E. C. L. 591....................i. 399
Keck *v.* Halstead, 3 Lutw. 481....................i. 17
Keeble *v.* Hickeringill, 11 East 574, *note*, Holt K. B. 14, 11 Mod. 74, 3 Salk. 9....................i. 357, 358
Keffe *v.* Milwaukee, etc., R. Co., 21 Minn. 207....................i. 159
Keighley *v.* Durant, (1901) A. C. 240....................ii. 490
Keith *v.* Goodwin, 31 Vt. 268....................ii. 244
Keleher *v.* Putnam, 60 N. H. 30....................i. 9
Kelk *v.* Pearson, L. R. 6 Ch. 809....................i. 209
Kelley *v.* Davis, 49 N. H. 187....................ii. 205
Kelley *v.* New York, 6 Misc. (N. Y.) 516....................i. 203
Kelley *v.* Owens, 30 Pac. Rep. 596....................i. 414
Kellogg *v.* Richards, 14 Wend. (N. Y.) 116....................ii. 103
Kellogg Bridge Co. *v.* Hamilton, 110 U. S. 108....................i. 386
Kelly *v.* Metropolitan R. Co., (1895) 1 Q. B. 944....................iii. 274
Kelly *v.* Solari, 9 M. & W. 54....................ii. 211, 213
Kendall *v.* Boston, 118 Mass. 234....................i. 108
Kenicot *v.* Bogan, Yelv. 198....................iii. 170
Kennedy *v.* Ashcraft, 4 Bush (Ky.) 530....................ii. 282
Kennedy *v.* Brown, 13 C. B. N. S. 677, 106 E. C. L. 677....................ii. 85
Kennedy *v.* Merrimack Paving Co., 185 Mass. 442....................i. 170
Kenny *v.* Gillet, 70 Md. 574....................i. 426
Kenrick *v.* Burges, Moo. K. B. 126, pl. 273....................i. 385
Kenrick *v.* Pargiter, Cro. Jac. 208, Yelv. 129....................iii. 310
Kenrig *v.* Eggleston, Aleyn 93....................ii. 267
Kensit *v.* Great Eastern R. Co., 27 Ch. D. 122....................i. 200, 204
Kent *v.* Bongartz, 15 R. I. 72....................i. 315
Kent *v.* Deaubeny, 3 Keb. 757....................iii. 185
Kent *v.* Shuckard, 2 B. & Ad. 803, 22 E. C. L. 186....................ii. 295
Kenyon *v.* Hart, 6 B. & S. 252, 118 E. C. L. 252....................i. 19
Ketchum *v.* Evertson, 13 Johns. (N. Y.) 359....................ii. 227
Keyse *v.* Keyse, 11 P. D. 100....................i. 487

Keyworth *v.* Hill, 3 B. & Ald. 685, 5 E. C. L. 422............i. 233; iii. 160
Kidder *v.* Dunstable, 7 Gray (Mass.) 104............i. 123
Kidney *v.* Persons, 41 Vt. 386............ii. 216
Kilby *v.* Wilson, R. & M. 178, 21 E. C. L. 409............i. 259
Kimball *v.* Bangs, 144 Mass. 321............i. 386
Kimball *v.* Harman, 34 Md. 407............i. 372
Kimber *v.* Barber, L. R. 8 Ch. 56............ii. 492
Kimber *v.* Press Assoc., (1893) 1 Q. B. 65............i. 310
Kimmans *v.* Chandler, 13 Iowa 327............i. 416
Kinaston *v.* Moor, Cro. Car. 89............iii. 164
King *v.* Duluth, etc., R. Co., 61 Minn. 482............ii. 129
King *v.* Haley, 86 Ill. 106............i. 172
King *v.* Kline, 6 Pa. St. 318............i. 17
King *v.* Lake, Hardres 470............i. 291, 292, 293
King *v.* Leith, 2 T. R. 144............iii. 197
King *v.* Patterson, 49 N. J. L. 417............i. 311
King *v.* Williams, 4 D. & R. 206............iii. 139
Kingsford *v.* Merry, 1 H. & N. 503............i. 260
Kingsley *v.* Brooklyn, 78 N. Y. 216............ii. 224
Kingsley *v.* Davis, 104 Mass. 178............ii. 480
Kingston *v.* Preston, (13 Geo. III.) referred to in 2 Dougl. 689............ii. 138
Kinlyside *v.* Thornton, 2 W. Bl. 1111............iii. 124, 270
Kinney *v.* Koopman, 116 Ala. 310............i. 218
Kintzing *v.* McElrath, 5 Pa. St. 467............i. 399
Kirk *v.* Gregory, 1 Ex. D. 55............i. 242; iii. 171
Kirkham *v.* Marter, 2 B. & Ald. 613............ii. 184, 185
Kirkman *v.* Booth, 11 Beav. 273............ii. 491
Kirkman *v.* Hamilton, 6 Pet. (U. S.) 20............iii. 143
Kirkman *v.* Philips, 7 Heisk. (Tenn.) 222............ii. 218; iii. 198
Kirkman *v.* Shawcross, 6 T. R. 14............i. 186
Kirkpatrick *v.* Eagle Lodge No. 32, 26 Kan. 390............i. 307
Kline *v.* Kline, 158 Ind. 602............i. 460
Knapp *v.* Alvord, 10 Paige (N. Y.) 205............ii. 492
Knight *v.* Bean, 22 Me. 531............ii. 224
Knight *v.* Farnaby, 2 Salk. 670............iii. 93
Knott *v.* Digges, 6 Har. & J. (Md.) 230............iii. 265
Knott *v.* Morgan, 2 Keen 213............i. 421
Koch *v.* Lyon, 82 Mich. 513............i. 259
Kohn *v.* Consolidated Butter, etc., Co., 30 Misc. (N. Y.) 725............ii. 534
Kolka *v.* Jones, 6 N. Dak. 461............i. 333
Kountze *v.* Kennedy, 147 N. Y. 124............i. 400
Krauss *v.* Jos. R. Peeble's Sons Co., 58 Fed. Rep. 585............i. 426
Krebs *v.* Oliver, 12 Gray (Mass.) 239............i. 308
Krewson *v.* Purdom, 13 Oregon 563............i. 252
Kriger *v.* Leppel, 42 Minn. 6............ii. 227
Kroeger *v.* Pitcairn, 101 Pa. St. 311............i. 406
Kroessin *v.* Keller, 60 Minn. 372............i. 265
Kromer *v.* Hein, 75 N. Y. 574............ii. 95
Kroppf *v.* Furst, 94 Fed. Rep. 150............i. 431
Kuhn *v.* Jewett, 32 N. J. Eq. 647............i. 113, 117
Kurtz *v.* Frank, 76 Ind. 594............i. 464

Lacon *v.* Page, 48 Ill. 499 .... i. 115
La Coursier *v.* Russel, 82 Wis. 265 .... ii. 227
Ladd *v.* Granite State Brick Co., 68 N. H. 185 .... i. 212
Ladd *v.* Moore, 3 Sandf. (N. Y.) 589 .... i. 259
Laflin, etc., Powder Co. *v.* Tearney, 131 Ill. 322 .... i. 220
La Fortune *v.* Jolly, 167 Mass. 170 .... i. 170
Laidlaw *v.* Sage, 158 N. Y. 73 .... i. 119
Laird *v.* Eichold, 10 Ind. 212 .... ii. 296
Lakeman *v.* Pollard, 43 Me. 463 .... ii. 224
Lake Shore, etc., R. Co. *v.* Hessions, 150 Ill. 556 .... i. 148
Lalance, etc., Mfg. Co. *v.* National Enameling, etc., Co., 109 Fed. Rep. 317 .... i. 431
Lalande *v.* Aldrich, 41 La. Ann. 307 .... ii. 203
Lamb *v.* Burnett, 1 Cromp. & J. 291 .... i. 39
Lambert, *Ex p.*, 13 Ves. Jr. 179 .... ii. 556
Lambert *v.* Bessey, T. Raym. 421 .... i. 79
Lambert *v.* Oakes, 1 Ld. Raym. 443, 1 Salk. 127, 12 Mod. 244, Holt 118 .... ii. 379
Lamine *v.* Dorrell, 2 Ld. Raym. 1216 .... ii. 216; iii. 195
Lampet's Case, 10 Coke 48*a* .... iii. 82
Lampleigh *v.* Brathwait, Hob. 105, Moo. K. B. 866 .... ii. 84
Lampleigh *v.* Brathwait, Hob. 105, 1 Smith Lead. Cas. (8th Am. ed.) 268 .... ii. 87
Lanark *v.* Dougherty, 153 Ill. 163 .... i. 148
Lancaster County Bank *v.* Allbright, 21 Pa. St. 228 .... i. 412
Lander *v.* Seaver, 32 Vt. 114 .... i. 39
Landon *v.* Emmons, 97 Mass. 37 .... i. 253
Land Title, etc., Co. *v.* Northwestern Nat. Bank, 196 Pa. St. 230 .... ii. 520
Lane *v.* Cotton, 12 Mod. 488 .... ii. 453
Lane *v.* Cotton, 1 Ld. Raym. 646 .... i. 36; ii. 306
Lane *v.* Cotton, 1 Salk. 17, 18 .... i. 185; ii. 441, 466
Lane *v.* Cox, (1897) 1 Q. B. 415 .... i. 93
Lang *v.* Smyth, 7 Bing. 284, 20 E. C. L. 130 .... ii. 421
Langridge *v.* Levy, 2 M. & W. 519 .... i. 58, 397
Lansing *v.* Stone, 37 Barb. (N. Y.) 15 .... i. 56
Lantry *v.* Parks, 8 Cow. (N. Y.) 63 .... ii. 225, 227
Larrabee *v.* Lewis, 67 Ga. 561 .... i. 424
Larson *v.* Berquist, 34 Kan. 334 .... i. 267
Larson *v.* Chase, 47 Minn. 307 .... i. 461
Lary *v.* Cleveland, etc., R. Co., 78 Ind. 323 .... i. 156
Lattimore *v.* Harsen, 14 Johns. (N. Y.) 330 .... ii. 128, 129
Lattin *v.* McCarty, 41 N. Y. 107 .... iii. 57
Laugher *v.* Pointer, 5 B. & C. 547, 12 E. C. L. 311 .... ii. 465
Lavell *v.* Richings, (1906) 1 K. B. 480 .... iii. 306
Lawrence *v.* Davey, 28 Vt. 264 .... ii. 128
Lawrence *v.* Fox, 20 N. Y. 268 .... ii. 157
Lawrence *v.* Jenkins, L. R. 8 Q. B. 274 .... i. 157
Lawrence *v.* Martin, 22 Cal. 174 .... iii. 86
Lawrence Mfg. Co. *v.* Lowell Hosiery Mills, 129 Mass. 325 .... i. 423
Lawrence Mfg. Co. *v.* Tennessee Mfg. Co., 138 U. S. 537 .... i. 423, 431

Lawson *v.* Weston, 4 Esp. 56..............................ii. 404, 406
Layng *v.* Stewart, 1 W. & S. (Pa.) 222..............................i. 405
Laythoarp *v.* Bryant, 2 Bing. N. Cas. 735, 29 E. C. L. 469..........ii. 108
Lazard *v.* Wheeler, 22 Cal. 139..............................iii. 87
Lazell *v.* Lazell, 12 Vt. 443..............................ii. 375
Lea *v.* Collins, 4 Sneed (Tenn.) 393..............................ii. 73
League *v.* Waring, 85 Pa. St. 244..............................ii. 390
Leake *v.* Young, 5 El. & Bl. 955, 85 E. C. L. 955..................ii. 131
Leame *v.* Bray, 3 East 593..............................i. 16, 79, 190; iii. 259
Leather Cloth Co. *v.* American Leather Cloth Co., 4 DeG. J. & S. 137.i. 421
Leather Manufacturer's Bank *v.* Morgan, 117 U. S. 115............ii. 248
Leavitt *v.* Putnam, 3 N. Y. 494..............................ii. 524
Lebby *v.* Ahrens, 26 S. Car. 275..............................i. 415
Le Clear *v.* Perkins, 103 Mich. 131..............................i. 331
Lee *v.* Ashbrook, 14 Mo. 379..............................ii. 226
Lee *v.* Atkinson, Yelv. 172..............................i. 256; ii. 314
Lee *v.* Bayes, 18 C. B. 599, 86 E. C. L. 599..............................i. 239
Lee *v.* Burnham, 82 Wis. 209..............................i. 414
Lee *v.* Flemingsburg, 7 Dana (Ky.) 28..............................ii. 82
Lee *v.* Lemert, 26 Kan. 111..............................i. 395
Lee *v.* Muggeridge, 5 Taunt. 46, 1 E. C. L. 14..................ii. 144, 146
Lee *v.* Whitney, 149 Mass. 447..............................ii. 408
Legallee *v.* Blaisdell, 134 Mass. 473..............................i. 331
Lehigh Zinc, etc., Co. *v.* Bamford, 150 U. S. 665....................i. 407
Leidy *v.* Tammany, 9 Watts (Pa.) 353..............................ii. 387
Leith *v.* Trott, 16 Nova Scotia 120..............................i. 39
Le Lievre *v.* Gould, (1893) 1 Q. B. 499..............................i. 403
Lemmon *v.* Webb, (1894) 3 Ch. 1..............................i. 216
Lenox *v.* Cook, 8 Mass. 460..............................ii. 552
Leonard *v.* Mason, 1 Wend. (N. Y.) 522..............................ii. 387
Leonard *v.* New York, etc., Electro Magnetic Tel. Co., 41 N. Y. 544.. i. 450, 451
Leonard *v.* Wilkins, 9 Johns. (N. Y.) 233..............................i. 18
Leopold *v.* Salkey, 89 Ill. 412..............................ii. 224
Leroux *v.* Brown, 12 C. B. 801, 74 E. C. L. 801..................ii. 177, 178
Lester *v.* Mahan, 25 Ala. 445..............................i. 390
Lethbridge *v.* Phillips, 2 Stark. 544, 3 E. C. L. 523....................i. 237
Leveson *v.* Kirke, 1 Rolle Abr. 105, pl. 10..............................iii. 166
Levi *v.* Milne, 4 Bing. 195, 13 E. C. L. 396..............................i. 294
Levy *v.* McCan, 44 La. Ann. 528..............................i. 311
Leward *v.* Basely, 1 Ld. Raym. 62..............................i. 8
Lewis *v.* Bruton, 74 Ala. 317..............................ii. 223
Lewis *v.* Levy, El. Bl. & El. 537, 96 E. C. L. 537....................i. 310
Lewis *v.* Mobley, 4 Dev. & B. L. (20 N. Car.) 323....................i. 260
Lewis *v.* Nicholson, 18 Q. B. 503, 83 E. C. L. 503....................i. 405
Lewis *v.* Price, cited in 2 Saund. 175*a*..............................i. 208
Lewis *v.* Western Union Tel. Co., 57 S. Car. 325....................i. 467
Lewisohn *v.* Kent, etc., Co., 87 Hun (N. Y.) 257....................ii. 514
Leyman *v.* Latimer, 3 Ex. D. 15, 352..............................i. 302
Lichtenstein *v.* Goldsmith, 37 Fed. Rep. 359..............................i. 424

Lickbarrow *v.* Mason, 2 T. R. 73 ii. 398
Liening *v.* Gould, 13 Cal. 598 ii. 75
Lightly *v.* Clouston, 1 Taunt. 112 ii. 215; iii. 199
Lilley *v.* Barnsley, 2 M. & Rob. 548 ii. 314
Limpus *v.* London General Omnibus Co., 1 H. & C. 526 ii. 457
Lincoln *v.* Com., 164 Mass. 368 i. 493
Lincoln *v.* Hapgood, 11 Mass. 350 i. 38
Lincoln *v.* Parr, 2 Keb. 781 iii. 190
Lincoln *v.* Topcliff, Cro. Eliz. 644 iii. 109
Lindon *v.* Hooper, 1 Cowp. 419 iii. 197
Lindsey *v.* Lindsey, 34 Miss. 432 i. 415
Lingenfelder *v.* Wainwright Brewing Co., 103 Mo. 578 ii. 128, 129
Linsley *v.* Bushnell, 15 Conn. 225 i. 482
Linville *v.* Rhoades, 73 Mo. App. 223 i. 323
Lipscomb *v.* Shofner, 96 Tenn. 112 i. 333
Litchfield *v.* Hutchinson, 117 Mass. 195 i. 407
Littauer *v.* Goldman, 72 N. Y. 506 ii. 415, 535
Little *v.* Hackett, 116 U. S. 366 i. 141
Littlefield *v.* Shee, 2 B. & Ad. 811, 22 E. C. L. 187 ii. 146
Livermore *v.* Batchelder, 141 Mass. 179 i. 18
Livermore *v.* Peru, 55 Me. 469 ii. 214
Liversidge *v.* Broadbent, 4 H. & N. 603 ii. 125
Livingston *v.* Moingona Coal Co., 49 Iowa 369 i. 192
Livingston *v.* Woods, 20 Mont. 91 ii. 293
Livingstone *v.* Rawyards Coal Co., 5 App. Cas. 39 i. 483
Lloyd *v.* Hough, 1 How. (U. S.) 160 ii. 217
Lloyd *v.* Sigourney, 5 Bing. 525, 15 E. C. L. 527, 3 M. & P. 229, 3 Y. & J. 220 ii. 399
Lloyd's *v.* Harper, 16 Ch. D. 290 ii. 159
Locke *v.* Bradstreet Co., 22 Fed. Rep. 771 i. 315
Lockenour *v.* Sides, 57 Ind. 360 i. 332
Lockhart *v.* Bear, 117 N. Car. 298 i. 334
Lockhart *v.* Lichtenthaler, 46 Pa. St. 151 i. 141
Lodie *v.* Arnold, 2 Salk. 458 i. 215
Loeschman *v.* Machin, 2 Stark. 311, 3 E. C. L. 423 i. 239, 248
Loewer *v.* Harris, 57 Fed. Rep. 368 i. 412
Logan *v.* Wallis, 76 N. Car. 416 ii. 216
Loker *v.* Damon, 17 Pick. (Mass.) 284 i. 130
London *v.* Gorry, 2 Lev. 174 iii. 189
London Brewery Co. *v.* Tennant, L. R. 9 Ch. 220 i. 204
London, etc., R. Co. *v.* Truman, 11 App. Cas. 45 i. 43
London Guarantee, etc., R. Co. *v.* Horn, 206 Ill. 493 i. 370
Long *v.* Fitzimmons, 1 W. & S. (Pa.) 530 i. 31
Long *v.* Tribune Printing Co., 107 Mich. 207 i. 298
Longchamp *v.* Kenny, 1 Dougl. 137 iii. 192
Longridge *v.* Dorville, 5 B. & Ald. 117, 7 E. C. L. 43 ii. 78
Lonsdale *v.* Nelson, 2 B. & C. 311, 93 E. C. L. 98 i. 216
Look *v.* Dean, 108 Mass. 116 i. 9
Loomis *v.* Ruck, 56 N. Y. 465 ii. 531
Loop *v.* Litchfield, 42 N. Y. 359 i. 60

Lord *v.* Carbon Iron Mfg. Co., 42 N. J. Eq. 157....................i. 192
Lord *v.* Houstoun, 11 East 62....................................iii. 135
Lord *v.* Price, L. R. 9 Exch. 54..............................i. 253, 254
Lord Derby, The, 17 Fed. Rep. 265.................................i 5
Loring *v.* Boston, 7 Met. (Mass.) 411..............................ii. 82
Lorillard *v.* Pride, 28 Fed. Rep. 434...............................i. 423
Losee *v.* Buchanan, 51 N. Y. 476...................................i. 63
Louisiana *v.* New Orleans, 109 U. S. 285...........................ii. 207
Louisville Coal Min. Co. *v.* International Trust Co., 18 Colo. App. 345..i. 558
Louisville, etc., R. Co. *v.* Barkhouse, 100 Ala. 543.................i. 248
Louisville, etc., R. Co. *v.* Caldwell, 98 Ind. 245....................ii. 504
Louisville, etc., R. Co. *v.* Hall, 113 Ky. 561.......................i. 474
Louisville, etc., R. Co. *v.* Willis, 83 Ky. 57........................i. 267
Loveless *v.* Fowler, 79 Ga. 134.....................................i. 239
Loverett *v.* Townesend, 1 Rolle Abr. 104, pl. 8....................iii. 272
Lowry *v.* Bourdieu, 2 Dougl. 468...................................ii. 214
Loyd *v.* Lee, 1 Stra. 94..ii. 77
Lucas *v.* Godwin, 3 Bing. N. Cas. 737, 32 E. C. L. 309.............ii. 221
Lucas *v.* Trumbull, 15 Gray (Mass.) 306............................ii. 287
Lucke *v.* Clothing Cutters', etc., Assembly No. 7507, 77 Md. 396.... i. 369, 371
Lucker *v.* Iba, 54 N. Y. App. Div. 566..........................ii. 531, 532
Ludden *v.* Buffalo Batting Co., 22 Ill. App. 415......................i. 255
Ludington *v.* Bell, 77 N. Y. 138....................................ii. 125
Luke *v.* Lyde, 2 Burr. 887..ii. 331
Lukens *v.* Freiund, 27 Kan. 664.....................................i. 388
Lumley *v.* Gye, 2 El. & Bl. 216, 244, 75 E. C. L. 216......i. 265, 266, 342, 343, 344, 345, 346; iii. 56
Lumley *v.* Musgrave, 4 Bing. N. Cas. 9, 33 E. C. L. 265............ii. 390
Lunsford *v.* Dietrich, 93 Ala. 565..............................i. 330, 331
Lyman *v.* Boston, etc., R. Corp., 4 Cush. (Mass.) 288................i. 57
Lyman *v.* U. S. Bank, 12 How. (U. S.) 225...........................ii. 390
Lymbe *v.* Hockly, 1 Lev. 205..i. 283
Lynch *v.* Knight, 9 H. L. Cas. 577..........................i. 285, 286, 290
Lynch *v.* Nurdin, 1 Q. B. 29, 41 E. C. L. 422.........................i. 66
Lyne *v.* Western Union Tel. Co., 123 N. Car. 129.....................i. 472
Lynn *v.* Bruce, 2 H. Bl. 317.....................................ii. 92, 101
Lyon *v.* Fishmongers' Co., 1 App. Cas. 662......................i. 199, 229
Lyons *v.* Desotelle, 124 Mass. 387..................................i. 180
Lyons *v.* Wilkins, (1899) 1 Ch. 255.................................i. 366
Lyons First Nat. Bank *v.* Ocean Nat. Bank, 60 N. Y. 278.............i. 100
Lyth *v.* Ault, 7 Exch. 669..ii. 125
Lytle *v.* Bowdon, 107 Ala. 361......................................iii. 197

M. Groh's Sons Co. *v.* Schneider, 34 Misc. (N. Y.) 195.............ii. 530
Mabry *v.* City Electric R. Co., 116 Ga. 624..........................i. 460
McAleer *v.* Horsey, 35 Md. 439......................................i. 415
McAllen *v.* Western Union Tel. Co., 70 Tex. 343.....................i. 454
McAndrew *v.* Bassett, 4 DeG. J. & S. 380............................i. 424

McAndrews *v.* Thatcher, 3 Wall. (U. S.) 347....................i. 19
McArthur *v.* Green Bay, etc., Canal Co., 34 Wis. 139....................iii. 87
McBee *v.* Fulton, 47 Md. 403....................i. 310
McCall *v.* Crousillat, 3 S. & R. (Pa.) 7....................iii. 111
M'Cance *v.* London, etc., R. Co., 7 H. & N. 477....................ii. 243
McCarty *v.* Hampton Bldg. Assoc., 61 Iowa 287....................ii. 129
McClamrock *v.* Flint, 101 Ind. 278....................i. 387
McClary *v.* Lowell, 44 Vt. 116....................i. 179
McClay *v.* Hedge, 18 Iowa 66....................ii. 226
McColl *v.* Western Union Tel. Co., 44 N. Y. Super. Ct. 487....................i. 450
M'Combie *v.* Davies, 6 East 538....................i. 239
M'Corkle *v.* Binns, 5 Binn. (Pa.) 340....................i. 294
McCullough *v.* Baker, 47 Mo. 401....................ii. 222
McCurdy *v.* Rogers, 21 Wis. 197....................i. 406
McDaniels *v.* Robinson, 26 Vt. 316....................ii. 296
McDermott *v.* Evening Journal Assoc., 43 N. J. L. 488....................i. 310
McDonald *v.* Lynch, 59 Mo. 350....................ii. 211
McDonald *v.* Snelling, 14 Allen (Mass.) 290....................i. 114
Macdonald *v.* Tacquah Gold Mines Co., 13 Q. B. D. 535, 539....................iii. 57
MacDougall *v.* Knight, 17 Q. B. 636....................i. 310
McDowall *v.* Great Western R. Co., (1903) 2 K. B. 331....................i. 120
McDowell *v.* Cook, 6 Smed. & M. (Miss.) 420....................ii. 556
McEntee *v.* New Jersey Steamboat Co., 45 N. Y. 34....................i. 246
McEntire *v.* Potter, 22 Q. B. D. 438....................i. 243
Macfadzen *v.* Olivant, 6 East 387....................i. 264
McFarland *v.* Newman, 9 Watts (Pa.) 55....................i. 391
Macfarlane *v.* Taylor, L. R. 1 H. L. Sc., 245....................i. 388
McGaughey *v.* Richardson, 148 Mass. 608....................i. 386
McGee *v.* Sodusky, 5 J. J. Marsh. (Ky.) 185....................i. 290
McGlinchy *v.* Hall, 58 Me. 152....................iii. 86
M'Gowan *v.* Windham, 25 Conn. 86....................ii. 224
McGrath *v.* Merwin, 112 Mass. 467....................i. 179, 180
McGreer *v.* Stone, 53 Pa. St. 436....................i. 102
MacGregor *v.* Rhodes, 6 El. & Bl. 266, 8 E. C. L. 266....................ii. 412
M'Gregor *v.* Thwaites, 3 B. & C. 24, 10 E. C. L. 6....................i. 310
McGrew *v.* Forsythe, 31 Iowa 179....................i. 386
McGuire *v.* Grant, 25 N. J. L. 356....................i. 195, 196
McIntire *v.* Kennedy, 29 Pa. St. 448....................ii. 390
McIntire *v.* Plaisted, 57 N. H. 606....................i. 18
Mackay *v.* Western Union Tel. Co., 16 Nev. 222....................i. 450
McKee *v.* Judd, 12 N. Y. 625....................iii. 86
McKee *v.* Tourtellotte, 167 Mass. 69....................i. 170
McKee *v.* Wilson, 87 N. Car. 300....................i. 277
McKersie *v.* McLean, 6 Ont. 428....................i. 271
McKinnon Mfg. Co. *v.* Alpena Fish Co., 102 Mich. 221....................i. 387
McKinsey *v.* Squires, 32 W. Va. 41....................i. 465
M'Kone *v.* Wood, 5 C. & P. 1, 24 E. C. L. 187....................i. 54
McLane *v.* Piaggio, 24 Fla. 72....................ii. 94
M'Laughlin *v.* Pryor, 4 M. & G. 48, 43 E. C. L. 34....................i. 81
McLean *v.* Fleming, 96 U. S. 245....................i. 421

McLeod v. Hunter, 29 Misc. (N. Y.) 558, 49 N. Y. App. Div. 131....ii. 510
McMann v. Walker, 31 Colo. 261....ii. 532
M'Manus v. Crickett, 1 East 106........ii. 453, 459, 469, 470; iii. 262, 265
McMurray v. Basnett, 18 Fla. 609....i. 489
McMurtry v. Brown, 6 Neb. 368....ii. 475
McNair v. Cleave, 10 Phila. (Pa.) 155....i. 426
McNamara v. Jose, 28 Wash. 461....ii. 530
McNamara v. King, 7 Ill. 432....i. 481
McNamee v. Minke, 49 Md. 122....i. 333
McPeek v. Western Union Tel. Co., 107 Iowa 356....i. 451
McPherson v. Daniels, 10 C. & B. 272, 21 E. C. L. 74....i. 275
McQueen v. Fulgham, 27 Tex. 463....i. 291
M'Quillin v. Cox, 1 H. Bl. 249....iii. 135
McQuire v. Western Morning News, (1903) 2 K. B. 109........i. 304, 306
McVey v. Brendel, 144 Pa. St. 235....i. 423
Maddison v. Alderson, 8 App. Cas. 488....ii. 177
Maddox v. Fisher, 14 Moo. P. C. 103....i. 145
Madras R. Co. v. Zemindar of Carvatenagarum, L. R. 1 Indian App. 364....i. 41
Madraza v. Willes, 3 B. & Ald. 353, 5 E. C. L. 313....i. 36
Magee v. Badger, 34 N. Y. 247....ii. 408
Magoon v. Reber, 76 Wis. 392....ii. 531
Mahoney v. Dore, 155 Mass. 513....i. 167, 169
Mahurin v. Harding, 28 N. H. 128....i. 390
Maitland v. Citizens' Nat. Bank, 40 Md. 540....ii. 408
Malachy v. Soper, 3 Bing. N. Cas. 371, 3 E. C. L. 161....i. 322
Malbon v. Birney, 11 Wis. 107....ii. 225
Malcom v. Spoor, 12 Met. (Mass.) 279....i. 46
Mallalieu v. Hodgson, 16 Q. B. 689, 71 E. C. L. 689....ii. 131
Manchester Bonded Warehouse Co. v. Carr, 5 C. P. D. 507......i. 31, 32
Mandeville v. Riddle, 1 Cranch (U. S.) 290....iii. 203
Manger v. Shipman, 30 Neb. 352....i. 55
Manhattan Brass Co. v. Reger, 168 Pa. St. 644....i. 415
Manhattan Medicine Co. v. Wood, 108 U. S. 218....i. 426
Manier v. Western Union Tel. Co., 94 Tenn. 448........i. 438, 443
Manker v. Western Union Tel. Co., 137 Ala. 292....i. 437
Manley v. St. Helens Canal, etc., Co., 2 H. & N. 840....i. 152
Manly v. Field, 7 C. B. N. S. 96, 97 E. C. L. 96....i. 269
Mann v. Locke, 11 N. H. 246....iii. 198
Mann v. Springfield Second Nat. Bank, 30 Kan. 412....ii. 408
Manning v. Sprague, 148 Mass. 18....i. 341
Manning's Case, Rolle Abr. 28, pl. 57....ii. 77
Mansfield v. Lynch, 59 Conn. 320....ii. 214
Manvell v. Thomson, 2 C. & P. 303, 12 E. C. L. 136....i. 270
Manwood v. Burston, 2 Leon. 203........ii. 61; iii. 183
Manzoni v. Douglas, 6 Q. B. D. 145....i. 105
Mapes v. Sidney, Cro. Jac. 683....ii. 34
Marbury v. Madison, 1 Cranch (U. S.) 166....i. 36
March v. Pigot, 5 Burr. 2802........ii. 111, 166

Marentille *v.* Oliver, 2 N. J. L. 358....i. 17
Marion County *v.* Clark, 94 U. S. 286....ii. 408
Marker *v.* Kenrick, 13 C. B. 188, 76 E. C. L. 188....iii. 124
Markham *v.* Cob, Latch 144, Noy 82....i. 495
Marks *v.* Baker, 28 Minn. 162....i. 309
Marlow *v.* Weeks, Barnes Notes 452....i. 16
Marriot *v.* Lister, 2 Wils. C. Pl. 142....ii. 47
Marriott *v.* Hampton, 7 T. R. 265....ii. 231
Mars *v.* Delaware, etc., Canal Co., 54 Hun (N. Y.) 625....i. 120
Marsh *v.* Astrie, 1 Rolle Abr. 93, pl. 16....i. 184
Marsh *v.* Cook, 32 N. J. Eq. 262....i. 416
Marshall *v.* Welwood, 38 N. J. L. 339....i. 63
Marshal's Case, 33 Hen. VI....ii. 300
Marston *v.* Bigelow, 150 Mass. 45....ii. 157
Martin *v.* Boure, Cro. Jac. 6....ii. 347, 348, 358
Martin *v.* Martin, 1 Ves. 211, 1 Will. IV., c. 47....iii. 138
Martin *v.* Stilwell, 1 Show. 156....ii. 211
Martinez *v.* Gerber, 21 Hen. VI....i. 265
Martinez *v.* Gerber, 3 M. & G. 88, 42 E. C. L. 55....i. 266
Martyn *v.* Burlings, Cro. Eliz. 589....i. 282
Martyn *v.* Hind, 2 Cowp 437, 443....ii. 155
Marvin *v.* Chicago, etc., R. Co., 79 Wis. 140....i. 121
Mary's Case, 9 Coke 112*b*....i. 266; iii. 310
Marzetti *v.* Williams, 1 B. & Ad. 415, 20 E. C. L. 412....iii. 274
Masham *v.* Bridges, Cro. Car. 223....i. 282
Mason *v.* Hill, 5 B. & Ad. 1, 27 E. C. L. 11....i. 198
Mason *v.* Keeling, 12 Mod. 332, 1 Ld. Raym. 608....i. 53, 54
Mason *v.* Thompson, 9 Pick. (Mass.) 280....ii. 296
Master *v.* Hansard, 4 Ch. D. 718....iii. 122
Master *v.* Miller, 4 T. R. 320....i. 340; iii. 86
Masters *v.* Ibberson, 8 C. B. 100, 65 E. C. L. 100....ii. 408; iii. 202
Mateer *v.* Brown, 1 Cal. 221....ii. 296, 297
Mathews *v.* London St. Tramways Co., 60 L. T. N. S. 47....i. 122
Matson *v.* Wharam, 2 T. R. 80....ii. 186, 188
Matthew *v.* Croze, 1 Rolle Abr. 34 (D.), pl. 5....i. 283, 285
Matthews *v.* Bloxsome, 33 L. J. Q. B. 209....ii. 533
Matthews *v.* Fiestel, 2 E. D. Smith (N. Y.) 90....i. 18
Matthews *v.* Jenkins, 80 Va. 463....ii. 227
Matthews *v.* Milton, 4 Yerg. (Tenn.) 576....ii. 186
Matthews *v.* Poythress, 4 Ga. 287....ii. 408
Matthews *v.* Warner, 29 Gratt. (Va.) 570....i. 181
Mawbrey *v.* Cunningham, cited in 1 Cowp. 228....ii. 188
Maxwell *v.* Day, 45 Ind. 509....ii. 390
May *v.* Burdett, 9 Q. B. 101, 58 E. C. L. 101....i. 55
May *v.* Chapman, 16 M. & W. 355....ii. 407, 408; iii. 202
May *v.* Cooper, Fortescue 376....ii. 387
May *v.* Western Union Tel. Co., 112 Mass. 90....i. 455
Mayer *v.* Walter, 64 Pa. St. 283....i. 334
Maylard *v.* Kester, Moo. K. B. 711....ii. 63; iii. 178, 183
Meacham *v.* Galloway, 102 Tenn. 415....ii. 296

Meagher v. Driscoll, 99 Mass. 281 ....i. 461
Means v. Hendershott, 24 Iowa 78 ....ii. 121
Mears v. London, etc., R. Co., 11 C. B. N. S. 850, 103 E. C. L. 850...i. 260
Medhurst v. Balam, 1 Rolle Abr. 35, pl. 7 ....i. 285
Mediana, Steamship, The, v. Comet Lightship, The, (1900) A. C. 116..i. 476
Medina v. Stoughton, 1 Salk. 210, 1 Ld. Raym. 503 ....i. 383, 385
Meech v. Smith, 7 Wend. (N. Y.) 315 ....i. 405
Meek v. Keene, 47 Ind. 77 ....i. 414
Megowan v. Peterson, 173 N. Y. 1 ....ii. 518
Mehlberg v. Fisher, 24 Wis. 607 ....ii. 503
Mellen v. Whipple, 1 Gray (Mass.) 322 ....iii. 206
Mellor v. Leather, 1 El. & Bl. 618, 72 E. C. L. 618 ....iii. 218
Mellor v. Merchants' Mfg. Co., 150 Mass. 362 ....i. 170
Melms v. Werdehoff, 14 Wis. 19 ....ii. 244
Melson v. Western Union Tel. Co., 72 Mo. App. 111 ....i. 450
Membery v. Great Western R. Co., 14 App. Cas. 179 ....i. 166
Meneely v. Meneely, 62 N. Y. 427 ....i. 432, 433, 434
Menendez v. Holt, 128 U. S. 514 ....i. 424
Mennie v. Blake, 6 El. & Bl. 849, 88 E. C. L. 849 ....iii. 219, 220, 221
Mentzer v. Western Union Tel. Co., 93 Iowa 752 ....i. 440, 466, 472
Mercer v. Corbin, 117 Ind. 450 ....i. 5
Mercer v. Sparks, Owen 51, Noy 35 ....i. 316
Merchants' Nat. Bank v. Guilmartin, 88 Ga. 797 ....ii. 277
Merchants' Nat. Bank v. National Bank of Commonwealth, 139 Mass. 513 ....ii. 213
Merest v. Harvey, 5 Taunt. 442, 1 E. C. L. 150 ....i. 484
Merivale v. Carson, 20 Q. B. D. 275 ....i. 303, 304, 306
Merriam v. Field, 24 Wis. 640, 29 Wis. 590 ....i. 388
Merriam v. Rockwood, 47 N. H. 81 ....ii. 408
Merrick v. Giddings, 1 Mackey (D. C.) 394 ....ii. 113
Merrit v. Rane, 1 Stra. 458 ....ii. 137
Merritt v. Claghorn, 23 Vt. 177 ....ii. 296
Merritt v. Jackson, 181 Mass. 69 ....ii. 559
Merryweather v. Nixan, 8 T. R. 186 ....i. 490; ii. 240
Messinger's Appeal, 109 Pa. St. 285 ....i. 200, 202
Metcalf v. Hess, 14 Ill. 129 ....ii. 296
Metcalfe v. Dickman, 43 Ill. App. 284 ....i. 239
Metropolitan Asylum Dist. v. Hill, 6 App. Cas. 193 ....i. 43
Metropolitan Bank v. Pooley, 10 App. Cas. 210 ....i. 332
Metropolitan Board of Works v. McCarthy, L. R. 7 H. L. 243 ....i. 494
Metropolitan R. Co. v. Jackson, 3 App. Cas. 193 ....i. 106
Meuer v. Phenix Nat. Bank, 42 Misc. (N. Y.) 341 ....ii. 523
Meux v. Cobley, (1892) 2 Ch. 253 ....i. 28
Mew v. Russel, 2 Show. 284 ....i. 380
Meyer v. Haworth, 8 Ad. & El. 467, 35 E. C. L. 442 ....ii. 146
Meyer v. Richards, 163 U. S. 385 ....ii. 413, 415
Michael v. Alestree, 2 Lev. 172, 3 Keb. 650 ....ii. 450
Middleton v. Fowler, 1 Salk. 282 ....ii. 453, 465
Mielenz v. Quasdorf, 68 Iowa 726 ....i. 314
Mighell v. Johore, (1894) 1 Q. B. D. 149 ....i. 37

Miles *v.* Furber, L. R. 8 Q. B. 77 .... iii. 306
Milford *v.* Com., 144 Mass. 64 .... ii. 208
Milhau *v.* Sharp, 27 N. Y. 611 .... i. 226
Millen *v.* Fandrye, Popham 161 .... i. 53, 54, 55
Miller *v.* Biddle, 13 L. T. N. S. 334 .... ii. 504
Miller *v.* Hancock, (1893) 2 Q. B. 177 .... i. 152
Miller *v.* Johnson, 79 Ill. 58 .... i. 298
Miller *v.* Miller, 7 Pick. (Mass.) 134 .... ii. 216
Miller *v.* Newell, 20 S. Car. 123 .... iii. 86
Miller *v.* Parish, 8 Pick. (Mass.) 384 .... i. 277
Miller *v.* Race, 1 Burr. 452 .... ii. 393
Milliken *v.* Thorndike, 103 Mass. 382 .... i. 394
Milliken *v.* Western Union Tel. Co., 110 N. Y. 403 .... i. 437
Millington *v.* Fox, 3 Myl. & C. 338 .... i. 420, 427
Millington *v.* Loring, 6 Q. B. D. 190 .... i. 272
Mills *v.* Armstrong, 13 App. Cas. 1 .... i. 142
Mills *v.* Guardians of Poor, 3 Exch. 590 .... ii. 211
Mills *v.* Martin, 19 Johns. (N. Y.) 34 .... iii. 219
Mills *v.* Wyman, 3 Pick. (Mass.) 207 .... ii. 146
Mills Pub. Co. *v.* Larrabee, 78 Iowa 97 .... i. 36
Milton's Case, Hardres 485 .... iii. 140
Milwaukee, etc., R. Co. *v.* Arms, 91 U. S. 489 .... i. 482
Milwaukee, etc., R. Co. *v.* Kellogg, 94 U. S. 469 .... i. 112, 115
Miner *v.* Gilmour, 12 Moo. P. C. 131 .... i. 198, 201
Minet *v.* Gibson, 3 T. R. 481 .... ii. 403
Mitchel *v.* Reynolds, 1 P. Wms. 181, 1 Smith Lead. Cas. (8th Am. ed.) 756 .... ii. 165
Mitchell *v.* Foster, 12 Ad. & El. 472, 40 E. C. L. 98 .... i. 38
Mitchell *v.* Fuller, 15 Pa. St. 268 .... ii. 515
Mitchell *v.* Great Works Milling, etc., Co., 2 Story (U. S.) 648 .... iii. 111
Mitchell *v.* Jenkins, 5 B. & Ad. 588, 27 E. C. L. 131 .... i. 331
Mitchell *v.* Rochester R. Co., 15 N. Y. 107 .... i. 458
Mitchell *v.* Rome, 49 Ga. 19 .... i. 196
Mitchell *v.* Rome R. Co., 17 Ga. 574 .... ii. 504
Mitchell *v.* Southwestern R. Co., 75 Ga. 398 .... i. 333
Mitchell *v.* Tarbutt, 5 T. R. 649 .... i. 490
Mitchil *v.* Alestree, 1 Vent. 295, 2 Lev. 172 .... i. 189
Mobile, etc., R. Co. *v.* Ashcraft, 48 Ala. 15 .... i. 482
Mibile, etc., R. Co. *v.* McKellar, 59 Ala. 458 .... iii. 263
Mody *v.* Gregson, L. R. 4 Exch. 49 .... i. 388
Moens *v.* Heyworth, 10 M. & W. 147 .... i. 399
Moffatt *v.* Bateman, L. R. 3 P. C. 115 .... i. 159
Mogadara *v.* Holt, 1 Show. 318 .... ii. 351
Mogul Steamship Co. *v.* McGregor, (1892) A. C. 25 .... i. 355, 359, 360, 363, 367, 417
Mogul Steamship Co. *v.* McGregor, 23 Q. B. D. 612 .... i. 314, 353
Mohney *v.* Cook, 26 Pa. St. 342 .... i. 179
Money *v.* Leach, 3 Burr. 1742 .... i. 36
Monnahan *v.* Judd, 165 Mass. 93 .... ii. 117
Monson *v.* Lathrop, 96 Wis. 386 .... i. 297

Monson *v.* Tussaud, (1894) 1 Q. B. 671........................i. 294, 319
Montacute *v.* Maxwell, 1 P. Wms. 618........................ii. 192
Monticello Bank *v.* Dooly, 113 Wis. 590........................ii. 521
Moody *v.* Baker, 5 Cow. (N. Y.) 351........................i. 290
Moody *v.* Drown, 58 N. H. 45........................i. 259
Moody *v.* McClelland, 39 Ala. 45........................i. 194
Moody *v.* Newmark, 121 Cal. 446........................ii. 73
Moody *v.* Walker, 89 Ala. 619........................iii. 197
Moon *v.* Martin, 122 Ind. 211........................ii. 94
Mooney *v.* Davis, 75 Mich. 188........................i. 412
Mooney *v.* Miller, 102 Mass. 217........................i. 394
Moore *v.* Appleton, 26 Ala. 633........................ii. 240
Moore *v.* Clementson, 2 Campb. 22........................ii. 479
Moore *v.* Detroit Locomotive Works, 14 Mich. 266........................ii. 128
Moore *v.* Francis, 121 N. Y. 199........................i. 294
Moore *v.* Meagher, 1 Taunt. 39........................i. 279, 286
Moore *v.* Moore, 1 Bulst. 160........................iii. 188
Moore *v.* Mourgue, 2 Cowp. 480........................ii. 279
Moore *v.* Paine, Lee t. Hardw. 288........................ii. 387
Moore *v.* Tate, 87 Tenn. 725........................i. 35
Moore *v.* Townshend, 33 N. J. L. 284........................i. 31
Moore *v.* Turbeville, 2 Bibb (Ky.) 602........................i. 413
Moore *v.* Webb, 1 C. B. N. S. 673, 87 E. C. L. 673........................i. 203
Mooring *v.* Mobile Marine Dock, etc., Ins. Co., 27 Ala. 254........................ii. 390
Moran *v.* Dunphy, 177 Mass. 485........................i. 346
Mordant *v.* Wats, Brownl. & Goldes. (pt. i.) 19........................iii. 120
More *v.* Massini, 32 Cal. 590........................iii. 87
Moreton *v.* Hardern, 4 B. & C. 223, 10 E. C. L. 316........................i. 190; iii. 264
Morey *v.* Hoyt, 65 Conn. 516........................i. 252
Morgan *v.* Cox, 22 Mo. 373........................i. 83
Morgan *v.* Hughes, 2 T. R. 225........................i. 329
Morgan *v.* Ide, 8 Cush. (Mass.) 420........................i. 254
Morgan *v.* Morris, 9 Exch. 145........................i. 240
Morgan *v.* Pike, 14 C. B. 473, 78 E. C. L. 473........................iii. 122, 123
Morgan *v.* Raney, 6 H. & N. 265........................ii. 295
Morison *v.* Cade, Cro. Jac. 162........................i. 285
Morison *v.* Thompson, L. R. 9 Q. B. 480........................ii. 492
Morison's Case, Jenk. 347, Cro. Jac. 163........................i. 283
Morley *v.* Attenborough, 3 Exch. 500........................i. 384; ii. 334
Morley *v.* Gaisford, 2 H. Bl. 442........................i. 16; iii. 260
Morrell *v.* Quarles, 35 Ala. 544........................ii. 121
Morrice *v.* Baker, 3 Bulst. 196, 1 Rolle 394........................i. 20
Morris *v.* Cheney, 51 Ill. 451........................iii. 86
Morris *v.* Morris, 5 Mich. 171........................iii. 87
Morris *v.* Nugent, 7 C. & P. 572, 32 E. C. L. 635........................i. 18
Morris *v.* Platt, 32 Conn. 75........................i. 7
Morris, etc., Canal Co. *v.* Van Vorst, 21 N. J. L. 100........................ii. 125
Morrison *v.* Belcher, 3 F. & F. 614........................i. 305
Morrison *v.* Davis, 20 Pa. St. 171........................i. 118
Morrison *v.* Marquardt, 24 Iowa 35........................i. 207, 208
Morrison's Case, 1 Broun (Scotch) 394........................i. 12

Mors *v.* Slew, 2 Keb. 866, 3 Keb. 72, 112, 135, 2 Lev. 69, 1 Vent. 190, 1 Mod. 85 .... ii. 268
Morse *v.* Nixon, 6 Jones L. (51 N. Car.) 293 .... i. 18
Morse *v.* Toppan, 3 Gray (Mass.) 412 .... ii. 206, 207
Morton *v.* Badley, 27 Ala. 640 .... i. 495
Morton *v.* Burn, 7 Ad. & El. 19, 34 E. C. L. 18 .... ii. 52
Morton *v.* Gloster, 46 Me. 520 .... ii. 286
Morton *v.* Lamb, 7 T. R. 121 .... ii. 139
Morton *v.* Shoppee, 3 C. & P. 373, 14 E. C. L. 355 .... i. 11
Morton *v.* Western Union Tel. Co., 53 Ohio St. 431 .... i. 467
Moses *v.* Arnold, 43 Iowa 187 .... iii. 198
Moses *v.* Katzenberger, 84 Ala. 95 .... i. 413
Moses *v.* Macferlan, 2 Burr. 1005 .... ii. 213, 231; iii. 193
Moses *v.* Stevens, 2 Pick. (Mass.) 332 .... ii. 226
Moses *v.* Trice, 21 Gratt. (Va.) 556 .... ii. 375
Moshcuvel *v.* District of Columbia, 191 U. S. 247 .... i. 132
Mosley *v.* Fosset, Moo. K. B. 543 .... ii. 262
Moss *v.* Pardridge, 9 Ill. App. 492 .... i. 55
Mostyn *v.* Fabrigas, 1 Smith Lead. Cas. (8th Am. ed.) 1027, *note* .... ii. 178
Moule *v.* Garrett, L. R. 7 Exch. 101 .... ii. 234
Moulton *v.* Sanford, 51 Me. 134 .... i. 110
Mounteagle *v.* Worcester, 2 Dyer 121*a* .... iii. 165
Mountney *v.* Watton, 2 B. & Ad. 673, 22 E. C. L. 164 .... i. 301
Mouse's Case, 12 Coke 63 .... i. 18, 23; ii. 301
Mowse *v.* Edney, 1 Rolle Abr. 20, pl. 12 .... iii. 81
Moxie Nerve Food Co. *v.* Beach, 33 Fed. Rep. 248 .... i. 425
Muetze *v.* Tuteur, 77 Wis. 236 .... i. 297
Muldoon *v.* Rickey, 103 Pa. St. 110 .... i. 333
Mulgrave *v.* Ogden, Cro. Eliz. 219 .... i. 237; iii. 165
Mullen *v.* Ensley, 8 Humph. (Tenn.) 428 .... i. 258
Mullen *v.* St. John, 57 N. Y. 567 .... i. 107
Mulligan *v.* Cole, L. R. 10 Q. B. 549 .... i. 299
Mullin *v.* Martin, 23 Mo. App. 537 .... ii. 131
Mulliner *v.* Florence, 3 Q. B. D. 484 .... i. 240, 257
Munns *v.* Dupont, 3 Wash. (U. S.) 31 .... i. 330
Munroe *v.* Bordier, 8 C. B. 862, 65 E. C. L. 862 .... ii. 389
Munroe *v.* Perkins, 9 Pick. (Mass.) 298 .... ii. 128
Munroe *v.* Pritchett, 16 Ala. 785 .... i. 394, 407
Munster *v.* Lamb, 11 Q. B. D. 588 .... i. 307, 498
Murdock *v.* Walker, 152 Pa. St. 595 .... i. 367
Murphy *v.* Deane, 101 Mass. 455 .... i. 138, 140
Murray *v.* McAllister, 38 Vt. 167 .... i. 277
Murray *v.* Moultrie, 6 C. & P. 471, 25 E. C. L. 493 .... i. 39, 40
Murray *v.* South Carolina R. Co., 1 McMull. L. (S. Car.) 385 .... ii. 471
Murray *v.* Tolman, 162 Ill. 417 .... i. 395
Musgrove *v.* Newell, 1 M. & W. 582 .... i. 331
Muspratt *v.* Gregory, 1 M. & W. 650 .... iii. 308
Musselman *v.* Barker, 26 Neb. 737 .... i. 464
Myer *v.* Hobbs, 57 Ala. 175 .... i. 196
Myer *v.* Wheeler, 65 Iowa 390 .... i. 389

N. K. Fairbank Co. *v.* R. W. Bell Mfg. Co., 77 Fed. Rep. 869........i. 431
Nabob of Carnatic *v.* East India Co., 1 Ves. Jr. 371, 2 Ves. Jr. 56....i. 37
Nash *v.* Minnesota Title Ins., etc., Co., 163 Mass. 574................i. 411
Nashua Iron, etc., Co. *v.* Brush, 91 Fed. Rep. 214....................i. 387
Nashville, etc., R. Co. *v.* McConnell, 82 Fed. Rep. 65................i. 346
National Bank of Republic *v.* Young, 41 N. J. Eq. 531..............ii. 408
National Citizens' Bank *v.* Toplitz, 81 N. Y. App. Div. 593..........ii. 522
National Enameling, etc., Co. *v.* Haberman, 120 Fed. Rep. 416.......ii. 164
National L. Ins. Co. *v.* Jones, 59 N. Y. 649.........................ii. 212
Nations *v.* Hawkins, 11 Ala. 859.......................................i. 260
Nautilus, The, 1 Ware (U. S.) 529......................................i. 146
Neate *v.* Harding, 6 Exch. 349..ii. 216
Nehr *v.* State, 35 Neb. 638..i. 17
Nelson *v.* Allen, 1 Yerg. (Tenn.) 360.................................iii. 111
Nelson *v.* Macintosh, 1 Stark. 237, 2 E. C. L. 96....................ii. 279
Nelson *v.* Whitman, 1 Rich. L. (S. Car.) 318.........................i. 235
Nesbitt *v.* Drew, 17 Ala. 379...ii. 225
Nevill *v.* Fine Arts, etc., Co., (1895) 2 Q. B. 156....................i. 315
Nevill *v.* Loadman, 2 F. & F. 313......................................i. 330
Newark Coal Co. *v.* Upson, 40 Ohio St. 17.............................i. 333
Newcomb *v.* Boston Protective Dept., 146 Mass. 596...................i. 176
New Haven Mfg. Co. *v.* New Haven Pulp, etc., Co., 76 Conn. 126...ii. 558
Newman *v.* Phillipsburg Horse Car Co., 52 N. J. L. 446..............i. 143
New Providence Tp. *v.* McEachron, 33 N. J. L. 339, 35 N. J. L. 528..ii. 293
Newton *v.* Chicago, etc., R. Co., 66 Iowa 422.........................ii. 120
Newton Mfg. Co. *v.* White, 53 Ga. 395...............................iii. 198
New World, Steamboat, *v.* King, 16 How. (U. S.) 469...............ii. 50
New York Cent. R. Co. *v.* Lockwood, 17 Wall. (U. S.) 357.........i. 100
New York, etc., Printing Tel. Co. *v.* Dryburg, 35 Pa. St. 303........i. 456
New York, etc., R. Co. *v.* Steinbrenner, 47 N. J. L. 161..............i. 141
New York Nat. Banking Assoc. Bank *v.* American Dock, etc., Co., 143 N. Y. 559..ii. 483
Nicholls *v.* More, 1 Sid. 36..ii. 267
Nicholls *v.* More, 1 Sid. 425, 1 Mod. 8, 1 Vent. 44, 2 Keb. 552.......iii. 187
Nichols *v.* Marsland, 2 Ex. D. 1, L. R. 10 Ex. 255...........i. 55, 63, 85
Nichols *v.* Newsom, 2 Murph. (6 N. Car.) 302.........................i. 237
Nichols *v.* Raynbred, Hob. 88..ii. 135
Nicholson *v.* Rust, 52 S. W. Rep. 933..................................i. 299
Nicholson *v.* Sedgewick, 1 Ld. Raym. 180, 3 Salk. 67.................ii. 379
Nicoll *v.* Burke, 78 N. Y. 581..ii. 480
Nicolls *v.* Bastard, 2 C. M. & R. 659............................i. 252, 254
Nightingale *v.* Chafee, 11 R. I. 609....................................ii. 390
Nitro-Glycerine Case, 15 Wall. (U. S.) 524.............................i. 84
Nix *v.* Goodhill, 95 Iowa 285...i. 334
Noble *v.* Adams, 7 Taunt. 59, 2 E. C. L. 59...........................i. 259
Noddleburn, The, 28 Fed. Rep. 857......................................i. 174
Noke's Case, 4 Coke 80*b*...iii. 125
Noonan *v.* Orton, 34 Wis. 259...iii. 86
Nordenfelt *v.* Maxim-Nordenfelt Guns, etc., Co., (1894) A. C. 535, 548...ii. 165

Norfolk v. Howard, 2 Show. 235....ii. 371
Norfolk, etc., R. Co. v. Ormsby, 27 Gratt. (Va.) 455....i. 144
Norfolk, etc., Steamboat Co. v. Davis, 12 App. Cas. (D. C.) 328....i. 308
Norman v. Thompson, 4 Exch. 756....ii. 131
Norrice's Case, Hardres 178....iii. 121
Norris v. Litchfield, 35 N. H. 271....i. 178
Norris v. Pine, cited in 2 Lev. 211....ii. 153
North v. Turner, 9 S. & R. (Pa.) 248....iii. 86
Northam v. Bowdon, 11 Exch. 70....i. 252
North Eastern R. Co. v. Wanless, L. R. 7 H. L. 12....i. 132
North Vernon v. Voegler, 103 Ind. 314....i. 492
Norton v. Coons, 6 N. Y. 33....ii. 239
Norton v. Eastern R. Co., 113 Mass. 366....i. 115
Norton v. Jason, Style 398....i. 163, 269
Norton v. Marden, 15 Me. 46....ii. 214
Norton v. Scholefield, 9 M. & W. 665....i. 202
Norton v. Sewall, 106 Mass. 143....i. 61
Norwich University v. Denny, 47 Vt. 13....ii. 476
Norwood v. Read, 1 Plowd. 180....ii. 55, 60, 62; iii. 68
Noseworthy v. Wildman, 2 Keb. 615....iii. 195
Noyes v. Colby, 30 N. H. 143....i. 52
Nugent v. Smith, 1 C. P. D. 27....ii. 306
Nugent v. Smith, 1 C. P. D. 423....i. 64; ii. 303, 318
Nye v. Western Union Tel. Co., 104 Fed. Rep. 628....i. 298

Oakes v. St. Louis Candy Co., 146 Mo. 391....i. 422
Oakland R. Co. v. Fielding, 48 Pa. St. 320....i. 268
Oaste v. Taylor, Cro. Jac. 306....ii. 348; iii. 139
O'Brien v. McGlinchy, 68 Me. 552....i. 143
O'Brien v. Vaill, 22 Fla. 627....ii. 296
O'Brien v. Young, 95 N. Y. 428....ii. 206
Oddy v. Paulet, 4 F. & F. 1009....i. 314
Odiham v. Smith, Cro. Eliz. 589....iii. 297
Ogden v. Claycomb, 52 Ill. 365....i. 7
Ogilvie v. Hallam, 58 Iowa 714....ii. 95
Ogle v. Barnes, 8 T. R. 188....i. 16; iii. 263
Olcott v. Rathbone, 5 Wend. (N. Y.) 491....iii. 203
Oldershaw v. King, 2 H. & N. 399, 517....ii. 34
Oliver Ditson Co. v. Bates, 181 Mass. 455....i. 254
Olmstead v. Beale, 19 Pick. (Mass.) 528....ii. 220
Olmstead v. Brush, 27 Conn. 530....ii. 149
Olson v. Solveson, 71 Wis. 663....i. 464
O'Maley v. South Boston Gas Light Co., 158 Mass. 135....i. 170
Onely v. Kent, 3 Dyer 355*b*....ii. 90
Onondaga County Bank v. Bates, 3 Hill (N. Y.) 53....iii. 143
Oppenheim v. White Lion Hotel Co., L. R. 6 C. P. 515....ii. 295
Oppenheimer v. Farmers', etc., Bank, 97 Tenn. 33....ii. 505
Ormrod v. Huth, 14 M. & W. 651....i. 385
Orr v. Home Mut. Ins. Co., 12 La. Ann. 255....i. 373
Ortiz v. Navarro, 10 Tex. Civ. App. 195....i. 464

Osborn *v.* Gillett, L. R. 8 Exch. 88 .... iii. 74
Osborne *v.* London, etc., R. Co., 21 Q. B. D. 220 .... i. 166, 167
Osborne *v.* O'Reilly, 42 N. J. Eq. 467 .... ii. 128
Osborne *v.* Veitch, 1 F. & F. 317 .... i. 12
Osborn's Case, 10 Coke 130*b* .... i. 266
Otis *v.* Janesville, 47 Wis. 422 .... i. 140
Oulds *v.* Harrison, 10 Exch. 572 .... ii. 389
Overdeer *v.* Lewis, 1 W. & S. (Pa.) 90 .... i. 8
Overend, *In re*, L. R. 6 Eq. 344 .... ii. 556
Owen *v.* Hyde, 6 Yerg. (Tenn.) 334 .... i. 27
Owen *v.* J. S. Ogilvie Pub. Co., 32 N. Y. App. Div. 465 .... i. 297
Owen *v.* Lewyn, 1 Vent. 223 .... i. 238; iii. 169
Owston *v.* Ogle, 13 East 538 .... iii. 110
Oxford *v.* Cross, 4 Coke 18 .... i. 283

Pacific Mail Steamship Co. *v.* Joliffe, 2 Wall. (U. S.) 450 .... ii. 208
Packard *v.* Windholz, 88 N. Y. App. Div. 365 .... ii. 535
Padmore *v.* Piltz, 44 Fed. Rep. 104 .... i. 39
Page *v.* Bent, 2 Met. (Mass.) 371 .... i. 407
Page *v.* Crosby, 24 Pick. (Mass.) 211 .... iii. 221
Page *v.* Cushing, 38 Me. 523 .... i. 334
Page *v.* Moulton, 3 Dyer 296*b* .... ii. 42
Paine *v.* Partrich, Carth. 194 .... i. 226
Palmer *v.* Fleshees, 1 Sid. 167 .... i. 207, 208
Palmer *v.* Fletcher, 1 Lev. 122 .... i. 207
Palmer *v.* Harris, 60 Pa. St. 156 .... i. 426
Palmer *v.* Pratt, 2 Bing. 185, 9 E. C. L. 373 .... ii. 508
Palmer *v.* Stavely, 12 Mod. 510 .... iii. 195
Palmer *v.* Thorpe, 4 Coke 20*b* .... i. 282
Palmer *v.* Wick, etc., Steam Shipping Co., (1894) A. C. 324 .... i. 490
Palmer Sav. Bank *v.* Insurance Co. of North America, 166 Mass. 189 .... ii. 149
Pangburn *v.* Patridge, 7 Johns. (N. Y.) 140 .... iii. 218
Paramour *v.* Payne, Moo. K. B. 703 .... ii. 63; iii. 183
Parcell *v.* McComber, 11 Neb. 209 .... ii. 226
Parker *v.* Foote, 19 Wend. (N. Y.) 309 .... i. 208
Parker *v.* Godin, 2 Stra. 813 .... i. 242
Parker *v.* Kennedy, 1 Bay (S. Car.) 404 .... iii. 86
Parker *v.* McKenna, L. R. 10 Ch. 96 .... ii. 492
Parker *v.* Smith, 5 C. & P. 438, 24 E. C. L. 401 .... i. 210
Parkersburg First Nat. Bank *v.* Johns, 22 W. Va. 520 .... ii. 408
Parkes *v.* Prescott, L. R. 4 Exch. 169 .... i. 298
Parkins *v.* Scott, 1 H. & C. 153 .... i. 287, 288, 290
Parkinson *v.* Lee, 2 East 314 .... i. 385
Parlement Belge, The, 5 P. D. 197 .... i. 37
Parmelee *v.* Thompson, 45 N. Y. 58 .... ii. 75
Parmiter *v.* Coupland, 6 M. & W. 105 .... i. 309
Parrott *v.* Barney, Deady (U. S.) 405 .... i. 31
Parsons *v.* Harper, 16 Gratt. (Va.) 64 .... iii. 265
Partridge *v.* Bank of England, 9 Q. B. 396, 58 E. C. L. 396 .... ii. 420

Partridge *v.* Scott, 3 M. & W. 220 ... i. 195
Pasley *v.* Freeman, 3 T. R. 51 ... i. 343, 385, 392, 409, 415; iii. 56
Pasnett *v.* Marble, 62 Vt. 48 ... i. 300
Passinger *v.* Thorburn, 34 N. Y. 634 ... i. 448, 449
Pastene *v.* Adams, 49 Cal. 87 ... i. 122
Paterson *v.* Gandasequi, 15 East 62 ... ii. 479
Paterson *v.* Wilcox, 20 U. C. C. P. 385 ... i. 270
Patnote *v.* Saunders, 41 Vt. 66 ... ii. 221
Patterson *v.* Lippincott, 47 N. J. L. 457 ... i. 406
Patterson *v.* Prior, 18 Ind. 440 ... ii. 215; iii. 199
Paul *v.* Frazier, 3 Mass. 71 ... i. 272
Paul *v.* Summerhayes, 4 Q. B. D. 9 ... i. 21
Pavesich *v.* New England L. Ins. Co., 122 Ga. 190 ... i. 320
Paxton *v.* Boyer, 67 Ill. 133 ... i. 7
Payne *v.* Western, etc., R. Co., 13 Lea (Tenn.) 507 ... i. 366, 368
Payne *v.* Zell, 98 Va. 294 ... ii. 522
Paynter *v.* Williams, 1 Cromp. & M. 810 ... ii. 85, 151
Payson *v.* Macomber, 3 Allen (Mass.) 69 ... i. 13
Payton *v.* Snelling, (1901) A. C. 310 ... i. 431
Peace *v.* Stennet, 4 J. J. Marsh. (Ky.) 449 ... ii. 94
Peacock *v.* Rhodes, 2 Dougl. 633 ... ii. 394
Peake *v.* Oldham, 1 Cowp. 275 ... i. 284
Pearson *v.* Garrett, Comb. 227, 4 Mod. 242 ... ii. 379, 383, 508
Pearson *v.* Skelton, 1 M. & W. 504 ... ii. 240
Peasley *v.* Boatwright, 2 Leigh (Va.) 196 ... ii. 504
Peay *v.* Western Union Tel. Co., 64 Ark. 538 ... i. 466
Pechell *v.* Watson, 8 M. & W. 691 ... i. 339, 340
Peck *v.* Ellis, 2 Johns. Ch. (N. Y.) 131 ... i. 490
Peck *v.* Michigan City, 149 Ind. 670 ... i. 45
Peck *v.* Requa, 13 Gray (Mass.) 407 ... ii. 76
Pecke *v.* Redman, 2 Dyer 113*a* ... ii. 55
Peek *v.* Derry, 14 App. Cas. 337 ... i. 400
Peek *v.* Derry, 37 Ch. D. 541 ... i. 400, 402
Peek *v.* Gurney, L. R. 6 H. L. 377, 43 L. J. Ch. 19 ... i. 397
Peers *v.* Sampson, 4 Dowl. & R. 636, 16 E. C. L. 216 ... ii. 291
Pelletreau *v.* Rathbone, 18 Johns. (N. Y.) 428 ... ii. 148
Peltier *v.* Babillion, 45 Mich. 384 ... ii. 514
Pender *v.* Robbins, 6 Jones L. (51 N. Car.) 207 ... ii. 306
Pendlebury *v.* Greenlagh, 1 Q. B. D. 36 ... ii. 472
Penn *v.* Flack, 3 Gill & J. (Md.) 369 ... iii. 203
Penniman *v.* Elliot, 27 Barb. (N. Y.) 315 ... ii. 131
Pennington *v.* Brinsop Hall Coal Co., 5 Ch. D. 769 ... i. 203
Pennsylvania Coal Co. *v.* Sanderson, 113 Pa. St. 126 ... i. 63, 202
Pennsylvania, etc., R. Co. *v.* Langendorf, 48 Ohio St. 316 ... i. 133
Pennsylvania R. Co. v. Angel, 41 N. J. Eq. 316 ... i. 44
Pennsylvania R. Co. *v.* Aspell, 23 Pa. St. 147 ... i. 127
Pennsylvania R. Co. *v.* Kerr, 62 Pa. St. 353 ... i. 117
Pennsylvania R. Co. *v.* Miller, 112 Pa. St. 34 ... i. 200, 201
Pennsylvania R. Co. *v.* Righter, 42 N. J. L. 181 ... i. 128, 140
Pennsylvania R. Co. *v.* Roney, 89 Ind. 453 ... i. 133

Penny *v.* State, 88 Ala. 105....i, 236
Penny *v.* Wimbledon Urban Dist. Council, (1899) 2 Q. B. 72....i. 155
Penruddock *v.* Monteagle, 1 Rolle Abr. 7 (N), pl. 3....iii. 192
Penruddock's Case, 5 Coke 101....i. 215
Penson *v.* Hickbed, Cro. Eliz. 170, 4 Leon. 99....iii. 84
People *v.* Detroit White Lead Works, 82 Mich. 471....i. 220
People *v.* Doe, 1 Mich. 451....i. 7
People *v.* Pearl, 76 Mich. 207....i. 8
People *v.* Peckens, 153 N. Y. 576....i. 395
People *v.* Tioga C. Pl., 19 Wend. (N. Y.) 73....iii. 86
Pepper *v.* Western Union Tel. Co., 87 Tenn. 554....i. 450, 456
Percival *v.* Hickey, 18 Johns. (N. Y.) 257....i. 5; iii. 265
Perkins *v.* Hersey, 1 R. I. 493....i. 465
Perkins *v.* New York Cent. R. Co., 24 N. Y. 196....i. 100
Perkins *v.* Pendleton, 90 Me. 166....i. 346, 367, 371
Perkins *v.* Smith, cited in 4 M. & S. 259....i. 243
Perkins *v.* Smith, Say. 41....iii. 160
Perley *v.* Muskegon County, 32 Mich. 132....ii. 293; iii. 112
Perley *v.* Spring, 12 Mass. 297....ii. 188
Perrault *v.* Gauthier, 28 Can. Sup. Ct. 241, 6 Quebec Q. B. 65, 10 Quebec Super. Ct. 224....i. 365
Perrine *v.* Taylor, 43 N. J. Eq. 128....i. 220
Perry *v.* Fitzhowe, 8 Q. B. 757, 55 E. C. L. 757....i. 216
Perry *v.* Truefitt, 6 Beav. 66....i. 420
Peter *v.* Beverly, 10 Pet. (U. S.) 532....ii. 390
Peter *v.* Compton, Skin. 353....ii. 193
Peters *v.* Farnsworth, 15 Vt. 155....ii. 485
Peterson *v.* Haffner, 59 Ind. 130....i. 5
Peterson *v.* Western Union Tel. Co., 65 Minn. 18, 72 Minn. 41, 75 Minn. 368....i. 297, 298
Petrel, The, (1893) P. 320....ii. 471
Petre *v.* Heneage, 12 Mod. 519....i. 238
Pettyjohn *v.* National Exch. Bank, 101 Va. 111....ii. 510
Peytoe's Case, 9 Coke 79*a*....ii. 88, 90, 93
Pfleger *v.* Browne, 28 Beav. 391....ii. 131
Phelan *v.* Moss, 67 Pa. St. 59....ii. 408
Phelps *v.* Gilchrist, 28 N. H. 277....i. 249
Phelps *v.* Nowlen, 72 N. Y. 39....i. 355, 366
Pheteplace *v.* Eastman, 26 Iowa 446....i. 416
Philadelphia, etc., R. Co. *v.* Philadelphia, etc., Steam Towboat Co., 23 How. (U. S.) 209....i. 179
Philbrick *v.* Foster, 4 Ind. 442....i. 7
Philip, etc., Ebling Brewing Co. *v.* Reinheimer, 32 Misc. (N. Y.) 594..ii. 542
Philips *v.* Martiney, 10 Gratt. (Va.) 333....i. 260
Philips *v.* Thompson, 3 Lev. 191....iii. 195
Phillips *v.* Homfray, 24 Ch. D. 439....ii. 217; iii. 61, 65, 70, 88, 200
Phillips *v.* Im Thurn, 18 C. B. N. S. 694, 114 E. C. L. 694....ii. 412
Phillips *v.* Low, (1892) 1 Ch. 47....i. 207
Phillips *v.* Wilpers, 2 Lans. (N. Y.) 389....i. 103
Philpott *v.* Kelley, 3 Ad. & El. 106, 30 E. C. L. 40....i. 238

Philpott *v.* Wallet, 3 Lev. 65 .... ii. 176, 190, 191
Phœnix Ins. Co. *v.* Rink, 110 Ill. 538 .... ii. 75
Phœnix Mut. L. Ins. Co. *v.* Arbuckle, 52 Ill. App. 33 .... i. 334
Pickard *v.* Sears, 6 Ad. & El. 469, 33 E. C. L. 115 .... ii. 242, 247
Pickard *v.* Smith, 10 C. B. N. S. 470, 100 E. C. L. 470 .... i. 153
Pickering *v.* Ilfracombe R. Co., L. R. 3 C. P. 235 .... iii. 86
Pickering *v.* Rudd, 1 Stark. 56, 2 E. C. L. 32, 4 Campb. 210 .... i. 19, 216; iii. 232
Pidding *v.* How, 8 Sim. 477 .... i. 426
Pierce *v.* Crafts, 12 Johns. (N. Y.) 90 .... iii. 203
Pierson *v.* Dunlop, 2 Cowp. 571 .... ii. 401
Pierson *v.* Hutchinson, 2 Campb. 211 .... ii. 375
Pike *v.* Brown, 7 Cush. (Mass.) 133 .... ii. 173
Pillans *v.* Van Mierop, 3 Burr. 1663 .... ii. 57, 141, 142, 143, 173, 389, 399, 400, 401
Pinches *v.* Swedish Evangelical Lutheran Church, 55 Conn. 183 .... ii. 221
Pinchon's Case, 9 Coke 86*b*, 89*a*, ... iii. 68, 178, 184
Pincombe *v.* Rudge, Hob. 3, 4 .... iii. 125
Pine *v.* New York, 103 Fed. Rep. 337, 112 Fed. Rep. 98 .... i. 199
Pinkerton *v.* Woodward, 33 Cal. 557 .... ii. 294, 296
Pinkney *v.* Hall, 1 Ld. Raym. 175 .... ii. 351, 379
Pinnel's Case, 5 Coke 117*a* .... ii. 88, 98, 99, 100, 102, 103
Piollet *v.* Simmers, 106 Pa. St. 96 .... i. 179
Piper *v.* Fosher, 121 Ind. 407 .... ii. 176
Piper *v.* Pearson, 2 Gray (Mass.) 120 .... i. 38
Pippin *v.* Sheppard, 11 Price 400 .... i. 187
Pitman *v.* Woodbury, 3 Exch. 4 .... iii. 122
Pitts *v.* Hale, 3 Mass. 321 .... iii. 222
Pittsburgh, etc., R. Co. *v.* Lyon, 123 Pa. St. 150 .... i. 482
Pixler *v.* Nichols, 8 Iowa 106 .... ii. 226
Plant *v.* Woods, 176 Mass. 499 .... i. 366, 367, 372
Planters' Rice-Mill Co. *v.* Merchants' Nat. Bank, 78 Ga. 574 .... ii. 482
Platt *v.* Waterbury, 72 Conn. 531 .... i. 45
Platz *v.* Cohoes, 89 N. Y. 219 .... i. 178
Playford *v.* Union Kingdom Electric Co., L. R. 4 Q. B. 707 .... i. 438
Pledall *v.* Knap, Anderson 65, pl. 139 .... i. 46
Plets *v.* Johnson, 3 Hill (N. Y.) 112 .... ii. 513
Plumer *v.* Smith, 5 N. H. 553 .... ii. 73
Plummer *v.* Bucknam, 55 Me. 105 .... ii. 227
Poeppers *v.* Missouri, etc., R. Co., 67 Mo. 715 .... i. 121
Poess *v.* Twelfth Ward Bank, 43 Misc. (N. Y.) 45 .... ii. 517, 544
Pointing *v.* Noakes, (1894) 2 Q. B. 281 .... i. 155
Poland *v.* Miller, 95 Ind. 387 .... i. 387
Pole *v.* Leask, 28 Beav. 562 .... ii. 485
Polhill *v.* Walter, 3 B. & Ad. 114, 23 E. C. L. 38 .... i. 396, 405, 455
Pollasky *v.* Minchener, 81 Mich. 280 .... i. 311
Pollock *v.* Cohen, 32 Ohio St. 514 .... ii. 487
Pomfret *v.* Ricroft, 1 Saund. 321 .... iii. 125
Pool *v.* Horner, 64 Md. 131 .... ii. 87
Pooly *v.* Gilberd, 2 Bulst. 41 .... ii. 34

Pope *v.* Lewyns, Cro. Jac. 630 .... i. 380
Pope *v.* Pollock, 46 Ohio St. 367 .... i. 333
Pope *v.* Tunstall, 2 Ark. 209 .... ii. 95
Poplett *v.* Stockdale, 2 C. & P. 198, 12 E. C. L. 87 .... ii. 73
Poplewell *v.* Wilson, 1 Stra. 264 .... ii. 391
Poppa *v.* Rose, L. R. 7 C. P. 32 .... i. 38
Pordage *v.* Cole, 1 Sid. 423, 1 Saund. 320 .... ii. 133; iii. 124
Porter *v.* Jackson, 95 Ind. 210 .... ii. 149
Port Jervis *v.* Port Jervis First Nat. Bank, 96 N. Y. 550 .... ii. 240
Portland Bank *v.* Stubbs, 6 Mass. 422 .... iii. 220, 221
Portsmouth Brewing Co. *v.* Portsmouth Brewing, etc., Co., 67 N. H. 433 .... i. 423
Postal Tel. Cable Co. *v.* Barwise, 11 Colo. App. 328 .... i. 450, 454
Postal Tel. Cable Co. *v.* Lathrop, 131 Ill. 575 .... i. 450
Postlethwaite *v.* Parks, 3 Burr. 1878 .... i. 269
Post Pub. Co. *v.* Hallam, 59 Fed. Rep. 530 .... i. 309
Post Pub. Co. *v.* Maloney, 50 Ohio St. 71 .... i. 309
Potter *v.* Green, 6 Allen (Mass.) 442 .... ii. 75
Potter *v.* Hall, 3 Pick. (Mass.) 368 .... iii. 308
Potter *v.* Pearson, 2 Ld. Raym. 759 .... ii. 384
Potter Drug, etc., Corp. *v.* Pasfield Soap Co., 106 Fed. Rep. 914 .... i. 424
Powell *v.* Ancell, 9 Dowl. 893 .... iii. 142
Powell *v.* Birmingham Vinegar Brewery Co., (1896) 2 Ch. 79 .... i. 428
Powell *v.* Dayton, etc., R. Co., 16 Oregon 33 .... i. 31
Powell *v.* Fall, 5 Q. B. D. 597 .... i. 57
Power *v.* Barham, 4 Ad. & El. 473, 31 E. C. L. 115 .... i. 383
Powtuary *v.* Walton, 1 Rolle Abr. 10, pl. 5 .... iii. 251
Powys *v.* Blagrave, 4 DeG. M. & G. 448 .... i. 31
Pozzi *v.* Shipton, 8 Ad. & El. 963, 35 E. C. L. 574 .... iii. 273
Pratt *v.* Gardner, 2 Cush. (Mass.) 63 .... i. 37
Prentice *v.* Brimhall, 123 Mass. 293 .... ii. 149
Preston *v.* Boston, 12 Pick. (Mass.) 7 .... ii. 230
Preston *v.* Frey, 91 Cal. 107 .... i. 314
Preston *v.* Mann, 25 Conn. 118 .... ii. 248
Preston *v.* Mercer, Hardres 60 .... iii. 255
Preston *v.* Prather, 137 U. S. 604 .... ii. 277
Prettyman *v.* Williamson, 1 Penn. (Del.) 224 .... i. 163
Price *v.* Easton, 4 B. & Ad. 433, 24 E. C. L. 96 .... ii. 154
Price *v.* Grantz, 118 Pa. St. 402 .... i. 221
Price *v.* Hartshorn, 44 N. Y. 94 .... i. 19
Price Baking Powder Co. *v.* Fyfe, 45 Fed. Rep. 799 .... i. 425
Prickett *v.* Badger, 1 C. B. N. S. 296, 87 E. C. L. 296 .... ii. 222
Priddy *v.* Henbrey, 1 B. & C. 674, 8 E. C. L. 284 .... iii. 142
Prideaux *v.* Mineral Point, 43 Wis. 513 .... i. 141
Priester *v.* Augley, 5 Rich. L. (S. Car.) 44 .... i. 18
Priestley *v.* Fowler, 3 M. & W. 1 .... i. 171; ii. 471
Priestly *v.* Fernie, 3 H. & C. 977 .... ii. 480
Primrose *v.* Western Union Tel. Co., 154 U. S. 1 .... i. 435, 452
Prince *v.* Brooklyn Daily Eagle, 16 Misc. (N. Y.) 187 .... i. 317
Pringle *v.* Vesta Coal Co., 172 Pa. St. 438 .... i. 192

Printing, etc., Registering Co. *v.* Sampson, L. R. 19 Eq. 462..........ii. 190
Proctor *v.* Spratley, 78 Va. 254..........i. 389
Proctor *v.* Webster, 16 Q. B. D. 112..........i. 314
Prussak *v.* Hutton, 30 N. Y. App. Div. 60..........i. 59
Pryce *v.* Monmouthshire Canal, etc., Co., 4 App. Cas. 215..........i. 42
Pugh *v.* Barnes, 108 Ala. 167..........ii. 124
Pullman *v.* Hill, (1891) 1 Q. B. 524..........i. 296, 297
Purslow *v.* Baily, 2 Ld. Raym. 1039..........iii. 192
Putnam *v.* Payne, 13 Johns. (N. Y.) 312..........i. 18
Putnam *v.* Woodbury, 68 Me. 58..........ii. 120
Pynchon *v.* Stearns, 11 Met. (Mass.) 304..........i. 27

Quartz Hill Consol. Gold Min. Co. *v.* Eyre, 11 Q. B. D. 674..i. 332, 333
Quigley *v.* Thompson, 53 Ind. 317..........i. 341
Quimby *v.* Blackey, 63 N. H. 77..........i. 495
Quincy *v.* Jones, 76 Ill. 231..........i. 196
Quinn *v.* Leathem, (1901) A. C. 495...i. 344, 350, 351, 358, 359, 361, 363

Rabone *v.* Williams, 7 T. R. 356, *note*..........ii. 479
Raborg *v.* Peyton, 2 Wheat. (U. S.) 385..........iii. 143
Radley *v.* London, etc., R. Co., 1 App. Cas. 754..........i. 135
Rae *v.* Hulbert, 17 Ill. 572..........ii. 207
Ralston *v.* Steamboat State Rights, The, Crabbe (U. S.) 33, 20 Fed. Cas. No. 11,540..........i. 146
Ramsay *v.* People, 197 Ill. 572..........ii. 293; iii. 112
Ramuz *v.* Crowe, 11 Jur. 715..........ii. 375
Randall *v.* Hazelton, 12 Allen (Mass.) 412..........i. 415, 416
Randall *v.* Jacksonville, etc., R. Co., 19 Fla. 409..........i. 44
Randall *v.* Newson, 2 Q. B. D. 102..........i. 387
Randall *v.* Sanderson, 111 Mass. 114..........i. 208
Randell *v.* Trimen, 18 C. B. 786, 86 E. C. L. 786..........i. 406
Ranger *v.* Goodrich, 17 Wis. 78..........i. 277
Rann *v.* Hughes, 7 T. R. 346..........ii. 85, 142, 143, 174, 380
Rapier *v.* London Tramways Co., (1893) 2 Ch. 588..........i. 218
Rashdall *v.* Ford, L. R. 2 Eq. 750..........i. 395
Rasin *v.* Conley, 58 Md. 59..........i. 385
Ratcliffe *v.* Evans, (1892) 2 Q. B. 524..........i. 280, 321
Ratcliffe's Case, 3 Coke 38..........i. 267
Ravenga *v.* Mackintosh, 2 B. & C. 693, 9 E. C. L. 225..........i. 330, 331
Rawson *v.* Clark, 70 Ill. 656..........ii. 224
Rawson *v.* Johnson, 1 East 112..........ii. 139
Rawstron *v.* Taylor, 11 Exch. 369..........i. 198
Ray *v.* State Bank, 3 B. Mon. (Ky.) 510..........ii. 214
Ray *v.* Sweeney, 14 Bush (Ky.) 1..........i. 208
Raycroft *v.* Tayntor, 68 Vt. 219..........i. 366, 368
Raymond *v.* Fish, 51 Conn. 80..........i. 38
Read *v.* Friendly Soc., etc., (1902) 2 K. B. 88..........i. 345
Read *v.* Legard, 6 Exch. 636..........ii. 204
Read *v.* Nash, 1 Wils. C. Pl. 305..........ii. 185
Reade *v.* Johnson, Cro. Eliz. 242, 1 Leon. 155..........iii. 180

Reade *v.* Lamb, 6 Exch. 130....ii. 177
Reading *v.* Clarke, 4 B. & Ald. 268, 6 E. C. L. 479....iii. 185
Ream *v.* Watkins, 27 Mo. 516....ii. 222
Reardon *v.* Thompson, 149 Mass. 267....i. 156
Rearick *v.* Wilcox, 81 Ill. 77....i. 309
Rector *v.* Smith, 11 Iowa 302....i. 307
Reddaway *v.* Banham, (1896) A. C. 199....i. 429, 430, 432
Redgrave *v.* Hurd, 20 Ch. D. 1....i. 413, 414
Redway *v.* Gray, 31 Vt. 292....i. 277
Reece *v.* Taylor, 4 N. & M. 469, 30 E. C. L. 388....i. 7
Reech *v.* Kennegal, 1 Ves. 125....ii. 147
Reed *v.* Eldredge, 27 Cal. 347....ii. 207
Reed *v.* Harrison, 2 W. Bl. 1218....i. 46
Reed *v.* Ingraham, 3 Dall. (Pa.) 505....ii. 371
Reed *v.* Murphy, 1 Ga. 236....ii. 503, 504
Reed *v.* Roark, 14 Tex. 329....ii. 501
Reed *v.* Western Union Tel. Co., 135 Mo. 661....i. 100
Reedie *v.* London, etc., R. Co., 4 Exch. 244....ii. 472
Reese *v.* Harris, 27 Ala. 30....iii. 152
Reeves *v.* Hearne, 1 M. & W. 323....ii. 92
Reg. *v.* Cornish, Dears. 425....ii. 310
Reg. *v.* Cotesworth, 6 Mod. 172....i. 6
Reg. *v.* Daniel, 1 Salk. 380....i. 265
Reg. *v.* Eastern Counties R. Co., 10 M. & W. 58....i. 51
Reg. *v.* Heppinstale, 7 W. R. 178....i. 24
Reg. *v.* Labouchere, 14 Cox C. C. 419....i. 30
Reg. *v.* Poyser, 2 Den. C. C. 233....ii. 310
Reg. *v.* Pratt, 4 El. & Bl. 860, 82 E. C. L. 860....i. 22
Reg. *v.* Treasury Com'rs, L. R. 7 Q. B. 387....i. 36
Regnault *v.* Hunter, 4 W. Va. 257....iii. 143
Reif *v.* Paige, 55 Wis. 496....ii. 121
Relf *v.* Rapp, 3 W. & S. (Pa.) 21....i. 89
Renfro *v.* Prior, 25 Mo. App. 402....iii. 86
Reniger *v.* Fagossa, 1 Plowd. 1....ii. 179
Renner *v.* Canfield, 36 Minn. 90....i. 459
Rennyson's Appeal, 94 Pa. St. 147....i. 208
Respublica *v.* De Longchamps, 1 Dall. (Pa.) 114....i. 6
Respublica *v.* Sparhawk, 1 Dall. (Pa.) 357....i. 23
Reubens *v.* Joel, 13 N. Y. 488....iii. 58
Rex *v.* Abingdon, 1 Esp. 226....i. 307, 314
Rex *v.* Amphlitt, 4 B. & C. 35, 10 E. C. L. 275....i. 297
Rex *v.* Banks, R. & R. C. C. 441....ii. 309
Rex *v.* Brazier, R. & R. C. C. 337....ii. 310
Rex *v.* Carlile, 3 B. & Ald. 167, 5 E. C. L. 252....i. 309
Rex *v.* Cotton, Parker 121....iii. 292
Rex *v.* Creevey, 1 M. & S. 273....i. 307
Rex *v.* Dover, 6 How. St. Tr. 547....i. 298
Rex *v.* Fletcher, 4 C. & P. 545, 19 E. C. L. 519....ii. 310
Rex *v.* Hertford, 2 Show. 172....ii. 269
Rex *v.* Jones, 7 C. & P. 151, 32 E. C. L. 474....ii. 310

Rex *v.* Longnor, 4 B. & Ad. 467, 24 E. C. L. 131 .... ii. 475
Rex *v.* Madox, R. & R. C. C. 92 .... ii. 310
Rex *v.* Neil, 2 C. & P. 483, 12 E. C. L. 226 .... i. 221
Rex *v.* Pease, 4 B. & Ad. 30, 24 E. C. L. 17 .... i. 42
Rex *v.* Robinson, Cro. Eliz. 79 .... i. 376
Rex *v.* Rosewell, 2 Salk. 459 .... i. 215
Rex *v.* S. Asaph, 21 How. St. Tr. 1022 .... i. 77
Rex *v.* Salisbury, 1 Ld. Raym. 341 .... i. 309
Rex *v.* Walsh, 2 Leach C. C. 1054, 4 Taunt. 258 .... ii. 311
Rex *v.* Wright, 8 T. R. 293 .... i. 310
Reynell *v.* Lewis, 15 M. & W. 527 .... ii. 486
Reynell *v.* Sprye, 1 DeG. M. & G. 660 .... i. 412, 415
Reynolds *v.* Clarke, 2 Ld. Raym. 1402 .... iii. 253, 256
Reynolds *v.* Clarke, 1 Stra. 636 .... iii. 252
Reynolds *v.* Hussey, 64 N. H. 64 .... i. 53
Reynolds *v.* Nugent, 25 Ind. 328 .... ii. 113
Reynolds *v.* Phillips, 13 Ill. App. 557 .... i. 17
Reynolds *v.* Pinhowe, Cro. Eliz. 429 .... ii. 106
Reynolds *v.* Roberts, 57 Vt. 392 .... i. 385
Rhea *v.* White, 3 Head (Tenn.) 121 .... i. 490
Rheel *v.* Hicks, 25 N. Y. 289 .... ii. 211
Rhodes, *In re*, 44 Ch. D. 94, 107 .... ii. 204
Rice *v.* Manley, 66 N. Y. 82 .... i. 346
Rice *v.* Yocum, 155 Pa. St. 538 .... i. 239
Rich *v.* Basterfield, 4 C. B. 783, 56 E. C. L. 783 .... i. 223
Rich *v.* Kneeland, Hob. 17, Cro. Jac. 330 .... ii. 267, 300
Rich *v.* Lowenthal, 99 Ala. 487 .... iii. 218
Rich *v.* Pilkington, Carth. 171 .... i. 490
Richard *v.* Jenkins, 18 L. T. N. S. 437 .... i. 192
Richards *v.* Bartlet, 1 Leon. 19 .... ii. 90, 97, 99
Richards *v.* Tobert, 3 Houst. (Del.) 172 .... i. 27
Richardson *v.* Atkinson, 1 Stra. 576 .... i. 258
Richardson *v.* Dukes, 4 McCord L. (S. Car.) 156 .... i. 18
Richardson *v.* Duncan, 3 N. H. 508 .... ii. 229
Richardson *v.* Hardwick, 106 U. S. 255 .... ii. 53
Richardson *v.* Williamson, L. R. 6 Q. B. 276 .... i. 406
Richels *v.* State, 1 Sneed (Tenn.) 606 .... i. 12
Richmond *v.* Smith, 8 B. & C. 9, 15 E. C. L. 144 .... ii. 295
Richmond Second Nat. Bank *v.* Smith, 118 Wis. 18 .... ii. 541
Ricket *v.* Metropolitan R. Co., L. R. 2 H. L. 175 .... i. 229, 494
Riddle *v.* Welden, 5 Whart. (Pa.) 10 .... iii. 308
Ridley *v.* Mobile, etc., R. Co., 8 S. W. Rep. 606 .... i. 133
Rigaut *v.* Gallisard, 7 Mod. 78 .... i. 264
Riggs *v.* Bullingham, Cro. Eliz. 715 .... ii. 83
Right *v.* Cuthell, 5 East 491 .... ii. 488
Rigney *v.* Chicago, 102 Ill. 64 .... i. 44, 493
Riley *v.* Allen, 23 Fed. Rep. 46 .... i. 39
Rippy *v.* State, 2 Head (Tenn.) 217 .... i. 8
Ritenour *v.* Mathews, 42 Ind. 7 .... ii. 113
Roach *v.* Quick, 9 Wend. (N. Y.) 238 .... ii. 205

Roach *v.* Turk, 9 Heisk. (Tenn.) 708....i. 244
Robb *v.* Mann, 11 Pa. St. 300....ii. 120
Roberson *v.* Rochester Folding Box Co., 171 N. Y. 538....i. 319, 320
Roberts *v.* Eldridge, 1 Sprague (U. S.) 54....i. 39
Roberts *v.* Evans, 43 Cal. 380....iii. 198
Roberts *v.* Gwyrfai Dist. Council, (1899) 2 Ch. 608....i. 198
Roberts *v.* Roberts, 5 B. & S. 384, 117 E. C. L. 384....i. 279
Roberts *v.* Stuyvesant Safe Deposit Co., 123 N. Y. 57....ii. 291
Roberts *v.* Wyatt, 2 Taunt. 268....i. 254
Robertson *v.* Broadfoot, 11 U. C. Q. B. 407....ii. 74
Robertson *v.* Frank Brass Co., 132 U. S. 17....ii. 230
Robertson *v.* Kensington, 4 Taunt. 30....ii. 527
Robinson *v.* Bird, 158 Mass. 357....i. 254
Robinson *v.* Chamberlain, 34 N. Y. 389....i. 36
Robinson *v.* Jewett, 116 N. Y. 40....ii. 113
Robinson *v.* Jones, 4 L. R. Ir. 391....i. 297
Robinson *v.* McDonald, 2 Ga. 116....i. 239
Robinson *v.* State, 1 Coldw. (Tenn.) 120....iii. 241
Rock *v.* Rock, Yelv. 175....iii. 188
Rodgers *v.* Niles, 11 Ohio St. 48....i. 387
Roe *v.* Haugh, 12 Mod. 133, 1 Salk. 29....ii. 124
Rogers *v.* Barnes, 169 Mass. 179....i. 262
Rogers *v.* Clifton, 3 B. & P. 587....i. 311, 314
Rogers *v.* Dutton, 182 Mass. 187....i. 260
Rogers *v.* Elliot, 146 Mass. 349....i. 221
Rogers *v.* Greenbush, 57 Me. 441....iii. 199
Rogers *v.* Head, Cro. Jac. 262....ii. 267
Rogers *v.* Huie, 2 Cal. 571....i. 244
Rogers *v.* Imbleton, 2 B. & P. N. R. 117....i. 16; iii. 264
Rogers *v.* Rajendro Dutt, 8 Moo. Indian App. 103....i. 493
Rogers *v.* Rogers, 53 Conn. 121....i. 432
Rogers *v.* Rogers, 139 Mass. 440....ii. 128
Rogers *v.* Snow, Dalison 94....ii. 25, 135
Rogers *v.* Stephens, 2 T. R. 713....ii. 553
Rogers *v.* Taylor, 2 H. & N. 828....i. 193
Rogers *v.* Waite, 44 Me. 275....i. 7
Rokwood's Case, Cro. Eliz. 163....ii. 155
Romney Marsh *v.* Trinity House, L. R. 5 Exch. 204....i. 112
Rooke *v.* Rooke, Cro. Jac. 245....iii. 188
Rooney *v.* Sewall, etc., Cordage Co., 161 Mass. 153....i. 170
Roope *v.* D'Avigdor, 10 Q. B. D. 412....i. 495
Rooth *v.* Wilson, 1 B. & Ald. 59....ii. 315
Roscorla *v.* Thomas, 3 Q. B. 234, 43 E. C. L. 713....ii. 86, 87
Rose *v.* Des Moines Valley R. Co., 39 Iowa 246....ii. 50
Rose *v.* Hurley, 39 Ind. 77....i. 398
Rose *v.* Miles, 4 M. & S. 101....i. 226, 228
Rose *v.* Poulton, 2 B. & Ad. 828, 22 E. C. L. 193....iii. 123
Roseman *v.* Mahony, 86 N. Y. App. Div. 377....ii. 521
Rosewell *v.* Pryor, 6 Mod. 116....i. 207
Rosling *v.* Muggeridge, 16 M. & W. 181....ii. 131

Ross *v.* Butler, 19 N. J. Eq. 294 .... i. 218, 219, 220
Ross *v.* Fitch, 58 Tex. 148 .... i. 290
Ross *v.* Hill, 2 C. B. 877, 52 E. C. L. 877 .... ii. 264
Ross *v.* Johnson, 5 Burr. 2825 .... i. 237; iii. 169
Rossiter *v.* Minnesota Brandner-Smith Paper Co., 37 Minn. 296 ..... i. 334
Roswel *v.* Vaughan, Cro. Jac. 196 .... i. 378, 380
Rosyer *v.* Langdale, Style 248 .... ii. 77
Rotch *v.* Hawes, 12 Pick. (Mass.) 136 .... ii. 286
Rotherham, *In re,* 14 Ch. D. 585 .... i. 424
Rotherham Alum, etc., Co., *In re,* 25 Ch. D. 103 .... ii. 158
Rothholz *v.* Dunkle, 53 N. J. L. 438 .... i. 311
Roundtree *v.* Smith, 108 U. S. 269 .... ii. 223
Rowand *v.* De Camp, 96 Pa. St. 493 .... i. 309
Rowbotham *v.* Wilson, 8 H. L. Cas. 348 .... i. 191, 192, 194
Rowe *v.* Hawkins, 1 F & F. 91 .... i. 7
Rowell *v.* Lowell, 7 Gray (Mass.) 100 .... i. 123
Rowell *v.* Western Union Tel. Co., 75 Tex. 26 .... i. 471
Royal Aquarium, etc., Soc. *v.* Parkinson, (1892) 1 Q. B. 431 .... i. 315
Royal Baking Powder Co. *v.* Royal, 122 Fed. Rep. 337 .... i. 434
Rublee *v.* Davis, 33 Neb. 779 .... ii. 408
Ruff *v.* Jarrett, 94 Ill. 475 .... i. 414
Rumford Chemical Works *v.* Muth, 35 Fed. Rep. 524 .... i. 424
Rumsey *v.* New York, etc., R. Co., 133 N. Y. 79 .... i. 44
Rushworth *v.* Taylor, 3 Q. B. 699, 43 E. C. L. 932 .... i. 249
Russell *v.* Barrow, 7 Port. (Ala.) 106 .... i. 17
Russell *v.* Corne, 2 Ld. Raym. 1032 .... i. 264, 269
Russell *v.* Shenton, 3 Q. B. 449, 43 E. C. L. 814, 2 Gale & D. 573 .... i. 223
Russell *v.* Stewart, 44 Vt. 170 .... ii. 121
Russell *v.* Western Union Tel. Co., 3 Dak. 315 .... i. 467
Russell *v.* Western Union Tel. Co., 57 Kan. 230 .... i. 443
Ruter *v.* Foy, 46 Iowa 132 .... i. 181
Rutherford *v.* Paddock, 180 Mass. 293 .... i. 290
Rutland's Case, 6 Coke 52*b* .... i. 38
Ryalls *v.* Leader, L. R. 1 Exch. 296 .... i. 310
Ryan *v.* New York Cent. R. Co., 35 N. Y. 210 .... i. 116
Rylands *v.* Fletcher, L. R. 3 H. L. 330 .... i. 41, 62, 63

Sadler *v.* Henlock, 4 El. & Bl. 570, 578 .... ii. 468
Safe Deposit Co. *v.* Pollock, 85 Pa. St. 391 .... ii. 291
Sage *v.* Wilcox, 6 Conn. 81 .... ii. 179, 181
St. Albans Steamboat Co. *v.* Wilkins, 8 Vt. 54 .... ii. 225
St. Helen's Smelting Co. *v.* Tipping, 11 H. L. Cas. 642 ...... i. 219, 220, 221, 222
St. Ores *v.* McGlashen, 74 Cal. 148 .... i. 481
Salford *v.* Lever, (1891) 1 Q. B. 168 .... ii. 492
Salisbury *v.* Herchenroder, 106 Mass. 458 .... i. 173
Salisbury *v.* Keigher, 47 Minn. 367 .... iii. 86
Salter *v.* Butler, Noy 46 .... iii. 170
Salter *v.* Howard, 43 Ga. 601 .... i. 346
Salter *v.* Pearce, 4 Ala. 669 .... iii. 157

Saltonstall *v.* Gordon, 33 Ala. 149 .... i. 414
Salvin *v.* North Brancepeth Coal Co., L. R. 9 Ch. 713 .... i. 221
Sampson *v.* Smith, 15 Mass. 368 .... i. 39
Sanborn *v.* Goodhue, 28 N. H. 48 .... ii. 104
Sanders *v.* Palmer, 55 Fed. Rep. 217 .... i. 330
Sanders *v.* Spencer, 3 Dyer 266*b* .... ii. 294, 295
Sanders *v.* Stuart, 1 C. P. D. 326 .... i. 452
Sanderson *v.* Collman, 4 M. & G. 209, 43 E. C. L. 115 .... ii. 412
Saner *v.* Bilton, 7 Ch. D. 815 .... i. 33
Sanford *v.* Abrams, 24 Fla. 181 .... ii. 95
Sard *v.* Rhodes, 1 M. & W. 153 .... ii. 94, 100
Sargent *v.* Gile, 8 N. H. 325 .... i. 240
Sarrazin *v.* W. R. Irby Cigar, etc., Co., 93 Fed. Rep. 624 .... i. 422
Satterthwaite *v.* Dewhurst, 4 Dougl. 315, 26 E. C. L. 378 .... i. 269
Saunders *v.* Baxter, 6 Heisk. (Tenn.) 369 .... i. 298, 314
Saunders *v.* City, etc., R. Co., 99 Tenn. 130 .... i. 148
Saunders *v.* Jackson, 2 B. & P. 238 .... ii. 182
Saunders *v.* Mills, 6 Bing. 213, 19 E. C. L. 60 .... i. 309
Saunders *v.* Sun L. Assur. Co., (1894) 1 Ch. 537 .... i. 432
Saunders *v.* Wakefield, 4 B. & Ald. 595, 6 E. C. L. 616 .... ii. 180
Saunderson *v.* Baker, 3 Wils. C. Pl. 317 .... ii. 466
Saunderson *v.* Griffiths, 5 B. & C. 909, 12 E. C. L. 404 .... ii. 490
Saunderson *v.* Jackson, 2 B. & P. 238 .... ii. 501
Savage *v.* Gregg, 150 Ill. 161 .... iii. 86
Savage *v.* Stevens, 126 Mass. 207 .... i. 407
Savannah, etc., R. Co. *v.* Quo, 130 Ga. 125 .... i. 461
Savannah Nat. Bank *v.* Haskins, 101 Mass. 370 .... ii. 376
Saveland *v.* Green, 40 Wis. 431 .... i. 456
Savignac *v.* Roome, 6 T. R. 125 .... iii. 258, 262, 265
Savile *v.* Roberts, 1 Ld. Raym. 374 .... i. 329, 332, 372
Sawyer *v.* Corse, 17 Gratt. (Va.) 230 .... ii. 307
Sawyer *v.* Davis, 136 Mass. 239 .... i. 57
Sawyer *v.* Goodwin, 34 Me. 419 .... iii. 265
Saxlehner *v.* Apollinaris Co., (1897) 1 Ch. 900 .... i. 428
Saxlehner *v.* Eisner, etc., Co., 179 U. S. 19 .... i. 424
Scheffer *v.* Washington City, etc., R. Co., 105 U. S. 249 .... i. 118
Schelling *v.* Bischoff, 59 N. Y. Super. Ct. 562 .... i. 415
Schemerhorn *v.* Vanderheyden, 1 Johns. (N. Y.) 140 .... ii. 157
Schenck *v.* Schenck, 20 N. J. L. 208 .... i. 298
Schermerhorn *v.* Van Volkenburgh, 11 Johns. (N. Y.) 529 .... i. 252
Schilling *v.* Rominger, 4 Colo. 100 .... i. 201
Schlencker *v.* Moxsy, 3 B. & C. 789, 10 E. C. L. 227 .... iii. 123, 180
Schmidt *v.* Durnham, 46 Minn. 227 .... i. 464
Schneider *v.* Heath, 3 Campb. 506 .... i. 394
Schneider *v.* Heinsheimer, 26 Misc. (N. Y.) 11 .... ii. 75
Schneider *v.* Norris, 2 M. & S. 286 .... ii. 181
Schneider *v.* Williams, 44 N. J. Eq. 391 .... i. 423
Schnell *v.* Nell, 17 Ind. 29 .... ii. 69
Schoener *v.* Lissauer, 107 N. Y. 111 .... ii. 230
Scholey *v.* Halsey, 72 N. Y. 578 .... ii. 231

School Dist. No. 46 *v.* Lund, 51 Kan. 731 .... ii. 226
Schroeder *v.* Trubee, 35 Fed. Rep. 652 .... i. 386
Schultz *v.* Griffin, 121 N. Y. 294 .... ii. 485
Schwartz *v.* Wilmer, 90 Md. 137 .... ii. 542
Schwartzman *v.* Post, 94 N. Y. App. Div. 475 .... ii. 544
Schweider *v.* Lang, 29 Minn. 254 .... ii. 95
Scioto, The, 2 Ware (U. S.) 360, 21 Fed. Cas. No. 12,508 .... i. 146
Scotson *v.* Pegg, 6 H. & N. 295 .... ii. 68, 113, 116, 117, 119, 120
Scott *v.* Donald, 165 U. S. 58 .... i. 481
Scott *v.* Hix, 2 Sneed (Tenn.) 192 .... i. 384
Scott *v.* Hunter, 46 Pa. St. 192 .... i. 114
Scott *v.* London, etc., Docks Co., 3 H. & C. 596 .... i. 107
Scott *v.* M'Intosh, 2 Campb. 238 .... iii. 191
Scott *v.* Shelor, 28 Gratt. (Va.) 891 .... i. 331
Scott *v.* Shepherd, 2 W. Bl. 892, 3 Wils. C. Pl. 403 .... i. 79; iii. 257
Scott *v.* Stansfield, L. R. 3 Exch. 220 .... i. 37, 307
Scott *v.* Surman, Willes 405 .... ii. 478
Scranton *v.* Baxter, 4 Sandf. (N. Y.) 5 .... ii. 282
Scranton *v.* Clark, 39 N. Y. 220 .... i. 384
Scranton *v.* Phillip, 94 Pa. St. 15 .... i. 192
Scrimshire *v.* Alderton, 2 Stra. 1183 .... ii. 478
Scroggin *v.* Wood, 87 Iowa 497 .... i. 394
Scruggs *v.* Gibson, 40 Ga. 518 .... iii. 308
Scudder *v.* Union Nat. Bank, 91 U. S. 406 .... ii. 178
Seale *v.* Baker, 70 Tex. 283 .... i. 411
Seaman *v.* Cuppledick, Owen 150 .... i. 8
Seaman *v.* Netherclift, 2 C. P. D. 53 .... i. 307
Sears *v.* Lyons, 2 Stark. 317, 3 E. C. L. 426 .... i. 485
Seaver *v.* Dingley, 4 Me. 315 .... iii. 221
Secretary of State *v.* Kamachee Boye Sahaba, 13 Moo. P. C. 22 .... i. 37
Seeley *v.* Brush, 35 Conn. 419 .... i. 204
Seignior *v.* Wolmer, Godb. 361 .... ii. 453
Selby *v.* Carrier, Cro. Jac. 345 .... i. 282
Selser *v.* Roberts, 105 Pa. St. 242 .... i. 389, 391
Semple *v.* Pink, 1 Exch. 74 .... ii. 34
Senior *v.* Ward, 1 El. & El. 385, 102 E. C. L. 385 .... i. 164
Sepp *v.* McCann, 47 Minn. 364 .... iii. 86
Sesler *v.* Montgomery, 78 Cal. 486 .... i. 297
Settles *v.* Bond, 49 Ark. 114 .... iii. 219
Severin *v.* Keppel, 4 Esp. 156 .... i. 237
Sewell *v.* New York, etc., R. Co., 171 Mass. 302 .... i. 125
Sewell *v.* Webster, 59 N. H. 586 .... i. 178
Seymore *v.* Goodrich, 80 Va. 304 .... ii. 103
Seymour *v.* Butterworth, 3 F. & F. 372 .... i. 309
Seymour *v.* Greenwood, 7 H. & N. 355 .... ii. 470
Shackell *v.* Rosier, 2 Bing. N. Cas. 634, 29 E. C. L. 438 .... ii. 73
Shadwell *v.* Shadwell, 9 C. B. N. S. 159, 99 E. C. L. 159 .... ii. 113, 114
Shafer *v.* Ahalt, 48 Md. 171 .... i. 290
Shalmer *v.* Slingsby, Aleyn 17 .... iii. 137
Shannon *v.* Shannon, 1 Sch. & Lef. 324 .... iii. 218, 220, 221

Sharington *v.* Strotton, 1 Plowd. 298............ii. 19, 36, 37, 43, 44, 45
Sharp *v.* Powell, L. R. 7 C. P. 253............i. 104
Sharp *v.* Pratt, 3 C. & P. 34, 14 E. C. L. 197............i. 249
Sharpe *v.* Fowlkes, 7 Humph. (Tenn.) 512............iii. 142
Sharrod *v.* London, etc., R. Co., 4 Exch. 581........ii. 456, 459; iii. 260
Shattuck *v.* Green, 104 Mass. 42............i. 385
Shaw *v.* Boston, etc., R. Co., 159 Mass. 597............i. 229
Shaw *v.* Railroad Co., 101 U. S. 557............ii. 408, 500
Shaw *v.* Smith, 150 Mass. 166............ii. 514
Shea *v.* Milford, 145 Mass. 525............i. 242
Sheehan, etc., Transp. Co. *v.* Sims, 28 Mo. App. 64............ii. 207
Sheffill *v.* Van Deusen, 13 Gray (Mass.) 304............i. 296
Shelden *v.* Hentley, 2 Show. 161............ii. 370, 371, 394
Shelton *v.* Jackson, 20 Tex. Civ. App. 443............ii. 102
Shepard *v.* Chicago, etc., R. Co., 77 Iowa 58............i. 460
Shepard *v.* Milwaukee Gas Light Co., 6 Wis. 539............i. 186
Shepherd *v.* Kain, 5 B. & Ald. 240, 7 E. C. L. 82............i. 383
Sheppard *v.* Furniss, 19 Ala. 760............iii. 265
Sheppard *v.* Shoolbred, C. & M. 61, 41 E. C. L. 39............i. 259
Sheridan *v.* Furbur, Blatchf. & H. Adm. 423............i. 40
Sherley *v.* Riggs, 11 Humph. (Tenn.) 53............i. 341
Sherman *v.* Elder, 24 N. Y. 381............iii. 87
Sherman *v.* Rawson, 102 Mass. 395............i. 272, 464
Sherrington's Case, Savile 40............iii. 71
Sherry *v.* Perkins, 147 Mass. 212............i. 365
Shiells *v.* Blackburne, 1 H. Bl. 158............ii. 279
Shingleur *v.* Western Union Tel. Co., 72 Miss. 1030............i. 456
Shipman *v.* State Bank, 126 N. Y. 318............ii. 512, 513
Shippen *v.* Bowen, 122 U. S. 581............i. 386
Shipwick *v.* Blanchard, 6 T. R. 298............i. 236; iii. 171
Shoemaker *v.* Keeley, 1 Yeates (Pa.) 245............iii. 87
Short *v.* Lovejoy, cited in Bull. N. P. 16............i. 9
Short *v.* Stotts, 58 Ind. 29............ii. 190
Shrewsbury's Case, 5 Coke 13*b*............i. 30; iii. 242
Shurtleff *v.* Parker, 130 Mass. 293............i. 290
Shurtleff *v.* Stevens, 51 Vt. 501............i. 311
Shuttleworth *v.* Garrett, Comb. 151............iii. 180
Shutts *v.* Fingar, 100 N. Y. 539............ii. 545
Sibley *v.* Aldrich, 33 N. H. 553............ii. 296, 297
Sibree *v.* Tripp, 15 M. & W. 23............ii. 94, 100
Sidenham *v.* Worlington, 2 Leon. 224............ii. 60, 84, 86
Sigourney *v.* Lloyd, 8 B. & C. 622, 15 E. C. L. 319, 3 M. & R. 58....ii. 399
Sillars *v.* Collier, 151 Mass. 50............i. 299
Silvers *v.* Reynolds, 17 N. J. L. 275............ii. 102
Simar *v.* Canaday, 53 N. Y. 298............i. 395
Simmonds, *Ex p.*, 16 Q. B. D. 308............ii. 214
Simmonds *v.* Parminter, 1 Wils. C. Pl. 185............iii. 140
Simmons *v.* Lillystone, 8 Exch. 431............i. 241
Simmons *v.* More, 100 N. Y. 140............i. 406
Simon *v.* Metivier, 1 W. Bl. 599, 3 Burr. 1921, Bull. N. P. 280......ii. 175

Simpson v. Hartopp, Willes 512....iii. 304, 306
Simpson v. McFarland, 18 Pick. (Mass.) 427....iii. 221
Simpson v. Moore, 5 Lea (Tenn.) 372....ii. 244
Simpson v. State, 59 Ala. 1....i. 69
Simson v. Brown, 68 N. Y. 355....ii. 159
Sinclair v. Bowles, 9 B. & C. 92, 17 E. C. L. 340....ii. 225
Sinclair v. Hathaway, 57 Mich. 60....i. 388
Singer v. Schilling, 74 Wis. 369....i. 414
Singleton v. Bolton, 3 Dougl. 293, 26 E. C. L. 114....i. 419
Sioux City, etc., R. Co. v. Stout, 17 Wall. (U. S.) 657....i. 160
Sippora v. Basset, 1 Sid. 225....i. 269
Six Carpenters Case, 8 Coke 146....i. 46, 47; ii. 203; iii. 187, 242, 295
Skinner v. Gunton, 1 Saund. 230....i. 329
Skinner v. London, etc., R. Co., 5 Exch. 787....i. 108
Skipp v. Eastern Counties R. Co., 9 Exch. 223....i. 164
Skowhegan First Nat. Bank v. Maxwell, 83 Me. 576....i. 415
Skyring v. Greenwood, 4 B. & C. 281, 10 E. C. L. 335....ii. 213
Slack v. Bowsal, Cro. Jac. 668....iii. 180
Slade v. Mutrie, 156 Mass. 19....ii. 101
Slade's Case, 4 Coke 92....ii. 60, 62, 63, 64, 160; iii. 68, 138, 178, 184
Slater v. Jones, L. R. 8 Exch. 186....ii. 94
Slater v. Swann, 2 Stra. 872....i. 17
Slaughter v. Gerson, 13 Wall. (U. S.) 379....i. 413
Sleath v. Wilson, 9 C. & P. 607, 38 E. C. L. 249....ii. 456, 469
Sloan v. McCarty, 134 Mass. 245....ii. 507
Sloane v. Southern California R. Co., 111 Cal. 668....i. 460
Slone v. Slone, 2 Met. (Ky.) 339....i. 7
Smale v. Hammon, 1 Bulst. 40....i. 283
Smalley v. Greene, 52 Iowa 241....ii. 176
Smart v. Sandars, 5 C. B. 895, 57 E. C. L. 895....ii. 492
Smart v. Wolff, 3 T. R. 348....ii. 332
Smeed v. Foord, 1 El. & El. 602, 102 E. C. L. 602....i. 447, 449
Smith v. Airey, 2 Ld. Raym. 1034, 6 Mod. 128, Holt K. B. 329....ii. 165; iii. 185
Smith v. Baker, (1891) A. C. 325....i. 163, 166, 169
Smith v. Ballou, 1 R. I. 496....ii. 103
Smith v. Chadwick, 9 App. Cas. 187....i. 399, 413
Smith v. Chadwick, 20 Ch. D. 27....i. 396
Smith v. Clarke, Peake N. P. (ed. 1795) 225....ii. 514, 527
Smith v. Easton, 54 Md. 138....i. 456
Smith v. Emery, 12 N. J. L. 53....iii. 122
Smith v. Fairbanks, 27 N. H. 521....i. 385
Smith v. Follansbee, 13 Me. 273....i. 32
Smith v. Foran, 43 Conn. 244....ii. 240
Smith v. Harrison, 33 Ala. 706....ii. 207
Smith v. Hays, 23 Ill. App. 244....i. 60
Smith v. Holcomb, 99 Mass. 552....i. 487
Smith v. Houston, 16 Ala. 111....ii. 217
Smith v. Howard, 28 Iowa 51....i. 308
Smith v. Jones, Owen 133, Yelv. 184....ii. 34, 77

Smith *v.* Kay, 7 H. L. Cas. 775 ... i. 414
Smith *v.* Kendall, 6 T. R. 123 ... ii. 387, 504
Smith *v.* Kennett, 18 Mo. 154 ... iii. 87
Smith *v.* Land, etc., Property Corp., 28 Ch. D. 15 ... i. 395
Smith *v.* London, etc., Docks Co., L. R. 3 C. P. 326 ... i. 152
Smith *v.* London, etc., R. Co., L. R. 6 C. P. 14 ... i. 102
Smith *v.* Lowell First Cong. Meetinghouse, 8 Pick. (Mass.) 178 ... ii. 200
Smith *v.* Matthews, 152 N. Y. 152 ... i. 481
Smith *v.* Mattingly, 96 Ky. 228 ... i. 32
Smith *v.* Mercer, 6 Taunt. 76, 1 E. C. L. 312 ... ii. 213
Smith *v.* People, 141 Ill. 447 ... i. 172
Smith *v.* Richardson, Willes 24 ... i. 317
Smith *v.* Shephard, Cro. Eliz. 710 ... ii. 465
Smith *v.* Smith, 110 Mass. 302 ... iii. 232
Smith *v.* Smith, 73 Mich. 445 ... i. 294
Smith *v.* Spooner, 3 Taunt. 246 ... i. 323
Smith *v.* Thompson, 94 Mich. 381 ... iii. 87
Smith *v.* Tripp, 13 R. I. 153 ... i. 129
Smith *v.* Utley, 92 Wis. 133 ... i. 298
Smith *v.* Weguelin, L. R. 8 Eq. 198 ... i. 37
Smith *v.* Westall, 1 Ld. Raym. 317 ... ii. 193
Smith *v.* Western Union Tel. Co., 83 Ky. 104 ... i. 450
Smith *v.* Woodfine, 1 C. B. N. S. 660, 87 E. C. L. 660 ... i. 464
Smith *v.* Young, 1 Campb. 439 ... i. 236
Smyth *v.* Tankersley, 20 Ala. 212 ... i. 46
Smythe *v.* U. S., 188 U. S. 156 ... ii. 293; iii. 112
Snag *v.* Gee, 4 Coke 16 ... i. 282
Sneed *v.* Coleman, 7 Gratt. (Va.) 200 ... ii. 148
Sneeden *v.* Harris, 109 N. Car. 357 ... i. 334
Sneesby *v.* Lancashire, etc., R. Co., L. R. 9 Q. B. 263, 1 Q. B. D. 42 ... i. 88, 112
Snow *v.* Peacock, 3 Bing. 444, 13 E. C. L. 44 ... ii. 406
Soane *v.* Knight, M. & M. 74, 22 E. C. L. 255 ... i. 305
Soane *v.* Knight, M. & M. 187 ... i. 304
Sollers *v.* Lawrence, Willes 413, 421 ... iii. 60
Solomons *v.* Bank of England, 13 East 135 ... ii. 405
Soltau *v.* De Held, 2 Sim. N. S. 133 ... i. 221
Solverson *v.* Peterson, 64 Wis. 198 ... i. 294
Some *v.* Barwish, Cro. Jac. 231 ... iii. 271
Somerville *v.* Hawkins, 10 C. B. 583, 70 E. C. L. 583 ... i. 311
Soprani *v.* Skurro, Yelv. 18 ... iii. 123
So Relle *v.* Western Union Tel. Co., 55 Tex. 308 ... i. 466
Southampton *v.* Brown, 6 B. & C. 718, 13 E. C. L. 303 ... iii. 122
Southby *v.* Wiseman, 3 Keb. 625 ... ii. 453
Southcote *v.* Stanley, 1 H. & N. 247 ... i. 157
Southcote's Case, 4 Coke 83*b* ... ii. 257, 259, 261, 263, 266, 283, 299
Southcott *v.* Bennett, 13 Harv. L. Rev. 43 ... ii. 263
Southern *v.* How, Popham 144 ... i. 418
Southern *v.* How, 2 Rolle 5, 26 ... ii. 449
Southern R. Co. *v.* Pugh, 97 Tenn. 624 ... i. 148

South, etc., Alabama R. Co. *v.* Donovan, 84 Ala. 141................i. 155
South Hetton Coal Co. *v.* North-Eastern News Assoc., 1 Q. B. 143..i. 303
South Wales Miners' Federation *v.* Glamorgan Coal Co., (1905) A. C. 239 ....i. 345
Southwick *v.* Memphis First Nat. Bank, 84 N. Y. 420..............ii. 212
Spade *v.* Lynn, etc., R. Co., 168 Mass. 285..........................i. 458
Spalding *v.* Oakes, 42 Vt. 343...i. 490
Speake *v.* Richards, Hob. 206, pl. 260, 1 Rolle Abr. 598, pl. 17......iii. 133
Spencer *v.* Parry, 3 Ad. & El. 331, 30 E. C. L. 107..................ii. 233
Spinula *v.* Camby, 22 Zeitschrift fuer Handelsrecht 22............ii. 341
Spokane Truck, etc., Co. *v.* Hoefer, 2 Wash. 45.....................i. 481
Spooner *v.* Delaware, etc., R. Co., 115 N. Y. 34.....................i. 133
Spooner *v.* Manchester, 133 Mass. 270...............................ii. 286
Sprat *v.* Agar, referred to in 1 Vent. 6.............................ii. 153
Springfield *v.* Harris, 4 Allen (Mass.) 494..........................i. 200
Springwell *v.* Allen, 2 East 448, *note,* Aleyn 91.....................i. 382
Spurraway *v.* Rogers, 12 Mod. 517....................................iii. 105
Squire *v.* Grevett, 2 Ld. Raym. 961...................................iii. 192
Squire *v.* Western Union Tel. Co., 98 Mass. 232..............i. 450, 456
Squire's Case, Jenk. 350...i. 282
Stacker *v.* Hewitt, 2 Ill. 207..ii. 504
Stainback *v.* Rae, 14 How. (U. S.) 532...............................i. 145
Stamey *v.* Western Union Tel. Co., 92 Ga. 613.......................i. 443
Stamper *v.* Temple, 6 Humph. (Tenn.) 113.........................ii. 82
Standard Oil Co. *v.* Doyle, 82 S. W. Rep. 271..................i. 366, 367
Stanley *v.* Jones, 7 Bing. 369, 20 E. C. L. 165........................ii. 164
Stanley *v.* Powell, (1891) 1 Q. B. 86..................................i. 82
Stannard *v.* Whittlesey, 9 Conn. 556................................iii. 111
Stansell *v.* Western Union Tel. Co., 107 Fed. Rep. 668.............i. 454
Stanton *v.* Metropolitan R. Co., 14 Allen (Mass.) 485..............i. 179
Stapleton's Case, 29 Edw. III..i. 183
Star *v.* Rookesby, 1 Salk. 335...i. 184
Stark *v.* Parker, 2 Pick. (Mass.) 267..................................ii. 227
Starke *v.* Cheesman, Carth. 509.......................................ii. 379
Starke *v.* Cheeseman, 1 Ld. Raym. 538..............................iii. 140
Starkey *v.* Bank of England, (1903) A. C. 114.......................i. 406
Starkey *v.* Mill, Style 296...ii. 155
State *v.* Avery, 7 Conn. 266...i. 296
State *v.* Balch, 31 Kan. 465...i. 309
State *v.* Bartlett, 170 Mo. 658..i. 8
State *v.* Brady, 44 Kan. 435...i. 294
State *v.* Burnham, 9 N. H. 34..i. 314
State *v.* Copeland, 96 Tenn. 296...ii. 293
State *v.* Fairclough, 29 Conn. 47.......................................iii. 241
State *v.* Gramm, 7 Wyo. 329..ii. 293
State *v.* Grinstead, 10 Kan. App. 78.....................................i. 309
State *v.* Holcomb, 68 Iowa 107..i. 206
State *v.* Houston, 78 Ala. 576...ii. 293
State *v.* Lanier, 31 La. Ann. 423..ii. 293
State *v.* Lonsdale, 48 Wis. 348..i. 311

State *v.* Louisville, etc., R. Co., 86 Ind. 114........................i. 44
State *v.* Moore, 31 Conn. 479..i. 69
State *v.* Pendergrass, 2 Dev. & B. L. (19 N. Car.) 365.................i. 39
State *v.* Sears, 86 Mo. 169..i. 12
State *v.* Shepard, 10 Iowa 126...i. 12
State *v.* Stockford, 77 Conn. 227......................................i. 367
State Bank *v.* Soloman, 84 N. Y. Supp. 976............................ii. 541
State University *v.* Keller, 1 Ala. 406...............................ii. 214
Staub *v.* Van Benthuysen, 36 La. Ann. 467..............................i. 299
Steamboat New World, The, *v.* King, 16 How. (U. S.) 474................i. 100
Stearns *v.* Sampson, 59 Me. 568..i. 11
Stebbins *v.* Palmer, 1 Pick. (Mass.) 71...........................i. 464, 465
Steele *v.* Burkhardt, 104 Mass. 59................................i. 176, 180
Steele *v.* McKinlay, 5 App. Cas. 754..................................ii. 549
Steiglitz *v.* Egginton, Holt 141, 3 E. C. L. 63........................ii. 474
Stein *v.* Hauck, 56 Ind. 65...i. 208
Steinmetz *v.* Kelly, 72 Ind. 442..i. 181
Stephen *v.* Myers, 4 C. & P. 349, 19 E. C. L. 414......................i. 11
Stephens *v.* Baird, 9 Cow. (N. Y.) 274.................................ii. 242
Stephens *v.* Elwall, 4 M. & S. 249.....................................i. 243
Stephenson *v.* Hart, 4 Bing. 476...................................i. 248, 260
Stephenson *v.* Little, 10 Mich. 433....................................i. 252
Sterling *v.* Jackson, 69 Mich. 488......................................i. 21
Stetson *v.* Faxon, 19 Pick. (Mass.) 147.................................i. 227
Stevens *v.* Dudley, 56 Vt. 158......................................i. 89, 113
Stevens *v.* Fassett, 27 Me. 280...i. 39
Stevens *v.* Fitch, 11 Met. (Mass.) 248.................................ii. 231
Stevens *v.* Lynch, 12 East 38..ii. 214
Stevens *v.* Rainwater, 4 Mo. App. 292...................................i. 398
Stevens *v.* Rose, 69 Mich. 259.................................i. 31; iii. 270
Stevens *v.* Sampson, 5 Ex. D. 55..i. 314
Stevens *v.* Stevens, 11 Met. (Mass.) 251................................i. 202
Stevenson *v.* Belknap, 6 Iowa 103.......................................i. 461
Stevenson *v.* Newnham, 13 C. B. 297, 76 E. C. L. 297...................i. 355
Stevenson *v.* Wallace, 27 Gratt. (Va.) 77..............................i. 195
Steward *v.* Gromett, 7 C. B. N. S. 191, 97 E. C. L. 191................i. 329
Stewart *v.* Casey, (1892) 1 Ch. 115....................................ii. 85
Stewart *v.* Houston, etc., R. Co., 62 Tex. 246........................iii. 88
Stewart *v.* Maddox, 63 Ind. 51..i. 460
Stewart *v.* Sonneborn, 98 U. S. 187...............................i. 331, 332
Stewart *v.* Swift Specific Co., 76 Ga. 280..............................i. 294
Stewart *v.* Wyoming Cattle Ranche Co., 128 U. S. 388..............i. 394, 399
Stilk *v.* Myrick, 2 Campb. 317...ii. 75
Stock *v.* Mawson, 1 B. & P. 290...i. 105
Stockdale *v.* Hansard, 9 Ad. & El. 1, 36 E. C. L. 13....................i. 311
Stockport Waterworks Co. *v.* Potter, 7 H. & N. 167......................i. 218
Stone *v.* Boston, etc., R. Co., 7 Gray (Mass.) 539....................iii. 86
Stone *v.* Hooker, 9 Cow. (N. Y.) 154...................................ii. 74
Stone *v.* Marsh, 6 B. & C. 551, 13 E. C. L. 249.........................i. 495
Stone *v.* Withipool, Latch 21..ii. 147

Stone *v.* Wythipol, Cro. Eliz. 126 .... ii. 68, 77
Stonehouse *v.* Bodvil, T. Raym. 67 .... ii. 47
Storey *v.* Wallace, 60 Ill. 51 .... i. 298
Stoudenmeier *v.* Williamson, 29 Ala. 558 .... ii. 128
Strafford *v.* Pell, Clayton 151, pl. 276 .... iii. 168
Strangborough *v.* Warner, 4 Leon. 3 .... ii. 55
Stratton *v.* Dole, 45 Neb. 472 .... i. 464
Stratton *v.* Hill, 3 Price 253 .... iii. 142
Stretch *v.* Parker, 1 Rolle Abr. 22, pl. 20 .... i. 463
Strickland *v.* Henry, 66 N. Y. App. Div. 23 .... ii. 522, 530
Strickler *v.* Todd, 10 S. & R. (Pa.) 63 .... i. 202
Stronge *v.* Watts, 1 Rolle Abr. 518, pl. 2 .... iii. 120
Stroyan *v.* Knowles, 6 H. & N. 454 .... i. 192, 193, 197
Struthers *v.* Dunkirk, etc., R. Co., 87 Pa. St. 282 .... i. 43, 44
Stuart *v.* Bell, (1891) 2 Q. B. 341 .... i. 312
Stuart *v.* F. G. Stewart Co., 91 Fed. Rep. 423 .... i. 431
Stuart *v.* Lander, 16 Cal. 372 .... ii. 207
Stuart *v.* Sears, 119 Mass. 143 .... ii. 211
Stuart *v.* Western Union Tel. Co., 66 Tex. 580 .... i. 466, 471
Stuart *v.* Wilkins, 1 Dougl. 18 .... i. 389, 390
Stucley *v.* Ballard, 4 Coke 16 .... i. 282
Sturlyn *v.* Albany, Cro. Eliz. 67 .... ii. 70
Sturton *v.* Richardson, 13 M. & W. 17 .... iii. 110, 111
Stye *v.* Mordant, 1 Rolle Abr. 104, pl. 7 .... iii. 272
Suit of Court and Services, 3 Salk. 332 .... iii. 297
Sullivan *v.* Boston, etc., R. Co., 156 Mass. 378 .... i. 155
Sullivan *v.* Creed, 2 Ir. R. 317 .... i. 58
Sullivan *v.* Strathan-Hutton-Evans Commission Co., 152 Mo. 268 .... i. 315
Sullivan *v.* Zenier, 98 Cal. 346 .... i. 106
Summerfield *v.* Western Union Tel. Co., 87 Wis. 1 .... i. 467
Summit, Schooner, The, 2 Curt. (U. S.) 150 .... i. 146
Sunderlin *v.* Bradstreet, 46 N. Y. 188 .... i. 311
Surocco *v.* Geary, 3 Cal. 69 .... i. 23
Sury *v.* Pigot, Popham 170 .... i. 206
Susquehanna Fertilizer Co. *v.* Malone, 73 Md. 268 .... i. 220
Sutton *v.* Bonnett, 114 Ind. 243 .... i. 83
Sutton *v.* Grey, (1894) 1 Q. B. 288 .... ii. 183
Sutton *v.* Tatham, 10 Ad. & El. 27, 37 E. C. L. 25 .... ii. 485
Sutton *v.* Wauwatosa, 29 Wis. 21 .... i. 178
Swan *v.* Tapping, 5 Cush. (Mass.) 104 .... i. 324
Swansborough *v.* Coventry, 9 Bing. 305, 23 E. C. L. 286 .... i. 207
Swasey *v.* Little, 7 Pick. (Mass.) 299 .... ii. 148
Swatman *v.* Ambler, 8 Exch. 72 .... iii. 122
Swett *v.* Shumway, 102 Mass. 365 .... i. 388
Swift, *In re*, 106 Fed. Rep. 65 .... ii. 538, 542
Swift *v.* Pierce, 13 Allen (Mass.) 136 .... ii. 186
Swift *v.* Tyson, 16 Pet. (U. S.) 1 .... ii. 408, 522
Swift, etc., Co. *v.* U. S., 111 U. S. 22 .... ii. 231
Swim *v.* Wilson, 90 Cal. 126 .... i. 244
Swindon Waterworks Co. *v.* Wilts, etc., Canal Nav. Co., L. R. 7 H. L. 697 .... i. 200

Swire *v.* Leach, 18 C. B. N. S. 479, 114 E. C. L. 479................iii. 306
Syeds *v.* Hay, 4 T. R. 260..i. 248
Sykes *v.* Lawlor, 49 Cal. 236.......................................i. 268
Sykes *v.* Sykes, 3 B. & C. 541, 10 E. C. L. 176.....................i. 419
Sykes *v.* Walls, 3 Keb. 282...iii. 168
Symmes *v.* Frazier, 6 Mass. 344.....................................ii. 82
Symons *v.* Darknoll, Palmer 523.....................................ii. 300

Tabor *v.* Hutson, 5 Ind. 322..i. 481
Tabor *v.* Peters, 74 Ala. 96...i. 386
Talbot *v.* Stemmons, 89 Ky. 222.....................................ii. 72, 76
Tally *v.* Ayres, 3 Sneed (Tenn.) 681.................................i. 83
Talmage *v.* Smith, 101 Mich. 370....................................i. 5
Tapley *v.* Butterfield, 1 Met. (Mass.) 515...........................ii. 474
Tapling *v.* Jones, 11 H. L. Cas. 290.................................i. 209
Tarleton *v.* M'Gawley, Peake N. P. (ed. 1795) 207...................i. 346, 352
Tarlton *v.* Fisher, 2 Dougl. 671.....................................i. 38
Tarry *v.* Ashton, 1 Q. B. D. 314.....................................i. 154
Tate *v.* Bates, 118 N. Car. 287......................................i. 411
Tatlock *v.* Harris, 3 T. R. 180......................................ii. 124
Taylor *v.* Bowers, 1 Q. B. D. 291....................................ii. 223
Taylor *v.* Dobbins, 1 Stra. 399......................................ii. 501
Taylor *v.* Doremus, 16 N. J. L. 473..................................i. 37
Taylor *v.* Hall, 2 Stra. 1189..i. 279
Taylor *v.* Hare, 1 B. & P. N. R. 260.................................ii. 213
Taylor *v.* Hilary, 1 C. M. & R. 741, 5 Tyrw. 373.....................ii. 126
Taylor *v.* Jaques, 106 Mass. 291.....................................ii. 229
Taylor *v.* Jones, 42 N. H. 25..i. 46
Taylor *v.* Lambertville, 43 N. J. Eq. 107............................ii. 203
Taylor *v.* Manners, L. R. 1 Ch. 48...................................ii. 71
Taylor *v.* Markham, Cro. Jac. 224....................................i. 8
Taylor *v.* Perkins, Cro. Jac. 144, 1 Rolle Abr. 4, pl. 4.............i. 277, 283
Taylor *v.* Rainbow, 2 Hen. & M. (Va.) 423............................i. 190; iii. 259
Taylor *v.* Whitehead, 2 Dougl. 745...................................i. 23
Teague *v.* Irwin, 127 Mass. 217......................................i. 407
Telephone Mfg. Co. *v.* Sumter Telephone Mfg. Co., 63 S. Car. 313...i. 424
Temperton *v.* Russell, (1893) 1 Q. B. 715............................i. 344
Tenant *v.* Goldwin, 6 Mod. 314.......................................i. 215
Tenant *v.* Goldwin, 1 Salk. 360, 2 Ld. Raym. 1089....................i. 289, 203
Tennessee Chemical Co. *v.* Henry, 85 S. W. Rep. 401..................i. 157
Tennessee Coal, etc., Co. *v.* Hamilton, 100 Ala. 252.................i. 203
Tercese *v.* Geray, Finch 301...ii. 376
Terre Haute, etc., R. Co. *v.* Graham, 95 Ind. 287.....................i. 181
Terry *v.* Fellows, 21 La. Ann. 375...................................i. 310
Terry *v.* Hooper, 1 Lev. 115...i. 282
Terry *v.* Munger, 121 N. Y. 101......................................ii. 219
Tewkesbury *v.* Bennett, 31 Iowa 83...................................i. 386
Thain *v.* Old Colony R. Co., 161 Mass. 353...........................i. 170
Thayer *v.* Hutchinson, 13 Vt. 504....................................i. 252
Thayer *v.* Wadsworth, 19 Pick. (Mass.) 349...........................ii. 225, 227

Thicknesse *v.* Bromilow, 2 Cromp. & J. 425 .... ii. 412
Thomas *v.* Churton, 2 B. & S. 475, 110 E. C. L. 475 .... i. 37
Thomas *v.* Cook, 8 B. & C. 728, 15 E. C. L. 333 .... ii. 186, 187
Thomas *v.* Heathorn, 2 B. & C. 477, 9 E. C. L. 152 .... ii. 104
Thomas *v.* Quartermaine, 18 Q. B. D. 685 .... i. 165, 166, 169, 170
Thomas *v.* Sylvester, L. R. 8 Q. B. 368 .... iii. 134
Thomas *v.* Thomas, 5 Exch. 28 .... iii. 110, 191
Thomas *v.* Thomas, 2 Q. B. 851, 42 E. C. L. 945 .... ii. 72
Thomas *v.* Winchester, 6 N. Y. 409 .... i. 60
Thomason *v.* Gray, 82 Ala. 291 .... i. 7
Thompson *v.* Banks, 43 N. H. 540 .... iii. 198
Thompson *v.* Beacon Valley Rubber Co., 56 Conn. 493 .... i. 330
Thompson *v.* Button, 14 Johns. (N. Y.) 84 .... iii. 219
Thompson *v.* Cumming, 2 Leigh (Va.) 321 .... ii. 554
Thompson *v.* Howard, 31 Mich. 309 .... ii. 217
Thompson *v.* Montgomery, 41 Ch. D. 35 .... i. 422
Thompson *v.* Perrine, 106 U. S. 593 .... ii. 371
Thompson *v.* Rose, 16 Conn. 71 .... i. 415
Thompson *v.* Shackell, M. & M. 187, 22 E. C. L. 286 .... i. 304
Thomson *v.* Davenport, 9 B. & C. 78, 17 E. C. L. 335 .... ii. 479
Thorley *v.* Kerry, 4 Taunt. 355 .... i. 293
Thorley's Cattle Food Co. *v.* Massam, 14 Ch. D. 763 .... i. 324
Thorn *v.* Knapp, 42 N. Y. 474 .... i. 464, 465
Thorne *v.* Deas, 4 Johns. (N. Y.) 84 .... i. 187; ii. 49
Thorns, Case of, 6 Edw. IV .... i. 21
Thorogood *v.* Bryan, 1 C. B. 115, 65 E. C. L. 115 .... i. 141
Thorp *v.* Burling, 11 Johns. (N. Y.) 285 .... i. 243
Thorp *v.* Thorp, 12 Mod. 455 .... ii. 134, 137
Thrall *v.* Lathrop, 30 Vt. 307 .... i. 239
Thursby *v.* Plant, 1 Sid. 401 .... iii. 134
Thursby *v.* Warren, W. Jones 208 .... iii. 186
Thurston *v.* Blanchard, 22 Pick. (Mass.) 18 .... i. 258
Thurston *v.* Hancock, 12 Mass. 220 .... i. 194, 197
Thweatt *v.* Jones, 1 Rand. (Va.) 328 .... i. 490
Tiffany *v.* Anderson, 55 Iowa 405 .... ii. 248
Tighe *v.* Morrison, 116 N. Y. 263 .... ii. 187
Tillett *v.* Ward, 10 Q. B. D. 17 .... i. 53
Tillinghast *v.* McLeod, 17 R. I. 208 .... i. 314
Tillinghast *v.* Merrill, 151 N. Y. 135 .... ii. 293
Tillson *v.* Robbins, 68 Me. 295 .... i. 294
Tilton *v.* Alcott, 16 Barb. (N. Y.) 598 .... ii. 95
Tilton *v.* Beecher, 59 N. Y. 176 .... i. 301
Tindal *v.* Brown, 1 T. R. 167 .... ii. 387, 540
Tinkler *v.* Poole, 5 Burr. 2657 .... iii. 171
Tithes, Case of, 21 Hen. VII .... i. 20
Tobin *v.* Western Union Tel. Co., 146 Pa. St. 375 .... i. 441, 442
Todd *v.* Dun, 15 Ont. App. 85 .... i. 311
Todd *v.* Flight, 9 C. B. N. S. 377, 99 E. C. L. 377 .... i. 223
Todd *v.* Hawkins, 8 C. & P. 88, 34 E. C. L. 304 .... i. 311
Todd *v.* Old Colony, etc., R. Co., 3 Allen (Mass.) 18 .... ii. 50

Toledo, etc., R. Co. *v.* Chew, 67 Ill. 378......iii. 198
Toledo, etc., R. Co. *v.* Pennsylvania Co., 54 Fed. Rep. 730......i. 366
Tolman *v.* American Nat. Bank, 22 R. I. 462......ii. 520
Tomkins *v.* Willshear, 5 Taunt. 431, 1 E. C. L. 145, 1 Marsh. 115...iii. 191
Tonawanda R. Co. *v.* Munger, 5 Den. (N. Y.) 267......i. 52
Toogood *v.* Spyring, 1 C. M. & R. 181......i. 315
Tooley *v.* Windham, Cro. Eliz. 206......ii. 77
Toothaker *v.* Conant, 91 Me. 438......i. 315
Tootle *v.* Clifton, 22 Ohio St. 247......i. 202
Topham *v.* Braddick, 1 Taunt. 572......iii. 110
Tottenham *v.* Bedingfield, 3 Leon. 24......iii. 196
Toussaint *v.* Martinnant, 2 T. R. 100......ii. 239; iii. 123, 201
Townsend *v.* Crowdy, 8 C. B. N. S. 477, 98 E. C. L. 477......ii. 212
Townsend *v.* Hargraves, 118 Mass. 334......ii. 177
Tozer *v.* Child, 7 El. & Bl. 377, 90 E. C. L. 377......i. 38; iii. 55
Tracy *v.* Veal, Cro. Jac. 223......i. 376
Trade Mark Cases, 100 U. S. 82......i. 422, 423
Trail *v.* Baring, 4 DeG. J. & S. 318......i. 412
Train *v.* Gold, 5 Pick. (Mass.) 380......ii. 52
Trainer *v.* Trumbull, 141 Mass. 530......ii. 204
Traylor *v.* Hughes, 88 Ala. 617......i. 248
Traywick *v.* Keeble, 93 Ala. 498......i. 259
Trent *v.* Hunt, 9 Exch. 20......iii. 284
Trent Nav. Co. *v.* Wood, 3 Esp. 127, 4 Dougl. 287, 26 E. C. L. 358...ii. 303
Trever *v.* Roberts, Hardres 366......iii. 181
Trewinian *v.* Howell, Cro. Eliz. 91......ii. 147
Tripe *v.* Potter, cited in 6 T. R. 128......iii. 258
Trow *v.* Vermont Cent. R. Co., 24 Vt. 487......i. 127
Trueman *v.* Fenton, 2 Cowp. 544......ii. 145
Tubbs *v.* Richard, 6 Vt. 442......i. 240
Tucker *v.* Bartle, 85 Mo. 114......ii. 75
Tucker *v.* White, 125 Mass. 347......i. 407
Tuff *v.* Warman, 2 C. B. N. S. 740, 89 E. C. L. 740, 5 C. B. N. S. 573, 94 E. C. L. 573......i. 135, 137, 139, 140
Tufts *v.* Matthews, 10 Fed. Rep. 609......iii. 87, 88
Tullay *v.* Reed, 1 C. & P. 6, 1 E. C. L. 297......i. 9
Tullidge *v.* Wade, 3 Wils. C. Pl. 18......i. 269, 484
Tunney *v.* Midland R. Co., L. R. 1 C. P. 296......ii. 471
Tunstall *v.* Christian, 80 Va. 1......i. 195, 196
Turbervell *v.* Savadge, 2 Keb. 545......i. 6
Turberville *v.* Stamp, 1 Comyns 32......i. 56
Turberville *v.* Stampe, Comb. 459......ii. 451
Turberville *v.* Stampe, 1 Ld. Raym. 264......ii. 452, 458
Turges *v.* Beacher, Moo. K. B. 694......ii. 63; iii. 178, 183
Turnbull *v.* Bird, 2 F. & F. 508......i. 309
Turner *v.* Ambler, 10 Q. B. 252, 59 E. C. L. 252......i. 330
Turner *v.* Buck, 22 Vin. Abr. 523, pl. 9......i. 31
Turner *v.* Davies, 2 Esp. 479......ii. 239
Turnor *v.* Goodwin, Fortescue 145, 10 Mod. 153......ii. 137
Turton *v.* Turton, 42 Ch. D. 128......i. 432

Tweddle *v.* Atkinson, 1 B. & S. 393, 101 E. C. L. 393................ii. 154
Twelfth Ward Bank *v.* Brooks, 63 N. Y. App. Div. 220..............ii. 545
Twycross *v.* Grant, 4 C. P. D. 40.............................iii. 69
Tyler *v.* Salley, 82 Me. 128.....................................i. 465
Tyler *v.* Western Union Tel. Co., 54 Fed. Rep. 634...................i. 467
Tyrrell *v.* London Bank, 10 H. L. Cas. 26, 2 Eng. Rul. Cas. 496......ii. 492
Tyson *v.* McGuineas, 25 Wis. 656...............................iii. 87

Ulery *v.* Jones, 81 Ill. 403.......................................i. 18
Uline *v.* New York Cent., etc., R. Co., 101 N. Y. 98..................i. 43
Ullrich *v.* New York Press Co., 23 Misc. (N. Y.) 168................i. 317
Underhill *v.* Wilton, 32 Vt. 40....................................i. 291
Underwood *v.* Brockman, 4 Dana (Ky.) 309.........................ii. 214
Underwood *v.* Green, 42 N. Y. 140.................................i. 38
Underwood *v.* Hewson, 1 Stra. 596.................................i. 79
Ungley *v.* Ungley, 5 Ch. D. 887..................................ii. 192
Union Associated Press *v.* Heath, 49 N. Y. App. Div. 247............i. 297
Union Bank *v.* U. S. Bank, 3 Mass. 74.............................ii. 213
Union Bank *v.* Warren, 4 Sneed (Tenn.) 167.......................ii. 376
Union Cotton Manufactory *v.* Lobdell, 13 Johns. (N. Y.) 462.......ii. 200
Union Credit Bank *v.* Mersey Docks, etc., Board, (1899) 2 Q. B. 216..i. 244
Union Pac. R. Co. *v.* Rollins, 5 Kan. 174...........................i. 52
U. S. *v.* Appleton, 1 Sumn. (U. S.) 492..........................iii. 232
U. S. *v.* Bryan, 82 Fed. Rep. 290..................................ii. 293
U. S. *v.* Colby, 1 Sprague (U. S.) 119..............................i. 39
U. S. *v.* Collins, 2 Curt. (U. S.) 194..............................i. 39
U. S. *v.* Humason, 6 Sawy. (U. S.) 199............................ii. 293
U. S. *v.* Hunt, 2 Story (U. S.) 120.................................i. 39
U. S. *v.* Lynah, 188 U. S. 474...................................iii. 199
U. S. *v.* Ortega, 4 Wash. (U. S.) 531...............................i. 6
U. S. *v.* Prescott, 3 How. (U. S.) 578................ii. 292, 293; iii. 112
U. S. *v.* Richardson, 5 Cranch (C. C.) 348..........................i. 12
U. S. *v.* Thomas, 15 Wall. (U. S.) 337.......................ii. 292, 293
U. S. *v.* Tynen, 11 Wall. (U. S.) 88...............................ii. 499
U. S. *v.* Zabriskie, 87 Fed. Rep. 714..............................ii. 293
U. S. Bank *v.* Daniel, 12 Pet. (U. S.) 33..........................ii. 214
U. S. Tel. Co. *v.* Gildersleeve, 29 Md. 232..........................i. 452
Usill *v.* Hales, 3 C. P. D. 319.....................................i. 310
Uther *v.* Rich, 10 Ad. & El. 784, 37 E. C. L. 232...................ii. 407

Vaiden *v.* Bell, 3 Rand. (Va.) 448.............................iii. 216, 218
Vale *v.* Egles, Yelv. 70, Cro. Jac. 69............................iii. 188
Valentine *v.* Duff, 7 Ind. App. 196................................i. 239
Valentine *v.* Piper, 22 Pick. (Mass.) 85...........................ii. 485
Valley Sav. Bank *v.* Mercer, 97 Md. 458..........................ii. 531
Valparaiso *v.* Hagan, 153 Ind. 337..................................i. 44
Van Bracklin *v.* Fonda, 12 Johns. (N. Y.) 468.......................i. 387
Vandenburgh *v.* Truax, 4 Den. (N. Y.) 464...........................i. 89
Vanderbeck *v.* Rochester, 122 N. Y. 285..........................ii. 214
Vanderbilt *v.* Schreyer, 91 N. Y. 392.............................ii. 129

Van Deusen *v.* Blum, 18 Pick. (Mass.) 229................ii. 200; iii. 136
Vandrink *v.* Archer, 1 Leon. 222..............................iii. 165
Van Duzer *v.* Howe, 21 N. Y. 531..............................i. 495
Vanheath *v.* Turner, Winch 24..............................ii. 346, 349
Van Ness *v.* Hamilton, 19 Johns. (N. Y.) 349..................i. 301
Van Orden *v.* Van Orden, 10 Johns. (N. Y.) 30..................ii. 148
Van Valkinburgh *v.* Watson, 13 Johns. (N. Y.) 480..............ii. 205
Varley *v.* Leigh, 2 Exch. 446..................................iii. 134
Vaspor *v.* Edwards, 12 Mod. 658............................iii. 311, 313
Vaughan *v.* Ellis, Cro. Jac. 213................................i. 278
Vaughan *v.* Menlove, 3 Bing. N. Cas. 468, 32 E. C. L. 208..i. 96, 101; ii. 275
Vaughan *v.* Taff Vale R. Co., 5 H. & N. 679....................i. 42, 57
Vaughan *v.* Watt, 6 M. & W. 492................................i. 246
Vaux *v.* Mainwaring, Fortescue 197............................iii. 135
Vaux *v.* Sheffer, 8 Moo. P. C. 103..............................i. 145
Vegelahn *v.* Guntner, 167 Mass. 92........................i. 366, 367, 372
Vere *v.* Ashby, 10 B. & C. 288, 21 E. C. L. 79..................ii. 490
Vere *v.* Smith, 2 Lev. 5..iii. 106
Vere *v.* Smith, 1 Vent. 121......................................ii. 266
Vermilye *v.* Adams Express Co., 21 Wall. (U. S.) 138............ii. 424
Vernon *v.* Boverie, 2 Show. 296..................................ii. 390
Verry *v.* Watkins, 7 C. & P. 308, 32 E. C. L. 520.................i. 271
Vicars *v.* Wilcocks, 8 East 1..................................i. 286, 290
Victorian R. Com'rs *v.* Coultas, 13 App. Cas. 222..............i. 289, 458
Villers *v.* Beamont, 2 Dyer 146*b*................................ii. 41
Villers *v.* Monsley, 2 Wils. C. Pl. 403........................i. 277, 293
Villet *v.* Parkhurst, 2 Dyer 250*b*, *note*........................iii. 272
Vinal *v.* Core, 18 W. Va. 1..i. 488
Vinkinstone *v.* Ebden, Carth. 358................................iii. 305
Vizetelly *v.* Mudie's Select Library, (1900) 2 Q. B. 170...........i. 299
Volkmar *v.* Manhattan R. Co., 134 N. Y. 418........................i. 108
Von Fragstein *v.* Windler, 2 Mo. App. 598..........................i. 482
Voorhis *v.* Childs, 17 N. Y. 354..................................iii. 58
Vosburg *v.* Putney, 80 Wis. 523.....................................i. 5
Vredenburg *v.* Behan, 33 La. Ann. 627..............................i. 55

Wabash, etc., R. Co. *v.* Shacklet, 105 Ill. 364.....................i. 141
Wabash R. Co. *v.* Hannahan, 121 Fed. Rep. 563.......................i. 366
Wachter *v.* Quenzer, 29 N. Y. 552...................................i. 301
Wade *v.* Bemboe, 1 Leon. 2.......................................iii. 118
Wade *v.* Simeon, 2 C. B. 548, 52 E. C. L. 548...................ii. 77, 78
Wadhurst *v.* Damme, Cro. Jac. 45....................................i. 18
Wadsworth *v.* Reg., 1 Q. B. 171, 79 E. C. L. 171....................i. 37
Wadsworth *v.* Tillotson, 15 Conn. 366...............................i. 199
Wadsworth *v.* Western Union Tel. Co., 86 Tenn. 695......i. 466, 473, 475
Wagner *v.* Bissell, 3 Iowa 396......................................i. 52
Wagworth *v.* Halyday, 29 Edw. III.................................iii. 147
Wain *v.* Warlters, 5 East 17......................ii. 169, 174, 179, 180
Wainwright *v.* Straw, 15 Vt. 215...................................ii. 186

Waite *v.* North Eastern R. Co., El. Bl. & El. 719, 96 E. C. L. 719....i. 142
Wakelin *v.* London, etc., R. Co., 12 App. Cas. 41....................i. 138
Wakeman *v.* Robinson, 1 Bing. 213, 8 E. C. L. 478....................i. 81
Wakley *v.* Cooke, 4 Exch. 511..i. 301
Wales *v.* Miner, 89 Ind. 118...i. 264
Walgrave *v.* Ogden, 1 Leon. 224....................................iii. 163
Walker *v.* Baird, (1892) A. C. 491....................................i. 36
Walker *v.* British Guarantee Assoc., 18 Q. B. 277, 83 E. C. L. 277..ii. 292
Walker *v.* Cronin, 107 Mass. 555..............................i. 346, 366
Walker *v.* Duncan, 68 Wis. 624.....................................iii. 198
Walker *v.* Macdonald, 2 Exch. 527....................................ii. 515
Walker *v.* Walker, Holt K. B. 328, 5 Mod. 13, Comb. 303...ii. 165; iii. 185
Walker *v.* Witter, 1 Dougl. 1.................................iii. 180, 194
Walker's Case, Clayton 127, pl. 227.................................iii. 168
Wall *v.* State, 10 Ind. App. 530......................................i. 172
Wallace *v.* Cannon, 38 Ga. 199..i. 177
Wallace *v.* Floyd, 29 Pa. St. 184....................................ii. 203
Wallace *v.* Long, 105 Ind. 522.......................................ii. 223
Wallis *v.* Bazet, 34 La. Ann. 131.....................................i. 310
Wallis *v.* Portland, 3 Ves. Jr. 494...................................i. 340
Wallis *v.* Wallis, 4 Mass. 135..ii. 43
Walsh *v.* Fitchburg R. Co., 145 N. Y. 301............................i. 160
Walter *v.* James, L. R. 6 Exch. 124..................................ii. 488
Walter *v.* Selfe, 4 DeG. & Sm. 315....................................i. 221
Waltham *v.* Mulgar, Moo. K. B. 776...................................ii. 449
Walton *v.* Booth, 34 La. Ann. 914.....................................i. 60
Wamsley *v.* Atlas Steamship Co., 168 N. Y. 533.......................i. 237
Wamsley *v.* Child, 1 Ves. 341...............................ii. 376, 385
Wanamaker *v.* Bowes, 36 Md. 42..i. 481
Warbrook *v.* Griffin, Brownl. & Goldes. 254 (pt. ii.)...............iii. 187
Ward *v.* Carp River Iron Co., 47 Mich. 65..............................i. 26
Ward *v.* Dampskibselskabet Kjoebenhaven, 136 Fed. Rep. 502.......i. 167
Ward *v.* Evans, 2 Ld. Raym. 928......................................ii. 389
Ward *v.* Evans, 2 Salk. 442..ii. 465
Ward *v.* Lloyd, 7 Scott N. R. 499.....................................i. 495
Ward *v.* Macauley, 4 T. R. 489.....................................iii. 239
Ward *v.* Neal, 37 Ala. 500...i. 208
Ward *v.* Sheppard, 2 Hayw. (3 N. Car.) 283.............................i. 27
Ward *v.* Weeks, 7 Bing. 211, 20 E. C. L. 104...............i. 287, 288, 290
Warner *v.* Grace, 14 Minn. 487.......................................ii. 121
Warner *v.* Riddiford, 4 C. B. N. S. 180, 93 E. C. L. 180..........i. 13
Warner *v.* Tallerd, 1 Rolle Abr. 91, pl. 7............................i. 382
Warner *v.* Vallily, 13 R. I. 483......................................i. 259
Warren *v.* Batchelder, 15 N. H. 129..................................ii. 155
Warren *v.* Hodge, 121 Mass. 106.......................................ii. 75
Warwick *v.* Foulkes, 12 M. & W. 507...................................i. 485
Wason *v.* Walter, L. R. 4 Q. B. 73...........................i. 303, 310
Watbroke *v.* Griffith, Moo. K. B. 876...............................iii. 187
Waterman *v.* Robinson, 5 Mass. 303...................................ii. 313
Waterman *v.* Shipman, 130 N. Y. 301...................................i. 424

Waters *v.* Van Winkle, 3 N. J. L. 154 .... i. 259
Watkins *v.* Wake, 7 M. & W. 488 .... iii. 142
Watson *v.* Brainard, 33 Vt. 88 .... ii. 217
Watson *v.* Cheshire, 18 Iowa 202 .... ii. 415
Watson *v.* King, 4 Campb. 272 .... ii. 492
Watson *v.* Poulson, 7 Eng. L. & Eq. 588 .... i. 393
Watson *v.* Swann, 11 C. B. N. S. 756, 103 E. C. L. 756 .... ii. 490
Watson *v.* Turner, Bull. N. P. 147*a*, Selwyn N. P. 53, *note* 4 .... ii. 150
Watson *v.* Watson, 9 Conn. 140, 10 Conn. 75 .... iii. 218
Watteau *v.* Fenwick, (1893) 1 Q. B. 346 .... ii. 480
Watton *v.* Brinth, 2 Hen. IV .... i. 187; ii. 29; iii. 175
Watts *v.* Fraser, 7 C. & P. 369, 32 E. C. L. 544 .... i. 298
Watuppa Reservoir Co. *v.* Fall River, 147 Mass. 548 .... i. 199
Weare *v.* Gove, 44 N. H. 196 .... i. 406
Weatherston *v.* Hawkins, 1 T. R. 110 .... i. 311
Weaver *v.* Bachert, 2 Pa. St. 80 .... i. 163
Weaver *v.* Jones, 24 Ala. 420 .... ii. 217
Weaver *v.* Lapsley, 43 Ala. 224 .... ii. 207
Weaver *v.* Lawrence, 1 Dall. (Pa.) 156 .... iii. 215, 221
Weaver *v.* Ward, Hob. 134 .... i. 78
Webb *v.* Beavan, 11 Q. B. D. 609 .... i. 277
Webb *v.* Bell, 1 Sid. 440 .... iii. 305
Webb *v.* Bird, 13 C. B. N. S. 841, 106 E. C. L. 841 .... i. 205
Webb *v.* Drake, 52 La. Ann. 290 .... i. 369
Webb *v.* Jiggs, 4 M. & S. 119 .... ii. 149
Webbe *v.* Western Union Tel. Co., 169 Ill. 610 .... i. 441, 443
Webster *v.* Drinkwater, 5 Me. 319 .... ii. 217
Webster *v.* Webster, 53 N. H. 18 .... i. 27
Weeks *v.* Currier, 172 Mass. 53 .... i. 407
Weeks *v.* Mays, 87 Tenn. 442 .... i. 465
Weeks *v.* Propert, L. R. 8 C. P. 427 .... i. 406
Weinstein *v.* National Bank, 69 Tex. 38 .... ii. 248
Weire *v.* Davenport, 11 Iowa 49 .... iii. 87
Weisser *v.* Denison, 10 N. Y. 69 .... ii. 248
Welch *v.* Durand, 36 Conn. 182 .... i. 5, 481
Welch *v.* Geneva, 110 Wis. 388 .... i. 176
Welch *v.* Wesson, 6 Gray (Mass.) 505 .... i. 181
Weld *v.* Oliver, 21 Pick. (Mass.) 559 .... i. 240
Weldon *v.* Buck, 4 Johns. (N. Y.) 144 .... ii. 552
Welfare *v.* London, etc., R. Co., L. R. 4 Q. B. 693 .... i. 109
Wellington *v.* Downer Kerosene Oil Co., 104 Mass. 64 .... i. 60
Wellington *v.* Wentworth, 8 Met. (Mass.) 548 .... i. 242
Wellman *v.* Sun Printing, etc., Assoc., 66 Hun (N. Y.) 331 .... i. 294
Wellock *v.* Constantine, 2 H. & C. 146 .... i. 327, 495
Wells *v.* Abrahams, L. R. 7 Q. B. 554 .... i. 327, 495
Wells *v.* Crew, 5 U. C. Q. B. O. S. 209 .... i. 249
Wells *v.* Head, 4 C. & P. 568, 19 E. C. L. 531 .... i. 18
Wells *v.* Howell, 19 Johns. (N. Y.) 385 .... i. 52
Wells *v.* Wells, 1 Vent. 41 .... ii. 147
Welsbach Light Co. *v.* Adams, 107 Fed. Rep. 463 .... i. 424

Welsh *v.* Bell, 1 Vent. 37 ... iii. 295
Welsh *v.* Craig, 8 Mod. 373 ... iii. 140, 141
Wenman *v.* Ash, 13 C. B. 836, 76 E. C. L. 836 ... i. 297
Wennall *v.* Adney, 3 B. & P. 247 ... ii. 146
Wennhak *v.* Morgan, 20 Q. B. D. 635 ... i. 297
Wenona Coal Co. *v.* Holmquist, 152 Ill. 581 ... i. 148
Wentworth *v.* Day, 3 Met. (Mass.) 352 ... ii. 82
Wentworth *v.* Jefferson, 60 N. H. 158 ... i. 178
Weshbourn *v.* Mordant, 2 Leon. 103 ... i. 214
West *v.* Houghton, 4 C. P. D. 197 ... ii. 158
West *v.* Western Union Tel. Co., 39 Kan. 93 ... i. 467
Westberg *v.* Chicago Lumber, etc., Co. 117 Wis. 589 ... ii. 501, 549
Westbury-on-Severn Rural Sanitary Authority *v.* Meredith, 30 Ch. D. 387 ... iii. 57
Westerfield *v.* Levis, 43 La. Ann. 63 ... i. 144
Western Assur. Co. *v.* Towle, 65 Wis. 247 ... ii. 217
Western Counties Manure Co. *v.* Lawes Chemical Manure Co., L. R. 9 Exch. 218 ... i. 324
Western, etc., R. Co. *v.* Lewis, 84 Ga. 211 ... i. 489
Western Union Tel. Co. *v.* Allgood, 125 Ala. 712 ... i. 437
Western Union Tel. Co. *v.* Ayers, 131 Ala. 391 ... i. 468, 472
Western Union Tel. Co. *v.* Blanchard, 68 Ga. 299 ... i. 450
Western Union Tel. Co. *v.* Broesche, 72 Tex. 654 ... i. 453
Western Union Tel. Co. *v.* Church, 90 N. W. Rep. 882 ... i. 451, 459
Western Union Tel. Co. *v.* Crocker, 135 Ala. 492 ... i. 468, 472
Western Union Tel. Co. *v.* Crumpton, 138 Ala. 632 ... i. 466, 468
Western Union Tel. Co. *v.* Cunningham, 99 Ala. 314 ... i. 468
Western Union Tel. Co. *v.* Edsall, 74 Tex. 329 ... i. 450
Western Union Tel. Co. *v.* Eubanks, 100 Ky. 604 ... i. 453
Western Union Tel. Co. *v.* Fatman, 73 Ga. 285 ... i. 452
Western Union Tel. Co. *v.* Ferguson, 157 Ind. 64 ... i. 467
Western Union Tel. Co. *v.* Frith, 105 Tenn. 167 ... i. 472
Western Union Tel. Co. *v.* Henderson, 89 Ala. 510 ... i. 466, 471
Western Union Tel. Co. *v.* Hyer, 22 Fla. 637 ... i. 452, 453
Western Union Tel. Co. *v.* J. A. Kemp Grocer Co., 28 S. W. Rep. 905 ... i. 450
Western Union Tel. Co. *v.* Krichbaum, 132 Ala. 535 ... i. 468
Western Union Tel. Co. *v.* Longwill, 5 N. Mex. 308 ... i. 443
Western Union Tel. Co. *v.* McCall, 9 Kan. App. 886, 56 Pac. Rep. 797 ... i. 459
Western Union Tel. Co. *v.* McKibben, 114 Ind. 511 ... i. 441
Western Union Tel. Co. *v.* Mellon, 96 Tenn. 66 ... i. 473
Western Union Tel. Co. *v.* Millsap, 135 Ala. 415 ... i. 437
Western Union Tel. Co. *v.* Reynolds, 77 Va. 173, 186 ... i. 451, 453
Western Union Tel. Co. *v.* Rogers, 68 Miss. 748 ... i. 467
Western Union Tel. Co. *v.* Shotter, 71 Ga. 760 ... i. 456
Western Union Tel. Co. *v.* Simpson, 64 Kan. 309 ... i. 454
Western Union Tel. Co. *v.* Smith, 76 Tex. 253 ... i. 454
Western Union Tel. Co. *v.* Uvalde Bank, 97 Tex. 219 ... i. 455
Western Union Tel. Co. *v.* Valentine, 18 Ill. App. 57 ... i. 450

Western Union Tel. Co. *v.* Waters, 139 Ala. 652..............i. 441, 468
Western Union Tel. Co. *v.* Watson, 94 Ga. 202..................i. 454
Western Union Tel. Co. *v.* Way, 83 Ala. 542................i. 452, 453
Western Union Tel. Co. *v.* Williford, 27 S. W. Rep. 700..........i. 451
Western Union Tel. Co. *v.* Wilson, 93 Ala. 32....................i. 468
Western Union Tel. Co. *v.* Wilson, 32 Fla. 527..................i. 452
Western Union Tel. Co. *v.* Wood, 57 Fed. Rep. 471..........i. 439, 467
West Ham Cent. Charity Board *v.* East London Waterworks Co., (1900) 1 Ch. 624..i. 29
Westlake *v.* St. Louis, 77 Mo. 47..................................ii. 231
West London Commercial Bank *v.* Kitson, 13 Q. B. D. 360........i. 395
Weston *v.* Downes, 1 Dougl. 23.................................iii. 192
West Virginia Transp. Co. *v.* Standard Oil Co., 50 W. Va. 611....i. 366
Wetmore *v.* Mellinger, 64 Iowa 741..............................i. 333
Weymouth *v.* Penobscot Log Driving Co., 71 Me. 29............i. 186
Whalley *v.* Lancashire, etc., R. Co., 13 Q. B. D. 131..............i. 23
Wheatley *v.* Chrisman, 24 Pa. St. 298......................i. 201, 204
Wheatly *v.* Lowe, Cro. Jac. 668..................................iii. 151
Wheatly *v.* Miscal, 5 Ind. 142.....................................ii. 226
Wheaton *v.* Beecher, 66 Mich. 307..............................i. 309
Wheeden *v.* Fiske, 50 N. H. 125...................................ii. 221
Wheeler *v.* Nesbitt, 24 How. (U. S.) 544..........................i. 330
Wheelock *v.* Cozzens, 6 How. (Miss.) 279.......................iii. 218
Wheelock *v.* Wheelwright, 5 Mass. 104..................i. 257, 286, 287
Whelan *v.* Ansonia Clock Co., 97 N. Y. 293.......................ii. 224
Whelen *v.* Watmough, 15 S. & R. (Pa.) 153.......................iii. 111
Whipple *v.* Gilpatrick, 19 Me. 427................................i. 239
Whipple *v.* Parker, 29 Mich. 369..................................ii. 176
Whirley *v.* Whiteman, 1 Head (Tenn.) 610........................i. 148
White *v.* Bigelow, 154 Mass. 593..................................ii. 192
White *v.* Carroll, 42 N. Y. 161......................................i. 308
White *v.* Cuyler, 6 T. R. 176...ii. 474
White *v.* France, 2 C. P. D. 308.....................................i. 151
White *v.* Lang, 128 Mass. 598.......................................i. 181
White *v.* Mellin, (1895) A. C. 154..................................i. 324
White *v.* Nicholls, 3 How. (U. S.) 266.............................i. 308
White *v.* Spettigue, 13 M. & W. 603...............................i. 495
White *v.* Twitchell, 25 Vt. 620......................................i. 103
White *v.* Vermont, etc., R. Co., 21 How. (U. S.) 575............ii. 423
Whitehead *v.* Harrison, 6 Q. B. 423, 51 E. C. L. 423........iii. 149, 152
Whitehead *v.* Tuckett, 15 East 400...............................ii. 481
Whitehead *v.* Walker, 9 M. & W. 514.............................ii. 360
Whitehill *v.* Western Union Tel. Co., 136 Fed. Rep. 499..........i. 438
Whiteley *v.* Adams, 15 C. B. N. S. 392, 109 E. C. L. 392......i. 312, 317
Whitely *v.* Pepper, 2 Q. B. D. 276...................................i. 153
White's Case, 2 Dyer 158*b*...i. 185
Whitfield *v.* Le Despencer, 2 Cowp. 754....................i. 36; ii. 307
Whitford *v.* Panama R. Co., 23 N. Y. 465.........................iii. 74
Whiting *v.* Hill, 23 Mich. 399.......................................i. 414
Whitsett *v.* Clayton, 5 Colo. 476...................................ii. 95

Whitworth v. Hall, 2 B. & Ad. 695, 22 E. C. L. 173..........i. 329, 332
Wichals v. Johns, Cro. Eliz. 703..............................ii. 55
Wickham v. Taylor, T. Jones 168..............................ii. 92
Wiedeman v. Keller, 171 Ill. 93..............................i. 387, 388
Wiggin v. Wiggin, 43 N. H. 561..............................ii. 149
Wilbraham v. Snow, 2 Saund. 47a, 1 Sid. 438..................i. 252, 254
Wilby v. Elston, 8 C. B. 142, 65 E. C. L. 142.....................i. 287
Wilcox v. Moore, 69 Minn. 49..............................i. 309
Wild v. Fisher, 4 Pick. (Mass.) 421..............................iii. 203
Wild v. Harris, 7 C. B. 999, 62 E. C. L. 999................ii. 109, 110
Wilde v. Baker, 14 Allen (Mass.) 349..............................ii. 214
Wildes v. Dudlow, L. R. 19 Eq. 198..............................ii. 187
Wildes v. Savage, 1 Story (U. S.) 27..............................ii. 401
Wilds v. Hudson River R. Co., 24 N. Y. 430.....................i. 124
Wiley v. Keokuk, 6 Kan. 94..............................i. 482
Wiley v. West Jersey R. Co., 44 N. J. L. 247.....................i. 130
Wilkes v. Hungerford Market Co., 2 Bing. N. Cas. 281, 29 E. C. L. 336..............................i. 229
Wilkes v. Lenson, 2 Dyer 169..............................ii. 42
Wilkes v. Wood, 19 How. St. Tr. 1167, Lofft (3 Geo. III.) 19..i. 477, 479
Wilkinson v. Coverdale, 1 Esp. 75..............................ii. 50
Wilkinson v. Drew, 75 Me. 360..............................i. 482
Wilkinson v. Fairrie, 1 H. & C. 633..............................i. 158
Wilkinson v. Kirby, 15 C. B. 430, 80 E. C. L. 430.................i. 261
Wilkinson v. Oliveira, 1 Bing. N. Cas. 490, 27 E. C. L. 468........ii. 71
Wilkinson v. Proud, 11 M. & W. 33..............................i. 191
Wilkinson v. Searcy, 74 Ala. 243..............................ii. 244
Wilkyns v. Wilkyns, Carth. 89..............................iii. 191
Willard v. Crook, 21 App. Cas. (D. C.) 237..................ii. 522, 532
William J. Moxley Co. v. Braun, etc., Co., 93 Ill. App. 183........i. 423
Wm. Rogers Mfg. Co. v. Rogers, 84 Fed. Rep. 639...............i. 432
Williams v. Birmingham Battery, etc., Co., (1899) 2 Q. B. 338..i. 166, 168
Williams v. Cowardine, 4 B. & Ad. 621, 24 E. C. L. 126........ii. 81, 82
Williams v. Currie, 1 C. B. 841, 50 E. C. L. 841.................i. 489
Williams v. Eady, 9 Times L. Rep. 637, 10 Times L. Rep. 41......i. 59
Williams v. Field, 3 Salk. 68..............................ii. 378
Williams v. Germaine, 7 B. & C. 468, 14 E. C. L. 84.............ii. 555
Williams v. Gesse, 3 Bing. N. Cas. 849, 32 E. C. L. 353...........i. 237
Williams v. Hide, Palmer 548, W. Jones 179...............ii. 265, 269
Williams v. Holland, 10 Bing. 112, 25 E. C. L. 50......i. 16, 190; iii. 264
Williams v. Hollingsworth, 6 Baxt. (Tenn.) 12....................i. 464
Williams v. Jones, 3 H. & C. 256..............................ii. 281
Williams v. Jones, 3 H. & C. 602..............................ii. 469
Williams v. Karnes, 4 Humph. (Tenn.) 9..............................i. 294
Williams v. Merle, 11 Wend. (N. Y.) 80..............................i. 239
Williams v. Nichol, 47 Ark. 254..............................ii. 149
Williams v. Stanton, 1 Root (Conn.) 426..............................ii. 95
Williams v. Walsby, 4 Esp. 220..............................ii. 174
Williams v. West Chicago St. R. Co., 191 Ill. 610..................ii. 82
Williams v. Williams, Carth. 270......................ii. 351, 357, 503

Williamson *v.* Allison, 2 East 446....i. 390
Williamsport, etc., R. Co. *v.* Com., 33 Pa. St. 288....i. 35
Willis *v.* Maclachlan, 1 Ex. D. 376....i. 38
Willmot *v.* Prigget, 1 Rolle Abr. 29, pl. 60....iii. 89
Willoughby, Matter of, 11 Paige (N. Y.) 257....ii. 192
Wilmarth *v.* Crawford, 10 Wend. (N. Y.) 341....iii. 143
Wilson, Matter of, 1 Sch. & Lef. 320....iii. 219
Wilson *v.* Brett, 11 M. & W. 113....i. 97, 100
Wilson *v.* Brig Mary, The, Gilp. (U. S.) 31....i. 39
Wilson *v.* Chambers, Cro. Car. 262....iii. 167
Wilson *v.* Edmonds, 24 N. H. 517....ii. 87
Wilson *v.* Merry, L. R. 1 Sc. & D. 326....ii. 471
Wilson *v.* New Bedford, 108 Mass. 261....i. 63
Wilson *v.* People, 19 Colo. 199....ii. 292, 293
Wilson *v.* Phœnix Powder Mfg. Co., 40 W. Va. 413....i. 59
Wilson *v.* Reed, 3 Johns. (N. Y.) 175....i. 240
Wilson *v.* Stripe, 4 Greene (Iowa) 551....iii. 219
Wilson *v.* Stump, 103 Cal. 255....ii. 82
Wilson *v.* Tumman, 6 M. & G. 236, 46 E. C. L. 236....ii. 490
Wilson *v.* Young, 31 Wis. 574....i. 480
Wimer *v.* Worth Tp., 104 Pa. St. 319....ii. 120
Windbiel *v.* Carroll, 16 Hun (N. Y.) 101....ii. 212
Windham *v.* Chetwynd, 1 Burr. 414, 418....ii. 168
Wing *v.* Mill, 1 B. & Ad. 105....ii. 151
Winkfield, The, (1902) P. 42....i. 255, 314, 315, 317
Winsmore *v.* Greenbank, Willes 577....iii. 56
Winter *v.* Henn, 4 C. & P. 494, 10 E. C. L. 491....i. 163
Winterbottom *v.* Derby, L. R. 2 Exch. 316....i. 225, 227
Winterbottom *v.* Wright, 10 M. & W. 109....i. 58
Wirt *v.* Stubblefield, 17 App. Cas. (D. C.) 283....ii. 498, 531
Wisconsin Freewill Baptists *v.* Babler, 115 Wis. 289....ii. 508
Wiswell *v.* Doyle, 160 Mass. 42....i. 143
Withers *v.* Richardson, 5 T. B. Mon. (Ky.) 94....ii. 190
Wolfe *v.* Howes, 20 N. Y. 197....ii. 224
Wolffe *v.* Eberlein, 74 Ala. 99....ii. 207
Wonsettler *v.* Lee, 40 Kan. 367....ii. 223
Wood *v.* Amory, 105 N. Y. 278....i. 399
Wood *v.* Erie R. Co., 72 N. Y. 196....i. 176
Wood *v.* Gaynon, Ambl. 395....i. 31
Wood *v.* Graves, 144 Mass. 365....i. 334
Wood *v.* Lane, 6 C. & P. 774, 25 E. C. L. 645....i. 13
Wood *v.* Waud, 3 Exch. 748....i. 198, 202
Woodbury *v.* Thompson, 3 N. H. 194....i. 290
Woodford *v.* Deacon, Cro. Jac. 206....iii. 181
Woodhouse *v.* Walker, 5 Q. B. D. 404....i. 30; iii. 65, 270
Woodleife *v.* Curties, 1 Rolle Abr. 2 (C), pl. 4....ii. 305
Woodlife's Case, Moo. K. B. 462....ii. 299
Woodlife's Case, Owen 57....ii. 262
Woodman *v.* Hubbard, 25 N. H. 67....i. 257; ii. 286
Woodrop-Sims, The, 2 Dods. 83....i. 145

Woods *v.* Caledonian Ry. Co. (Scotch), 13 Rettie 1118..............i. 133
Woods *v.* Rose, 135 Ala. 297..............i. 239
Woods *v.* Wiman, 122 N. Y. 445..............i. 308
Woodward *v.* Anderson, 9 Bush (Ky.) 624..............i. 272
Woodward *v.* Aston, 2 Mod. 95..............iii. 191
Woodward *v.* Rowe, 2 Keb. 105, 132..............ii. 350, 370
Woodward *v.* Walton, 2 B. & P. N. R. 476..............i. 264, 271
Woodward *v.* Washburn, 3 Den. (N. Y.) 369..............i. 267
Wookey *v.* Pole, 4 B. & Ald. 1, 6 E. C. L. 365..............ii. 404
Woolaston *v.* Webb, Hob. 18..............ii. 34, 77
Wooley *v.* Batte, 2 C. & P. 417, 12 E. C. L. 198..............ii. 240
Woolf *v.* Chalker, 31 Conn. 121..............i. 18, 69
Woolvil *v.* Young, 5 Mod. 367..............ii. 379
Wootton *v.* Dawkins, 2 C. B. N. S. 412, 89 E. C. L. 412..............i. 68
Works *v.* Hershey, 35 Iowa 342..............ii. 103
Worrall *v.* Munn, 5 N. Y. 229..............ii. 474
Worth *v.* McConnell, 42 Mich. 473..............i. 386
Worthington, The, 19 Fed. Rep. 836..............i. 146
Wren *v.* Weild, L. R. 4 Q. B. 213, 38 L. J. Q. B. 88..............i. 301
Wren *v.* Weild, L. R. 4 Q. B. 730..............i. 323
Wright *v.* Lothrop, 149 Mass. 385, 390..............i. 308
Wright *v.* Pearson, L. R. 4 Q. B. 582..............i. 52
Wright *v.* Ramscot, 1 Saund. 84..............i. 18
Wright *v.* Woodgate, 2 C. M. & R. 573..............i. 315
Wyatt *v.* Harrison, 3 B. & Ad. 871, 23 E. C. L. 205..............i. 195
Wyndham *v.* Chetwynd, 1 W. Bl. 97..............ii. 169 170

Yahoola River, etc., Hydraulic Hose Min. Co. *v.* Irby, 40 Ga. 479..iii. 263
Yard *v.* Eland, 1 Ld. Raym. 368..............ii. 155
Yarmouth *v.* France, 19 Q. B. D. 647..............i. 167, 168
Yates *v.* Milwaukee, 10 Wall. (U. S.) 497..............i. 199
Yates *v.* Nash, 8 C. B. N. S. 581, 98 E. C. L. 581..............ii. 510
Yellowly *v.* Gower, 11 Exch. 274..............i. 31
Yevance *v.* Holcomb, Dyer 250*b*, 3 Leon. 13..............iii. 271
York *v.* Toun, 5 Mod. 444, 1 Ld. Raym. 502..............iii. 189
York County *v.* Watson, 15 S. Car. 1..............ii. 293
Youl *v.* Harbottle, Peake N. P. (ed. 1795) 49..............i. 248
Youmans *v.* Smith, 153 N. Y. 214..............i. 296
Young *v.* Ashburnham, 3 Leon. 161..............ii. 200; iii. 186
Young *v.* Western Union Tel. Co., 107 N. Car. 370..............i. 466
Youngblood *v.* Lowry, 2 McCord L. (S. Car.) 39..............iii. 308

Zabriskie *v.* Smith, 13 N. Y. 322..............iii. 87, 88
Zander *v.* New York Security, etc., Co., 178 N. Y. 208..............ii. 501
Zenobio *v.* Axtell, 6 T. R. 162..............i. 300
Zierenberg *v.* Labouchere, (1893) 2 Q. B. 183..............i. 301
Zimmer *v.* Sennott, 134 Ill. 505..............ii. 149

INDEX

OF VOLUMES I, II, AND III.

ABBOTT, C. J.

See TENTERDEN, LORD.

Approves exemplary damages in case of poisoning poultry, i. 485.

Charge to jury in Gill *v.* Cubitt, ii. 406.

Conversion by person plying public calling, i. 244.

Foreign bonds held to be transferable, ii. 420.

Trespasser assumes risk of injury from spring gun, i. 69.

ABDUCTION.

Abduction of heir or ward, guardian's action, i. 267.

Abduction of heir, parent's action, i. 267.

Abduction of servant, master's action, i. 265.

Abduction of wife, husband's action, i. 263.

ABINGER, J.

Maintenance, definition of, ii. 164.

ABUSE OF LEGAL AUTHORITY.

Privilege destroyed by, i. 45.

ABUSE OF PROCESS.

See MALICIOUS ABUSE OF PROCESS.

ACCEPTANCE.

See BILLS AND NOTES.

ACCIDENT.

Blow to person standing behind, i. 82.

Carrier not liable for loss occasioned by inevitable accident, when, ii. 301.

Early law, accident no excuse for injury, i. 77.

Fire, accidental, what is, i. 56.

Firearms —

Accidental injury in military practice, i. 78, 80.

Gun, careless handling of, i. 78, 79.

Unavoidable necessity sole defense, i. 79.

Glancing shot, injury caused by, i. 82.

Inevitable accident, what is, ii. 303.

Innkeeper not responsible for accidental loss, when, ii. 296.

Runaway horse, accident caused by, i. 82.

Unavoidable accident no defense in trespass, i. 79.

ACCORD AND SATISFACTION.
Accord as alternative of formal release, ii. 88.
Accord must be executed, ii. 89.
American authorities, ii. 95.
Conflict of authority, ii. 94.
Rule based on considerations of policy and convenience, ii. 93.
Accord without satisfaction nugatory, ii. 90.
Antiquity of accord, ii. 88.
Composition with creditors, ii. 94, 95, 105.
Consideration as affecting law of accord, ii. 99.
Executory accord repudiated, ii. 92.
Executory accord theoretically good bilateral contract, ii. 91.
Executory accord valid, ii. 90.
Historical explanation, ii. 89, 92, 93.
Negotiable note given for part of debt good satisfaction of whole, ii. 100.
Parol discharge of negotiable instrument, ii. 101.
Part payment —
Brian's view as to effect of, ii. 97.
Good satisfaction in early law, ii. 96.
Part payment in satisfaction of debt not due, ii. 98.
Part payment in satisfaction of whole, analogy to executed gift, ii. 104.
Part payment not good satisfaction, when, ii. 98, 102.
Part payment of debt in satisfaction of whole invalid, unpopularity of doctrine, ii. 103.
Promise to pay part in satisfaction of whole, ii. 101.
Repudiation of idea that part payment is good satisfaction, ii. 97.
Want of consideration for promise to forego residue, ii. 98, 99.
Payment for collateral promise, ii. 106.
Promissory note given in satisfaction, ii. 94.
Recognition of validity of executory accord, ii. 91.
Satisfaction good where original contract is varied, ii. 98.
Two mysteries of common law, ii. 89.

ACCOUNT.
Account concurrent with detinue, when, iii. 107.
Account obsolete legal remedy, iii. 99.
Action of account, early history, iii. 102.
Action of account perishes with person, iii. 103.
Action of account render in Pennsylvania, iii. 111.
Auditors of account, iii. 107, 108.
Bailee liable in action of account, when, ii. 265, 266.
Bill in equity supersedes account, iii. 110.
Count for money had and received supersedes account, iii. 190.
Debt maintainable in lieu of account, when, iii. 109.
Equitable jurisdiction over matters of account, iii. 110, 111.
Equitable nature of action of account, iii. 107.
Indebitatus assumpsit supersedes action of account, iii. 110.
Obligation to render account, iii. 99.

ACCOUNT — *Continued.*
Partners, accounting among, iii. 103.
Privity of relation essential to right of account, iii. 103.
Procedure in account —
Accounting before the auditor, iii. 108.
Issue on question of liability to account, iii. 107.
Judgment, iii. 108.
Promise to account, effect of, iii. 106.
Ratification gives right to accounting, when, iii. 105.
Revival of account in nineteenth century, iii. 110.
Statutory extension of remedy, iii. 103.
Stranger, right of, to enforce accounting, iii. 105.
Writ of account, form of, iii. 99.

ACCOUNTANT.
Bailiff distinguished from accountant, iii. 100.
Common-law accountant —
Bailiff, iii. 100, 101.
Guardian, iii. 100.
Receiver, iii. 100, 102.
Custodian of public funds liable as accountant, iii. 112.
Possessory title of, iii. 100.
Receiver of public moneys liable for official fund, iii. 112.
Servant not subject to account to master, iii. 100.
Wager of law, when available to accountant, iii. 108.

ACTIO FURTI, iii. 229.
Analogy to *actio sacramenti,* iii. 23.
Nature of remedy, iii. 49.
Scope of remedy, iii. 229.
Supplanted by appeal of larceny, iii. 49.

ACTIO IN FACTUM PRÆSCRIPTIS VERBIS, ii. 21.

ACTION.
See Right of Action.
Abolition of actions, iii. 57.
Action *ex contractu,* iii. 41.
Action *ex delicto,* iii. 41.
Actio sacramenti earliest formal action, iii. 13.
Assignee, when suit to be brought in name of assignor, ii. 503; iii. 84.
Blackstone's division of actions, iii. 43.
Bracton's division of actions —
Action *in personam,* iii. 37.
Action *in rem,* iii. 37.
Genesis of Bracton's classification, iii. 38.
Mixed actions, iii. 37.
Classification of common-law actions, iii. 36.
Considerations of convenience as affecting, iii. 36.
Types of actions —
Præcipe, iii. 36.
Si te fecerit securum, iii. 36.

ACTION — *Continued.*
Common-law scheme of actions a natural growth, iii. 37.
Common-law theory of actions, iii. 29.
Forms of action —
Abolition of, as affecting right of stranger to sue on contract, ii. 158, 160.
Formless civil action goal of remedial law, iii. 56.
Forms in early English law, iii. 26.
Function of form, iii. 2, 3, 9.
Golden age of forms, iii. 31.
Importance of form in early law, iii. 1.
Inelasticity of forms, iii. 48, 53.
Substantive and adjective law, interplay between, iii. 2.
Issuance of new writs, iii. 248.
Local and transitory action distinguished, iii. 91.
Mixed action, iii. 43. 44.
Ownership, action based on, iii. 41.
Personal action, iii. 42, 43.
Enumeration of, iii. 46.
Process in, iii. 43.
Prominence of law of actions in early jurisprudence, iii. 1.
Real action, iii. 42, 43.
Debt maintainable for rent after abolition of real actions, iii. 134.
Obsolescence of, iii. 46.
Process in, iii. 42.
Real and personal action, origin of distinction between, iii. 42.
Recuperatory action, iii. 63, 64.
Technical limits of actions not strictly observed, iii. 259.
Transitory action, nature of, iii. 91, 92.
Venue of action.
See VENUE.

ACTION *IN PERSONAM*, iii. 37–41.

ACTION *IN REM*, iii. 37–41
Action for recovery of chattel not action *in rem*, iii. 40.
Bracton restricts action *in rem* to recovery of immovables, iii. 39.

ACTION OF THEFT.
See ACTIO FURTI.

ACTION ON CASE.
In general—
Analogy of case to bill in equity, iii. 54.
Case a formless action, iii. 246.
Definition, iii. 247.
Function of case in preserving balance between right and remedy, iii. 51.
Principle of growth embodied in case, iii. 52, 247.
Residuary remedy available where damages only are sought, iii. 55. 56, 246.
Scope of remedy, iii. 245, 246, 247.
Action on case for breach of contract, iii. 272–277.

ACTION ON CASE — *Continued.*
Action on case for negligence concurrent with trespass, when, iii. 259–264.
Action on case for negligent direct injury, iii. 263, 264.
Appearance of special actions in case —
Action of slander, iii. 250.
Deceit on case, iii. 250.
Nuisance, action on case for, iii. 271.
Trespass on case, iii. 249, 250.
Trover, iii. 250.
Waste, action on case for, iii. 268.
Assumpsit and case —
Case concurrent with special assumpsit, when, iii. 275.
Criticism of Brown *v.* Boorman, iii. 277.
Election of remedy, iii. 273.
Respective limits, iii. 272–277.
Bailee —
Case as remedy against, ii. 267.
Case available for negligent injury by, iii. 162, 163.
Conversion by bailee actionable in case, iii. 162.
Unlawful detention of bailee not actionable in case, iii. 163.
Breach of contract —
Case maintainable for, when, iii. 272.
Plaintiff not in privity with contract sues in case, iii. 273.
Breach of duty incident to employment, case as remedy for, iii. 276.
Breach of duty incident to public calling, case as remedy for, iii. 273.
Debt, influence of case on development of, iii. 51.
Detinue —
Case as substitute for, iii. 162.
Influence of case on development of, iii. 51.
General action on case —
Action against officer for breach of official duty, iii. 251.
Action against person plying common calling, iii. 251.
Action for false return, iii. 251.
Action for fire, iii. 251.
Action for slander, early instances of, iii. 251.
Interference with domestic relations, case supersedes trespass as remedy for, iii. 266.
Master and servant —
Master liable in case for trespass of servant, iii. 260.
Master not responsible for wilful act of servant, iii. 262.
Negligence —
Injury consequential on negligent act, iii. 258, 260.
Injury directly following from negligent act, iii. 258, 262–264.
Nuisance, case supplants other remedies for, iii. 271.
Obligation in nature of assumpsit, case as remely for breach, iii. 274.
Parliament authorizes issuance of writs in case, iii. 34.
Pleading —
Declaration, iii. 252.
Formlessness of action, iii. 252.

ACTION ON CASE — *Continued.*
Principle of growth embodied in action on case, iii. 52, 247.
Provisions of Westminster II. concerning writs in case, iii. 248.
Secondary trespass, trespass on case as remedy for, iii. 254.
Trespass —
Extension of case into field of trespassory injury, iii. 263-265.
Influence of case on development of action of trespass, iii. 51.
Trespass and trespass on case —
Consequential and direct damage distinguished, iii. 252-254.
Election of remedy, iii. 264, 265.
General action on case distinguished from, iii. 245, 246.
Limits of respective remedies, iii. 252-266.
Tossing of lighted squib, iii. 257, 258.
Trespass on case as remedy for secondary trespass, iii. 245, 254.
Turning water on land of neighbor, iii. 256.
Trover, influence of case on development of, iii. 51.
Waste, action on case supplants writ of waste, iii. 270.

ACTIO PERSONALIS, iii. 61.

ACTIO PERSONALIS MORITUR CUM PERSONA.
Doctrine applies to all personal obligations, iii. 61.
Final scope of maxim, iii. 71.
Maxim not limited to penal actions, iii. 61.
Maxim not limited to tort law, iii. 60.
Modern law repudiates principle, iii. 60.
Origin of maxim uncertain, iii. 60.
State of law in time of Bracton, iii. 63.

ACTIO SACRAMENTI, iii. 13.
Antiquity of, iii. 13.
Proceedings in —
Award of *judex,* iii. 14.
Deposit of stake, iii. 14.
Feigned combat, iii. 13.
Intervention of pretor, iii. 14.
Reference to *judex,* iii. 14.
Symbolic elements antedate historic knowledge, iii. 16.
Technical and formal remedy, iii. 16.

ACT OF GOD.
Carrier not responsible for loss caused by, ii. 300.
Cockburn's discussion of, ii. 303.
Extraordinary downpour of rain, i. 63.
Innkeeper not responsible for loss caused by, ii. 296.
Lord Mansfield's view of act of God, ii. 302.
Meaning of term 'act of God,' ii. 301.
Storm at sea, ii. 303.

ACT OF STATE, DOCTRINE OF, i. 36, 37.

ACTON BURNELL, STATUTE OF, ii. 326.

ADDISON, C. G.
Treatise on Torts, i., p. xxii.

ADDRESSEE.
Right of action for negligent transmission of telegram, i. 437.
Who is addressee of telegram, i. 436.

ADEQUACY OF CONSIDERATION.
See CONSIDERATION.

ADJUDICATION.
First step in legal evolution, iii. 3.

AID.
Incident of military tenure abolished by statute, iii. 296.

ADMIRALTY, COURT OF.
Contest with common-law courts, ii. 332.
Mercantile law administered in, ii. 332.
Waning influence of, ii. 332, 333.

ADPROMISSOR, ii. 435.

ADSTIPULATION.
Roman substitute for agency, ii. 435.

ADSTIPULATOR, ii. 435.

AËRONAUT.
Liability for damage incident to descent of balloon, i. 88.

AGENCY.
See also PRINCIPAL AND AGENT.
Agency a relation not a contract, ii. 432.
Agency associated with contractual relation, ii. 433.
Agency coupled with interest, ii. 491.
Agency imports relation of confidence, ii. 491.
Basis of law of, ii. 429.
Consent, bearing of, on agency, ii. 432.
Death, effect of, ii. 491.
Definition, ii. 433.
Fiction of, in transaction by bill of exchange, ii. 350.
Historical difficulties, ii. 429.
Kinship between law of service and law of agency, ii. 453.
Principle of equivalence in law of, ii. 473.
Requisites of true agency, ii. 434.
Roman law of agency, ii. 433.
St. Germain on law of agency, ii. 448, 449.
Scope of term, ii. 430.
Status, early law of agency implicated with, ii. 431.
Transition from status to consent in law of agency, ii. 431, 432

AGENT OF HARM.
Liability for maintenance of, i. 149.
Maintainer of dangerous agent relieved on surrendering harmful agent, i. 50.
Origin of conception of responsibility for damage done by, i. 51.
Responsibility for, i. 49, 50.

AGISTOR.
Agistor has no lien at common law, ii. 290.
Care required of agistor, ii. 296.
Not liable as person plying common calling, ii. 290.

AGREEMENT.
See STATUTE OF FRAUDS.

ALDERSON, B.
Definition of negligence, i. 96.
Measure of damage in breach of contract, i. 445.

ALTERATION.
Effect of alteration of negotiable instruments, ii. 546.
What constitutes alteration, ii. 546, 547.

AMES-BREWSTER.
Controversy over Negotiable Instruments Law, ii. 497.

AMES, PROF. J. B.
Considers bill of exchange a specialty, ii. 389.
Criticism of Lynn *v.* Bruce, ii. 101.
Criticism of Negotiable Instruments Law —
Section 64, ii. 533.
Section 65, ii. 534.
Sections 89, 135, ii. 539.
Section 175, ii. 556.
Interpretation of Negotiable Instruments Law —
Section 9, subs. 5, ii. 515.
Section 37, ii. 526.
Section 40, ii. 527.
Observation on scope of replevin, iii. 217.
Supposes part payment of debt may be good satisfaction of whole, ii. 99.
Theory of bilateral contract, ii. 107.

ANCIENT LIGHT, INTERFERENCE WITH.
See COGNATE NUISANCE.

ANDERSON, J.
Sanctions trover against innocent purchaser of vendee having no title, iii. 166.

ANGUISH, MENTAL.
See MENTAL DISTRESS.

ANIMALS.
Cattle, chasing, a ground of action in trespass, when, i. 15.
Dog —
Damage done by, i. 54.
Right to kill dog destroying poultry, i. 18.
Dog, vicious —
Action of person injured not affected by violation of Sunday law, i. 181.
Right to kill, i. 17.

ANIMALS — *Continued.*
Escaped animal, responsibility for injury to, i. 112, 114, 116.
Horse, damage done by kicking horse, i. 53.
Justification of trespass in pursuit of noxious animals, i. 21.
Negligence as affecting liability for injury by wild beast, i. 85.
Responsibility of owner of domestic animals, i. 51.
Responsibility of owner of wild beast, i. 55.
Right to kill dangerous trespassing beast, i. 17, 18.
Stallion, damage done by, i. 52.

ANIMUS CONTRAHENDI AS AFFECTING FORMATION OF CONTRACT, ii. 71.

ANSON, SIR WILLIAM.
Observation on Scotson *v.* Pegg, ii. 117, 118.
Validity of promise to pay barred debt, ii. 145.

APPEAL.
Appeal of felonious assault —
Predecessor of action of trespass, iii. 226.
Scope of remedy, iii. 229.
Appeal of larceny —
Predecessor of writ of trespass, iii. 226.
Scope of remedy, iii. 228.

APPLETON, C. J.
Observation on meaning of proximate cause, i. 110.

APPRENTICE.
Enticement of apprentice —
Basis of *quasi*-contractual duty, ii. 215.
Indebitatus assumpsit as remedy for, iii. 199.

ARBITRATION.
Adjudication of arbitrators creates duty in nature of debt, ii. 91.
Indebitatus assumpsit available as remedy to enforce performance of award, iii. 192.

ARBITRATOR.
Delegation of function not permitted, ii. 476.
Privilege of, i. 38.

ARRHA.
See EARNEST.

ART.
Fair comment and criticism on work of art. i. 303.

ARYAN.
Development of legal institutions among Aryan people, iii. 4.

ASCOGHE, J.
Breach of parol promise not actionable, i. 188.

ASPORTATION.
Conversion by, i. 231, 241.

ASSAULT AND BATTERY.
See TRESPASS ON PERSON.

ASSIGNMENT.
Assignability determined by reference to question of survivability, iii. 87.
Assignee may maintain suit in name of assignor, when, iii. 83.
Chose in action, development of law pertaining to assignment of, iii. 88.
Debt not assignable at common law, iii. 81.
King may assign chose in action, iii. 81.
King may sue as assignee of chose in action, iii. 81.
Lack of privity on part of assignee as affecting question of assignment, iii. 77.
Maintenance as affecting assignment of chose in action, iii. 82.
Novation as affecting assignment, iii. 88, 89.
Novation distinguished from assignment, iii. 89.
Personal right of action not assignable, iii. 76.
Property and property rights, transferable character of, iii. 78.
Right of action *ex contractu* assignable, when, iii. 86, 87.
Right of action *ex delicto* assignable, when, iii. 84–89.
Right of action founded on deceit not assignable, iii. 87.
Right of action founded on personal wrong not assignable, iii. 86.

ASSIGNOR AND ASSIGNEE.
Action in name of assignor to use of assignee, iii. 83–85.
Assignee of chose in action, present status of, iii. 85.
Assignee of instrument lacking words of negotiability sues in name of assignor, ii. 503.
Assignee of lease liable to assignor for breach of covenant, when, iii. 274, 275.
Bill or note payable to assignee negotiable, ii. 501.
Covenant binding on assignee, when, iii. 126.

ASSIGNS.
Appears as term of negotiability in bills of exchange, ii. 360.

ASSIZE.
See ASSIZE OF NUISANCE; ASSIZE UTRUM; DARREIN PRESENTMENT; MORTE D'ANCESTOR; NOVEL DISSEISIN.

ASSIZE OF NUISANCE.
Early remedy for nuisance, i. 213.
Scope of remedy, iii. 271.

ASSIZE UTRUM, iii. 37.

ASSOCIATION, UNINCORPORATED.
See UNINCORPORATED ASSOCIATION.

ASSUMPSIT.
Assumpsit an action in nature of deceit, iii. 173.
Assumpsit a specialized form of action on case, iii. 172.
Becomes purely contractual remedy, iii. 178.

ASSUMPSIT — *Continued.*
Case and assumpsit —
Election of remedies, iii. 273.
Respective limits, iii. 272, 277.
Covenant, assumpsit not maintainable on, iii. 123, 179.
Debt, assumpsit maintainable on simple debt, iii. 178.
Debt evidenced by seal, assumpsit not maintainable on, iii. 180.
Detriment to promisee as basis of liability in, iii. 173, 175, 176.
Early limits of assumpsit, ii. 200.
Fundamental notion underlying action, iii. 173.
Genesis of action, iii. 172–175.
Implied warranty in chattel sale, action of assumpsit as remedy on, i. 389, 390.
Misfeasance and nonfeasance distinguished, iii. 177.
Mutual promises, iii. 178.
Negligent performance of lawful undertaking, iii. 173.
Obligations in nature of assumpsit, ii. 235.
Plaintiff must unite in himself both promise and consideration, ii. 154.
Pleading —
Allegation of assumpsit, iii. 174.
Super se assumpsit, function of, in action against bailee, ii. 268.
Promise, emergence of idea of obligation of, iii. 174.
Promise supported by executed consideration, iii. 177.
Promise to pay existing debt, ii. 61; iii. 177.
Rent, assumpsit not maintainable for, iii. 180.
Sealed obligation, assumpsit not maintainable on, iii. 123, 179, 180.
Special assumpsit not maintainable without proof of promise in fact, iii. 186.
State of assumptual law at beginning of sixteenth century, iii. 176.
Super se assumpsit, allegation of, ii. 268.
Survival of action in assumpsit, iii. 68, 179.

ASSUMPTION OF RISK.
Concrete cases discussed —
Breaking of defective rope in colliery, i. 164.
Falling into vat of brewery, i. 165.
Injury received in making up train, i. 164.
Injury received in shunting trucks, i. 166.
Open hatchway of ship, i. 167.
Slippery approach to railroad station, i. 167.
Spring-gun case, i. 163.
Consent to incur risk takes away injurious character of act, i. 162.
Contributory negligence, analogy with, i. 150.
Contributory negligence distinguished, i. 165.
Contributory negligence identical with assumption of risk, when, i. 164.
Danger must be appreciated as well as perceived, i. 165.
Dangerous employment, risk assumed by person engaged in, i. 166.
Doctrine of assumed risk, i. 150.
Doctrine of assumption of risk in America, i. 169.
Employers' Liability Act as affecting assumption of risk, i. 170.

ASSUMPTION OF RISK — *Continued.*
Essentials to assumption of risk, i. 166.
Fellow-servant doctrine, i. 170.
Guest, risk assumed by, when, i. 157.
Implied assumpsit of risk, i. 157.
Involuntary submission to risk, i. 168.
Driving dangerous horse under protest, i. 167.
Exposure of servant to unnecessary risk, i. 168.
Knowledge of danger not conclusive of assumption of risk, i. 169.
Licensee —
Defective carriage, i. 159.
Falling from roof, i. 158.
Falling into quarry, i. 158.
Falling through bridge over private way, i. 158.
Going into dark warehouse, i. 158.
Spectator killed by collapse of steam crane, i. 159.
Licensee, risk assumed by, when, i. 157.
Question for jury, when, i. 166, 167.
Servant —
Risk assumed by, when, i. 157.
Servant assumes risks naturally incident to employment, i. 164.
Trespasser —
Collapse of old structure, i. 156.
Falling into pit, i. 156.
Injury from electric wire, i. 155.
Injury from spring gun, i. 163.
Risk of injury assumed by trespasser, i. 155.
Trespassing animals —
Eating yew leaves, i. 156, 157.
Stray animal eating injurious substance, i. 157.
Stray horse falling into pit, i. 156.
Turntable cases, i. 159.
Volenti non fit injuria, import of maxim, i. 162.

ATTORNEY.
Arguments absolutely privileged, when, i. 307.
Communication with client privileged, when, i. 311.
Power of attorney authorizing assignee to sue in name of assignor, iii. 84.

ATTORNEY'S FEE.
Clause providing for collection of, does not destroy negotiability, ii. 505.

AUCTION.
Statute of frauds as affecting sale at, ii. 505.

AUCTIONEER.
Conversion, when auctioneer liable for sale in course of business, i. 244.
Right to recover auction tax of person whose property is sold, ii. 233.
Statute of frauds, auctioneer agent of buyer or seller for making memorandum, ii. 175.

AUDITORS.
Accounting before, iii. 107, 108.

AUSTIN, JOHN.
Criticism of Blackstone's theory of function of judge, i. 498.
Theory of master's responsibility for negligence of servant, ii. 459.

AVIGNON, STATUTE OF, ii. 335.

AVOWANT, iii. 212.

AVOWRY IN REPLEVIN, iii. 212.

AXIOM.
Axiom of representation, ii. 463, 464.

BACON, MATTHEW.
Explanation of doctrine of trespass *ab initio*, iii. 243.
Theory of law of master and servant, ii. 466, 467.

BAD FAITH.
Bad faith essential to liability in slander of title, i. 323.

BAILEE.
Allegation of assumpsit in action against, ii. 267, 268.
Bailee a debtor for chattel bailed, ii. 25, 263.
Bailee for hire, liability of, ii. 254.
Bailee's action against stranger a corollary from right of possession, ii. 316.
Bailee's action against stranger supposed to depend on responsibility to owner, ii. 315.
Repudiation of this notion, ii. 315.
Conversion by bailee, iii. 162.
Debtor, bailee ceases to be liable as debtor, ii. 267.
Diligence used in caring for own goods no criterion for determining liability of, ii. 275.
Embezzlement by, made criminal by statute, ii. 311.
Gratuitous bailee —
May sue stranger in trover, when, i. 252.
Replevin not maintainable by, iii. 313.
Larcenous conversion by, ii. 310.
Liability for jewels delivered in sealed chest, ii. 256.
Liability of bailee when sued in account, ii. 265.
Negligence essential to liability when bailee sued in case, ii. 265.
Negligent keeping of goods by bailee not conversion, i. 237.
Possession —
Bailee's possession good against bailor, ii. 311.
Possession equivalent to property as against stranger, ii. 314.
Possessory right of bailee, ii. 309.
When possession of bailee ceases, ii. 309.
Robbery as defense for factor, ii. 262.
Robbery or theft of chattel no defense for bailee, when, ii. 255.
Special property of bailee, ii. 311, 313, 314.
Special property of bailee for term, ii. 314.

BAILEE — *Continued.*
Special property, right of possession identified with, ii. 311, 312.
Trover maintainable by bailee because of special property, ii. 313.
Unpreventable loss, ii. 255.
Wrongdoer cannot plead want of title in bailee, ii. 316.

BAILIFF.
Accountant distinguished from bailiff, iii. 100.
Accountant, responsibility of bailiff as, iii. 106.
Account as remedy against bailiff, iii. 100, 102.
Bailee distinguished from, iii. 101.
Bailiff defined, iii. 101.
Bailiff of own wrong, extent of liability, iii. 106.
Implied authority, ii. 448.
Power to bind principal, ii. 447.

BAILMENT.
Antiquity of, ii. 251.
Bailee, bailment for benefit of, ii. 273.
Bailee liable as debtor, rule peculiar to detinue, ii. 265.
Bailee liable for gross negligence, ii. 275.
Bailment at request of bailee, ii. 280.
Bailment for safe keeping —
Liability of bailor, ii. 263.
Mode of declaring on duty to keep, ii. 264.
Bailor, bailment for benefit of, ii. 273.
Bailor has no action against stranger, when, ii. 258.
Bonion's Case, doctrine of, ii. 256, 257.
Bractonian epoch in law of, ii. 15.
Carriage, bailment for, ii. 298.
Colorable bailment, ii. 309.
Contract *re*, bailment identified with, ii. 1, 251.
Definition of, ii. 308.
Degree of care required of bailee, i. 99.
Early law of bailment, ii. 251.
Strictness of doctrine, ii. 253.
English character of law of bailment, ii. 318.
Foreign influence on law of bailment, ii. 318.
Gratuitous bailment —
Gratuitous bailment distinguished from bailment for hire, ii. 269.
Liability of bailee for act of servant, ii. 277.
Misfeasance on part of bailee, ii. 270.
Negligence makes bailee liable, ii. 270.
Liability of bailee for mutilation of chattel, ii. 256.
Lord Holt's classification of bailments, genesis of, ii. 271.
Lost goods, finder a *quasi*-depositary, ii. 278.
Meaning of term, ii. 251.
Modern law of bailment, ii. 270, 294.
Mosaic law of bailment, ii. 274.
Mutual benefit of parties, bailment for, ii. 273.
Ownership and possession, severance of, ii. 252, 308.

BAILMENT — *Continued.*
Readjustment incident to development of conception of obligation of promise, ii. 47.
Sale distinguished from bailment, ii. 290.
Sealed package, when custodian liable as bailee for contents of, ii. 257.
Special proviso against absolute liability, ii. 260.
Stranger, bailee's action against, ii. 258.

BAILOR.
Action for recovery of chattel, ii. 252.
Bailor is owner, ii. 317.
General property of bailor, ii. 318.
Incomplete remedy of bailor as against third person, iii. 50.
Trover maintainable by owner against sub-bailee, when, ii. 313.

BALDWIN, C. J.
Observation on remedy for public nuisance, i. 224.

BANK.
Bankers' lien, ii. 421.
Check on early bank of deposit not transferable, ii. 338.
Early bank of deposit, ii. 337.
Florentine bankers —
Exchange business conducted by, ii. 336.
Financially damaged by repudiation of debts of Edward III., ii. 336.
London goldsmiths engage in banking, ii. 367.

BANKING.
Estoppel of depositor by negligent failure to examine returned checks, ii. 248.
Liability of bank for embezzlement of special deposit, ii. 276.

BANK OF ENGLAND.
Transferability of dividend warrants, ii. 420.

BANK OF VENICE.
First bank of deposit, ii. 337.

BARCELONA, ORDINANCE OF, ii. 337.

BARGAIN AND SALE.
Assumpsit as remedy for breach of contract of sale, ii. 33.
Bargain and sale ceases to be contract *re*, ii. 27.
Bracton, bargain and sale in time of, ii. 15.
Conditions of validity of contract of sale in early law, ii. 5.
Debt and detinue as remedies of seller and buyer, ii. 26.
Early law, bargain and sale in, ii. 4.
Extension of early doctrine, ii. 26.
Fraud and false warranty in chattel sale, see DECEIT.
Independence of reciprocal duties resulting from, ii. 133.
Payment, effect of, ii. 27.
Risk of loss with person having possession, ii. 5.
Title passes on agreement of sale without payment, ii. 27.
Vendee cannot maintain trover for conversion by seller, when, i. 252.
Vendee may maintain detinue, when, iii. 145.
Warranty given after sale invalid, ii. 86.

BARREL.
Implied warranty of fitness for particular purpose, i. 387.

BARTER, ANTIQUITY OF, ii. 2.

BATHURST, J.
Circumstances of time and place of injury as affecting exemplary damages, i. 484.

BATTERY.
See TRESPASS ON PERSON.

BATTLE.
Analogy of trial by battle to *actio sacramenti*, iii. 25.
Early mode of trial, iii. 25.

BAY, J.
Observation on law of distress, iii. 308.

BAYLEY, J.
Application of maxim *volenti non fit injuria*, i. 163.
Originates idea of malice in law, i. 317.

BEALE, PROF. J. H.
Manuscript report of Chandelor *v.* Lopus, i. 381.
Manuscript report of Southcott *v.* Bennett, ii. 263.
Theory concerning liability of bailee, ii. 66.
Theory concerning liability of carrier, ii. 302.

BEARER.
See BILLS AND NOTES.
Bill payable to, held good, ii. 394.
Negotiable Instruments Law, when instrument payable to bearer under, ii. 510.
Term descriptive of person taking under contract, ii. 394.

BELTING.
Camel-hair belting, secondary signification of, i. 429.

BENEFIT TO PROMISOR.
See CONSIDERATION.

BENJAMIN, JUDAH P.
Modern English doctrine of implied warranty in chattel sales, i. 384.

BENNETT, PROF. E. H.
Supposes benefit to promisor to be good consideration, ii. 69.

BENTHAM, JEREMY.
Theory of responsibility of master for negligent act of servant, ii. 459.

BERREWIK, J.
Observation on origin of plea *de vetito namio*, iii. 210.

BEVEN, T.
Theory of liability for negligence, i. 90.

BIGELOW, C. J.
Observation on duty of telegraph company to use care, i. 440.

BIGELOW, PROF. M. M.
Antiquity of tort of malicious prosecution, i. 328.
Definition of tort, i., p. xxvi.
Observation on forms of action in early English law, iii. 26, 27.
BILATERAL CONTRACT.
In general —
Consensual nature of bilateral contract, ii. 59, 107.
Effect of recognizing, ii. 56.
Need for recognition of, ii. 56.
Origin and nature, ii. 52, 55.
Scope of bilateral contract, ii. 59, 107, 122.
Scope of bilateral contract broader than scope of unilateral contract, ii. 111.
Consideration in, ii. 55, 57, 110.
Consists of mutual parol promises or of mutual covenants, ii. 132.
Content of mutual promises, ii. 110.
Character of thing promised, ii. 110.
Dependence of mutual promises, ii. 132, 135.
Dilemma of legal theory, ii. 137.
Doctrine of mutual dependence, ii. 136.
General dependence, ii. 140.
Holt's statement of doctrine of mutual dependence, ii. 136.
Intention of parties, ii. 138.
Macclesfield's solution of problem of dependence, ii. 137.
Mutual concurrent conditions, doctrine of, ii. 138–140.
Readiness to perform, ii. 139.
Limitations imposed by doctrine of consideration, ii. 60.
Mutuality of promises gives validity to both, ii. 109.
Mutual promises in furtherance of existing obligation valid, ii. 116.
American authorities, ii. 117.
Conflict of authority, ii. 119.
Explanation of validity of bilateral contract, ii. 118.
Qualification of doctrine, ii. 120.
Promise given for discharge of statutory or official duty invalid, ii. 120.
Promise of performance of existing obligation, ii. 112.
Scotson *v.* Pegg, doctrine of, ii. 116.
Theory of bilateral contract in unsatisfactory state, ii. 107.
Theory that contract is based on consideration in sense of detriment —
View of Prof. Ames, ii. 108.
View that each party incurs detriment in assuming or promising, ii. 108.
Unilateral contract distinguished from, ii. 53.
Validity not recognized in early law, ii. 20, 36.
Wager, validity of, ii. 110.
BILLÆ NUNDINALES.
Bill of exchange payable at fair, ii. 507.
BILL OF DEBT.
See Bills and Notes.
Identified with promissory note, ii. 354, 355.
Modes of negotiation in seventeenth century, ii. 357.

BILLS AND NOTES.
Absence of words of negotiability —
Distinction between English and American law, ii. 387.
Effect of, stated by Marius, ii. 361.
Acceptance, ii. 374
Acceptance not according to tenor of bill, ii. 374.
Acceptor becomes primarily liable, ii. 397.
Constructive acceptance by retention of bill, ii. 411.
Honor, acceptance for, ii. 374.
Irrevocability of acceptance, ii. 374.
Oral acceptance invalid under Negotiable Instruments Law, ii. 548.
Promise to accept equivalent to acceptance, when, ii. 400.
Provisions of Ordinance of Barcelona, ii. 337.
Qualified acceptance, ii. 374.
Signature of acceptor, when necessary, ii. 549.
Verbal acceptance, ii. 401.
Virtual acceptance, ii. 401.
Requisites, ii. 402.
Acceptor —
Obligation to payee, ii. 340, 345.
Undertaking of, ii. 412.
Action on bill, nature of, ii. 349.
Adaptation of bills to common-law theory of contract, ii. 343.
Agency, relation between remitter and payee, ii. 346.
Agent, liability of purported agent, ii. 410.
Alteration, effect of, ii. 546.
Ambulatory character of bill of exchange, ii. 325.
Assignee of non-negotiable instrument sues in name of assignee, ii. 341.
Attorney's fee, effect on negotiation of note, ii. 505.
Bank note, innocent purchaser gets good title, ii. 393.
Bearer cannot maintain action, when, ii. 379.
Bearer, term formerly not used as word of negotiability, ii. 372, 380.
Bill becomes transferable, ii. 359.
Bill executed in blank, ii. 359.
Bill given for precedent debt treated as conditional payment, ii. 390.
Bill need not originate in trading transaction, ii. 379.
Bill not to be made payable to bearer or bringer, ii. 356, 357.
Bill of debt not negotiable in early period, ii. 329.
Bill of exchange —
Drawer —
No longer primarily liable after acceptance, ii. 397.
Bill or note given for debt operates as absolute payment, when, ii. 390.
Bill payable on contingency not negotiable, ii. 392.
Bill supposed to be good without consideration, ii. 141, 383.
Notion repudiated in House of Lords, ii. 142.
Blank indorsement of bill payable to order, ii. 394, 511.
Common-law principles ingrafted on law merchant, ii. 409.
Consideration —
Burden of showing want of, on defendant, ii. 389.
Consideration essential to validity of bill, ii. 387–389.

BILLS AND NOTES — *Continued.*
Consideration — *Continued.*
Consideration not alleged in early declaration, ii. 382.
From whom consideration to move, ii. 389.
Presumption of consideration, ii. 382.
Recital of consideration in early bill of exchange, ii. 382.
Courts take judicial notice of custom of merchant, ii. 351.
Currency of the bill, ii. 395.
Currency theory contrasted with mercantile theory, ii. 395.
Custom need not be specially pleaded, ii. 351.
Custom of merchants comes to apply to all foreign bills, ii. 350.
Death, instrument payable at fixed time after, ii. 507.
Decisive epoch in law of bills and notes, ii. 393.
Deposit, assignment of, in bank of deposit, ii. 355.
Difficulty incident to use of special assumpsit as remedy on, ii. 347.
Drawee, liability on destroyed bill, ii. 411.
Drawer —
Obligation to remitter, ii. 340, 344.
Undertaking of drawer, ii. 412.
Earliest reported action on bill of exchange, ii. 347.
Early action by assignee against payee of bill, ii. 341.
Early bill, ii. 337.
Early bill not negotiable, ii. 339.
Early bill not payable to order, ii. 356.
Early bill sanctioned by business custom only, ii. 355, 357.
Exchequer bill, negotiability of, ii. 404.
Fair, instrument payable at particular fair negotiable, ii. 507.
Fiction of agency between remitter and payee, ii. 350.
Fictitious party, bill payable to, treated as payable to bearer, ii. 403.
Foreign bill only instrument approved by early custom of merchants, ii. 344, 355.
Forgery, effect on rights of parties, ii. 520.
French and English law compared, ii. 396.
Grace —
Grace before protest for nonpayment, ii. 373, 374.
Instrument entitled, though lacking words of negotiability, ii. 387.
Historical treatment of bills and notes a desideratum, ii. 323.
Holder of negotiable instrument not mere assignee, ii. 394.
Holder of office, instrument payable to, negotiable, ii. 510.
Immaturity of English contract law in sixteenth century, ii. 340.
Indorsement —
Anomalous indorsement, ii. 533.
Form of indorsement, ii. 361.
Indorsement in blank, effect stated by Marius, ii. 361.
Indorsement in blank makes bill payable to bearer, ii. 394
Indorsement of non-negotiable bill, ii. 377.
Indorsement operates as drawing of new bill, ii. 377, 378.
Special indorsement does not affect negotiability, ii. 398.
Indorser —
Becomes drawer of new bill, ii. 362.
Estoppel of, ii. 412.

BILLS AND NOTES — *Continued.*
Indorser — *Continued.*
Indorser discharged by non-presentment, ii. 378.
Liability of indorser, ii. 361, 362.
Liability placed on equitable grounds, ii. 376.
Liable to holder before exhaustion of remedies against party primarily liable, ii. 378.
Undertaking of indorser, ii. 412.
Warranties of indorser, ii. 414.
Warranties pass to subsequent holder, ii. 414.
Warranty of indorser without recourse, ii. 415.
Inland bill —
Inland bill comes into commercial use, ii. 368.
Inland bill held to be within custom of merchants, ii. 360, 369.
Inland bill of equal validity with foreign bill, ii. 370.
Promissory note contemporary with inland bill, ii. 369.
Promissory note placed on same footing, ii. 385.
Protest for nonacceptance permitted by statute, ii. 380.
Protest for nonpayment permitted, ii. 380.
Protest unnecessary at common law, ii. 380.
Innocent purchaser —
Bad faith necessary to defeat title, ii. 407.
Carelessness tending to show bad faith, ii. 407.
Circumstances giving rise to imputation of fraud, ii. 405.
Gill *v.* Cubitt, radical doctrine of, ii. 405, 406.
Gross negligence necessary to deprive of rights of *bona fide* holder, ii. 406.
Notice of defects, ii. 404.
Purchaser not bound to inquire into antecedents of paper, ii. 404.
Innocent purchaser transmits good title to one having knowledge of defects, when, ii. 408.
Instrument lacking words of negotiability —
Assignee must sue in name of assignor, ii. 503.
Assignee, rights acquired by, ii. 503.
Consideration presumed, ii. 504.
Grace attached to, ii. 387.
Indorsement, ii. 503.
Instrument payable to bearer, early illustration of, ii. 329.
Interplay between custom and law, ii. 409.
Italian origin of bill of exchange, ii. 337.
Legal relations of parties to early bill of exchange, ii. 339.
Lost instrument —
Action not maintainable on, ii. 375.
Marius's opinion, ii. 375.
Marius's treatise on bills of exchange, ii. 360.
Marriage, instrument payable at future marriage not negotiable, ii. 508.
Method of growth, ii. 416.
Negotiability —
Features incident to, ii. 500.
Requisites under Negotiable Instruments Law, ii. 500.
Stipulation for retention of title to secure purchase price, ii. 506.

BILLS AND NOTES — *Continued.*
Negotiability defined, ii. 500.
Negotiable Instruments Law —
Acceptance —
Acceptance necessary to discharge drawee (§ 127), ii. 548.
Acceptance to be written on the bill, when (§ 133), ii. 549.
Acceptance written on paper other than bill (§ 134), ii. 549.
Conditional acceptance (§ 141), ii. 550.
Constructive acceptance by retention of bill (§ 137), ii. 549.
Incomplete bill (§ 138), ii. 550.
Joint acceptance (§§ 139, 140), ii. 550.
Local acceptance (§ 141), ii. 550.
Overdue and dishonored bill (§ 138), ii. 550.
Partial acceptance (§ 141), ii. 550.
Promise in writing to accept bill (§ 135), ii. 549.
Qualified acceptance (§ 142), ii. 551.
Qualified acceptance, right of holder to refuse (§ 142), ii. 551.
Qualified acceptance, what is (§§ 139, 141), ii. 550.
Requisites of acceptance and mode of making same (§ 132), ii. 548.
Time within which acceptance to be given (§ 136), ii. 549.
Acceptance for honor —
Acceptance for honor, *supra* protest must be in writing (§ 162), ii. 554.
Acceptor for honor, engagement of (§ 165), ii. 555.
Acceptor for honor, to whom liable (§ 164), ii. 554.
Drawer, acceptance for honor in behalf of (§ 163), ii. 554.
Instrument payable after sight, maturity of (§ 166), ii. 555.
Party for whose benefit acceptance for honor may be made (§ 161), ii. 554.
Reference in case of need (§ 167), ii. 555.
Accommodation party, liability of (§ 29), ii. 522.
Agent, when personally liable (§ 20), ii. 518.
Ambiguous instrument, construction of (§ 17), ii. 518.
Antedating, effect of (§ 12), ii. 515.
Assignment, bill does not operate as assignment of fund (§ 127), ii. 548.
Attorneys' fees, instrument payable with (§ 2), ii. 505.
Bank, making instrument payable at bank authorizes payment by bank (§ 87), ii. 538.
Bearer, when instrument payable to (§ 9), ii. 510.
Bill of exchange —
Definition (§ 126), ii. 547.
Promissory note, when bill of exchange may be treated as (§ 130), ii. 548.
Bills in set —
Acceptance, how to be made (§ 181), ii. 557.
Acceptor, liability of (§ 182), ii. 557.
Discharge of one part discharges all (§ 183), ii. 557.

BILLS AND NOTES — *Continued.*
Negotiable Instruments Law — *Continued.*
Bills in set — *Continued.*
Negotiation of separate parts to different holders —
General effect of (§ 179), ii. 557.
Indorser, liability of (§ 180), ii. 557.
Several parts constitute one bill (§ 178), ii. 557.
Blank in negotiable instrument operates as notice of limitation of holder's authority, when, ii. 516, 517.
Blanks, authority of holder to supply (§ 14), ii. 515.
Collateral securities, provision for sale of (§ 5), ii. 508.
Confession of judgment, provision for (§ 5), ii. 508.
Consideration, failure of, made a defense (§ 28), ii. 522.
Consideration in negotiable instruments, ii. 521.
Construction of language of statute (§ 17), ii. 518.
Contingency, instrument payable on (§ 4), ii. 507.
Date, presumption in undated instrument (§ 17), ii. 518.
Date stated in instrument assumed as *prima facie* true (§ 11), ii. 515.
Debt, antecedent or pre-existing (§ 25), ii. 521.
Delivery, by whom and when to be made (§ 16), ii. 517.
Delivery essential to make instrument complete (§ 16), ii. 517.
Demand, when instrument payable on (§ 17), ii. 509.
Determinable future time (§ 4), ii. 507.
Discharge of negotiable instruments —
Act sufficient to discharge simple contract (§ 119), ii. 544.
Alteration —
Effect (§ 124), ii. 546.
Material alteration, what is (§ 135), ii. 547.
Cancellation, burden of proof (§ 123), ii. 546.
Cancellation by holder (§ 119), ii. 544.
Cancellation by mistake (§ 123), ii. 546.
Parties secondarily liable, when discharged (§ 120), ii. 544.
Payment by accommodated party (§ 119), ii. 544.
Payment by party secondarily liable (§ 121), ii. 545.
Payment in due course (§ 119), ii. 543.
Principal debtor becoming holder in own right (§ 119), ii. 544.
Renunciation by holder —
Effect (§ 122), ii. 546.
How made (§ 122), ii. 546.
Election to require something to be done in lieu of payment of money (§ 5), ii. 508.
Election to take stock in corporation, effect of provision for (§ 5), ii. 508.
Estate of deceased person, instrument payable to, ii. 514.
Exchange, instrument payable with (§ 2), ii. 505.
Exemptions —
Waiver of, effect of provision for (§ 5), ii. 508.
Fictitious or non-existing person, instrument payable to (§ 9), ii. 510–513.

BILLS AND NOTES — *Continued.*
Negotiable Instruments Law — *Continued.*
Fictitious or non-existing person, instrument payable to, is payable to bearer without being indorsed, ii. 513.
Forgery, effect of, on rights of parties (§ 23), ii. 519.
Form and interpretation of negotiable instruments, ii. 500.
Gambling contract, effect of statute on, ii. 498.
General principles of construction, ii. 498.
Holder of office, instrument payable to (§ 8), ii. 510.
Holder, when deemed holder for value (§ 26), ii. 522.
Incomplete instrument, negotiation of (§ 15), ii. 517.
Indorsement —
Indorsement in blank (§ 9), ii. 511, 514, 515.
Want of capacity on part of corporation or infant (§ 22), ii. 519.
Indorser —
Presumption from signature (§ 17), ii. 518.
Who is (§ 63), ii. 532.
Inland bill (§ 129), ii. 548.
Instalments, instrument payable in (§ 2), ii. 505.
Interest, when begins to run (§ 17), ii. 518.
Joint drawee (§ 128), ii. 548.
Kind of money stipulated for (§ 6), ii. 509.
Law merchant, instrument not falling within statute governed by (§ 196), ii. 559.
Liabilities of parties —
Acceptor —
Admissions (§ 62), ii. 532.
Engagement (§ 62), ii. 532.
Agent for undisclosed principal (§ 69), ii. 536.
Drawer, engagement of (§ 61), ii. 532.
Indorser —
Indorser of instrument negotiable by delivery (§ 67), ii. 535.
Order of liability (§ 68), ii. 535.
To whom and how liable (§ 64), ii. 533.
Warranties (§ 66), ii. 535.
Joint indorsers liable as if indorsing severally (§ 68), ii. 535.
Maker, engagement of (§ 60), ii. 532.
Person negotiating by delivery or qualified indorsement, warranties of (§ 65), ii. 533.
Lienholder a holder for value (§ 27), ii. 522.
Negotiation, ii. 523.
Blank indorsement (§ 34), ii. 524.
By delivery (§ 30), ii. 523.
By indorsement (§ 31), ii. 523.
Conditional indorsement, ii. 527.
Holder may convert blank indorsement into special indorsement (§ 35), ii. 525.
Holder may strike out indorsement, when (§ 48), ii. 528.

BILLS AND NOTES — *Continued.*
Negotiable Instruments Law — *Continued.*
Negotiation — *Continued.*
Indorsement by person acting in representative capacity (§ 44), ii. 528.
Indorsement by person whose name misspelled (§ 43), ii. 528.
Indorsement, how made, ii. 523.
Instrument payable to fiscal officer (§ 42), ii. 528.
Instrument payable to two or more payees (§ 41), ii. 528.
Overdue paper, presumption regarding (§ 45), ii. 528.
Partial indorsement invalid (§ 32), ii. 524.
Place of indorsement, presumption concerning (§ 46), ii. 528.
Qualified indorsement (§ 38), ii. 526.
Recourse, indorsement without, ii. 526.
Reissue of paper negotiated back to prior party (§ 50), ii. 529.
Restrictive indorsement (§ 36), ii. 525.
Special indorsement (§ 34), ii. 524.
Special indorsement of instrument payable to bearer (§ 40), ii. 527.
Striking out indorsement (§ 48), ii. 528.
Transfer without indorsement (§ 49), ii. 529.
New York State enacts Negotiable Instruments Law, ii. 496.
Notice of dishonor —
Address, when notice to be sent to (§ 108), ii. 542.
Agent, notice given by (§§ 91, 94), ii. 540.
Bankrupt, giving notice to (§ 101), ii. 541.
Delay in giving notice, when excused (§ 113), ii. 543.
Delivery of notice, how made (§ 96), ii. 540.
Dispensed with, when (§ 112), ii. 542.
Drawer entitled to (§ 89), ii. 538.
Drawer of check entitled to, ii. 539.
Drawer, when notice unnecessary to (§ 114), ii. 543.
Indorser entitled to (§ 89), ii. 538.
Indorser, when notice of dishonor unnecessary (§ 115), ii. 543.
Joint parties, giving of notice to (§ 100), ii. 541.
Nonacceptance, failure to give notice of dishonor by (§ 117), ii. 543.
Nonpayment, notice unnecessary when paper dishonored by nonacceptance (§ 116), ii. 543.
Oral notice, requisites of (§ 96), ii. 540.
Partners, giving of notice to (§ 99), ii. 541.
Party by whom notice may be given (§ 90), ii. 540.
Party to whom notice to be given (§ 97), ii. 541.
Personal representative, when notice to be given (§ 98), ii. 541.
Place to which notice to be sent (§ 108), ii. 542.
Post, notice sent by (§§ 105, 106), ii. 541.
Time when notice to be given (§§ 102–104, 107), ii. 541.
To whose benefit giving of notice inures (§§ 92, 93), ii. 540.

BILLS AND NOTES — *Continued.*
Negotiable Instruments Law — *Continued.*
Notice of dishonor — *Continued.*
Waiver embodied in instrument (§ 110), ii. 542.
Waiver of protest includes waiver of notice (§ 111), ii. 542.
Waiver, when may be made (§ 109), ii. 542.
Written notice (§ 95), ii. 540.
Order, to whose order instrument may be drawn (§ 8), ii. 510.
Order, when instrument payable to (§ 8), ii. 510.
Origin of Negotiable Instruments Law, ii. 495, 496.
Overdue paper payable on demand (§ 7), ii. 509.
Particular fund, instrument payable from (§ 3), ii. 506.
Payment for honor —
Effect (§ 175), ii. 555.
Notarial attestation of payment for honor (§§ 172, 173), ii. 555.
Party for whose benefit intervention may be made (§ 171), ii. 555.
Party making payment for honor, rights of (§ 177), ii. 556.
Party who may intervene (§ 174), ii. 555.
Refusal to receive payment for honor, effect of (§ 176), ii. 556.
Payment in due course, what is (§ 88), ii. 538.
Person not intended to have interest in proceeds of bill, instrument payable to, ii. 511, 512.
Place where drawn, absence of recital immaterial (§ 6), ii. 509.
Place where payable, absence of recital immaterial (§ 6), ii. 509.
Post-dating, effect of (§ 12), ii. 515.
Presentment for acceptance —
Delay, when excused (§ 147), ii. 552.
Dishonor for nonacceptance (§ 149), ii. 552.
Holder's right of recourse against drawer or indorser (§ 151), ii. 552.
Failure to accept (§ 150), ii. 552.
Party by whom presentment must be made (§ 145), ii. 551.
Presentment for payment excused on dishonor by nonacceptance (§ 151), ii. 552.
Presentment to be made in reasonable time (§ 144), ii. 551.
Time when presentment to be made (§§ 145, 146), ii. 551.
When necessary (§ 143), ii. 551.
When presentment excused (§ 148), ii. 552.
Presentment for payment —
Acceptor for honor, when and where presentment must be made to (§ 168), ii. 555.
Accommodation paper, presentment not necessary to charge indorser, when (§ 80), ii. 537.
Bank, instrument payable at (§ 75), ii. 537.
By whom to be made (§ 72), ii. 536.
Certificate of deposit, presentment necessary to charge indorser, ii. 536.
Delay in making presentment, when excused (§ 81), ii. 537.

BILLS AND NOTES — *Continued.*
Negotiable Instruments Law — *Continued.*
Presentment for payment — *Continued.*
Delay in presentment to acceptor for honor or referee in case of need (§ 169), ii. 555.
Demand paper, when presentment to be made (§ 71), ii. 536.
Drawer —
Presentment necessary to charge (§ 70), ii. 536.
Presentment not necessary to charge, when (§ 79), ii. 537.
Grace not allowed on paper payable at fixed time (§ 85), ii. 538.
Holiday, instrument maturing on (§ 85), ii. 538.
Indorser, presentment necessary to charge (§ 70), ii. 536.
Instrument not payable on demand, when presentment to be made (§ 71), ii. 536.
Instrument to be exhibited to person of whom payment is demanded (§ 74), ii. 537.
Nonpayment, effect of dishonor by (§ 84), ii. 538.
Parties severally liable, presentment to (§ 78), ii. 537.
Partners, presentment to (§ 77), ii. 537.
Personal representative, presentment to (§ 76), ii. 537.
Person primarily liable, presentment not necessary to charge (§ 70), ii. 536.
Person to whom presentment to be made (§ 72), ii. 536.
Place at which to be made (§ 73), ii. 536.
Saturday, instrument maturing on (§ 85), ii. 538.
Sunday, instrument maturing on (§ 85), ii. 538.
Time of maturity, computation of (§ 86), ii. 538.
Time when to be made (§ 72), ii. 536; (§ 75), ii. 537.
Waiver of presentment (§ 82), ii. 538.
When presentment for payment dispensed with (§ 82), ii. 537.
Presumption of value, ii. 521.
Procuration, signature by (§ 21), ii. 519.
Promise to do act in addition to payment of money, effect of (§ 5), ii. 508.
Promissory notes and checks —
Check —
Assignment of fund, check does not operate as (§ 189), ii. 558.
Certification (§ 187), ii. 558.
Definition (§ 185), ii. 557.
Drawer and indorser discharged by certification, when (§ 188), ii. 558.
Presentment for payment (§ 186), ii. 558.
Promissory note, definition of (§ 184), ii. 557.
Protest —
Circumstances excusing protest (§ 159), ii. 554.
Contents of protest (§ 153), ii. 553.
Delay in protest (§ 159), ii. 554.
Failure to make, effect of (§ 152), ii. 553.

BILLS AND NOTES — *Continued.*
Negotiable Instruments Law — *Continued.*
Protest — *Continued.*
Foreign bill (§ 118), ii. 543.
Inland bill, protest unnecessary (§ 152), ii. 552.
Lost instrument, mode of protesting (§ 160), ii. 554.
Nonacceptance, protest for (§ 152), ii. 552.
Nonpayment, protest following protest for nonacceptance (§ 157), ii. 553.
Nonpayment, protest for (§ 152), ii. 552.
Nonpayment, protest on dishonor by acceptor for honor (§ 170), ii. 555.
Place where protest to be made (§ 156), ii. 553.
Protest for better security (§ 158), ii. 554.
Protest, how made (§ 154), ii. 553.
Requisites of protest (§ 153), ii. 553.
Time when protest to be made (§ 155), ii. 553.
Waiver, effect of (§ 111), ii. 542.
Referee in case of need (§ 131), ii. 548.
Retention of title by seller, effect of stipulation for, ii. 506.
Rights of holder —
Burden of proof on question of innocent purchase (§ 59), ii. 532.
Demand paper negotiated after unreasonable time (§ 53), ii. 530.
Holder in due course —
Extent of right (§ 57), ii. 531.
Who is (§ 52), ii. 529.
Holder may sue in own name (§ 51), ii. 529.
Holder receiving notice of infirmity after part payment (§ 54), ii. 530.
Holder's title as affected by fraud or duress (§ 55), ii. 530.
Holder's title defective, when (§ 55), ii. 530.
Notice of infirmity (§ 56), ii. 531.
When instrument subject to defenses (§ 38), ii. 532.
Seal, presence does not destroy negotiability (§ 6), ii. 509.
Several drawees (§ 128), ii. 548.
Signature made by authorized agent (§ 19), ii. 518.
Signature on blank paper authority to complete note, when (§ 14), ii. 515.
Statement of transaction, effect of (§ 3), ii. 506.
States where statute in force, ii. 496.
Statute not applicable to negotiable instruments delivered prior to passage (§ 195), ii. 559.
Statute requiring nature of consideration to be stated (§ 6), ii. 509.
Successive drawees (§ 128), ii. 548.
Sum certain (§ 2), ii. 505.
Sunday, act required to be done on Sunday or holiday to be done on next succeeding business day (§ 194), ii. 559.

BILLS AND NOTES — *Continued.*
Negotiable Instruments Law — *Continued.*
Terms of instrument, sufficiency of (§ 10), ii. 515.
Time for payment, effect of omission to state (§ 7), ii. 509.
Trade name, effect of use (§ 18), ii. 518.
Unconditional promise (§ 3), ii. 506.
Undated instrument —
Right of holder to insert true date (§ 13), ii. 515.
Unincorporated association, instrument payable to, ii. 514.
Usage of trade or business as affecting 'reasonable time' (§ 193), ii. 559.
Value received, absence of recital immaterial (§ 6), ii. 509.
Waiver of benefit, provision for (§ 5), ii. 508.
Words and phrases —
Acceptance (§ 191), ii. 558.
Bank (§ 191), ii. 558.
Bearer (§ 191), ii. 558.
Bill (§ 191), ii. 558.
Delivery (§ 191), ii. 558.
Holder (§ 191), ii. 558.
Indorsement (§ 191), ii. 558.
Instrument (§ 191), ii. 558.
Issue (§ 191), ii. 558.
Note (§ 191), ii. 558.
Person (§ 191), ii. 558.
Primarily liable (§ 192), ii. 559.
Reasonable time (§ 193), ii. 559.
Secondarily liable (§ 192), ii. 559.
Unreasonable time (§ 193), ii. 559.
Value (§ 191), ii. 558.
Writing (§ 191), ii. 558.
Written (§ 191), ii. 558.
Negotiation of bill before issuance, ii. 358.
Recourse on prior parties, ii. 358.
Origin of bill, ii. 335.
Origin of negotiability of bill, ii. 354.
Overdue paper —
Assignee affected with notice of defect, ii. 501.
Incidents to negotiation, ii. 501.
Negotiability of, ii. 528.
Parol discharge without consideration, ii. 410.
Parties to bill of exchange, ii. 339.
Payee, rights against acceptor, ii. 340, 345.
Payment for honor, ii. 374.
Pleading —
Debt and assumpsit as remedy on bills, iii. 140, 143.
Effect of statute on declaration, iii. 202.
Normal mode of declaring on bill, ii. 348, 349; iii. 139.
Simplification of pleading incident to acceptance of law merchant as part of common law, ii. 348.

BILLS AND NOTES — *Continued.*
Practice of specially pleading custom of merchants abandoned, ii. 352.
Presentment for acceptance —
Instrument drawn on two or more parties, ii. 374.
Presentment necessary to charge drawee, ii. 373.
Presentment to be made, when, ii. 373.
Presentment, reasonable time for, ii. 378.
Prior parties, recourse on, ii. 358.
Procuration, signature by, ii. 519.
Promise of drawer, ii. 344.
Promise to accept, ii. 400.
Promise to accept undrawn bill, ii. 399, 400.
Criticism of Pillans *v.* Van Mierop, ii. 400, 401.
Promissory note —
Ambulatory bill of debt not limited to use among merchants, ii. 364.
Appearance contemporary with inland bill, ii. 368.
Bearer of note must show himself holder for value, when, ii. 371.
Bearer takes as successor in title, when, ii. 371.
Bill of debt as common-law contract, ii. 366.
Bill of debt negotiable by delivery, when, ii. 365.
Bill of debt negotiated by re-execution of instrument to transferee, ii. 365.
Characteristics of early bill of debt, ii. 364.
Confusion between inland bill and promissory note, ii. 369.
Demand supposed essential to right of action on unsealed promissory note, ii. 371.
Distinction as regards negotiability between note to order and to bearer, ii. 379.
Early note authorizing payment to creditor or attorney producing instrument, ii. 363.
Form of promissory note in time of Malynes, ii. 365.
Delivery presumed, ii. 366.
Recital of consideration, ii. 366.
Recital that business transaction took place between merchants, ii. 365.
Recital that instrument originated in mercantile transaction, ii. 365.
Recital that one of parties was foreigner, ii. 365.
Seal unnecessary, ii. 366.
Indorsee of note payable to bearer may recover as indorsee, ii. 372.
Joint makers formerly liable *pro rata* by custom of merchants, ii. 366.
Lord Holt holds promissory note not within the custom of merchants, ii. 383.
Lost note, ii. 375.
Note given as collateral security, when conditional, ii. 506.
Note given for debt of another not within statute of Anne, ii. 391.
Note given for precedent debt a conditional payment, ii. 389.
Note payable on contingency not negotiable, ii. 392.
Note payable out of particular fund not negotiable, ii. 392.

BILLS AND NOTES — *Continued.*
Promissory note — *Continued.*
Note payable to bearer held not negotiable, ii. 372.
Promissory note comes into general use, ii. 367.
Promissory note comes within custom of merchants, ii. 363.
Promissory note first ambulatory contract, ii. 363.
Promissory note first extensively used by goldsmiths, ii. 368.
Recital of value received made unnecessary by statute of Anne, ii. 391.
Release of one party releases all, ii. 366.
Rescounter in payment, ii. 365.
Rights of assignee, ii. 367.
Sealed note, negotiability of, ii. 370, 371.
Statute of Anne makes note negotiable though lacking words of negotiability, ii. 386.
Value of early bill of debt as circulating credit, ii. 364.
Protest —
Effect of, ii. 341.
Protest for better security, ii. 375.
Protest for nonpayment does not discharge acceptor, ii. 373.
Protest for nonpayment following protest for nonacceptance, ii. 553.
Protest for want of due acceptance, ii. 374.
Protest of inland bill, ii. 380.
Recital of value received becomes unnecessary in bill, ii. 391.
Remedy —
Action on case in nature of special assumpsit, ii. 348, 349.
Debt, iii. 139–143.
Indebitatus assumpsit, iii. 201–206.
Special assumpsit, ii. 343, 344, 347; iii. 202.
Remitter, action against drawee, ii. 344.
Remitter, rights against drawer, ii. 339.
Renunciation to be in writing, when, ii. 410.
Restrictive indorsement —
Effect of, ii. 399.
What is, ii. 399.
Special indorsement, effect of, ii. 398.
Specialty —
Bill treated as specialty, ii. 381, 383.
Idea that bill is specialty disappears, ii. 387, 388, 409.
Specimens of early bill of exchange, ii. 338.
State of law of bills and notes when Malynes wrote, ii. 359.
State of law pertaining to bills and notes at close of 17th century, ii. 253, 378.
State of literature pertaining to bills and notes, ii. 323.
Suits concerning, not entertained in common-law courts during 15th and 16th centuries, ii. 341.
Transferability not characteristic of early bill, ii. 354.
Transferee acquires title free from defenses against prior holders, ii. 395.

BILLS AND NOTES — *Continued.*
Transferor —
Liability of, as vendor of chattel, ii. 413.
Warranty of one who transfers by delivery only, ii. 414.
Warranty inures to immediate vendee only, ii. 415.
Warranty of title, ii. 413.
Untrue recital of consideration avoids bill, French rule, ii. 382.
Usage, modern, ii. 416.
Value received, presumption of, ii. 391.
Warranties incident to transfer of commercial paper, ii. 411.
Warranty of ordinary indorser distinguished from that of transferor by delivery or qualified indorsement, ii. 415.
Words of negotiability first appear in bill, ii. 360.

BILLS OF EXCHANGE ACT (1882).
Acceptance to be written on bill, ii. 548.
A codification of law of bills and notes, ii. 495.
Alteration, provision concerning, ii. 546.
Bill payable to fictitious or nonexisting person to be treated as payable to bearer, ii. 511, 513.
Bills and notes lacking words of negotiability made negotiable, ii. 387, 502.
Conditional indorsement, provision concerning, ii. 527.
Indorsement by infant or corporation, effect of, ii. 519.
Innocent purchaser, duress no defense against, ii. 530, 531.
Notice of dishonor, provision concerning, ii. 539.
Unfilled blank operates as notice of limitation on authority, ii. 516.

BILLS OF EXCHANGE ACT (GERMAN).
Provisions incorporated in Negotiable Instruments Law, ii. 517, 519.

BISHOP, PROF. J. P.
Treatise on Noncontract Law, i., p. xxii.

BLACK, J.
Malice not a constitutive element of legal wrong, i. 366.

BLACKBURN, LORD.
Denies negotiability of domestic debentures, ii. 422.
Discussion of law of undisclosed principal, ii. 480.
False statement made with eyes shut actionable in deceit, when, i. 403.
Fraudulent character of ambiguous statement, i. 399.
Observation on conversion by bailee, i. 248.
Observation on implied malice, i. 318.
Principle underlying assessment of damages, i. 483.
Propounds test on question of liability of broker for conversion, i. 245.

BLACKSMITH.
See SMITH.

BLACKSTONE, SIR WM.
Bailment defined, ii. 308.
Classification of actions in common-law system, iii. 43.
Nuisance defined, i. 211.

BLACKSTONE, SIR WM.—*Continued.*
Observation on technical nature of distress, iii. 295.
Primary classification of wrongs based on conception of violence, i. 2.
Recognizes implied warranty of title in chattel sales, i. 383.
Scope of replevin, iii. 217.
Statement of law of master and servant, ii. 454, 455.
Theory of function of judge, i. 498.
Waste defined, i. 26.

BLAME.
Blameworthiness a necessary factor in non-violent injury, i. 3.
Element of blame essential to liability in secondary trespass, i. 84.
Element of blame essential to liability in trespass, i. 80.
Relation between blame and legal liability, i. 3.

BLECKLEY, C. J.
Observation on mental distress as element of recoverable damage, i. 474.

BOARD OF HEALTH, PRIVILEGED CHARACTER OF, i. 38.

BONDS.
See TRANSFERABLE SECURITIES.

BOSANQUET AND PULLER.
Criticism of doctrine of moral consideration, ii. 146.

BOWEN, L. J.
Actionability of words injurious in respect of business, i. 324.
Assumption of risk distinguished from contributory negligence, i. 165.
Deceit not maintainable without proof of fraud, i. 403.
Defines 'maliciously,' i. 314.
Discussion of effect of Employers' Liability Act on assumption of risk, i. 170.
Fair comment and criticism, i. 303.
Maxim *volenti non fit injuria,* i. 169.
Observation on difficulty of defining *actio personalis,* iii. 61.
Observation on law of interference with air, i. 205.
Observation on survival of rights of action originating in tort, iii. 70.
Privileged character of competition in business, i. 360.
Seller of newspaper not necessarily responsible for libelous matter, i. 298, 299.

BOYCOTT.
Interference with trade or calling characterized by, i. 367.

BRACTON, HENRY.
Agency in time of, ii. 440.
Competition by erection of rival mill not actionable, i. 217.
Contributes little to English law of contract, ii. 14.
Exposition of law of bailment, ii. 254.
Illustration of *damnum absque injuria,* i. 492.
Influenced by Italian legists, ii. 15.
Scheme of remedial justice in time of, iii. 32.

BRAMWELL, B.

Considers detinue to be action *ex delicto,* iii. 156.
Criticises doctrine denying action for damage consequential on death by wrongful act, iii. 74.
Definition of conversion, i. 233.
Factor of malice as destructive of legal privilege, i. 313.
Threat to convert not a conversion, i. 237.

BREACH OF PROMISE.

Action contractual in form only, i. 465.
Common-law action for, i. 463.
Damage for breach of promise, i. 463.
Parasitic element of damage in action for, i. 464, 465.

BREACH OF STATUTORY DUTY.

Extent of liability —
Omissive illegal act, i. 173.
Positive illegal act, i. 173.
Negligence, violation of statutory duty amounts to, when, i. 172.
Omissive violation of statute —
Concrete cases discussed —
Failure to keep sufficient water pressure, i. 175.
Failure to medicine ship, i. 174.
Improper arrangements for shipping live stock, i. 174.
Positive illegal act and omissive breach of duty distinguished, i. 173.
Violation of law by party defendant —
Concrete cases discussed —
Maintaining sign over street, i. 173.
Sale of explosive to child, i. 173.
Sale of intoxicants, i. 172.
Sale of liquor to slave, i. 173.
Train run at unlawful speed, i. 172.
Violation of law by person injured —
Concrete cases discussed —
Blocking of street, i. 176.
Driving at unlawful speed, i. 177.
Illegal use of firm name, i. 176.
Imposing unlawful weight on bridge, i. 176.
Injury received in stringing electric wires across street, i. 180.
Injury sustained while assisting in war against government, i. 177.
Riding on platform of moving car, i. 176.
Springing of bridge from trotting, i. 178.
Conduct contrary to public policy, i. 177.
Illegal conduct concurring with negligence of other party, i. 178.
Illegal conduct on part of person injured analogous to contributory negligence, i. 175.
Illegal conduct on part of plaintiff a bar to an action, when, i. 176.

BREACH OF STATUTORY DUTY — *Continued.*
Violation of Sunday ordinance —
Concrete cases discussed —
Collapse of bridge, i. 178.
Collision of vehicle at camp meeting, i. 180.
Defective highway, i. 178.
Traveling on Sunday on other business than necessity or charity, i. 178, 179.
Doctrine of majority courts, i. 178, 179.
New England rule criticised, i. 180.

BREAKING OF BULK.
Breaking of bulk by bailee constitutes larcenous conversion, when, iii. 241.
Possession of bailee terminated by, ii. 309, 310.

BRETT, M. R.
See ESHER, LORD.
Discussion of negligence in aspect of breach of implied duty, i. 92.
Right to turn threatened injury on neighbor, i. 24.
Statement concerning function of judges, i. 498.

BREWERY.
Assumption of risk by person working in, i. 165.

BREWSTER, L. D.
Interpretation of Negotiable Instruments Law, § 124, ii. 546.
Replies to Ames's criticism on Negotiable Instruments Law, ii. 497.

BRIAN, C. J.
Debt for service rendered not maintainable save where price fixed beforehand, iii. 186.
Detinue not available against trespasser, iii. 150.
Intention irrelevant in early theory of trespass, i. 77.
Observation on bailee's right of action against disseisor, ii. 256.
Observation on effect of claim on property in replevin suit, iii. 214, 215.
Part payment of debt not a satisfaction, ii. 96, 97.
Recognizes right of action for misfeasance of parol promise, ii. 32.
Strictness of liability in theory of trespass, i. 76.
Trespassory violation of possession essential to larceny, iii. 241.
Violation of possessory right essential to maintenance of trespass, ii. 236.

BRIDGE.
Collapse of bridge, plaintiff precluded by violation of Sunday law, i. 178.
Failure to repair —
Liability for injury caused by, i. 183.
Remedy for, i. 182.
Springing of bridge —
Plaintiff precluded by violation of statute prohibiting trotting of horse, i. 178.

BRITTON.
Statement concerning law of bailment, ii. 256.

BROKER.
Action on case against deceitful real-estate broker, iii. 175.
When broker liable for conversion by act done in course of business, i. 245.

BROMLEY, SERJEANT.
Argument in favor of sufficiency of consideration of love and affection, ii. 44.

BRONSON, J.
Observation on English law of light, i. 208.

BROOKE, R.
Observation on assignment of chose in action, iii. 84.
Observation on *nudum pactum*, ii. 29, 30.
Responsibility of principal for act of agent, ii. 447.
Right of executors to maintain replevin, iii. 222.
Right to pursue noxious animal on land of another, i. 21.
Supposes detinue available for any unlawful detention, iii. 149.

BROTHER.
Mental distress occasioned by inability to attend funeral of brother, i. 471.

BROUGHAM, LORD.
Observation on liability of master for negligent act of servant, ii. 461.

BROWNLOE.
Precedents of actions on bill, ii. 352.

BRUMPTON, J.
Observation on plea *de vetito namio*, iii. 210.

BRUNNER, DR.
Law of representation among Germanic people, ii. 437.
Strictness of early law of liability, i. 77.

BRYNCHESLEY, J.
Recognizes right of action for negligent misfeasance, i. 187.

BULLER, J.
Common-law remedy for seduction of daughter, i. 271.
Observations on state of commercial law, ii. 398.
Repudiates idea that implied warranty of title arises only where seller has possession, i. 385.
Statement of rule as to novation by change of debtor, ii. 124.

BURNELL.
See ACTON BURNELL.

BUSINESS.
Defamatory words injurious in respect of business, i. 324.

BUTCHER.
Implied warranty of wholesomeness of food, i. 387.

CABLE.
Warranty of quality, measure of damage for breach of, i. 446.

CALLING, INTERFERENCE WITH.
See INTERFERENCE WITH TRADE OR CALLING.

CAMPBELL, LORD.
Doctrine of imputed negligence, i. 142.
Judicial notice of principles of law merchant, ii. 421.

CAMPBELL'S ACT, LORD, iii. 71.

CANAL.
Bridge over private way, responsibility of owner for defect, i. 158.
Unlighted swing bridge, responsibility of company for injury caused by, i. 152.

CANDISH, J.
Recognizes validity of parol promise, ii. 174.

CANON LAW.
Influence of ecclesiastical courts, ii. 11.

CARE.
See DILIGENCE.
Breach of implied duty to take care, i. 186.
Conduct of prudent man furnishes standard of, i. 96.
Degrees of care, i. 98.
Foresight of harm ultimate criterion of reasonable care, i. 97.

CARRIER, COMMON.
See COMMON CARRIER.

CARRIER, PRIVATE, ii. 298.
Degree of care required of, ii. 298.

CARTA MERCATORIA, ii. 6, 326.

CASE.
See ACTION ON CASE.

CASH.
Instrument payable to 'Cash' payable to bearer, ii. 514.

CASUALTY, INEVITABLE.
Excuse for nonperformance of contract, ii. 224.

CATLIN, C. J.
Action of debt lies only for recovery of sum certain, iii. 135.
Upholds consideration of love and affection, ii. 45.

CATTLE.
Horses and pigs included under term, i. 52.

CATTLEGUARD.
Negligence of railroad company in failing to maintain, i. 127.

CAUSA, CAUSE.
Analogy to consideration, ii. 37.

CAUSE.
Effective legal cause, see PROXIMATE CAUSE.
Want of probable cause in malicious prosecution, i. 329.
Want of probable cause, what is, i. 330.

CAUSE, PROXIMATE.
See PROXIMATE CAUSE.

CAVEAT EMPTOR.
Doctrine strictly applied by common-law courts, i. 378.
Maxim does not apply, when, i. 388.
Opportunity to inspect as affecting application of doctrine, i. 378, 379.
Origin of doctrine, ii. 334.
Scope of doctrine in modern English law, i. 384, 385.

CERTIFICATE OF DEPOSIT.
When not negotiable, ii. 501.

CESSIO BONORUM, iii. 20.

CHALMERS, M. D.
Contrasts English and French theories of negotiable instrument, ii. 396.
Digest of the English Law of Bills, Notes, and Cheques, ii. 495.
Framer of English Bills of Exchange Act, ii. 495.

CHAMPERTY.
Assignment of right of action as affected by, iii. 85.
Champerty a form of maintenance, ii. 164.
Champerty as affecting legality of contract, ii. 163.
Prosecution of claim for alien not champerty, when, iii. 85.

CHANCELLOR.
Writs issued by chancellor as royal secretary, iii. 28, 248.

CHANCERY COURT.
Bill in equity analogous to action on case, iii. 54.
Forms of action not recognized in chancery, iii. 53.
Jurisdiction over equitable assumpsit, iii. 186.
Law judges stimulated by rivalry of chancery court, iii. 54.
Origin of chancery jurisdiction, iii. 53.
Procedure in court of chancery, iii. 53.
Recognizes validity of simple promise, ii. 34, 35.

CHANNELL, B.
Approves exemplary damages in wanton injury, i. 486.

CHATTELS.
Disseisin of, see CONVERSION.

CHEATING.
Cheating at cards, i. 376.
Cheating by means of forged documents, i. 376.

CHECK.
Conditional payment of precedent debt, ii. 390.
Drawer entitled to notice of dishonor under Negotiable Instrument Law, ii. 539.

CHEMIST.
See DRUGGIST.

CHEVAUX DE FRISE.
Responsibility for injury done by, i. 65.

CHILDREN.
Contributory negligence in playing on turntable, i. 160.
Turntable cases involving injury to children, i. 159.

CHOKE, J.
Observation on larcenous conversion by bailee, ii. 309, 310.
Observation on law of breaking bulk, iii. 241.
Statement of principle of immunity of servant who acts at instance of master, ii. 444.
Strictness of liability in trespass, i. 76.

CHOSE IN ACTION.
Chose in action equivalent to right of action, iii. 78.
Chose in action inclusive of intangible property rights, iii. 78.
Confusion as to meaning of term, iii. 79.
Definition, iii. 79.
Nontransferability of chose in action, iii. 79.
Right of action distinguished from fruits of suit, iii. 81.
Right of action founded on personal wrong not assignable, iii. 86.

CHRISTIANCY, J.
Basis of rule denying action for damage consequential on death by wrongful act, iii. 74.

CIPHER.
Measure of damages for negligent transmission of telegram in cipher, i. 452, 453.

CIRCUMSPECTE AGATIS.
Statute or ordinance of, ii. 13.

CIVIL DAMAGE ACT.
Rumseller's liability for damage caused by drunken man, i. 172.

CLASSIFICATION.
Blackstone's classification of wrongs, i. 2.
Classification of actions in common-law system, iii. 36.
Negligence, Lindley's division of cases involving, i. 126.
Primary division of wrongs suggested, i. 87.
Right as basis of legal classification, iii. 7.

CLERGYMAN.
Communication between clergyman and parishioner privileged, when, i. 311.

COCKBURN, C. J.
Account of evolution of English law merchant, ii. 417.
Discussion concerning meaning of term 'Act of God,' ii. 303.
Forbearance to prosecute invalid claim good consideration, when, ii. 79.
Recognizes modern usage as sufficient to impart negotiability to instrument, ii. 423.

COGNATE NUISANCE.
Consumption of water —
Contract rights in water, i. 201.
Domestic and barnyard use, i. 201.
Irrigation, right of appropriation for purposes of, i. 201.
Manufacturing uses, i. 201.
Prescriptive right of consumption, i. 202.
Reasonable use, what is, i. 200.
Diversion of water —
General principle of liability, i. 198.
Percolating waters, i. 199.
Reasonable use, special damage as affecting, i. 204.
Interference with air —
Brewery, unwholesome vapors from, i. 206.
Easement for maintenance of ventilating flue, i. 205.
Grant of right to ventilation presumed from lapse of time, i. 205.
Light, law of, distinguished from law pertaining to air, i. 204.
Limekiln built near dwelling house, i. 206.
Maintenance of pigsty near dwelling, i. 206.
Pollution amounting to nuisance, i. 206.
Structure causing chimney to smoke, i. 205.
Ventilation, right to, i. 204.
Interference with lateral support —
Application of maxim *sic utere tuo,* etc., i. 193.
Easement of support —
Acquired by lapse of time, i. 195.
Acquired by prescription, American doctrine, i. 196.
Lateral support distinguished from subjacent support, i. 193.
Lateral support of building distinguished from lateral support of land, i. 195.
Malice destructive of legal privilege, when, i. 196.
Mitigation of principle of liability, i. 193, 194.
Nature of right to lateral support, i. 195.
Negligent interference with support, i. 196.
Prescriptive right distinguished from right of support, i. 195.
Recoverable damage —
English rule, i. 197.
Massachusetts rule, i. 197.
Right of lateral support, i. 193.
Right of support for land in natural state not dependent on contiguity, i. 194.
Right to lateral support of house a right of easement, i. 195.
Support of artificial structures, i. 194.
Support of land in natural state, i. 194.
Trespassory interference with support, i. 196.
Interference with light —
Ancient light, what is, i. 208.
Angle of forty-five degrees, presumption from, i. 209.
English doctrine repudiated in America, i. 208.
English law of light peculiar, i. 296.

COGNATE NUISANCE — *Continued.*
Interference with light — *Continued.*
Gist of the tort, i. 209.
Loss of prospect not actionable, i. 206.
Modes of acquiring right to light in England, i. 209.
Nuisance, English law of light reaches basis of, i. 210.
Period of prescription, i. 208.
Remedy —
Action on case, iii. 271.
Writ of nuisance, i. 210.
Stoppage of ancient light first becomes actionable, i. 207.
Stoppage of light, ancient law concerning, i. 206, 207.
Structure on old foundation, custom of London concerning, i. 207.
Substantial diminution of light essential to right of action, i. 209.
Interference with subjacent support —
Negligence as bearing on liability, i. 192.
Right of support not limited to reasonable support, i. 192.
Support of artificial structures, i. 192.
Support of land in natural state, i. 191, 192.
Support of superior tenement, i. 193.
Theory and extent of right of support, i. 192.
Obstruction of water —
Common property in running water, i. 200.
Easement distinguished from riparian right, i. 199.
General principle of liability, i. 198.
Nature of riparian right, i. 199.
Owner of spring, right of, i. 199.
Percolating water, i. 198.
Water falling in artificial channel, i. 198.
Place of cognate nuisance in legal theory, i. 191.
Pollution of water —
Deposit of dyestuffs in stream, i. 203.
Discharge of poisons and corrosive substances, i. 203.
Grant and prescription, effect of, i. 203.
Pollution from reasonable use, i. 202.
Pollution of underground water, i. 203.
Previous pollution, effect of, i. 203.
Special damage not essential to right of action, i. 204.
Tanyard, offensive matter from, i. 203.

COHEN, ARTHUR.
Interpretation of Negotiable Instruments Law, § 29, ii. 522.
Interpretation of Negotiable Instruments Law, § 137, ii. 550.

COKE, LORD.
Approves allegation of fictitious finding in action of trover, iii. 164.
Approves assumpsit as remedy on simple debt after death of debtor, iii. 68.
Detinue maintainable on allegation of *devenerunt ad manus*, iii. 147.
Explanation of Bonion's Case, ii. 257.
Hostile attitude to action for defamation, i. 284.

COKE, LORD — *Continued.*
Interpretation of Southcote's Case, ii. 264.
Interpretation of Statute of Marlborough on subject of waste, i. 29.
Leads in contest against Court of Admiralty, ii. 332.
Observation on accord and satisfaction, ii. 98.
Observation on refusal by bailee to surrender possession, iii. 167, 168.
Statement of essentials of conversion. iii. 160.
Theory of trespass *ab initio*, i. 47.

COLERIDGE, LORD.
Discountenances action for interference with contract relation, i. 343.
Doctrine of maintenance in modern law, i. 338.
Violation of possessory right essential in action of replevin, iii. 219.

COLLATERAL LIABILITY.
See STATUTE OF FRAUDS.

COLLIERY.
Miner assumes risk of injury from defective hoisting apparatus, when, i. 164.

COLLINS, M. R.
Discussion of bailee's right of action against stranger, ii. 316.
Observations on fair criticism, i. 304.

COLLISION.
Passenger not identified with crew of vessel in respect of negligence, i. 142.
Pilot, liability where steamer runs foul of sailing vessel, i. 135.

COLLOQUIUM.
Allegation of *colloquium* in action for defamation, i. 300.

COLONEL.
Liability for injury incurred at target practice, i. 80.

COLTMAN, J.
Doctrine of identification in negligence, i. 141.

COMBINATION.
Unlawful combination as affecting liability for interference with trade or calling, i. 362.

COMITY.
Immunity of sovereign recognized by, i. 37.

COMMENT, FAIR.
See FAIR COMMENT AND CRITICISM.

COMMERCIAL PAPER.
See BILLS AND NOTES.

COMMISSIONERS ON UNIFORMITY OF LEGISLATION.
American law of bills and notes codified at instance of, ii. 496.

COMMODATARY.
Borrower absolutely liable as debtor, ii. 261.
Commodatary held to strictest diligence, ii. 281.

COMMODATARY — *Continued.*
Commodatary must not deviate from terms of bailment, ii. 282.
Has no authority to delegate, ii. 282.
Inevitable accident releases, ii. 282.
Liability of commodatary in time of Bracton, ii. 254.
Loan, antiquity of, ii. 2.

COMMODATE.
Definition, ii. 271.
Deviation on part of bailee from bailment, ii. 282.
Essentials of commodate, ii. 281.
Loan for definite period not revocable, ii. 281.

COMMON.
Commoner may distrain beasts of lord, when, iii. 310.
Surcharge of common, iii. 310.
Writ for admeasurement of common, iii. 310.

COMMON CARRIER.
Act of God as affecting liability, ii. 304.
Assumpsit, allegation unnecessary in declaration against, ii. 267.
Breaking bulk terminates bailment, ii. 309.
Carrier by sea, liability of, ii. 268, 305.
Compensation as affecting character of carrier, ii. 305.
Compensation for expenditure incident to keep of horse, right of carrier to recover, ii. 234.
Compensation supposed to be at basis of carrier's liability, ii. 269.
Conversion —
Conversion in course of business, when carrier liable for, i. 244.
Delivery to wrong consignee operates as conversion, i. 248.
Negligent keeping of goods by carrier not a conversion, i. 237.
Defective coach, liability of proprietor for injury resulting from, i. 132.
Delay in transportation followed by loss from other cases, i. 118.
Diligence to be exercised by, ii. 304.
Ejection of passenger not proximate cause of loss, when, i. 119.
Exceptions to liability, ii. 300.
Failure to provide seats not proximate cause of injury, when, i. 119.
Form of remedy against common carrier where goods are lost or stolen, iii. 169.
Implied duty incident to public calling, i. 185.
Liability as affected by payment of compensation, ii. 305.
Live stock, liability of carrier for damage resulting from improper shipping facilities, i. 175.
Loss of goods in transit, liability of company not affected by shipment to consignor under illegal name, i. 176.
Mental distress of husband caused by failure of carrier to transport body of deceased wife, i. 474.
Negligence as basis of liability in early law, ii. 299.
Negligence renders carrier liable for loss caused by act of God, when, ii. 304.
Policy and necessity as basis of strict liability, ii. 300.

COMMON CARRIER — *Continued.*
Positive *quasi*-contractual duty to convey for public, ii. 237.
Private carrier distinguished, ii. 298.
Public calling as affecting character of carrier, ii. 306.
Public enemy, origin of exception arising from act of, ii. 300.
Scope of occupation, carrier's right to limit, ii. 306.
Servant, liability of carrier for loss caused by, ii. 436.
Stowage of goods, consent of shipper as affecting liability, i. 162.
Trover not available where carrier loses goods, iii. 169.
Writ against, form of, ii. 302.

COMMON COUNT.
See COUNT.

COMMON LAW.
Beginning, ii. 1.
Characteristics, i., pp. xxiii, xxv.
Law merchant —
Assimilation into common law, ii. 324, 332.
Common law distinguished, ii. 330.
Effect of assimilation by common law, ii. 333, 334.
Law merchant modificative of common-law principle in commercial law, ii. 419, 424.

COMMON-LAW PROCEDURE ACT (1852), i. 234; iii. 24, 93, 155, 202.

COMMON-LAW PROCEDURE ACT (1854), iii. 158.

COMPARATIVE NEGLIGENCE.
Degrees of negligence —
Gross, i. 147.
Ordinary, i. 147.
Slight, i. 147.
Origin and statement of doctrine of comparative negligence, i. 147
Unsoundness of doctrine, i. 147.

COMPENSATION.
Measure of damages as affected by idea of compensation, i. 477.

COMPETITION.
Business competition not actionable as private nuisance, i. 217.
Privileged character of business competition, i. 359.

COMPOSITION WITH CREDITORS, ii. 94, 95.
Composition agreement defined, ii. 130.
Nonperformance on part of debtor, effect of, ii. 95.
Original claim enforceable where debtor fails to pay, ii. 131.
Payment of part in satisfaction of whole, ii. 105.
Theoretical difficulty in recognizing validity of composition agreement, ii. 130.
Validity of composition agreement explained, ii. 130.

COMPURGATION.
Trial by, iii. 24.

CONCEALMENT.
Fraudulent concealment, when actionable, i. 394.

CONCURRING CONTRIBUTORY NEGLIGENCE.
See CONTRIBUTORY NEGLIGENCE.

CONCURRING NEGLIGENCE.
Concurring negligence of third person —
Concrete cases discussed —
Collision of vehicles, i. 122.
Defective gas fittings, i. 123.
Defective sidewalk, i. 122.
Timber insecurely piled, i. 122.

CONDICTIO, iii. 16.

CONDUCTOR, ii. 274.

CONQUEST, NORMAN.
See NORMAN CONQUEST.

CONSENT.
Agency as affected by consent of parties, ii. 432.
Consent of owner as factor in bailment, ii. 252.
Consent to incur risk, effect of, i. 162.

CONSIDERATION.
Accord and satisfaction, consideration in, ii. 98, 99.
Adequacy, ii. 69.
Size of detriment of benefit immaterial, ii. 69, 70.
Assets as consideration to support promise of devisee or representative, ii. 148.
Benefit to promisor —
Benefit to promisor not good consideration, ii. 68, 104.
Persistence of notion that benefit to promisor is good consideration, ii. 68.
Bilateral contract not based on consideration in sense of detriment, ii. 57.
Bill of exchange, recital of consideration in early bill, ii. 382.
Bill of exchange supposed to be good without consideration, ii. 381, 382.
Causa distinguished from consideration, ii. 37.
Consideration and promise go together, ii. 81.
Consideration and right of action, ii. 152.
Stranger to consideration has no right of action, ii. 152.
Exception in favor of parties related by blood, ii. 153.
Consideration legal equivalent for the promise, ii. 70.
Consideration moved by previous request, ii. 83.
Fiction of relation, ii. 84.
Obsolescence of doctrine of previous request, ii. 85.
Subsequent promise necessary, ii. 84.
Conveyance —
Consideration in conveyancing, ii. 40.
Consideration necessary to pass use in equity, ii. 40.
Consideration necessary to pass use in law court, ii. 42.
Consideration unnecessary to pass title at common law, ii. 40.

CONSIDERATION — *Continued.*
Court of chancery hastens development of doctrine, ii. 34.
Deed imports consideration, ii. 44.
Definition of consideration by Lush, J., ii. 68.
Definitions, early, ii. 38.
Detriment lacking in case of forbearance to sue on invalid claim, ii. 78.
Detriment lacking in unilateral promise based on legal duty, ii. 150.
Detriment may be good consideration though parties do not treat it as such, ii. 71.
Detriment to promisee basis of consideration in unilateral assumpsits, ii. 32, 33, 57, 68.
Detriment to promisee true test of sufficiency of consideration, when, ii. 105.
Doctrine of consideration at beginning of 16th century, ii. 33.
Early history of consideration, ii. 29, 36.
Executed consideration, ii. 33.
Forbearance after institution of suit on invalid claim, ii. 77.
Forbearance as consideration, ii. 34.
Forbearance good consideration where claim based on reasonable ground, ii. 79.
Forbearance to institute suit on invalid claim, ii. 77.
Forbearance to institute suit on unenforceable claim, ii. 77.
Forbearance to prosecute invalid claim, history of, ii. 76–80.
Forbearance to prosecute invalid claim, modern doctrine, ii. 78.
Forbearance to prosecute invalid claim treated as incompetent consideration, ii. 76.
Formative period in doctrine of consideration, ii. 67.
Frowike's summary of doctrine of consideration, ii. 33.
Good consideration, ii. 42.
Doing of act one is legally bound to do, ii. 75.
Leading virtuous life good consideration, when, ii. 72.
Performance of existing contract not consideration, ii. 76.
Illegality, ii. 73.
Illustrations of illegal consideration, ii. 73.
Knowledge of illegality of consideration, ii. 74.
Incompetent consideration, ii. 74.
Payment of part of debt in satisfaction of whole, ii. 100, 102.
Quitting vicious habit not incompetent consideration, ii. 76.
Intention of parties as affecting question of consideration, ii. 70, 71.
Legal obligation, ii. 147.
Consideration of legal duty not based on detriment, ii. 63.
Disappearance of consideration of legal obligation, ii. 63, 64.
Doctrine supplanted by doctrine of implied promise, ii. 149.
Insurance company's promise to beneficiary of policy, ii. 148.
Obligation of overseer of poor to compensate one who attends pauper, ii. 150.
Promise implied from existence of legal obligation, ii. 149.
Promise of bank to pay check, ii. 148.
Promise of devisee to pay legacy, ii. 148.

CONSIDERATION — *Continued.*
Legal obligation — *Continued.*
Promise of representative to pay debt of decedent, ii. 148.
Promise to do act one is legally bound to do, ii. 147.
Promise to pay debt due, ii. 61.
Promise to pay for doing of act which promisor was legally bound to perform, ii. 150.
Reappearance of the consideration of legal obligation, ii. 147.
Love and affection sufficient consideration to support use in equity, ii. 42.
Love and affection sufficient to support action on promise in favor of blood, ii. 153.
Love and affection sufficient to support covenant to stand seized, ii. 43, 45.
Mansfield's opinion of function of consideration, i. 141.
Marriage sufficient consideration to support conveyance, ii. 45.
Moral consideration —
Genesis and scope of doctrine, ii. 143, 144.
Moral consideration criticised and limited, ii. 146.
Promise of discharged bankrupt, ii. 145.
Promise to pay barred debt, ii. 145.
Promise to pay money lent at usury, ii. 145.
Repudiation of doctrine of moral consideration, ii. 146.
Nominal consideration, ii. 72.
Origin of term consideration, ii. 37.
Past consideration —
Past consideration insufficient to support promise though coupled with moral obligation, ii. 146.
Past consideration invalid, ii. 83, 86.
Past distinguished from executed consideration, ii. 83.
Privity of blood gives right of action to beneficiary, ii. 153.
Promise as consideration for counter-promise, ii. 57.
Promise to increase wages of sailor invalid, when, ii. 75.
Promise to support former mistress, ii. 72, 73.
Promissory note, burden of proving want of consideration, ii. 388.
Rewards, ii. 81.
Statute of Frauds does not dispense with consideration, ii. 173, 174.
Types of consideration, ii. 61, 62, 67.
Unlawful act —
Doing of unlawful act not good consideration, ii. 73.
Promise to indemnify against consequences of unlawful act, ii. 74.
Vicious habit, abandonment of, ii. 72.

CONSIGNEE.
Conversion resulting from indorsement of delivery order, i. 234.

CONSPIRACY.
Bearing on liability for interference with trade or calling, i. 362, 366, 372.
Conspiracy not a substantive tort, i. 372.
Conspiracy to prosecute on false charge, i. 328.

CONSPIRACY — *Continued.*

Conspiracy to prosecute on groundless charge of felony, i. 372.
Statutory definition of conspiracy, i. 329.
Writ, i. 328, 329, 372.

CONSTANS, EMPEROR.

Establishes extraordinary process throughout empire and abolishes formulary system, iii. 21.

CONTINGENCY.

Instrument payable on contingency not negotiable, ii. 507.

CONTRACT.

Agency distinguished from contract, ii. 432, 433.
Aleatory contract, see WAGER.
Assumpsit, contract in early law distinguished from, ii. 60.
Assumptual tie, conception of, ii. 199.
Bilateral contract —
  Effect of recognition, ii. 56.
  Exceptional character of consideration, ii. 57.
Bractonian epoch, ii. 14, 19.
Champerty and maintenance as affecting, ii. 163.
Classification, ii. 174.
Consensual contract, ii. 4.
Consensual contract in Roman law, ii. 58.
Consideration essential to validity of, when, ii. 142.
Contract distinguished from assumpsit, ii. 60.
Contract for benefit of third person —
  Assumpsit, limits of, ii. 156.
  Indebitatus assumpsit, limits of, ii. 156.
  Indebitatus assumpsit supplies remedy for third person, when, ii. 156.
  Intention to confer benefit on third person, ii. 159.
  Modern American doctrine, ii. 157.
  Modern English doctrine, ii. 158.
  Perversion of indebitatus, ii. 157.
  Quasi-contractual nature of obligation, ii. 237.
  Question of right of stranger to sue one of procedure, ii. 156, 158.
  Recognition of right of stranger to sue, ii. 157.
  Right of stranger to sue in equity, ii. 159.
  State of controversy as to right of stranger to sue, ii. 160.
  Stranger to consideration has no action at common law, ii. 152–155.
Debt, occultation of, ii. 199.
Deceit, affinity of, to contract theory, i. 374.
Double basis of English contract law, ii. 64.
Early history, ii. 1, 21, 29, 36.
Formal contract, covenant becomes, iii. 118.
Formality in contract tends to disappear, ii. 56.
Guaranty and surety as affected by Statute of Frauds, ii. 184.
Illegality fatal to all forms of contract, ii. 162.

CONTRACT — *Continued.*
Implied contract —
Contract implied on facts of case, ii. 203.
Obligation of principal to indemnify surety, ii. 238.
Promise an inference of fact, when, ii. 202.
Promise an inference of law, ii. 202.
Special assumpsit remedy on promise implied of fact, ii. 202.
Implied contract and *quasi*-contract, ii. 205.
Implied contract excluded by special contract, ii. 220.
Implied contract to compensate for benefit conferred, ii. 201.
Implied contract to compensate for expenditure for benefit of other, ii. 233.
Implied promise to pay debt, ii. 62.
Indivisible contract, sailors' contract for wages, ii. 224.
Innominate contract —
Innominate contract in early common law, ii. 22.
Innominate real contract, ii. 21.
Paulus's formula, ii. 21.
Personal service, ii. 23.
Remedy —
Assumpsit, ii. 34.
Debt, ii. 25.
Roman law, ii. 21.
Do ut des, ii. 22.
Do ut facias, ii. 22, 25.
Facio ut des, ii. 22, 24.
Facio ut facias, ii. 22, 24, 25.
Facio ut non facias, ii. 22.
Interference with contract relation, see INTERFERENCE WITH CONTRACT RELATION.
Judgment included among contracts, ii. 207.
Legality a condition precedent to validity of contract, ii. 162.
Liability, extent of in field of contract, i. 88.
Measure of damages for breach of contract, i. 445–447.
Mode of contract —
Bilateral, ii. 53.
Unilateral, ii. 52, 53.
Mode of contract determined at inception of contractual relation, ii. 54.
Obligation —
Emergence of idea of obligation of promise, ii. 10, 60; iii. 174.
Obligation results from acts of law, ii. 162.
Performance excused by death or inevitable casualty, ii. 224.
Performance excused by destruction of property, ii. 224.
Performance excused by existence of epidemic, when, ii. 224.
Personal service, innominate contract for, ii. 23.
Promise to accept bill of exchange, ii. 400.
Promissory note held to be simple common-law contract, ii. 388.
Readjustment incident to development of idea of obligation of promise, ii 46.

CONTRACT — *Continued.*
Remedy —
Account, iii. 99.
Assumpsit, iii. 172, 182, 272.
Case, iii. 272, 277.
Covenant, iii. 114.
Debt, iii. 127.
Detinue, iii. 154.
Restraint of trade as affecting legality of contract, ii. 163.
Simplicity of English contract law, ii. 195.
State of law at close of Bractonian period, ii. 19.
State of law at close of 15th century, ii. 28.
State of law in early 16th century, ii. 36.
Tort, arbitrary nature of distinction between contract and, i. 87.
Validity of simple contract, ii. 142.

CONTRACTOR, INDEPENDENT.
See INDEPENDENT CONTRACTOR.

CONTRACT *RE,* ii. 1.
Bargain and sale ceases to be, ii. 27.
Commodatum, ii. 3.
Depositum, ii. 3.
Jurisdiction of local courts, ii. 7.
Mutuum, ii. 3.
Readjustment incident to development of assumpsit, ii. 48.
Vadium, ii. 4.

CONTRA PACEM.
Function of allegation in action of trespass, iii. 230.

CONTRA PROHIBITIONEM REGIS.
Function of allegation in writ of waste, iii. 269.

CONTRIBUTION.
Sureties, contribution among, ii. 239.
Tortfeasors, contribution among, ii. 240.
Tortfeasors, no contribution among, when, i. 490.

CONTRIBUTORY NEGLIGENCE.
Basis of doctrine, i. 125.
Both parties at fault, i. 126.
Burden of proof, i. 138.
Butterfield *v.* Forrester, i. 125.
Classification of Lindley, L. J., i. 126.
Concurring contributory negligence, i. 136.
Concrete cases discussed —
Going into place of danger, i. 138.
Pedestrian run down by carriage, i. 137.
Riding on bumper of engine, i. 138.
Plaintiff disabled from recovery where negligence contributes to injury, i. 137.
Concurring negligence of plaintiff not a bar, when, i. 148.

CONTRIBUTORY NEGLIGENCE — *Continued.*
Conduct not amounting to contributory negligence —
Concrete cases discussed —
Defective sidewalk, i. 132.
Driving on wrong side of highway, i. 131.
Insecure door to passenger car, i. 131.
Use of dangerous exit into street, i. 131.
Danger incurred in rescue of third person —
Rushing in front of train, i. 133.
Standing at post of danger, i. 133.
Dangerous alternative —
Jumping from position of danger, i. 132, 133.
Risk on person primarily to blame, i. 132.
Party threatened with injury must try to escape hurt —
Failure to put out fire, i. 130.
Failure to restore fence, i. 130.
Representation in contributory negligence, i. 140.
Rusticum judicium —
Degree of fault of respective parties not considered, i. 146.
Division of loss between colliding vessels, i. 144.
Doctrine as applied in admiralty courts, i. 144.
Inscrutable fault, i. 146.
Lord Stowell's statement of doctrine, i. 145.
Mutual fault necessary, i. 146.
Origin of doctrine, i. 144.
Servant, plaintiff chargeable with contributory negligence of, i. 140.
Successive negligence, concurring negligence distinguished from, i. 139.
Successive negligent acts —
Doctrine of last chance, i. 136.
Injury caused by defendant's negligence —
Concrete cases discussed —
Drinking of polluted water, i. 128.
Jamming of wharf, i. 136.
Negligent management of ill-laden car, i. 135.
Passenger jumping from moving train, i. 128.
Passenger, negligence in alighting from train, i. 127.
Pedestrian run down by cart, i. 134.
Railroad crossing, injury received at, i. 128.
Steamer running afoul of sailing vessel, i. 135.
Stray cattle killed by train, i. 127.
Tethered donkey hurt on highway, i. 134.
Test of contributory negligence, i. 139, 140.
Turntable, contributory negligence of child playing on, i. 160.
Wanton injury, defense of contributory negligence unavailable, i. 181.
CONVERSION.
Adverseness of possession as affecting, i. 246.
Agent —
Agent plying common calling not liable for conversion, when, i. 245.
When liable for conversion by principal, i. 242.

CONVERSION — *Continued.*
Asportation, conversion by, i. 231, 241.
Assumption of property by converter, i. 233.
Bailee at will converts by transferring interest, i. 240.
Bailee for hire for limited period converts by transferring interest, i. 240.
Bailment, conversion of chattel by departure from, ii. 286.
Clerk, when liable for conversion in course of employment, i. 242.
Confusion as to meaning of term conversion, i. 233.
Contract of hire, conversion by departure from, i. 257.
Conversion in law, what is, i. 234.
Damage to property, conversion does not involve idea of, i. 232.
Definition of conversion, i. 231, 232, 233.
Demand and refusal —
Bailee —
Demand necessary to charge bailee, when, i. 248.
Property consumed or destroyed by bailee, i. 247.
Property unaccountably lost, i. 247.
Property wrongfully withheld by bailee, i. 247.
Refusal by bailee, effect of, i. 247.
Demand ineffective when accompanied by improper condition, i. 249.
Nature of demand, i. 249.
Qualified refusal, effect of, i. 246.
Refusal of *prima facie* conversion, i. 247.
Refusal to surrender possession operates as conversion, when, i. 246.
Unreasonable condition imposed, effect of, i. 246.
Detention, conversion by, i. 231.
Dilution of liquor, when a conversion, i. 258.
Disseisin, conversion viewed as, i. 232.
Finder of chattel may maintain trover against wrongdoer, when, i. 251.
Fraud, seller's right of action against vendee, i. 258, 259.
Gist of conversion, i. 231.
Hirer of chattel converts by sending to auctioneer, when, i. 239.
Indebitatus assumpsit as remedy for recovery of proceeds of conversion, iii. 196.
Intent to convert —
Absence of intent, effect of, i. 235.
Proof of intention, when material, i. 236, 242.
Relevancy of intent to convert, i. 234, 235.
Lienor converts chattel by transferring interest, i. 240.
Loss of goods by gratuitous bailee not conversion, i. 237.
Measure of damages —
Carrier may recoup to extent of charge for carriage, i. 255.
Distinction as between general and special owner, i. 255.
Mortgagee against mortgagor, i. 255, 256.
Mortgagor against mortgagee, i. 256.
Pledgor against pledgee, i. 255.
Value of goods, i. 255.

CONVERSION — *Continued.*
Mortgagee, when guilty of conversion, i. 239.
Negligent keeping by bailee, i. 237.
Nonfeasance does not work conversion, i. 237.
Outstanding title, available by defendant, when, i. 252.
Overt act essential to conversion, i. 236.
Ownership and possession —
Conversion not a wrong against ownership but against right of control, i. 250.
Conversion violative of possession or right of possession, i. 250.
Deprivation of property as element in conversion, i. 233.
Interference with dominion and control incident to ownership, i. 232.
Mere claim of ownership not a conversion, i. 236.
Plaintiff must show possession or right of possession, i. 251.
Partial abridgment of right of control, i. 237.
Pledgee does not convert by transferring interest, i. 240.
Pledgee, when guilty of conversion, i. 239.
Positive act which works a conversion —
Appropriation of converter to own use, i. 238.
Consumption by wrongdoer, i. 238.
Creation of adverse lien, i. 239.
Damaging property amounts to conversion, when, i. 241.
Destruction of chattel a conversion, when, i. 241.
Intermeddling with goods of deceased person, i. 242.
Sale and delivery to third person, i. 238.
Sale or pledge by person having assignable interest, i. 240.
Wrongful removal, i. 241.
Purchaser, when innocent purchaser guilty of conversion, i. 239.
Quasi-contractual duty incident to appropriation of chattel, ii. 215.
Real property —
Doctrine of conversion not extended to, i. 261.
Misappropriation by trustee, i. 261.
Mortgagee, abuse of trust by, i. 261, 262.
Wrongful diversion of title, i. 261.
Resale by seller, vendee cannot maintain trover, i. 252.
Servant —
Cutting of grass by servant, i. 243.
When liable for conversion by master, i. 242.
When servant not personally liable for conversion in master's employment, i. 243.
Sub-pledgee, effect of, i. 253.
Suit for conversion, who may maintain —
Bailee's action against owner, i. 254.
Bailee, when entitled to action, i. 253.
Bailor and bailee, concurrent right of action against stranger, i. 255.
Finder of chattel, i. 251.
Owner's right of action against stranger, i. 254.
Person having possession, i. 251, 252.

CONVERSION — *Continued.*
Suit for conversion, who may maintain — *Continued.*
Remainderman, i. 260.
Reversioner, i. 260.
Survival of action for conversion, iii. 71.
Tenant in common converts by selling entire property, i. 240.
Tenant in common does not convert by transferring interest, i. 240.
Threat to convert not sufficient to make conversion, i. 236.
Trover, perversion of, when used against vendor of chattel, i. 256.
Unauthorized sublease of chattels, i. 258.
Unlawful detention, conversion by, i. 233.
Unlawful disposal, conversion by, i. 231.
Vendor and vendee —
Resale by vendor, i. 252, 253.
Right of action against fraudulent vendee, i. 258, 259.
Taking possession under fraudulent sale a conversion, when, i. 259, 260.
Vendor's lien, effect of, i. 253.

CONVEYANCE.
Common-law requisites to passage of title, ii. 40, 42.
Consideration in law of conveyance, ii. 40.
Consideration necessary to pass use in equity, ii. 41.

CORPORAL PUNISHMENT.
Words tending to subject to corporal punishment defamatory, i. 276.

COSTS.
Court costs as affecting action for malicious civil proceeding, i. 333.

COTESMERE, J.
Approves action on case in nature of deceit for breach of parol promise, iii. 175.
Statement concerning invalidity of executory accord, ii. 123.

COUNT.
Anglo-Saxon law, form of count in, iii. 26.
Common count available in suit on bill or note, when, iii. 203.
Common counts, origin of —
Account stated, iii. 188.
Count for materials furnished, iii. 187.
Count for work and labor, iii. 187.
Money had and received, iii. 188.
Money lent, iii. 188.
Money paid, iii. 188.
Quantum meruit, iii. 185, 187.
Quantum valebant, iii. 185, 188.
Count for money paid to defendant's use, iii. 201.
Count for service wrongfully appropriated, iii. 199.
Count on fictitious sale, iii. 197.
Formality of count in early English law, iii. 26, 27.

COUNT — *Continued.*
Money had and received —
Count for, supersedes action of account, iii. 190.
Equitable nature of count for, iii. 189.
Failure of consideration, iii. 192.
Form of count for, iii. 194.
Limitation of count as used against converter, iii. 197.
Lord Mansfield's exposition of nature of count, iii. 193.
Nature of common count, iii. 188.
Quantum meruit —
Abandonment of entire contract by plaintiff precludes recovery on, ii. 225.
Joinder with count in debt on specialty, ii. 200.
Right to recover on part performance of contract, ii. 224.

COUNTY COURT ACT (1850), iii. 155.

COUPONS.
See TRANSFERABLE SECURITIES.

COURSE OF EMPLOYMENT.
See MASTER AND SERVANT.

COURT.
Common-law courts acquire jurisdiction of commercial causes, ii. 333.
Contest of common-law and admiralty courts, ii. 322.
Deception of court a ground of deceit, i. 375.
Innovation, courts have no power of direct innovation, i. 499.
King's court, unifying effect on English judicial system, iii. 28.
Local courts, waning influence of, ii. 332.
Theory of function of court, i. 498.

COURT OF PIEPOUDRES, ii. 327.

COVENANT.
See SPECIALTY.
Action of covenant —
Assumpsit not concurrent remedy, iii. 123.
Case available in lieu of covenant, when, iii. 124.
Debt not concurrent remedy, iii. 120.
Lies only at instance of party to covenant, iii. 121.
Party may sue though covenant not signed by him, iii. 122.
Privity essential to maintenance of action, iii. 121.
Promise to pay debt, when covenant maintainable on, iii. 120.
Scope of remedy, iii. 114, 120.
Sounds in contract, iii. 115.
Third person for whose benefit covenant is made has no action, iii. 122.
Writ, iii. 114.
First appearance, iii. 114.
Form, iii. 115.
Contract of covenant —
Basis for levy of fine, ii. 17; iii. 117.
Condition precedent to performance of mutual covenant, ii. 134.

COVENANT -- *Continued.*
Contract of covenant — *Continued.*
Consideration not necessary to support, iii. 119.
Covenant does not perish with person, iii. 125.
Covenant in consideration of performance distinguished from covenant in consideration of other covenant, ii. 134.
Covenant in early law, ii. 9; iii. 114, 116.
Covenant must be evidenced by writing, iii. 117.
Covenants mutually independent unless made mutually dependent, ii. 134.
Covenants real and personal, iii. 117.
Dependence of mutual covenants, ii. 143.
Doctrine of mutual independence, ii. 134.
Form —
Implied covenant, iii. 125.
No particular words necessary to make covenant good, iii. 124.
Words importing covenant in law —
Concessi, iii. 125.
Dedi, iii. 125.
Demisi, iii. 125.
Formal contract, covenant becomes, ii. 18; iii. 118.
Nature, ii. 17.
Analogy to parol promise, ii. 132.
Parol promise distinguished from covenant, ii. 133.
Sealed obligation of debt distinguished, iii. 119.
Personal service, covenant stipulating for, abrogated by death, iii. 126.
Remedy —
Action of covenant, iii. 114.
Action on case, iii. 123.
Assumpsit, iii. 123.
Scope, iii. 120.
Seal essential to creation of covenant, iii. 18.
Specific performance of covenant, iii. 115.
Subsidiary covenant fails when principal contract fails, iii. 122.

COVENANT TO STAND SEIZED.
Consideration of love and affection, ii. 43.
Consideration of love and affection for illegitimate child, ii. 45.
Marriage sufficient consideration, ii. 45.
Nature of covenant, i. 43.

CRANCH, WM.
Contribution to history of bills and notes, ii. 323.

CRANE.
Collapse of steam crane, responsibility of contractor, i. 159.

CRANWORTH, LORD.
Master's liability for negligent act of servant, ii. 461, 462.

CRAWFORD, J. J.
Codifier of American law of bills and notes, ii. 496.

CRIME.
Justification of battery in prevention of crime, i. 10.

CRIMINAL CONVERSATION.
Husband's action for criminal conversation with wife, i. 264.

CRIMINAL OFFENSE.
Imputation of criminal offense defamatory, i. 277.

CRITICISM.
See FAIR COMMENT AND CRITICISM.

CROKE, J.
Existence of debt sufficient consideration to support promise to pay same, ii. 63.
Fraud coupled with damage gives cause of action, i. 393.
Refusal of bailee to surrender chattel does not constitute conversion, iii. 167.

CUSTODY.
Diligence required of bailee for custody, ii. 289.

CUSTOM.
Customary duties, ii. 206, 207.
Remedy —
Debt, iii. 132.
Indebitatus assumpsit, iii. 189.
Custom of merchants —
Applies only to foreign bills, ii. 344.
Comes to apply to all bills, ii. 350.
Good only in transactions among merchants, ii. 349.
Held not to extend to promissory note, ii. 384.
Judicial notice of, ii. 349, 421.
Need not be specially pleaded, ii. 351, 352.
Not pleadable at law, when, ii. 347.
Provable by witnesses, when, ii. 253.
Sanctioned by business integrity, ii. 359.
Source of legal duty, ii. 347.
Debts created by custom, ii. 207.
Evidence of usage in commercial cases, ii. 398.
Fire, responsibility of keeper of fire, i. 56.
Function of business usage in evolution of commercial law, ii. 397.
Modern usage as source of liability in commercial law, ii. 416.
Privilege incident to performance of duty imposed by, i. 40.
Settled custom judicially known, ii. 353.
Usage of business as affecting authority of agent, ii. 485.
Usage of business as affecting right of agent to appoint substitute, ii. 477.

DALLAS, C. J.
Liability of bailee for theft of servant, ii. 277.

DAMAGE.
Consequential damages —
Consequential damages associated with secondary trespass, iii. 253, 254.
Direct damage distinguished from, iii. 252, 253.
Defamation —
Pecuniary damage as basis of action for injurious words, i. 278.
Direct damage, iii. 253, 254.
Elements of recoverable damage —
Compensatory damages, assessment of, i. 488.
Danger of recognizing new damage elements, i. 470.
Exemplary damage, amount left to discretion of jury, i. 488.
Injury to person, i. 457.
Injury to reputation, i. 457.
Jury, freedom of, in dealing with damage, i. 488.
Law of damage outstrips theory of civil wrong, i. 488.
Mental distress, i. 460.
Right of action arising *ex contractu,* i. 471.
Right of action arising *ex delicto,* i. 472.
Mental distress as element of recoverable damage in telegraph cases, i. 466–469.
Mental distress not an element of recoverable damage, when, i. 474.
Nervous shock, i. 457.
Injury considered remote, when, i. 458.
Nervous shock associated with physical injury, i. 459.
Nervous shock without impact, i. 458.
Physical suffering engendered by nervous shock, i. 458.
Parasitic damage characteristic of transition stage, i. 470.
Parasitic damage, nature of, i. 461.
Pecuniary loss, i. 457.
Physical suffering, i. 457, 459.
Proximity and remoteness of damage, i. 489.
Mental attitude of wrongdoer as affecting proximity, i. 489.
Exemplary damages, see MEASURE OF DAMAGES.
Meaning of damage, i. 457.
Measure of damage, see MEASURE OF DAMAGES.
Ordinary damage —
Ordinary damage presumed to have been in contemplation of parties, i. 446.
Special damage distinguished from, i. 446, 447.
Remoteness of damage in law of defamation, i. 289.
Special damage —
Illustrations of, i. 447, 448.
Notice of antecedent condition as affecting liability, i. 447.
Remote and speculative damage distinguished from special damage, i. 449.
Remote damage not recoverable as special damage, i. 448.
Special pecuniary damage as basis of action of slander, i. 287.
Speculative damage, what is, i. 449.

DAMAGE — *Continued.*
Telegraph company, liability for consequential damage incident to negligent transmission, i. 444.
Trespass on personal property, actual damage essential to liability in, i. 16.
Vindictive damages, see MEASURE OF DAMAGES.

DAMAGE AND INJURY.
Damage not a universal element of wrong, i. 491.
Damnum absque injuria, i. 492.
Injury said to import damage, i. 491.
Injury the sole universal element of legal wrong, i. 491.
Nonactionable damage, i. 493.
Nonactionable injury, i. 493, 494.

DAMNUM ABSQUE INJURIA, i. 432.
Damage consequential on exercise of legal right, i. 369.
Illustrations of *damnum absque injuria*, i. 492, 493.

DAMPIER, J.
Sanctions indebitatus assumpsit as remedy on running account, iii. 191.

DANBY, J.
Observation on liability of bailee, ii. 260.

DANGER.
Obviousness of danger as connected with responsibility, i. 67.

DANGEROUS PREMISES.
In general —
Assumption of risk by person injured, i. 150.
Responsibility of person maintaining, i. 149.
Delegation of repair, effect on liability of maintainor, i. 154.
Person responsible for —
Occupant, i. 153.
Person guilty of actual shortcoming, i. 153.
Primary risk incident to maintenance —
Concrete cases discussed —
Bales insecurely piled, i. 151.
Broken gas main, i. 154.
Displaced plate over coal cellar, i. 152.
Fall of stand at steeplechase, i. 151.
Insecure gangway, i. 152.
Insecure lamp over street, i. 154.
Obstacle left in roadway pending repairs, i. 155.
Open chute in manufacturing establishment, i. 151.
Slippery stairs, i. 152.
Trap in passageway, i. 151.
Unguarded area, i. 153.
Unlighted swing bridge, i. 152.

DANVERS, J.
Recognizes doing of any act as sufficient *quid pro quo* to support debt, ii. 24.

DARREIN PRESENTMENT.
Assize of, iii. 37.

DATE.
Absence of does not affect negotiability, ii. 509.
Antedating of negotiable instrument, ii. 515.
Date stated in negotiable instrument assumed to be *prima facie* true, ii. 515.
Fixed period after date, ii. 507.
Insertion of wrong date in negotiable instrument, ii. 515.
Postdating of negotiable instrument, ii. 515.
Undated negotiable instrument, right of holder to insert true date, ii. 515.

DAVEY, LORD.
Observation on English law of light, i. 209.

DEAD.
Libel tending to blacken memory of dead person indictable, i. 294.

DEALER'S TALK.
Not sufficient foundation for action of deceit, i. 386.

DEATH.
Action of account perishes with person, iii. 103, 104.
Action of debt perishes with person, when, iii. 63, 65, 66.
Agency terminated by, ii. 491.
Assumpsit survives death of party, iii. 68.
Covenant unaffected by death of party, iii. 125.
Death by wrongful act gives no cause of action, when, iii. 73, 74.
Death of person injured as affecting right of action of third person for consequential damage, iii. 71.
Detinue survives death of party, iii. 64.
Instrument payable at fixed period after death negotiable, ii. 507.
Personal obligation as affected by death of party, iii. 60.
Right of action in tort survives, when, iii. 70, 71.
Right of representative to recover on contract partly performed by decedent, ii. 224.
Trover perishes with person, iii. 64.

DEBENTURES.
See TRANSFERABLE SECURITIES.

DEBT.
Action of debt as remedy on early contract *re*, iii. 128.
Action of debt lies to recover on duty created by contract, custom, or record, iii. 127.
Action of debt maintainable for recovery of rent charge, when, iii. 56.
Action of debt on simple contract superseded by assumpsit, iii. 138.
Antiquity of, ii. 1.
Assignment of debt valid, when, iii. 84.
Assumpsit available for recovery of simple debt, iii. 138.
Assumpsit maintainable on debt after death of debtor, iii. 68.

DEBT — *Continued.*
Bills and notes —
Acceptor liable in action of debt, when, iii. 140, 142.
Acceptor liable in indebitatus, when, iii. 141.
American doctrine concerning debt as remedy on bills and notes, iii. 142.
English doctrine, iii. 139, 142.
Indorser liable to action of debt, when, iii. 142.
Maker liable to action of debt, when, iii. 141.
Customary and statutory duties constitute debts, ii. 207.
Customary duties, action of debt as remedy on, iii. 132.
Debt and assumpsit, ii. 61.
Confusion between conception of debt and obligation of promise, ii. 64, 65.
Two conceptions distinguished, ii. 64.
Debt follows person of debtor, iii. 91.
Debt for service rendered not maintainable unless price fixed, iii. 186.
Debt in *debet et detinet,* iii. 129.
Debt in *detinet,* iii. 129.
Debt maintainable in lieu of account, when, iii. 109.
Duty in nature of debt, see QUASI-CONTRACT.
Early limits of action of debt, ii. 200.
Heir liable for debt of ancestor —
Alienation of land of heir, iii. 138.
Descended lands, iii. 137.
Extent of liability of heir, iii. 137.
Implied promise to pay debt, ii. 62.
Judgment, action of debt as remedy for recovery of, iii. 132.
Jurisdiction of common-law courts, iii. 132.
Jurisdiction of local courts, iii. 132.
Master's responsibility for debt created by servant, ii. 446.
Money debt distinguished from chattel debt, iii. 129.
Money debt, nature of, iii. 129.
Mutual promises distinguished from debt, ii. 133.
Permanence of conception of debt, ii. 65.
Personal character of obligation of debt, iii. 136.
Pleading —
Defect of venue pleadable in abatement only, iii. 136.
Fictitious venue, iii. 136, 137.
Heir's plea of *riens per descent,* iii. 138.
Joinder of counts for money and chattels, iii. 130.
Joinder of counts on simple debt and specialty debt not permitted, iii. 131.
Proof of debt in early law, ii. 8.
Proprietary character of action of debt, iii. 130.
Quasi-contract, action of debt as remedy on, iii. 133.
Rent, action of debt as remedy for, iii. 133.
Scope of debt, iii. 127.
Sealed obligation of indebtedness distinguished from covenant, iii. 119.

DEBT — *Continued.*
Specialty debt distinguished from simple debt, iii. 131.
Specialty debt, nature of, iii. 131, 132.
Statute of Frauds, liability for debt of another, ii. 184.
Statutory penalty, action of debt as remedy for, iii. 132.
Sum certain —
Action of debt lies only for recovery of, iii. 135.
Indebitatus assumpsit maintainable where debt reducible to certainty, iii. 135.
Survival —
Action of debt destroyed by death of party, iii. 63.
Action of debt does not perish where heir or successor bound, iii. 65.
Detinue and debt distinguished on point of survival, iii. 131.
Explanation of perishability of simple debt, iii. 66.
Specialty debt survives death of party, iii. 66.
Wager of law as explanatory of non-survival of debt, iii. 66, 67.
Transitory character of obligation of debt, iii. 136.
Unilateral nature of the debt, ii. 133.
Venue of debts, iii. 136.
Incorrect venue pleadable in abatement only, iii. 136.
Wager of law in action on simple debt, iii. 138.
Writ of debt for money and chattels, form of, iii. 129, 130.

DECEIT.
Abuse of legal process formerly ground of action in deceit, i. 376.
Action on the case in nature of deceit, scope of, i. 375, 376.
Affinity of deceit to contract theory, i. 374.
Ancient writ superseded by action on the case, i. 376.
Cheating, i. 376.
Deceitful promise to enfeoff, ii. 32.
Early history of deceit —
Deception in judicial proceedings, i. 375.
Extended use of writ of deceit, i. 375.
False personation, i. 375.
Extension of action, ii. 31.
False warranty in chattel sale —
Affirmation of ownership not equivalent to warranty, i. 382.
Breach of warranty conceived as breach of contract, i. 389.
Caveat emptor, i. 378.
Different conceptions of liability, i. 377, 389, 390.
False representation as to title, i. 382.
False representation of quality, i. 380.
False warranty of title or quality in early law, i. 377.
Implied warranty of title, i. 382.
American doctrine, i. 384.
Modern English doctrine, i. 384.
Personalty in possession of seller, i. 384.
Possession of seller not proper criterion for raising implied warranty, i. 385.
Warranty implied from possession, i. 383.

DECEIT — *Continued.*
False warranty in chattel sale — *Continued.*
Scienter unnecessary to be alleged, i. 382.
Seller liable for breach of warranty, when, i. 379.
Warranty must be express, i. 379.
Warranty must induce sale, i. 380.
Warranty of quality, i. 385.
Description, goods must answer to, when, i. 388.
Goods supplied for particular purpose —
Copper sheathing for vessel, i. 387.
Crane rope for hoisting barrels, i. 386.
Hair restorer, i. 387
Intention of party as affecting question of warranty, i. 386.
Opportunity to inspect as affecting question of implied warranty, i. 388.
Representation operating as warranty, i. 385.
Dealer's talk, i. 386.
Expression of opinion, i. 386.
Prediction of future yield, i. 386.
Sample, sale by, i. 389.
Wholesomeness of food and drink —
Scienter of unwholesomeness, when necessary to be proved, i. 388.
When warranty of, arises, i. 387.
Fraud in chattel sales —
Action by disappointed purchasers disfavored at common law, i. 378.
Actual knowledge of falsity essential to fraud, i. 380.
Caveat emptor, i. 378.
Chandelor *v.* Lopus, doctrine of, i. 380.
Different conceptions of liability for, i. 377, 389.
Fraudulent sale in early law, i. 377.
Scienter, allegation of, i. 381.
Scienter, gist of action, when, i. 382.
Seller liable for fraud, when, i. 379.
What constitutes fraud on part of seller, i. 379, 480.
Fraudulent imposition of pecuniary loss as ground of liability in deceit, i. 374.
Fraudulent misrepresentation, see MISREPRESENTATION.
Trademark, action on case in nature of deceit as remedy for counterfeiting of, i. 418.
Unauthorized agent not liable for deceit where he believes himself to have authority, i. 406.
Warrantizando vendidit, form of declaration in declaring on, i. 380.
Writ of deceit, i. 375.

DECEPTION.
See DECEIT; also MISREPRESENTATION; UNFAIR COMPETITION.

DEED.
Debt evidenced by sealed obligation, iii. 131, 132.
Requisites of, as affected by Statute of Frauds, ii. 172.
Signature to deed necessary under Statute of Frauds, when, ii. 172.

DEEMER, J.

Duty of telegraph company to use reasonable care in transmission of telegram, i. 440, 441.

DEFAMATION.

Anomalous state of this branch of law, i. 273.
Common-law doctrine —
Aspersion in respect of one's profession, i. 277.
Criminal offense, words imputing, i. 276.
Disherison, words of, i. 278.
Imputation of loathsome disease, i. 277.
Pecuniary damage, words followed by, i. 278.
Written defamation or libel, i. 278.
Contract, interference with, by publication of defamatory statement, i. 346.
Essentials of wrong —
Communication must be defamatory, i. 275.
Falsity, i. 274, 275.
Fair comment and criticism, i. 302.
Foresight of damage as test of defamatory words, i. 286, 287.
Gist of defamation, i. 273.
History and general state of law of slander and libel, i. 275.
Insult, words of insult not necessarily defamatory, i. 285.
Interference with contract relation by means of defamatory words, i. 346.
Interpretation of defamatory words —
Construed *in mitiori sensu,* when, i. 299.
Hypothetical and metaphorical language, i. 299, 300.
Interrogative insinuation, i. 300.
Words taken in sense intended by defamer, i. 299.
Justification —
Defamatory written statement, when may be justified, i. 301.
Pleading matter of justification, i. 301.
Justification must go to whole of charge, i. 301.
Particularity required, i. 301.
Plea of justification disfavored, i. 302.
Unsuccessful justification indicative of malice, i. 302.
Libel —
Dead person, libel to blacken memory of, indictable, i. 294.
Distinction between libel and slander established, i. 293.
Gist of libel, i. 279.
History of law of libel —
Political aspects of subject, i. 291.
Severance of libel from slander, i. 291.
Libelous effigy or sign, i. 294.
Offensiveness of the libel, i. 294.
Representation leading to false inference as to character actionable, when, i. 320.
Severity of law of libel, explanation of, i. 292.
Special damage not required in libel, i. 295.

DEFAMATION — *Continued.*
Libel — *Continued.*
Writing supposed to show malice, i. 292.
Malice —
Function of malice in theory of defamation, i. 313.
Malice in law, i. 316.
Tort of defamation not founded on malice, i. 316.
Measure of damages, extent of circulation of defamatory matter relevant on, i. 296.
Mode —
Effigy, i. 274.
Picture or sign, i. 274.
Words, spoken or written, i. 274.
Pleading —
Colloquium, i. 300.
Inducement, i. 300.
Innuendo, i. 300.
Privacy, infringement of right of, i. 318.
Privilege —
Absolute privilege —
Argument of attorney, i. 307.
Communication relating to affairs of state, i. 307.
Official utterances of administrative functionary, i. 307.
Person acting in judicial capacity, i. 37.
Proceedings of jurors, i. 307.
Report made in obedience to military duty, i. 307.
Testimony of witness, i. 307.
Utterance of judge, i. 307.
Utterance of member of Parliament, i. 307.
Abuse of privilege takes away privilege, i. 314, 315.
Basis of doctrine of privilege, i. 313.
Factors destructive of legal privilege —
Heated and exaggerated language, i. 315.
Malice, i. 313.
Burden of proving malice, i. 316.
Recklessness of statement, i. 315.
Want of probable cause, i. 315.
Qualified privilege —
Communication between parties occupying confidential relation, i. 311.
Communication concerning fitness of applicant for office, i. 308, 309.
Communication concerning official conduct, i. 309.
Communication containing reflection on servant, i. 311, 312.
Communication made in obedience to social duty, i. 312.
Mistake as to existence of duty, effect of, i. 312.
Complaint addressed by private citizen to public functionary, i. 308.
Criticism of public official, i. 308, 309.
Mercantile agencies, statements given out by, i. 311.

DEFAMATION — *Continued.*
Privilege — *Continued.*
Qualified privilege — *Continued.*
Report of legislative proceedings, i. 310.
Report of proceedings of inferior legislative body, i. 310.
Unofficial account of judicial proceedings, i. 309, 310.
Publication —
Assisting publication, when actionable, i. 298.
Communication between husband and wife, i. 297.
Communication to husband or wife by third person, i. 297.
Communication to person defamed, i. 296.
Delivery to telegraph company, i. 297.
Extent of dissemination immaterial, i. 296.
Mail, transmission through, i. 297.
Printing, i. 297.
Procuring publication of defamatory matter, i. 298.
Publication by person libeled, i. 296.
Publication essential in libel and slander, i. 296.
Repetition of defamatory matter constitutes new publication, i. 299.
Republication of slanderous words actionable, when, i. 288.
Stenographer, dictation to, i. 297.
Telegraph, transmission by, i. 297.
Remedy, appearance of action on case for slanderous words, iii. 250.
Slander —
Authorized republication, i. 288.
Employment lost as result of slander, i. 286.
Gist of slander, i. 279.
Repetition of slanderous words, when actionable, i. 287.
Unchastity, words imputing, i. 289, 290.
Slander, history of, i. 280.
Common-law courts assume jurisdiction over slander, i. 282.
Common-law courts overrun by actions for defamatory words, i. 283.
Common-law courts refuse to entertain suits for slander, i. 281.
Defamation originally punished in local courts, i. 281.
Ecclesiastical jurisdiction over slander, i. 282.
Hostile attitude of King's Bench, i. 284.
Scandalum magnatum, i. 281.
State of law in America, i. 290.
State of law in time of Coke, i. 282.
Statutory improvement of law of slander, i. 290.
Special pecuniary damage, doctrine of, i. 285.
Temporal damage ground of common-law jurisdiction, i. 283.
Truthful communication gives no cause of action, i. 275.
Truth, justification by proof of, i. 300.

DEFAMATION OF GOODS.
Disparagement of manufactured goods, i. 323.
Fair comment and criticism, application of doctrine of, i. 324.

DEFAMATION OF GOODS—*Continued.*
Reckless disregard of truth, i. 324.
Words injurious in respect of business, i. 324.
Actual damage necessary to be shown, i. 324.

DEFAULT.
Liability for default of another under statute of frauds, ii. 184.

DEFECTUS.
Meaning as used in writ against carrier, ii. 302.
Meaning as used in writ against innkeeper, ii. 297.

DE GREY, C. J.
Approves use of action on case as remedy for breach of covenant, iii. 124.

DELEGATION.
Act of discretion cannot be delegated, ii. 476.
Agent may delegate authority, when, ii. 475.
Delegation of performance of ministerial act, ii. 475.

DELICT.
Delict and *quasi*-delict distinguished, i., p. xxvi.

DELICTUM, i., p. xxii.

DELIVERY.
Delivery of negotiable instrument, requisites and effect, ii. 517.

DEMAND.
Conversion, when demand necessary to make purchaser guilty of, i. 239.

DENISON, J.
Observation on effect of special indorsement, ii. 398.

DENMAN, J.
Observation on contractual character of action of detinue, iii. 155, 156.
Responsibility for harm done by dangerous agent, i. 66.
Statement of doctrine of equitable estoppel, ii. 242.

DEODAND.
Historical account of deodand, i. 50.
Illustrations of deodand, i. 50, 51.

D'EON, CHEVALIER.
Wager on sex of, ii. 166.

DE PLAGA FACTA.
Criminal appeal, iii. 229.

DEPOSIT.
Definition, ii. 271.

DEPOSITARY.
Bracton, liability of depositary in time of, ii. 254.
Debtor, depositary treated as, ii. 254, 263.

DEPOSITARY — *Continued.*
Finder of lost goods a *quasi*-depositary, ii. 278.
Good faith required of depositary, ii. 274.
Gross neglect makes depositary liable, ii. 275.
Liability for act of servant or agent, ii. 277.
Special deposit with bank, ii. 276.
When entitled to use chattel for own benefit, ii. 278.

DE PREROGATIVA REGIS.
Statute, iii. 296.

DETENTION.
Conversion by unlawful detention, i. 231.

DETINUE.
Action for recovery of specific chattel, iii. 144.
Ascription of property to trespasser retards extension of detinue, iii. 238.
Asportation, detinue available as remedy, iii. 149.
Bailment, detinue chiefly used in field of, iii. 144.
Bailor and bailee —
Detinue defective remedy for bailor, ii. 253.
Detinue falls into disuse as remedy against bailee, ii. 266.
Detinue superseded by case as remedy of bailor, iii. 150, 151.
Bargain and sale, detinue as remedy of vendee, iii. 145.
Contractual character of early action, iii. 154.
Debt, detinue derived from action of, iii. 144.
Detinue *sur bailment*, iii. 145.
Bailor's action against bailee, iii. 146.
Fictitious bailment, iii. 152.
Joint bailor cannot maintain action without demand in behalf of all, iii. 154.
Joint owner other than actual bailor cannot maintain action against bailee, iii. 154.
Limitations of early action, iii. 147.
Pleading —
Allegation of trover, iii. 147, 148.
Devenerunt ad manus, iii. 147.
Representative of deceased bailee liable at suit of bailor, iii. 146.
Sub-bailee liable at suit of bailee, iii. 146, 147.
Third person not liable at suit of bailor, iii. 146.
Writ, form of, iii. 146.
Detinue *sur trover*, iii. 147.
Action on case *sur trover* supersedes detinue *sur trover,* iii. 151.
Fictitious finding, iii. 148, 149.
Trover distinguished from, iii. 159.
Fictions of trover, iii. 160.
Finder of lost goods liable in detinue, iii. 148.
Nature of action —
Bracton treats detinue as action *in personam,* iii. 41.
Change incident to extension of scope of action, iii. 155.
Conflicting views —

DETINUE — *Continued.*
Nature of action — *Continued.*
Conflicting views — *Continued.*
Contract theory, iii. 156.
Tort theory, iii. 156.
Contractual character of early action, iii. 154.
Detinue comes to be classed as delictual action, iii. 155.
Difficulty of placing detinue in common-law system, iii. 42.
Proprietary character of action, iii. 157, 158.
Remedy sometimes sounds in contract, sometimes in tort, iii. 156.
Period of atrophy in development of action, iii. 150.
Plaintiff must show general or special ownership and right of immediate possession, iii. 152, 153.
Pleading, allegation of fictitious bailment, iii. 152.
Rehabilitation of detinue in modern times, iii. 153.
Scope of action, iii. 145.
Scope of modern action, iii. 153.
Sealed obligation, detinue as remedy on, iii. 145.
Summary of steps in development of detinue, iii. 153.
Survival of detinue, iii. 64.
Trespasser, detinue as remedy against, iii. 149, 152.
Trover supersedes action of detinue, iii. 151.
Unlawful detention as gist of action, iii. 149, 152, 153.

DETRIMENT TO PROMISEE.
See CONSIDERATION.

DICEY, A. V.
Interpretation of conspiracy cases, i. 364.

DILAPIDATIONS.
Obligation of assignee of lease to compensate lessee for money paid in respect of dilapidations, ii. 234.

DILIGENCE.
Agistor, diligence required of, ii. 290.
Bailee for custody, diligence required of, ii. 289.
Bailee for hire, diligence required of, ii. 285.
Bailee for service, diligence required of, ii. 289.
Commodatary, diligence exacted of, ii. 281.
Common carrier, diligence required of, ii. 304.
Depositary, diligence required of, ii. 275.
Finder of lost goods, diligence required of, ii. 278.
Mandatary, degree of care required of, ii. 279.

DIOCLETIAN, EMPEROR.
Authorizes use of extraordinary process by provincial magistrates, iii. 20.

DIRECTORS' LIABILITY ACT, i. 403.

DISEASE, LOATHSOME.
Words imputing affliction of loathsome disease defamatory, i. 277.

DISHERISON.
Words tending to disherison defamatory, when, i. 278.

DISPOSAL.
Conversion by wrongful disposal of goods, i. 231.
DISSEISIN OF CHATTELS.
See CONVERSION.
DISSEISIN OF REAL PROPERTY.
See CONVERSION.
DISTRESS.
See MENTAL DISTRESS.
In general —
Analogy of distress to *legis actio sacramenti*, iii. 291.
Definition, iii. 278.
Distress falls into disuse, iii. 294.
Origin of right to distrain, iii. 279.
Place of distress in legal theory, iii. 278.
Survival from early legal formation, iii. 23.
American law of distress, iii. 308.
Care required of distrainor, iii. 313.
Distrainable things —
Exemption —
Beasts of plough, iii. 304.
Cab in hand of hirer, iii. 306.
Chattel in hand of pawnbroker, iii. 306.
Cock or sheaf of corn, iii. 304.
Goods in hand of auctioneer, iii. 306.
Goods in hand of carrier, iii. 306.
Instrument of husbandry, iii. 304.
Instrument of trade, iii. 304.
Thing annexed to freehold, iii. 304.
Thing delivered to person exercising public calling, iii. 304.
Goods of stranger subject to be taken, when, iii. 306.
Implement of trade, iii. 305.
Slave, iii. 307.
Distrainor —
Acquires no property in thing distrained, iii. 292.
Cannot use thing distrained, iii. 292.
Not required to furnish sustenance, iii. 292.
Use of distress by, constitutes trespass, iii. 293.
Distress damage feasant, iii. 309–313.
Antiquity of, iii. 309.
Care required of distrainor, iii. 313.
Commoner may distrain beasts of lord, when, iii. 310.
Damage —
Each beast to answer for own damage, iii. 311.
Uncertainty of the damage, iii. 312.
Distrainable things —
Cattle, iii. 309–311.
Inanimate things —
Railroad engine, iii. 312.
Turves, iii. 312.

DISTRESS — *Continued.*
Distress damage feasant — *Continued.*
Exemption, iii. 311.
Technical strictness of law concerning, iii. 311.
Time when beasts must be taken, iii. 311.
Who may distrain —
Commoner, iii. 310.
Owner of soil, iii. 310.
Early law of distress resembles Salic law, iii. 283.
Exemption —
Absolute exemption, iii. 304.
Qualified exemption, iii. 304.
Reason for exemption, iii. 304–305.
Fealty, feudal distress inseparable from, iii. 302.
Feudal organization as affecting remedy of distress, iii. 287–288.
Feudal service, distress as remedy for, iii. 288–297.
Heriot, right to distrain for heriot custom, iii. 297.
History —
Archaic features of distress, iii. 291.
Distress among Teutonic people, iii. 282–283.
Distress for feudal service, iii. 288.
Distress in early England, iii. 283.
Distress in Irish law, ii. 283.
Distress in Roman law, iii. 280–282.
Distress sinks to level of auxiliary process, iii. 285.
Early law, iii. 278–280.
Gradual obsolescence of distress, iii. 285–286.
Revival of substantive distress, iii. 285.
Irish law, iii. 283–284.
Judicial distress, iii. 278.
Jurisdiction of manorial courts, iii. 288.
Money paid to prevent wrongful distress recoverable, when, ii. 230.
Notice —
Notice of intention to distrain not necessary at common law, iii. 284.
Statutory requirement of notice, iii. 284.
Proceedings in distress —
Impounding, iii. 292.
Seizure, iii. 291.
Provisions of statute of Marlborough, iii. 210, 290.
Rent, distress as remedy for, iii. 298–303.
Assignee of rent may distrain, when, iii. 302.
Conditions of right to distrain, iii. 303.
Connection between distress and rent, iii. 300, 301.
Rent-charge, iii. 299.
Rent granted, iii. 300.
Rent must be reducible to certainty, iii. 301.
Rent reserved, iii. 299, 300.
Rent reserved to stranger not distrainable, iii. 301.
Rent-seck, iii. 299.
Rent-service, iii. 299.

DISTRESS — *Continued.*
Roman law —
Pignoris capio, iii. 280–281.
Nature of remedy, iii. 280–281.
Scope of remedy, iii. 281.
Salic law, iii. 282–283.
Proceedings in distress —
Caption, iii. 283.
Demand, iii. 282.
Second demand, iii. 282.
Summons, iii. 282.
Third demand, iii. 282.
Self-help, idea of, as basis of distress, iii. 279.
Suit-real, right of distress incident to, iii. 297.
Suit-service, right of distress incident to, iii. 297.
Technicalities, distress becomes burdened with, iii. 295.
Teutonic law, iii. 282–283.

DIVERSION.
Diversion of threatened injury as ground of justification in trespass, i. 23.

DIVIDEND WARRANTS.
See TRANSFERABLE SECURITIES.

DIVINE SERVICE.
Liability for failure to maintain, i. 184.

DOCTOR AND STUDENT, DIALOGUE OF.
See SAINT GERMAIN.

DODDERIDGE, J.
Supposes trover not maintainable against bailee on allegation of fictitious finding, iii. 166, 167.

DOLUS, i. 374.

DOMESTIC RELATIONS.
See INTERFERENCE WITH DOMESTIC RELATIONS.
Relation of master and servant classed among, ii. 430.

DOOMS.
Awards of early judges, iii. 4, 5.

DOWER.
Writ for admeasurement of dower, iii. 45.
Writ of dower, iii. 44, 45.
Writ of dower *unde nihil habet*, iii. 45.

DRINK.
Implied warranty of quality in sale of food and drink, i. 387, 388.

DRUGGIST.
Negligence of in compounding prescription, i. 60, 61.
Poison, responsibility for injury done by, i. 60.
Poison sold under innocent label, i. 60.

DRUNKENNESS.
Duty of drunken person to compensate for necessaries, ii. 204.
Justification of battery committed in handling drunken man, i. 9.

DURESS.
Effect on negotiability of instrument, ii. 530, 531.
Undue pressure, duress distinguished from, ii. 229, 230.

DUTY.
Conception of duty, iii. 6.
Origin of, iii 5, 6.
Determinate person as obligee of duty, i. 94.
Privity of relation, i. 94; iii. 60, 61, 77.
Right correlative with duty, iii. 7.

DYNAMITE.
See Explosive.

EARNEST.
Analogy to Roman *sacramentum*, ii. 6.
Forfeiture by breach of bargain, ii. 5.
Forfeiture of double earnest, ii. 6.
Function of earnest in early law, ii. 5.
Giving of earnest does not make contract *re*, ii. 6.
Mercantile law, earnest in, ii. 6, 330.

EASEMENT.
Easement of support, how acquired, i. 195.

ECCLESIASTICAL COURTS.
Compromise with common-law courts, ii. 13.
Jurisdiction over contract, ii. 11.
Jurisdiction over contracts limited, ii. 13.
Pledge of faith, ii. 11.

EDGE, C. J.
Observation on customary right of privacy in Indian law, i. 320.

EDITOR.
Managing editor subject to action for publication of libelous matter, i. 298.

EFFIGY.
Defamation by means of, i. 274, 294.
Effigy representing one as perpetrator of murder, i. 290.

EJECTMENT WRIT, iii. 45.

ELDON, LORD.
Recognizes principle of unfair competition in trade, i. 419.
Sanctions debt as remedy against maker of note, iii. 141.

ELECTION.
Action against returning officer, iii. 55.

ELECTRICITY.
Live wire, responsibility of keeper of premises for injury caused by, i. 155.

ELLENBOROUGH, LORD.
Approves rule that money paid under mistake of law is not recoverable, ii. 214.
Holds that words imputing malicious mischief are not defamatory, i. 286.
Meaning of 'agreement' in Statute of Frauds, ii. 179.
Observation on liability of occupant for injury resulting from dangerous premises, i. 153.
Originates doctrine of constructive acceptance, ii. 411.
Part payment of debt not good consideration for accord and satisfaction, ii. 99, 100.
Person jumping from position of danger not chargeable with contributory negligence, when, i. 133.

EMPLOYERS' LIABILITY ACT, i. 168.

EMPTIO-VENDITIO.
See Bargain and Sale.

ENTERPRISE, PUBLIC.
Fair comment and criticism on, i. 303.

ENTRY, WRIT OF.
See Writ of Entry.

EQUITY.
Distinction between law and equity not abolished by modern procedure acts, iii. 58.

EQUIVALENCE.
Principle of equivalence in relation of master and servant, ii. 465.

ERLE, J.
Meaning of maxim *Sic utere tuo*, etc., i. 211.
Recognizes implied warranty of title in chattel sale, i. 384.

ERSKINE, THOMAS.
Observation on strictness of liability in trespass, i. 77.

ESCHEAT.
Incident of military tenure abolished by statute, iii. 296.

ESHER, LORD.
See Brett.
Generalization of theory of negligence, i. 92, 93, 149, 150.
Summary of law of equitable estoppel, ii. 245.

ESTATE.
Instrument payable to estate of deceased person, ii. 514.

ESTOPPEL.
Acquiescence of principal in unauthorized act of agent, effect of, ii. 245.
Analogy of estoppel to law of deceit, ii. 246.
Conduct calculated to mislead reasonable man, effect of, ii. 246.
Equitable estoppel, ii. 241.
Estoppel by negligence, ii. 248.

ESTOPPEL — *Continued.*
Estoppel *in pais*, ii. 241.
Estoppel of principal arising from holding out of agent as authorized to do particular business, ii. 486.
Failure to assert ownership in self, ii. 243.
Maker of note estopped from asserting defense, ii. 244.
Misrepresentation as basis of equitable estoppel, ii. 241.
Misrepresentation as to title and boundary of land, effect, ii. 244.
Modernness of law of equitable estoppel, ii. 242.
Negligence, effect of, ii. 246.
Owner estopped from asserting title, when, ii. 242, 243.
Quasi-contractual nature of law of estoppel, ii. 246.
Renunciation of title to land, ii. 243.
Undervaluation by shipper, ii. 243.
Wilful misrepresentation, ii. 245.

EVOLUTION.
Process of legal development in field of tort, i. 496, 497.

EWART, J. S.
Estoppel, theory of liability of master for unauthorized act of agent, ii. 486, 487.
Negotiability and estoppel, ii. 424.

EXCEPTIONS.
See Qualifications and Exceptions.

"EXCHANGE."
Instrument payable to exchange treated as payable to bearer, ii. 511, 514.

EXCHEQUER CHAMBER, COURT OF.
Refuses to entertain assumpsit for breach of promise to pay specialty debt, iii. 181.

EXECUTORS AND ADMINISTRATORS.
Action of account conceded to, iii. 104.
Promise to answer damages out of own estate, ii. 184.
Right of action for trespass done to estate of decedent, iii. 69.
Right of executor to recover of legatee tax paid by executor, ii. 232.

EXEMPTION.
Clause in negotiable instrument providing for waiver of exemption, ii. 508.

EXERCITOR.
Representative of owner of ship, ii. 434.

EXONERATION.
Principal and agent, exoneration as between, ii. 240.
Servant's duty to exonerate master, ii. 449.
Surety, exoneration of, ii. 238.

EXPERT.
Assumption of professional skill, i. 97.
Care required of highly skilled person, i. 97.

EXPLOSIVE.
Nitro-glycerine, responsibility for damage done by, i. 84.
Responsibility of owner, keeper, and vendor, i. 59, 60.
Sale of loaded cartridges to small boy, liability of seller, i. 172, 173.

EYRE, C. B.
Arguments against negotiability of bill payable to fictitious party, ii. 403.
Basis of rule denying validity of executory accord, ii. 93.

FACTOR.
Factor originally a common-law accountant, iii. 102.
Factor treated as bailee in modern law, iii. 101.
Liability of factor acting for undisclosed principal, ii. 478.
Robbery by stranger as defense for, ii. 262.
When factor liable for conversion in course of business, i. 244.

FACTORAGE.
Fiction of factorage in transactions by bill of exchange, ii. 346.

FAIR COMMENT AND CRITICISM.
Book criticism, i. 304.
Criticism must be honest and relevant, i. 304.
Defense of fair comment distinct from defense of privilege, i. 303.
Fact and comment on fact distinguished, i. 303.
Fair criticism, what is, i. 304.
Limits of the defense of fair comment, i. 305.
Malice, effect of, i. 305.
Naval plans, scientific attainments of author of naval plans open to criticism, i. 305.
Strictures on work of art and public enterprise, i. 302, 303.
Theatrical performance, criticism of, i. 304.

FAIR, COURT OF.
See Piepoudres.

FAIRFAX, J.
Approves extension of action of assumpsit, iii. 54.
Civil and criminal liability in trespass distinguished, i. 76.
Detinue as remedy against finder of lost goods, iii. 147.
Favors the extension of action on the case on assumpsit, ii. 34.

FAITH, PLEDGE OF.
See Pledge of Faith.

FALSE IMPRISONMENT.
See Trespass on Person.

FALSE PERSONATION.
False personation in court proceedings a ground of liability in deceit, i. 375.

FALSE PRETENSES.
False pretenses as ground of action in deceit, i. 376.

FARRELL, J. L.
Interpretation of Negotiable Instruments Law, § 9, subs. 5, ii. 515.

FEALTY.
Incident of military tenure, iii. 296, 297.

FELLOW SERVANT.
See MASTER AND SERVANT.

FELONY.
Civil action merged in felony, when, i. 494; iii. 72.
Conviction of felony operates as forfeiture of goods —
American doctrine, i. 495.
English doctrine, i. 494, 495.
Justification of libel charging previous conviction of felony, i. 302.

FENCE —
Contributory negligence of person failing to restore, i. 130.
Liability for damage resulting from failure to maintain, i. 127, 183, 184.

FERÆ NATURÆ.
See ANIMALS.

FERRY.
Interference with exclusive franchise of ferry, i. 217.
Overloading of boat, liability of ferryman for, i. 187.

FEUDALISM.
Feudal organization as affecting history of distress, iii. 287, 288.
Feudal services, distress as remedy for, iii. 288, 297.
Feudal tenure —
Nature of, iii. 287.
Principal incidents of, iii. 296.
Right to distrain an incident of feudal jurisdiction, iii. 290.

FICTITIOUS PERSON —
Instrument payable to fictitious or nonexisting person treated as payable to bearer, ii. 510–513.

FIDEIUSSOR.
See PLEDGE OF FAITH.

FIDES FACTA.
See PLEDGE OF FAITH.

FIELD, J.
Observation on liability of bank for special deposit, ii. 277.

FIGURES.
Discrepancy between words and figures of negotiable instrument, ii. 518.

FINCH, SIR HENRY.
Summary of law of bailment, ii. 262.

FINDER.
Liability of finder of lost goods, ii. 278.

FINE.
Covenants used as means of levying, iii. 117.

FINEUX, J.
Notes consequences of extension of action of assumpsit, ii. 35.
Observation on maxim *actio personalis*, etc., iii. 68.
Recognizes action for nonfeasance of parol promise, ii. 33.
Supposes part payment of debt may be good satisfaction, ii. 96.

FIRE.
Communicated fire —
Responsibility for damage caused by, i. 115, 116, 117.
Responsibility for damage done by flame conveyed by wind, i. 121.
Householder, responsibility for fire caused by guest, ii. 443.
Keeper of premises, responsibility of, i. 56, 57.
Responsibility for fire communicated by burning oil, i. 113, 117.
Responsibility of master for fire caused by negligence of servant, ii. 443.
Sparks from locomotive engine, responsibility for damage, i. 130.

FIREARMS.
Pointing of unloaded gun constitutes assault, when, i. 12.
Relaxation of the principle of liability for injury done by, i. 79–82.
Responsibility of owner or keeper for injury done by, i. 57.
Strictness of liability for injury done by, i. 78, 79, 80, 82, 83.

FITZHERBERT, ANTHONY.
Observation on law of assignment, iii. 84.
Observation on scope of detinue, iii. 145.
Perishability of action of debt, iii. 67.
Public and private nuisance distinguished, i. 224.

FLEETWOOD AND WRAY.
Argument against consideration of love and affection, ii. 43.

FOOD.
Implied warranty of quality in sale of, i. 387, 388.

FOREIGN BONDS.
See TRANSFERABLE SECURITIES.

FORE-OATH.
Function of, in early remedial law, iii. 24.

FORESIGHT OF HARM.
Antecedent condition of liability for negligence, i. 91.
Assumption of risk by trespasser as affected by foresight of harm, i. 155.
Determinative of responsibility in secondary trespass, when, i. 67.
Reasonable foresight of harm the test of responsibility, i. 68.
Test of liability for negligent injury, i. 89, 104.
Test of responsibility for injury done by domestic animals, i. 52.

FORFEITURE.
Conviction of felony does not operate as forfeiture of goods in America, i. 495.
Conviction of felony works forfeiture of goods, when, i. 494.

FORGERY.
When party to negotiable instrument precluded from raising defense, ii. 520.

FORM.
Formalism in early English law, iii. 24.
Formalism in Roman and Teutonic law, iii. 10.
Formality a necessary phenomenon in early law, iii. 9.
Function of form, iii. 9.
Problem of adjudication simplified by formality, iii. 9.
Prominence of form in early law due to absence of professional lawyer, iii. 9.

FORMATION.
Successive legal formations in tort law, i. 496.

FORMEDON IN DESCENDER.
Writ of, iii. 50.

FORTESCUE, C. J.
Title passes on agreement to sell without payment, ii. 27.

FORTESCUE, J.
Immediate and consequential injury distinguished, iii. 252.

FORWARDING MERCHANT.
Liability of forwarding merchant as bailee for custody, ii. 290.

FOSTER, J.
Recognizes right of innkeeper to recover on *quantum meruit,* iii. 187.

FRANK-PLEDGE, INSTITUTION OF, ii. 438.

FRAUD.
See DECEIT; MISREPRESENTATION.
Fraudulent intent as affecting liability in unfair competition, i. 426, 427.
Gross negligence distinguished from, ii. 279.
Implied warranty, conception of, suppletory to law of fraud, i. 404.
Malice distinguished from fraud, i. 356.
Negligence compared with fraud, i. 72.
Recession of fraud as constitutive element of liability, i. 427.

FROWIKE, C. J.
Distinguishes between misfeasance and nonfeasance as ground of liability, iii. 176, 177.
Sanctions debt as concurrent with action of account, iii. 108.
Summary of law of assumpsit, ii. 33.

FRY, J.
Right of individual to use own name in business, i. 434.

FULLER, C. J.
Fraudulent intent as affecting liability for unfair competition, i. 431.

GAIUS, INSTITUTES OF, iii. 13.

GAMBLING CONTRACTS.
See Wager.

GASCOIGNE, C. J.
Action of replevin as concurrent with trespass, iii. 216.

GAS COMPANY.
Implied duty incident to public calling, i. 186.

GAWDY, J.
Observation on assignment accompanied by letter of attorney, iii. 84.

GENERAL WARRANT.
Illegal commitment under ground for exemplary damages, i. 484.

GIBBS, C. J.
Approves exemplary damages in case of insulting trespass, i. 485.
Sanctions indebitatus as remedy on running account, iii. 191.

GIBSON, C. J.
Observation on right to distrain property of stranger, iii. 306.
Statement of relation between consideration and right of action, ii. 154.

GLANVILL, J.
Observation on father's right of action for abduction of child, i. 267.

GLANVILL, R.
Authorship of writ of replevin attributed to, iii. 208.
State of English contract law in time of, ii. 1.
Writ process in time of, iii. 30.

GLOUCESTER, STATUTE OF, i. 29; iii. 249, 269.

GOLDSMITHS.
Advance money on public revenue, ii. 367.
Failure of goldsmiths, ii. 368.
Goldsmiths' notes, ii. 368.
London goldsmiths engage in business of banking, ii. 367.

GOODS, DEFAMATION OF.
See Defamation of Goods.

GOULD, J.
Observations on one's duty to care for self, i. 124.

GRACE.
Note entitled to grace though lacking words of negotiability, ii. 387.
Sight paper deprived of grace by Negotiable Instruments Law (§ 7), ii. 509.

GRAIN ELEVATOR.
Grain depositors treated as tenants in common, ii. 291.
Grain elevator company treated as bailee with special authority, ii. 291.
Liability of elevator company as bailee for custody, ii. 290.

GRANT.
Right of support acquired by grant, i. 195.

GREEN, N. ST. JOHN.
Contribution to history of law of defamation, i. 273.

GREENLEAF, PROF. SIMON.
Theory of damages, i. 479.

GRIER, J.
Principle underlying assessment of exemplary damages, i. 482.

GUARANTORS AND SURETIES.
Collateral liability of, ii. 183.

GUARANTY.
Origin of contract of guaranty, ii. 47.
Place of contract in modern law, ii. 48.
Statute of Frauds as affecting contract, ii. 184.

GUARDIAN.
Accountant, responsibility of guardian as, iii. 106.
Guardian in socage required to account for estate of ward, iii. 102.

GUARDIAN AND WARD.
See INTERFERENCE WITH DOMESTIC RELATIONS.

GUEST.
Assumption of risk by, see ASSUMPTION OF RISK.
Householder's responsibility for fire due to guest, ii. 443.

GUILFORD, LORD KEEPER.
Connection with authorship of Statute of Frauds, ii. 169.

GUN.
See FIREARMS.

HALE, LORD.
Authorship of Statute of Frauds attributed to, ii. 168.
Distinguishes libel from slander, i. 291.
Holds debt not to be available as remedy on accepted bill, iii. 140, 141.
Observation on liability of carrier by sea, ii. 269.
Trover not available against carrier who loses goods, iii. 169.

HALSBURY, LORD.
Delict and *quasi*-delict distinguished, i., p. xxvi.
Distinguishes venue from question of jurisdiction, iii. 94.
Intimidation, obstruction, and molestation as affecting liability for interference with trade or calling, i. 350.
Statement of the *rationale* Allen *v.* Flood, i. 351.

HAMMOND, PROF. W. G.
Approves Blackstone's theory of function of judge, i. 499.

HANKFORD, J.
Competition in business not actionable, i. 217.
Gives illustration of *damnum absque injuria*, i. 493.
Small trespasses not actionable in early common-law court, i. 15.

HANNEN, SIR JAMES.
Bearing of combination on liability for interference with trade or calling, i. 363.
Observation on principle of compensation as affecting assessment of damages, i. 487.

HARDWICKE, LORD.
Approves distinction between slander and libel, i. 293.
Law of unfair competition in time of, i. 418, 419.
Puts law of interference with light on basis of nuisance, i. 210.

HARTMANN.
Opinion as to date of origin of negotiability of bill, ii. 354.

HAUGHTON, J.
Existence of debt sufficient consideration to support promise to pay same, ii. 63.
Sanctions allegation of fictitious finding in trover against bailee, iii. 167.

HAWKINS, J.
Intimidation and coercion as affecting liability for interference with trade or calling, i. 349.

HEATH, J.
Approves exemplary damages in case of assault and battery, i. 485.

HEBREW LAW.
Development of Hebrew code, iii. 10.
Judge precedes legislator, iii. 4.
Procedure in Hebrew law not characterized by formality, iii. 10.
Rapidity of growth, iii. 10.

HEIR.
Heir bound by covenant of ancestor, when, iii. 126.
Heir liable for debt of ancestor, when, iii. 65, 66, 137.

HENGHAM, J.
Formulates axiom of agency, ii. 464.

HERESY.
Imputation of heresy not defamatory, i. 277.

HERIOT.
Heriot custom, iii. 297.
Heriot service, iii. 297.

HERSCHELL, LORD.
Interference with trade or calling brought about by persuasion and warning, i. 350.
Observation on jurisdiction of court over local action arising from trespass on realty, iii. 95.

HERSCHELL, LORD — *Continued.*
Opposes recognition of malice as constitutive element of legal wrong, i. 356.
Principle of vengeance not admitted in administration of civil justice, i. 478.
Secondary signification of words not subject of trademark right, i. 429.
Statement of function of malice in tort of defamation, i. 318.
Summary of the law of deceit, i. 401.

HIGHWAY.
See BRIDGE.
Contributory negligence of person driving on wrong side of highway, i. 131.
Improper use of highway constitutes trespass, when, i. 21, 22.
Justification of trespass incident to detour from impassable highway, i. 23.
Obstruction —
Contributory negligence of traveler, i. 125.
Loss of patronage incident to, arises, i. 226.
Modern English doctrine concerning, i. 229.
Plaintiff precluded from recovering for injury, when, i. 177.
Public nuisance distinguished from private nuisance, i. 225.
Responsibility for damage done by horse frightened on highway, i. 111, 113.
Responsibility for damage incident to collision of sleigh, i. 114.
Stray animals run down by vehicle, when driver liable, i. 134.
Violation of statute by plaintiff as affecting right of action for injury, i. 178, 179.

HILARY RULES (1833).
Effect on pleading in action on bill of exchange, iii. 202.

HILLIARD, FRANCIS.
Treatise on Torts, i., p. xxii.

HIRING.
Diligence required of bailee for hire, ii. 285.
Hiring in early law, ii. 4.
Hiring in time of Bracton, ii. 15.
Letting of chattel to hire, ii. 284.
Care exacted of bailee, ii. 284.
Colorable hiring made with intent to convert, ii. 288.
Departure from terms of bailment, ii. 286.
Driving horse beyond destination, ii. 286.
Right of bailee to retain, ii. 284.
Place of contract in modern theory, ii. 48.

HOLMES, JUDGE O. W.
Notes ancient equitable jurisdiction over parol promises, ii. 35.
Observation on validity of contract of wager, ii. 111.
Recognizes privileged character of competitive labor, i. 371.

HOLMES, JUDGE O. W. — *Continued.*
Theory of agency, ii. 441, 460, 461.
Theory of liability of bailee, ii. 258.
Theory of origin of legal responsibility, i. 51.

HOLROYD, J.
Observation on payment of part in satisfaction of entire debt, ii. 104.

HOLT, LORD.
Argument in Ashby *v.* White, iii. 55.
Becomes Chief Justice of King's Bench, ii. 378.
Classification of bailments, ii. 271.
Criticism of Bonion's Case, ii. 257.
Damage element in malicious prosecution, i. 332.
Definition of conversion, i. 233.
Entertains opinion that bill of exchange is specialty, ii. 381.
Holds promissory note not to be within custom of merchants, ii. 383, 384.
Indebitatus assumpsit held not maintainable for recovery of rent, iii. 180.
Influence on law of bills and notes, ii. 378.
Influence on law of master and servant, ii. 451.
Injury imports damage in law, i. 491.
Master liable for negligent trespass of servant, iii. 260.
Notes date of appearance of promissory note and inland bill, ii. 368.
Observation on duty incident to public calling, i. 185.
Observation on form of declaration in action on bill, iii. 140.
Observation on special damage in public nuisance, i. 226.
Opposes extension of indebitatus assumpsit, iii. 189.
Originates doctrine that note given for precedent debt is conditional payment, ii. 389.
Sanctions trover as remedy in case of unlawful detention, iii. 168.
Statement of doctrine of mutual dependence, ii. 136.
Submission to arbitration involves mutual implied promises to perform award, iii. 192.
View concerning liability of postmaster, ii. 306, 307.
Warranty of title implied from possession, i. 383.

HOMAGE.
Incident of military tenure abolished by statute, iii. 296.

HORSE.
Conversion by departure from terms of hiring, i. 257; ii. 286, 287; iii. 162.

HOUSEHOLDER.
Responsibility of householder in early law for acts of members of household, ii. 437, 440.

HOWARD, J.
Ownership not triable in replevin suit, iii. 213.

HULL, J.
Denounces contract in restraint of trade as illegal, ii. 164.
Recognizes actionability of permissive waste, i. 32.

HUSBAND AND WIFE.
See INTERFERENCE WITH DOMESTIC RELATIONS.
Consent of husband as affecting right of action for adulterous conduct, i. 163.
Husband has no right of action for damages resulting from injury to wife where wife instantly killed, iii. 74.
Husband's action for seduction of wife unaffected by death of wife, ii. 72.
Husband's right of action for negligent injury to wife as affected by death of wife, iii. 73.
Justification of battery by one spouse in defense of other, i. 8.
Mental distress of husband occasioned by failure of physician to attend wife, i. 471.
Mental distress of wife occasioned by nondelivery of information of husband's death, i. 471, 472.
Obligation of husband to compensate for necessaries furnished wife, ii. 204.
Wife acting as agent of husband in commission of trespass, ii. 442.

IDENTIFICATION IN NEGLIGENCE.
See NEGLIGENCE.

ILLEGALITY.
Benefit conferred in furtherance of illegal purpose, ii. 223.
Illegality as affecting validity of contract, ii. 162.
Illegality of consideration, ii. 73.
Innocent party may recover for benefit conferred in furtherance of illegal purpose, ii. 223.

IMPRISONMENT, FALSE.
See TRESPASS ON PERSON.

IMPUTED NEGLIGENCE.
Basis of doctrine, i. 142.
Doctrine disfavored in America, i. 144.
Infant, negligence of custodian imputed to infant, when, i. 142.
Limitations of doctrine, i. 143.

INANIMATE THING, DAMAGE DONE BY.
See SECONDARY TRESPASS.

IN CONSIMILI CASU.
Parliament authorizes issuance of writs *in consimili casu*, iii. 34.

INDEBITATUS ASSUMPSIT.
Acceptor of bill liable in indebitatus assumpsit, when, iii. 141.
Account partially superseded by, iii. 109, 110.
Award, indebitatus available to enforce performance of, iii. 192.
Common count, see COUNT.
Consideration —
  Limits of indebitatus, iii. 206.
  Stranger to, may maintain indebitatus, when, iii. 205.
Count for money had and received available in case of conversion, iii. 195.

INDEBITATUS ASSUMPSIT — *Continued.*

Count for money had and received not available where accounts are complicated, iii. 190.

Count for money had and received supersedes action of account, iii. 190.

Count for money paid to defendant's use, when available, iii. 201.

Count on fictitious sale as remedy against tortfeasor, iii. 198.

Count on fictitious sale available in case of conversion, iii. 197.

Customary duty, indebitatus lies for recovery, iii. 189.

Debt and indebitatus, iii. 193, 194.

Duty in nature of debt —

Indebitatus as remedy, iii. 201.

Enticement of apprentice, recovery of profits incident to, iii. 199.

Express promise to pay existing debt, indebitatus as remedy, iii. 183, 184.

Failure of consideration, indebitatus as remedy, iii. 192.

Guaranty, indebitatus not maintainable for breach of, iii. 185.

Implied promise to pay simple debt, iii. 184.

Judgment, indebitatus as remedy on foreign judgment, iii. 194.

Mutual promises, indebitatus not available on, iii. 185.

Nature of action —

Affinity to assumpsit, iii. 205.

Affinity to case, iii. 205.

Affinity to debt, iii. 205.

Reversion to primitive type, iii. 204.

Obligation in nature of assumpsit, indebitatus not available on, iii. 201.

Origin of action, ii. 61; iii. 183.

Penalty, indebitatus as remedy for, iii. 189.

Pleading —

Form of count for money had and received, iii. 194.

Form of count in indebitatus, iii. 185.

Money had and received, allegation of receipt to plaintiff's use, iii. 195.

Simplicity of pleading in indebitatus, iii. 188.

Running accounts, indebitatus as remedy on, iii. 191.

Service rendered by person unlawfully imprisoned, indebitatus as remedy for, iii. 199.

Stages in development of action —

Indebitatus on common count, iii. 183.

Indebitatus on simple debt, iii. 182.

Tenant in common, indebitatus not available as remedy against co-tenant, iii. 191.

Wager of law, action of indebitatus not subject to, iii. 184.

INDEPENDENT CONTRACTOR.

Servant distinguished from, ii. 471.

INDE PRODUCIT SECTAM.

Meaning of allegation in common-law declaration, iii. 24.

INDIAN CIVIL WRONGS BILL, c. VI., § 44, i. 233.

INDUCEMENT.
Allegation of inducement in action for defamation, i. 300.

INFAMOUS PUNISHMENT.
Words tending to subject to infamous punishment defamatory, i. 277.

INFANT.
Express promise to pay for necessaries, ii. 204.
Indorsement of negotiable instrument by, effect of, ii. 519.
Infant husband liable for necessaries furnished wife, ii. 205.
Necessaries, *quasi*-contractual duty of infant to compensate for, ii. 203.
Negligence of custodian imputed to, i. 142, 143.
Street car company liable for injury to, i. 143.

INFANTS' RELIEF ACT, ii. 145.

INFRINGEMENT OF TRADEMARK.
See TRADEMARK; UNFAIR COMPETITION.

INJURY.
See DAMAGE AND INJURY.

INNKEEPER.
Allegation of assumpsit unnecessary in action against, ii. 267.
Custom of realm the basis of liability of innkeeper, ii. 298.
Exceptions to liability of, ii. 296.
Implied duty incident to public calling, i. 185.
Liability enforced in action on the case, ii. 294.
Liability for accidental loss, ii. 296.
Liable as insurer of guest's goods, ii. 294.
Measure of damages in case of conversion by, i. 257.
Negligence as basis of liability, ii. 295.
Negligent keeping of goods by, not a conversion, i. 237.
Not responsible for loss occasioned by negligence of guest, ii 295.
Positive *quasi*-contractual duty to entertain wayfarer, ii. 236.
Quantum meruit, right of innkeeper to recover on, iii. 187.
Relaxation of doctrine of strict liability, ii. 295.
Strict liability of, not a survival from early law, ii. 295.
When innkeeper not a true bailee, ii. 298.
Writ against innkeeper, form of, ii. 296.

INNOCENT PURCHASER.
See PURCHASER, INNOCENT.

INNOMINATE CONTRACT.
See CONTRACT.

INNUENDO.
Allegation of innuendo in action for defamation, i. 300.

IN PERSONAM, ACTION.
See ACTION IN PERSONAM.

IN REM, ACTION.
See ACTION IN REM.

INSANE.

Duty of insane person to compensate for necessaries, ii. 204.

INSCRUTABLE FAULT, i. 146.

INSIMUL COMPUTASSENT.

See COUNT.

INSTITOR.

Representative of owner in management of business, ii. 434.

INSULT.

Exemplary damages recoverable in case of wrong characterized by insult, i. 484, 486.
Insult conceived as aggravative of legal injury, i. 487.
Words of personal insult not necessarily defamatory, i. 285.

INSURANCE.

Aleatory character of contract, ii. 165.

INTEGRATION.

Integration and disintegration in tort law, i. xxi.

INTENTION.

Adequacy of consideration as affected by intention of contracting parties, ii. 70, 71.
Bearing on liability in trespass, i. 2, 4.
Defamation, bearing of malice on liability for, i. 317.
Hostile intent, bearing on liability for assault, i. 10, 11, 12.
Intent in sense of motive irrelevant on question of legality of act, i. 355.
Intention in law of estoppel, ii. 247.
Intention irrelevant in battery, when, i. 4.
Intention to compass particular harm, effect on liability for slander, i. 289.
Intent to convert, i. 234, 238, 241.
Misrepresentation, intention as affecting liability for, i. 396.
Presumption that one intends natural consequences of acts, i. 5.

INTERFERENCE WITH CONTRACT RELATIONS.

Bad faith essential to right of action, i. 344.
Contract for performance of personal service, i. 342, 343.
Contract unconnected with personal service, i. 344.
Discharge by employer without breach of contract on his part, i. 349.
Knowledge of existence of contract relation, bearing on liability of wrongdoer, i. 344.
Legal justification —
- Disinterested persuasion and advice, i. 345.
- Equal or superior right necessary to justification, i. 345.

Malice not essential to right of action, i. 344.
State of law in America, i. 346.
Use of means unlawful *per se*, i. 346.

INTERFERENCE WITH DOMESTIC RELATIONS.
Guardian and ward —
Loss of marriage of heir, i. 267.
Loss of marriage of ward, i. 267.
Husband and wife —
Abduction of wife, i. 263.
Derivative trespass, i. 263.
Loss of *consortium* gist of wrong, i. 263.
Criminal conversation with wife, i. 264.
Trespass originally proper remedy, i. 264.
Wife's consent irrelevant, i. 264.
Disability of wife to sue for criminal conversation with husband, i. 264, 265.
Rape of wife, i. 264.
Master and servant —
Abduction of servant, i. 265.
Battery of servant, i. 266.
Double right of action against wrongdoer, i. 266.
Remedy of master, i. 266.
Enticement of servant, i. 265, 266.
Harboring of servant, i. 265, 266.
Interference with relation of service, i. 265.
Master's right to service, i. 265.
Negligent personal injury, i. 267.
Retention of servant after notice of service due to previous employer, i. 266.
Seduction of female dependent, i. 268, 271.
Measure of damages, i. 268.
Unlawful imprisonment of servant, i. 266.
Parent and child —
Abduction of daughter, parent's right of action unaffected by death of daughter, iii. 72.
Action for loss of service, i. 268.
Measure of damages, i. 268.
Presumption of service from relation of parent and child, i. 268.
Parent's right of action for loss of marriage of heir, i. 267.
Person *in loco parentis,* right of action for seduction of female dependent, i. 270.
Seduction of daughter, i. 268.
Action limited to relations of service, i. 269.
Trespass for assault and battery, when maintainable, i. 269.
Trespass *quare clausum fregit,* when maintainable, i. 269.
Seduction of self-supporting girl, i. 270.
Remedy —
Action on case, iii. 266.
Trespass, iii. 266.

INTERFERENCE WITH LIGHT.
See COGNATE NUISANCE.

INTERFERENCE WITH SUPPORT.
See Cognate Nuisance.

INTERFERENCE WITH TRADE OR CALLING.
Allen *v.* Flood —
Discussion of principles underlying decision, i. 349.
Facts, statement of, i. 347.
Maliciously procuring employer to discharge workman held not to give right of action, i. 348.
Point of view of dissenting judges, i. 349, 350, 352.
Point of view of prevailing judges, i. 350–352.
Theory of the decision criticised, i. 351.
American doctrine, i. 365, 371.
Boycott, interference characterized by unlawful, i. 367.
Combination and coercion as affecting liability, i. 362, 366.
Conspiracy, bearing on liability for interference with trade or calling, i. 362, 363.
Discharge of employee at instigation of labor union, i. 369.
Discharge of employee procured by threat to violate contract, i. 370.
Driving wild fowl from decoy, i. 357.
Employee prohibited by employer from trading with plaintiff, i. 368.
Gist of the wrong, i. 372.
Intimidation and coercion as affecting liability, i. 349.
Labor union, discharge of employee at instance of, i. 367.
Malice —
Act otherwise lawful does not become actionable by reason of malice, i. 355.
Privilege destroyed by, when, i. 359.
Malice not an independent ground of action, i. 366.
Moral coercion resulting from combination, i. 367.
Nuisance, interference characterized by, i. 365.
Picketing, interference characterized by, i. 366.
Privilege —
Bearing of the doctrine of privilege on the question of liability, i. 358.
Competition in labor, privileged character of, i. 361.
Privilege incident to competition in labor market, i. 359.
Procuring discharge of employee in exercise of legal right, i. 368.
Quinn *v.* Leathem —
Discussion of principles underlying decision of, i. 361, 362.
Malice as affecting liability for interference with trade or calling, i. 363.
Representation, warning, and persuasion as affecting liability for interference with trade or calling, i. 350.
Unlawful means —
Conspiracy, i. 353.
Defamation, i. 353.
Duress, i. 354.
Fraud, i. 353.
Menaces and threats of bodily harm, i. 353.

INTERFERENCE WITH TRADE OR CALLING — *Continued.*
Unlawful means — *Continued.*
Moral intimidation and coercion, i. 353.
Riot, i. 353.
Violence, i. 352.
Void contract, interference in conformity with terms of, i. 370.

INTERVENING CAUSE.
Act of young child not an intervening cause, i. 121.
What is intervening cause —
Concrete cases discussed —
Conveyance of flame by ordinary wind, i. 121.
Conveyance of flame by whirlwind, i. 121.
Insecure opening into cellar, i. 121.
Open pit maintained near sidewalk, i. 121.
Starting of locomotive by meddlesome third person, i. 120.

INTOXICATING LIQUORS.
Rum seller, liability for damage resulting from illegal sale of liquor, i. 172, 173.

JAILER.
Liability for escape, ii. 260.

JENKINS, J.
Inveighs against use of assumpsit for recovery of simple debt, iii. 138.

JENKINS, SIR LEOLINE.
Reputed author of Statute of Frauds, ii. 169.

JESSEL, M. R.
Observation on doctrine of accord and satisfaction, ii. 89.

JETTISON.
Average, contribution in general average, i. 19.

JEWEL.
Responsibility of principal for sale of counterfeit jewel by agent, ii. 450.

JONES, SIR WILLIAM.
Classification of bailments, ii. 271.
Definition of bailment, ii. 308.
View regarding liability of innkeeper, ii. 297.

JUDEX.
Function in *actio sacramenti,* iii. 14.

JUDGE.
Early judge, place and function of, iii. 4.
Fiction of divine inspiration in early law, iii. 4.
Function of judge in modern law, i. 497, 498.
Judge and legislator, iii. 4.
Malicious and oppressive act privileged, when, i. 37.
Privileged character of utterances, i. 307.

JUDGMENT.

Action of debt as remedy for recovery of, iii. 132.

Confession of, effect of provision for in negotiable instrument, ii. 508.

Debt, judgment comes within conception of, ii. 206.

Judgment treated as contract, when, ii. 206, 207.

Nature of obligation created by, ii. 206, 207.

Quasi-contractual duty to refund money paid on judgment subsequently reversed, ii. 231.

Specialties, judgments are, ii. 207.

JUDICIAL NOTICE.

Courts refuse to take judicial notice of custom of merchants, ii. 349.

Custom of merchants judicially known when once established, ii. 353.

Established usage in commercial world, ii. 421.

JUDICIAL PRECEDENT.

Common-law doctrine. i. 499.

Doctrine not recognized in continental countries of Europe, i. 500.

JUDICIAL PROCEEDINGS.

Account of privileged, when, i. 309, 310.

JUDICIS POSTULATIO, iii. 16.

JURY.

Assize turned into jury, iii. 228.

Jury *de medietate linguæ*, ii. 327.

Venue of actions as affected by jury system, iii. 90.

JUS.

Meaning in maxim *ubi jus ibi remedium,* iii. 48.

JUS IN PERSONAM.

Action *in personam* used to vindicate, iii. 38.

JUS IN REM.

Action *in rem* used to vindicate, iii. 38.

JUSTA CAUSA DEBENDI, ii. 4, 10.

JUSTIFICATION.

Justification in actions of defamation, see DEFAMATION.

JUYN, C. J.

Sanctions action on case for breach of parol promise, ii. 30.

KEBLE, J.

Observation on death of party as affecting contract of covenant, iii. 126.

KEKEWICH, J.

Deception or likelihood of deception basis of action for unfair competition, i. 428.

KELLY, C. B.

Observations on proximate cause, i. 112.

KENNEDY, J.
Sanctions negotiability of conditional debentures payable to bearer, ii. 423.

KENT, J.
Considers factor not to be bailee, iii. 101.
Controversy with Story over question of consideration in negotiable instruments, ii. 522.
Statement of law of mandate, ii. 49.

KENYON, LORD.
Denies validity of executory accord, ii. 92.
Distinguishes between trespass and trespass on case, iii. 253.
Master is not liable where servant quits sight of employment, ii. 470.
Questions validity of moral consideration, ii. 144.
Theory of master's liability for negligence of servant, ii. 459.

KING.
King can do no wrong, basis of maxim, i. 35.

KING'S BENCH.
Extends assumpsit into field of simple debt, ii. 63.
Favors assumpsit for breach of promise to pay specialty debt, iii. 181.
Hostile attitude to action for defamation, i. 284.

LABORERS, STATUTE OF, i. 265, 343; ii. 23.

LABOR UNION.
Employee discharged at instigation of, i. 367, 368, 369.

LANDLORD AND TENANT.
Defective roof, landlord not responsible for injury, when, i. 158.

LANGDALE, M. R.
Statement of principle underlying law of trademark, i. 420.
Statement of principle underlying unfair competition, i. 420.

LANGDELL, PROF. C. C.
Benefit to promisor not a good consideration, ii. 68.
Criticism of Bradford *v.* Roulston, ii. 86.
Statement of common-law rule concerning consideration and right of action, ii. 152.

LARCENY.
Appeal of larceny supplants *actio furti,* iii. 49.
Conversion by bailee constitutes larceny, when, ii. 310.
Trespassory violation of possession essential to larceny, iii. 240, 241.

LAST CHANCE, DOCTRINE OF, i. 136.

LAW.
First appearance of conception of law, iii. 5.
Ideals of the law, i., p. xxiv.
Justice the end of law, i. 477.
Method of legal research, i., p. xxiv.

LAW — *Continued.*
Order of historical development, iii. 8.
Adjudication embodies first step in legal evolution, iii. 3.
Concrete precedes abstract, iii. 9.
Court first legal institution, iii. 5.
Path of the law, iii. 8.
Substantive and adjective law, iii. 1, 2.
Unity of law, i., p. xxviii.

LAW, MERCANTILE.
Lex mercatoria supplies basis of, ii. 324.

LAW MERCHANT.
Characteristic features of law merchant, ii. 328, 416.
Common-law principles ingrafted on, ii. 409.
Custom contrary to settled rule of law invalid, ii. 397.
Deceptive nature of term, ii. 417.
Development retarded by common-law courts, ii. 333.
Difference between law merchant and common law, ii. 330.
Doctrine of *caveat emptor* derived from, ii. 334.
English law merchant not an exotic, ii. 416.
Fiction of immemorial usage, ii. 416.
Identified with universal law of nature, ii. 331.
Law merchant accepted as part of common law, ii. 348.
Law merchant not an unmixed product of civil law, ii. 381.
Method of growth, ii. 416.
Promissory note supposed not to be within custom of merchants, ii. 383, 384.
Universality of law merchant, ii. 328, 330.

LEGAL AUTHORIZATION.
Blasting, liability for damage resulting from, i. 44.
Doctrine as applied in America, i. 43, 44.
Presumption against legislative intent to legalize nuisance, i. 43.
Privilege as defense against claim for consequential damage, i. 45.
Privilege cannot be invoked where damage is direct, i. 45.
Privilege incident to performance of authorized act, i. 41.

LEGALITY OF CONTRACT.
See CONTRACT.

LEGES JULIÆ, iii. 18.

LEGIS ACTIONES, iii. 13.

LEGISLATIVE PROCEEDINGS.
Account of, privileged, when, i. 310.

LEPROSY.
Words imputing affliction of leprosy defamatory, i. 277.

LEX ÆBUTIA, iii. 18.

LEX FORI.
Application of Statute of Frauds as affected by, ii. 178.

LEX LOCI CONTRACTUS.
Bearing on application of Statute of Frauds, ii. 178.

LEX MERCATORIA.
Assimilation into common law, ii. 324.
Characteristic features, ii. 328.
Dissolution and absorption into common law, ii. 332.
Effect of assimilation into common law, ii. 324.
Special courts for administration of, ii. 324, 331.

LEX NATURÆ.
See NATURE.

LIABILITY.
Extent of liability in tort and contract, i. 88.
Qualifications and exceptions, i. 35.
Responsibility distinguished from liability, i. 49.
Strict theory of civil liability in early stages of law, i. 77.

LIBEL AND SLANDER.
See DEFAMATION.

LICENSEE.
Assumption of risk by, see ASSUMPTION OF RISK.

LIEN.
Conversion from creation of adverse lien, i. 239.

LIGHT, INTERFERENCE WITH.
See COGNATE NUISANCE.

LINDLEY, LORD.
Bearing of conspiracy on liability for interference with trade or calling, i. 363.
Classification of cases involving negligence, i. 126.
Persuasion and coercion as affecting liability for interference with trade or calling, i. 351.

LIQUOR.
Dilution operates as conversion, when, i. 258.

LITIS CONTESTATIO, iii. 19.

LITTLEDALE, J.
Observation on limits of case and assumpsit, iii. 275.
Observation on principle underlying law of master and servant, ii. 465.
Observation on scope of action on case, iii. 247.

LITTLETON, SERJEANT.
Approves detinue as remedy against finder, iii. 148.
Recognizes principle that covenant is not abrogated by death of party, iii. 125.

LIVELIHOOD.
Wrongful interference with, i. 357.

LOAN.
See COMMODATARY.

LOCATIO CUSTODIÆ, ii. 298.

LOCATIO, LOCATUM.
See HIRING.

LOCATIO OPERIS, ii. 268.

LOCATIO OPERIS FACIENDI.
Definition, ii. 271.

LOCATIO OPERIS MERCIUM VEHENDARUM, ii. 298.

LOCATIO REI, ii. 271.

LOCATOR, ii. 274.

LOG DRIVING COMPANY.
Implied duty incident to public calling, i. 186.

LOMBARD.
Trading guild of Lombard bankers, ii. 335.

LOPES, L. J.
Observation on trespass resulting from abuse of highway, i. 22.
Summary of the law of deceit, i. 402.

LOST INSTRUMENT.
Action not maintainable in common-law court on lost instrument, ii. 375, 376.

LOVE AND AFFECTION.
See CONSIDERATION.

LUKE, J.
Disapproves action of debt in lieu of account, iii. 109.

LURTON, J.
Discountenances allowances of damages for mental distress, i. 472.

LUSH, J.
Definition of valuable consideration, ii. 68.

LUSHINGTON, RIGHT HON. DR.
Nonactionable damage, i. 493.

MACCLESFIELD, LORD.
Solution of problem of dependence of mutual promises, ii. 147.

McKEAN, C. J.
Extends remedy of account to all cases of partnership affairs, iii. 111.

McKEEHAN, PROF. C. L.
Interpretation of Negotiable Instruments Law, § 9, subs. 5, ii. 515.
Interpretation of Negotiable Instruments Law, § 40, ii. 527.

McMURTRIE, R. C.
Discussion of doctrine of Chandelor *v.* Lopus, i. 381.

MACNAGHTEN, LORD.
Ratification where agent's intention to act for another is not revealed, ii. 490.

MADMAN.
Justification of battery in restraint of, i. 9.

MAGNA CARTA.
Guardians made liable for waste, iii. 269.
Provisions for encouragement of commerce, ii. 325.

MAINE, PROF. H. S.
Archaic features of distress, iii. 291.
Explanation of *actio sacramenti*, iii. 14, 15.

MAINTENANCE.
American doctrine, i. 340, 341.
Assignee may lawfully maintain suit in name of assignor, when, iii. 83.
Assignment of right of action bad for maintenance, when, iii. 82.
Assisting prosecution of *qui tam* proceedings, ii. 338.
Charity, assistance given in cause of, i. 340.
Common interest in subject-matter of suit, i. 339.
Instigation of groundless suit, i. 339.
Maintenance as affecting validity of contract, ii. 163.
Maintenance defined, i. 337; ii. 164.
Malicious prosecution, analogy to maintenance, i. 337.
Prominence in former ages, i. 338.
Relative, right to maintain suit in favor of, i. 340.
Termination of suit wrongfully maintained, i. 339.

MAITLAND, PROF. F. W.
Characterization of *lex mercatoria*, ii. 328, 329.
'Select Pleas of Manorial Courts,' ii. 328.

MALICE.
Anger distinguished from, i. 314.
Comment and criticism, effect of malice in, i. 305.
Defamation —
Presumption of malice from putting of slanderous words into writing, i. 292.
Tort of defamation not founded on malice, i. 316.
Discussion of nature and function of malice, i. 313, 335, 356.
Exemplary damages, malice as affecting, i. 481.
Fraud distinguished from malice, i. 356.
Malice in law, i. 316.
Notion of malice in law gives trouble in defamation, i. 317.
Origin of doctrine, i. 317.
Malice will not convert lawful act into unlawful act, i. 355, 356.
Malicious prosecution —
Burden of proof in, i. 316, 331.
Liability as affected by presence of malice, i. 331.
Misrepresentation, malice not essential ingredient in, i. 396.

MALICE — *Continued.*
Mode of proof, i. 314.
Negligence compared with, i. 72, 356.
Privilege, when malice destructive of, i. 39, 40, 313.
Recession of malice as constitutive element in legal wrong, i. 335.
Slander of title, malice not essential to liability for, i. 323.
Spite and hatred, malice distinguished from, i. 331.
Truthful communication not defamatory though coupled with malice, i. 275.

MALICIOUS ABUSE OF PROCESS.
Analogue of trespass *ab initio,* ii. 334.
Gist of wrong, i. 336.
Malice in wrong of malicious abuse, i. 334.

MALICIOUSLY.
Definition of, i. 314.

MALICIOUS MISCHIEF.
Words imputing malicious mischief held not to be defamatory, i. 286.

MALICIOUS PROSECUTION.
Malicious civil proceedings —
Bankruptcy proceedings, malicious institution of, i. 331.
Conflict of authority concerning actionability of, i. 332.
Corporation, malicious petition to wind up, i. 331.
Court costs as affecting right of action, i. 333.
Lunacy, malicious inquisition of, i. 332.
Special damage as affecting liability for, i. 332, 333.
Malicious criminal proceedings —
Absence of probable cause, i. 329.
Antiquity of the wrong, i. 328.
Conspiracy to prosecute on false charge, i. 328.
Criminal proceedings ordinarily privileged in law, i. 326, 327.
Essentials to right of action for, i. 329.
False criminal charge *prima facie* actionable, i. 326.
Good faith of prosecutor as affecting liability for, i. 330.
Malice as affecting right of action, i. 331.
Malicious prosecution a branch of defamation, i. 327.
Privilege, basis of, i. 326.
Privilege of criminal proceedings a qualified privilege, i. 327.
Statutory recognition of tort of malicious prosecution, i. 328.
Termination of proceedings as affecting right of action, i. 329.
Obligation of individuals to prosecute criminals where accusation is well founded, i. 326, 327.
Special damage as basis of liability for, i. 332.

MALYNES, GERARD.
Author of Treatise on *Lex Mercatoria,* ii. 354.
Form of bill of exchange, ii. 356.
State of law of bills and notes in time of, ii. 359.

MANDATE.
Definition, ii. 271.
Diligence required of mandatary, ii. 279.
Misfeasance in performance of mandate, when actionable, ii. 49, 50.
Nonfeasance of gratuitous commission not actionable, ii. 49.

MANDATUM.
Substitute for agency in Roman law, ii. 435.

MANSFIELD, LORD.
Approves assessment of exemplary damages, i. 479.
Becomes Chief Justice of King's Bench, ii. 141.
Currency theory of money, ii. 394.
Defines liability of common carrier as that of insurer, ii. 301.
Denies actionability of permissive waste, i. 31.
Doctrine of virtual acceptance, ii. 401.
Favors action of stranger to consideration on contract made for his benefit, ii. 155.
Favors extension of indebitatus in form of count for money had and received, iii. 192.
Influence on contract law, ii. 141.
Influence on development of law of bills and notes, ii. 393.
Interpretation of clause 2, section 4, of Statute of Frauds, ii. 188.
Mutual covenants and promises, classification of, i. 138.
Observation on distinction between slander and libel, i. 293.
Observation on universality of mercantile law, ii. 331.
Recognizes principle of unfair competition in use of trademark, i. 419.
Sanctions action of surety to recover money paid to benefit of principal, ii. 238.

MANUS INJECTIO, iii. 16.

MANUUM CONSERTIO, iii. 13, 14.

MARIUS, JOHN.
Advice Concerning Bills of Exchange, ii. 359, 360.
Recognizes bill as being within custom of merchant, ii. 360.
Statement of law of bills and notes in time of, ii. 373, 376.

MARKBY, PROF. WILLIAM.
Observation on terms right and duty, iii. 7.

MARKET.
Interference with exclusive franchise of market, i. 217.
Market overt, origin of doctrine concerning, ii. 334.

MARLBOROUGH, STATUTE OF, i. 29; iii. 102, 103, 210, 289, 290.

MARRIAGE.
Deceitful promise of marriage, i. 376.
Instrument payable at future marriage not negotiable, ii. 508.
Marriage contract, ii. 192.
Mutual promises to marry not within Statute of Frauds, ii. 175,
Promises supported by consideration of, ii. 190, 192.
Right of marriage as incident of tenure abolished, iii. 296.

MARSEILLES, STATUTE OF, ii. 336.

MARTIN, B.
Definition of conversion, i. 233.
Observation on meaning of conversion, iii. 161.
Supposed benefit to promisor a good consideration, ii. 68.

MARTIN, J.
Denies action for breach of parol promise, ii. 30.
Observation on liability of master for fraudulent sale by servant, ii. 443, 444.

MASTER AND SERVANT.
See INTERFERENCE WITH DOMESTIC RELATIONS.
Abandonment of service precludes right to recovery of compensation, when, ii. 225.
Abduction, lord not responsible for wrongful abduction accomplished by retainers, ii. 442.
Act of servant, act of master, ii. 464-466.
Authority of servant presumed from course of employment, ii. 451, 452.
Authorization of act, what is, ii. 455.
Authorization of end authorizes necessary means, ii. 452.
Axiom underlying law of, ii. 464.
Branch of law of agency, ii. 430.
Civil responsibility of master in early law, ii. 439.
Commanded act, master alone liable for consequences of, ii. 445.
Communication between, privileged, when, i. 311.
Consent as element in relation of master and servant, ii. 468.
Conversion, when servant liable for conversion in employment of master, i. 242, 243.
Course or scope of employment as test of responsibility of master, ii. 435-437.
Departure of servant from course of duty, effect of, ii. 450, 469; iii. 265.
Equivalence of act of servant to act of master, ii. 464.
Exposure of servant to unnecessary risk, liability of master for injury resulting from, i. 168.
Fellow-servant doctrine, ii. 470.
Assumption of risk of employee, ii. 470.
Servant makes business of master his own, ii. 471.
Fiction of identity of legal *personæ*, ii. 441.
Fraudulent sale by servant, ii. 443.
General command implied from scope of employment, ii. 454.
General command inferred from conduct or usage, ii. 455.
Identification of act of servant as act of master, ii. 441.
Immunity of servant —
Servant liable for consequences of wrongful act done at instance of master, ii. 445.
Servant not answerable for consequences of commanded act, ii. 444.

MASTER AND SERVANT — *Continued.*
Incompetent servant, responsibility of master for employment of, ii. 458, 459.
Independent contractor, ii. 471, 472.
Influence of Lord Holt on development of law, ii. 451.
Interference with relation of personal service, master's right of action for, i. 342.
Maiming of servant ground of action at instance of master, i. 15.
Maintenance, servant may maintain controversy of master, when, i. 340.
Master and servant both liable to injured person where servant is negligent, ii. 451.
Master an insurer against harms of servant, ii. 462.
Master chargeable with contributory negligence of servant, i. 140.
Master not responsible for positive misfeasance of servant, ii. 446.
Master represented by servant, in what sense, ii. 463.
Master responsible for foreseeable consequence of commanded act, ii. 456.
Master's responsibility for crimes of retainers disappears, ii. 439.
Master, who is, ii. 468, 472.
Misfeasance, servant's liability for consequences of, ii. 445.
Negligence of servant —
Master responsible for consequences of, when, ii. 443, 451, 457.
Principle underlying responsibility of master for, ii. 458, 463, 465.
Theories concerning responsibility of master, ii. 448, 458, 459, 460, 461.
Particular command —
Absence of particular command relieves master, when, ii. 444.
Distinguished from general command, ii. 444.
Particular command, as applied in 17th century, ii. 449.
Personal injury of servant —
Master has no action where servant instantly killed, iii. 74.
Master's action for consequential damage, i. 265, 266.
Power of discharge as affecting master's responsibility for acts of servant, ii. 461.
Private instructions of master irrelevant, ii. 456.
Quitting sight of employment, effect of, ii. 470.
Reflection on character of servant privileged, when, i. 311, 312.
Remedy —
Master liable in case for trespass of servant, when, iii. 260.
Master liable in trespass for trespass of servant, when, iii. 260, 261.
Respondeat superior, doctrine of, i. 171.
Responsibility of master for commanded acts, ii. 442.
Responsibility of master for negligence of servant in respect of fire, ii. 443.
Responsibility of master for tortious act of servant, ii. 439.
Responsibility of master supposedly based on negligence in choice of incompetent servant, ii. 448, 458, 459.
Right to control as criterion of relation of master and servant, ii. 468.

MASTER AND SERVANT — *Continued.*

Risk incident to employment, assumption of, by servant, i. 164.
Secret instructions inconsistent with general authority, effect of, ii. 457.
Seduction of servant, master's right of action for, i. 271.
Servant distinguished from agent, ii. 430.
Servant, independent contractor is not, ii. 471.
Servant liable to master for negligent misfeasance, i. 187.
Servant's departure from employment, ii. 469.
Mental attitude of servant as affecting liability of master, ii. 469.
Wanton act aside from purpose of employment, ii. 469.
Servant's duty to exonerate master for consequence of wrongful act of servant, ii. 449.
Servant, who is, ii. 468.
Theft of servant, master's responsibility for, ii. 277.
Vicarious responsibility of the lord in early English law, ii. 437.

MASTER OF SHIP.

Abuse of power, liability incident to, i. 40.
Agent of owner in Roman law, ii. 434.
Privilege of, i. 39.

MAULE, J.

Observation on justification in libel, i. 301.

MAXIMS.

Acta exteriora indicant interiora secreta, i. 47.
Actio personalis moritur cum persona, iii. 60, 75.
A man is presumed to intend natural consequences of his act, i. 5, 75
Caveat emptor, i. 334, 378, 379, 384, 385, 388.
Cujus est solum ejus est usque ad cœlum, ii. 20, 207.
Culpa est rei se immiscere ad se non pertinenti, i. 338.
Debitum et contractus sunt nullius loci, iii. 92, 136.
Delegata potestas non potest delegari, ii. 475.
Delegatus non potest delegare, ii. 475, 476.
Ex nudo pacto non oritur actio, ii. 36.
Expressum facit cessare tacitum, ii. 220.
Ex turpi causa non oritur actio, i. 490; ii. 163.
King can do no wrong, i. 35.
Nulla injuria est quæ in volentem fiat, i. 162.
Omnis ratihabitio retrotrahitur et mandato comparatur, ii. 487.
Qui facit per alium facit per se, ii. 464; iii. 260, 261.
Qui inscienter peccat scienter emendet, i. 77.
Res loquitur ipsa, i. 107, 109.
Respondeat superior, i. 171.
Sic utere tuo ut alienum non lædas, i. 193, 211, 218.
Suppressio veri suggestio falsi, i. 399.
Ubi jus ibi remedium, iii. 48, 59.
Vicini vicinorum facta præsumuntur scire, iii. 90.
Volenti non fit injuria, i. 162, 171.

MEASURE OF DAMAGES.
Amount of damages as affected by idea of compensation, i. 477.
Amount of damages as affected by idea of prevention, i. 477.
Amount of damages as affected by idea of punishment, i. 477.
Assessment, controversy over principle governing, i. 479.
Breach of contract —
Anticipated profits not recoverable, i. 445.
Doctrine of Hadley *v.* Baxendale, i. 445.
Recoverable damage limited to such as might be foreseen, i. 446.
Difficulties of law concerning measure of damages, i. 476.
Exemplary damages, i. 479, 481, 483.
Compensatory damages for mental suffering substantially same as exemplary damages, i. 480.
Conflicting theories, i. 479, 480.
Fraud, malice, or oppression as affecting, i. 481.
Illegal commitment under general warrant justifies assessment, i. 484.
Jury, amount of exemplary damages left to the discretion of, i. 488.
Principle underlying assessment of, i. 482.
Meaning of term measure of damage, i. 476.
Punishment, recession of idea of punishment in theory of civil wrong, i. 478.

MELIORATING WASTE.
Equity will not enjoin, when, i. 28.

MEMBER OF PARLIAMENT.
Privileged character of utterances of, i. 307.

MEMORANDUM.
See Statute of Frauds.

MENACES.
Interferences with contract relation by means of, i. 346.

MENTAL ANGUISH.
See Mental Distress.

MENTAL DISTRESS.
Aggravative element of damage, i. 460.
Damage incident to, when recoverable, i. 460.
Insult, mental distress caused by, conceived as aggravative of legal injury, i. 487.
Mental distress as element of damage in telegraph cases, i. 466.
Liability based on breach of contract, i. 467.
Liability based on tort, i. 467.
Telegraph company liable for —
Right of action arising *ex contractu*, i. 471, 473.
Right of action arising *ex delicto*, i. 471.

MERCANTILE AGENCY.
Communication concerning credit and character of individual privileged, when, i. 311.

MERCANTILE LAW AMENDMENT ACT (1856).
Acceptance of bill of exchange, provision concerning, ii. 548, 549.
Dispenses with necessity for stating consideration in memorandum of agreement, ii. 181.

MERCHANT.
Carta mercatoria, ii. 6, 326.
Custom of merchant, ii. 324.
Equity court open to mediæval merchant, ii. 327.
Foreign merchant in mediæval England, ii. 325.
Local regulations hamper foreign traders, ii. 326.
Mediæval merchant not subject to common-law jurisdiction, ii. 327.
Mercantile transactions require speedy justice, ii. 328.
Merchant traders averse from suing in common-law court, ii. 342, 358.
Privileges conferred by *carta mercatoria,* ii. 327.
Special courts for administration of justice, ii. 327.
Speedy process for collection of debts, ii. 326.
Status of mediæval merchant in England, ii. 325, 326.
Statute of Acton Burnell *de mercatoribus,* ii. 326.
Statuto dell' Universita della Mercatanzia, ii. 336.

MERGER.
Civil wrong merges in felony, when, i. 494; iii. 72.
Obsolescence of doctrine of merger, iii. 73.

MERTON, COUNCIL OF, iii. 33.

METHOD.
Scientific method, safeguards of, i., p. xxiv.

MILL.
Loss of toll incident to competition gives no right of action, i. 217.

MINE.
Flooding from artificial accumulation of water, i. 62.

MINING.
Interference with lateral support by mining operations in noncontiguous soil, i. 194.
Subjacent support of surface not to be interfered with, i. 191.

MISCARRIAGE.
Liability for miscarriage of another, ii. 184.
Meaning of term as used in Statute of Frauds, ii. 184.

MISFEASANCE.
Case as remedy for negligent misfeasance, ii. 29.
Mandate, misfeasance of, when actionable, ii. 49, 50.
Negligent misfeasance of lawful undertaking, i. 187; ii. 29.

MISREPRESENTATION.
Estoppel by, ii. 241.
Fraudulent representation —
Action for, i. 392.
Ambiguous statement fraudulent, when, i. 398.

MISREPRESENTATION — *Continued.*
Fraudulent representation — *Continued.*
Belief, misrepresentation of, gives no right of action, i. 394.
Concealment, misrepresentation by, i. 394.
Conduct, misrepresentation by, i. 394.
Damage —
Contingent liability, i. 416.
Damage essential to liability, i. 415.
Present pecuniary loss, i. 415.
Subjection to legal obligation leading to future loss, i. 415.
Deception —
Material inducement, what is, i. 414.
Plaintiff must be misled, i. 413.
Representation as inducing cause, i. 413.
Representation not actionable where person claiming to be misled acted from other motive, i. 414.
Subsequent representation, i. 415.
Uncommunicated representation, i. 415.
Essential elements of wrong, i. 393.
Existing fact, representation must concern, i. 394.
Falsity of representation, i. 398.
Fraud coupled with damage gives cause of action, i. 393.
Future event, misrepresentation of supplies no ground for action, i. 394, 395.
Intention as affecting liability of person making false representation, i. 396.
Knowledge of falsity of representation —
Absence of honest belief, i. 399.
Assumption of knowledge, i. 407.
Giving of gratuitous information, i. 408.
Changed conditions, effect of, i. 411.
Confidential relation, positive duty arising from, i. 411.
Criticism of Derry *v.* Peek, i. 403.
Duty to correct erroneous statement when falsity of discovered, i. 412.
False statement honestly believed to be true, i. 400.
Gratuitous voluntary statement, i. 408.
Haycraft *v.* Creasy, discussion of, i. 409, 410.
Implied warranty, doctrine of, as applicable to cases like Derry *v.* Peek, i. 407.
Implied warranty of truth of representation, i. 404.
Negligence of statement relevant on question of honest belief, i. 402.
Negligent statement not actionable, i. 402.
Reckless statement, i. 399, 400.
Recommendation of solvency, i. 409.
Representation as to existence of knowledge, i. 400.
Request that representation shall be acted upon, effect of, i. 409.
Scienter, i. 399.

MISREPRESENTATION — *Continued.*
Fraudulent representation — *Continued.*
Knowledge of falsity of representation — *Continued.*
Self-serving information, i. 408.
Social and business courtesy, i. 409.
Statement believed to be true, but without sufficient grounds, i. 401.
Law, misrepresentation concerning state of the law not actionable, i. 395.
Material fact —
Representation must involve statement concerning, i. 396.
What constitutes material fact, i. 396.
Motive, statement of, immaterial, i. 396.
Opinion —
Misrepresentation of, gives no right of action, i. 395.
What constitutes matter of, i. 395.
Person intended to be influenced, i. 397.
Representation not made directly to person who acts upon same, i. 397.
Silence, i. 399.
Subsequent representation, i. 415.
Suppressio veri, i. 394, 399.
Uncommunicated representation, i. 415.
Words, misrepresentation by, i. 393.
Implied warranty of truthfulness of statement, i. 404, 411.
Principal and agent —
Agent's implied warranty of authority, i. 406.
Pretended agent liable in action for deceit if he knows he has no authority, i. 406.
Unauthorized agent not liable for misrepresentation of authority, when, i. 406.
Telegram, liability of telegraph company for erroneous transmission, i. 454.

MISSIO IN POSSESSIONEM, iii. 20.

MISTAKE.
Mistake of fact as basis of *quasi*-contractual duty, ii. 212.
Mistake of law, when given same effect as mistake of fact, ii. 214.

MOILE, B.
Observation on past consideration, ii. 86.
Observation on *quid pro quo* in debt, ii. 24, 27.

MONEY.
Agreements for exchange of, ii. 69.
Currency of, ii. 394.
Kind of money as affecting negotiability, ii. 509.

MONEY HAD AND RECEIVED.
Equitable nature of count, iii. 189.
Money paid under undue pressure recoverable as money had and received, ii. 228.
Origin of count, iii. 188.

MONEY LENT.
Count for, iii. 188.

MONEY PAID.
Count for, iii. 188.
Count on *quasi*-contractual duty to compensate for benefit conferred, ii. 213.
Criterion of action for money paid under pressure, ii. 229.
Equitable nature of action for, ii. 213.
Failure of consideration, available in case of, ii. 214.
Mistake of law, ii. 214.
Quasi-contractual obligation to compensate for money paid to defendant's use, ii. 233, 241.
Right of recovery as affected by changed position of party receiving payment, ii. 213.
Right of recovery not barred by negligent payment, ii. 213.

MORAL TURPITUDE.
Words imputing moral turpitude defamatory, i. 276.

MORDANT, J.
Observation on death of party as affecting contract of covenant, iii. 126.

MORTE D'ANCESTOR.
Assize of, iii. 37, 44.

MORTGAGE.
Conversion, when mortgage of chattels amounts to, i. 239.

MORTGAGOR AND MORTGAGEE.
Abuse of trust by mortgagee, measure of damages for, i. 261, 262.
Mortgagor estopped to foreclose, when, ii. 245.

MOSAIC LAW.
Provisions concerning bailment, ii. 274.

MOTIVE.
Motive irrelevant on question of the legality of act, i. 355.

MUTUAL PROMISES.
See BILATERAL CONTRACT.

MUTUUM.
Place of contract in legal theory, ii. 272.

NATURE.
Law merchant identified with law of nature, ii. 331.

NAVIGABLE WATERS.
Bargeman, liability for damage caused by mooring boat in swift current, i. 102.
Responsibility for damage incident to blocking of, i. 114.

NECESSARIES.
Quasi-contractual duty of insane or drunken person to compensate for, ii. 203.

NEGLIGENCE.
In general —
Affinity to contract theory, i. 87.
Affinity to tort law, i. 87.
Association of negligence with primary and secondary trespass, i. 71.
Criterion of negligence found in foresight of harm, i. 101.
Definition of negligence, i. 73, 96.
Dispute whether negligence has reference to state of mind, i. 95.
Fraud compared with, i. 72.
Fusion of tort and contract conceptions of liability, i. 87, 89.
Latitude in meaning of negligence, i. 73.
Malice compared with, i. 72, 73.
Modernness of the law of negligence, i. 182.
Negligence not a specific tort, i. 72.
Negligence represents state of mind, i. 72.
Place of conception of negligence, i. 71.
Twofold aspect of the conception of negligence —
Negligence viewed as omissive wrong, i. 86.
Negligence viewed as positive wrong, i. 86.
Breach of duty —
Determinate legal duty, i. 182, 183, 184.
Duty incident to public calling, i. 185.
Duty to care for self, i. 124.
Duty to take care not to injure person or property of other, i. 91, 92, 186.
Statutory duty, i. 172.
Comparative negligence, see COMPARATIVE NEGLIGENCE.
Concurring negligence of third person, see CONCURRING NEGLIGENCE.
Contributory negligence, see CONTRIBUTORY NEGLIGENCE.
Dangerous premises, see DANGEROUS PREMISES.
Degrees —
Fallacy of recognizing degrees in negligence, i. 99.
Gross negligence, i. 98.
Ordinary negligence, i. 98.
Repudiation of idea of degrees in negligence, i. 100.
Slight negligence, i. 98.
Duty to care for self, i. 124.
Concrete cases discussed —
Customer at restaurant, failure to observe care in making exit, i. 125.
Failure to heed whistle at railroad crossing, i. 124.
Riding bicycle over railroad crossing, i. 125.
Estoppel by negligence, ii. 246.
Estoppel resulting from negligent failure to speak, ii. 243.
Exemplary damages, gross negligence or recklessness of conduct as affecting assessment of, i. 481.
Extent of liability for established negligence, i. 89-91, 109, 111, 112.
False representation not fraudulent if made in honest belief, i. 402.
Foresight of harm as criterion of negligence, i. 101.

NEGLIGENCE — *Continued.*
Foresight of particular harm not essential to charge wrongdoer with negligence, i. 104.
Gross negligence, ii. 279, 280.
Harm, foresight of, charges wrongdoer with negligence —
Concrete cases discussed —
Crowd listening to public harangue, damage done by, i. 103.
Mooring boat in swift current, i. 102.
Scaffold, loosening support of, i. 103.
Ship's steering apparatus defective, i. 102.
Sparks from locomotive, i. 102.
Spontaneous combustion of hayrick, i. 101.
Harm, inability to foresee, relieves of liability —
Crossing street at unaccustomed place, i. 106.
Injury done by runaway horse, i. 104, 105.
Passenger injured by falling girder, i. 105.
Ship, unmanageable, i. 106.
Thumb crushed by door of railway carriage, i. 106.
Unexpected freezing of water turned on street, i. 104.
Unforeseeable freezing of water main, i. 104.
History of negligence —
Breach of determinate duty, i. 182.
Concrete cases discussed —
Breach of duty to keep up restraining wall, i. 183.
Failure to keep up fence, i. 183.
Failure to maintain divine service, i. 184.
Failure to repair bridge, i. 183.
Negligent keeping of fence, i. 184.
Negligent maintenance of wall, i. 183.
Breach of implied duty incident to public calling, i. 184.
Breach of implied duty to take care, i. 186.
Broader conception of liability, i. 189.
Neglect in office, i. 184.
Negligent misfeasance, i. 187.
Trespass, late appearance of negligence in field of, i. 190.
Identification in negligence, i. 141.
Doctrine of Thorogood *v.* Bryan, i. 141.
Passenger identified with driver, when, i. 141.
Repudiation of doctrine, i. 142.
Implied duty to take care, negligence viewed as breach of, i. 186.
Imputed negligence, see IMPUTED NEGLIGENCE.
Innkeeper, negligence as basis for liability of, ii. 295, 297.
Intervening cause, see INTERVENING CAUSE.
Liability for established negligence extends to all consequences not remote, i. 89–91.
Concrete cases discussed —
Blocking stream with boat, i. 114.
Burning of noncontiguous premises, i. 116.
Burning oil, i. 113.
Collision of sleigh, i. 114.

NEGLIGENCE — *Continued.*
Liability for established negligence extends to all consequences not remote — *Continued.*
Concrete cases discussed — *Continued.*
Communicated fires, i. 112.
Failure to signal approach of train, i. 115.
Fire communicated by burning oil, i. 117.
Fire communicated to neighboring structure, i. 115.
Harm befalling lost cattle, i. 112.
Horse frightened at spouting of water on highway, i. 111.
Injury to escape animal, i. 114.
Leaving team in hands of inexperienced person, i. 114.
Machinery left near highway, i. 113.
Negligent collision of train, i. 117.
Sheep, escaped, destroyed by bears, i. 116.
Turning team off fairground, i. 114.
Unsafe street, i. 115.
Vessel, drifting and unmanageable, i. 112.
Liability for established negligence limited to foreseeable consequences, i. 117.
Negligence in trespass —
Trespass, intentional, absolute liability for, i. 74.
Trespass, unintentional, negligence essential to liability in, i. 74.
Omissive act not violative of positive duty —
Failure of city to keep street in repair, i. 129.
Failure of landowner to mow thistles, i. 129.
Failure of railroad company to detain train, i. 129.
Positive duty, negligence viewed as breach of, i. 183.
Proximate cause, see PROXIMATE CAUSE.
Public calling —
Breach of implied duty arising from, i. 184.
Implied duty on part of person pursuing public calling to use due care, i. 188.
Public office, neglect in, i. 184.
Remedy —
Trespass for injury directly following from negligent act, i. 190; iii. 258, 259.
Trespass on case for injury consequential on negligent act, i. 189; iii. 258, 260.
Trespass on case sanctioned as remedy for negligent direct injury, i. 190; iii. 263.
Res loquitur ipsa —
Concrete cases discussed —
Bags falling from warehouse, i. 107.
Collapse of wall, i. 107.
Fall of bust in concert hall, i. 108.
Landslide in railway cut, i. 108.
Objects falling from insecure structures, i. 107, 108, 109.
Foresight test, applicability of, i. 109.
Maxim inapplicable, when, i. 108.
Negligence presumed on facts of case, i. 107.

NEGLIGENCE — *Continued.*
- Secondary trespass, negligence essential to liability in, i. 84.
- Standard of care —
  - Conduct of the prudent man, i. 96.
  - External standard, i. 96.
  - Highly skilled person, care required of, i. 97.
  - Personal equation disregarded, i. 96.
  - Test of existence of negligence, i. 96.
- Violation of law by person injured, see BREACH OF STATUTORY DUTY.

NEGLIGENT TRANSMISSION OF TELEGRAM.
- In general —
  - Contract conception of liability, i. 435.
  - Fusion of tort and contract conceptions of liability, i. 441.
  - Negligence, extension of doctrine to law of telegram, i. 436.
  - Place of tort in legal theory, i. 435.
  - Telegraphic message, nature of, i. 435.
  - Tort conception of liability, i. 436.
- Damage —
  - Cipher messages, i. 452.
  - Contents of message as affecting liability of company for, i. 450, 451.
  - Contract aspect of liability, i. 444.
  - Failure to send message, i. 452.
  - Mental distress in action arising *ex contractu*, i. 471.
  - Mental distress in action arising *ex delicto*, i. 472.
  - Nominal damages only recoverable, when, i. 452.
  - Remote damages, i. 454.
  - Special damage, when telegraph company liable for, i. 450.
  - Telegraph company liable only for foreseeable damage, i. 450, 451.
  - Tort aspect of liability, i. 444.
- Foresight of harm as affecting liability for, i. 439.
- Misrepresentation, when telegraph company liable for, i. 454.
- Negligence essential to liability of company, i. 455, 456.
- Sendee —
  - Sendee in privity with contract has right of action for negligent transmission, i. 437.
  - Sendee not in privity with contract —
    - American doctrine, i. 438.
    - English doctrine, i. 438.
- Telegraph company —
  - Obligation incident to public calling, i. 440, 441.
  - Right of company to determine conditions of responsible service, i. 443.
  - Theory underlying liability of, i. 440, 451, 454, 456.

NEGOTIABLE INSTRUMENTS.
- See BILLS AND NOTES.

NEGOTIABLE INSTRUMENTS LAW.
See BILLS AND NOTES.

NERVOUS SHOCK.
Damage incident to, recoverable, when, i. 457.

NEWSDEALER.
Subject to action for defamatory matter appearing in paper, when, i. 298.

NEWSPAPER.
Proprietor liable for publication of defamatory matter, i. 298.
Seller responsible for libelous matter, when, i. 298.

NEWTON, J.
Observation on right of election between trespass and replevin, iii. 216.

NIEBUHR, B. G.
Recovers lost Institutes of Gaius, iii. 13.

NITRIC ACID.
Responsibility of seller for injury done by, i. 60.

NITRO-GLYCERINE.
Express company responsible for injury done by nitro-glycerine, when, i. 84.

NOISE.
Nuisance created by, i. 217.

NON FACIO NE FACIAS, ii. 22.

NONFEASANCE.
Liability for failure to enter on undertaking, ii. 29.
Nonfeasance not sufficient to operate as conversion, i. 237.
Parol promise, nonfeasance of not actionable in early law, ii. 29.

NORMAN CONQUEST.
Centralizing effect of Norman rule, iii. 27, 28.
Political organization in England as affected by, iii. 27.

NOTE.
See BILLS AND NOTES; PROMISSORY NOTE.

NOTTINGHAM, LORD.
Connection with passage of Statute of Frauds, ii. 169.

NOVATION.
Accord and satisfaction, compromise with principle of, ii. 126.
Accord and satisfaction, conflict with doctrine of, ii. 126.
Agreement to discharge necessary, ii. 124.
Assignment distinguished from novation, iii. 89.
Assignment of chose in action as affected by principle of novation, iii. 88, 89.
Bad faith or coercion renders novation nugatory, ii. 128.
Bilateral contract, novation of, ii. 128.
Change of parties, novation by, ii. 122.

NOVATION — *Continued.*
Change or substitution of contract, ii. 126.
Composition with creditors, see COMPOSITION WITH CREDITORS.
Debtor, novation by discharge of, ii. 125.
Discharge by necessary implication, ii. 124.
Discharge must be present discharge, ii. 125.
Forms of, ii. 122.
Mutual executory obligations, novation of, ii. 127.
Novation an executory accord, ii. 122.
Novation invalid in early law, ii. 123.
Promise given to secure performance of pre-existing obligation, ii. 128.
Bilateral contract valid, ii. 130.
Unilateral promise invalid, ii. 129.
Public policy as affecting validity of, ii. 128.
Recognition of bilateral contract as affecting validity of novation, ii. 123.
Unilateral duty, novation of, ii. 127.

NOVEL DISSEISIN.
Assize of, iii. 37, 44.
Nature of remedy, iii. 445.
Assize of *novel disseisin* as predecessor of writ of trespass, iii. 226, 228.
Assize turned into jury, iii. 228.
Inquiry into matter of trespass, iii. 228.
Possessory character of remedy, iii. 228.
Proceedings in action of, iii. 227.
Scope and function of remedy, iii. 227.

NOXÆ DEDITIO, i. 50.

NOXAL SURRENDER, i. 50.

NOXIOUS VAPORS.
Nuisance resulting from, i. 217, 221.

NOY, ATTORNEY-GENERAL.
'Grounds and Maxims of English Laws,' ii. 262, 450.

NUDUM PACTUM, ii. 23, 30.
Accord executory is *nudum pactum*, ii. 91.
Contract wanting consideration, ii. 142.
English law concerning nude pact, ii. 37.
Mediæval doctrine of civilians, ii. 36.
Novation treated as *nudum pactum* in early law, ii. 123.
Nudum pactum invalid at law and in equity, ii. 35.
Part payment of debt in satisfaction of whole, ii. 99, 100.
Roman law, ii. 36.

NUISANCE.
In general —
Affinity to trespass, i. 191.
Continuance of wrong essential in nuisance, i. 222.
Extension of conception of trespass on realty, i. 211.

NUISANCE — *Continued.*
In general — *Continued.*
Gist of nuisance, i. 211.
Interference with occupant right, i. 212.
Law of nuisance not founded on idea of responsibility, i. 230.
Nuisance an interference with incorporeal real rights, i. 211.
Nuisance involving interference with right appurtenant to realty, i. 230.
Nuisance not personal wrong, i. 212.
Place of nuisance in legal theory, i. 191, 192.
Comfort of existence, interference with, i. 220, 221.
Conduct creating evidence against a right, action maintainable for, i. 222.
Damage to property as affecting question of nuisance, i. 221.
Diminution of value or impairment of personal comfort, i. 220.
Enterprise carried on under legislative authority, i. 44.
Health, injury to, not essential to constitute nuisance, i. 221.
History —
Ancient nuisance —
Exclusion of commoner, i. 213.
Interference with right of pasturage, fishery, and the like, i. 213.
Raising dike or pond, i. 213.
Antiquity of conception of nuisance, i. 212.
Criminal character of early nuisance, i. 213.
Genesis of conception of civil liability for nuisance, i. 213.
Interference with trade or calling characterized by nuisance, i. 365.
Justification of trespass in abatement of nuisance, i. 23.
Noxious vapors, i. 221.
Nuisance in conduct of business, 216.
Annoyance incident to urban life, i. 219.
Competition in business not actionable as private nuisance, i. 217.
Conduct of manufacturing enterprises, i. 219, 220.
Ferry, interference with, i. 217.
Franchise, exclusive, interference with, i. 247.
General principles, application of, i. 218.
Location of business as bearing on question of nuisance, i. 218–220.
Market, interference with, i. 217.
Moving into neighborhood of nuisance, i. 220.
Prescriptive right to carry on offensive business, i. 220.
Smoke, gases, noises, filthy residues, i. 217.
Presumption against legislative intent to authorize, i. 43.
Private nuisance —
Actual damage essential to private right of action, i. 228.
Public nuisance distinguished from, i. 224, 225, 227.
Public nuisance —
Criminal offense, i. 223.
Highway, obstruction of, amounts to private nuisance, when, i. 225.

NUISANCE — *Continued.*
Public nuisance — *Continued.*
Obstruction of public ways and waters, i. 224.
Private nuisance distinguished from, i. 224.
Remoteness of damage, when fatal to recovery for nuisance, i. 227.
Special damage essential to private right of action, i. 244.
Special damage, what is, in public nuisance, i. 225.
Remedy —
Abatement by act of person injured, i. 215.
Antiquity of remedy by abatement, i. 215.
Illustrations from early period, i. 215.
Qualifications of right to abate, i. 216.
Who may abate, i. 216.
Action on case, i. 214; iii. 271.
Assize of *novel disseisin,* i. 213.
Assize of nuisance, i. 213; iii. 271.
Bill in equity, i. 214.
Ground of equitable interference, i. 214.
Quod permittat prosternere, writ of, i. 214; iii. 271.
Who is liable for —
Landlord liable, when, i. 223.
Tenant or occupant primarily liable for nuisance, i. 222, 223.

NUISANCE, COGNATE.
See COGNATE NUISANCE.

OBLIGATION.
Bilateral character of personal obligation, iii. 61.
Death of party as affecting personal obligation, iii. 63.
Meaning in Roman law, iii. 61.

OBLIGATION IN NATURE OF ASSUMPSIT.
See QUASI-CONTRACT.

OBSTRUCTION AND DIVERSION OF WATERS.
See COGNATE NUISANCE.

OCCUPATION.
Wrongful interference with, i. 357.

OFFICE.
Neglect in performance of official duty, i. 184.
Words involving injurious imputation in respect of office defamatory, i. 277.

OFFICER.
Election officer, privilege of, i. 38.
Negligent failure of attaching officer to keep goods safely not a conversion, i. 238.

OFFICER OF STATE.
Privileged character of communication from, i. 307.
Privilege of, i. 35, 36.

OIL.
Responsibility for damage done by burning oil, i. 113, 117.

OMNIBUS.
Unfair competition in establishment of rival line, i. 421.

OPPRESSION.
Exemplary damages, oppression as affecting assessment of, i. 481.

OVERDUE PAPER.
Payable on demand, when, ii. 509.

OVERSEER OF POOR.
See PAUPER.

OVERT ACT.
Conversion involves overt act, i. 236.

OWNERSHIP.
Ascription of property to tortfeasor, iii. 237.
Origin of doctrine, iii. 49, 50.

OWNERSHIP AND POSSESSION, ii. 308.
See POSSESSION.
Claim of ownership not sufficient to make conversion, i. 236.
Conversion as affecting ownership and possession, i. 250.
Interference with dominion and control constitutes conversion, when, i. 232.
Plaintiff in detinue must show general or special ownership and right of immediate possession, iii. 153.
Severance of ownership from possession in bailment, ii. 252.

OXFORD.
See PROVISIONS OF OXFORD.

PACKER.
Conversion, when packer not liable for, i. 245.

PACT.
Pretor recognizes validity of, ii. 58.
Roman consensual contract, ii. 58.

PAINTING.
Fair comment and criticism on, i. 304.

PARASITIC DAMAGE.
Action for breach of promise, i. 463.
Contract, parasitic element of damage as incident to breach of, i. 462.
Tort, parasitic element of damage as incident to, i. 461.

PARDA.
Custom of *parda* in Indian province, i. 320, 321.

PARENT AND CHILD.
See INTERFERENCE WITH DOMESTIC RELATIONS.
Battery —
Child may justify battery committed in defense of parent, i. 8.
Parent may justify battery committed in defense of child, i. 8.

PARENT AND CHILD—*Continued.*
Communication between privileged, when, i. 311.
Duty of parent to compensate for necessaries furnished to child, ii. 204.
Mental distress of daughter occasioned by failure to receive telegram informing of mother's convalescence, i. 471.
Mental distress of father occasioned by inability of mother-in-law to attend sick child, i. 472.
Mental distress of father occasioned by nondelivery of telegram informing of child's death, i. 472.
Mental distress of son occasioned by inability to attend funeral of mother, i. 472.
Parent not liable for unauthorized trespass of son, ii. 442.

PARKE, B.
Distinguishes malice from spite, i. 331.
Form of action against master for negligent trespass of servant, iii. 260.
Limits of case and assumpsit, iii. 274.
Malice as affecting legality of act otherwise lawful, i. 355.
Observation on doctrine of 'last chance,' i. 136.
Sanctions debt as remedy against indorser, iii. 142, 143.
Theory of responsibility of master for negligence of servant, ii. 459.
View concerning origin and nature of law merchant, ii. 410.

PARKER, C. J.
Indebitatus assumpsit maintainable where debt reducible to certainty, iii. 135.
Liability of bank for special deposit, ii. 276, 277.

PARKER, PROF. J. A.
Definition of bailment, ii. 308.

PAROL DISCHARGE OF BILL OR NOTE, ii. 410.

PARTNERSHIP.
Accounting between partners, ii. 334.
Influence of law merchant on law of survivorship, ii. 334.
Modern procedure acts as affecting action among partners, iii. 58.
Roman law not based on agency in true sense, ii. 436.
Unfair competition by misrepresentation concerning continuation of business, i. 433.

PART PAYMENT.
See ACCORD AND SATISFACTION.

PASTON, J.
Marriage held not to be sufficient *quid pro quo* to support debt, ii. 24.
Sanctions action on case for breach of parol promise, ii. 30.

PATENT RIGHT.
Note given for patent right to show consideration, ii. 509.

PATERFAMILIAS.
Fiction of identity of legal *personæ* of head of household and dependents, ii. 441.
Legal status in Roman law, ii. 434.

PAUPER.
Obligation of overseers to compensate one who attends, ii. 150, 151.

PAWN.
See PLEDGE.

PAYEE.
Certainty required in description of, ii. 510.
Joint payees, instrument payable to, ii. 510.
Several payees, instrument payable to, ii. 510.

PAYMENT.
Note given for precedent debt treated as conditional payment, when, ii. 389.

PECUNIARY DAMAGE.
See SPECIAL DAMAGE.
Doctrine of special pecuniary damage in law of slander, i. 285.
Fraudulent imposition of, i. 374.
Intention to compass particular harm makes damage special, i. 289.
Pecuniary damage gist of slander, when, i. 280.
Proof of special damage not necessary where words impute want of chastity, i. 290.
Risk of pecuniary loss gist of slander, when, i. 279.
Special damage basis of action for slander, when, i. 287.
Special damage in slander must be direct and immediate, i. 286.
Special damage not required in libel, i. 295.
When damage remote in slander, i. 289.

PEGOLETTI.
Treatise on Mercantile Law, ii. 337.

PEMBERTON, C. J.
Bearer of promissory note required to show value given, ii. 383.

PENALTY.
Statutory penalty, action of debt as remedy for recovery of, iii. 132.

PERKINS, JOHN.
Statement concerning law of resulting uses, ii. 41.
Supposes part payment of debt may be good in satisfaction of whole, ii. 97.

PERSAY, J.
Observation on action against person taking chattel from bailee, ii. 259, 260.

PERSONAL INJURY.
Death of person injured as affecting action of third person for consequential damage, iii. 71, 75.

PERSONAL INJURY — *Continued.*
Involuntary interposition of other person not proximate cause of latter's injury from explosion, when, i. 119.
Not proximate cause of subsequent suicide, when, i. 119.

PERSONAL PROPERTY.
Distinction between real and personal property, origin of, iii. 42.

PERSONAL REPRESENTATIVE.
Collateral liability of, ii. 183.

PERSONATION, FALSE, see FALSE PERSONATION.

PHOSPHORUS, see EXPLOSIVE.

PHOTOGRAPH.
Publication of photograph of another not actionable, i. 319.

PHYSICAL SUFFERING.
Element of recoverable damage, when, i. 457, 459.

PIACENZA, ORDINANCE OF, ii. 337.

PICKETING.
Interference with trade or calling characterized by picketing unlawful, i. 366.

PICTURE.
Defamation by means of, i. 274, 294.
Publication of photograph of another not defamatory, when, i. 319, 320.

PIEPOUDRES, COURT OF, ii. 327.
Administration of justice in, ii. 327.
Universality of law administered in, ii. 328.

PIGNORIS CAPIO, iii. 16, 17, 280, 281.

PIGOT, C. B.
Observation on past consideration, ii. 86.

PILOT.
Running steamer afoul of sailing vessel, i. 135.

PLAGUE.
Words imputing affliction of plague defamatory, i. 277.

PLEDGE.
Antiquity of pledge, ii. 283.
Conversion, when pledge of goods amounts to, i. 239.
Definition, ii. 271.
Pledge in early law, ii. 4.
Presumption of negligence in case chattel is stolen, ii. 284.
Relaxation of law of pledge, ii. 259.

PLEDGEE.
Acquires property in thing pledged, ii. 283.
'are required of pledgee, ii. 283.
Liability of pledgee in time of Bracton, ii. 254.
Not liable for injury to pledge unless negligent, ii. 283.
Special property of, ii. 313.

PLEDGE OF FAITH.
Controversy between temporal and spiritual authorities, ii. 12.
Enforcement in spiritual courts, ii. 12.
Nature of, ii. 12.
Repudiation by common-law courts, ii. 14.

PLENE COMPUTAVIT.
Plea of, in action of account, iii. 107.

PLOWDEN, EDMUND.
Argument in favor of sufficiency of consideration of love and affection, ii. 44.

POISON.
Liability of druggist for negligence in compounding prescription, i. 60.
Nitrate of soda, responsibility of keeper for injury to neighbor's cattle, i. 157.
Yew leaves, responsibility of keeper of premises for injury to neighbor's cattle, i. 156, 157.

POLICY.
See PUBLIC POLICY.

POLLEXFEN, C. J.
Takes judicial notice of custom of merchants, ii. 351.

POLLOCK, C. B.
Approves exemplary damages in case of wanton injury, i. 486.
Estoppel of principal by representation of authority, ii. 486.
Observation on danger of recognizing new damage elements, i. 470.
Question of nuisance determined on facts of case, i. 218.
Sanctions debt for recovery of rent reserved after abolition of real action, iii. 134.
View concerning extent of liability for negligence, i. 90.

POLLOCK, SIR F.
Criticism of Derry *v.* Peek, i. 403.
Definition of private nuisance, i. 223.
Definition of tort, i. 26.
Discussion of fellow-servant doctrine, ii. 471.
Nature of right of possession, ii. 312.
Observation concerning malice in slander of title, i. 323.
Observation on meaning of *cause* in French contract law, ii. 37.
Paradox of promise and performance, ii. 118.
Performance of duty as consideration, ii. 113.
Statement of doctrine of contributory negligence, i. 136.
Theory of liability of master for negligent act of servant, ii. 460, 462, 463.

POLLOCK AND MAITLAND.
Master's liability in time of Bracton, ii. 440.
Nature of pledge of faith described, ii. 12.
Statement of doctrine of representation in old English law, ii. 437.
Theory of liability of master for negligent act of servant, ii. 460.
Theory of noxal surrender, i. 51.

PONE, WRIT OF, iii. 211.

POPHAM, C. J.
Defines undertaking of carrier, ii. 299.
Disfavors action for fraudulent sale, i. 378.
Recognizes implied warranty of title in chattel sales, i. 383.
Responsibility of master for commanded act, ii. 450.

POSSESSION.
As against wrongdoer possession is title, ii. 317.
Conversion as violative of, i. 250.
Implied warranty of title incident to possession by seller, i. 384, 385.
Possession a sort of title, ii. 312.
Possession equivalent to property right, when, ii. 314.
Possessory right of bailee, ii. 308, 309, 312.
Severance of ownership and possession characteristic of bailment, ii. 252.

POSTMASTER.
Gratuitous nature of postal service, ii. 307.
Official privilege exempts from liability, ii. 306.
Postmaster a bailee, ii. 306.

POSTOFFICE DEPARTMENT.
See POSTMASTER.

POUND.
Antiquity of village pound, iii. 291.

POWDER.
See EXPLOSIVE.

POWELL, J.
Gratuitous bailee liable for negligent misfeasance, ii. 270.
Nothing in law that is not reason, ii. 267.

PRÆCIPE.
Præcipe quod faciat, iii. 36.
Præcipe quod permittat, iii. 36.
Præcipe quod reddat, iii. 36.

PRATT, L. C. J.
Approves exemplary damages for illegal commitment under general warrant, i. 484.

PRECEDENT.
See JUDICIAL PRECEDENT.

PREMISES, DANGEROUS.
See DANGEROUS PREMISES.

PRESCRIPTION.
Right of support for house acquired by, i. 195.

PRESCRIPTION ACT (1832).
Provision concerning ancient light, i. 209.

PRESUMPTION.
Tendency of presumption of fact to harden into rule of law, ii. 452.

PRETENSES, FALSE.
See FALSE PRETENSES.

PRETOR.
Devises formulary process as substitute for *legis actiones*, iii. 17.
Extra-ordinariæ cognitiones, iii. 20.
Extraordinary and summary process supplants formulary system, iii. 20, 21.
Influence on development of Roman law of agency, ii. 436
Jurisdiction —
Administration of trust, iii. 20.
Restitutio in integrum, iii. 20.
Procedure before pretor —
Decree, iii. 20.
Missio in possessionem, iii. 20.
Recognizes validity of formless consensual pact, ii. 58, 59.

PREVENTION.
Idea of prevention as affecting assessment of damages, i. 477.

PREVIOUS REQUEST.
See CONSIDERATION.

PRICE.
Price of goods as affecting application of Statute of Frauds, ii. 194.
When to be stated in memorandum, ii. 195.

PRIMER SEISIN.
Incident of military tenure abolished by statute, iii. 296.

PRINCIPAL AND AGENT.
See also AGENCY.
Agency, place of in legal theory, ii. 430.
Agent —
Account of profits, liability of agent to render, ii. 491.
Classification of agents, ii. 483.
General agent, ii. 484.
Special agent, ii. 484.
Value of distinction between general and special agents questioned, ii. 484, 485.
Distinguished from servant, ii. 430.
Function of agent, ii. 473.
Implied warranty of authority of agent, i. 406.
Power of agent acting within scope of apparent authority, ii. 480.
Broker binds principal by selling at lower price than authorized, ii. 481.
Manager binds principal by acceptance of bill, ii. 481.
Salesman binds employer by pledging credit for transportation, ii. 482.

PRINCIPAL AND AGENT — *Continued.*
Agent — *Continued.*
Right to delegate, ii. 475.
Act of discretion cannot be delegated, ii. 476.
Complete delegation, ii. 476.
Delegation of ministerial acts, ii. 475.
Special authority to delegate, ii. 476.
Substitute, appointment of, ii. 476.
Unforeseen emergency, ii. 477.
Usage of trade as affecting, ii. 477.
Agent, scope of term, ii. 430.
Authority —
Authority implied from relation of principal and agent, ii. 474.
Form of authority, ii. 474.
Instrument under seal, ii. 474.
Parol authority, sufficiency of, ii. 475.
Principal bound by act within apparent authority of agent, when, ii. 481.
Authority to do act includes authority to do things necessary to carry power into effect, ii. 485.
Axiom of agency, ii. 464.
Bailiff, power of, to bind principal, ii. 447.
Communication between principal and agent privileged, when, i. 311.
Consent as affecting relation of, ii. 474.
Conversion, when agent liable for conversion made in master's business, i. 242, 243.
Death —
Agency coupled with interest, ii. 491.
Agency terminated by, when, ii. 491.
Agency unaffected by, where contract so provides, ii. 491.
Estoppel —
Acquiescence in unauthorized act of agent, ii. 245.
Estoppel theory of liability of principal for unauthorized act of agent, ii. 485, 486.
Holding out of agent as authorized to do particular act, ii. 485.
Fraudulent act of agent —
Bogus receipts in name of fraudulent officer, ii. 482.
Bogus warehouse receipts, ii. 482.
Fraudulent bills of lading, ii. 482.
Principal bound by, when, ii. 482.
Theory underlying responsibility of principal, ii. 483.
Identification of act of agent as act of principal, ii. 441.
Immunity of agent from liability for consequences of authorized act, ii. 473, 474.
Implied authority of bailiff as agent, ii. 448.
Principal —
Agent's theft of bailed chattel, when principal liable for, ii. 276, 277.
Legal consequences of agent's act attach to principal exclusively, when, ii. 473.
Principal bound by act violative of specific instruction, when, ii. 481

PRINCIPAL AND AGENT — *Continued.*

Principal — *Continued.*

Principal bound by act within scope of apparent authority, ii. 453.

Principal chargeable with contributory negligence of agent, when, i. 140.

Purchase of goods by servant, when master bound by, ii. 447.

Quasi-contractual obligation of agent to reimburse principal, ii. 240.

Quasi-contractual obligation of principal to exonerate agent, ii. 240.

Responsibility of principal for act of agent in early law, ii. 446.

Responsibility of principal for fraudulent sale by agent, ii. 450.

Ratification —

Agent must have assumed to act for another, ii. 489.

Fiction of relation, ii. 487.

No ratification possible of act which must be valid when done, ii. 487.

Ratification equivalent to prior authority, ii. 487.

Rescission, ratification impossible where assumed agent and other party rescind, ii. 488.

Right of third party to retreat before ratification, ii. 488, 489.

Rights of stranger unaffected by, ii. 487.

Undisclosed intention on part of assumed agent, ii. 490.

Unauthorized agent not liable on contract made by him as agent, i. 405.

Undisclosed principal, ii. 477.

Contract in writing, ii. 480.

Election of party dealing with agent of undisclosed principal, ii. 479.

Factor acting for, ii. 478.

Leading authorities, ii. 479.

Rights and liabilities of parties to contract, ii. 479, 480.

PRINTER.

Printer of libelous matter subject to action, i. 298.

PRISOT, C. J.

Approves principle of *stare decisis* in connection with interpretation of statutes, i. 500.

Sanctions detinue as remedy against finder of lost goods, iii. 148.

PRIVACY, RIGHT OF.

Infringement of privacy, analogy to defamation, i. 319.

Infringement of privacy by publication of photograph not actionable, i. 319.

Right of privacy sanctioned by immemorial custom in Indian provinces, i. 320.

PRIVATEER.

Owner of privateer authorized to prey on enemy's commerce not liable when crew fall on ship of friendly nation, ii. 450.

PRIVATE INSTRUCTIONS.

Liability of master unaffected by, when, ii. 456.

Liability of principal unaffected by, when, ii. 481.

PRIVILEGE.
Absolute privilege, i. 35-37, 307.
Account of judicial proceedings, privilege of, i. 309.
Act authorized by statute, privilege of, i. 41.
Barrister, privilege of, i. 38.
Basis of doctrine of privilege, i. 313.
Board of health, privilege of, i. 38.
Churchwarden, privilege of, i. 38.
Communication between parties in confidential relation, i. 311.
Communication concerning official conduct, i. 309.
Communication made in obedience to social duty, i. 312.
Competition in business —
Highly privileged character of, i. 359.
Malice as affecting liability for, i. 360.
Rivalry in shipping trade, i. 359, 360.
Rival schoolmasters, case of, i. 359.
Competition in labor market, privilege of, i. 371.
Custom, privilege incident to performance of duty imposed by, i. 40, 41.
Defamatory matter privileged, when, i. 307, 312.
Definition of privilege, i. 307.
Executive officer liable for purely tortious acts, when, i. 36.
Executive officer, privilege of, i. 36.
Fair comment and criticism distinguished from privilege, i. 303.
Judges, privilege of, i. 37.
Labor organization not specially privileged, i. 371.
Legislative proceedings, when report of privileged, i. 310.
Malice destructive of qualified privilege, i. 39, 40, 313.
Malicious prosecution, bearing of doctrine of privilege on, i. 326, 327.
Master of ship, privilege of, i. 39.
Member of Parliament, privilege of, i. 307.
Negligence destructive of, when, i. 445.
Officer of state acting in political capacity, i. 35.
Parents, privilege of, i. 38.
Person acting in *quasi*-judicial capacity, privilege of, i. 38.
Person executing legal process, privilege of, i. 38.
Person *in loco parentis,* privilege of, i. 38.
Qualified privilege, i. 38, 308.
Servants of crown, privilege of, i. 35.
Sovereign —
Immunity of domestic sovereign, i. 35.
Immunity of foreign sovereign, i. 37.
State, immunity of sovereign state, i. 35.
Status, idea of as affecting doctrine of privilege, i. 40.

PRIVITY OF BLOOD.
Privity of blood as affecting right of action of stranger to consideration, ii. 153.

PROBABLE CAUSE.
Probable cause in malicious prosecution, i. 330.

PROCESS.
Malicious abuse of, see MALICIOUS ABUSE OF PROCESS.

PROCURATION.
Effect of signature by, ii. 519.

PROFESSION.
Words involving injurious imputation on professional standing defamatory, i. 277.

PROHIBITION.
Writ used to limit ecclesiastical jurisdiction, ii. 13.

PROMISE.
Action on deceitful promise in early law, ii. 31.
Chancery court recognizes validity of simple promise, ii. 34.
Conception of obligation of promise —
As basis of contract law, ii. 64.
Emergence of notion, ii. 32.
Modernness of notion, ii. 2.
Obligation of promise in bilateral contract, ii. 59.
Implied promise —
Implied promise of overseers of poor to compensate for attention to pauper, ii. 151.
Implied promise supplants promise supported by previous request, ii. 85.
Implied promise to pay debt, ii. 62.
Statute of Frauds does not affect, ii. 173.
Legal duty —
Promise given in consideration of performance of, ii. 113.
Promise to compensate for act which promisor was bound to do, ii. 150.
Marriage, promise given to bring about marriage between other parties, ii. 114.
Misfeasance in performance of gratuitous promise, ii. 50.
Origin of conception of obligation of promise, iii. 174, 177.
Parol promise —
Analogy to covenant, ii. 132.
Parol promise not actionable in early law, ii. 29, 30.
Parol promise supported by executed consideration, ii. 32.
Past consideration will not support, ii. 85.
Promise and performance, paradox of, ii. 118.
Promise as consideration for counter-promise, ii. 55.
Promise made good by doing of any act, ii. 24.
Promise to accept undrawn bill irrevocable, when, ii. 399.
Promise to pay debt, ii. 61.
Promise to pay sealed debt, ii. 62.
Unconditional promise under Negotiable Instruments Law, what is, ii. 506.
Written promise supposed to be good formal contract, ii. 141.

PROMISEE.
Promisee distinguished from beneficiary, ii. 154.
Promisee distinguished from person to whom promise is communicated, ii. 154.
Who is promisee in law, ii. 154.

PROMISSORY NOTE.
See BILLS AND NOTES.
Bill of debt identified with early promissory note, ii. 354, 355.
Custom of merchants, promissory note held not to be within, ii. 384.
Form of action on promissory note at beginning of 18th century, ii. 385.
Negotiability under statute of 3 and 4 Anne, ii. 385.
Note given for precedent debt treated as conditional payment, ii. 389.
Payment to bearer as agent, ii. 364.

PROPERTY.
Transferability of property and property rights, iii. 78.
Trial of right of property, iii. 214.
Proceedings in, iii. 214, 215.
Alias replevin, iii. 215.
Issuance of writ, iii. 215.
Pluries replevin, iii. 215.
Who entitled to writ, iii. 215.

PROSECUTION.
Danger of prosecution gist of slander, when, i. 279.

PROSECUTION, MALICIOUS.
See MALICIOUS PROSECUTION.

PROSPECTUS.
False representation in, who may maintain action for, i. 397.
Person intended to be influenced by, i. 397.
Statement believed to be true but without sufficient grounds, actionability of, i. 401.

PROVISIONS OF OXFORD (1258).
Chancery deprived of power to issue new writs without approval of council, iii. 34.

PROXIMATE CAUSE.
In general —
Discussion of meaning and principle underlying, i. 109–111.
Question of proximity, how determined, i. 110.
Remote cause distinguished from, i. 110.
Concurring negligence of third person, i. 122.
Intervening independent cause relieves original actor of responsibility, i. 120.
Negligence a proximate cause of damage —
Concrete cases discussed —
Blocking stream with boat, i. 114.
Collision of sleighs, i. 114.
Communicated fires, i. 112, 115.

PROXIMATE CAUSE — *Continued.*
Negligence a proximate cause of damage — *Continued.*
Concrete cases discussed — *Continued.*
Drifting or unmanageable vessels, i. 112.
Failure to signal approach of train, i. 115.
Harm befalling lost cattle, i. 112.
Leaving team in hands of inexperienced person, i. 114.
Machinery left near highway, i. 113.
Oil, damage from burning of, i. 113.
Spouting of water on highway, i. 111.
Turning team off fairground, i. 114.
Unsafe street, i. 115.
Negligence not proximate cause of damage —
Concrete cases discussed —
Delay in transportation followed by loss for other reasons, i. 118.
Failure of carrier to provide seats, i. 119.
Suicide of injured person, i. 119.
Violation of Sunday ordinance not proximate cause of injury, when, i. 179, 180.
Wrongful act not proximate cause of damage —
Concrete cases discussed —
Ejection of passenger, i. 119.
Interposing other person to prevent injury to self, i. 119.

PROXIMATE DAMAGE.
Mental attitude of wrongdoer as affecting proximity and remoteness of damage, i. 489.

PRUDENT MAN.
Carrier held to standard of ordinary prudence, ii. 304.
Conduct of as criterion of negligence, i. 96, 97.

PUBLICATION.
Publication of defamatory matter, see DEFAMATION.

PUBLIC CALLING.
Action on case as remedy for breach of duty incident to, iii. 273.
Assumpsit as remedy for breach of duty incident to, iii. 273.
Basis and limits of implied duty incident to public calling, i. 184, 185.
Implied duty incident to —
Carrier, i. 185.
Gas company, i. 186.
Innkeeper, i. 185.
Log driving company, i. 186.
Smith, i. 185.
Telegraph company, i. 440.
Victualer, i. 185.
Water company, i. 186.

PUBLIC ENEMY.
Act of, as defense for bailee, ii. 260.
Common carrier not responsible for loss caused by, ii. 300.

PUBLIC ENEMY — *Continued.*
Innkeeper not responsible for loss caused by, ii. 296.
Justification of trespass incident to invasion of country by public enemy, i. 22.

PUBLIC OFFICER.
Criticism of character or conduct of privileged, when, i. 308, 309.
Custodian of public fund —
Bailee distinguished from, ii. 290.
Extent of liability for loss of fund, ii. 290.
Robbery or theft no defense for, when, ii. 292.
Statutory liability of, ii. 293.
Quasi-contractual obligation to perform duties of office, ii. 236.

PUBLIC POLICY.
Common carrier, liability of as affected by, ii. 300.
Influence of considerations of policy on growth of legal doctrine, i. 342, 497.
Innkeeper, liability of as affected by, ii. 294.
Legality of contract as affected by, ii. 163, 164.
Mental distress, recovery of damages for, as affected by public policy, i. 475.

PUNISHMENT.
Idea of punishment as affecting assessment of damages, i. 477.

PUNITORY DAMAGE.
See MEASURE OF DAMAGES.

PURCHASE MONEY.
Part payment of purchase money, effect of, ii. 5.

PURCHASER, INNOCENT.
Conversion, when innocent purchaser guilty of, i. 239.
Doctrine of Gill *v.* Cubitt, ii. 405, 406.
Gross negligence of, ii. 407.
Innocent purchaser of lost bill payable to bearer, rights of, ii. 394.
Innocent purchaser of stolen bank note, rights of, ii. 393, 394.
Notice of defects, effect of, ii. 404.

QUAIN, J.
Observation on extent of liability in field of tort, i. 88.

QUALIFICATIONS AND EXCEPTIONS TO LEGAL LIABILITY, i. 35.

QUANTUM MERUIT.
See COUNT.

QUANTUM VALEBANT.
See COUNT.

QUARE EJECIT INFRA TERMINUM.
Writ of, iii. 45.

QUARRY.

Open quarry near highway, responsibility of quarryman for injury caused by, i. 158.

QUASI-CONTRACT.

In general —
  Classification —
    Duties in nature of debt, ii. 199, 211, 220, 228.
    Obligations in nature of assumpsit, ii. 235.
  Discussion of nature and theory of *quasi*-contract, ii. 199, 210, 235.
  Elements of *quasi*-contract, ii. 203, 208.
  Kinship between debt and *quasi*-contract, ii. 208.
  Scope of term, ii. 206.
Benefit conferred under unenforceable contract, ii. 218.
  Abandonment of divisible contract, ii. 225.
  Abandonment of entire contract, ii. 225.
  Basis of recovery on *quasi*-contractual duty, ii. 221.
  Contract abrogated by law, ii. 224.
  Contract modified by mutual consent, ii. 221.
  Defective performance, ii. 221.
  Destruction of property pending performance of contract, ii. 224.
  Distinction between complete but defective performance and unfinished performance, ii. 226.
  Illegal purpose, benefit conferred in furtherance of, ii. 223.
  Locus pœnitentiæ, ii. 223.
  Original contract materially modified —
    Compensation for defective work, ii. 220.
    Relation of service terminated at election of one, ii. 221.
  Part performance, ii. 223, 226.
  Performance prevented by act of God or rule of law, ii. 223.
  Performance prevented by default of defendant, ii. 222.
    Extent of recovery, ii. 222.
  Repudiation based on violation of Statute of Frauds, ii. 222, 227.
  Repudiation of contract by infant, ii. 226.
Conversion of chattel as basis of *quasi*-contractual duty, ii. 215, 216.
Duty in nature of debt, ii. 199, 211, 220, 228.
  Assumptual obligation distinguished from, ii. 202.
  Quasi-assumptual obligation distinguished from, ii. 235, 236.
  Remedy —
    Debt, limitations of, ii. 200.
    Indebitatus assumpsit, ii. 200.
Duty to compensate for benefit conferred, iii. 200.
  Benefit conferred under mistake of fact —
    Mistake in account rendered, ii. 212.
    Recovery of money paid in mistake as to existence of obligation, ii. 211.
    Recovery of overpayment resulting from mistake in sale, ii. 211.
  Early limits of duty, ii. 200.
  General principles underlying, ii. 201.

QUASI-CONTRACT — *Continued.*
Duty to compensate for benefit conferred — *Continued.*
Money paid in honest but mistaken belief, ii. 211.
Money paid upon moral obligation, ii. 213.
Money recoverable where retention would be against conscience, ii. 212.
Remedy —
Debt, ii. 200.
Indebitatus assumpsit, ii. 200.
Duty to compensate for chattels or service wrongfully appropriated, ii. 215.
Conversion of chattel, ii. 215, 216.
Enforced service, ii. 215.
Enticement of apprentice, ii. 215.
Extension of doctrine, ii. 215.
Limitation on right of recovery, ii. 215.
Duty to make reparation for damage done, iii. 210.
Enforced service as basis of *quasi*-contractual duty, ii. 215.
Judgment not a *quasi*-contract, ii. 207.
Money paid —
Money paid in legal proceedings —
Judgment, effect of reversal, ii. 231.
Right of person not party to record to recover, ii. 231.
Money paid to defendant's use, ii. 232.
Payment in obedience to legal or moral duty, ii. 232.
Money paid under mistake of law, ii. 214.
Money paid under undue pressure —
Extortion by public officer, ii. 231.
General principle underlying right of recovery, ii. 230.
Involuntary payment, ii. 228.
Payment to avoid unlawful arrest, ii. 229.
Payment to obtain enlargement after illegal arrest, ii. 228.
Payment to obtain release of property, ii. 230.
Payment to secure immunity from wrongful interference with business, ii. 231.
Obligation in nature of assumpsit —
In general —
Duty in nature of debt distinguished from, ii. 236.
Nature and characteristics of, ii. 235, 236.
Agent's implied warranty of authority, ii. 237.
Contract for benefit of third person, ii. 161, 237.
Contribution among sureties, ii. 239.
Contribution among tortfeasors, ii. 240.
Duty to use care as incident to undertaking, ii. 237.
Equitable estoppel, see ESTOPPEL, EQUITABLE.
Exoneration as between principal and agent, ii. 240.
Exoneration of surety, ii. 238.
Implied promise of contracting party not to prevent performance of contract, ii. 238.
Implied warranty of title, i. 389; ii. 237.

QUASI-CONTRACT — *Continued.*
Obligation in nature of assumpsit — *Continued.*
Negligence as founded on breach of, i. 91; ii. 237.
Obligation to indemnify for expenditures made for the benefit of another, ii. 233.
Positive duty of person plying common calling, ii. 236.
Positive obligation of public officer to perform duties of office, ii. 236.
Promise to pay for act which promisor was bound to do, ii. 150.
Obligation of overseers of poor to compensate one who attends pauper, ii. 150.
Statutory obligation in nature of assumpsit, ii. 236.
Telegraph company, duty to use reasonable care, i. 439, 440.
Remedy —
Action on case, iii. 201.
Debt, iii. 133.
Indebitatus, ii. 200, 206; iii. 201.
Roman law of *quasi*-contract, ii. 209, 210.
Unjust enrichment, principle of, as basis of *quasi*-contract, ii. 209.

QUASI-DELICT.
See Delict.

QUIA EMPTORES.
Statute of, ii. 41; iii. 296.

QUID PRO QUO.
Basis of debt, ii. 10.
Illustrations, ii. 24.
Justa causa debendi identified with *quid pro quo,* ii. 25.
Marriage as *quid pro quo,* ii. 24.
Nature of *quid pro quo,* ii. 25, 26.
Origin of term, ii. 25.
Personal service as *quid pro quo,* ii. 23.
Type of consideration, ii. 39.

QUI FACIT PER ALIUM, FACIT PER SE, ii. 464; iii. 260, 261.

QUI TAM PROCEEDINGS.
Maintenance in assisting prosecution of, i. 338.

QUOD COMPUTET.
Interlocutory judgment against accountant, iii. 107.

QUOD PERMITTAT.
Remedy for disturbing common, iii. 45.
Writ for abatement of nuisance, i. 214; iii. 271.

RAILROAD.
Alighting passenger, liability of company for injury happening to, i. 127.
Bumper of engine, company not liable for injury to person riding on, when, i. 138.
Contributory negligence of person jumping from moving train, i. 128.

RAILROAD — *Continued.*
Incompetent employees, liability of company for injury resulting from, i. 133.
Insecure door to passenger car, liability of company for injury resulting from, i. 131.
Negligence in loading cars, liability of company for damage resulting from, i. 135.
Nuisance, liability for damage caused by nuisance incident to operation, i. 43, 44.
Privilege incident to operation of trains, i. 42, 43.
Slippery approach to station, liability of company for injury caused by, i. 167.
Smoke, liability for damage caused by, i. 43.
Spark from locomotive, liability of company for damage caused by, i. 43, 57, 102.
Statutory signal, liability of company for injury resulting from failure to give, i. 133.
Stray cattle killed by train, liability of company for, i. 127.
Turntable, liability of company for injury to children, i. 159.
Unattended engine, liability of company for damages done by, i. 120.
Unlawful speed, liability of railroad company for injury resulting from, i. 172.
Vibration, liability of company for damage caused by, i. 42.

RAILROAD CROSSING.
Contributory negligence of person injured at, i. 124, 128.
Failure to signal approach of train, liability of company for damage caused by, i. 115.

RAPE.
Rape of wife, husband's right of action for, i. 264.

RASTELL, JOHN.
Precedents of early actions on bills, ii. 343, 345.

RATIO DECIDENDI.
Binding force of, i. 500.

RAYMOND, C. J.
Immediate and consequential injury distinguished, iii. 252, 253.

REAL ACTION.
Abolition of, iii. 56.

REAL CONTRACT.
See CONTRACT RE.

REAL PROPERTY.
Distinction between real and personal property, origin of, iii. 42.

RECEIVER.
Accountant, responsibility of receiver as, iii. 106.
Obligation to account arises, when, iii. 102.
Receiver as common-law accountant, iii. 102.

RECUPERATORES.
Function of, in Roman writ process, iii. 18.

RECUPERATORY ACTION.
Death of party as affecting survival of right of action founded on property, iii. 64.

REDDIE, MR.
Account of origin of bill of exchange, ii. 335.

REDE, C. J.
Intention irrelevant in early law of trespass, i. 76.
Master not responsible for positive misfeasance of servant, when, ii. 446.
Observation on relation between intent and legal liability in trespass, i. 4.

REDESDALE, LORD.
Observation on scope of replevin, iii. 218, 219.

REGISTER.
Account of origin, iii. 28, 29.
Contents of early Register, iii. 30, 31.
Order of writs in Register, iii. 30.

REGISTRUM BREVIUM.
See REGISTER.

RELEASE.
Effect of release of one of several joint parties to negotiable instrument, ii. 366.

RELIEF.
Incident of military tenure abolished by statute, iii. 296.

REMAINDER.
Innominate tort against owner of reversionary and remainder interest in chattel, i. 260.
Remainder interest in chattel not recognized at common law, iii. 50.

REMEDIAL LAW.
Action on facts goal of remedial law, iii. 11, 12.
Civil action on facts of case —
Formulary process in Roman law supplanted by, iii. 21.
Simplicity of procedure, iii. 21.
English remedial law at accession of Edward I., state of, iii. 32.
Epochs of legal development —
Action on the facts, iii. 11.
Formal action, iii. 11.
Judicial writs, iii. 11.
Factors tending to liberalize procedure, iii. 54.
Fiction, influence on development of remedial law, iii. 11.
Formless civil action on facts of case, iii. 56.
Formulary (or writ) process, iii. 17.
Comparison of formulary process with English writ system, iii. 19.

REMEDIAL LAW — *Continued.*
Formulary (or writ) process — *Continued.*
Formulary process becomes hardened, iii. 19.
Formulary system, advantages of, iii. 19.
Nature of formula or writ, iii. 18.
Supplants legal actions, iii. 18.
Formulary remedies, crystallization of, iii. 11.
History of remedial law in England —
Complexity of historical factors, iii. 22.
English common law reproduces history of Roman remedial law, iii. 22.
Stages of legal development —
Abolition of forms, iii. 22.
Actions based on writ process, iii. 22.
Formalism in actions, iii. 22.
Legal actions, iii. 13.
Actio sacramenti, iii. 13.
Condictio, iii. 16.
Legal actions applicable only between Roman citizens, iii. 17.
Manus injectio, iii. 16, 17.
Obsolescence of legal actions, iii. 17.
Relics of ancient procedure, iii. 18.
Legal growth —
Case, principle of as affecting growth of remedial law, iii. 52.
Exhaustion of the principle of growth embodied in case, iii. 52.
Legislation, influence of, iii. 11.
Principle underlying remedial growth, iii. 52.
Process of growth in English law, iii. 46, 47.
Written record as impediment to legal growth, iii. 52.
Modern procedure acts, iii. 57.
Assignee of chose sues in own name, iii. 58.
Partnership may sue firm having common member, iii. 58.
Relation between right and remedy, iii. 57, 58.
Theory and application of, iii. 57.
Modes of trial in early English law —
Battle, iii. 25.
Inquest of jury, iii. 25.
Oath of defendant, iii. 24.
Ordeal, iii. 25.
Witnesses, iii. 25.
Natural history of, iii. 1, 13, 22, 36, 48.
Power of issuing new writs vests in Parliament, iii. 249.
Right and remedy —
Absence of remedy negatives existence of right, iii. 50.
Relation between, iii. 48.
Writ process, defects of, iii. 33.

REMEDY.
See RIGHT AND REMEDY.

REMOTE CAUSE, i. 110.

REMOTE DAMAGE, i. 110.

RENT.
- Charge on land created by, iii. 298.
- Obligation to pay rent assignable, iii. 302.
- Remedy —
  - Action for use and occupation, ii. 217.
  - Debt, iii. 133, 134.
  - Distress, iii. 298–303.
    - Conditions of right to distrain, iii. 303.
    - Rent must be reducible to certainty, iii. 301.
    - Rent reserved to stranger not distrainable, iii. 301.
  - Real action, iii. 134.
- Rent a real obligation, iii. 298.
- Rent reserved an incident to reversion, iii. 302.
- Rent reserved for life, iii. 134.
- Rent reserved or charged in fee, iii. 134.
- Types of rent —
  - Rent-charge, iii. 299.
  - Rent granted, iii. 300.
  - Rent reserved, iii. 299.
  - Rent-seck, iii. 299.
  - Rent-service, iii. 299.

REPLEGIARI FACIAS, WRIT OF, iii. 208.

REPLEVIN.
- In general —
  - Derivation of term, iii. 208.
  - Genesis of action, iii. 207.
  - Nature of remedy, iii. 52.
- Bailee, right of action against trespasser, iii. 213.
- Carrier not subject to replevin for nondelivery of goods, iii. 220.
- Claim of property, iii. 212.
  - Jurisdiction of sheriff destroyed by, iii. 212, 213.
- Custody of law, replevin not available to recover chattels in, iii. 218.
- Detinue, replevin concurrent with, iii. 216.
- Executors and administrators —
  - Replevin maintainable by, when, iii. 221, 222.
  - Replevin not available against, iii. 222.
- Fraudulent vendee, replevin not available against, iii. 220.
- Ownership not triable in replevin suit, iii. 213, 214.
- Plaintiff —
  - Must show prior possession, iii. 220.
  - Who is plaintiff in replevin suit, iii. 212.
- Pleading —
  - Claim of property, iii. 212, 213.
  - *De vetito namio*, iii. 210.
  - *Non cepit*, iii. 221.
- Possessory right essential to maintenance of, iii. 213, 220.

REPLEVIN — *Continued.*
Proceedings in action of replevin, iii. 208.
Avowry, iii. 212.
Hue and cry, iii. 209.
Process of attachment, iii. 209.
Removal to king's court, iii. 211.
Replevin by sheriff, iii. 209.
Second replevin, iii. 211.
Sureties for return of property, iii. 211.
Trial of property, iii. 214.
Vetitum namium, iii. 209.
Withernam, iii. 209.
Writ *de retorno habendo*, iii. 212.
Property right not necessary to support action, iii. 213.
Provisions of Westminster II. concerning replevin, iii. 210.
Scope of action, iii. 207.
Blackstone's statement, iii. 217.
Modern doctrine, iii. 218.
Remedy for unlawful distress, iii. 215, 217.
Remedy for unlawful taking, iii. 216.
Second replevin final, iii. 211.
Sheriff, jurisdiction of, iii. 208.
Suggestion of nontenure, in distress for rent, iii. 210.
Taking under legal process, replevin not available in case of, iii. 218.
Tortious taking as ground for action, iii. 217.
Trespass, replevin concurrent with, iii. 216, 218.
Unauthorized seizure under process, replevin available when, iii. 219.
Unlawful detention, anomalous extension of remedy to cases of, iii. 221.
Unlawful taking essential, when, iii. 219.
Vendee of bailee not subject to action at instance of owner, iii. 220.
Wager of law available by defendant in, iii. 217.
Writ of replevin, iii. 208.
Writ of second deliverance, iii. 212.

REPORTERS.
Inaccuracy of reporters of 17th century commented on, ii. 379.

REPRESENTATION.
Axiomatic basis of law of representation, ii. 463.
Conception of responsibility as basis of law of representation, ii. 429.
History of law of representation —
Modern law of master and servant, ii. 456.
Modern law of principal and agent, ii. 473.
Old English law, ii. 437.
Principle of representation in Roman law, ii. 433.
Year-book period, ii. 442–449.

REPRESENTATION, FRAUDULENT.
See MISREPRESENTATION.

REPRESENTATION *INTER VIVOS.*
See REPRESENTATION.

RESCOUS, WRIT OF, iii. 293.

RESCUE.
Right of resçue by person distrained upon, iii. 292.

RESERVOIR.
Responsibility of owner for damage done by dangerous accumulation of water, i. 62, 63.

RESIDUES.
Nuisance created by filthy residues, i. 217.

RES LOQUITUR IPSA, i. 107, 108.

RESPONSIBILITY.
Axiomatic basis of motion, i. 67.
Conception of, as basis of secondary trespass, i. 49, 67, 68.
'Liability' distinguished from 'responsibility,' i. 49.
Place of conception in legal theory, i. 49.

RESTITUTIO IN INTEGRUM, iii. 20.

RESTRAINT OF TRADE.
See TRADE.

REVERSION.
Innominate tort against owner of reversionary interest in chattel, i. 260.
Reversionary interest in chattel not recognized at common law, iii. 50.

REWARD.
Contract right to reward. ii. 81, 82.
Knowledge of existence of offer as affecting right of recovery, ii. 82.
Statutory right to reward, ii. 82.

RIGHT.
Conception of right in modern classification, iii. 6, 7.
Conception of right not familiar in early law, iii. 6, 7.
Duty correlative with, iii. 7.
Existence of right, how proved, iii. 8.

RIGHT AND REMEDY.
Relation between, iii. 49, 51, 55.
Ubi jus ibi remedium, iii. 48–59.

RIGHT OF ACTION.
Assignment of right of action, iii. 76–89.
Death of party as affecting right of action, iii. 60–71.
Debt perishes with person, iii. 60, 63, 65.
Detinue survives death of party, iii. 64.
Intangibility of right of action, iii. 77.
Nontransferability of right of action, iii. 62, 77.
Right of action in assumpsit survives death of party, iii. 68.
Subversion of doctrine of nontransferability, iii. 62.

RIGHT OF ACTION — *Continued.*
Survival —
Ancient rule, iii. 60.
Modern doctrine, iii. 64.
Transferability of right of action founded on property, iii. 63.
Trespass perishes with person, iii. 69.
Trover perishes with person, iii. 64.
Wager of law as explanatory of nonsurvival of debt, iii. 67.
Waste, action perishes with person, when, iii. 65.

RIGHT OF PRIVACY.
See PRIVACY, RIGHT OF.

RIGHT, WRIT OF.
See WRIT OF RIGHT.

RIPARIAN RIGHT, INTERFERENCE WITH.
See COGNATE NUISANCE.

RISK.
Assumption of risk by person injured, i. 150.
Primary risk of author or maintainer of harmful agent, i. 149.

ROBBERY.
Bailee, robbery as defense for ordinary bailee, ii. 255, 256, 259, 282.
Carrier by sea, robbery not good defense for, ii. 268, 269.
Pledgee, robbery as defense for, ii. 259.

ROLFE, B.
Repudiates idea of 'degrees' in negligence, i. 100.
Supposes abolition of real actions to leave owner of rent charge in fee without remedy, iii. 134.

ROLLE, C. J.
Favors action of stranger to consideration on contract made for his benefit, ii. 155.
Observation on adequacy of consideration, ii. 70.
Particular command —
Statement of doctrine of, ii. 444.
Sustains civil action for damage resulting from breach of marriage promise, i. 463.

ROMER, L. J.
Observation in regard to liability of auctioneer for conversion, i. 244.
Observation on conspiracy and combination in tort of interference with trade or calling, i. 365.

RUSTICUM JUDICIUM.
See CONTRIBUTORY NEGLIGENCE.

RUTLEDGE, C. J.
Recognizes right to distrain slave for rent, iii. 307.

RYAN, C. J.
Compensatory and exemplary damages compared, i. 480.

SACRAMENTUM.
See ACTIO SACRAMENTI.

SAFE-DEPOSIT COMPANY.
Bailee distinguished from, ii. 290.
Liability of, as affected by terms of contract, ii. 291.

SAILOR.
Promise to increase wages of invalid, when, ii. 75.

SAINT GERMAIN.
Doctrine of consideration as presented by, ii. 38.
Observations on *nudum pactum*, ii. 39.
Past consideration invalid, ii. 83.
Statement concerning duty of servant to exonerate master, ii. 448.
Statement concerning liability of common carrier, ii. 299.
Summary of law of bailment, ii. 261.
Summary of law of representation at close of year-book period, ii. 448, 449.

SALE.
See BARGAIN AND SALE.
Bailment distinguished from sale, ii. 290.
Conversion, when sale of goods amounts to, i. 238.
Failure to deliver at time stipulated, measure of damage for, i. 447-449.
Fictitious sale as basis of action against converter, ii. 216.
Master, responsibility for fraudulent sale by servant, ii. 443, 450.
Sale of goods as affected by section 17 of Statute of Frauds, ii. 194.
Sale of land as affected by Statute of Frauds, ii. 193.

SALE OF GOODS ACT.
Re-enacts 17th section of Statute of Frauds, ii. 177, 195.

SALMOND, PROF. J. W.
Theory concerning notions of punishment and compensation in law of damage, i. 477.
Theory of damage and injury, i. 491.

SAMPLE.
Implied warranty in sale by, i. 389.
What constitutes sale by, i. 389.

SANBORN, J.
Fraudulent intent as affecting liability for unfair competition, i. 431.

SATISFACTION.
See ACCORD AND SATISFACTION.

SAVIGNY, FRIEDRICH KARL VON.
Theory of representation in Roman law, ii. 435.

SCANDALUM MAGNATUM, i. 281.

SCHOOL.
Competition by erection of rival school not actionable, i. 217.

SCHOOLMASTER.
Immoderate punishment of pupil, i. 39.
Reasonable correction of pupil, i. 38.

SCIENTER.
Allegation in action of fraud, i. 381.
Knowledge of falsity of statement necessary in slander of title, i. 323.
Scienter as affecting liability for false representation, i. 399.

SCOPE OF EMPLOYMENT.
See MASTER AND SERVANT.

SCOTT, SIR WILLIAM.
See STOWELL, LORD.

SCROGGS, C. J.
Privity of blood as basis for action of assumpsit in favor of stranger, ii. 153.

SCROPE, J.
Observation on connection between injury and right of action, i. 493, 494.

SEAL.
Authority of agent, when required to be under seal, ii. 474.
Conclusiveness of seal, ii. 8.
Consideration, seal does not import, ii. 19.
Covenant required to be evidenced by, iii. 118.
Effect in early law, ii. 8.
Sealed contracts unaffected by Statute of Frauds, ii. 172.
Sealed instrument, negotiability of, ii. 509.
Sealed obligation becomes transitory, iii. 91, 92.
Seal makes specialty contract, ii. 8, 9.

SEAMAN.
Right of shipmaster to punish, i. 39.

SECONDARY TRESPASS.
In general —
Agents of harm, conception of responsibility for as basis of secondary trespass, i. 49.
Negligence, place in theory of secondary trespass, i. 67, 84.
Obviousness of danger as bearing on question of responsibility, i. 67.
Principle underlying secondary trespass, i. 49, 67, 149.
Trespass distinguished from, i. 67, 70.
Consequential damage as associated with secondary trespass, iii. 253, 254.
Dangerous accumulation of water —
Act of God and *vis major* as defenses against claim for damages, i. 63, 64.
Artificial lake flooded by extraordinary downpour, i. 63.
Responsibility of person collecting water in artificial body, i. 62.
Rylands *v.* Fletcher, basis of decision, i. 62.
Strict principle of liability enforced, i. 62.

SECONDARY TRESPASS — *Continued.*
Dangerous premises, see Dangerous Premises.
Domestic animals —
Casual and unpreventable damage, owner not responsible for, i. 53.
Cattle driven in public thoroughfare, i. 53.
Kicking horse, i. 53.
Knowledge of vicious propensities, when essential, i. 53.
Negligence basis of owner's responsibility, i. 52.
Owner not responsible for act of stranger, i. 53.
Remedy for damage done by, i. 55.
Stallion, injury done by, i. 52.
Trespasses committed by, responsibility of owner for, i. 51.
Vicious dog —
Knowledge of vicious propensities, i. 54.
Responsibility of owner for injury done by, i. 54.
Explosives —
Dangerous explosive left accessible to children, i. 59.
Explosion by lightning no defense, when, i. 59.
Owner or keeper, responsibility of, for damage done by dangerous explosives, i. 59.
Seller, duty to give notice of dangerous character of thing sold, i. 60.
Selling explosive to child, i. 59.
Steam boiler, explosion of, i. 63.
Fire —
Accidental fires, responsibility for damage done by, i. 56.
Negligence essential to cause of action in modern times, i. 57.
Negligence formerly essential to responsibility for fire, i. 56.
Premises, responsibility for fire originating on, i. 56.
Firearms —
Defective gun sold with false warranty, i. 58, 59.
Loaded gun negligently left in hands of immature child, i. 58.
Loaded gun negligently left near pathway, i. 58.
Owner or keeper responsible for damage done by, when, i. 57.
Strictness of law regarding injury by, i. 58.
Inanimate agent not dangerous *per se* —
Concrete cases discussed —
Barrier across road, i. 65.
Vehicle left unattended in crowded thoroughfare, child hurt while playing on, i. 66.
Vehicle left unattended in crowded thoroughfare, damage done by backing of horse caused by interference from stranger, i. 66.
Responsibility of keeper or maintainer for harm done by, i. 65.
Intended harms done by dangerous things —
Spring-gun cases —
Assumption of risk by trespasser, i. 68.
Notice, necessity for giving of, i. 68, 69.

SECONDARY TRESPASS — *Continued.*
Poisonous drugs —
Negligence on part of druggist essential to cause of action, i. 61.
Responsibility of druggist or chemist for injury done by, i. 60.
Remedy —
No specific writ for torts of responsibility, iii. 255.
Trespass on the case, iii. 245, 254.
Wild animals —
Responsibility of owner for injuries done by, i. 55.
Strict rule of liability, i. 55.

SECRETARY.
Negotiability of instrument payable to secretary, ii. 510.

SECTA.
Function of, in early law, iii. 24.

SECURITIES, TRANSFERABLE.
See TRANSFERABLE SECURITIES.

SEDGWICK, THEODORE.
Theory concerning measure of damage, i. 479.

SEDUCTION.
Consent of female as affecting right of action against seducer, i. 163.
Exemplary damages assessable in action for, when, i. 484.
Parent has right of action for seduction of daughter, when, i. 268.
Person *in loco parentis* has right of action for seduction of female dependent, when, i. 268.
Seduced female has cause of action against seducer who is guardian, i. 272.
Seduced female has no cause of action against seducer, when, i. 272.
Self-supporting girl, parent has no right of action for seduction of, i. 270.
Servant, master's right of action for seduction of, i. 271.

SEED.
Warranty of quality, measure of damage for breach of, i. 448, 449.

SELBORNE, LORD.
Benefit to promisor as consideration, ii. 105.

SELF-DEFENSE.
Ground of justification for battery, i. 7.

SELF-HELP.
Distress based on idea of, iii. 286.
Self-help in early English law, iii. 286.

SENDEE.
Action of, for negligent transmission of telegram, i. 437.
Sender of telegram acting as agent of sendee, i. 437.
Sendee ratifies by paying for message, i. 437.
Who is sendee of telegram, i. 436.

SERVANT.
See Master and Servant.

SERVICE.
Action on contract for personal service, ii. 23.
Procuring of service to be done on chattel, ii. 288, 289.
Care required of bailee, ii. 289.
Delivery of possession necessary, ii. 289.
Survival of action founded on loss of service, iii. 71.

SHAND, LORD.
Statement of theory underlying Allen *v.* Flood, i. 359.

SHAW, C. J.
Statement of principle underlying master's responsibility for negligent act of servant, ii. 462.

SHERIFF.
Jurisdiction over replevin, iii. 208, 209, 212.

SHIP.
Failure to medicine ship, liability of owner for damage resulting from, i. 174.
Open hatchway, liability of vessel for injury caused by, i. 167.

SHOWER, SIR B.
Argument on liability of indorser, ii. 376, 377.

SIC UTERE TUO UT ALIENUM NON LÆDAS, i. 193, 211, 218.

SIDEWALK.
Contributory negligence of pedestrian in passing obstruction, i. 138.
Contributory negligence of person using defective sidewalk, i. 132.

SIGHT.
Instrument payable at fixed period after, ii. 507.
Instrument payable at sight, effect of Negotiable Instruments Law on, ii. 509.

SIGNATURE.
See Statute of Frauds.
Party to covenant may sue though covenant not signed by him, iii. 122.

SIGNS, DEFAMATION BY MEANS OF, i. 274, 294.

SILENCE.
Estoppel resulting from failure to speak, ii. 243.

SI TE FECERIT SECURUM, WRIT, iii. 37.

SKILL.
Assumption of professional skill, i. 97, 98.

SKYNNER, L. C. B.
Twofold classification of contracts, ii. 174.

SLANDER AND LIBEL.
See Defamation.

SLANDER OF TITLE.
Bad faith necessary to liability for, i. 323.
Definition of, i. 322.
Injurious words may be either spoken or written, i. 322.
Knowledge of falsity, i. 323.
Malice in fact not essential to liability, i. 323.
Special damage as basis of liability, i. 322.

SLANDER OF WOMEN ACT (1891), i. 290.

SLAVE.
Conversion of, by use in hazardous employment, i. 258.
Distrainable for rent, when, iii. 307.
Master's responsibility for act of, in early law, ii. 437.
Responsibility of master avoided by surrender of slave, ii. 438.

SMART MONEY, i. 479, 482, 483.

SMITH.
Implied duty incident to public calling, i. 184.
Negligent injury to horse, i. 187.
Quasi-contractual obligation to shoe horse of person desiring service, ii. 237.
Responsibility for negligent act of servant in shoeing horse, ii. 445.

SMITH, J. W.
Benefit to promisor as consideration for promise, ii. 105.
Discussion of limits of case and assumpsit, iii. 276.

SMITH, L. J.
Discussion of subject of ratification, ii. 490.

SMOKE.
Nuisance created by, i. 217.

SOCIAL INTERCOURSE.
Infringement of right to social intercourse gist of slander, when, i. 279.

SOCIETAS, ii. 435, 436.

SPECIAL DAMAGE.
See PECUNIARY DAMAGE.
Breach of contract—
Distinction between special and remote damage, i. 449.
Notice of antecedent condition as affecting recovery of special damage, i. 447.
Remote damage not recoverable as special damage, i. 448.
Special damage may be recovered for when, i. 446–448.
Defamation of goods, actual damage essential to right of action for, i. 324.
Malicious prosecution, special damage as affecting liability for, i. 332.
Nuisance, nature of special damage in law of, i. 225, 227, 228.

SPECIALTY.
Bills and notes held not to be specialty contracts, ii. 387, 388.
Consideration not necessary in, ii. 19.

SPECIALTY — *Continued.*
Covenant, history of, ii. 8; iii. 114.
High nature of specialty contract, ii. 9.
Sealed debt —
Early history, ii. 8.
Nature of, iii. 131.
Validity of, derived from form, ii. 19.

SPELLMAN, J.
Action on case concurrent with detinue as remedy against bailee, iii. 151.

SPRING.
Right of owner to divert water to exclusion of owner below, i. 199.

SPRING GUN.
Application of maxim *volenti non fit injuria*, i. 163.
Liability for personal injury done by, i. 8.
Responsibility of person placing, i. 68.

SQUIB CASE, iii. 257.
Nature of problem involved in, iii. 257.
Proper form of remedy, iii. 257, 258.

STALLION.
Responsibility of owner for injury done by, i. 52.

STARE DECISIS.
Antiquity of doctrine, i. 500.
Principle of, i. 500.

STATE, ACT OF.
See Act of State.

STATUS.
Agency as connected with conception of status, ii. 431, 434.
Conception of status loses vitality in English law, ii. 440.
Interference with relations of status, see Interference with Domestic Relations.
Legal privilege as affected by, i. 40.
Obsolescence of status and transition to contract, ii. 436.

STATUTE.
Breach of statutory duty, see Breach of Statutory Duty.

STATUTE OF FRAUDS.
In general —
Authorship, ii. 168, 169.
Criticism of form and wording of statute, ii. 170.
Criticism of policy and wisdom, ii. 196–198.
Effect of statute —
Dispenses with no common-law requirement, ii. 173.
Only simple contracts affected by, ii. 171.
Statute operates on remedy only, ii. 178.
Origin of statute, ii. 168.
Purpose and method of statute, ii. 169.
Statute meets with general approval, ii. 169, 170.

STATUTE OF FRAUDS — *Continued.*
Agreement, meaning of, ii. 178, 179.
Agreement or memorandum to be reduced to writing, ii. 178.
Agreement to be performed on one side within year, valid, ii. 176.
Classification adopted in, basis of, ii. 170.
Collateral liability of personal representatives of guarantors and sureties, ii. 183, 185.
Contracts not performable within one year, ii. 193.
Validity of contract determined at time contract is made, ii. 193, 194.
Debt, default, or miscarriage, promise to answer for, ii. 184.
Evidence, abolition of exclusionary rules as affecting policy of statute, ii. 198.
Failure to comply with statute renders contract voidable only, ii. 176.
Implied promises not within statute, ii. 172.
Interpretation of statute —
Agreements to be performed within one year, ii. 176.
Attitude of modern courts, ii. 175.
Different rules of interpretation necessary in dealing with different provisions, ii. 174.
Liberal interpretation at first adopted, ii. 174.
Lord Mansfield's view as to principle of interpretation, ii. 174.
Section 17 construed *in pari materia* with section 4, ii. 177.
Lex fori as determining applicability of statute, ii. 178.
Lord Tenterden's Act, ii. 194.
Value of goods, ii. 194.
Memorandum —
Consideration must appear in writing, ii. 179.
American courts repudiate this rule, ii. 180.
Criticism of this doctrine, ii. 179, 180.
Rule in question abrogated by statute, ii. 181.
Memorandum to be signed by party to be charged, ii. 181.
Perjury, danger of, as affecting policy and wisdom of statute, ii. 189.
Place of statute in modern contract law, ii. 195.
Competency of witnesses as affecting policy and wisdom of statute, ii. 197, 198.
Reactionary character of statute, ii. 196.
Temporary makeshift in evolution of contract law, ii. 196.
Promise supported by consideration of marriage —
American doctrine, ii. 192.
Mutual promises of marriage not within statute, ii. 190.
Other bilateral agreements involving promises of marriage left within statute, ii. 190, 191.
Promise of third party in consideration of marriage of B and C within statute, ii. 191.
Promise to settle property in consideration of marriage within statute, ii. 191.
Repudiation of contract violative of Statute of Frauds originates *quasi*-contractual duty, when, ii. 222, 223.
Repudiation of contract violative of Statute of Frauds, right to recover on *quantum meruit*, ii. 227.

STATUTE OF FRAUDS — *Continued.*

Roman law, principles underlying Statute of Frauds not adopted in, ii. 197.

Sale of goods —

Contract for purchase of goods to be made to order, ii. 194.

Memorandum required, ii. 195.

Sale of Goods Act re-enacts 17th section of Statute of Frauds, ii. 177.

Sale of land, contract for, ii. 193.

Section 4, clause 2 —

Collateral liability as clue to application of, ii. 185.

Coming in aid to procure credit, ii. 186.

General principle stated, ii. 187.

Original and independent promise not within statute, ii. 185.

Original liability must be continuing one, ii. 185.

Policy of, general observations concerning, ii. 188, 189.

Promise made to debtor by third person not within statute, ii. 187.

Promise to indemnify, when not within statute, ii. 186.

Statute probably intended to apply only to promises collateral to existing liability, ii. 188.

Section 4, clause 5 —

Interpretation of, ii. 193.

Prospective character of provision, ii. 193.

Section 4, language of, ii. 171.

Section 17, language of, ii. 171.

Signature —

By whom to be made, ii. 181.

Mode of signing, ii. 182.

Signature to deed of conveyance unnecessary under Statute of Frauds, ii. 172.

Where must appear, ii. 181.

Witnesses, competency of, as affecting policy of statute, ii. 197, 198.

STATUTES.

52 Hen. III., c. 1, iii. 289.

52 Hen. III., c. 1–4, iii. 210.

52 Hen. III., c. 17, iii. 102.

52 Hen. III., c. 24, i. 29.

3 Edw. I., c. 34, i. 281.

6 Edw. I., c. 5, i. 29; iii. 269.

6 Edw. I., c. 7, iii. 249.

6 Edw. I., c. 8, iii. 233.

12 Edw. I., c. 6, iii. 115.

13 Edw. I., c. 1, iii. 50.

13 Edw. I., c. 2, iii. 107, 108, 211.

13 Edw. I., c. 3, ii. 326.

13 Edw. I., c. 12, i. 328.

13 Edw. I., c. 17, iii. 294.

13 Edw. I., c. 22, iii. 269.

13 Edw. I., c. 23, iii. 104.

STATUTES — *Continued.*

13 Edw. I., c. 24, i. 214; iii. 34, 35, 248.
13 Edw. I., c. 36, 37, i. 328; iii. 294.
18 Edw. I., c. 1, i. 41; iii. 296.
33 Edw. I., c. 1, i. 329.
17 Edw. II., c. 6, iii. 296.
1 Edw. III., Stat. 2, c. 12, iii. 296.
4 Edw. III., c. 7, iii. 69.
25 Edw. III., Stat. 5, c. 5, iii. 69, 104.
27 Edw. III., Stat. 2, c. 8, ii. 327.
27 Edw. III., Stat. 2, c. 19, ii. 443.
28 Edw. III., c. 13, ii. 327.
31 Edw. III., c. 11, iii. 104.
34 Edw. III., c. 15, iii. 296.
2 Rich. II., c. 5, i. 281.
5 Rich. II., Stat. 1, c. 2, ii. 337.
6 Rich. II., c. 2, iii. 93, 136.
12 Rich. II., c. 11, i. 281.
4 Hen. IV., c. 18, iii. 93.
27 Hen. VIII., c. 10, ii. 42.
32 Hen. VIII., c. 34, iii. 126.
1 & 2 Phil. & Mary, c. 12, iii. 294.
13 Eliz., c. 5, ii. 40.
12 Chas. II., c. 24, iii. 296, 297.
29 Chas. II., c. 3, § 4, ii. 40, 168, 171, 227.
29 Chas. II., c. 3, § 17, ii. 171.
2 Will. & Mary, Sess. 1, c. 5, iii. 294.
9 & 10 Will. III., c. 17, ii. 380; iii. 140.
3 & 4 Anne, c. 9, ii. 380, 385, 386, 388, 391, 502; iii. 140.
3 & 4 Anne, c. 16, iii. 302.
4 Anne, c. 16, § 27, iii. 104.
6 Anne, c. 31, i. 56.
9 Anne, c. 16, ii. 144, 145.
11 Geo. II., c. 19, iii. 296.
11 Geo. II., c. 19, § 14. ii. 217.
11 Geo. II., c. 19, § 18, iii. 181.
59 Geo. III., c. 46, iii. 23.
7 & 8 Geo. IV., c. 18, i. 69.
9 Geo. IV., c. 14, ii. 194.
1 Will. IV., c. 47, iii. 138.
2 Will. IV., c. 39, § 16, iii. 43.
3 & 4 Will. IV., c. 27, § 36, iii. 46.
3 & 4 Will. IV., c. 42, iii. 65, 69, 93, 139.
3 & 4 Will. IV., c. 71, § 3, i. 209.
9 & 10 Vict., c. 93, iii. 71.
13 & 14 Vict., c. 61, § 11, iii. 155.
15 & 16 Vict., c. 71, § 49, iii. 202.
15 & 16 Vict., c. 76, i. 234; iii. 24, 155.
17 & 18 Vict., c. 78, iii. 158.
17 & 18 Vict., c. 90, i. 145.

STATUTES — *Continued.*
23 & 24 Vict., c. 126, § 26, iii. 46.
24 & 25 Vict., c. 100, § 31, i. 69.
37 & 38 Vict., c. 62, ii. 145.
46 & 47 Vict., c. 57, i. 422.
51 & 52 Vict., c. 50, i. 422.
53 & 54 Vict., c. 64, i. 403.
54 & 55 Vict., c. 51, i. 290.
56 & 57 Vict., c. 71, § 4, ii. 177, 195.
Statutum Incerti Temporis, i. 328.

STEAM-BOILER.
Explosion due to inherent and undiscoverable defect, responsibility for damage resulting from, i. 63.
Implied warranty in sale of, i. 387.

STEAMSHIP.
Defective steering apparatus, liability of steamship company for damage resulting from, i. 102.

STENOGRAPHER.
Dictation to stenographer constitutes publication of defamatory matter, when, i. 297.

STINESS, C. J.
Interpretation of Negotiable Instruments Law, § 23, ii. 520.

STIPULATION.
A formal contract, ii. 16.
Bracton on law of, ii. 16.
Judicial stipulation identified with recognizance, ii. 17.

STONE, J.
Mere recommendation of solvency not actionable as false representation, i. 409.

STORY, J.
Bearer of negotiable instrument takes as nominee under contract, ii. 371.
Classification of bailments, ii. 271.
Considers factor a bailee, iii. 101.
Controversy with Kent, J., over consideration in negotiable instrument, ii. 522.
Distinguishes between general and special agents, ii. 484.
Observation on application of standard of care to bailment, i. 99.
Sanctions debt as remedy against acceptor, iii. 143.

STOWELL, LORD.
Statement of doctrine of *rusticum judicium*, i. 145.

STREET.
City responsible for damage resulting from unsafe street, i. 115.
Damage to wagon improperly placed in street, plaintiff not precluded by unlawful conduct, i. 176.

STREET — *Continued.*
Defective sidewalk, responsibility of city for injury resulting from, i. 132.
Injury resulting from dangerous exit into street, responsibility for, i. 131.
Insecure lamp over street, responsibility of keeper of premises, i. 154.

SUBAGENT.
Right of agent to appoint, ii. 477.

SUBSTITUTE.
Right of agent to appoint, ii. 476.

SUIT OF COURT.
Suit-real, iii. 297.
Suit-service, iii. 297.

SUMMA ANGELICA, ii. 448.

SUPPORT.
Interference with support, see COGNATE NUISANCE.

SUPPRESSIO VERI, i. 399.

SURETY, ii. 4.
Contribution among sureties —
Contract of several sureties evidenced by separate bonds, ii. 239.
Quasi-contractual obligation to contribute, ii. 239.
Successive suretyship, ii. 239.
Estoppel of surety incident to holding self out as a principal debtor, ii. 244.
Money paid for benefit of principal, right of surety to recover, ii. 238.
Surety a debtor, ii. 8.

SURETYSHIP.
Early law of suretyship, ii. 7.
Formal nature of contract, ii. 7.
Guaranty, contract of, recognized as valid, ii. 47.
Guaranty distinguished from suretyship, ii. 184.
Readjustment in law of suretyship incident to growth of assumptual law, ii. 46, 47.
Seal becomes essential in early contract of suretyship, ii. 46.
Surety a principal debtor, ii. 47.

SURGEON.
Negligence in treatment of patient, i. 187.

SURVIVAL.
Account, iii. 104.
Application of maxim *actio personalis,* iii. 60–75.
Assumpsit, iii. 68.
Covenant, iii. 125.
Debt, iii. 66.
Detinue, iii. 64.
Trespass, iii. 69, 70.
Trover, iii. 64.
Waste, iii. 65.

SWAYNE, J.
Observation on estoppel by renunciation of title, ii. 243.

TAFT, J.
Distinguishes between contract and agency, ii. 433.

TAVERNER.
Implied warranty of wholesomeness of food and drink, i. 387.

TELEGRAM, NEGLIGENT TRANSMISSION OF.
See NEGLIGENT TRANSMISSION OF TELEGRAM.

TELEGRAPH COMPANY.
See NEGLIGENT TRANSMISSION OF TELEGRAM.

TEMPEST.
Loss by, as defense for bailee, ii. 261.

TENANT AT WILL.
Permissive waste, tenant at will not liable for, i. 30.

TENEMENT.
Superior tenement, right of, to subjacent support, i. 193.

TENTERDEN, LORD.
Considers effect of restrictive indorsement, ii. 399.
Lord Tenterden's Act, ii. 194.
Observation on effect of restrictive indorsement, ii. 399.

TENURE.
Abolition of military tenure, iii. 296, 297.
Copyhold tenure as affected by statute, iii. 296.
Incidents of military tenure, iii. 296.
Tenure in frankalmoign as affected by statute, iii. 296.

TERTIARY TRESPASS.
Nuisance viewed as tertiary trespass formation, i. 191.

THEFT.
Theft by stranger as defense for bailee, ii. 255, 256, 259.

THEFT, ACTION OF.
See ACTIO FURTI.

THEMISTES.
Awards of the early judges, iii. 4, 5.

THESIGER, L. J.
Observations on right of agent to delegate authority, ii. 476.

THIEF.
Ascription of property to thief and trespasser, origin of doctrine, iii. 49.

THORPE, J.
Notes relaxation of law of pledge, ii. 259.
Recognizes wrong of simple assault, i. 11.

THREAT.
Interference with contract by means of, i. 346.
Money paid on threat of prosecution and imprisonment, ii. 229.
Money paid on threat of prosecution on well-grounded charge, ii. 230.
Threat to convert not sufficient to work a conversion, i. 236.

TIME.
Determinable future time, what is, ii. 507.
Negotiability of instrument not dependent on length of time stipulated for, ii. 508.
Negotiable instrument payable on demand when time for payment not expressed, ii. 509.

TIME-TABLE.
Railroad liable for misrepresentation contained in, when, i. 398.

TINDAL, C. J.
Concurring contributory negligence a bar to plaintiff's action, i. 137, 138.
Forbearance as consideration, ii. 77.
Negligence not determined by reference to capacity of particular individual, i. 96; ii. 275.
Observation on implied promise incident to drawing and accepting bill, iii. 202.
Observation on responsibility for harm done by dangerous agent, i. 66.

TIRWIT, J.
Denies right of action for breach of simple promise, i. 187.

TORT.
Arbitrary nature of distinction between contract and tort, i. 87.
Breach of contract distinguished from, i., p. xxviii.
Classification based on distinction between trespass and case, i., pp. xxi–xxiii.
Crime distinguished from, i., p. xxviii.
Definitions of, i., pp. xxvi, xxvii.
Equitable injury distinguished from, i., p. xxviii.
Extent of liability in field of tort, i. 88.
First treatise on "Torts," i., p. xxii.
Generic and derivative torts distinguished, i. 496.
Legal formations in law of, i. 496.
Modern treatment of torts, i., p. xxii.
Primary types of legal wrong, i. 497.
Process of legal growth —
Illustration in law of interference with contract relation, i. 343.
Illustration in law of privacy, i. 318–321.
Influence of considerations of policy and justice, i. 343.
Stages in development of legal theory, i., p. xxi.
Scope of subject of torts, i., p. xxviii.
Spiritual offense distinguished from, i., p. xxviii.
Waiver of tort —
Conversion of chattel, ii. 215, 217; iii. 196.
Election of remedy, ii. 218.

TORTFEASORS, JOINT.
Contribution among, when permitted, i. 490; ii. 240, 241.
Election of remedy by plaintiff, effect on liability of joint tortfeasor, ii. 218.
Ex turpi causa non oritur actio, i. 490.
Joint and several, liability of, i. 490.

TOWER OF LONDON.

Charles I. forces compulsory loan from merchants depositing funds in Tower, ii. 367.
London merchants use king's mint in Tower as place of deposit, ii. 367.

TRADE.

Contract in restraint of trade —
Early rule, ii. 164.
Modern doctrine, ii. 165.
Reasonable restraint, ii. 165.
Interference with trade or calling, see INTERFERENCE WITH TRADE OR CALLING.

TRADEMARK.

Clean hands, plaintiff must come into court with, i. 426.
Infringement of trademark —
Counterfeiting, i. 418.
Intent of infringer immaterial, i. 420.
Scienter unnecessary to be shown, i. 420, 421.
Simulation, i. 419.
Registration of trademark, statutory regulation of, i. 422, 423.
Requisites of valid trademark —
Legality of business, i. 423.
Mark must be attached to article sold, i. 423.
Novelty, how far essential, i. 423.
Secondary signification of words not subject to trademark right, i. 429.
Trademark represents property right, i. 421.
Unfair competition —
Infringement of trademark and unfair competition confused, i. 422.
Trademark law supplemented by law of unfair competition, i. 425.
What constitutes trademark —
Arbitrary devices, i. 423.
Symbols, i. 423.
Words, i. 423.
Descriptive combination of words arbitrarily used, i. 424, 425.
Descriptive words, i. 424.
Familiar words used arbitrarily, i. 424.
Foreign words, i. 424.
Geographical term, i. 424.
Newly coined words, i. 424.

TRADE NAME.

Colorable name, i. 432.
Misrepresentation as to continuation of business after dissolution of partnership, i. 433.
Negotiable instrument, effect of using trade name in, ii. 518.
Own name —
Conditions imposed on use of, i. 434.
Form in which name to be used, i. 432.
Right to use, i. 432.

TRANSFERABLE SECURITIES.
Bonds, coupons, and debentures, ii. 419.
Bonds payable to holder, ii. 420.
Conditional debentures payable to bearer, ii. 423.
Debentures, pledgee of, does not convert by sub-pledging, when, i. 240.
Dividend warrants of Bank of England, ii. 420.
Domestic debentures, ii. 422.
Ambulatory intent as criterion of transferability, ii. 424.
Modern usage as affecting negotiability, ii. 422.
Foreign bonds —
Foreign bonds passing from hand to hand, ii. 420.
Neapolitan bonds, ii. 421.
Negotiability a question of fact for jury, ii. 421.
Government scrip made negotiable by modern commercial usage, ii. 423.
Sealed bonds payable to assigns, ii. 419.

TRANSITORY ACTION.
Contractual obligation becomes transitory, iii. 92.
Sealed obligation gives rise to transitory cause of action, iii. 92.

TRAP.
Coal cellar, responsibility for injury incident to insecurity of, i. 152, 153.
Digging of pit on common, responsibility for injury to stray animal, i. 156.
Insecure gangway, responsibility for personal injury resulting from, i. 152.
Old structure, responsibility for injury resulting from collapse of, i. 156.
Open shoot in manufacturing establishment, i. 151.
Pit near pathway, i. 156.
Passageway, trap in, i. 151.
Slippery stairs, i. 152.
Unguarded area, i. 153.
Unlighted staircase, i. 158.

TREASURER.
Liability of public treasurer for funds held in official custody, ii. 292, 293.
Negotiability of instrument payable to, ii. 510.

TREBY, C. J.
Summary of history of law of bills at close of seventeenth century, ii. 351, 352.

TREE.
Overhanging boughs, right to lop off, i. 20.

TREMAYLE, J.
Observation on writ of action by bailor against disseisor of bailee, iii. 239.

TRENCHANT, JOHN.
Validity of inland bill not recognized in time of, ii. 360.

TRESPASS.
Action of trespass, see TRESPASS, ACTION OF.
Amelioration of principle of trespass, i. 3, 79.
Ascription of property to trespasser, origin of, iii. 49.
Basis of strict liability in trespass, i. 78.
Blame essential to liability in modern times, i. 80.
Civil and criminal liability distinguished, i. 75.
Civil liability absolute in early law —
Accidental fall of timber, i. 76.
Accidental glancing of arrow, i. 76.
Accidental striking, i. 76.
Felling thorns on neighbor's land, i. 76.
Disseisin distinguished from trespass, iii. 227.
Exemplary damages —
Trespass accompanied by insult, i. 485.
Trespass characterized by wanton disregard of legal right, i. 486.
Wilfulness of trespass as affecting assessment of, i. 483.
Extent of liability in trespass, i. 74.
Intent —
Presumption of intent as regards natural consequences, i. 75.
Trespassory intent essential to criminal liability, i. 75.
Trespassory intent not essential to civil liability, i. 75.
Jurisdiction of king's court based on violence, iii. 230.
Jurisdiction of local courts over early trespass, iii. 225.
Justification —
Menaces from others not sufficient to justify trespass on third person, i. 78.
Self-defense, i. 7.
Various grounds of, i. 7–9.
Moral ingredient in law of trespass, i. 2, 3.
Negligence —
Negligence essential to liability in trespass —
Accidental blow to person standing behind, i. 82.
Accidental damage happening without fault not actionable, i. 81.
Glancing shot, injury caused by, i. 82.
Runaway horse, unavoidable accident caused by, i. 82.
Original theory of trespass excludes conception of negligence, i. 74.
Possession —
Trespass violative of possession, i. 34; iii. 234.
Waste distinguished from trespass, i. 33.
Remedy —
Action of trespass proper remedy in primary trespass, iii. 254.
Trespass on case normal remedy in secondary trespass, iii. 254.
Right of action for trespass perishes with person, iii. 69.
Secondary trespass distinguished, i. 70.
Survival of right of action against estate of deceased trespasser, iii. 70.
'Trespass' equivalent to 'tort,' iii. 224.

TRESPASS — *Continued.*

Trespass on case —
Negligent misfeasance —
Barber, iii. 251.
Ferryman, iii. 250, 251.
Surgeon, iii. 251.
Veterinarian, iii. 251.
Violence —
First trespass a wrong of intentional violence, i. 74.
Moral ingredient not considered in wrongs of violence, i. 2.
Violent accidental injury, liability for, i. 78–83.

TRESPASS *AB INITIO.*

Abuse of legal authority makes one trespasser *ab initio,* i. 45.
Basis of doctrine, iii. 242, 243.
Distress as associated with trespass *ab initio,* iii. 295.
Essentials of trespass *ab initio,* i. 48.
Finder of lost chattel treated as trespasser *ab initio,* when, iii. 244.
Illustrations of trespass *ab initio,* i. 46.
Intent —
Fictitious intent ascribed to wrongdoer, function of, i. 48.
Presumption of wrongful intent, i. 47.
Malicious abuse of process, analogy of, to trespass *ab initio,* ii. 334.
Misfeasance essential to trespass *ab initio,* i. 46.
Nonfeasance cannot make one trespasser *ab initio,* i. 47.
Person entering inn, when trespasser *ab initio,* i. 46.
Remedy —
Action of trespass, i. 47.
Obstacle to use of, i. 47.
Wrongful sale of distrained goods, i. 46.

TRESPASS, ACTION OF.

Action lies for forceful damage of any kind, iii. 232.
Analogy to criminal appeal, iii. 231.
Criminal appeal supplanted by, iii. 230.
Criminal aspects of action of trespass, iii. 231.
Early substitutes for action of trespass, iii. 226–229.
Finder of lost property subject to action of trespass, when, iii. 244.
Interference with domestic relations, trespass superseded by case as remedy for, iii. 266, 267.
Kinds of writs —
Returnable writ, iii. 230.
Vicontiel writ, iii. 230.
Master and servant —
Master liable in trespass for commanded act of servant, iii. 260, 261.
Master liable in trespass for natural consequences of commanded act, iii. 261.
Negligence —
Injury consequentially resulting from negligent act, iii. 252, 253, 258.
Injury directly resulting from negligent act, iii. 252, 253, 258, 259.

TRESPASS, ACTION OF — *Continued.*
Pleading —
Contra pacem, iii. 230.
Vi et armis, iii. 230.
Scope of trespass, iii. 223, 224.
Case and trespass supplemental remedies, iii. 223.
Difficulty of defining, iii. 223.
Statute of Gloucester restricts use of remedy, iii. 233.
Threefold function of remedy, iii. 229.
Trespass and trespass on case —
Direct and consequential damage distinguished, iii. 252, 253.
Limits of respective actions, iii. 252–264.
Trespass normal remedy in primary trespass, iii. 254.
Trespass on case normal remedy in secondary trespass, iii. 254.
Trespass *de bonis asportatis,* iii. 229–231.
Action not maintainable unless goods taken worth forty shillings, iii. 233.
Common-law remedy for asportation of chattels, i. 15.
Plaintiff must show violation of possessory right, ii. 236.
Remedy not available against disseisor of bailee, when, iii. 239.
Remedy not available by bailor against vendee of bailee, iii. 238, 239.
Trespass for assault and battery, iii. 232, 233.
Damage to live chattel, i. 16.
Personal injury, i. 4–9.
Simple assault, i. 10.
Trespass for assault and battery maintainable for injury to live thing, when, i. 16.
Trespass for mesne profits, i. 261.
Trespass *quare clausum* —
Origin of remedy, iii. 231, 232.
Plaintiff must show possession in fact, iii. 236.
Remedy for seduction of daughter, when, i. 269.
Strictness of principle of liability in, i. 24.
Trespass *vi et armis,* iii. 230–234.
Common-law remedy for injury to chattels, i. 15.
Turning water on land of neighbor, when actionable in trespass, iii. 256, 257.
Violation of possession essential to right of action, iii. 235–240.
Consequences of rule, iii. 237.
Historical explanation, iii. 235, 236, 240.
Violence as affecting right of action, iii. 232.
Voluntary waste by lessee actionable in trespass, iii. 242.
Waste, trespass as remedy for destructive waste, iii. 270.
Wilful direct injury, trespass exclusive remedy for, iii. 265.
Writ of trespass —
Appearance of, iii. 225, 226.
Contents, iii. 230.
Form of returnable writ, iii. 226, 230.
Form of vicontiel writ, iii. 230.

TRESPASSER.
Assumption of risk by trespasser, see Assumption of Risk.

TRESPASS ON CASE.
See Action on Case.

TRESPASS ON PERSON.
Assault —
Action of trespass maintainable for simple assault, i. 10.
Antiquity of wrong, i. 10.
Assault derived from battery, i. 10.
Display of hostile force coupled with apparent ability to do hurt, i. 10.
Intent —
Bearing of intent on liability for assault, i. 10.
Manifestation of hostile purpose, i. 11, 12.
Pointing unloaded gun, i. 12.
Assault and battery —
Contributory negligence not a defense in action for, i. 181.
Battery —
Accidental contact in crowded place, i. 6.
Actor liable for accidental result of unlawful act, i. 4.
Breach of peace, tendency of hostile touching to provoke, i. 6.
Caressing of non-consenting woman, i. 6.
Drunk man, handling of, i. 9.
Excessive force, use of, in ejection of trespasser, i. 9.
Excessive force, use of, in self-defense, i. 7.
Exemplary damages recoverable in action for wanton battery, i. 485, 486.
Hostile touching actionable, though no hurt is done, i. 6.
Injuries included within, i. 5.
Injury by independent agent not included in battery, i. 5.
Intention irrelevant where actual bodily injury is inflicted, i. 4.
Intent material in considering damages, when, i. 4.
Justification —
Defense of possession of chattels, i. 8.
Defense of relatives, i. 8.
Ejection of trespasser, i. 9.
Prevention of crime, i. 10.
Recaption, i. 8.
Self-defense, i. 7.
Self-defense not good justification in early law, i. 7.
Taking of life justifiable, when, i. 8.
Madman, restraint of, i. 9.
Parish officers cutting off hair of pauper, i. 6.
Presumption that one intends natural consequences, i. 5.
Spitting in face of another, i. 6.
Types of battery, i. 4.
False imprisonment —
Antiquity of wrong, i. 12.
Coercion essential in, i. 13.

TRESPASS ON PERSON — *Continued.*
False imprisonment — *Continued.*
Deduced from battery, i. 13.
Detention contrary to will of person imprisoned, i. 13.
Exemplary damages recoverable in action for, when, i. 485.
Incarceration not essential to constitute, i. 13.
Obstruction of locomotion in particular direction not, i. 14.
Physical contact and forceful constraint unnecessary, i. 13.
Surveillance by detectives constitutes false imprisonment, when, i. 14.
Violence —
Obnoxious character of element of violence, i. 1.
Place of conception of violence in legal theory, i. 1.
Recession of violence as constitutive factor in tort, i. 3.
Violent and non-violent injury distinguished, i. 2.
Violent trespass, i. 1.

TRESPASS ON PERSONAL PROPERTY.
Asportation of chattels, i. 15.
Destruction of chattels, i. 15.
Justification —
Jettison, i. 19.
Justification under war power, i. 23.
Self-defense, i. 17.
Trespassing animals, i. 17, 18.
Trespassing fowls, i. 18.
Injury to chattel short of destruction, i. 15.
Actual damage essential to cause of action, i. 16, 17.
Common-law courts at first take no account of wrong, i. 15.
Common-law courts obtain jurisdiction over this tort, i. 15.
Justification, grounds of, i. 17, 19.
Scratching of panel of carriage, i. 17.

TRESPASS ON REALTY.
Entry on soil of another actionable, i. 19.
Firing into field of another, i. 19.
Highway —
Improper use of highway as ground of trespass, i. 21, 22.
Unlawful interference by person moving along highway, i. 22.
Unlawful interference by person stationed on highway, i. 22.
Inadvertent intrusion, i. 19.
Intrusion by hunter, i. 21.
Justification —
Destruction of house in path of flames, i. 23.
Erection of fortification against public enemy, i. 22, 23.
Impassable highway justifies detour over private property, i. 23.
Necessity and policy as ground of justification, i. 22.
Nuisance, abatement of, i. 23.
Pursuit of beast of chase, i. 21.
Recaption, entry for purpose of, i. 21.
Rescuing property from flames, i. 20.

TRESPASS ON REALTY — *Continued.*
Rule of liability —
Strictness of, i. 19.
Trespass on realty and trespass on person, comparison between, i. 24.
Tree, obtrusion of, on premises of another, i. 19, 20.
Unauthorized entry, i. 19.
Unauthorized entry on friendly mission not justified, when, i. 20.
Waste distinguished from trespass, i. 33.

TRIAL BY BATTLE.
Criminal appeal subject to, iii. 231.

TRIAL OF PROPERTY.
See PROPERTY.

TROVER.
Action on case in nature of detinue, iii. 159.
Analogy to detinue *sur trover*, iii. 159.
Ascription of property to trespasser retards extension of trover, iii. 238.
Asportation of chattel actionable in trover, iii. 164.
Bailee —
Fictitious finding alleged in action against, iii. 166.
Not chargeable for wrongful detention contrary to contract, i. 248.
Carrier not liable in trover for lost goods, i. 238.
Characteristics of trover, iii. 161.
Conversion, trover as remedy for, iii. 160.
Detinue *sur trover* superseded by action on case *sur trover*, iii. 151.
Disseisin of chattel gist of tort for which trover lies, iii. 160.
Distress, trover as remedy for unlawful distress, iii. 170.
Essentials of right of action —
Plaintiff must show possession or right of possession, i. 251.
Property right not essential, i. 251.
Finder of chattel may maintain trover against wrongdoer, i. 251.
Finder of goods liable in trover upon failure to surrender, iii. 163, 164.
Genesis of trover, iii. 159.
Case as remedy against bailee, iii. 161, 162.
Case *sur trover* as remedy against bailee, iii. 161, 166.
Case *sur trover* as remedy against finder, iii. 161, 163.
Case *sur trover* as remedy against trespasser *de bonis asportatis*, iii. 161, 164.
Modern action of trover, iii. 165.
Pleading —
Conversion to defendant's use, iii. 160.
Fictitious allegations, iii. 160, 161.
Process, trover as remedy for unlawful seizure under legal process, iii. 170, 171.
Refusal by bailee to surrender chattel, iii. 167.
Refusal by trespasser or finder to surrender chattel, iii. 167.
Replevin, trover concurrent with, iii. 171.
Scope of action of trover, iii. 171.

TROVER — *Continued.*
Seller's action against fraudulent vendee, i. 258, 259.
Trespass *de bonis asportatis*, trover concurrent with, iii. 164–166.
Unlawful detention, trover available for, iii. 168, 169.

TRUTH.
Truthful communication not defamatory, i. 275.

TURLEY, J.
Denies recovery of reward where act is done in ignorance of offer, ii. 82.

TURNTABLE.
Basis of doctrine underlying turntable cases, i. 161.
Children injured while playing on turntable, responsibility of railroad company for, i. 159.
Immature child not competent to assume risk, i. 160.
Implied invitation of the company, i. 160.

UBI JUS IBI REMEDIUM, iii. 48, 51.
Doctrine of Ashby *v.* White, iii. 55.
Principle of action on case as affecting, iii. 247.
Right and remedy, relation between, iii. 48–59.

UNDISCLOSED PRINCIPAL.
See PRINCIPAL AND AGENT.

UNDUE PRESSURE.
Duress distinguished, ii. 229.
Quasi-contractual duty incident to payment of money under undue pressure, ii. 229.

UNFAIR COMPETITION.
Clean hands, plaintiff must come into court with, i. 426.
Deception —
Ambiguous statement intended to deceive, i. 430, 431.
Deception or likelihood of deception as affecting liability, i. 427, 428.
Definition of unfair competition, i. 425.
Fraudulent intent, i. 426, 427.
American doctrine, i. 430.
English doctrine, i. 428, 430.
Fraudulent intent immaterial except as bearing on question of deception, i. 428.
Fraud, unfair competition a wrong of fraud, i. 421.
Gist of unfair competition, i. 417.
Deception or likelihood of deception, i. 427.
History of law pertaining to —
Counterfeiting trademark, i. 418.
Simulation of trademark, i. 419.
Simulation of wrapper, i. 419.
Misrepresentation —
Ingredients, false statement concerning, i. 426.
Place of manufacture, false statement concerning, i. 426.

UNFAIR COMPETITION — *Continued.*
Misrepresentation — *Continued.*
Plaintiff must be free from charge of misrepresentation, i. 426.
Purity, false statement concerning, i. 426.
Omnibus, unfair competition in establishment of rival line, i. 421.
Remedy —
Action at law, i. 417, 418.
Bill in equity, i. 417.
Ground of equitable interference, i. 418.
Selling goods as and for goods of another, i. 419, 420.
Trademark —
Confusion of doctrine underlying trademark law and unfair competition, i. 422.
Secondary signification of words not subject to trademark right, i. 429.

UNIFORM STATE LAWS.
Committee on, ii. 496.

UNILATERAL CONTRACT.
Bilateral contract distinguished, ii. 52.
Nature of unilateral contract, ii. 52, 53.
Performance of offer, condition precedent to existence of contract, ii. 52.
Shadwell *v.* Shadwell, doctrine of, ii. 115.
Unilateral duty characteristic of early contract law, ii. 20.
Unilateral promise given to secure performance of existing obligation, ii. 112.

UNINCORPORATED ASSOCIATION, INSTRUMENT PAYABLE TO, ii. 514.

UNION, LABOR.
See Labor Union.

UNJUST ENRICHMENT.
Quasi-contract arising from, ii. 208, 209; iii. 199–201.
Appropriation of chattel, ii. 215, 216; iii. 195–198, 200.
Appropriation of service, ii. 215; iii. 199.
Benefit conferred under mistake of fact, ii. 211.
Benefit conferred under unenforceable contract, ii. 220.
Failure of consideration, ii. 214; iii. 192.
Money paid to defendant's use, ii. 232.
Money paid under pressure, ii. 228.
Survival of action, iii. 200.
Roman law —
Dare ob causam, ii. 209.
Enrichment *ex injusta causa,* ii. 209.
Enrichment *sine causa,* ii. 209.
Solutio indebiti, ii. 209.

USAGE.
See Custom.

USANCE.
Meaning of term in early law merchant, ii. 356.

USE.
Reasonable use of riparian water, what is, i. 200.

USE AND OCCUPATION.
Action on case for use and occupation, iii. 180.
No implied contract to compensate for, ii. 217.
Statutory action, ii. 217.
Trespass for mesne profits, i. 261.

USES.
Chancery jurisdiction over, ii. 40.
Resulting use, ii. 41.

USES, STATUTE OF, ii. 42.

USURY.
Effect on negotiability of instrument, ii. 535.
Promise to pay debt void for usury, ii. 144, 145.

VADE MECUM, ii. 346.
Precedents of actions on bills, ii. 352.

VALUE.
Antecedent or pre-existing debt, ii. 521.
Value in negotiable instruments, ii. 521.
Value of goods as affecting application of Statute of Frauds, ii. 194.

VALUE RECEIVED.
Presumption in bills and notes, ii. 391.
Recital in early bill, ii. 339.
Recital of, unnecessary under Negotiable Instruments Law, ii. 509.

VAPORS, NOXIOUS.
See NOXIOUS VAPORS.

VASTUM.
See WASTE.

VAUGHAN, C. J.
Observation on nature of common-law debt, ii. 27.
Questions decision in Slade's Case, iii. 138.

VAVISOR, J.
Approves use of detinue as remedy against trespasser, iii. 150.
Supposes replevin maintainable in case of wrongful taking, iii. 216.

VEHICLE.
Defective carriage, responsibility of owner for injury done by, i. 159.
Driving at unlawful speed, when not a bar to plaintiff's action, i. 177.
Passenger chargeable with contributory negligence of driver, when, i. 140.
Pedestrian run down, driver liable, when, i. 134, 137.

VENICE, BANK OF.
See BANK OF VENICE.

VENUE.
Actions triable in county where cause of action arises, iii. 90.
Change of venue not permitted in local actions, iii. 93, 94.
English court devoid of jurisdiction over trespass committed in foreign country, iii. 94.
Fictitious venue, iii. 92.
Pleading, certainty required in, iii. 91.
Statutory provisions concerning, iii. 92, 93.
Venue as question of jurisdiction, iii. 94.
Venue to be laid in writ, iii. 90.

VESSEL.
Responsibility for damage done by drifting vessel, i. 112.

VETITUM NAMIUM, iii. 209.

VICIOUS HABIT.
Abandonment of vicious habit good consideration for promise, ii. 72.

VICTUALER.
Implied duty incident to public calling of, i. 185.
Implied warranty of wholesomeness of food and drink, i. 387.

VI ET ARMIS.
Function of allegation in action of trespass, iii. 230.

VIOLENCE.
See TRESPASS ON PERSON.
Conception of violence as basis of legal classification, i. 2.
Initial point in theory of civil liability, i. 1.

VIRTUAL ACCEPTANCE.
Common-law contract ingrafted on law merchant, ii. 409.
Doctrine of, ii. 401, 402.
Requisites of, ii. 402.

VIS MAJOR.
See ACT OF GOD.

VOLENTI NON FIT INJURIA.
Applicability of maxim to negligence cases, i. 163.
Appreciation of danger as affecting applicability of maxim, i. 163.
Knowledge of danger as affecting applicability of maxim, i. 163.
Origin of maxim, i. 162.

VON REUMONT.
Account of origin of bill of exchange, ii. 335.

WAGER.
Consensual nature of agreement of wager, ii. 111.
Courts begin to discountenance wagers, ii. 166.
Election, wager on, invalid, ii. 166.
Gambling contracts made void by statute, ii. 167.
Idle wagers formerly enforced, ii. 166.
Stakeholder, duty to refund money before payment to winner, ii. 223.
Validity of contract of wager, ii. 111, 165.
Validity of wager on past event, ii. 111.

WAGER OF LAW.
Abolition, iii. 139.
Assumpsit not subject to, iii. 68.
Debt subject to, ii. 61, 62; iii. 138.
Detinue, ii. 266.
Law merchant does not recognize, ii. 330.
Replevin subject to, iii. 217.
Trial by wager of law, iii. 24.
Wager of law as explanatory of non-survival of debt, iii. 66, 67.

WAIVER.
Effect of clause in negotiabl instruments providing for waiver of exemption, ii. 508.
Waiver of tort, ii. 215; iii. 196.

WALES, STATUTE OF, ii. 17; iii. 116.

WALL.
Neglect in maintenance of, i. 183.

WAMBAUGH, PROF. E.
Theory of ratification, ii. 489.

WANTON ACT.
Exemplary damages —
Wanton assault and battery, i. 486.
Wantonness of conduct as affecting assessment of, i. 481.
Wanton poisoning of poultry, i. 485.

WAR.
Justification of trespass resulting from exercise of war power, i. 22, 23.

WARDEN.
Churchwarden, privilege of, i. 38.

WARDSHIP.
Incident of military tenure abolished by statute, iii. 296.

WAREHOUSEMAN.
Bailee for custody, ii. 290.
Negligent keeping of goods by warehouseman not a conversion, i. 237.

WARRANTY.
Bills and notes, warranties incident to transfer of, ii. 411.
False warranty in chattel sale, i. 377.
Conception of liability —
Breach of warranty conceived as breach of contract, i. 389.
Breach of warranty conceived as tort, i. 389.
Transition from tort to contract conception of liability, i. 389, 390.
Implied warranty of title, i. 382.
Measure of damages, i. 446–449.
Warranty of quality, i. 385.
Implied warranty —
Application of doctrine to case of Derry *v.* Peek, i 407.

WARRANTY — *Continued.*
Implied warranty — *Continued.*
Estoppel as manifestation of implied warranty, ii. 246.
Essential elements of estoppel, ii. 247.
Estoppel forestalls damage, ii. 247.
Giving of gratuitous information, i. 408.
Implied warranty suppletory to law of fraud, i. 404.
Pennsylvania doctrine, i. 391.

WASTE.
Ameliorating waste, i. 28.
Criteria of waste —
Changing character of inheritance, i. 27.
Diminution of value, i. 28.
Injury to inheritance, i. 27.
Death, effect of, on right of action, iii. 65.
Definition of waste, i. 26.
Equity courts, attitude of, in modern times, i. 28, 30, 31.
Guardian liable for waste, iii. 268.
Permissive waste —
American doctrine concerning actionability of, i. 31, 32.
Covenant to keep in repair, effect of, i. 30.
Deterioration from reasonable use, i. 33.
Equity repudiates idea that permissive waste is actionable, i. 30, 33.
Law courts reach conclusion permissive waste not actionable, i. 31, 33.
Permissive waste not actionable in early common law, i. 29.
Statutes of Marlborough and Gloucester, i. 29.
Tenant at will not answerable for permissive waste, i. 29.
Tenant from year to year not answerable for, i. 30.
Positive waste —
Alteration of premises, i. 28.
Destruction by reasonable use, i. 33.
Estovers, right to take, i. 26.
Exile of men, i. 26.
Fixtures, removal of, i. 26.
Husbandry, changing course of, i. 27.
Mines, opening of, i. 26.
Timber, unauthorized cutting of, i. 26, 27.
Remedy —
Action on case in nature of waste, iii. 270.
Prohibition of waste, iii. 269.
Statutory action of waste, iii. 269, 270.
Trespass lies for destructive waste, when, iii. 270.
Writ of waste, iii. 268.
Social conditions as affecting, i. 27.
Special exceptions to liability —
Act of God, i. 32.
Act of public enemy, i. 32.
Tenant for life liable for waste, iii. 268.

WASTE — *Continued.*
Tenant in common liable to cotenant, iii. 269.
Tenant in dower liable for waste, iii. 268.
Trespass distinguished from waste, i. 33.
Waste violative of property right, i. 34.
Writ of waste, scope of remedy, iii. 268.

WATER.
Artificial accumulation of, responsibility of owner for damage done by, i. 62–64.
Interference with water rights, i. 198–204.
Obstruction and diversion of, see COGNATE NUISANCE.

WATER COMPANY.
Failure to keep sufficient water pressure, liability for damage caused by, i. 175.
Implied duty incident to public calling, i. 186.
Polluted water, contributory negligence of person drinking, i. 128.

WESTBURY, LORD.
Observations on law of nuisance in business, i. 219.

WEST, WM.
Form of bill of exchange at beginning of seventeenth century, ii. 356, 357, 382.

WESTMINSTER, PROVISIONS OF, iii. 102.

WESTMINSTER II., STATUTE OF, i. 214, 328; ii. 31; iii. 3, 34, 35, 50, 103, 104, 108, 210–212, 248, 269.

WESTMINSTER III., STATUTE OF.
See QUIA EMPTORES.

WHARF.
Jamming of wharf, liability of steamer for damage incident to, i. 136.

WHARFINGER.
Bailee for custody, ii. 290.
Negligent keeping of goods by, not a conversion, i. 237.

WIGHTMAN, J.
Observation on effect of contributory negligence, i. 140.

WILCOX, H. C.
Concerned with drafting of Negotiable Instruments Law, ii. 496.

WILDE, B.
Approves exemplary damages in high-handed trespass, i. 486.

WILDE, J.
Statement of nature of unilateral contract, ii. 52.

WILLES, J.
Observation on meaning of *actio personalis*, iii. 60.
Principle underlying law of master and servant, ii. 465.

WILLIAMS, JOSHUA.
Meaning of chose in action, iii. 80.

WILLIAMS, T. C.
Exposition of nature of chose in action, iii. 80.

WILLISTON, PROF. SAMUEL.
Criticism of theory of bilateral contract, ii. 107, 108, 119.

WILLS, J.
Application of maxim *volenti non fit injuria*, i. 167.

WILMOT, J.
Discussion of right of 'bearer' to sue on negotiable instrument, ii. 394.
Effect of restrictive indorsement considered, ii. 399.
Judicial notice of principles of law merchant, ii. 398.

WILMOT, L. C. J.
Approves revival of action of account, iii. 110.
Sanctions exemplary damages in case of seduction, i. 484.
Validity of contract as affected by illegality, ii. 163.

WINDMILL.
Implied warranty of quality in sale of, i. 387.

WITHERNAM, iii. 209.
Goods seized in withernam may be used by distrainor, iii. 293.

WITNESS.
Complaint witness, see SECTA.
Policy of Statute of Frauds as affected by modern enactments making parties competent, ii. 197.
Trial by witnesses in early English law, iii. 25.

WOODS, J.
Observation on unilateral contract, ii. 53.

WORDS OF NEGOTIABILITY.
Effect of statute of 3 and 4 Anne on notes not containing, ii. 386, 387.
English Bills of Exchange Act makes bills and notes negotiable though lacking words of negotiability, ii. 387.
Instrument lacking words of negotiability entitled to grace, ii. 503.
Words of negotiability necessary to make instrument negotiable under American Negotiable Instruments Law, ii. 387, 500.

WRAPPER.
Simulation of wrapper, i. 419.

WRIT OF RIGHT.
Remedy for recovery of proprietary interest in land, iii. 44.

WRIT PROCESS.
Bracton's scheme of remedial justice, iii. 32, 33.
Centralizing effect of writ process, iii. 28.
Chancery as source of writs, iii. 28.
Common-law theory of actions, iii. 29.
Defects of remedial system, iii. 33.
Importance of wording of the writ, iii. 28.
Judicial writ distinguished from original writ, iii. 32.

WRIT PROCESS — *Continued.*

Kinds of writs —

Magisterial writs, iii. 29, 32.

Writ of course, iii. 29, 32.

Nature and function of writ, iii. 28.

New writs —

Chancery deprived of power to issue, iii. 34.

Mode of issuance, iii. 31.

Parliament authorizes issuance of writs in case, iii. 34.

Right and remedy, iii. 29, 30, 32, 33.

Right of action as affected by nonexistence of appropriate writ, iii. 29.

Roman formulary system, analogy to English writ process, iii. 29.

Scheme of writs becomes settled, iii. 34.

Tale of writs in thirteenth century, iii. 31.

Types of writ —

Præcipe —

Si te fecerit securum, iii. 36.

WRITS.

Account (*de computo*), iii. 99, 100.

Admeasurement of common, iii. 45.

Admeasurement of dower, iii. 45.

Assize of nuisance, i. 213; iii. 271.

Assumpsit (case *sur* assumpsit), iii. 173-175, 177.

Covenant (*de convencione*), iii. 115.

Darrein presentment, iii. 37.

Debt (in the *debet et detinet*), iii. 129.

Debt (in the *detinet*), iii. 129.

De manso obsesso, i. 265.

De nativis abductis, i. 265.

De parco fracto, iii. 292, 293.

De proprietate probanda, iii. 214, 215.

De rationabili parte, iii. 44.

De reparatione facienda, i. 182.

De retorno habendo, iii. 212.

Detinue (debt in the *detinet*), iii. 144, 146.

Detinue (*devenerunt ad manus*), iii. 147.

Detinue *sur bailment*, iii. 146.

Detinue *sur trover*, iii. 146.

De uxore abducta, i. 263.

Dower, iii. 44, 45.

Dower *unde nihil habet*, iii. 45.

Ejectione firmæ, iii. 45.

Ejectment, iii. 45.

Entry, iii. 45.

Entry *in casu proviso*, iii. 249.

Formedon in descender, iii. 50.

Formedon in remainder, iii. 44.

Formedon in reverter, iii. 44, 50.

Indebitatus assumpsit, iii. 182, 185.

WRITS — *Continued.*
Morte d'ancestor, iii. 37, 44.
Novel disseisin, iii. 37, 44, 277.
Nuisance (*de nocumento*), iii. 271.
Pone, iii. 211.
Power of English Chancery to issue new writs, iii. 248.
Prohibition, ii. 13.
Prohibition of waste, iii. 269.
Quare ejecit infra terminum. iii. 45.
Quare impedit, iii. 45.
Quod permittat, i. 214; iii. 45, 271.
Replevin (*replegiari facias*), iii. 208, 215.
Rescous, iii. 293.
Second deliverance, iii. 212.
Trespass (*de transgressione*), iii. 225, 230.
Trespass *de bonis asportatis,* iii. 231.
Trespass *de equo interfecto,* iii. 234.
Trespass *quare clausum fregit,* iii. 232.
Trespass *vi et armis,* iii. 230, 233.
Trover (action on case *sur trover*), iii. 159, 161.
Venue of action to be laid in writ, iii. 90.
Waste (*de vasto*), iii. 268, 269.
Writ against carrier, ii. 302.
Writ against innkeeper, ii. 296, 297.
Writ *in consimili casu,* iii. 34.
Writ of right, iii. 44.
Writ of right of advowson, iii. 45.

WRONG.
Nature of conception of wrong, iii. 6.
Origin, iii. 5, 6.

ZEMINDAR.
Privilege incident to performance of customary duty by, i. 40, 41.

www.ingramcontent.com/pod-product-compliance
Lightning Source LLC
LaVergne TN
LVHW090254210926
848480LV00001B/18
* 9 7 8 1 8 9 3 1 2 2 2 5 3 *